MOON

EDINBURGH,
GLASGOW &
THE ISLE OF SKYE

SALLY COFFEY

Contents

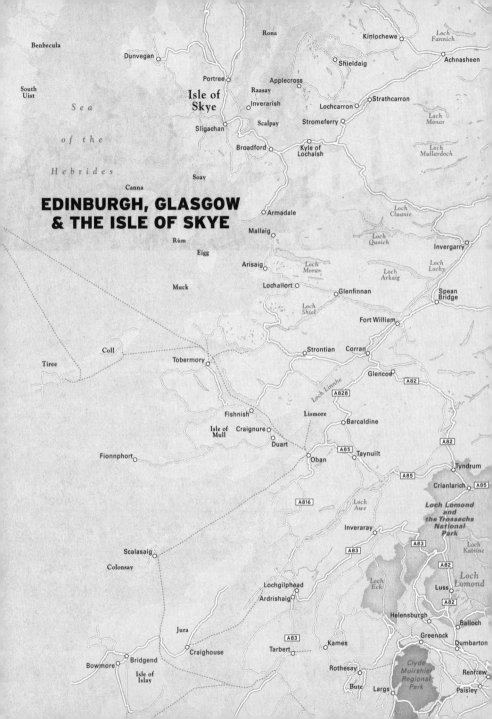

EDINBURGH, GLASGOW & THE ISLE OF SKYE

Benbecula

South Uist

Sea

of the

Hebrides

Rona

Dunvegan

Portree

Isle of Skye

Applecross

Raasay

Inverarish

Sligachan

Scalpay

Broadford

Soay

Canna

Rùm

Eigg

Muck

Armadale

Mallaig

Arisaig

Lochailort

Coll

Tiree

Tobermory

Fishnish

Isle of Mull

Craignure

Duart

Fionnphort

Scalasaig

Colonsay

Bowmore

Bridgend

Isle of Islay

Jura

Craighouse

Kinlochewe

Loch Fannich

Shieldaig

Achnasheen

Strathcarron

Lochcarron

Stromeferry

Kyle of Lochalsh

Loch Monar

Loch Mullardoch

Loch Cluanie

Loch Quoich

Invergarry

Loch Morar

Loch Arkaig

Loch Lochy

Glenfinnan

Spean Bridge

Loch Shiel

Fort William

Strontian

Corran

Glencoe

A82

Loch Linnhe

A828

Lismore

Barcaldine

A82

Oban

Taynuilt

A85

A85

Tyndrum

Crianlarich

A85

A816

Loch Awe

Loch Lomond and the Trossachs National Park

Inveraray

A83

Loch Katrine

A82

Luss

Loch Lomond

Lochgilphead

Ardrishaig

Loch Eck

Helensburgh

Balloch

A82

Tarbert

A83

Kames

Rothesay

Bute

Largs

Greenock

Dumbarton

Renfrew

Paisley

Clyde Muirshiel Regional Park

DISCOVER

Edinburgh, Glasgow & the Isle of Skye

With the good looks, history, and intrigue of Edinburgh, the buzzy, post-industrial reinvention of Glasgow, and the sheer drama of Skye, Scotland can't be accused of being a one-trick pony.

In Edinburgh and Glasgow, you can find high culture and heritage behind the venerable facades of eminent museums and galleries as well as boundary-pushing art shows and pulsating, pioneering music in the underground clubs and thrilling pop-ups that form the beating hearts of both cities.

But if what you're looking for is peace and solitude, you don't have to travel far. The Highlands, a huge region that covers much of the north and west of Scotland, is home to some of the country's most remote communities, magnificent mountains that sweep down to glittering blue lochs, and a truly breathtaking array of wildlife.

The Isle of Skye is surely the Highlands' showpiece. This prehistoric land still bears evidence of its former dinosaur residents, along with scars from the last Ice Age, when melting ice tore through the island, leading to landslips that left jagged peaks, soaring spires, and steep drops. The result is a land of stark

Clockwise from top left: National Wallace Monument, Stirling; the rural village of Torrin on the shores of Loch Slapin; puffins can be seen off the coast of Mull and its neighboring isles; Edinburgh Old Town; Riverside Museum, Glasgow; Highland cattle on Islay

contrasts—conical hillsides meet sharp crevices, barren-looking munros (Scottish mountains higher than 3,000 ft/914 m) hide glistening lochs—and only folklore can explain the incomprehensible.

Scotland is a country of juxtapositions. Although the cities are undoubtedly dynamic and vibrant, what attracts travelers time and time again is the sense that the country has remained largely unchanged for eons—making it the ultimate destination for slow travel. A blank canvas for outdoor adventure, the Highlands offers trekkers the opportunity to camp under skies unpolluted by urban lights, to spot puffins, whales, red deer, and red squirrels in the wild, and to wander through abandoned villages. Or you can just take your time working through the country's many single malt whiskies, preferably in a cozy old inn.

Whether you want to spend never-ending summer days exploring new sights, or "coorie doon" and escape the brooding winter nights by a fire, you'll find that Edinburgh, Glasgow, and the Isle of Skye represent the best of all that Scotland has to offer. Hence the answer to the common question, "How long are you here for?," is oft "For as long as possible."

Clockwise from top left: The Old Man of Storr, Isle of Skye; Edinburgh Castle; University of Glasgow; Highland wildflowers.

13 TOP EXPERIENCES

1 Sampling the best Scottish whisky and gin, from single malts produced by **Islay's whisky distilleries** (page 235) to **craft gin at Pickering's** (page 71), one of Edinburgh's coolest hangouts.

2 Trekking to cut-off and deserted villages such as **Boreraig** on Skye, where the impact of the Highland Clearances can truly be felt, and stopping to take in the spectacular views en route (page 343).

3 Scaling the 822-foot-high (251-meter-high) peak of **Arthur's Seat** to view the ancient yet cosmopolitan city of Edinburgh in relative peace (page 54).

<<<

4 Kicking back in one of the many beautiful **parks and green spaces in Glasgow**, such as the Victorian-landscaped Kelvingrove Park bordered by grand buildings (page 154).

>>>

5 Breaking away from the contemporary music scene for a traditional jam at **Glasgow's Ben Nevis** (page 166) or **Edinburgh's Sandy Bell's** (page 76).

<<<

6 Riding the **Jacobite Steam Train** over the iconic Glenfinnan Viaduct and catching a glimpse of the Glenfinnan Monument on the banks of Loch Shiel (page 318).

>>>

7 Bagging a munro (Scottish hills higher than 3,000 feet/914 meters), such as **Bla Bheinn** on the Isle of Skye, and feeling like you've conquered Everest (page 341).

>>>

8 Pitching up for the night in the wilds of Scotland, whether in the middle of **Loch Lomond and the Trossachs National Park** (page 215) or by a stream in **Glencoe** (page 307), and embracing the freedom afforded by this vast landscape.

>>>

9 Exploring the cliffs of the **Quiraing** on the Isle of Skye and afterward perfecting the art of coorie (getting snug, Scottish-style) with a wee dram by the fire in a cozy inn (page 352).

<<<

10 **Kayaking on Loch Ness** and basking in the serenity of Scotland's deepest—and most mysterious—loch (page 291).

>>>

11 **Spotting Mull's wildlife,** such as red deer, killer whales, and both white-tailed and golden eagles (page 228).

<<<

12 **Driving through Glencoe** and being utterly humbled by the sheer majesty of the giant mountains that loom over the valley floor that drops below you (page 305).

>>>

13 Soaking up the history of the **Culloden Battlefield**, where the Jacobites took their last stand against the Duke of Cumberland's government troops in what became one of the most pivotal days in Scottish history (page 279).

<<<

Planning Your Trip

Where To Go

Edinburgh

Edinburgh, Scotland's handsome capital, is full of **history,** and a visit here isn't complete without exploring both the sophisticated 18th-century **New Town** and the crumbling but atmospheric **Old Town,** where medieval wynds (narrow lanes between houses) will bring you to the **Royal Mile,** a thoroughfare flanked by two of the city's most celebrated attractions: **Edinburgh Castle** and the **Palace of Holyroodhouse**. The latter is overlooked by the volcanic peak of **Arthur's Seat,** which stands in its own windswept hilly park—a small promise of what the Highlands might offer, right here in the city.

Glasgow

Cool, edgy, and with its tongue firmly in its cheek, Glasgow is a place that reveals a little more of itself on every visit. It has some beautiful architecture—including the old warehouses of the **Merchant City** and Charles Rennie Mackintosh's Art Nouveau buildings, which epitomized the "Glasgow Style"—but it's for the non-stop energy that one should visit Scotland's most populous city. In the city center, taking a tour of the **City Chambers** is a must, as is a visit to the **Gallery of Modern Art**, if only to grasp the scale of wealth that once poured through the city and straight into the pockets of Edinburgh's tobacco lords. To the south you'll find beautiful **green spaces**, whereas in the **East End** you can visit the famous **Barras Market**, **Glasgow Cathedral,** and the **Necropolis**. However, for a little bit of everything, from cultural houses and

Edinburgh from Calton Hill

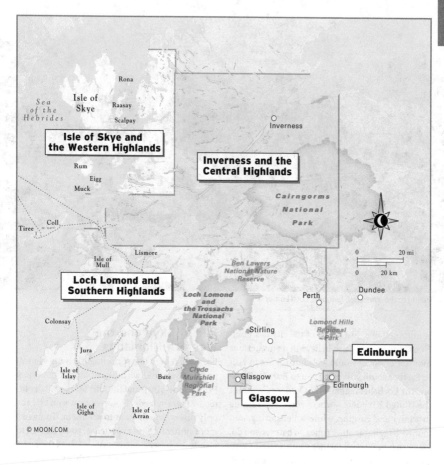

Isle of Skye and the Western Highlands

Inverness and the Central Highlands

Loch Lomond and Southern Highlands

Edinburgh

Glasgow

Sea of the Hebrides

Rona

Isle of Skye

Raasay

Scalpay

Rum

Eigg

Muck

Coll

Tiree

Isle of Mull

Lismore

Colonsay

Jura

Isle of Islay

Bute

Isle of Gigha

Isle of Arran

Clyde Muirshiel Regional Park

Inverness

Cairngorms National Park

Ben Lawers National Nature Reserve

Loch Lomond and the Trossachs National Park

Stirling

Perth

Dundee

Lomond Hills Regional Park

Glasgow

Edinburgh

0   20 mi

0   20 km

© MOON.COM

stunning architecture to cool thrift stores and great nightlife, head straight to the **West End**.

Loch Lomond and the Southern Highlands

Dominated by the expansive **Loch Lomond and the Trossachs National Park**—an outdoor playground where you can go **kayaking** on Scotland's biggest loch, cycle along shaded woodland trails, or climb one of the many **munros**—this region is easily accessible from both Glasgow and Edinburgh. To the east of the park lies the historic city of **Stirling**, home to arguably Scotland's finest castle, and a little

further north will bring you to the "Fair City" of **Perth**—Scotland's ancient capital. To the west of Loch Lomond, you'll find **Oban** and its isles, including **Mull**; you need to travel a little farther south to reach the wildlife and whisky wonderland of **Islay**.

Inverness and The Central Highlands

Gateway to the Highlands, **Inverness** is an attractive enough city, but most people come here to go somewhere else. For a history lesson, a visit to Culloden just east of the city and scene of one of the most brutal battles on Scottish soil,

Hiking to the top of Ben Lomond, Loch Lomond

is unforgettable. Just south of the city lies **Loch Ness**, and whether you believe in its mysterious monster or not, it would feel churlish not to visit it. Farther south will bring you to **Fort William** and the Lochaber region—the Outdoor Capital of the United Kingdom—where you can go skiing in winter and gorging, white-water rafting, and munro-bagging at other times. Whatever you do, make sure you travel farther south again to visit **Glencoe**, an epic landscape that will leave you open-mouthed in awe.

Isle of Skye and the Western Highlands

For good reason this sprawling isle is top of most people's Scotland wish list; photos of the **Fairy Pools**, **Quiraing**, and the **Old Man of Storr** litter Instagram feeds. However, you won't be the only one who will want to see them. To have a more authentic Skye experience, you'd do well to visit some lesser-known spots, such as the **road from Broadford to Elgol**, which takes you down and through the **Cuillin mountain range** and which is one of the best road trips with which few are familiar.

If You Have...

- **Three days**: Stick to the two main cities. In Edinburgh, see the historic sights of the Old Town before going for a gin tasting at Pickering's or embarking on a pub crawl. A second day in Edinburgh could be spent exploring the New Town and catching a comedy show. If you have just one day in Glasgow, spend it wandering around the Merchant City and the city center before dancing the night away to an up-and-coming band at one of the city's clubs.

- **One week**: Extend your trip by traveling up to Loch Lomond and spend a few days kayaking, hiking, and camping in the park.

- **Two weeks**: From Loch Lomond, head to Fort William and catch the Jacobite Steam Train to Mallaig for the ferry over to Skye, where you should base yourself for at least a week to do it justice.

- **Three weeks**: If you have an extra week, you could cross back to the mainland from Skye via the Kyle of Lochalsh bridge and travel east to the shores of Loch Ness and then south to Glencoe. Alternatively, you could spend some time on the Isle of Mull after your stay in Loch

Merchant City, Glasgow

Lomond, before heading north to Mallaig for the ferry to Skye.

Before You Go

When To Go

When you visit depends on what you plan to do here. In **August** there is no other place on Earth like Edinburgh—a heady art, comedy, and music pageant at which you can wander from show to show making new friends. But for some, Edinburgh's atmosphere in August is overwhelming, so if you want to explore Edinburgh's historic attractions, it's probably best to avoid this month.

Spring in Scotland is when many of the wild flowers come into bloom, bringing the hillsides and meadows to life with vibrant displays. It is also a time when the weather is reasonably clement (though you never really can tell in Scotland), and you'll get good daylight hours for attempting any of the many munros on Skye, in Loch Lomond, or elsewhere in the Highlands.

For many, **autumn** is a favored time of year when a sea of reds, auburns, browns, and purples appears to glow in each sunset's golden haze. Cool temperatures give you a good excuse to wrap yourself in a cashmere or lamb's wool blanket and snuggle up by the fire in a traditional cottage or an old inn with a wee dram in hand.

And who can forget **Hogmanay**, a lively celebration of the year's end, when Scottish

Though they are more of a Victorian invention than a genuine Scottish tradition, the Highland games are nevertheless colorful and lively celebrations of Highland culture that pay homage to historic sporting events played out among clan members in past centuries.

Originally, Highland games were a way for the clan chieftain to select the best fighters and couriers and to audition the best pipers and dancers to add an air of prestige to his clan. The games as we know them today began in earnest when Queen Victoria endorsed the fledgling practice of racing and competing on a local level in the mid-19th century (after the original games had stalled following the Battle of Culloden in 1746). Soon the events were turned into huge spectacles, with participants dressed in full Highland garb, including kilts made of the tartan specific to each clan (a late 18th- or early 19th-century creation), all played out against the sound of the massed pipers.

Once the preserve of the wealthy country house residents of Scotland and their guests, today the games welcome everyone, and often you will find the whole community at a local event. Some 100 events take place annually across the Highlands, usually **May-September**. The events include traditions such as the **caber toss** (the throwing of a large tapered pole, often made from a larch tree), the **tug of war**, and the **hammer throw**.

Inverness Highland Games

INVERNESS HIGHLAND GAMES

Every July, this show-stopper of an event attracts more than 10,000 spectators. It includes all the usual games as well as a display of shinty (an old Scottish game played with sticks and a ball), a mass Highland fling, and even a wheelbarrow "Grand Prix."

LOCH LOMOND HIGHLAND GAMES

Every July, the village of Balloch at the southern entry to the park holds a Highland games with the ubiquitous piping, dancing, and caber toss. It also hosts two tug of wars, along with the 80-meter (262 feet) Scottish Sprint Championship.

MALLAIG AND MORAR HIGHLAND GAMES

On the first Sunday in August, this small but inclusive local gathering includes piping, dancing, athletics, heavy-lifting, and a cross-country race. It's worth attending for the stunning views across to Skye and the Small Isles alone.

hospitality and geniality comes into its own. Other major events worth visiting for include **Burns Night**, a celebration of the Scottish poet Robert Burns held on his birthday of January 25 each year, when traditional suppers are hosted throughout Scotland, and **Halloween**, the Celtic origins of which can be traced back here.

Transportation

Both **Glasgow** and **Edinburgh** are well connected with international flights from the United States, Canada, and Europe, and they are accessible via numerous flights and trains from **London** and other parts of the **United Kingdom**. However, traveling within Scotland can take a good deal of planning if you are using public transport. Despite Edinburgh being the capital, **Glasgow** is by far the most **well-connected hub,** with direct trains and buses to all main towns and cities. If you are traveling from Edinburgh, you will often have to pick up a connection in Glasgow.

The main train operator is **Scotrail** (www.scotrail.co.uk), and the main bus operators are **Scottish Citylink** (www.citylink.co.uk) and **Stagecoach** (www.stagecoachbus.com).

Passports and Visas

There are few visa restrictions if you are visiting Scotland for no more than six months. If you are an **EU citizen** or come from Switzerland or one of the non-EU member states of the **EEA** (Norway, Liechtenstein, and Iceland), you do not need a visa. Nor do you need a visa if you are a member of the **Overseas Countries and Territories (OCT).**

Currently, there is **no visa requirement** for citizens of the **United States, Canada, Australia,** or **New Zealand** who plan to visit Scotland for six or fewer months. Anyone planning to come for **more than six months** will need to get an **entry clearance certificate** from the British Embassy in their home country before they travel.

To enter the United Kingdom, travelers from **South Africa** do need a **Standard visitor visa** (www.gov.uk/standard-visitor-visa), which currently costs £93 and allows stays of up to six months.

You will of course need a **passport** if you are traveling here from outside the United Kingdom (unless you are traveling from an EEA country, in which case you can travel with a **National Identity Card,** at least until Brexit, which could result in new passport requirements).

For the latest advice on travel documents, check the U.K. and Foreign and Commonwealth Office's website (www.gov.uk/government/organisations/uk-visas-and-immigration).

Best of Edinburgh, Glasgow & the Isle of Skye

Day 1: Edinburgh

Spend your first day in Scotland's capital, **Edinburgh**. Start with a hike up to **Arthur's Seat** in the morning, when you'll likely have more space to enjoy the panoramic views of the city. After your hike, head to the **Palace of Holyroodhouse** at the bottom of the Royal Mile to learn about the royal history of Edinburgh. Have lunch in the café in the palace before browsing the shops of the **Grassmarket,** at the top of the Royal Mile. If you have time, you can take a tour of **Edinburgh Castle**, or you can just snap a photo of its exterior from the Grassmarket. Don't leave the city before you've sampled a few whiskies and heard some traditional music in one of its many historic taverns, such as **Sandy Bell's.**

Day 2: Glasgow

After an early breakfast at your hotel, take a morning train to **Glasgow Queen Street.** Join a free tour of the **City Chambers,** and afterward walk up to **Glasgow Cathedral.** Stroll amid the aging headstones of the **Necropolis,** which looks out over the city from above the cathedral and keep an eye out for the overblown statue of the divisive leader of the Scottish Reformation, John Knox. Head back to the city center for a hearty afternoon tea at **Mackintosh at the Willow,** where you can admire the designs of Charles Rennie Mackintosh while sipping tea and eating finger sandwiches. For art of a more subversive nature, head to the **Gallery of Modern Art**—be sure to snap a picture with the cone-headed Duke of Marlborough outside. After dinner, spend the night dancing and rocking out to whatever band is playing at the **Barrowland** in the East End.

Glasgow Cathedral

Loch Lomond

Day 3: Loch Lomond and Glencoe

Rent a car and drive north out of Glasgow to the **Loch Lomond and the Trossachs National Park**. Rent a **kayak** from **Loch Lomond Leisure** in Luss and spend the morning paddling along the shore or exploring one of the isles. After lunch in the old slate village of Luss, head north out of the park, past the desolate and raw landscape of Rannoch Moor and up through the mountainous **Glencoe**. Stop to take photos of the **Three Sisters** before pitching up for the night at the **Red Squirrel Campsite** and having dinner and drinks at the **Clachaig Inn.**

Day 4: Fort William to Skye

After breakfast, drive 45 minutes to **Fort William** and ride the **Nevis Range** mountain gondola for great views of Britain's highest mountain, Ben Nevis. After lunch at the **Ben Nevis Inn,** drive the **Road to the Isles**, stopping at the **Glenfinnan Monument** that stands on the shores of Loch Shiel (near the iconic Glenfinnan Viaduct), all the way to **Mallaig,** where you can have a delicious seafood supper at the **Cornerstone Restaurant** before catching the ferry over to **Skye** and staying the night at **Eilean Iarmain** on Sleat, in the south of the isle.

Days 5-6: Isle of Skye

Spend your first morning on Skye driving the **Broadford to Elgol road** for incredible views of the Red Cuillin and Bla Bheinn, stopping for tea and cake at the **Blue Shed Cafe.** From Elgol, take a boat ride over to **Loch Coruisk**, an eerily still deep-blue loch surrounded by mountains, looking out for resident seals and the occasional visiting whale en route. Back on dry land, take a late afternoon whisky tour of **Talisker Distillery** before going for dinner at **Loch Bay** on the Waternish peninsula and bedding down for the night next door at the **Stein Inn,** Skye's oldest inn.

The next day, start early with a drive to the northeast of the isle to hike the ethereal and mind-boggling landscape of the **Quiraing**, carved out by landslips at the end of the last Ice Age. Have a hearty lunch at **Skye Restaurant** before paying a visit to **The Old Man of Storr.** You can view it from the road, but if lunch has restored your energy, walk out to the base of the pinnacle (about 1.5 hours round-trip). Afterward, treat yourself to a three-course supper at **Scorrybreac** in Portree before either staying the night in town or heading back to the mainland via the Kyle of Lochalsh bridge.

City-Hopping from Edinburgh to Glasgow

Days 1-2: Edinburgh

Start your day in **Edinburgh** with an early hike up through **Holyrood Park** to the summit of **Arthur's Seat.** The steep climb is tough at times but it's worth it: there are few cities you can peer over from atop an ancient volcano. Take your time descending to the city and head to the **National Museum of Scotland** to see the 12th-century Lewis Chessmen and more fabulous city views from the 7th-floor roof terrace. Book an afternoon tour of **Pickering's Gin Distillery** and, if it's a Saturday, pop into the **Captain's Bar** to listen to some afternoon live music. Alternatively, meander back to the Old Town and pop into **Edinburgh Castle** just before closing, when it should be relatively quiet. Afterward, head to **The Grain Store** for dinner before going for a nightcap in the **Bow Bar**.

Start your day at the **National Portrait Gallery** in the **New Town**—a visual feast of who's who in terms of Scotland's heroes and heroines. Stroll down to the **Scott Monument**, a Gothic masterpiece that overlooks Princes Street Gardens and that celebrates the man who shone the tourism spotlight on Scotland, Sir Walter Scott. Walk to **Charlotte Square** and see if the first minister is at home at **Bute House** and afterward pop into the **Oxford Bar**

Scott Monument in Princes Street Gardens

Whisky-making in Scotland dates back to at least the 15th century, though some believe it may have been introduced by the Celts long before that. It was originally a way of turning rain-soaked barley into something palatable. For centuries, there were thousands of illicit distilleries in Scotland, and they only began to be licensed from the 18th century onward.

Whisky-making is no quick process—Scotch whisky needs to age for a minimum of three years, though most distilleries prefer to age theirs for at least 5 or even 10 years. The protractedness of the aging process is one of the reasons that gin-making has become so popular here (70 percent of the UK's gin is produced in Scotland). Gin-making is a way for distilleries to make some money while they wait for their whisky to mature, so you will find a new generation of whisky makers that also make a very good gin.

WHISKY REGIONS

There are five main whisky making regions in Scotland: The Lowlands, Islay, Speyside, Campbeltown (on the Kintyre peninsula, Argyll), and the Highlands. Each has its own unique character, though you will find variations within each region. Whiskies from the Lowlands are quite light in color and dry (most end up in blended whiskies); Islay whiskies are generally peaty and smoky; Speyside whiskies are the sweetest; and Campbeltown whiskies are usually full bodied and have a slightly salty finish. Whiskies from the Highlands are the hardest to define and can range from full bodied and spicy to light and fruity.

A distillery tour is highly recommended. If you can't make it to a distillery, you can still buy spirits in bars across Scotland, though more rural locations tend to favor spirits from local distilleries.

ISLAY

This island in the southern Hebrides is renowned for its peaty style of whisky, which harks back to the days when the island's infinitite peat resources were used to heat pretty much everything, including the barley in the malt houses. The island's eight distilleries (a ninth is due to open any day) range from the peat-heavy **Laphroaig** and **Lagavulin** in the southeast to the lighter, more drinkable unpeated **Bruichladdich** whisky on the southwest peninsula. Bruichladdich is also known for its Botanist gin.

Edinburgh Gin ingredients

THE HEBRIDEAN WHISKY TRAIL

A stalwart of whisky-making, Skye's **Talisker Distillery**, Skye newcomer **Torabhaig**, and the **Isle of Raasay Distillery** (on Skye's neighboring isle to the east) are featured in the Hebridean Whisky Trail (https://hebrideanwhisky.com). Navigating from one to another is surprisingly easy.

SPEYSIDE

Southeast of Inverness, this region that runs along the River Spey has the largest concentration of distilleries in Scotland, including **Glenfiddich**, built by William Grant and his family in 1886 with the intention of creating the "best dram in the valley." The Grant family succeeded; today Glenfiddich is one of the most popular brands of Scotch whisky. If you're visiting Inverness, consider a detour through Speyside for a few wee drams before heading to Loch Ness or Fort William.

EDINBURGH AND GLASGOW

In Edinburgh you will find two excellent gin distilleries—**Pickering's** and **Edinburgh Gin**—and in Glasgow, a new whisky distillery called the **Clydeside Distillery**, which will be joined in late 2019 by another on the south side of the River Clyde, the Clutha Distillery.

for an afternoon pint or two. Well oiled, wander down to pretty **Stockbridge** to browse the many independent stores before having an intimate dinner at **The Stockbridge Restaurant**. End the night with one final cocktail at the **Last Word**.

Days 3-4: Glasgow

Get an early train from Edinburgh Waverley to **Glasgow Queen Street**. Stretch your legs after the train ride with a walk up to **Glasgow Cathedral**. Grab a coffee and a sandwich at the Tardis-style **Empire Coffee** and walk thorugh the Victorian "city of the dead," the **Necropolis**, which overlooks the city from above the cathedral.

Take the hop-on hop-off bus to the **West End** and visit **Kelvingrove Art Gallery and Museum**—you may be in time for an afternoon organ recital. Stroll through beautiful **Kelvingrove Park** on your way to **Ashton Lane**

for dinner and drinks. End your evening listening to some traditional Scottish music at one of the pubs that make up the Teuchters' Triangle—the **Ben Nevis**, **Islay Inn**, or the **Park Bar**—before spending the night at the **Alamo Guest House**.

Take the morning tour of the **University of Glasgow**, then head the **Ubiquitous Chip** for lunch. Afterward, jump on the hop-on hop-off bus from nearby Byres Road and get off at the **Clydeside Distillery**. After sampling Glasgow's single malt, hop back on the bus to the city center for afternoon tea at **Mackintosh at the Willow** and spend some time walking the **City Centre Mural Trail** and wandering around the old **Merchant City**—be sure to pop by the **Gallery of Modern Art** (GOMA) to see the cone-headed Duke of Marlborough. Try dishes from several stalls at the **Platform at Arglye Street Arches** food market for dinner and then check out some live music at **King Tut's Wah Wah Hut**.

From Lochs to Munros: Exploring the Highlands

Whether you want to bag a munro, go kayaking in a loch, spot wildlife, or camp under starry skies, Scotland's topography is tailor-made for adventure.

Day 1: Loch Lomond

Start your tour of the Highlands in **Loch Lomond and the Trossachs National Park**. Rent a kayak from **Loch Lomond Leisure** and spend the morning paddling to **Inchconnachan** and exploring the island, or rent a bike and cycle along the **West Loch Lomond Cycle Path**. Back in Luss, stop into **The Village Rest** for lunch, and then drive to the **Falls of Falloch** in the northern end of the park. If you're able to brave the cold, slip into the pools beneath the crashing waterfall for some **wild swimming**. The nearby **Drover's Inn** is a great place to have dinner and spend the night.

Day 2: Glencoe Road and Fort William

After breakfast, drive to **Fort William**, the outdoor capital of the UK, via Glencoe. The drive, though all on a main road, is not to be sniffed at; the road curves and twists up steep passes and along the edge of gut-wrenching gorges. Before you enter Glencoe itself, stop for lunch at the **Bridge of Orchy** and sit by the fireside for a traditional meal of Scottish beef with neeps and tatties. You'll need filling up for your afternoon expedition with **Vertical Descents**, which will take you **gorge-walking** in Fort William, where you'll slide down natural water flumes and take a dunk in icy pools. Book in for a night of pampered luxury at **Inverlochy Castle**, and get ready for some serious adventuring in the morning.

Scotland's Cleared Villages

Few experiences can be more moving than walking through forgotten townships in some of Scotland's most remote corners. Often these settlements were abandoned when inhabitants sought to start lives elsewhere on faraway shores, but more often entire populations were forcibly evicted—never to return—from ancestral lands by greedy landlords during the Highland Clearances of the 18th and 19th centuries.

BORERAIG, SKYE

In central Skye, about a third of the way down the Broadford to Elgol road, you can start a walk up through farmland over a hill to this village on the edge of a loch. In this once-busy township, long deserted, the walls of many houses remain.

HALLAIG, RAASAY

Raasay-born poet Sorley MacLean wrote powerfully about the lost people of Hallaig, forced from their homes when a new chief by the name of Rainy took ownership of their isle.

PEANMEANACH

With beautiful views out to the Small Isles, this abandoned village, situated above a sandy beach, is a lovely spot to visit. Depopulation began here in

the walk to the cleared village of Boreraig

the mid-18th century with the emigration of many families to Canada and America. Though more people were forced out during the Highland Clearances, some clung on to their homes until as late as the 1940s.

Day 3: Ben Nevis

Today is the day you will ascend Britain's highest mountain (and Scotland's loftiest munro), **Ben Nevis**. You can opt to do the **Pony Track** on your own if you are a competent hillwalker, or you can choose a tour guide, such as **Adventure Nevis**. The trek there and back, which is relentlessly uphill and involves some scrambling as well as navigating scree and boulders, should take 7-9 hours. After that, you'll be fully deserving of a hearty meal at the **Ben Nevis Inn**, followed by a very long soak in the bath back at the hotel.

Days 4-5: Isle of Skye

After a good night's sleep, set off early to **Mallaig,** where you will take the 30-minute ferry crossing to **Armadale** in south **Skye**. Book an excursion with **Skye Jeep Tours**, which will take you to some of the lesser-known spots on the Misty Isle before dropping you off at a beautiful location for some **wild camping** in a military pod, so you can make the most of the clear night skies.

After a night under the stars, head to the pretty port town of **Portree** for a good breakfast at **Café Arriba** and to stock up on any provisions. Stewart of **Skye High Wildlife** will pick you up from here and take you deep into the island for **wildlife spotting** (golden eagles and otters) and a photography lesson. Lunch will be taken in an out-of-the-way bothy (a small hut or cabin), where

Bella Jane runs boat trips to Loch Coruisk and the Small Isles

you can indulge in a **whisky tasting session**. End your day with some whisky-infused mussels at the **Red Skye Inn** near Broadford and spend a cozy night at **10 Torrin,** an old crofter's cottage.

Day 6: Eigg

In the morning, grab breakfast at the **Blue Shed Cafe** and drive to Elgol to catch a ride with **Bella Jane Boat Trips** to **Eigg**, one of the Small Isles. Spend the ride looking for wildlife. Once on Eigg, hike **An Sgurr** (3-4 hours) or book a kayaking trip or guided walk with **Eigg Adventures**. Head back to Skye in the late afternoon, or if you want to extend your trip on idyllic Eigg, you can stay for a couple of nights at **Sweeney's Bothy**.

Edinburgh

"Edina! Scotia's darling seat! All hail thy palaces and towers," declared Robert Burns, in his 18th-century *Address to Edinburgh.*

Today, millions of travelers descend on the medieval city of Edinburgh to see the very same noble buildings that so enraptured Scotland's most celebrated poet. They walk the historic Royal Mile at the center of the city's Old Town, beginning at Edinburgh Castle as it looks protectively over the metropolis from its ancient volcanic seat, before following it as it slopes down through the oldest part of the city all the way to the Palace of Holyroodhouse, the Queen's official home in Edinburgh.

But, while the history of the Old Town is fascinating, the allure of

Highlights

Look for ★ to find recommended sights, activities, dining, and lodging.

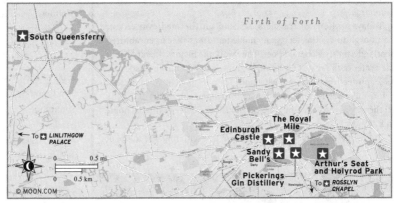

★ **Edinburgh Castle:** Perched high above the city, this iconic fortress—the most besieged castle in Britain—has stood to protect the city of Edinburgh for 900 years (page 42).

★ **The Royal Mile:** The epicenter of the Old Town, this thoroughfare is home to some of the city's most historic buildings as well as a network of intriguing closes that tell another side to the city's story (page 47).

★ **Arthur's Seat and Holyrood Park:** Hike this ancient volcano, the summit of a group of hills to the east of the city center, for panoramic views and a calm retreat from city life (page 54).

★ **Pickering's Gin Distillery:** This tiny distillery in Summerhall, one of the city's coolest cultural spaces, is the place to come to sample Scotland's fastest-growing spirit (page 71).

★ **Hear traditional music at Sandy Bell's:** Squeeze yourself into this busy bar where

there is fantastic folk music every night of the week and a lively, welcoming crowd (page 76).

★ **See side-splitting comedy:** Shows at The Stand are legendary, but festival favorites, such as Gilded Balloon, also have regular nights that will have you laughing out loud (page 84).

★ **South Queensferry:** For dramatic views of the Forth Bridge, this is the place to come—the area is regenerating following the opening of the new Queensferry Crossing in 2017 (page 115).

★ **Linlithgow Palace:** While the interiors of the birthplace of Mary, Queen of Scots, have been ravaged by fire and decay, the medieval walls are remarkably intact (page 119).

★ **Rosslyn Chapel:** Admire the intricate stone masonry of this 15th-century church and decide for yourself if the carvings hide clues from the notoriously secretive Knights Templar (page 123).

the neoclassical "New Town," which is not actually that new, is not to be overlooked. Built between the 18th and 19th centuries to cope with the city's growing population, it is an architectural masterpiece, with grand Georgian squares, avenues, and elegant townhouses. It is also the artistic center of Edinburgh, with three national galleries within strolling distance. It is little wonder that both the Old Town and New Town were classified a World Heritage Site by UNESCO in 1995.

A little further exploration to the northeast will bring you to the foodie hotspot of Leith, while the seaside suburb of Portobello east of Holyrood Park is where locals go to unwind. Meanwhile, pretty Stockbridge, just north of the New Town, and Bruntsfield on the Southside are fashionable urban villages that embrace a more bohemian vibe.

But, while the heritage sites and buzzy neighborhoods are undoubtedly enchanting, it is the city's maze-like closes, secret tunnels, and welcoming howffs (traditional pubs) that really reel you in. And perhaps most spellbinding of all, Edinburgh's gloomy beauty is contradicted by its jovial atmosphere and the friendliness of its people, who will charm you with their self-deprecating and disarming humor and make you feel much like Charles Dickens did, who famously said: "Coming back to Edinburgh is to me like coming home."

HISTORY

While people have lived around modern-day Edinburgh for millennia—evidence shows human habitation as long ago as 8,500 BC—it was the introduction of a hill fort in the early Middle Ages (presumably where Edinburgh Castle sits today) that truly established it as a settlement. Indeed, it is from the fort that the city gets its name: Edinburgh comes from Dunedin or Din Eidyn (fort of Eidyn). The "burgh" part came during the reign of King David I in the 12th century, who built burghs

(chartered towns) around some of Scotland's most significant castles. It was during David I's reign that there was first mention of the castle.

Both the castle's strategic location and its role as a royal seat for Scotland's kings and queens led to it being ransacked many times throughout its history, as English monarchs fought with Scottish armies for control over it. King of Scots Robert the Bruce ordered the castle's destruction shortly after reclaiming it from the English in 1314, and, though the castle was rebuilt, it suffered subsequent attacks right up until the English Civil War in the 17th century and the Jacobite rebellions of the 18th century.

The 16th century was marred by a period of huge religious conflict between Catholics and Protestants across Western Europe, and in Scotland, where the church was an integral part of everyday life, this was no exception. At the beginning of the century, Scotland was resolutely Catholic, but, with English King Henry VIII having converted to Protestantism, it was only a matter of time before he pushed these values on his neighbors north of the border.

In 1544, an attack on Edinburgh was the first in a series of assaults on Scotland by the English in an attempt to unite the two nations through the marriage of Henry's son, Prince Edward, and the infant queen, Mary, Queen of Scots. The campaign, known as the "Rough Wooing," was largely unsuccessful, but following the death of his father, King Edward VI continued the attacks on Scotland. Nevertheless, Mary, a Catholic, resisted and married Francis the Dauphin of France (himself a Catholic) and retreated to France.

However, the march toward Protestantism across Scotland and England proved unstoppable when Queen Elizabeth I came to the throne in 1558, giving reformers such as John Knox renewed confidence, and by 1560 the Scottish Reformation was complete:

Previous: view over Edinburgh from Calton Hill; Edinburgh Castle; The Royal Mile

Edinburgh

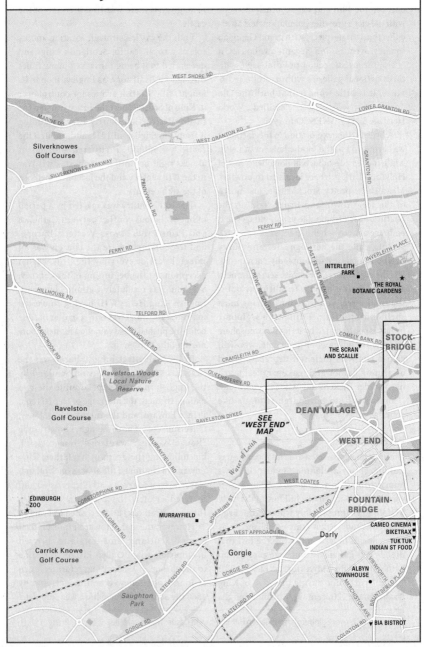

Silverknowes
Golf Course

WEST SHORE RD

MARINE DR

LOWER GRANTON RD

WEST GRANTON RD

SILVERKNOWES PARKWAY

PENNYWELL RD

GRANTON RD

FERRY RD

FERRY RD

CREWE RD SOUTH

EAST FETTES AVENUE

INVERLEITH PLACE

INTERLEITH
PARK

★ THE ROYAL
BOTANIC GARDENS

HILLHOUSE RD

TELFORD RD

HILLHOUSE RD

CRAIGCROOK RD

COMELY BANK RD

STOCK-
BRIDGE

CRAIGLEITH RD

THE SCRAN
AND SCALLIE ▾

QUEENSFERRY RD

Ravelston Woods
Local Nature
Reserve

RAVELSTON DYKES

DEAN VILLAGE

SEE
"WEST END"
MAP

Ravelston
Golf Course

MURRAYFIELD RD

Water of Leith

WEST END

EDINBURGH
ZOO ★

CORSTORPHINE RD

WEST COATES

BALGREEN RD

MURRAYFIELD ■

ROSEBURN ST

DALRY RD

FOUNTAIN-
BRIDGE

Carrick Knowe
Golf Course

WEST APPROACH RD

Darly

CAMEO CINEMA ■
BIKETRAX ■

TUK TUK ▾
INDIAN ST FOOD

STEVENSON RD

Gorgie

GORGIE RD

ALBYN
TOWNHOUSE ●

VIEWFORTH

MERCHISTON AVE

BRUNTSFIELD PLACE

Saughton
Park

SLATEFORD RD

GORGIE RD

COLINTON RD

▾ BIA BISTROT

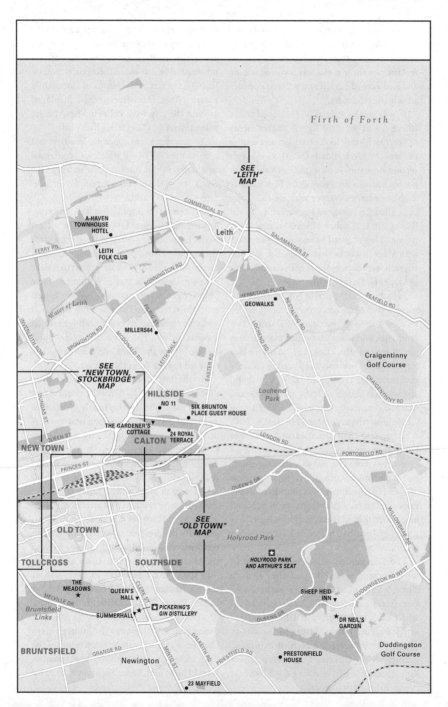

Scotland was a Protestant country, and more specifically, Presbyterian. By the time Mary returned into Leith, Edinburgh, in 1561 to reclaim her throne, she was a young widow and had earned herself some fierce enemies among the reformers.

It was at the Palace of Holyroodhouse where one of the most significant moments in Scottish history took place. On an evening in March 1566, Lord Darnley—Mary's second husband—and a gang of Protestant nobles burst in on the queen's bedchamber as she was having supper with a close group of confidantes, dragged her secretary David Rizzio out, and stabbed him 56 times. Their reason? They claimed he was having an affair with Mary in a bid to have influence over the court. It was the beginning of the unravelling of Mary and Darnley's marriage.

In truth, it was the Earl of Bothwell to whom many feared Mary was growing too close. He was implicated in the death of Darnley two years later, and when Mary then married him just three months after that, many nobles turned against her. She was forced to abdicate in favor of her young son, James VI, whom, after she was imprisoned, she never saw again. Mary was eventually executed at Fotheringhay Castle in Northamptonshire, England, in 1587. A century and a half later, it was at the Palace of Holyroodhouse that Bonnie Prince Charlie set up court as part of his bid to restore the Stuart line to the throne during the Jacobite Rebellion of 1745. His tenure there was short-lived, as the prince and his Jacobites left on their ill-fated and long march toward London, though legend has it not before he had hosted at least one lavish and victorious ball.

The 17th century saw the city mired in what became referred to as the "Killing Time." Thousands of Scots gathered in Greyfriars Kirkyard and made a covenant with God to take up arms in defiance against anyone accused of meddling in the affairs of the Presbyterian Church of Scotland, (namely King Charles I and later Stuart kings), resulting in some of the bloodiest events in Scottish history.

It was in the small Magdalen Chapel in the city's Cowgate that the bodies of many executed "Covenanters" as they were called, were returned to be dressed in their burial clothes. In 1689, the heads and hands of Covenanter martyrs that executioners had displayed around the city were collected here before being interred in Greyfriars Kirkyard.

At this time, most people lived in and around the Old Town, which was contained by a wall on three sides and the waters of the Nor Loch to the north, where today Princes Street Gardens stand.

But the city's population was growing. Towering tenements—the world's first high-rise housing—were built to cope with the rapidly rising population. By the end of the 17th century, some properties were nine stories high or more. Without suitable plumbing, sewage was often simply tossed onto the streets, and smoke from the wood and coal fires used to heat buildings created a dense smog. (The city's nickname "Auld Reekie" from the Scots word for smoke is believed to stem from this period.)

By the 18th century, the overcrowding problem was dire. By 1766 the council had bought farmland to the north of the Old Town and invited designs for a new town. A little-known architect by the name of James Craig won and began the mammoth task of designing the Georgian squares and streets that you still see today, such as well-heeled Ann Street in Stockbridge, today one of the most exclusive residential streets in Britain.

The New Town, as it became known, was generally the preserve of wealthy Edinburgh residents who could afford to leave behind the tenements of the Old Town and move into the grand residences in the north of the city. It soon became a meeting place for leading figures of the Scottish Enlightenment. Scottish poet and author Tobias Smollett described 18th-century Edinburgh as a "hotbed of genius" as the greatest minds of the time, including philosophers and economists David Hume and Adam Smith, met to share ideas.

Today, Edinburgh is still considered a center of intellectual and cultural excellence, home to one of the oldest universities in the English-speaking world as well as some of Scotland's best museums and art galleries.

Since 1947, it has also been the scene of one of the world's most exciting artistic extravaganzas, thanks to the endless fusion of events that make up the annual Edinburgh Festival each August.

ORIENTATION

The city center has two distinct areas: the Old Town and the New Town, once divided by Nor Loch. Though the loch is long gone, **Princes Street Gardens,** which stands in its place, acts as a boundary. To the north of the gardens, Princes Street, which runs east to west, marks the start of the **New Town:** look south from here and you'll be afforded striking vistas of the castle. To the south of the gardens, reached by passing over The Mound or Waverley Bridge, Market Street and the twisting roads, lanes, and steep steps that lead up to the Royal Mile form the entry point to the **Old Town.** Staying true to its medieval street plan, this oldest part of the city, includes the **Royal Mile, Canongate,** and the **Grassmarket,** all the way to Chambers Street in the south, home to the **National Museum of Scotland.**

Old Town

Most visitors make a beeline to the Royal Mile in the heart of the Old Town and for good reason. The bagpipes, tartan shops, and frisson of activity of this main drag are cornerstones of a visit here. At one end is the iconic **Edinburgh Castle,** Scotland's most visited attraction for which you need to pay; at the other end is the **Palace of Holyroodhouse,** an official residence of Her Majesty The Queen.

New Town

From the Old Town, a 10-minute walk north across Waverley Bridge or The Mound will bring you to the Georgian splendor of the New Town. Here you can see the towering **Gothic Scott Monument** up close, admire the exquisite design of **Charlotte Square,** and take in some culture at one of three world-class galleries (the Scottish National Gallery is on The Mound itself). **Broughton Street** in the northeast of the New Town is home to independent shops and also some of the city's best gay bars. More central are **Rose Street,** a narrow road running behind Princes Street that is renowned for its plethora of bars and restaurants, and, just behind it, **George Street** one of the city's more salubrious shopping areas, which is also popular after dark with well-dressed party-goers.

West End

The West End, which starts just past the western fringes of Princes Street Gardens where Princes Street meets Lothian Road, offers a quiet oasis from the bustle of city life. The dark stone buildings of this part of town, once a mix of dwellings and tailors' workshops, have latterly been home to offices and work places. However, with a smattering of boutiques, cafés, and bars, it's becoming a destination worth walking a few blocks west for. There's a lot of history here too: a short walk amid its neatly compact streets will bring you past the home of leading Suffragette Elsie Inglis (8 Walker Street), while at no. 2 Melville Crescent there is a plaque to former resident Joseph Bell, the physician whom Arthur Conan Doyle credited as having inspired his famous detective, Sherlock Holmes.

Farther west is the crossroads of **Haymarket,** most notable for its superb transport connections, including the Haymarket railway station, plus trams and bus routes. It's just about walking distance to the city center (20 minutes), and its proximity to the **Murrayfield Stadium** as well as the **Scottish National Gallery of Modern Art** and **Dean Village** make it a smart choice for travelers looking for less hefty hotel prices.

Stockbridge

Stockbridge is fast becoming the cool

neighborhood where Edinburgh natives—sometimes referred to as Dunedians after the city's old name, or the slightly less appealing Edinburghers, though there's a good chance neither term will be well received—retreat when they've had enough of Scottish clichés. With gastropubs and cafés and more sophisticated antiques shops replacing the former junk shops, it's been subject to gentrification in recent years, but it still retains a village-like atmosphere and a laid-back feel.

Southside

From Chambers Street south, you are in what is known as Edinburgh's Southside, which is largely a student area but none the less pleasant for it, with a string of attractive Victorian villas and tenement buildings. Historically, this area was the city's first suburb for the better-off residents—past inhabitants include Sir Walter Scott—and on the western side of George Square you'll find Georgian terraces that pre-date the New Town. Today, most visitors come to the neighboring districts of **Bruntsfield** and Morningside. The former is a low-key area, home to lots of well-priced restaurants and quirky gift shops as well as a generous offering of cafés. Just south of Bruntsfield, **Morningside** continues the theme but is slightly more affluent and is home to a number of quirky sites, including the **Bore Stone**—a rather nondescript stone memorial that marks the spot from where King James IV led his army to the infamous Battle of Flodden.

Leith

A short bus ride northeast of the city center will bring you to the historic Port of Leith where Mary, Queen of Scots, arrived back from her exile in France to stake her claim on the throne. Today it is a real foodie destination, with lots of good seafood restaurants and cafés lining the waterfront. It is also home to the **Royal Yacht Britannia**.

PLANNING YOUR TIME

Edinburgh isn't huge, and many of the real tourist draws can be explored on foot, including the countless closes and wynds (alleyways just wide enough to allow a horse and cart to wind their way through) that lead off from the Royal Mile and other parts of the Old Town.

Allow a full day to explore the attractions along the **Royal Mile** properly (more if you are venturing up to **Arthur's Seat** too). However, tourism is becoming a bit of a problem in the city center, and, as the Royal Mile becomes saturated with visitors, locals complain that it has become something of a theme park, particularly during festival season and Hogmanay (there are plans to further pedestrianize parts of the city).

A good compromise is to spend a day or two seeing the main sights in and around the **Old Town** and along or off **Princes Street** in the New Town before escaping to one of the cooler, less congested neighborhoods for a more authentic taste of Edinburgh life.

If you are planning to visit during Hogmanay (New Year's) or the Edinburgh Festival (most of the month of August), try to book accommodations around six months in advance to secure your top choice. January and February are generally quiet months but also very cold with a good chance of snow. Visitor season picks up from March onward when prices really start to rise, and the season then starts to slow down from September to November.

Popular restaurants such as **The Witchery by the Castle** need booking in advance, and, if you are planning on doing a tour of **The Real Mary King's Close** or one of the more popular ghost tours, then it would be prudent to book a couple of weeks ahead of your visit, particularly if you're coming in high season.

Itinerary Ideas

DAY 1

Spend your first day taking in the sights of the Royal Mile and Old Town.

1 Stop into **Luscious** on Canongate for a quick breakfast.

2 Take an early-morning hike up to **Arthur's Seat in Holyrood Park** (weather depending)—first thing is often the quietest time here and you may even find you have the place to yourself.

3 After your hike, head to the **Palace of Holyroodhouse** at the foot of Holyrood Park to learn about the royal history of Edinburgh, from Mary, Queen of Scots, to Bonnie Prince Charlie.

4 Allow a couple of hours to explore the palace and its grounds fully, and then have lunch or afternoon tea in the **Café at the Palace** in the Mews Courtyard.

5 Enjoy a leisurely stroll past the colorful shop fronts and bustling bars of **Grassmarket and Victoria Street** on your way to Edinburgh Castle.

6 Pay the entry fee to **Edinburgh Castle,** and join one of the free tours to hear tales of bloodshed and bitter rivalries and to view the famous Honours of Scotland and the ancient Stone of Destiny.

7 Have dinner at the legendary **The Witchery by the Castle** restaurant on Castlehill (book well ahead).

8 Round off your evening with a live folk session at **Sandy Bell's** pub.

DAY 2

Spend your second day in the New Town, seeing a different side of the city.

1 Start your morning at the **Scottish National Gallery of Modern Art**—home to Scotland's foremost contemporary art collection (allow 1-2 hours).

2 Wander around and admire the crowning glory of the New Town, **Charlotte Square,** and pop into the **Georgian House** museum to see what life was like in 18th-century Edinburgh.

3 Stop for a burger at **The Cambridge Bar** on Young Street.

4 For an after-lunch tipple, pop into the **Oxford Bar** just a few doors down, where Ian Rankin's famous detective Inspector Rebus regularly goes to mull over his cases.

5 Go to the majestic **Scottish National Portrait Gallery** and peer at some of the most recognizable faces in Scottish history.

6 Have a hearty and well-priced Indian meal at **Dishoom.**

7 Pop in for a drink at the ornate Circle Bar in the **Café Royal.**

8 End your night with a riotous introduction to Scottish humor at **The Stand Comedy Club.**

Edinburgh Itineraries

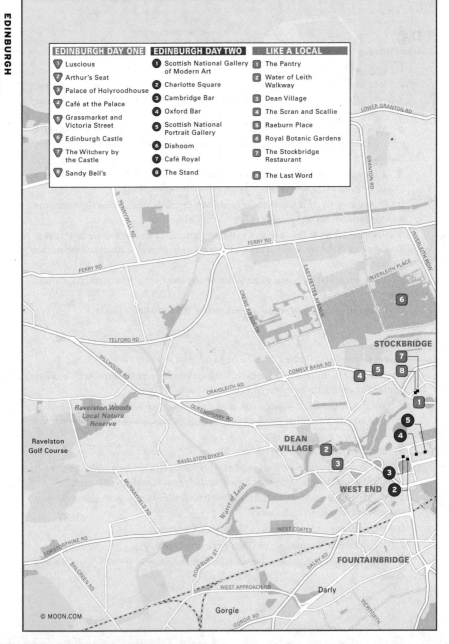

EDINBURGH DAY ONE
1. Luscious
2. Arthur's Seat
3. Palace of Holyroodhouse
4. Café at the Palace
5. Grassmarket and Victoria Street
6. Edinburgh Castle
7. The Witchery by the Castle
8. Sandy Bell's

EDINBURGH DAY TWO
1. Scottish National Gallery of Modern Art
2. Charlotte Square
3. Cambridge Bar
4. Oxford Bar
5. Scottish National Portrait Gallery
6. Dishoom
7. Café Royal
8. The Stand

LIKE A LOCAL
1. The Pantry
2. Water of Leith Walkway
3. Dean Village
4. The Scran and Scallie
5. Raeburn Place
6. Royal Botanic Gardens
7. The Stockbridge Restaurant
8. The Last Word

© MOON.COM

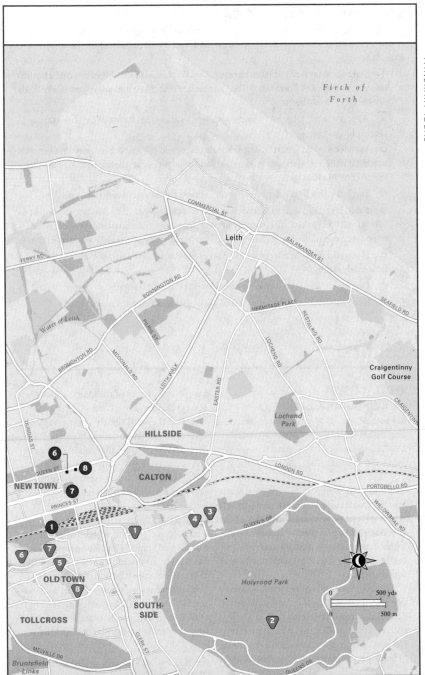

EDINBURGH LIKE A LOCAL

Spend your day in Stockbridge, one of the most fashionable hangouts in the city. Nevertheless, it still has an air of calm that is at odds with the frenetic tourist hubs of the Royal Mile and Princes Street.

1 Start your day lazily at modern bistro **The Pantry** with a waffle or the café's healthier spin on a cooked breakfast: grilled courgettes (zucchini) and sweet potato alongside poached eggs and chorizo.

2 Appetite sated, take the 15-minute walk or so along the **Water of Leith walkway** to Dean Village.

3 Wander around **Dean Village,** a picturesque old milling community that includes tenement buildings alongside grander red sandstone properties, before heading back along the river to Stockbridge.

4 Stop into **The Scran and Scallie** for some excellent and hearty pub grub.

5 Next, it's time for a little shopping, à la **Stockbridge:** if it's Sunday, pay a visit to **Stockbridge Market**. Alternatively browse the quirky, bohemian independent retailers or pop into one of the many charity shops, particularly those around **Raeburn Place.**

6 If you still have the energy and the day is nice, head to the **Royal Botanic Gardens** for a lovely stroll.

7 Finish your day with dinner at **The Stockbridge Restaurant.**

8 Head to **The Last Word** for a drink or two before calling it a night.

Sights

OLD TOWN
★ Edinburgh Castle

Castlehill; tel. 0131 225 9846; www.edinburghcastle. scot; 9:30am-6pm daily April.-Sept.; 9:30am-5pm daily Oct.-Mar.; adult £18.50 at gate/£17 in advance, child £11.50 at gate/£10.20 in advance, concessions £15/£13.60

Its position high atop an old craggy volcano assures that Scotland's most recognizable landmark can be seen from all parts of the city. But while it provides backdrops to many a photo and selfie, you really must pass the castle walls to get to grips with this icon of Scottish history.

Edinburgh Castle is by far Scotland's most celebrated attraction. Its stone walls guard Scotland's crown jewels, as well as the legendary Stone of Destiny, which for centuries was used in the coronation ceremonies of Scotland's monarchs. It is also the location

for the daily firing of the One O'Clock Gun (except Sundays).

Inside the walls there's a vast complex of historic buildings, including the city's oldest, St. Margaret's Chapel, interconnected by a series of batteries; you really need to give yourself at least two hours to explore it fully. Last entry is an hour before closing.

HISTORY

The volcanic rock on which the castle sits was formed some 340 million years ago and has been home to a hill fort for the past 2,000 years. Here embattled kings and queens of Scotland have sought refuge, while marauding forces under the leadership of Edward I, Oliver Cromwell, and Robert the Bruce have fought to snatch it back from enemy hands,

1: Edinburgh Castle from Grassmarket 2: The Royal Mile

Old Town

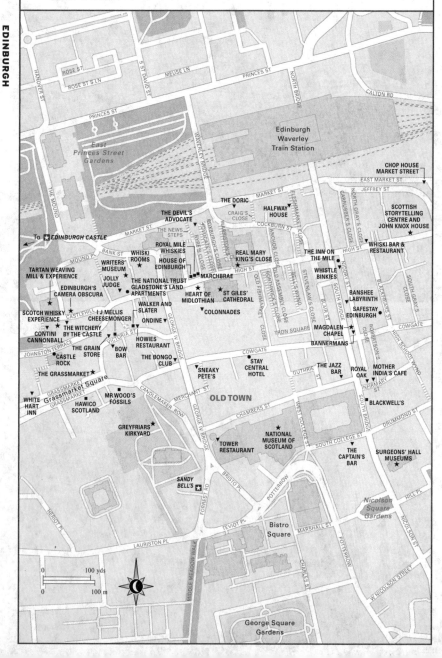

ROSE ST
ROSE ST S LN
HANOVER ST
S ST DAVID ST
MEUSE LN
PRINCES ST
NORTH BRIDGE
CALTON RD

PRINCES ST

East
Princes Street
Gardens

Edinburgh
Waverley
Train Station

THE MOUND

CHOP HOUSE
MARKET STREET

EAST MARKET ST
JEFFREY ST

MARKET ST
THE DORIC
CRAIG'S CLOSE
HALFWAY HOUSE

SCOTTISH
STORYTELLING
CENTRE AND
JOHN KNOX HOUSE

To ☐ EDINBURGH CASTLE

MARKET ST
THE DEVIL'S
ADVOCATE
THE NEWS STEPS

COCKBURN ST
FLESHMARKET CLOSE
CARRUBBER'S CLOSE
NORTH GRAY'S CLOSE
HIGH ST

WHISKI BAR &
RESTAURANT

BANK ST
MOUND PL
ROYAL MILE
WHISKIES
ROXBURGH'S CLOSE
ADVOCATE'S CLOSE
BYRE'S CLOSE
WARISTON'S CLOSE
ANCHOR CLOSE
OLD ASSEMBLY CLOSE

REAL MARY
KING'S CLOSE

THE INN ON
THE MILE

WHISTLE
BINKIES

TARTAN WEAVING
MILL & EXPERIENCE
WRITERS'
MUSEUM
WHISKI
ROOMS
HOUSE OF
EDINBURGH
MARCHBRAE
HIGH ST
OLD FISHMARKET CLOSE
BORTHWICK'S CLOSE
FISHMARKET CLOSE
STEVENLAW'S CLOSE
NIDDRY ST
SOUTH BRIDGE
BANSHEE
LABYRINTH

EDINBURGH'S
CAMERA OBSCURA
JOLLY
JUDGE
THE NATIONAL TRUST
GLADSTONE'S LAND
APARTMENTS
HEART OF
MIDLOTHIAN
ST GILES'
CATHEDRAL
BLACKFRIARS ST
SOUTH GRAY'S

SAFESTAY
EDINBURGH

SCOTCH WHISKY
EXPERIENCE
CASTLEHILL
I J MELLIS
CHEESEMONGER
WALKER AND
SLATER
COLONNADES
TRON SQUARE
BLAIR ST
COWGATE

ROBERTSON'S CLOSE
HIGH SCHOOL WYND

CONTINI
CANNONBALL
THE WITCHERY
BY THE CASTLE
ONDINE
MAGDALEN
CHAPEL
BANNERMANS

JOHNSTON TERRACE
THE GRAIN
STORE
VICTORIA ST
BOW
BAR
HOWIES
RESTAURANT
GEORGE IV BRIDGE

CASTLE
ROCK
THE BONGO
CLUB
COWGATE
STAY
CENTRAL
HOTEL
GUTHRIE
THE JAZZ
BAR
ROYAL
OAK
MOTHER
INDIA'S CAFE

THE GRASSMARKET
GRASSMARKET
SNEAKY
PETE'S
MERCHANT ST
INFIRMARY ST
SOUTH BRIDGE

WHITE
HART
INN
Grassmarket Square
GRASSMARKET
MR WOOD'S
FOSSILS
OLD TOWN
CHAMBERS ST
BLACKWELL'S
DRUMMOND ST

HAWICO
SCOTLAND
CANDLEMAKER ROW

GREYFRIARS
KIRKYARD
GEORGE IV BRIDGE
NATIONAL
MUSEUM OF
SCOTLAND
WEST COLLEGE ST
SOUTH COLLEGE ST

TOWER
RESTAURANT
THE
CAPTAIN'S
BAR
SURGEONS' HALL
MUSEUMS

SANDY
BELL'S
FOREST RD
BRISTO PL
POTTERROW
Nicolson
Square
Gardens
HILL PL
NICOLSON ST

HERIOT PL
Bistro
Square
TEVIOT PL
MARSHALL ST
POTTERROW
CHARLES ST
W NICOLSON STREET

LAURISTON PL
MIDDLE MEADOW WALK

0   100 yds
0   100 m

George Square
Gardens

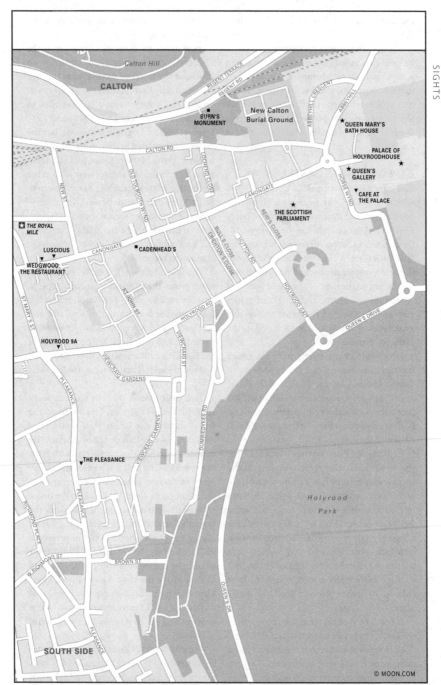

© MOON.COM

making it the most besieged castle in all of Britain.

Throughout its 900-year history the castle has served a variety of purposes: It has been a royal palace, an arsenal, a gun foundry, infantry barracks, and even a prison. Today it is still garrisoned, though this is largely for administrative purposes or to deliver the ceremonial pomp for which the castle is known.

EXPLORING THE CASTLE

You can pay for an audio guide (£3.50), which gives useful background on the history and architecture of the castle but is a tad dry. Alternatively, tag along on one of the free tours that set off from just inside the Portcullis Gate. A clock indicates the time of the next tour (usually around every half hour, depending on the time of year), and tours last 30-45 minutes. Funny and insightful guides give an overview of the most impressive aspects before allowing visitors to explore the castle for themselves.

Inside the castle itself there are many treasures to discover, not least the Scottish Crown Jewels, plus the **Stone of Destiny,** which kings of Scotland stood upon for centuries during their coronation ceremony. Both are housed on the first floor of the Royal Palace, to the east of Crown Square.

Esplanade: Pause on the esplanade before you enter the castle, where each August the spectacular Edinburgh Tattoo, a showcase of military ceremony, takes place. Laid out in 1753 as a place for troops to parade, some 200 years earlier this very area was used for altogether darker purposes. Between the 15th and 18th centuries, over 300 women were burned at the stake here—indeed in the 16th century more women were murdered here than in any other place in Scotland. Their crime? Witchcraft.

A small relic of this iniquitous episode in the castle's past can be seen in the **Witches' Well,** a small fountain that remembers those poor women who were tortured and killed. So discreet many miss it, the fountain is on the southeastern castle wall, just outside the Tartan Weaving Mill.

Scottish Crown Jewels: Dating from the 15th and 16th centuries, the Scottish Crown Jewels, or **Honours of Scotland** as they are more correctly known, comprise a scepter and sword, which were papal gifts presented to King James IV of Scotland in 1494 and 1507, respectively. Its origin is unknown, but the crown was first used in the coronation of King James V's wife Mary of Guise in 1540; three years later, it and the scepter were used at the coronation of their daughter Mary, Queen of Scots. Mary didn't actually wear the crown—aged just nine months when she was crowned, it was much too big for the infant queen, who by all accounts screamed her way through the coronation ceremony.

The Scottish Crown Jewels are composed of fewer pieces than their British counterparts, but they are a lot older. They became obsolete following the unification of England and Scotland in 1707 when the Crown Jewels of the United Kingdom—which had been remade in the late 17th century after Oliver Cromwell destroyed the originals—were used in their place.

The Great Hall: With its hammerbeam roof, just across Crown Square from the Royal Palace, the Great Hall is a feat of medieval majesty that once hosted elaborate banquets, but the oldest part of the castle is **St. Margaret's Chapel,** just a short walk away near Foog's Gate. When his forces recaptured the medieval castle in 1314, Robert the Bruce ordered its destruction (perhaps to deter the English from trying to reclaim it), but he spared the chapel, perhaps out of reverence to Queen Margaret, mother of David I, for whom the chapel was constructed around 1130. Outside the chapel you can see Mons Meg, a 15th-century bombard (cannon) that was fired to mark the wedding of Mary, Queen of Scots, and her first husband, the Dauphin of France.

Argyll Battery: Central to any visit should be witnessing the firing of the **One O'Clock gun,** a tradition that dates back to 1861 when it helped ships entering the Firth of Forth to set their chronometers, although you should still be able to hear it throughout the city. The firing takes place at 1pm at the Mills Mount Battery every day except Sundays, Christmas Day, and Good Friday.

Crown Square: Also worth a visit is the **Scottish National War Memorial,** opposite the Great Hall on the north side of Crown Square. It is an elaborate commemoration of the dead of both world wars, as well as remembering those who have died on military campaigns since 1945. Built in the 1920s on the highest point of the castle rock—the site of a former church and munitions store— the architectural detail (including beautiful stained glass and complex stone sculptures depicting symbols of peace, courage, and justice) shows a real respect for the men and women who lost their lives for Scotland. Inside, the Rolls of Honour contains the names of individual casualties, and the website that accompanies it (www.snwm. org/roll-search) is a good resource for people researching Scottish ancestry.

Grounds: As you walk around the castle grounds, look for carvings showing the rose and thistle, which celebrate the marriage of King James IV of Scotland (the thistle) and Princess Margaret Tudor of England (the rose—Margaret was Henry VIII's sister) in 1503 that was supposed to signify a reconciliation between the kingdoms of Scotland and England. In truth it didn't work, and warfare between the two nations continued.

TIPS

If you want to avoid the crowds at the castle, try to visit during the week and aim for morning (9:30am-10am) or later in the afternoon (just before last entry time—5pm in summer, 4pm in winter). Although, if you do come later in the day, you may find yourself a bit rushed to take everything in.

Whenever you plan to come, book your ticket in advance because not only will this save you money, but you will also save time queuing on arrival—at peak times it can take up to an hour to buy a ticket on the gate.

★ The Royal Mile
Castlehill, Lawnmarket, the High Street, Canongate, and Abbey Strand

This mile-long thoroughfare, made up of a series of streets that lead on to one another, runs all the way west to east from Edinburgh Castle to the Palace of Holyroodhouse; although, strictly speaking, it is a Scots mile, which is slightly over an English mile (by around 107 yards/98 meters).

There's no need to book a tour of the Royal Mile—it's easy to do on foot with a guidebook in hand. You can do the route from the castle to the palace or vice versa. Here I have chosen the former option.

It's an easy walk that should take no more than 20 minutes, but allow one to two hours if you want to stop by some of the historic attractions en route or pop into one of the many shops.

From the castle esplanade, descend down **Castlehill** past the **Scotch Whisky Experience** on your right and the **Camera Obscura** on your left. It is rather overrun with tourists here at most times of the day, and Scottish stereotypes are brashly displayed in the form of William Wallace caricatures and kilted bagpipers.

As you enter the **Lawnmarket** section, the crowds dissipate (ever so slightly) and you may be able to spot a plaque on the wall, near the entrance to Lady Stair's Close, on the left-hand side of the street, by **Gladstone's Land** (the best surviving 17th-century tenement building in Edinburgh). The **plaque** marks the site of a house in which Robert Burns lived for a period in 1786. Though the close in which the house once stood has long since been demolished, the plaque remembers the poet's connection to the city.

This section of the Royal Mile is integral to the growth of the city for it was to here in 1128 that King David I began granting trading rights for the supply of goods to the noblemen and soldiers based on the hill fort (the castle came later). David also set out the High Street, which was known as Via Regis (Way of the King) and so began the evolution of this once dormant volcano into a royal burgh.

Just east of Lawnmarket is the High Street where you will find **St. Giles' Cathedral,** founded during the reign of David I. With its distinct crown steeple, it is one of the most recognizable sights on the city's skyline, but it is perhaps best known for being home to the Order of the Thistle, Scotland's greatest order of chivalry. Here too you will find some good retailers (such as Marchbrae Clothing) in between the hackneyed souvenir shops.

As you head east, you'll reach **St. Mary's Street,** which once formed the border with Canongate, a separate burgh until 1856. **Canongate** takes you down all the way to the **Scottish Parliament** building before you eventually reach the **Palace of Holyroodhouse** on Abbey Strand.

Scotch Whisky Experience

354 Castlehill; tel. 0131 220 0441; www. scotchwhiskyexperience.co.uk; 10am-5pm daily Sept.-Mar., 10am-6pm daily Apr.-Jul., 10am-5pm daily Aug. (open until 5:40pm on weekends in Aug.); Silver Tour £15.50, Gold Tour £27, Morning Masterclass £40

Gin may be the spirit of the moment (some say rum will be next), but for many visitors a trip to Scotland wouldn't be complete without a few drams of the water of life, and this visitor attraction handily sited on the Royal Mile is only too happy to make full use of the fact. It is a bit of a tourist trap, it's true, but it's also a very fun way to spend a few hours and you're bound to walk away a bit more knowledgeable and perhaps a tad squiffy.

Part museum and part tasting room, all visitors must join a tour, most of which start aboard a bizarre but totally absorbing barrel ride that takes you on a visual journey through the history of Scotch and how it is made. With psychedelic imagery and strange sound effects, it's about as far removed from the slightly staid view many people have of whisky as it's possible to be.

There are several tour options. The 50-minute Silver Tour (£15.50) available all day every day promises to turn you into a one-hour whisky expert. However, I recommend paying an extra £11.50 to upgrade to a Gold Tour, which includes a chance to compare Scottish single malts from four of the five regions you'll learn about—The Highlands, The Lowlands, Islay, Campbeltown, and Speyside. The Taste of Scotland (£73) combines both an in-depth whisky tasting with a meal in the **Amber Restaurant,** where the food is so-so.

For whisky fans who have more than a passing interest (and a bit of prior knowledge), the Morning Masterclass (£40) is a chance to test your knowledge and maybe learn a new thing or two. It lasts just 90 minutes (no barrel ride on this tour) and starts with a viewing of the world's largest Scotch collection over tea and shortbread (visitors on other tours just have a brief visit). It also includes a comparative tasting of one blend, one single grain, and two single malt whiskies (from different distilleries) as well as a sensory test and a nosing of a new-make spirit.

Edinburgh's Camera Obscura

549 Castlehill; tel. 0131 226 3709; www. camera-obscura.co.uk; 9am-10pm daily Jul.-Aug., 9:30am-8pm daily Sept.-Oct., 10am-7pm daily Nov.-Mar., 9:30am-8pm daily Apr.-Jun.; adult £15.50, child (5-15) £11.50, under fives free

The city's oldest purpose-built visitor attraction is one of its biggest surprises 150 years on. Once you've trekked round the interesting but slightly morose castle and seen the cast-iron Witches' Well, this world of illusions offers some light relief.

The attraction was opened in the 1850s by the mysterious Maria Short, who arrived in the city from the West Indies in 1827 and claimed to be the daughter of the late Thomas Short, who had built the city's first public observatory on Calton Hill.

Maria inherited her supposed father's Great Telescope and opened a new observatory near his defunct one on Calton Hill. Soon after, she added Edinburgh's first major attraction, the Camera Obscura. Powered by just daylight, the part periscope and part pinhole camera enabled visitors to see moving images for the first time. Though simple by today's standards, for the Victorians, the Camera Obscura was quite literally like nothing they had ever seen before.

Unfortunately, Maria was forced to close the original building in 1849, but, undeterred, she relocated to a 17th-century tenement building on the Royal Mile, where she added two floors to give visitors some of the best views in Edinburgh.

Today there is lots more to see in the building besides the Camera Obscura. **The World of Illusions** with its maze of mirrors and bedazzling Bewilderworld is a great place for the whole family to enjoy. It's hard to keep a straight face as you walk through the spinning multicolored tunnel called The Vortex trying desperately not to fall over, and kids will love shrinking their parents in the Ames Room. Perhaps the biggest highlight though is the view from the rooftop, which very well might still offer the best panoramas in the whole of Edinburgh—you can even visit after dark.

Tickets are valid all day, which is great for families who may need to take an emergency food break or simply break the excitement up for the kids.

Tartan Weaving Mill and Experience

555 Castlehill; 0131 220 2477; shop 9am-6pm daily, demos 9am-4pm daily; free

If you want to see the work that goes into making the tartan that is omnipresent on the Royal Mile, then this free museum is worth half an hour of your time. Inside you will find working looms, and you can even get kitted out in full Highland dress and have your picture taken. It might be a bit naff for some, but for others it will be a fun and informative visit. There are also lots of wares for sale in the shop.

Gladstone's Land

477B Lawnmarket, Royal Mile; tel. 0131 226 5856; www.nts.org.uk/visit/places/gladstones-land; 10:30am-4pm Mon.-Tues., 12:30pm-4pm Weds., 10:30am-3pm Thurs., 10:30am-2pm Fri., 10:30am-3:30pm Sat., 11:30am-4pm Sun.; tour adult £7, child £5

For a sense of what the Royal Mile was like in medieval times, Gladstone's Land, one of its oldest buildings, is a good place to start. Built in 1550 and extended the following century, it is one of the few old tenement houses to remain and offers insight into the cramped conditions people (albeit of a slightly higher class) in Edinburgh lived in before the New Town was built.

Once owned by a merchant by the name of Thomas Gladstone, who extended the tall building to attract wealthy tenants, Gladstone's Land is notable for its opulent interiors that include incredible hand-painted Renaissance ceiling panels rich in symbolism. However, while it was more luxurious than most, the property was still subject to the same limitations of 16th- and 17th-century society: lack of running water, open fires for heat, and glass-less windows.

Most members of society in 17th-century Scotland hunted with birds, and, between noon and 4pm every day, handlers set up outside Gladstone's Land with birds of prey that you can hold for a donation (£4).

Entry is by guided tour only (about one hour) and must be booked in advance, either by phone or at the venue.

Real Mary King's Close

2 Warriston's Close, off the Royal Mile; tel. 0131 225 0672; www.realmaryskingsclose.com; 10am-9pm daily Apr.-Oct., 9am-5:30pm Mon.-Thurs., 9:30am-9pm Fri.-Sat., 9:30am-6:30pm Sun. Nov., 10am-5pm Sun.-Thurs., 10am-9pm Fri.-Sat. Dec.-Mar.; adult £15.50, child £9.50, family £42.50

This labyrinth of medieval underground streets and homes offers a slice of social history and tells the stories of real 17th-century residents, including Mary King, a local merchant burgess.

What remains of the close (a residential area that historically could be locked up at night to keep undesirables out) stays true to its origins. The narrow lanes are much as they were when they were surrounded by tenement buildings as the city's population swelled in the 17th century.

Prior to Mary King's time, Mary, Queen of Scots, is said to have spent a night in Stuart's Close, at the top of the warren of lanes, in 1567 following her abdication. A plaque nearby at the entrance to The Quadrant of the City Chamber marks the evening the disgraced queen spent here in a state of some distress before being taken to the Palace of Holyroodhouse the next night.

In 1644 the close was sealed off to prevent the spread of the plague. However, it was a decision to build the Royal Exchange over the top of the close, thus effectively turning it into a perfectly preserved ghost town, that led to some of its more enduring unsettling tales.

A one-hour tour with a costumed guide is mandatory with visits. Your guide will dispel some myths, while hamming up some of the spooky tales of the maze-like underground city, including the chilling story of Annie, a young girl who it is said was left to die by her parents when the plague took hold. Some visitors even leave gifts in the little girl's room.

In summer, you should book one of the tours a week or two in advance. Walk-ups may be available in quieter winter months.

St. Giles' Cathedral

High Street, Royal Mile; tel. 0131 226 0674; www.
stgilescathedral.org.uk; 9am-7pm Mon.-Fri.,
9am-5pm Sat., 1pm-5pm Sun. Apr.-Oct., 9am-5pm
Mon.-Sat., 1pm-5pm Sun. Nov.-Mar.; free (but
donations are encouraged)
This cathedral about a third of the way down the Royal Mile has been a popular place of worship since medieval times. Though entrance is free (donations are encouraged), there is a £2 charge for taking photos. Today, the cathedral's unusual steeple can be seen from across the city. While there may have been a church here as early as 1124, much

of the interior you see dates from the 14th century, although it was largely restored in the 19th century.

The stained glass is stunning, but the highlight is the **Thistle Chapel**—home to the Order of the Thistle, the highest order of chivalry in Scotland. Completed in 1911, it features elaborate carvings, stalls for each of the 16 knights, and an ornate stone vaulted ceiling with an intricate pattern of ribs and bosses.

Near the west door of St. Giles' Cathedral is a heart-shaped mosaic set in the pavement, known as the **Heart of Midlothian.** Many visitors step over it without realizing its significance, but this mosaic marks the site of the former 15th-century tolbooth building, which housed a prison and gallows. Conditions inside the prison were notoriously brutal—so much so that Mary, Queen of Scots, ordered the building of a new tolbooth, but executions and torture still took place here until the building was eventually demolished in the early 19th century. However, with the publication of Sir Walter Scott's *The Heart of Midlothian,* which told the tale of a woman desperately trying to get a pardon for a condemned prisoner, it was immortalized.

Some say the heart is positioned on the very spot where the executions once took place. One strange tradition adhered to is that of spitting on the heart. Today, it is supposed to bring good luck, but the tradition likely originated as a way of showing disdain toward the horrid events that unfolded within the prison walls.

Magdalen Chapel

41 Cowgate; tel. 0131 220 1450; www.
scottishreformationsociety.org/the-magdalen-
chapel; 10:30am-2:30pm, Tues., Thurs.-Fri. (but check
before visiting); free but donations encouraged
Built in the mid-16th century with the primary purpose of praying for the soul

---

1: Greyfriars Bobby outside Greyfriars Kirkyard
2: A plaque commemorates Mary, Queen of Scots' stay at Mary King's Close 3: St. Giles' is home to the Order of the Thistle

1

ON THIS SITE STOOD THE LODGING OF SIR SIMON PRESTON OF CRAIGMILLAR, PROVOST OF THE CITY OF EDINBURGH 1567, IN WHICH LODGING MARY QUEEN OF SCOTLAND AFTER HER SURRENDER TO THE CONFEDERATE LORDS AT CARBERRY HILL SPENT HER LAST NIGHT IN EDINBURGH 15 JUNE 1567. ON THE FOLLOWING EVENING SHE WAS CONVEYED TO HOLYROOD AND THEREAFTER TO LOCHLEVEN CASTLE AS A STATE PRISONER.

THIS TABLET WAS ERECTED BY THE LORD PROVOST MAGISTRATES AND COUNCIL OF EDINBURGH. 1898

2

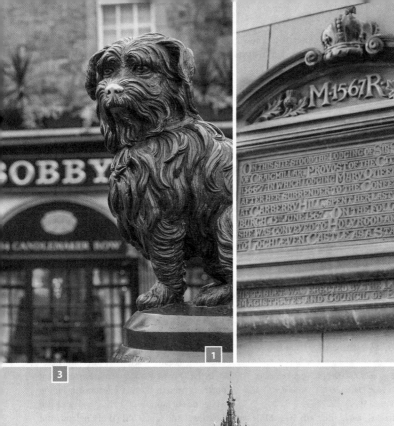

3

of Mary, Queen of Scots, this little-known church is a genuine hidden gem for history buffs.

Inside, you'll find engraved wooden panels as well as artifacts linked to the Hammermen, as the chapel was once their guildhall. It's also home to the only intact pre-Reformation stained glass in the whole of Scotland (located in the middle window on the chapel's south wall), and it was a favored meeting place for the Covenanters, who were fierce opposers to the interference of Stuart kings into matters of the Presbyterian Church. In fact, you can still see the table on which the bodies of some of the Convenanter martyrs were laid to be dressed in their grave clothes.

It's not huge—a half-hour visit will suffice—but you will probably come away with a profound understanding of the significant role of religion in Scotland's history.

Palace of Holyroodhouse

Canongate, Royal Mile; tel. 0303 123 7306; www. royalcollection.org.uk/visit/palace-of-holyroodhouse; 9:30am-6pm daily Apr.-Oct., 9:30am-6pm daily Nov.-Mar.; adult £14, under 17 £7.50, under-fives free, family £32.50

The official residence of Her Majesty The Queen in Edinburgh, the Palace of Holyroodhouse has been the principal home of the kings and queens of Scotland since the 16th century. The palace that you see today is largely the work of King Charles II who ordered a major overhaul of the palace in the 17th century.

It is in the forecourt, during the Ceremony of the Keys, that the Queen is welcomed into the city of Edinburgh each year. The spectacle occurs during Holyrood Week (usually late June or early July). From the forecourt, the palace looks symmetrical. Although the large tower to your left is original, the one on the right was added by Charles II, who created a new quadrangle layout.

Though he never visited the palace, Charles used it to show his status and the might of the Royal Family at a time when there was a power struggle between the church in Scotland and the Crown. Its classical style was later borrowed by much of the nobility in their houses and palaces around Scotland.

The quadrangle you see as you first step beyond the castle walls is a great place to view the architectural style, with Doric columns on the ground level, the slightly more decorative Ionic on the floor above, and finally the Corinthian columns on top.

A free audio guide will take you through the other rooms in the palace. The first room you reach at the top of the staircase is the **Royal Dining Room.** This is where the Queen and the Royal Family dine when they are in residence each summer and also where they host guests. It has been used in such a manner since the reign of Queen Victoria. Looking over everyone is a portrait celebrating the 1822 visit of King George IV. Stage managed by Sir Walter Scott, it was the first visit to Scotland by an English monarch in more than 200 years, and it served to underline the unification of both countries.

In the **Throne Room** are more magnificent portraits from the Royal Collection, including a huge one of James VI (I of England) and also Charles II and James VII (II of England) and their wives.

Charles II had the state apartments laid out so that they get progressively more opulent as you approach the **King's Bedchamber.** (This is a style copied from the Palace of Versailles, the famous French court designed by his cousin, King Louis XIV of France.) The state bed was made in the 17th century and adorned with crimson damask—a very expensive fabric of the time. The room was designed to impress. Paintings and tapestries were added to flatter the king by associating him with great classical heroes.

The **Great Gallery**—where the walls are lined with the portraits of the kings and queens of Scotland, all commissioned by Charles II—is a particular highlight of a tour. Here, When Bonnie Prince Charlie over-took Holyroodhouse for six weeks in 1745, he

Murder in the Palace

The Palace of Holyroodhouse

A heavily pregnant Mary, Queen of Scots, was dining in the small supper room off her bedchamber in the Palace of Holyroodhouse, accompanied by some ladies in waiting and her Italian secretary Rizzio, when a hugely significant event took place that would ultimately have tragic consequences for Mary.

Lord Darnley, Mary's second husband (she had been widowed some years earlier aged just 18), and some of his men burst in and demanded to see Rizzio, who they felt had too much influence over the queen—indeed, they may have even suspected the pair of having an affair. Mary tried to resist, but they held a gun to the queen's head and dragged Rizzio to the outer chamber where he was stabbed 56 times. Later, Darnley himself was murdered—many thought by the Earl of Bothwell—perhaps on the orders of Mary.

Mary did little to quell the rumors when she subsequently married Bothwell, and she soon lost respect among her subjects. She was forced to abdicate in favor of her son, James VI, and went to England under the supposed protection of her cousin Queen Elizabeth I never to see her son again.

Though they never actually met, Elizabeth didn't trust Mary—perhaps rightly so as many people considered her the rightful Queen of England—and so she kept her in captivity for 19 years before she was tried for treason and executed in 1587.

reputedly held lavish balls here, buoyed on by his triumphant return to the royal palace of his Stuart ancestors.

Almost 200 years earlier, Mary, Queen of Scots, had returned to Scotland from her exile in France and set up home here. It feels very much like the route through the state rooms is building up to a visit to her bedchamber, accessed via a narrow winding staircase in the northwest tower toward the end of the tour. Mary grew up around great Renaissance

opulence—a style she tried to recreate here in Holyroodhouse, as evidenced in her lavish bedchamber, complete with decorative oak ceiling and painted frieze. There is a four-poster bed and rich tapestries on the wall, but perhaps most revealing of all is the low doorway that Mary must have found a struggle—although most people in the 1500s were short compared with today, Mary grew to be almost six feet (1.8 m) tall.

Once you have finished the audio tour

inside, you can explore the ruins of **Holyrood Abbey** during palace opening hours and walk around the palace gardens for beautiful views of Holyrood Park and Arthur's Seat. All that's left of the original abbey, founded by King David I, is the east processional doorway. What you see today is the remains of a medieval Gothic abbey church built in its place; nevertheless, there is an eerie romance about the place.

Queen Mary's Bath House

3 Abbeyhill

It's easy to miss this small turreted structure to the northwest of the palace where Mary, Queen of Scots, is said to have bathed in sweet white wine. However, it's location close to the King's Privy Garden suggests it may have been a summer house instead or possibly one of the world's oldest tennis pavilions. Unfortunately, you can't actually enter the bath house, but there is a small path to it that you can access from Abbey Strand for a closer look. If it's closed, then you can only see it from the street on Abbeyhill.

Queen's Gallery

Canongate; tel. 0303 123 7306; www.royalcollection. org.uk/visit/the-queens-gallery-palace-of-

holyroodhouse; 9:30am-4:30pm Nov.-Mar., 9:30am-5pm Apr.-Oct.; adult £7.20, child £3.60, under-fives free, combined tickets with the palace adult £19.10, child £10.80

Located right next to the Palace of Holyroodhouse and featuring some incredible paintings from the Royal Collection, the gallery hosts a series of rolling exhibitions, including the recent Canaletto and the Art of Venice show, which displayed some of the finest works by the famous Italian view-painter, as well as touring shows from London, such as the exhibition celebrating the royal wedding of the Duke and Duchess of Sussex (14 June-6 October 2019). An hour-long multimedia guide will point out the biggest attractions, and you can also combine your visit with the Palace of Holyroodhouse for a reduced overall rate. The last admission is an hour before closing.

TOP EXPERIENCE

★ Arthur's Seat and Holyrood Park

Queen's Drive; www.walkhighlands.co.uk/lothian/ arthurs-seat.shtml

Visitors to Edinburgh can't avoid the gaze of Arthur's Seat, a hill left by a volcanic eruption

Arthur's Seat from Holyrood Park

350 million years ago, that looms over the city to the east from its position 822 feet (251 m) above sea level in Holyrood Park.

Arthur's Seat was once the site of one of four hill forts that date back 2,000 years. Today, ascending it is a rite of passage for visitors, and for locals. It's an Edinburgh tradition to climb Arthur's Seat on the first day of May and wash your face in the morning dew (although fewer people do it every year). Set amid the 640-acre (260-hectare) Holyrood Park, located adjacent to Holyrood Palace, it is a serene place that offers the chance to see a diverse range of fauna as well as overarching views of the city, including all the way to Leith and the Firth of Forth.

Entry to the park is just a few minutes stroll from the eastern end of the Royal Mile near the Palace of Holyroodhouse. This route follows a well-marked walkway from Queen's Drive (use the path that bears left) and takes you up behind Salisbury Crags via windswept fields, with bountiful yellow gorse in spring. Keep to the main path, and you'll soon bear right onto a grassy path that leads steeply to the top of the crags. Follow the escarpment with care; as it climbs up and to your east, you'll get a good view of the summit. As you near the end of the escarpment, take the muddy path just to your left and bear right to join the incoming path. To reach Arthur's Seat itself, cross over to a path of steps that zig-zag up. This section is steep but not too long, and from here you simply follow the path as it curves round the hill before bearing left and starting the final rocky climb to the summit of Arthur's Seat. In total, you cover a distance of three miles (4.75 km), and it should take you 2-2.5 hours to reach the summit and come back down on a different path to the east, where there is a metal chain to help you in your descent.

You are exposed here, so be sure to dress appropriately—sunblock is advisable in summer, and good walking shoes plus wind protection are recommended at all times. If you don't want to walk to Arthur's Seat on your own, then join a tour accompanied by a geologist with Geowalks.

Some say Arthur's Seat looks like a reclining lion, hence its nickname The Lion. There is also some debate over where it gets its actual name from. Contrary to what many assume, its moniker has nothing to do with the legendary King Arthur and is more likely a corruption of Àrd-na-Said, "Height of Arrows," which over time has evolved into "Arthur's Seat."

On the way back down you will pass St Margaret's Loch in the northeast of the park, from where there are wonderful views of the ruins of the 15th-century **St. Anthony's Chapel** above.

National Museum of Scotland

Chambers Street; tel. 0300 123 6789; www.nms. ac.uk; 10am-5pm daily; free

A huge museum of national and international significance and set across seven floors, this is the most visited attraction in Edinburgh and is more than worthy of a couple of hours of your time. Though admission is free, charges may apply for specific exhibitions.

Half of the museum, housed in a grand Victorian building, is very much geared toward younger people and families, with hanging planes and hands-on exhibits, while the other half shows a more serious side and will take you through the history of Scotland. Popular exhibits include the famous Dolly the Sheep, the Lewis Chessmen, and a T. rex skeleton cast. It's also here that you will find the rather macabre miniature coffins discovered in a cave on the northeast slopes of Arthur's Seat by a group of schoolboys in 1836. The eight surviving coffins (there were originally 17) are carved of wood and have remained a mystery. Were they related to witchcraft? Were they some form of surrogate burial for people who died abroad or at sea? Or maybe they were an eerie memorial to some of the people killed by grave-robbers and murderers Burke and Hare, who were convicted shortly before it is thought these coffins were made.

Avoid visiting the museum during school holidays, when it can get stiflingly busy. If you

The Haunted City

It's pretty much impossible to walk around Edinburgh without seeing at least one flyer promising an experience to scare the living daylights out of you. But while many of the tours are predictably gimmicky, the brooding passages that wind their way through the city, together with Edinburgh's very real bloody history, make it a ripe backdrop for spooky tales.

EDINBURGH CASTLE

There have been many supposed sightings of a ghost dog in Edinburgh Castle's dog cemetery (a dedicated resting place for soldiers' loyal canine friends), which many presume to be the famous Greyfriars Dog. There have also been numerous reports of a headless drummer boy, who if seen is supposed to be an ominous sign that the castle will soon come under attack.

The most eerie of all the castle's spirits, though, is that of the ghost piper, said to be the spirit of a small drummer boy who was sent into the warren of tunnels underneath Edinburgh Castle to see where they led. The story goes that the boy was instructed to play the bagpipes as he descended into the dark passageway so that those above ground could keep track of his whereabouts. He played loudly as he disappeared underground, but eventually the bagpipes stopped, and the boy was never seen again. To this day, visitors report hearing the muffled sound of bagpipes beneath Edinburgh Castle.

EDINBURGH VAULTS

The Edinburgh Vaults are a series of underground chambers found in the 19 arches of South Bridge just off the Royal Mile. Once home to 18th-century taverns, cobblers, and other businesses, it later became a crime-ridden slum. It is even claimed that notorious 19th-century serial

want to visit the rooftop terrace, enter via the tower entrance and take the lift or stairs to the seventh floor. It's a nice space with a different view over the city.

There is a useful **Highlights app** (www. nms.ac.uk/app) to help you narrow down the main exhibits of the museum, or join one of the free daily tours run by volunteers, which set off from the entrance hall at 11am, 1pm, and 3pm.

In spring 2019 three new galleries dedicated to ancient Egypt, East Asia, and the Art of Ceramics are due to open.

Greyfriars Kirkyard

Candlemaker Row; www.greyfriarskirk.com;
10:30am-4:30pm Mon.-Fri., 12pm-4pm Sat.
Apr.-Oct., 10:30am-3:30pm Thurs. Nov.-Mar.
This churchyard, where burials have been taking place since the late 16th century, is known for its historical links, not least for the dark period in the late 17th century when hundreds of Covenanters were caged here in a makeshift prison during the notorious "Killing Time."

Decades earlier, the Covenanters had met in the churchyard to sign their defiant Covenant.

In recent years its rows of aging headstones and weather-worn mausoleums with their faded epitaphs have been more associated with a certain J. K. Rowling, who is said to have taken inspiration from here for many of the characters in her Harry Potter tales. Tours aren't able to take you to the grave of the "real" Voldemort, Thomas Riddell Esq., but they may give you a nudge in the right direction; otherwise, look for one of the graves surrounded by other tourists.

Probably most famous of all, though, is the grave of **Greyfriars Bobby,** a Skye terrier whose loyalty to his owner made him one of Edinburgh's most beloved characters. According to local legend, when Bobby's owner died in the 19th century, the faithful dog guarded his grave until his own death 14 years later. More romanticized versions of the story tell how the dog would hear the firing of the One O'Clock gun each day and come running back to Greyfriars where he would

killers Burke and Hare came here to hide the bodies of their victims—or perhaps even hunt for victims—though there is no proof. Today the vaults are mainly the preserve of a handful of ghost tour companies, and visitors have reported receiving mysterious scratches and bruises as well as seeing a strange figure that some people call The Watcher.

MARY KING'S CLOSE

In the hidden streets of Mary King's Close, a subterranean world once walled up to prevent the spread of the plague, some people have reported being grabbed by the tiny hand of Wee Annie Plague—a little girl said to have been deserted by her parents and sealed up underground for ever more.

BRODIE'S CLOSE

And finally, does the ghost of the real-life Jekyll and Hyde haunt Brodie's Close?

William Brodie, often referred to as Deacon Brodie, was an affluent and respected Edinburgh cabinet maker who is said to have inspired the title character in Robert Louis Stevenson's Gothic novella *Strange Case of Dr. Jekyll and Mr. Hyde*.

A peer of Robert Burns, by day Brodie mingled with the city's gentry, but by night he is said to have used his skills as the city's leading locksmith to break into people's homes and rob them, presumably to fund his secret life of gambling and philandering. Brodie was hanged for his crimes in the Old Tolbooth in 1788. He supposedly can still be seen walking around Brodie's Close, just off the Royal Mile, carrying a lantern.

stay for the rest of the day. There is a statue dedicated to the dog outside the entrance to the graveyard, by the pub that bears his name, and as you enter the churchyard you can see his little grave.

Writers' Museum

Lady Stair's Close, Lawnmarket; tel. 0131 529 4901; www.edinburghmuseums.org.uk; 10am-5pm Weds.-Sat., noon-5pm Sun.; free

This small museum tucked into a close just off Lawnmarket pays homage to three of Scotland's most celebrated writers: Robert Burns, Robert Louis Stevenson, and Sir Walter Scott. Exhibits include first editions of Walter Scott's *Waverley* (from which Edinburgh's train station takes its name) and Robert Louis Stevenson's *A Child's Garden of Verses*.

Poignantly, there is even a cast of Burns' skull (one of only three made), plus the national poet's writing desk and his manuscript of "Scots Wha Hae" (also known as "Robert Bruce's Address to His Troops at Bannockburn"). This museum sheds some light on why Edinburgh has been granted City of Literature status by UNESCO.

Whiski Rooms

4-7 North Bank Street; tel. 0131 225 7224; www. whiskirooms.co.uk; 10am-10pm; tastings from £25

This tasting room is a more serious and grown-up place to partake in some whisky tasting compared with the Scotch Whisky Experience. Choose between introductory sessions, whisky and cheese pairings (yes, it is a thing), and even whisky and chocolate tastings (all of which must be booked in advance). You'll get to try whiskies from each of the main producing regions of Scotland, such as the Isle of Islay and Speyside, while seated in a semi-formal setting round a table with fellow tasters.

There is also a premium option for those already au fait with Scotch whisky but wanting to learn even more. With this option you'll get to sample rarer varieties, plus whiskies that have been aged that bit longer.

Scottish Storytelling Centre and John Knox House

43-45 High Street, Royal Mile; tel. 0131 556 9579; www.scottishstorytellingcentre.com; John Knox House £5 per adult, £1 for children seven and older, under-sevens free; tours from £120 plus house admission

These two attractions housed side by side on the Royal Mile mix medieval intrigue with live storytelling and exciting cultural events.

Dating from 1470, John Knox House is one of Edinburgh's oldest buildings and is notable for its association with one of the most turbulent periods in Scottish history: the Scottish Reformation. John Knox, who lived here for a short time before his death in 1572, was one of the leading figures of the Reformation. He was a Calvinist and the founder of Scottish Presbyterianism. He was openly opposed to Mary, Queen of Scots, and her Catholic leanings, calling for her execution following her enforced abdication. Before Knox, another inhabitant of the house was also a peer of the doomed queen's, although James Mosman was fiercely loyal to the queen—you can still see the initials of Mosman and his wife Mariotta Arries inscribed on the wall outside by the first-floor window.

Relics of John Knox's era (though not owned by him) are inside the house, including a rather grim scold's bridle (a humiliating iron muzzle that was used as an instrument of punishment in the 16th century). Without a doubt the most poignant artifact on display, though, is a 1572 printed copy of the 1557 Geneva Bible that Knox and his contemporaries translated into English. Inside are explanatory notes from Knox that sowed the idea that anyone who disobeyed God's word should be overthrown. These words contributed in no small way to the eventual downfall of Mary, Queen of Scots.

Tours of the house are run by the Scottish Storytelling Centre, a modern adjunct next door. They come at a hefty price, but they are run by highly qualified storytellers who will give genuinely fresh perspectives on Edinburgh's history and Scottish culture, and they can be tailored to specific interests. The Preacher and the Queen tour explores the bitter relationship between Knox and Mary.

The Scottish Storytelling Centre also runs other bespoke tours on Scottish politics and the city's literary links. It also hosts regular events, including the spring-time TradFest, an impassioned celebration of Scotland's folk arts.

The Scottish Parliament

Horse Wynd, Canongate; tel. 0131 348 5200; www. parliament.scot/visitandlearn; 10am-5pm Mon.-Sat.; free

Opened in 2004 following Scotland's devolution some seven years earlier—in which the UK government transferred powers to the Scottish Parliament to allow it to legislate on day-to-day matters that affect Scottish life—this is where Scotland's laws are made and debated.

Seated at the foot of the Royal Mile, just opposite the Palace of Holyroodhouse, the building, or rather complex of buildings, caused a lot of controversy because it was three years behind schedule and massively over budget. Nevertheless, the unique design—it's made of a mix of steel, oak, and granite and has features such as leaf-shaped structures, a turf roof, and solar panels in a bid to blend in with the surrounding landscape—has been largely embraced, or at least accepted by residents.

Self-government is a major issue for the people of Scotland, who for centuries following the union with England in 1707 felt frustrated that they were being dictated to by members of parliament (MPs) in London, many of whom had never ventured north of the border. With devolution in 1997 came a new sense of independence, one that the Scottish National Party wants to build on by fully separating from the UK, though the 2014 referendum on independence favored staying in the union. Visiting the Scottish Parliament building is an emotive experience and gives you a sense of just how important it is to the people of Scotland that they get to make their own laws.

Guided tours are free and are a good way of gaining insight into how the Scottish Parliament works. You can also book a seat in the public gallery of the Debating Chamber (Tues.-Thurs.). There is no need to book to go to the public areas, but for guided tours booking opens three months before and to sit in on debates you can book up to a week in advance. On the day tickets are sometimes available but not guaranteed and don't forget to check recess dates (when Parliament is not sitting) such as the summer holidays from late June to early September. Last entry is at 4:30pm.

The Grassmarket

Candlemaker Row, Victoria Street, West Bow, King's Stables Road, and West Port

Once the site of public hangings, this ancient marketplace in the hollow of Edinburgh Castle, which connects the streets that make up the Grassmarket area, is also a favored viewing point, offering photo opportunities of the oldest part of the castle. Today it's an animated spot with lots of pubs and cafés spilling onto the cobbles, and it can get a bit rowdy on weekends.

However, if it's a sense of history you're after, then it's a prime spot. Between 1661 and 1688, 100 Covenanters were hanged here for their religious beliefs in what became known as the Killing Time. A memorial near the site includes a plaque listing all the known names.

Elsewhere in the area, look around at the names of pubs, which will give some clues to the murky goings on here. Maggie Dickson's Pub (92 Grassmarket), for instance, is named after "Half-Hangit Maggie," a woman who was sentenced to the hangman's noose for killing her illegitimate child shortly after birth but who woke on her journey back home to be buried.

The area is also known for its live music, which can be heard in many of the pubs around the cobbles most nights of the week but particularly from Thursday to Saturday.

NEW TOWN
Princes Street Gardens and Scott Monument

Princes Street; gardens 7am-10pm late May-late Aug., 7am-8pm late April-late May and late Aug.-late Sept., 7am-7pm late Mar.-late April and late Sept.-late Oct., 7am-6pm late Oct.-late Mar.; monument 10am-9pm June-Aug., 10am-7pm May and Sept., 10am-4pm Oct.-April.; £5 to climb, cash only

These lovely gardens in the shadow of the castle, which effectively divide the Old Town from the New Town, are a popular place for Edinburghers to stroll and play host to many events during the year, from concerts in summer to an annual Christmas extravaganza.

The gargantuan monument to Sir Walter Scott, which stands proud over the gardens, is the largest monument in the world to a writer and gives some indication of just how much the writer is revered here. Built in the Victorian Gothic style, the monument is adorned with 64 figures representing characters from Scott's much-loved books and it was seen as a fitting tribute to the literary figure following his death in 1832.

If you're feeling brave, you can actually climb the 287 steps to the top of the 200-foot (61 m) monument for a view of the city's skyline, but be warned, the spiral staircase can be unforgiving.

The gardens will gradually start to close about an hour before full closing.

Scottish National Gallery and Royal Scottish Academy

The Mound; tel. 0131 624 6200; www. nationalgalleries.org/visit/scottish-national-gallery; 10am-5pm daily (except Sun., when the Royal Scottish Academy opens at mid-day, and Thurs. when both buildings are open until 7pm); free

Located on the Mound, a man-made hill that overlooks Princes Street Gardens, between the Old Town and New Town, the Scottish National Gallery is one of three art galleries in Edinburgh and home to world-class collections of Renaissance art, including Raphael, Titian, the Impressionists, and

New Town and Stockbridge

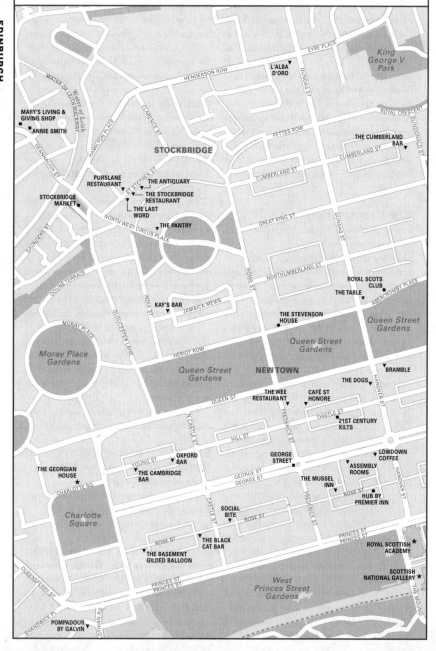

King George V Park

L'ALBA D'ORO

EYRE PLACE

HENDERSON ROW

DUNDAS ST

ROYAL CRESCENT

DUNDONALD ST

MARY'S LIVING & GIVING SHOP

ANNIE SMITH

WATER OF LEITH WALKWAY

Water of Leith

FETTES ROW

THE CUMBERLAND BAR

HAMILTON PLACE

CLARENCE ST

STOCKBRIDGE

CUMBERLAND ST

CUMBERLAND ST

DEANHAUGH ST

PURSLANE RESTAURANT

ST STEPHEN ST

THE ANTIQUARY

THE STOCKBRIDGE RESTAURANT

STOCKBRIDGE MARKET

THE LAST WORD

GREAT KING ST

SAUNDERS ST

NORTH WEST CIRCUS PLACE

THE PANTRY

DUNDAS ST

HOWE ST

NORTHUMBERLAND ST

DOUNE TERRACE

GLOUCESTER LANE

INDIA ST

KAY'S BAR

JAMAICA MEWS

ROYAL SCOTS CLUB

THE TABLE

ABERCROMBY PLACE

MORAY PLACE

THE STEVENSON HOUSE

Queen Street Gardens

Moray Place Gardens

HERIOT ROW

Queen Street Gardens

Queen Street Gardens

NEW TOWN

BRAMBLE

THE DOGS

HANOVER ST

QUEEN ST

THE WEE RESTAURANT

CAFÉ ST HONORE

N CASTLE ST

FREDERICK ST

THISTLE ST

21ST CENTURY KILTS

HILL ST

LOWDOWN COFFEE

YOUNG ST

OXFORD BAR

GEORGE STREET

ASSEMBLY ROOMS

HANOVER ST

THE GEORGIAN HOUSE

THE CAMBRIDGE BAR

GEORGE ST

GEORGE ST

THE MUSSEL INN

ROSE ST

HUB BY PREMIER INN

CHARLOTTE SQ

CASTLE ST

SOCIAL BITE

ROSE ST

FREDERICK ST

Charlotte Square

ROSE ST

THE BLACK CAT BAR

PRINCES ST

PRINCES ST

ROYAL SCOTTISH ACADEMY ★

THE BASEMENT GILDED BALLOON

PRINCES ST

PRINCES ST

West Princes Street Gardens

SCOTTISH NATIONAL GALLERY ★

QUEENSFERRY ST

SHANDWICK PL

LOTHIAN RD

POMPADOUR BY GALVIN

THE MOUND

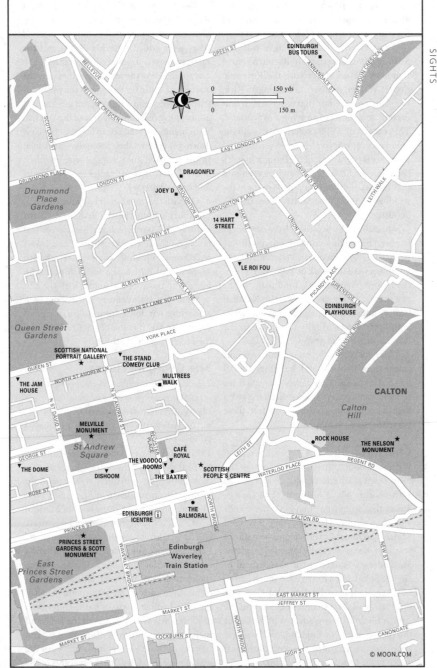

British landscape artists such as Turner. It's also a great introduction to the history of Scottish art, with pieces by Ramsay, Wilkie, McTaggart, and Raeburn. Seek out *The Skating Minister*, arguably Raeburn's most famous painting. Depicting the Reverend Robert Walker, minister of Canongate Kirk, ice-skating on Duddingston Loch, it has become something of an symbol of Scotland. The contrast of Walker's stern outfit with the wild landscape beyond is mesmerizing, and many Scots find a great deal of humor in it: it's been parodied many times and it's even said that Walker's outline inspired the shape of the windows in one of the Scottish Parliament's buildings.

Since 2004, the Scottish National Gallery has been linked by an underground walkway with the Royal Scottish Academy. Both buildings were the work of William Playfair, the renowned architect behind many of the city's finest buildings. The Scottish National Gallery houses permanent collections, while temporary shows usually take place in the Royal Scottish Academy.

There are currently 18 main gallery rooms across three floors in both buildings, but all this could change if proposals to create three times as much gallery space ever get the green light. Though general admission is free, there is a fee for some exhibitions.

Charlotte Square

Without a doubt, the crowning glory of the New Town is Charlotte Square, a dignified 18th-century plaza to the west of George Street that would put London's Grosvenor Square to shame. The swan song of revered Scottish architect Robert Adam, who died a year later, it was originally intended to mirror St. Andrew's Square at the eastern end of George Street, but it has aged so much better.

Interestingly, Charlotte Square was originally called St. George's Square, and the connection of the two squares named after the patron saints of England and Scotland signified the union of the new countries, which at the time was still in its infancy.

Sadly, the dome and portico to West Register House (formerly the church of St. George) were not what Adam envisioned (they were added after his death), but the mirrored palace-fronted edifices of the north and south side of the square, together with the statuesque sphinxes that guard the pyramid-shaped roofs, lend a resplendent air. You can almost picture leading figures of the Scottish Enlightenment, who set up home in the New Town, going about their business—gentlemen in their skirted knee-length coats, breeches, and silk stockings and ladies in their corsets and hooped dresses.

One of the most coveted addresses in Edinburgh both then and today is **Bute House** (6 Charlotte Square), the central house on the north side of the plaza. It was once home to John Crichton-Stuart, the 4th Marquess of Bute and a Scottish peer who bought up much of the square with the aim of removing 19th-century intrusions, such as dormer windows, from Adam's original design. Today, it is the official residence of the First Minister of Scotland.

The Georgian House

7 Charlotte Square; tel. 0131 225 2160; www.nts. org.uk/visit/places/georgian-house; 10am-5pm late Mar.-Oct., 11am-4pm Nov.-mid-Dec., closed mid-Dec.-late Mar.; adult £8, concessions £6, family £17.50

Taking pride of place in the exquisite surroundings of Charlotte Square is this museum of living history, right next door to the official residence of Scotland's First Minister. Step across its threshold for a taste of what life was like in 18th-century Edinburgh.

The striking townhouse, designed by Robert Adam, suggested wealth and good taste to those lucky enough to live here during the Scottish Enlightenment, including its first owner, John Lamont, the 18th-century chief of the Clan Lamont. Today it has been restored to represent a typical house of the time and includes period furniture, paintings, and silverware, as well as a glimpse into what life was like "below stairs" for the servants of the house. Kids (and more imaginative adults) will love dressing up in some of the costumes left out for this purpose—you can even tour the house in character if you like, which might make writing with one of the quill pens come more naturally.

Scottish National Portrait Gallery

1 Queen Street; tel. 0131 624 6200; www. nationalgalleries.org/visit/scottish-national-portrait-gallery; 10am-5pm daily; free

This collection of paintings of Scotland's great and good is housed in one of the city's most magnificent buildings—a neo-Gothic palace built of red sandstone, which, when it opened in 1889, became the world's first purpose-built portrait gallery.

Although the initial collection was bequeathed by David Erskine, 11th Earl of Buchan, who collected portraits of famous Scots in the late 18th century, it has been added to over the years by other gifts and the commissioning of portraits of contemporary Scots.

It's a chance look upon the faces of the men and women who have shaped Scotland, from Bonnie Prince Charlie to the woman who folklore says helped him escape the clutches of British forces, Flora Macdonald, and from Robert Louis Stevenson to Sir Walter Scott himself. Just as well, as the building's architect, Sir Robert Rowand Anderson, employed by philanthropist John Ritchie Findlay, owner of the *Scotsman* newspaper, designed it as a shrine to the nation's heroes and heroines, hence the elaborate friezes, sculptures, and murals.

Look up as you enter to see the faces of William Wallace and Robert Burns peering down at you. And don't miss the Great Hall where a painted frieze charts some of the most significant figures in Scottish history in reverse order. The building, which includes 17 gallery spaces across three floors, is also home to the National Photography Collection. Allow at least two to three hours

to appreciate it fully. Though admission is free, there is a fee for some exhibits.

The Nelson Monument

32 Calton Hill; tel. 0131 556 2716; www. edinburghmuseums.org.uk/venue/nelson-monument; 10am-4pm (open until 7pm in summer) Mon.-Sat.; £5 to climb the tower

For many, this memorial to Admiral Horatio Nelson, completed in 1808, offers the best views of Edinburgh. Commanding a prime position atop Calton Hill, it was constructed to commemorate Nelson's victory against the Spanish and French at the Battle of Trafalgar, in which the British naval hero was fatally wounded.

It stands at the highest point of Calton Hill, 561 feet (171 m) above sea level, and is said to resemble an upturned telescope, although the castellated design may have been added to fit in with some of the surrounding prisons that were in the area at the time.

In 1853 a large time ball was added, which acted as a timepiece for ships in the Port of Leith who set their chronometers by it. Its role was replaced by the One O'Clock gun fired at Edinburgh Castle from 1861 onward as the latter could be heard even in foggy conditions. The time ball was damaged in a storm in 2007; in 2009 it was brought back into service, but the mechanism is now operated manually, based on the firing of the One O'Clock Gun.

A **free museum** on the ground floor is worth nosing into if only to see the scale model of Nelson's ship *HMS Victory* and to see a piece of timber of the original ship. I recommend paying the £5 to climb the 143 steps to the **viewing gallery** too, for what some claim are the best views in Edinburgh.

Also on Calton Hill is the unfinished **Parthenon,** which was envisioned as a national monument to those who lost their lives in the Napoleonic Wars. However, for William Playfair this was an ambition too far and despite support from the likes of Sir Walter Scott, the project ran out of funds and stands as a stark reminder of the city's occasional folly.

Burns Monument

1759 Regent Road

This small circular temple at the southern foot of Calton Hill, just before the entrance to the New Calton Burial Ground, on the other side of Regent Road, pays homage to Scotland's national bard, Robert Burns. Construction on the temple began in 1831, and it once housed a white marble statue of the poet, which can now be seen in the Scottish National Portrait Gallery.

The monument looks out toward Arthur's Seat but also Canongate graveyard where Burns's close friend, Agnes Maclehose or "Clarinda," is buried. Burns was infatuated with Maclehose, as she was with him. He wrote her many songs, including "Ae Fond Kiss," but though separated she was still married and so their love affair remained unconsummated.

St. Andrew Square

Eastern end of George Street

Once the blueprint for the more celebrated Charlotte Square, this plaza is now the hub of the business district and has melded more with the modern world, with some contemporary office blocks and bars and restaurants. Some historic buildings remain, though, including the old **British Linen Bank** (now owned by the Bank of Scotland) where you can see Romanesque figures atop Corinthian columns.

The square's most prominent landmark is the 140-foot (43 m) **Melville Monument** in its center, which celebrates one of Scotland's most controversial figures, whose story has been largely forgotten: Henry Dundas, 1st Viscount Melville, had contradictory nicknames such as the "Uncrowned King of Scotland" and the "Great Tyrant," giving some indication of how divisive he was. Melville was a member of parliament (MP) in the late 18th and early 19th centuries until his impeachment in 1806 on the grounds of a misuse of public funds.

He was found not guilty, but the slur left a stain. Despite this slur, the column was erected in 1823, 12 years after his death—Dundas had some very rich and powerful friends in Georgian society. The statue of Melville was modeled by one of the leading sculptures of the day, Francis Chantrey. Each year many events take place around the imposing monument, including ice-skating.

Scottish People's Centre

2 Princes Street; tel. 0131 535 1314; www.nrscotland.
gov.uk/research/visit-us/scotlandspeople-centre;
9am-4:30pm Mon.-Fri. (except some public holidays);
fees start at £15 per day

This is a good port of call for anyone wanting to trace their Scottish ancestry. Set in the historic General Register House, built by Robert Adam, this is where many Scottish records are kept, including birth, death and marriage records, Catholic parish registers, coats of arms, census records, valuation rolls, and wills and testaments. There are even historic images, which you can save.

You can book a search room seat online and start researching your Scottish heritage. The fee will give you access all day with supervisors on site to get you started and give you direction. One important thing to remember is that you will need details of at least one event (such as a marriage, death, or birth) to get your search started.

WEST END

St. Mary's Cathedral

Palmerston Place; tel. 0131 225 6293; www.cathedral.
net; opening times vary

Built by Sir George Gilbert Scott (most famous for his masterpiece the Midland Grand Hotel at London's St. Pancras Station), this cathedral is an astonishing example of Gothic revival architecture, with a soaring central spire (plus two smaller ones by its western entrance added later), numerous lancet windows, and giant pointed arches adding drama along its nave.

1: view from the Nelson Monument on Calton Hill of the incomplete "Parthenon" 2: Scott Monument

West End

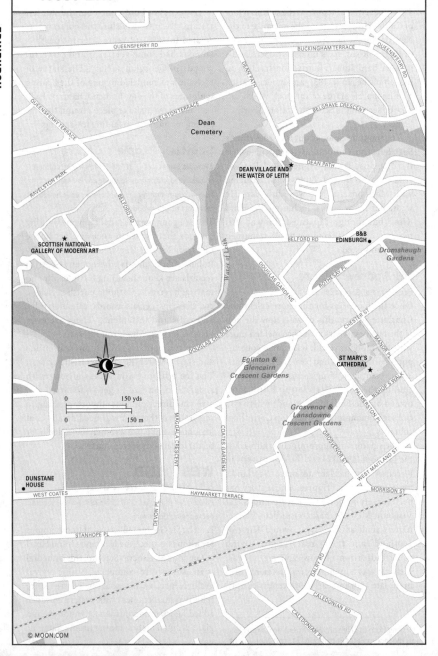

QUEENSFERRY RD

BUCKINGHAM TERRACE

QUEENSFERRY RD

DEAN PATH

BELGRAVE CRESCENT

QUEENSFERRY TERRACE

RAVELSTON TERRACE

Dean Cemetery

RAVELSTON PARK

DEAN PATH

★ DEAN VILLAGE AND
THE WATER OF LEITH

BELFORD RD

BELFORD RD

B&B
EDINBURGH ●

Drumsheugh
Gardens

★ SCOTTISH NATIONAL
GALLERY OF MODERN ART

Water of Leith

DOUGLAS GARDENS

ROTHESAY PL

CHESTER ST

MANOR PL

DOUGLAS CRESCENT

Eglinton &
Glencairn
Crescent Gardens

ST MARY'S
CATHEDRAL ★

BISHOP'S WALK

0   150 yds
0   150 m

MAGDALA CRESCENT

COATES GARDENS

Grosvenor &
Lansdowne
Crescent Gardens

GROSVENOR ST

PALMERSTON PL

● DUNSTANE
HOUSE

WEST COATES

HAYMARKET TERRACE

WEST MAITLAND ST

MORRISON ST

DEVON PL

STANHOPE PL

DALRY RD

CALEDONIAN RD

CALEDONIAN PL

© MOON.COM

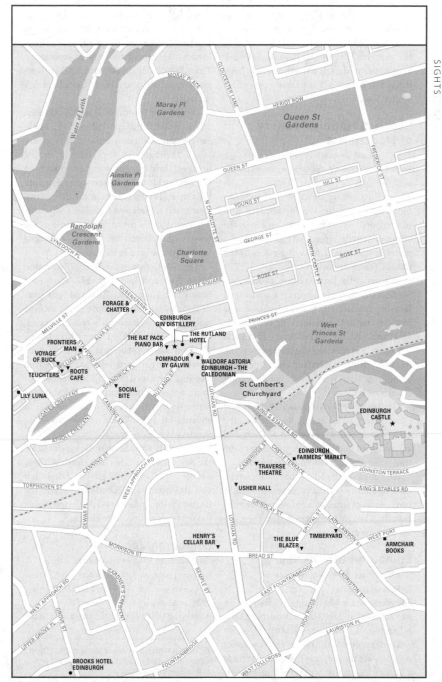

But while the building is stunning, the Charles I Chapel is sadly underwhelming with a few random bits of memorabilia related to the monarch that look as though they have been gathering dust. It is worth a peek in here, though, if only to see the family pew of Sir Walter Scott.

Scottish National Gallery of Modern Art

75 Belford Road; www.nationalgalleries.org/visit/ scottish-national-gallery-modern-art; 10am-5pm daily; free

This exciting gallery set across two handsome buildings is a must-see for modern and contemporary art lovers. It's set back from the Water of Leith in a peaceful location amid a pretty sculpture park featuring pieces by the likes of Tracey Emin.

In front of the first building, neoclassical Modern One, you can admire the landscaped lawn of postmodernist Charles Jencks. Inside Modern One are two unnerving early pieces by Francis Bacon (*Figure Study II* depicts a deformed screaming character emerging from beneath an umbrella), alongside some of the artist's later works, and a good selection of abstract art.

Head to Modern Two, housed in the former Dean Gallery, across Belford Road, to view the gallery's impressive collection of Dada and surrealist art and to see a re-creation of the studio of Scottish artist Eduardo Paolozzi.

An hour in each gallery should be enough time to admire the main pieces, though, if you're short of time, make Modern One your priority. Though admission is free, there is a fee for some exhibitions.

Edinburgh Gin Distillery

1a Rutland Place; www.edinburghgin.com; 9:45am-4:45pm daily

For years the award-winning Edinburgh Gin was actually produced in England, but now it is firmly back in its namesake city.

Underground tours of the compact distillery are the only way to visit and include a history lesson that will reveal the horrific

social fallout of the Gin Craze of the 18th century when sanitary conditions were so bad that people drank gin like it was water, which in turn led to a shockingly low life expectancy. Thankfully, today gin drinking is altogether a lot more refined, and it is a fashionable drink of choice.

On the Gin Discovery Tour (45 minutes; 10am, noon, and 2pm Mon.-Fri., 10am Sat., 10am and noon Sun.; £10) you are taken through the surprisingly simple process, including smelling and touching the botanicals used, before squeezing into the tiny still room to see the distillery's two copper stills, Flora and Caledonia, up close. Afterward you'll get to sample some of the wares with a gin and tonic in a booth tucked into one of the bare-brick alcoves.

The Gin Connoisseur Tour (75 minutes; 11am, 1pm, and 3pm Mon.-Fri., 11am-3pm hourly Sat., 11am, 1pm, 2pm, and 3pm Sun.; £25) includes all of the above plus a tutored tasting, so it is thoroughly recommended. During the Gin Making Tour (three hours; 12:15pm daily; £100), you can craft your own bespoke gin, even down to personalized labeling. Advanced booking is essential. All tours are busy, particularly on Saturdays when you may have to book three months in advance for a slot. Tours mid-week and on Sundays have more availability.

After dark, when the distillery is closed for the day, the venue turns into Heads & Tales, a bit of a speakeasy-style gin bar. Edinburgh Gin also now has a second distillery in the Biscuit Factory in Leith (4-6 Anderson Place), though tours are not yet available.

Edinburgh Zoo

134 Corstophine Road; www.edinburghzoo.org.uk; 10am-6pm daily Apr.-Sept., 10am-5pm daily Oct. and Mar., 10am-4pm daily Nov.-Feb.; adult £17.50, child £9.85, under threes free, concessions £15

A little out of the city center, this zoo is home

1: Scottish National Gallery of Modern Art 2: Dean Village 3: Bernard's Well along the Water of Leith 4: Edinburgh Gin Distillery

to the only giant **pandas** in the UK, the female Tian Tian (meaning sweetie) and the male Yang Guang (sunshine). At busy times you may need to book a timeslot to view the solitary creatures, which each have their own enclosure; they are only brought together once a year in mating season. The pandas are on loan from China until 2021, so time is running out to see them.

The zoo offers talks throughout the day, so you can learn a little more about the resident Sumatran tigers, the sun bears, and the chimpanzees. Don't miss the daily penguin parade (2:15pm) when the King, Gentoo, and Rockhopper penguins leave their enclosure and go on a stroll with their keeper—if they are in the mood, that is.

The fairly generous animal enclosures are set amid 80 acres (32 hectares) of hilly parkland, and, though there are clear paths, some of them involve steep slopes. It's easy to navigate your way round, but don't try to see everything as you'll only exhaust yourself. Do make sure you factor in a visit to see the pair of Scottish wildcats, which look like slightly larger versions of domestic cats (though you wouldn't want to stroke them) and are still found in remote parts of the Highlands.

The zoo is easily accessible from the city center. You can jump on either a number 12, 26, or 31 bus from the city center. Just remember to have the exact change of £1.70 for the journey. Make sure you book zoo tickets online for the reduced rates listed. Though open daily, hours are reduced on Christmas Day.

Dean Village

Edinburgh's secret water mill village looks more like it belongs in Amsterdam than Scotland. Just a 10-minute walk from the West End (20 minutes from Princes Street), it's the remains of a former thriving milling community, and relics from its heyday can be seen in the mill stones and plaques decorated with bread and pies that are hidden throughout the village.

In modern times the conservation area has been sensitively regenerated, and the old granaries are now home to offices and luxury flats. There's not much to do here as such, save taking in the views of the pretty preserved village hidden in a valley that feels very rural for its city setting; however, it's a calm sanctuary from city life. From here, it's a lovely walk along the Water of Leith into Stockbridge, via St. Bernard's Well—a well once said to have healing waters that is marked in a typically showy fashion with a pillared dome around a marble statue of Hygieia, the Roman and Greek Goddess of Health.

From street level, most visitors reach the village via Bells Brae, a small road that leads under the Thomas Telford-designed Dean Bridge and which leads on to Dean Path (bus no. 37 and bus no. 113 will take you to Drumsheugh Place from where it's just a five-minute walk). However, far more romantic is to arrive along the **Water of Leith**, a river that flows through the city, either from Stockbridge or the path that leads down to the river from Belford Road, just before the entrance to the Scottish National Gallery of Modern Art.

Royal Botanic Gardens

Arboretum Place; tel. 0131 248 2909; 10am-4pm daily Nov.-Jan., 10am-5pm daily Feb. and Oct., 10am-6pm daily Mar.-Sept.; glasshouse adult £6.60, children (under 15) free, concessions £5.50

This huge green space, which dates all the way back to 1670, is the perfect place to while away a leisurely Sunday afternoon and is just a short walk from the shops and restaurants of Stockbridge. Entrance to the garden, which includes 70 acres (28 hectares) of grounds, is free, but there is a charge to enter the glasshouses—worth it to see the sheer array of exotic plants.

Highlights include the largest collection of wild-origin Chinese plants outside China and the Scottish Heath Garden, where you can see plants native to the Scottish Highlands, and the Rock Garden, a popular Victorian addition. The glasshouses shut an hour before closure.

SOUTHSIDE

TOP EXPERIENCE

★ Pickering's Gin Distillery

1 Summerhall; www.pickeringsgin.com; tel. 0131 290 2124; 9am-5pm Mon.-Fri., 11am-7pm Sat., 11am-7pm Sun.; tours at 2pm Weds.-Sat.; tours £10

When it opened in 2013, Pickering's became Edinburgh's first exclusive gin distillery to open in the city for 150 years. However, judging by the rate at which gin distilleries are opening in the rest of the country, it will soon be joined by others. But that's beside the point. What makes Pickering's stand out—apart from its award-winning handcrafted gins—is its location in the very cool **Summerhall arts venue,** which becomes a fashionable hub come festival season. Interestingly, the distillery is also located on the site of an old animal hospital, but don't let that put you off.

Everything is done on site, from the distilling and diluting right through to the bottling and shipping, and this personal service shows. Though you should really book tours in advance, staff will accommodate you if they're quiet, and you can usually pop in for a chat or to buy a bottle and learn a little more.

Tours (allow 1.5 hours) meet in the buzzing Royal Dick bar (open to visitors outside tour times too) where you'll be met by a super helpful and enthusiastic member of staff who will have story upon story to tell you. There are one to two tours a day, but times vary.

Pickering's was set up by friends Marcus and Matt and is based on an old Bombay recipe shared by a friend of Marcus's late father. First things first—you'll be handed a gin and tonic to sip on as you're taken through to the miniscule distillery where you can see the two copper stills, Emily and Gertrude (named after Marcus and Matt's grandmothers). It's all very informal, with lots of time to hear anecdotes and ask questions. You'll also see the bottling room before being taken back to the bar for some more tasting.

Sadly, the original recipe has had to be tweaked to accommodate the changing taste of tonic water, but the distillery now makes three styles of gin, including the (slightly amended) Original 1947 Gin, which has a spicy after taste; Pickering's Gin (very smooth); and its Navy Strength, which is bottled at a punch-inducing 57 percent.

If you're visiting during the Edinburgh Festival, you are advised to book ahead; Summerhall is a very popular venue.

Pickering's Gin Distillery

Dr. Neil's Garden

Old Church Lane, Duddingston Village; www. drneilsgarden.co.uk; tel. 07849 187 995; 10am-6pm Mon.-Fri.; free

On the east side of Holyrood Park, where Arthur's Seat slopes down to the ancient Duddingston Loch, is this lovely garden that is one of Edinburgh's best-kept secrets.

The tranquil space is the work of husband and wife Nancy and Andrew Neil, who in the 1960s began the mission of transforming wild church land near the 12th-century kirk into a public place for all to enjoy. Both doctors, Nancy and Andrew encouraged their patients to help cultivate the garden and thus enjoy the health benefits of outdoor living. Plantings include three redwood sequoia trees, peonies, and irises. The couple's vision has been so brilliantly realized that today many people come here to meditate, paint, and write.

Though Nancy and Andrew both died in 2005, the garden is now a registered charity and is free to visit. There is a café on site, and in one corner stands the 19th-century **Thomson's Tower,** designed by William Playfair as a place to store curling stones. The tower tells the history of the sport in Scotland, plus the story of the garden and the ancient village of Duddingston.

Surgeons' Hall Museums

Nicolson Street; https://museum.rcsed.ac.uk; tel. 0131 527 1711; 10am-5pm daily; adult £7, under 16s and over 60s £4, under fives free

This building by William Playfair is located at the Royal College of Surgeons and houses one of the most comprehensive pathology collections in the world. Originally intended as a learning facility, with specimens collected from the late 17th century, the building is today open to the public.

The collection shows surgery procedure advancements over the past few hundred years, and contains many curiosities. One of the grisliest exhibits is a notepad said to be made out of the skin of William Burke, one of the city's notorious body snatchers (following his execution, Burke was dissected—like his victims—and his skin was used for grim souvenirs). Also here is a letter from Arthur Conan Doyle crediting Dr. Joseph Bell, who was a fellow of the Royal College of Surgeons, as the inspiration behind Sherlock Holmes. Last entry is at 4:30pm.

LEITH
Royal Yacht Britannia

Ocean Drive; tel. 0131 555 5566; www. royalyachtbritannia.co.uk; 10am-3:30pm Jan.-Mar.

Royal Yacht Brittania

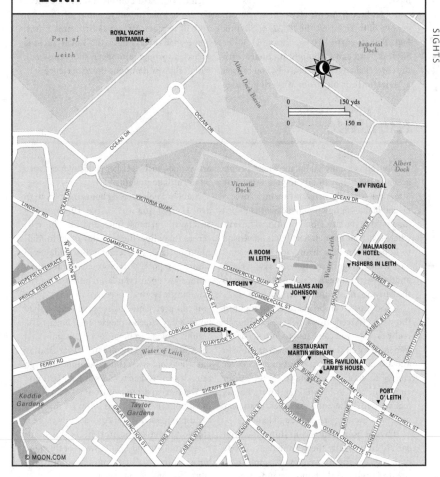

Leith

Port of Leith

ROYAL YACHT BRITANNIA ★

Imperial Dock

Albert Dock Basin

0   150 yds

0   150 m

Albert Dock

OCEAN DR

OCEAN DR

Victoria Dock

MV FINGAL

OCEAN DR

LINDSAY RD

OCEAN DR

VICTORIA QUAY

Water of Leith

TOWER PL

MALMAISON HOTEL

A ROOM IN LEITH ▼

FISHERS IN LEITH ▼

COMMERCIAL ST

HOPEFIELD TERRACE

PRINCE REGENT ST

N JUNCTION ST

COMMERCIAL QUAY

KITCHIN ▼

DOCK PL

WILLIAMS AND JOHNSON ▼

SHORE

TOWER ST

COMMERCIAL ST

COBURG ST

ROSELEAF ▼

QUAYSIDE ST

SANDPORT WAY

TIMBER BUSH

FERRY RD

Water of Leith

SANDPORT PL

RESTAURANT MARTIN WISHART ▼

BERNARD ST

CONSTITUTION ST

DOCK ST

SHORE

THE PAVILION AT LAMB'S HOUSE

BURGESS ST

PORT O' LEITH

Keddie Gardens

MILL LN

SHERIFF BRAE

WATER ST

MARITIME LN

MARITIME ST

Taylor Gardens

GREAT JUNCTION ST

KING ST

CABLES WYND

HENDERSON ST

GILES ST

GILES ST

TOLBOOTH WYND

QUEEN CHARLOTTE ST

CONSTITUTION ST

MITCHELL ST

© MOON.COM

---

and Nov.-Dec., 9:30am-4:30pm Apr.-Sept., 9:30am-4pm Oct.; adult £16, child £8.50, under fives free, family £45

Step aboard the Royal Yacht Britannia, one of Scotland's most popular attractions, for a glimpse into what life was like for Her Majesty the Queen and her nearest and dearest when they took their annual holiday around Scotland's Western Isles—the Queen once labeled it as the one place in which she could truly relax. Its lavish decks and staterooms have also accommodated and entertained world leaders, including Nelson Mandela, Rajiv Gandhi, and Ronald Reagan. Highlights of a tour include seeing the bedroom Her Majesty once slept in and taking afternoon tea on the Royal Deck Tea Room.

Royalists will love peeking into the Royal Family's private lives, but for everyone else it may be a bit sycophant. Steer clear of Britannia on wet days as it will spoil your enjoyment of the deck areas. The Royal Deck tearoom is a good place to rest and warm up with a cuppa, but it can get very busy.

To get here from the city center, you can get one of three buses: the 11, 22, or Skylink 200. Tickets cost £1.70 each way (£4.50 for Skylink) and can be bought on board with the correct change. Alternatively, you can get a Majestic Tour bus from Waverley Bridge (£15 per adult), which costs more but does include onboard commentary throughout the hour-long journey, a tour of the city, and 10 percent off Royal Britannia entry. Somewhat surprisingly, the Royal Yacht is accessed through a modern shopping mall, which slightly dampens the experience.

Nightlife

Edinburgh is a convivial place where people are only too happy to talk to you, especially after dark when the drink is flowing. There is no end of pubs or howffs (an old Scottish word for a pub) in the city, from traditional taverns where everyone from Robert Louis Stevenson to Robert Burns has drunk, to cool cocktail bars with vintage décor and quirky interiors, and late-night dive bars where dancing into the early hours is actively encouraged.

Good music can be heard every night of the week. Indeed, this is where Edinburgh really excels—you can listen to folk music for free in many city center pubs such as those in and around the **Grassmarket** or pay a cover charge to enter one of many subterranean clubs and bars to hear DJs spinning house, techno, and drum and bass tunes, or to hear genuinely exciting breakthrough bands.

If live performance is your thing, then you can see cutting-edge theater and dance in one of the city's many arts venues or sample some of Edinburgh's world-famous stand-up comedy gigs.

If you're looking to bar hop, then **Rose Street** in the New Town, which runs parallel with Princes Street, is a good shout as there is a pub every few yards for almost a mile. It also has a great comedy club in the shape of Gilded Balloon, and it's an easy walk from other notable pubs and bars, including the Café Royal and the Oxford Bar. **Lothian Road,** which runs from the West End down to the Southside, has a similarly high concentration of bars that are well located for some of Edinburgh's high-end arts venues, such as Usher Hall, but it can get a bit unruly late at night.

Standard pub opening hours in Edinburgh are 11am-11pm (or 12pm-10:30pm on Sundays), but most pubs and bars have licenses that allow them to stay open to midnight or 1am, particularly on Friday and Saturday nights. Numerous clubs and music venues are open even later, and during the Edinburgh Festival increased licenses mean you can pretty much get served alcohol 24 hours a day. Freebie magazines *The List* and *Skinny,* which can be picked up in pubs and cafes around the city, are useful for finding out what's on; www.timeout.com/edinburgh provides up-to-date reviews and gig listings.

You can expect to pay around £4 for a pint in Edinburgh, slightly less if you are drinking hand-pumped ales and considerably more if you go for one of the craft beers. Cocktails range from around £7-8 in some of the more hipster joints to £10 or more in some of the city's more glamorous venues.

Whiskies usually come in 25ml measures (though some pubs serve 35ml), and you can usually get a blended whisky for around £3 and a single malt from around £4. There is a surprisingly good amount of single-malt whiskies on offer for £4-5—as a rule of thumb the more aged the whisky the more you will pay, so stick to whiskies that have matured for 10-15 years.

It's thought that one of the reasons the Scottish Enlightenment, an intellectual movement that began in the 18th century, took off here is due to the large number of pubs where inquisitive minds could share ideas and debate the world's problems. True or not, it's certainly accurate to say that many of the historic pubs in and around both the Old Town and New Town have remained little changed for centuries, with many nooks and crannies to hide away in and pieces of memorabilia pointing to their past lives.

If you're visiting one of Edinburgh's more historic, pokey pubs, then be prepared to share a table with strangers, particularly if there's music playing—with few tables, if everyone sat on their own, there would be a lot of people standing (make sure you ask first, though, if you're going to join someone else). This rule doesn't apply in some of the swankier, more cavernous venues.

OLD TOWN
Bars
THE DEVIL'S ADVOCATE

9 Advocate's Close; tel. 0131 225 4465; devilsadvocateedinburgh.co.uk; noon-1am daily; cocktails £8-10, bottles of wine from £22

If you're looking for a smarter alternative to some of the Old Town's more historic pubs, then this bar is a good bet. With a cool industrial feel—walls are stripped back and spirits are stored in what could be former medical cabinets—it fuses the old and new seamlessly. The venue was once a Victorian pump house, but today it's known for its broad whisky collection (around 400 malts and blends), plus seasonal cocktails and a curated wine list. The best tables are on the mezzanine level, where food is also served.

HOLYROOD 9A

9a Holyrood Road; tel. 0131 556 5044; www. theholyrood.co.uk; 9am-midnight Mon.-Thurs. and Sun., 9am-1am Fri. and Sat.; cocktails £7.95-8.95, bottles of wine from £17.95

This upmarket joint at the eastern end of the Royal Mile serves a good cocktail, from firm favorites (old fashioned and whisky sour) to the delectable (and local) Edinburgh Royale, which includes Edinburgh Gin Liqueur

topped with prosecco. It also has a good line of craft beer (over 20 beers on tap) and is renowned for its tasty burgers, which go down extremely well after a trek up to Arthur's Seat.

Pubs
★ BOW BAR

80 West Bow; tel. 0131 226 7667; www.thebowbar. co.uk; noon-midnight Mon.-Sat., noon-11:30pm Sun.; from £3.70 a pint, whiskies from £4.50

Set amid the elegant facades of Victoria Street is this grown-up pub, all wood paneling with old pub signs. There are no gimmicks, just good beer, lots of whiskies, and a friendly welcome, but it is utterly charming. Take a seat and let the gentle hum of chatter wash over you. A selection of tasty pies is on offer (pheasant and pancetta, Moroccan lamb, etc.), but take note: the pies don't come with anything—this is a pub not a restaurant, after all—just pie on a plate. But at £3.50-4.50 a piece, it's an affordable and pleasant pit stop.

JOLLY JUDGE

7 James Court, Lawnmarket, Royal Mile; www. jollyjudge.co.uk; tel. 0131 225 2669; noon-midnight Fri.-Sat. and Mon., noon-11pm Tues.-Thurs. and Sun.; from £3.80 a pint, whiskies from £3.90

Tucked away on a close at the bottom of Castlehill, Jolly Judge is everything a pub should be: friendly, warm, and snug. Though some savvy tourists find their way here, it's mostly filled with locals who pop in for a pint of ale or one of the simple but delicious toasties or bowls of soup (served until 3pm). When the fire is lit, there are few places better to be perched than round a table here under its low beams, and the calm air is at odds with the hectic throb of tourists just yards away.

HALFWAY HOUSE

24 Fleshmarket Close; tel. 0131 225 7101; 11am-11pm Sun.-Thurs., 11am-1am Fri. & Sat.; from £4.20 per pint, whiskies from £3.95-4.95

For a long time this teeny one-room pub was

known as Edinburgh's smallest, though the slightly cynical opening of the Wee Pub on Grassmarket may have put paid to all that. Smallest or not, there's no doubt about it: with just four bar stools and a couple of tables, it's certainly cozy. It's also well placed, halfway up the steep steps that lead from Waverley Station to the Royal Mile, so you really do feel like you've earned a short refreshment break. Despite several changes in management over the years, it still retains the homely front-room feel of yesteryear and stocks good cask ales, plus a fine selection of whisky. Bar meals are available.

Traditional Music Pubs

TOP EXPERIENCE

★ SANDY BELL'S

25 Forrest Road; tel. 0131 225 2751; www.sandybells. co.uk; noon-1am Mon.-Sat., 12:30pm-12am Sun.; from £3.80 per pint, whiskies from £3.80 (35ml measures)

This is the most renowned spot in the city for traditional folk music sessions and is a great place to hear locals and tourists mingle happily, while those who want to hear the music proper have to squeeze themselves into the space at the back of the pub by the seated musicians.

Music sessions have been held in this former grocery store since the 1940s with the onus on Scottish and Irish folk music. Nightly evening sessions include fiddles, guitars, flutes, and "mouthies" (harmonicas) from 9:30pm, and there are afternoon sessions on Saturdays and Sundays at 2pm and 4pm respectively. Throughout August music all day every day coincides with the Edinburgh Festival. Locals embrace the in-the-know tourists who find themselves here, and the atmosphere is amiable. Table sharing is the norm, so find a seat or cram into a free space and let the music carry you away.

WHITE HART INN

32-34 Grassmarket; www.belhavenpubs.co.uk/ pubs/midlothian/white-hart; tel. 0131 226 2806; 11am-midnight Mon.-Thurs. and Sun., 11am-1am Fri.-Sat.; from £4.10 per pint, single malt whiskies from £4.95

The White Hart Inn in the Grassmarket area is one of the city's oldest pubs. It was here that Robert "Rabbie" Burns chose to lodge on his last visit to the city in 1791, and just over 10 years later English poet William Wordsworth stayed here with his sister Dorothy. The pub, now in the reputable chain of Belhaven, likes to play up to its past: the words of Burns can be seen on the pub's beams, and the faces of two of its other former patrons—the notorious body snatchers Burke and Hare—can be seen grinning down too.

★ ROYAL OAK

1 Infirmary Street; tel. 0131 557 2976; www. royal-oak-folk.com; 1pm-3am Mon.-Fri., 12pm-3am Sat. & Sun..; from £4.35 per pint, whiskies from £3.80

Forget bells and whistles at this musician's favorite: you're more likely to come across fiddles and accordions. Renowned for its folk music, this stripped-back late-night pub is where many a musician ends the night after playing in some of the other pubs around the city. There is music every night of the week and the atmosphere is very inclusive—if you arrive with a guitar or a song to sing, you will be invited into the fold. Otherwise, just bring good chat and be prepared to share your table in either the cramped bar downstairs or the slightly bigger bar upstairs, where it is often standing room around the piano only. During the Edinburgh Festival, proceedings are slightly more formal, so you may need to book a ticket through the Fringe Festival, though this can normally be done at quite short notice.

Other Live Music
WHISTLE BINKIES

4-6 South Bridge; tel. 0131 557 5114; whistlebinkies. com; 5pm-3am daily; free before midnight, £4 after, from £4.20 a pint, £4 a whisky

A bit rough round the edges and certainly not the place for a classy night out in Edinburgh, Whistle Binkies nevertheless draws a fun, carefree crowd and has fantastic music every night of the week. Live music ranges from ska to rock and indie, and the atmosphere is rambunctious, largely because people usually arrive fairly well lubricated having drunk elsewhere. The dance floor is always busy, if a little sticky, and the dark lighting helps people lose their inhibitions.

THE JAZZ BAR

1 Chambers Street; tel. 0131 220 4298; www. thejazzbar.co.uk; 5pm-3am daily (open at 1:30pm and 2pm on Sat. and Sun. if there is an afternoon gig); tickets from £4; from 4.50 a pint, bottle of wine £18-22,

If you've had your fill of folk music, this cool local favorite just off South Bridge is a great place to finish your night. It's the brainchild of Edinburgh musician Bill Kyle, who has worked tirelessly to build up its reputation as a happening and unpretentious music space. The devastating Cowgate fire in 2002 almost spelled the end for the venue, but fortunately, some loyal regulars loaned the club enough money to get back on its feet.

With as many as three to five bands playing a day, there is always something to listen to. While much of it is jazz, there is also blues, roots, acoustic, funk, and soul. Some events, particularly daytime gigs, are free.

HENRY'S CELLAR BAR

16a Morrison Street; tel. 0131 629 2992; www. henryscellarbar.co.uk; 9pm-3am daily (occasional earlier opening, depending on event); tickets from £5; pints of beer from £3.60, small glass of wine £3

Known as a bit of a spit and sawdust type of place, this basement bar is a little dingy but also a lot of fun. There are occasional gigs, but Henry's is mostly known for its sweaty club nights popular with students due to cheap drinks. Opening/closing times vary on nights other than Monday, Friday, and Saturday, depending on the event.

BANSHEE LABYRINTH

29-35 Niddry Street; tel. 0131 558 8209; www. thebansheelabyrinth.com; 7pm-3am daily; free-7.50; beers from £3.60, wine from £4.50

Not for everyone, this unapologetically "haunted" bar makes the most of its historic position. One part of the building was once part of the supposedly haunted Edinburgh Vaults, while the other was owned by one of the richest men in Edinburgh: Lord Nicol Edwards. Edwards was suspected of torturing women accused of witchcraft in dungeons beneath his house before they stood trial, and the pub's name derives from this gruesome legend. (In Gaelic folklore a banshee is a wailing woman.)

It's unlikely you'll hear the banshee yourself as music (more often than not, rock) blares across the seven rooms, which even include a 50-seater cinema. It's teeming with tourists and you may tire of seeing posed photo shoots of people looking terrified, but the cinema runs a cool program of events and screenings for horror fans.

SNEAKY PETE'S

73 Cowgate; tel. 0131 225 1757; www.sneakypetes. co.uk; 7pm-3am daily; ticket prices vary; beers £2.50-4/spirits with mixers £3.50

This grungy one-room venue is a popular spot for club nights and gigs by up-and-coming bands. Being small, it gets crowded, but it's one of the few places in the city that can rival the excitement of Glasgow's world-famous live music venues. Sneaky Pete's has an unapologetic dive-bar vibe (there are no beers on tap; cans are better for dancing with). It's had many incarnations since opening in the 1970s, but it now wears its original name with pride—you can even buy t-shirts emblazoned with it.

BANNERMANS

212 Cowgate; tel. 0131 556 3254; www. bannermanslive.co.uk; noon-1am Mon.-Sat., 12:30pm-1am Sun.; from £3.70 a pint/£2.95 bottled beer, whiskies from £2.80

This rock and indie bar is lively and loud but oh so fun. Tucked underneath Edinburgh's Cowgate, it's not the kind of place you're likely to stumble upon, meaning that the punters here have all come here looking for a similar type of vibe. It's not for the faint-hearted: shots at the bar are almost obligatory, and only the brave should venture to the cockpit at the front of the stage when metal bands are on. There's cheap pool and you may even be able to nab one of the free CDs featuring bands who have played here recently.

Nightclubs
THE BONGO CLUB

66 Cowgate; tel. 0131 558 8844; 11pm-3am daily; ticket prices vary; from £2.50 a beer (cans)

Run by a local arts charity, which saved this Edinburgh institution from closure in 2012, this city center venue hosts legendary club nights that attract some of the hottest DJs around. With drinks starting at just £1 a shot, Midnight Bass on Tuesday nights is a student favorite. Playing a mix of drum and bass, jungle and grime, the night has a real urban feel with clubbers dressed down in streetwear ready to rinse out.

NEW TOWN
Bars
★ CAFÉ ROYAL

19 West Register Street; tel. 0131 556 1884; www. caferoyaledinburgh.co.uk; 11am-11pm Sun.-Weds., 11am-midnight Thurs., 11am-1am Fri.-Sat.; pints from £4.35, bottle of wine from £20

You would be hard-pushed to find a more salubrious drinking venue in Edinburgh. With its high ceilings, Victorian plasterwork, stained-glass windows, and famed circular bar, Café Royal is a great place for a pre-dinner glass of champagne or even a whisky digestif. You may struggle to get a seat, and if you do, be prepared to share. The Parisian-style **oyster bar** upstairs was famously used in the dining scene in Oscar-winning film *Chariots of Fire* and has changed little over the years.

BRAMBLE

16A Queen Street; tel. 0131 226 6343; www. bramblebar.co.uk; 4pm-1am daily; cocktails from £6.50-9, wine from £16.50 a bottle

Not only does this decadent bar serve smashing cocktails in a cool subterranean venue, but it has a rolling lineup of cool DJs too. It's classier than a lot of modern joints as well—grab a seat in a high-backed leather armchair

then leaf through a book-bound menu to select your drink.

THE VOODOO ROOMS

19A West Register Street; tel. 0131 556 7060; www. thevoodoorooms.com; noon-1am Fri.-Sun., 4pm-1am Mon.-Thurs.; cocktails from £7.95-14.95, bottle of wine from £18

If you're looking for a slightly more glamorous night out, this cocktail bar with cabaret rooms above the Café Royal is a good option. The main bar with gold and black décor, booth seating, and huge arched windows shout decadence, and its team of mixologists serve up some of the best cocktails in the city while intimate event spaces host lively cabaret and music nights.

Pubs
★ KAYS BAR

39 Jamaica Street; tel. 0131 225 1858; www.kaysbar. co.uk; 11am-noon Mon.-Thurs., 11am-1am Fri.-Sat., 12:30pm-11pm Sun.; pints from £3.50, wine from £14 a bottle

This fantastic local's bar is set on a pleasant mews a short walk from Charlotte Square. While it has an impressive whisky collection (including rare bottlings), it's widely considered Edinburgh's premier cask ale house, with seven guest ales on tap. The pub was actually a reputable wine merchant during the Victorian era, and many of the features from its Victorian heyday remain, including signage around the frieze, cast-iron pillars, and old barrels. It also offers exceptionally good-value lunches such as haggis, neeps, and tatties or Scotch pie, chips, and beans for just £4.50.

★ OXFORD BAR

8 Young Street; tel. 0131 539 7119; www.oxfordbar. co.uk; noon-midnight Mon.-Thurs., 11am-1am Fri.-Sat., 12:30pm-11pm Sun.; pints from £3.50

"The Ox," just off Charlotte Square, is one of those places you always hope to find but assume have been confined to the memory bank. The back room, with its framed pictures, wooden seats built into the wall, and a fire lazily simmering, is the perfect place to have a pint, do the crossword, or exchange stories with your neighbor. For a bit more life, sidle into the bar near the entrance and wait for a local to bring you into their conversation. It will happen. And yes, this is the bar where Inspector Rebus, the fictional character in Ian Rankin's detective novels, likes to come.

THE CUMBERLAND BAR

1-3 Cumberland Street; tel. 0131 558 3134; www. cumberlandbar.co.uk; noon-midnight Mon.-Weds., noon-1am Thurs.-Sat., 11am-11pm Sun.; pints from £3.70, wine from £16 per bottle

A firm favorite in Edinburgh's New Town, the Cumberland is a traditional pub with a warren of snugs that was once frequented by the area's lawyers and judges and which today has been given a respectful uplift. Food is of the utmost importance—the DM Stewart family who own this and other Edinburgh pubs have a history of livestock farming alongside their wine and spirit merchant credentials, making the Cumberland a credible gastropub. The pub serves a mean Sunday roast, plus hearty dishes such as steak and ale pie. For snacks, it's pretty hard to resist the pork and haggis Scotch egg. If you like historic pubs with a touch of gloss, then this is for you.

THE BLACK CAT BAR

168 Rose Street; tel. 0131 225 3349; www. theblackcatbar.com; 10:30am-1am daily; pints of beer from £3.60, bottles of wine £13.95

Standing out on this popular street of bars and restaurants is no mean feat, but somehow this modern whisky bar has done it. It may have something to do with the traditional Scottish music sessions on Monday and Wednesday nights (from 9:30pm) and Sunday afternoons (from 4pm) or the whisky flights that are a great introduction to whisky tasting and a good excuse to have a natter with bar staff, who are only too happy to oblige. There are also a few tables out front, great for a spot of people watching.

Live Music
THE JAM HOUSE

5 Queen Street; tel. 0131 220 2321; www.thejamhouse. com; 6pm-3am Sat. and select Fri.; pints of beer from £4, spirit & mixer £4.95

The brainchild of jazz musician Jools Holland and designer Neil Tibbatt, this sultry club, which has sister venues in other UK cities, takes inspiration from the blues clubs of LA and Chicago. There is music on some Fridays, but Saturday is when the joint is really jumping. There are some low-key performances early on before things rev up with the main

Café Royal

live band at 10:30pm and DJs in between until 3am.

WEST END

Bars

★ VOYAGE OF BUCK

29-31 William Street; tel. 0131 225 5748; www. thevoyageofbuckedinburgh.co.uk; 10am-midnight Sun.-Weds., 10am-1am Thurs.-Sat.; cocktails £7.50-11, punch for sharing from £38 for four

This bar, which opened in 2017 in the smart West End, could so easily be dismissed as too gimmicky—it is all centered around the idea of a fictional Victorian philanthropist after all. But somehow it works. The cocktail menu is inspired by "Buck's" supposed travels. The reasonably priced cocktails (starting at £7.50) are served with finesse, and the low-lit, classy bar with cozy booths is reminiscent of a train station café circa 1920.

Pubs

THE BLUE BLAZER

2 Spittal Street; tel. 0131 229 5030; www. theblueblazer.co.uk; 11am-1am Mon.-Sat., 12:30pm-1am Sun.; from £3 a pint, whiskies from £3.80 (for 35ml measure)

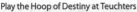

Not many tourists venture to this Victorian boozer on the far-side of Grassmarket. A lot less gimmicky than many of the pubs in the area, it's a straight-up traditional pub where chatty locals bunch round beer barrels drinking one of eight cask ales on tap or some of the fine whiskies on sale. The pub is also known for its rum collection and is even home to the Edinburgh Rum Club, which hosts master classes and tastings throughout the year.

Whisky Bars

★ TEUCHTERS

26 William Street; tel. 0131 225 2973; teuchtersbar. co.uk/teuchters-west-end-bar; 10.30am-1am daily; from £4.25 a pint, whiskies from £4, whisky flights from £11.75

While some people come to Teuchters for dinner in the downstairs restaurant, which serves Scottish dishes, the whisky bar upstairs is where the fun is really to be had. Pivotal to festivities is the Hoop of Destiny game: for £4 you get three goes at throwing a hoop over one of the many whiskies on display, and you win whichever one you land. If you don't land a single malt, don't fret, you'll still be rewarded with a glass of Sheep Dip—a good local blended whisky. It's a great ice-breaker for chatting to the sociable crowd.

Play the Hoop of Destiny at Teuchters

Live Music
THE RAT PACK PIANO BAR

9 Shandwick Place; tel. 0131 228 9147;
ratpackpianobars.com; 7pm-3am daily; cocktails
from £4.95, wine from £16.50 a bottle, beer from
£3.80 a bottle

With music from the 1950s, right up to the
present day, this late-night West End bar is
a great place to round off your night if you're
one of the last people standing. Cocktails are
expertly prepared, and the pianist takes requests, giving the place a bit of an off-Broad-
way feel. It's also had a recent makeover, which
was a long time coming.

STOCKBRIDGE
Bars
THE ANTIQUARY

72-78 St. Stephen Street; tel. 0131 225 2858;
theantiquarybar.co.uk; 4pm-11pm Mon.,
4pm-midnight Tues., noon-midnight Weds., noon-1am
Thurs.-Sat., 11am-11:30pm Sun.; beer from £3.40 a
pint, whiskies from £2.70

This basement bar in the hip neighborhood
of Stockbridge, which is a lot more youthful
than it appears, is all wooden floors and wood-
paneled walls. The bar takes its name from the
book of the same name by Sir Walter Scott.
The remains of a 19th-century bakery can be
found at the back of the bar, which is also said
to have its own resident ghost in the shape of
a female baker. There is a good folk session on
Thursdays at 8:30pm.

★ THE LAST WORD

44 St. Stephen Street; tel. 0131 225 9009; www.
lastwordsaloon.com; 4pm-1am daily, opens at 2pm
Sun.; cocktails from £6.50-8, wine from £14 a bottle

Everyone in Stockbridge knows that, if you
want good cocktails, this is where you come.
It's a bit on the grungy side compared to some,
but who said cocktails were only for glamour
pusses? Music plays at a good level in the dark
basement bar, and you can buy a measure of
the bar's "break even bottle" for the price

they paid for it if you fancy trying a more expensive whisky than the norm. I also recommend some of the quirkier single-pour drinks,
such as the Great King Street Glasgow Blend
Whisky, which comes with cream soda. Yum.

SOUTHSIDE
Pubs
SHEEP HEID INN

43-45 The Causeway; tel. 0131 661 7974; www.
thesheepheidedinburgh.co.uk; 11am-11pm Mon.-Thurs.,
11am-midnight Fri.-Sun.; beer from £3.95 a pint, wine
from £14.95 a bottle, cocktails from £7.50-8.50 (two
for £10 12pm-7pm Mon.-Fri.)

Possibly dating from the 14th century, the
Sheep Heid is one of the city's oldest surviving pubs. Once visited by King James VI (I
of England) and his mother, Mary, Queen
of Scots, who reputedly played skittles here,
today it is a cozy gastropub with plentiful
memorabilia on its walls, a good selection of
real ales, and even a Victorian bowling alley,
which is fully utilized.

★ THE CANNY MAN

237 Morningside Road; tel. 0131 447 1484; www.
cannymans.co.uk; 11am-11pm Sun.-Weds., 11am-12pm
Thurs., 11am-1am Fri. and 11am-12pm Sat.; whiskies
from £6 (35ml measure), wine from £13.50 per carafe

This Morningside pub, which has been in the
same family for generations, is a bona fide local's favorite, though its reputation for serving up the best bloody Mary in town ensures
it has a steady stream of tourists too. There
are two bars: the main bar, where you'll find
most of those tourists, and the back bar, where
locals hide away. The décor inside is gloriously
eclectic, with floral floor-length curtains, red
velvet bench seats, and walls chockablock
with memorabilia, from framed photos to old
clocks. The vibe is also very European—free
snacks are served with drinks (not the norm
at all), and there is even a free buffet from 5pm
to 6pm Monday to Thursday, much like the
Italian aperitivo hour.

Traditional Music Pubs
THE CAPTAIN'S BAR

4 South College Street; tel. 07493 555 702;
captainsedinburgh.webs.com; 2pm-1am daily; beer
from £3.80 a pint, whiskies from £4

A tiny pub with a big heart, this is one of the best places to catch an afternoon music session on the weekend. It's pretty informal, but it usually kicks off around 3pm and goes on until 6ish. There are a few regular musicians who turn up to keep proceedings ticking along but anyone can join in, and while the onus is on folk music, contemporary songs are welcome too. A highlight is when the bar man leaves his regular spot behind the bar, picks up his fiddle, and joins in the music. There are also sessions on Tuesday and Wednesday afternoons.

LEITH
Bars
ROSELEAF

23-24 Sandport Place; tel. 0131 476 5268; www.
roseleaf.co.uk; 10am-1am daily; beer from £3.60 a
pint, cocktails £5.50-7.75

This sweet bar-café is well known for its pottails (cocktails served in a tea pot). Gimmicky names aside, it's a coy bar that welcomes everyone, from babes in arms to fun young things and a more mature crowd. Cocktails are good and, at between £5.50 and £7.75, a lot cheaper than some city center bars. Try the Rhubarb and Custard, which stays true to its name. There is nice music on the stereo and board games to liven up lazy drinking days, but it's quiet enough to hear what your friend is saying, and the pub grub is not bad either.

Pubs
PORT O'LEITH

58 Constitution Street; tel. 0131 555 5503;
2:30pm-1am daily; beer from £3.60 a pint, wine from
£12 a bottle

Port O'Leith was once the domain of dockers and seafarers, and a traditional morning order here was for a whisky and a pony (a small glass of beer). The tight-knit locals' pub became renowned for its weekly discos and occasional Rocky Horror Show nights under previous landlady Mary Monarty. The jury is still out on its facelift in 2017 and whether the introduction of craft beers was a good idea. It's certainly lost some of its original flavor, but it's still a fun place to come on a Friday or Saturday night, particularly if you want some local chat.

Live Music
LEITH FOLK CLUB

221 Ferry Road; tel. 07833 135 399, texts only; www.
leithfolkclub.com; open at 7:30pm; tickets £8 (unless
stated otherwise); beer from £3.60, wine from £4

Despite its name, you don't have to be a member to attend one of the many folk, blues, or country gigs at the Leith Folk Club. The nonprofit venue exists to bring good world music to the local community, and the atmosphere is inclusive (you can even enter the local raffle) with a fully engaged audience, which is nice to see.

Performing Arts and Entertainment

CONCERT HALLS AND EVENT VENUES
USHER HALL

Lothian Road; tel. 0131 228 1155; www.usherhall.
co.uk; lunchtime concerts £4

First opening in 1914 and set in an Edwardian-modern hybrid building in the West End, Scotland's premier concert hall is renowned for its incredible acoustics. It has been the main venue for the Edinburgh International Festival since the festival first ran in 1947 and is used in Freedom of the City ceremonies. It also hosts visiting orchestras as well as respected jazz, blues, and world music musicians. The opulent **Usher Hall Organ,** covered in Spanish mahogany, takes center stage, and a lunchtime concert by city organist John Kitchen is not to be missed (Mondays at 1.10pm but check website for dates and tickets). Kitchen plays a mix of classical pieces and organ classics and even occasionally takes requests. Book in advance as often there is a huge queue on the day. Lunchtime concerts are £4; prices vary for other events.

SUMMERHALL

Summerhall Place; tel. 0131 560 1580; www. summerhall.co.uk; 9am-11pm Mon.-Thurs., 9am-1am Fri., 9:30am-1am Sat., 11am-11pm Sun.

One of the coolest places to hang out both during the Edinburgh Festival and at other times of the year, this multi-arts complex is considered something of a creative village and the go-to place for the city's hungry culture vultures looking for intimate events (none of the spaces are huge). It's set on the site of the old Royal Dick Veterinary College, and you'll see many artifacts from the building's former function on display. Shows here consistently attract critical acclaim and are held across several venues, from outside areas such as **The Terrace and the Roundabout** (particularly popular during the festival) and inside venues such as **The Dissection Room**—home to the regular funk DJ night, Soulsville, and the popular live music lineup of Nothing Ever Happens Here—which both gives a platform to new bands and hosts established artists. There is also a regular Ceilidh night every Tuesday from 8pm.

QUEEN'S HALL

85-89 Clerk Street; tel. 0131 668 2019; www. thequeenshall.net

This former church near Summerhall is now a 900-seat event space that hosts about 200 concerts a year and is the home of the Scottish Chamber Orchestra.

THE PLEASANCE

60 Pleasance Courtyard; tel. 0131 556 1513; www. pleasance.co.uk

One of the most revered venues during festival season, what started as a long bet on the eastern fringes of the city near Holyrood Park now attracts international performers of repute, so much so it even spawned an offshoot in London.

Throughout August the cobbled courtyard between the two main buildings becomes a huge beer garden for people attending one of the performances as they wander in and out of the main venues of **The Pleasance Bar** and the **Cabaret Bar,** which accommodate 320 and 164 people respectively. More popular shows can also be hosted in the 750-seater **Pleasance Grand,** and there is a kidzone for little ones. It's so well catered for that many people simply set up here for the day and don't venture elsewhere. Outside festival season, there are comedy and music events throughout the year, and the Edinburgh Festival previews in July are always worth a visit.

THEATER

TRAVERSE THEATRE

10 Cambridge Street; tel. 0131 228 1404; www. traverse.co.uk

Next door to Usher Hall, this theater dedicated to new writing is a revelation. It plays a pivotal role during the Edinburgh Festival, but its year-round commitment to producing and showcasing cutting-edge shows lead many to refer to it as the "Fringe venue that got away."

EDINBURGH PLAYHOUSE

18-22 Greenside Lane; tel. 0844 871 3014; www. atgtickets.com/venues/edinburgh-playhouse

This former cinema, modeled on New York's Roxy Cinema, hosts touring musicals and concerts from around the UK, including hit West End shows, at a snip of the London prices. Its authentic art deco facade gives it a vintage feel, but bar prices feel anything but old-fashioned, with drinks starting at around £4.50 for a can of beer.

ASSEMBLY ROOMS

54 George Street; tel. 0131 220 4248; www.
assemblyroomsedinburgh.co.uk

This New Town Georgian venue, with a grand portico (added in the first half of the 19th century) plays an integral role both in the city's annual Hogmanay celebrations and the Edinburgh Festival. At other times of the year it is a multi-use building worth visiting for a play or concert if only to see inside the stunning ballroom with its gigantic crystal chandeliers, rich damask curtains, and intricate gilt decorations.

★ COMEDY

THE STAND COMEDY CLUB

York Place; tel. 0131 558 7272; www.thestand.
co.uk; 7.30pm-12am Mon.-Weds., 7pm-12am
Thurs., 6pm-12am Fri. & Sat., 12:30pm-3:30pm
& 7:30pm-12am Sun.; box office open 10am-7pm
Mon.-Fri. & 12pm-7pm Sat.; tickets £3-15

With venues in Glasgow and Newscastle, The Stand is nevertheless the undisputed king of Edinburgh's comedy scene. There's comedy every night of the week, but tickets, particularly for the much-lauded Saturday night show, do sell out so book a few days before to avoid disappointment. If you want to dip your toe into Edinburgh comedy, then this New Town club is a good place to start. Many big touring acts choose here to perform; plus, with £3 tickets on Monday for The Stand's infamous Red Raw night of new talent and a free improv show on Sunday afternoons, it really won't break the bank.

THE BASEMENT GILDED BALLOON

204 Rose Street; tel. 0131 622 6552; gildedballoon.
co.uk

You can expect to see Fringe favorites most Wednesdays and Thursdays at this low-key but very welcoming little club. The Comedy Show each Friday and Saturday night features an eclectic lineup and is intimate enough that you really feel part of the show. That said, if you don't actually want to be part of the show, avoid the front row (and heckling). There's a small bar at the back of the room, and seating is round small tables without making you feel hemmed in. Afterward, head to **Dirty Dick's** pub across the road, where all the comedians go, for a chance to mingle with some of the stars.

CINEMA

CAMEO CINEMA

38 Home Street; tel. 0871 902 5723; www.
picturehouses.com/cinema/Cameo_Picturehouse;
£7.50 all day Monday, £12.20 peak, £10.40 off peak

Quentin Tarantino famously proclaimed this discrete art-house cinema—one of the oldest still in use in Scotland—as his favorite place to watch a movie. Whether he still stands by that statement following the acquisition of the former independent by the Picturehouse chain of cinemas in 2012, I don't know, but it's still the go-to cinema of choice for Edinburghers.

Festivals and Events

For the month of August, the whole of Edinburgh is taken over by festival fever as five major cultural events take place concurrently, more than doubling the number of visitors to the city. It's not for the faint-hearted, but it's when Edinburgh is at its best—a vibrant celebration of music, comedy, performance, and literature. The only other time that can perhaps live up to this period in terms of liveliness is the annual New Year's celebration of Hogmanay.

AUGUST

EDINBURGH FRINGE FESTIVAL

Various locations; tel. 0131 226 0026; www.edfringe.
com; August; ticket prices vary

When people talk about the Edinburgh Festival, they're usually referring to the Edinburgh

Fringe Festival. What began as a slight act of rebellion by a small number of theater groups has now grown into the largest arts festival in the world—thousands of performances take place across hundreds of venues each year. Pretty much anyone can perform, meaning that the quality ranges massively, but that's part of the fun: trying to choose what shows will be ground-breaking and which will leave you wishing the ground will swallow you up. There is everything, from comedy to music, cabaret and dance. You do need to book tickets for more well-known acts or hyped up performances, but for a lot of performances you can just turn up on the day. Some events may be free.

EDINBURGH INTERNATIONAL FESTIVAL
Various locations; tel. 0131 473 2000; www.eif.co.uk; August; ticket prices vary

The more mature sibling of the Fringe, this showcase of music, dance, and spoken word leans heavily toward the classical side of things and is often deemed a lot more serious than its little sister. Nevertheless, quality is assured as, unlike the Fringe Festival where anyone can apply for a slot, here top-class musicians, dancers, and visual artists are invited to perform. As it runs at the same time as the Fringe, there's no reason you can't do a little bit of both. Some events may be free.

EDINBURGH MILITARY TATTOO
Castle Esplanade; 9pm Mon.-Fri. and 7:30pm Sat. August; from £25

Each evening throughout festival season, this showcase of military pomp and ceremony takes place in front of the backlit Edinburgh Castle and is watched live by more than 200,000 people. Tightly choreographed routines are performed against a sea of pageantry and accompanied by the rousing battle tunes of Scotland's regiments played by the Massed Pipes and Drums and the Massed Military Bands. The pinnacle of the evening is when the lone piper plays his sorrowful lament from the castle walls, which is then followed by a chorus of "Auld Lang Syne," a riotous fireworks display, and a military flyby. It's rare to witness such a scene of unapologetic patriotism.

Tickets start at £25, but you will be positioned right at the back. There is a much wider choice of seats if you are willing to pay up to £58, while £80 will get you near the front, £150 will get you Premier Seats, and for a place in the Royal Gallery you'll need to fork out upward of £300 per ticket. Some Saturdays there is a second performance at 10:30pm.

EDINBURGH ART FESTIVAL
Various venues; tel. 0131 226 6558; edinburghartfestival.com; prices vary for special exhibitions

Since 2004 this festival, which usually kicks off just prior to the other festivals, has been providing some visual arts amid the forest of stand-up comics and avant-garde theatrics. Set across various galleries throughout the city, including the Dovecot Gallery and the City Art Centre, as well as incorporating some site-specific work in pop-ups designed with the festival in mind, it covers everything from photography to painting and textiles. Many events are free.

EDINBURGH INTERNATIONAL BOOK FESTIVAL
Charlotte Square; tel. 0345 373 5888; www. edbookfest.co.uk; free

For two weeks in the middle of August, this literary event set across a mini tented village in the center of Charlotte Square celebrates the printed form, with talks from novelists, comic-book creators, illustrators, biographers, and more. There are over 900 inspiring events to choose from—it has recently spread out to include parts of George Street too—from sessions to get young readers interested in books to creative writing workshops and discussions on everything from characterization to reporting ethics. The book festival also runs the **Unbound literary cabaret** in the Spiegel tent every night from 9pm to 11pm. Some special events have a fee.

Navigating the Edinburgh Festival

Although Edinburgh is a lively, fun city year-round, it really comes into its own in summer. Each August, hundreds of thousands of people arrive to witness the giant extravaganza that is the Edinburgh Festival.

Over the course of 25 days, the world's largest arts festival takes place in virtually every corner of the city. Arts houses, theaters, comedy clubs, and pubs become a living, breathing entertainment showcase, and acts are notoriously varied.

But that's not all: **Princes Street Gardens** becomes an outdoor concert space, and huge temporary structures are erected across the city to house the seemingly endless stream of performers, from comedians, to musicians, acrobatics, and artists. It's relentless, but in a good way. Performances start in the morning and go on until 5am with just a short closure before shenanigans start again— it's the only way it can fit in all 50,000 performances.

Though it's known collectively as the Edinburgh Festival, it is made up of several festivals that run at the same time—most significantly, the **Edinburgh International Festival**, which features a program of dance, opera, music, and theater, and the **Edinburgh Festival Fringe,** which, though it began as an unofficial sideshow to the Edinburgh International Festival, is now a festival of epic proportions. Also running at the same time as the main festivals are the Royal **Edinburgh Military Tattoo,** the **Edinburgh Art Festival,** and the **Edinburgh International Book Festival.** In truth, though, it's hard to know where one festival begins and the other ends.

PLANNING YOUR VISIT

You need to allow at least two days to have an enjoyable festival experience—the first day will be spent trying to navigate the crowds and figuring out the best places to go—but three to five days is better.

TICKETS

Many of the events are free, but some are ticketed. It can be a daunting prospect to decide what to see, and some shows will be better than others.

In terms of the Fringe, it's often easier to get tickets in the first week (before the reviews are in), but if you want to wait and see which ones have passed the critics' test, aim to visit from the second week on. Make sure you grab a copy of the official **Fringe Programme,** which is released online each June (www.edfringe.com) and can also be picked up at many outlets across the city. There's also a useful app released each year. In addition, it's worth following the festival's

DECEMBER
HOGMANAY

Various locations; tel. 0131 510 0395; www. edinburghshogmanay.com; street party tickets £31, concert in the Gardens from £65, other prices vary

During Hogmanay, one of the greatest New Year's celebrations in the world, the streets of Edinburgh come alive with festivities. Central to proceedings is the huge street party, plus there is a Ceilidh under the castle, a concert in Princes Street Gardens, and an incredible

fireworks display. Tickets sell out fast and so do hotels, so book well in advance.

The evocative torch procession, inspired by Viking tradition, that takes place down the Royal Mile to Holyrood Park is a memorable sight, but to truly make it an unforgettable experience, pay a little extra for the chance to join in with your own torch rather than remain a bystander. There is no overriding Hogmanay ticket to get you access to everything, but a ticket for the Concert in the Gardens will give you access to the street

social media channels throughout August for last-minute changes and surprise appearances. The *Scotsman* newspaper also does a good hour-by-hour listing of what is on at the festival each day. In addition, local freebie magazine *The List* publishes weekly during the festival (it's normally every other month), and reviews in the *Edinburgh Evening News* are really useful.

Although it is tempting to squeeze in as many shows as possible, you are in danger of falling victim to festival fatigue. Better still is to choose two to three shows you'd like to see and then leave a bit of time in your schedule to fit in an unexpected visit to the best new thing that your new pal at the bar just told you about.

ACCOMMODATIONS

Accommodation in Edinburgh books up fast in the lead up to the festival, so if you want a good choice of places to stay without having to remortgage your house, you need to book around six months in advance.

Throughout August the population of Edinburgh more than doubles—in addition to the many thousands of visitors, there are also around 27,000 performers and participants to house. Unsurprisingly, hotels in and around the Old Town book up first, so if you are looking for somewhere to stay just a couple of months prior, you do need to think smart.

The **Festival Partnership** (edinburghfestival.net), a letting agent focused on finding accommodation in the city in August, has lots of private apartments to rent, but you would be looking at paying upward of £750 per week for a studio apartment and a lot more for properties sleeping three or more.

The **Edinburgh International Festival's website** (eif.co.uk) has suggestions of places to stay—from premium hotels with prices as high as £400 per night, to much more affordable self-catering or Airbnb options, where you can pay as little as £40 per night.

One sensible alternative is to book a room in the University of Edinburgh's student digs of **Pollock Halls** (www.book.accom.ed.ac.uk), where you can get a basic en suite with buffet breakfast for £490 per week (less for a shared bathroom), or, for perhaps the best value for money, **Edinburgh Festival Camping,** near the airport, has pitches plus bell tents for hire at a snip of the price. The campsite is serviced by buses until 11:50pm (£1.80 or £2.80 each way, depending on the bus), after which you can try two late-night buses at 1:30am or 3am. Or you can get an Uber for around £25 if you want to stay out and head back to site when you choose.

And, if you are unlucky enough to find all accommodations booked up (unlikely), you could consider staying in Glasgow, which is just 50 minutes away by train, with trains running slightly later (until 12:30am) during the festival.

party where you'll be able to view the fireworks, so it's close. Don't forget, Hogmanay celebrations carry on to 1 January (2 January is a national holiday).

JULY
CEREMONY OF THE KEYS

Palace of Holyroodhouse

Each summer Her Majesty the Queen takes up residence in the Palace of Holyroodhouse during what is known as Holyrood Week (or Royal Week). Ancient tradition dictates that, before she does so, she must be handed the keys on the forecourt of the palace by the Lord Provost in the Ceremony of the Keys, which she then hands back—a symbolic gesture that shows she is entrusting the keys into the hands of elected officials. During the ceremony, the national anthem is played, and a 21-gun royal salute rings out from Edinburgh Castle at the other end of the Royal Mile.

Tours and Experiences

EDINBURGH LITERARY PUB TOUR

18-20 Grassmarket; tel. 0131 226 6665; www.
edinburghliterarypubtour.co.uk; £14 or £12 in
advance online

This lively two-hour tour, which starts inside the Beehive Inn in Grassmarket, is as much a pub tour as it is a literary one (feel free to buy drinks along the route). Told by two actors—one playing a bohemian, one an intellectual—who take visitors in and out of some of the city's oldest taverns, or howffs, gives invaluable insight into the writing habits of some of Scotland's literary greats. It was in the dark closes and far-from-wholesome drinking dens of the city that Robert Burns and Sir Walter Scott sought inspiration, and this tour will give you a taste of some of the colorful characters they met along the way.

AULD REEKIE TOURS

45 Niddry Street; tel. 0131 557 4700; www.
auldreekietours.com; from £12, concessions £10

Want to scare yourself witless? These ghost tours take place at some of the spookiest locations across the city, the Edinburgh Vaults (sometimes called the Niddry Street Vaults). The original Vaults Tour (about one hour) burrows beneath South Bridge Street where your guide will regale you with horrid tales of life in the slums and even bring you to an underground witches' temple.

EDINBURGH BUS TOURS

Waverley Bridge; tel. 0131 220 0770; www.
edinburghtour.com; Edinburgh Tour adult £15,
concessions £14, child £7.50, family £36; Royal
Edinburgh Ticket adult £55, concessions £48, child
£30

While by no means the cheapest way of traveling around the city, if time is short, then hopping on or off one of these bus tours with a knowledgeable guide can be a great way of cramming in as many sights as possible. The Edinburgh Tour takes in many of the main sights of the Old Town and New Town, and you can hop on and off at your leisure throughout the day; the Royal Edinburgh Ticket allows unlimited travel aboard three bus routes over two days, plus entry to Edinburgh Castle, the Royal Yacht Britannia, and the Palace of Holyroodhouse.

GEOWALKS

23 Summerfield Place; tel. 0131 555 5488; www.
geowalks.co.uk/iarthur.html; £25 for a two-hour tour

If you don't want to walk to Arthur's Seat on your own, then joining this tour with Geowalks, accompanied with a geologist, can be a good alternative. Setting off from Canongate, you can opt to do it on your own or in a group (the more people the cheaper it will be). Choose between a two-hour hike to Arthur's Seat or a gentle circular walk around Salisbury Crags for views of Edinburgh's most famous peak.

BOBCAT ALPACAS

Bonaly Road; tel. 07963 324 922; bobcat-alpacas.
co.uk; from £20

It may not be the most obvious choice of activity on a visit to Scotland, but this alpaca farm at the foot of the Pentland Hills consistently wins rave reviews. Visitors can take part in a 90-minute alpaca experience that includes learning how to handle the animals and even taking them for a walk in the surrounding countryside before returning to the farm to feed them. Weekend visits must be booked three months in advance. The farm is just a 20-minute drive from the city center, or you can catch either the no. 10 or no. 16 bus with Lothian Buses.

Sports and Recreation

Golf is a sport almost synonymous with Scotland, and while Edinburgh may not boast courses in quite the same league as those in and around St. Andrews, it nevertheless has a large number of courses for its size. The sport Edinburgh is probably best associated with, though, is rugby. **Murrayfield Stadium** to the west of the center is the largest of its kind in Scotland and home to Scottish Rugby Union. Most of the nation's test matches are played here. If you can get a ticket, watching a match alongside bona fide fans can be an exhilarating experience.

Elsewhere, Edinburgh has lots of green spaces in which to kick back and take in the views or to recover from the night before. With cycle routes, waterways, and its own nature park in the form of Holyrood Park, the city also offers opportunity for adventure.

PARKS

THE MEADOWS
Melville Drive

This park just south of the Old Town marks the boundary with the Southside and hosts many community events and festivals throughout spring and summer. It's also home to the largest play area in the city and is a good place to catch some rays when the sun does have its hat on, all while taking in views of Arthur's Seat.

INTERLEITH PARK
Arboretum Road

This is where Stockbridge locals come to walk off their Sunday lunch or laze about on warm afternoons. It also offers good views of Edinburgh Castle, so it's a good shout for watching the New Year's fireworks. There are several lakes to walk by, and the sundial garden is a lovely spot for a picnic.

HIKING AND CYCLING

Hiking to Arthur's Seat is an unmissable experience, but there are lots of other good walking and cycling routes in and around the city too.

WATER OF LEITH WALKWAY

The Water of Leith is a river that runs through Edinburgh, and this pedestrian pathway runs gently alongside it. The walk starts just outside the **Scottish National Gallery of Modern Art** and offers respite from busy city life with little more than the sound of rushing water and birdsong to keep you company, but be careful in wet weather because it can get slippery.

From the gallery you can continue along the Water of Leith all the way to **Stockbridge** where on Sundays you will find a bustling craft and food market (10am-5pm). En route you will pass by Dean Village—a remarkably well preserved old milling town—where you can see Dean Bridge, designed by renowned Scottish civil engineer Thomas Telford, and a little farther along, the elaborate temple around St. Bernard's Well, a natural spring once believed to have healing powers.

If you're feeling particularly energetic, you could follow the Water of Leith (around 4.3 mi/7km from the gallery) all the way to Leith itself, where there are plenty of lunchtime spots along the Shore, such as Fishers in Leith.

BIKETRAX
11 Lochrin Place; tel. 0131 228 6633; www.biketrax. co.uk; from £20 per day

While cycling in the city center can be tricky, getting on two wheels can be great for a little off-road exploration, including around Arthur's Seat and along the banks of the Union Canal. The rental office for this hire company is based in Tollcross in Southside.

ARTHUR'S SEAT CYCLE CIRCUIT

Circling Edinburgh's most famous crag, Arthur's Seat, this cycle route is reasonably strenuous. However, if you have the stamina for it, you'll be rewarded with breathtaking views across Holyrood Park, giving a taste of the wildness the Scottish Highlands has to offer, as well as the Pentland Hills and the Firth of Forth. Starting at St. Margaret's Loch, this route follows Queen's Drive, which loops all the way around the park, with the long-extinct volcano in the middle, until bringing you back to your start point. Be aware that the road is open to traffic, except on Sundays, and that the path that runs alongside it is also used by walkers.

Leaving St. Margaret's Loch (with the loch on your right-hand side), you'll ascend over the next mile to Dunsapie Loch. This is the toughest part of the route. Once you reach Dunsapie, there is a flat stretch from where you can enjoy the views over Duddingston Loch, south Edinburgh, and the Pentland Hills in the distance. Keep following Queen's Drive up a slight incline for views over Edinburgh's Old Town, and then it's the fun bit: downhill all the way down to the Palace of Holyroodhouse and back to where you started. In total, the route is about three miles (5 km) and should take around 30-40 minutes.

UNION CANAL CYCLE PATH

www.scottishcanals.co.uk/activities/cycling/
union-canal

The towpath along the Union Canal is a great place to cycle, although be aware that it does narrow to as little as 3.3 feet (1 m) wide in some places and is also a popular walking route, as well as busy with dog-walkers and anglers, so you'll need to make good use of your bell and display caution when it comes to speed. The good news, though, is that it is traffic-free and pretty much all level, meaning even novices should be able to manage it.

The access point for the start of cycling routes from the city center is at Edinburgh Quay in Fountainbridge, near Haymarket. From here, head west out of the city, riding over a mix of tarmac, cobblestones, and rougher terrain. After eight miles (13.5 km), you'll reach **The Bridge Inn** in Ratho—a charming pub with lots of Scottish ales on tap and good pub grub to replenish you. You could ride back from here or overnight and carry on to Linlithgow (a further 13 mi/21 km) the next morning to see the birthplace of Mary, Queen of Scots.

GOLF

MUSSELBURGH LINKS

Balcarres Road, Musselburgh; tel. 0131 653 5122; www.musselburgholdlinks.co.uk; green fees £15.30 Mon.-Fri., £16.30 Sat.-Sun.; concessions available

Also known as the "Old Golf Course," this historic course just seven miles (11km) out of the city center is reputedly one of the world's oldest—some say Mary, Queen of Scots, even played on it—and it hosted the Open six times in the late Victorian era. Today it is open to visitors year-round, its coastal location ensures you can enjoy sea views as you play, and it has many natural hazards to overcome, creating a real challenge. Buses to bring you here from the city include the no. 124 from Princes Street to Loretto Upper School from which the course is a seven-minute walk. There is even a £10m project underway to restore the course to its former Open condition.

MUIRFIELD OPEN COURSE

Duncur Road, Muirfield; tel. 01620 842 123; www.muirfield.org.uk; green fees £250 for one round and £350 for two rounds (groups of four)

Open to visitors on Tuesdays and Thursdays, this classic links course, which is home to The Honourable Company of Edinburgh Golfers—the oldest golf club in the world—has hosted 16 Open Championships (most recently in 2013). It's considered one of the fairest tests of all Open venues because it has few of the hidden obstacles that plague other courses and its two circuits of nine holes each that rotate in opposite directions means golfers don't have to face the same wind direction on two consecutive holes.

The course is only open to players with handicaps of 18 or less, with groups of four required; green fees are steep, plus you need to book around eight months in advance. The club house is very formal, and lunch for players (12:30pm-3pm) requires a jacket and tie for gentlemen and smart/casual attire for ladies. Indeed, the club is notoriously snooty and old-school—women members have only been permitted since 2017, a change that occurred after the club had its right to host the Open revoked in 2016. It has since had its right to host the Open reinstated.

To get here, take the X5 bus from Waverley Station to Muirfield House (45 minutes), from where it is a five-minute walk, or it's a 45-minute drive along the A1.

BRAID HILLS

*27 Braid Hill Approach; tel. 0131 447 6666; www.
edinburghleisure.co.uk/venues/braid-hills-golf-
course; green fees £25.30 on weekdays, £26.50 on
weekends*

Braid Hills, which occupies the southernmost of the seven hills in and around Edinburgh, offers views of Arthur's Seat, Edinburgh Castle, and the Forth all the way to Fife. It was once the testing ground for legendary Scottish golfers Tommy Armour and James Braid, who practiced hitting balls from one hilly crag to the next. There is a lot of gorse, and the natural sloping landscape can make play hard, but it's worth it, if only for the serene location. Looked after by Edinburgh Leisure, which also manages several other golf courses in and around the city, it's open to visitors seven days a week and is a lot less snooty than Muirfield.

ICE-SKATING

ST. ANDREW SQUARE

*St. Andrew Square; tel. 0844 545 8252; www.
edinburghschristmas.com; mid-Nov.-early Jan.; adult
£9, child £5, family £20*

Each Christmas from mid-November until early January, a giant ice rink encircles the Melville Monument in the center of St. Andrew Square. Skating is by booked time slot, and sessions last 45 minutes. St. Andrew Square is popular in the run up to Christmas, filled with festive families and raucous Christmas parties, and, though it is invariably very cold, the bar serves up hot cider and mulled wine to warm you through. There are usually rides around the rink, including a Merry Go Round and Helter Skelter. Lots of festive fun can also be had at the nearby East Princes Street Gardens.

SPECTATOR SPORTS
Rugby
MURRAYFIELD

*Roseburn Street; tel. 0131 346 5160; ticket.centre@
sru.org.uk; www.scottishrugby.org; match prices vary,
tours adult £10, child £5*

To the west of the city center, this sports stadium is the largest of its kind in Scotland and the home of Scotland's Rugby Union. Tickets to matches can be booked through Scottish Rugby, and those for more popular matches are released in batches over a few months.

Watching a rugby match here is a must for any fan—the atmosphere is electric with high-spirited fans and good-humored banter in the stands. Lots of spectators bring children, and there is food and drink available, though nothing special (burgers and hot dogs, etc.), or you can bring a small amount of food (no large hampers) or sealed bottles of water or soft drinks.

In the past, large concerts have been criticized for being poorly managed (though the rugby tends to go without a hitch). Some supporters can get a bit rowdy and bad-mouthed, but they are in the minority.

If you can't make a match, tours of the stadium are also good and give visitors the chance to see the Calcutta Cup, the trophy awarded to the winning team when England and Scotland play each other in February or March each year (at least until England wins it back), and visit the players' changing room before walking through the tunnel right up to the pitch. Tours are available Monday to Saturday at 11am with an extra tour on Thursdays and Fridays at 2:30pm and should be booked in advance.

Shopping

From boutique outlets to designer shops, high-street brands, and the ubiquitous tartan and whisky stores, Edinburgh has no shortage of places to spend your vacation money.

SHOPPING DISTRICTS

Old Town

The Old Town is the obvious place to shop for souvenirs and specialist Scottish gifts and produce.

ROYAL MILE

While the wares in some of the shops on the Royal Mile are overpriced and of questionable quality, there are still some reputable places to buy authentic items. Plus, it can be a good option if you're short of time and want to combine shopping with seeing some of the city's biggest attractions.

GRASSMARKET AND VICTORIA STREET

Just a few minutes' walk from the castle end of the Royal Mile, Grassmarket and the higgledy-piggledy shops of nearby Victoria Street, one of the places pinpointed as J. K. Rowling's inspiration for Diagon Alley and which curves all the way back up to George IV Bridge, are filled with independent and specialist proprietors, which are of a slightly higher caliber than some of the Scottish-themed gift shops elsewhere.

New Town

PRINCES STREET

You'll find high-street favorites such as Zara and Urban Outfitters on Princes Street and can gaze at views of the castle as you pop in and out of shops. Parallel to Princes Street and connecting Charlotte Square to St. Andrew Square, **George Street** is home to more upmarket and chic clothing stores, such as Hobbs and LK Bennett.

BROUGHTON STREET

Broughton Street a little northeast of George Street is fast becoming a hotspot for trendy independents. You'll find a high density of good food shops among alternative boutiques and slightly left-field gift shops.

Grassmarket shops

West End

The cobbled lanes of the West End, in and around William Street, hides some unique retailers such as Lily Luna, which sells handcrafted jewelry and is always worth a wander.

Stockbridge

This neighborhood is home to a variety of quirky, bohemian independent retailers and charity shops, particularly around **Raeburn Place.** On Sundays, it's almost compulsory to pop along to **Stockbridge Market** and browse the artisan stalls for gifts or nibbles.

Southside
BRUNTSFIELD

A 20-minute walk south from Grassmarket (or a ride on the no. 42 bus from outside the Scottish National Gallery) will bring you to Bruntsfield, an affluent neighborhood known for its unique gift shops and cafés.

OLD TOWN
Clothing
HAWICO SCOTLAND

71 Grassmarket; tel. 0131 225 8634; www.hawico. com; 10am-6pm Mon.-Sat.

Starting business in 1874 during the Industrial Revolution, Hawico has made a name for itself across the world for producing luxurious cashmere knitwear. Today, Hawico has stores in London, Milan, and Tokyo (and many places in between), yet every single piece in both its men's and women's collections is still made in its original factory in the Borders town of Hawick. If none of the pieces in the collection (which start upward of £100 for a cashmere scarf and around £300-plus for cashmere cardigans) quite tickle your fancy, you can make use of the Create Your Own special order service in store.

★ MARCHBRAE

375 High Street; tel. 0131 226 3997; marchbrae.com; 9:30am-6pm Mon.-Thurs., 9:30am-7pm Fri. and Sat., 10am-6pm Sun.

This shop matches traditional Scottish fabrics and designs with practical clothing for men and women that will actually come in handy should you venture to the Highlands. Choose from quilted Barbour jackets perfect for keeping the Scottish chill off, fitted tweed jackets, and cozy tartan slippers.

HOUSE OF EDINBURGH

2 St. Giles Street; tel. 0131 225 5178; 10am-6pm daily

House of Edinburgh offers a good selection of lambswool tartan scarves, alongside kilts, cashmere jumpers, and cardigans, and quality is higher than what you'll find in some Royal Mile shops. It's neatly laid out too, with rows of color-coded men's and women's sweaters making for a much more pleasurable browsing experience.

WALKER AND SLATER

16-20 Victoria Street; tel. 0131 220 9750; www. walkerslater.com/edinburgh-grassmarket-menswear-store; 10am-6pm Mon.-Weds., Fri. & Sat., 10am-7pm Thurs., 11am-5pm Sun.

Tweed is the order of the day at this smart tailor, which makes you feel a little like you've taken a time machine to the 19th century. Mannequins are adorned with double-breasted jackets and cravats, while there is a good choice of ready-to-wear apparel. If you have the time and budget, then you can't beat getting a made-to-measure jacket or suit (upward of £1200); the turnaround time is 10 weeks, and they do like to get you in for a fitting before finalizing (so good if you are making a return trip, but if needs be, it can be finished off back home). This is the men's shop; there is also a ladies' shop at 46 Victoria Street.

Whisky
WHISKI ROOMS

4-7 North Bank Street; tel. 0131 225 7224; www. whiskirooms.co.uk; 10am-10pm daily

This shop, which also has a good restaurant and offers whisky tasting courses, has over 500 whiskies on offer. If you know what you want, they should have it here. If you don't, the knowledgeable staff will be able to talk you through some choice buys. If you don't want to carry your purchases home with you, you could order online as the shop ships worldwide.

★ ROYAL MILE WHISKIES

379 High Street; tel. 0131 524 9380; www. royalmilewhiskies.com; 10am-8pm daily

This renowned whisky merchant is a good place to pick up a bottle of your favorite tipple. Its interior is a little more old-school than others in the area, with row upon row of wooden shelves crammed with whiskies and attentive staff to help guide your choice between single malts from well-established distilleries to those from smaller scale producers. There is also a good selection of Japanese whiskies, bourbons, and Irish brands. Plus, they ship worldwide if you haven't space to cart it home.

CADENHEAD'S

172 Canongate; tel. 0131 556 5864; www.cadenhead. scot; 10:30am-5:30pm Mon.-Sat.

A popular place among real whisky fans, Cadenhead's is the oldest independent bottler in the whole of Scotland. Though the company's Edinburgh shop is a mere bairn, the company has been operating since 1842, with its origins in Aberdeen. Never mind all that though, what you need to know is that in the cramped confines of Cadenhead's you'll be surrounded by bottles of limited and unique whiskies, and staff have an inexhaustible amount of knowledge to impart. You can try whisky straight from the cask, and there's also a good selection of gin and rum.

Food and Wine
I.J. MELLIS CHEESEMONGER

30a Victoria Street; tel. 0131 226 6215; www. mellischeese.net/stores; 9:30am-7pm Mon.-Sat., 11am-6pm Sun.

This artisan cheese seller specializes in Scottish farmhouse cheese made by small-scale producers, and, though there are now three shops across the city, this small outlet, which has tempting cheese piled high, is the original. If you like what you taste, make your way to the **Bruntsfield shop** (330

Morningside Road), which has its very own Cheese Lounge where you can pair your favorite cheeses with some good wine from small-scale producers.

Books
BLACKWELL'S

53-62 South Bridge; tel. 0131 622 8222; blackwells. co.uk/bookshop/shops; 9am-8pm Mon., Tues., Thurs., and Fri., 9:30am-8pm Weds., 9am-6pm Sat., 12pm-6pm Sun.

This huge bookshop just a short walk from the Royal Mile will keep even the hungriest of bibliophiles happy for hours. It's the largest bookshop in Edinburgh, and its Scottish Room is a great place to shop for books on Scottish history.

Gifts
MR WOOD'S FOSSILS

53-59 Cowgatehead; tel. 0131 220 1344; www. mrwoodsfossils.co.uk; 10am-5:30pm daily

This unique treasure trove began life selling the collections of renowned fossil hunter Stan Wood, who passed away in 2012. Self-taught Wood is best known for discovering the *Westlothiana lizziae*—"Lizzie"—which was thought at the time to be the oldest reptile ever discovered and now on display in the National Museum of Scotland. Alongside fossils, minerals, and meteorites, shoppers can also buy jewelry featuring the likes of ammonite spirals or even 500-million-year-old trilobites. Minerals start from as little as £2.50, while a meteorite pendant (in some cases dating back billions of years) will start from just £85.

NEW TOWN
Kilts
21ST CENTURY KILTS

48 Thistle Street; tel. 0131 220 9450; 21stcenturykilts. com; 11am-6pm Tues., Thurs., Fri., and Sat. although appointment required

This independent shop sells a mix of ready-to-wear kilts alongside bespoke kilts that can be made within eight weeks of your fitting. The store's aim is to make kilt-wearing fashionable once more, and, though they do look good, it comes at a price: off-the-rail kilts start at a wallet-bulging £650.

Clothing
JOEY D

54 Broughton Street; tel. 0131 557 6672; 10:30am-6pm daily

For couture clothing with a distinct Scottish edge, Joey D is hard to beat. He specializes in making cutting-edge fashion (for men and women) using old cast-offs of tweed, tartan, and army-wear. The end results have quite a punk feel, and Joey himself is quite a character—chatty yet humble. Don't be put off by the slightly dingy workshop; anyone is welcome to browse the shop and Joey is usually around, working on his next project.

Malls
MULTREES WALK

St. Andrew Square; tel. 0131 557 0050; www. multreeswalk.co.uk; 10am-6pm Mon.-Sat., 11am-5pm Sun.

Home to Scotland's only Harvey Nichols, this pleasant pedestrian square peppered with high-end shops is the place to go for designer brands, including Louis Vuitton, Burberry, Mulberry, Victoria Beckham, and Stella McCartney. If you're looking for luxury clothes and gifts, then hotfoot it here.

Gifts
DRAGONFLY

111a Broughton Street; tel. 0131 629 4246; www. thedragonflygifts.co.uk; 10am-6pm Mon., Tues., Weds., Fri., and Sat., 10am-7pm Thurs., 11am-5pm Sun.

If you need a bit of inspiration when it comes to gift-buying, let Louise, owner of this original little shop, guide you. There are quaint tea sets, local artworks, retro and vintage clothing (for kids and adults), and well-priced jewelry.

WEST END
Clothing
FRONTIERS MAN

18 Stafford Street; tel. 0131 538 3546; www. frontiers-man.com; 10:30am-6:30pm Mon.-Thurs., 10am-6pm Fri.& Sat., occasional Sun. opening

The nearby Frontiers Woman (16b Stafford Street) has been a favorite West End shop for years, and a couple of years ago they opened this, their brother shop. Both shops sell luxurious clothes from smaller labels with lines not sold in many high-street shops. The ethos is in creating individual style with a little flair, so bright colors and vibrant

Stockbridge Market

prints feature heavily. The lambswool hats and scarves made here in Scotland are particularly lovely.

Jewelry
★ LILY LUNA

43 William Street; 0131 467 8245; www.lilyluna.co.uk; 10:30am-6pm Mon.-Sat.

This jewelry shop is a great little find. Pieces are all handmade and sourced from across the world, and fairly priced they are, too. You can find ethical pieces from Ethiopia alongside delicate necklaces and rings made out of oxidized silver with unusual geometric designs, and they are pretty much all gorgeous.

Books
★ ARMCHAIR BOOKS

72 West Port; tel. 0131 229 5927; armchairbooks. co.uk; 10am-6:30pm daily

Located just above Grassmarket, this old second-hand bookstore is the stuff of book lovers' dreams. Its dusty shelves are stacked with all manner of tomes, and the joy is in taking your time and searching for unexpected finds.

STOCKBRIDGE
Markets
★ STOCKBRIDGE MARKET

1 Saunders Street; tel. 0131 261 6181; www. stockbridgemarket.com; 10am-5pm Sun.

This popular outdoor Sunday food and craft market isn't huge, but it's always bustling with locals and visitors looking to pick up organic goods or unusual gifts, such as framed prints of Scottish wildlife and handmade tweed bags, from small independent traders. It's a good, cheap lunchtime spot too. **Harajuku Kitchen** serves good Japanese street food, while the health conscious will want to stop by the **Edinburgh Fermentarium** stall for some Stoatin' Sauerkraut (including turmeric root and Himalayan salt) or the Braw Slaw—its version of coleslaw that includes beetroot, apple, cabbage, and star anise.

Clothing
MARY'S LIVING & GIVING SHOP

34a Raeburn Place; tel. 0131 315 2856; www. facebook.com/mlgstockbridge; 9:30am-5pm Mon. Sat., 11am-5pm Sun.

Stockbridge is overflowing with good secondhand shops, but this is perhaps the best when it comes to kitting yourself out. Part of fashion and retail expert Mary Portas's brainwave of transforming the high street by turning charity shops into places people actually want to go to, it feels more vintage boutique (think London's King's Road, circa 1969) than jumble sale, and the quality of clothing (particularly women's) is high, even though the prices are not.

Jewelry
ANNIE SMITH

12 Raeburn Place; tel. 0131 332 5749; www. anniesmith.co.uk; 10am-5:30pm Mon.-Sat., 12pm-5pm Sun.

This jewelry studio is the labor of love of husband-and-wife duo Annie and Ariel who dreamed of setting up their own jewelrymaking business. All of the pieces you see are handcrafted on site, and the range includes chunky pendants and earrings, beautiful pearl bracelets and necklaces (from £95), as well as diamond rings.

BRUNTSFIELD
Food and Drink
COCO OF BRUNTSFIELD

174 Bruntsfield Place; tel. 0131 290 2159; cocochocolatier.com; 10am-6pm Mon.-Sat., 12pm-4pm Sun.

If you like chocolate (at least dark chocolate), you'll like this place, but if you like chocolate and pretty things, you'll love it. It's pretty much a free-for-all in terms of creativity—the chocolatiers are free to create unique flavors, while local artists design the wrappers to make them really stand out. Recommended flavor combinations include haggis spice and gin and tonic, while the gorgeous tins of hot chocolate make for lovely gifts. There is also a branch in Stockbridge (20 Raeburn Place), which is open 10am-6pm daily.

PEKOETEA

20 Leven Street; tel. 0131 477 1838; www.pekoetea. co.uk; 10am-6pm Mon.-Sat., 12pm-5pm Sun.

This charming little tea shop has its own tea bar, so you can come and do a tasting before you choose what loose-leaf tea you want to buy to take home. It's a small enterprise with big ambitions, and its high-quality teas are imported direct from source in China. Next on its to-do list is to open a flavoring and blending room so it can flavor all its teas right here in Bruntsfield.

Jewelry
ROSIE BROWN

148 Bruntsfield Place; tel. 0131228 9269; www. rosiebrownjewellery.com; 9:30am-5:30pm Mon.-Sat., 11am-5pm Sun.

The lovely pieces in this shop are designed by owner Rosie herself and made in the shop's workshop by experienced jewelers. The range is very feminine and classic, with links featuring motifs such as butterflies and raindrops round pearl bracelets and silver and gold bangles and chains. The small shop is genteel with a calm ambience, and each piece is hallmarked and presented in a gift box wrapped in ribbon, which will make the receiver of your gift feel very special indeed.

Food

With no fewer than four Michelin-starred restaurants, food in Edinburgh is now serious business. Food provenance is of the utmost importance, so you will find that many restaurants only serve ingredients that are in season.

There are good restaurants in pretty much every corner of the city. In and around the Royal Mile and Old Town fine-dining restaurants make the most of the splendid views, while a slightly more glamorous crowd can be seen in the dining rooms of the New Town. The port district of Leith is understandably the go-to place for fresh seafood, while Stockbridge is hot on its heels as a foodie destination of note. Meanwhile, in the Southside, the village-style vibe is the perfect setting for an array of relaxed cafés and ethical coffee shops.

If you want to sample traditional Scottish fare while you're here, then haggis is the first dish you'll want to try. Most of the restaurants in the city will have some variation of this dish of sheep liver, lungs, and heart minced with lots of spices, onion, suet, and oatmeal, and, if it doesn't appear with your cooked breakfast, you are within your rights to send the breakfast back (the same applies if there is no black pudding or tattie scones).

If the sound of sheep entrails doesn't appeal, then vegetarian alternatives are available. The common accompaniment to haggis is neeps and tatties (swede, or rutabaga, and potato), usually mashed together.

You'd also be a fool not to try Scottish wild salmon (ideally smoked) or indeed roasted grouse (particularly when shooting season starts after the Glorious 12th, or August 12), which are bountiful on menus.

OLD TOWN
Traditional Fare
★ THE GRAIN STORE

30 Victoria Street; tel. 0131 225 7635; www. grainstore-restaurant.co.uk; noon-2:30pm and 6pm-9:45pm Mon.-Sat., noon-2:30pm and 6pm-9:30pm Sun.; entrées £14

Set beneath the stone archways of the original store rooms high above Victoria Street's shops, this intimate candlelit restaurant is a lovely setting for sampling Scottish produce with a creative flair. Absolutely everything is made on site—from the pasta to the freshly baked bread—and dishes include home-smoked Orkney salmon and a good selection of game, including pigeon and partridge. It's not cheap, but food this good does come at a price.

THE DORIC

15-16 Market Street; tel. 0131 225 1084; www. the-doric.com; 12pm-10pm daily; entrées £8

This bistro above a charming old pub serves hearty fare at middling prices. Comfort dishes include homemade shepherd's pie and steak and chips. Don't miss the Haggis Bons, deep-fried haggis balls served with a turnip and mustard sauce.

WHISKI BAR & RESTAURANT

119 High Street, Royal Mile; tel. 0131 556 3095; www.whiskibar.co.uk; 11am-10pm Mon.-Thurs., 10am-10:30pm Fri.-Sun.; entrées £8

This restaurant-cum-bar comes alive with Scottish music every night of the week, and the food is good, too. With all-day dining, it's a good lunchtime stop halfway down the Royal Mile, or a place to go at night for the house favorite Haggis Tower, served with neeps, tatties, and their very own whisky sauce.

CONTINI CANNONBALL

356 Castlehill; tel. 0131 225 1550; www.contini.com/cannonball; noon-3pm and 5:30pm-10pm Tues.-Sat.; entrées £8

On the top floor of a three-story building, this restaurant offers fine views of both the castle and the Royal Mile. It is renowned for its Scottish oysters, and other house specials include grilled lobster, Scotch beef, and Cannonballs—crumbed haggis balls with a homemade whisky marmalade served with a 10-year-old Glengoyne whisky and pickled turnip. Pay a visit to the **Whisky Bar** too, open from Tuesday to Saturday.

HOWIES RESTAURANT

10-14 Victoria Street; tel. 0131 225 1721; www. howies.uk.com/victoria-street-edinburgh; lunch noon-2:30pm Mon.-Thurs., noon-3pm Sat.-Sun., dinner 5:30pm-10pm daily; entrées £5.95

The flagship of this small family-owned portfolio (there is another Howies on Waterloo Place and one in Aberdeen, plus the family opened Scotts Kitchen on Victoria Terrace in 2017), Howies prides itself on using locally sourced produce from Scotland's natural larder. Venison comes from its estate in Perthshire, salmon from the Shetland Isles, and you can be assured that everything else on your plate is in season. The set lunches offer great value, and there is an early dining offer too. From Sunday to Thursday you can even bring your own wine or champagne.

Modern Scottish

★ WEDGWOOD THE RESTAURANT

267 Canongate; tel. 0131 558 8737; www. wedgwoodtherestaurant.co.uk; noon-3pm and 6pm-10pm daily; entrées £9.95

Though the food at this husband-and-wife-run restaurant is definitely of fine-dining quality, the service is anything but sniffy. The set lunch menus offer the best value, but for a real taste of what they are capable of, try the Wee Tour of Scotland tasting menu (£50). It's Scottish food, no doubt about it, but it has been influenced by Paul Wedgwood's love of travel. The Sound of Mull scallops come with a cauliflower korma with pistachio and peanut crust, while the Highland venison with West Calder black pudding has the surprise addition of smoked paprika. If you're feeling particularly flush, you could add a wine pairing (for an extra £35).

Fine Dining

★ THE WITCHERY BY THE CASTLE

352 Castlehill, Royal Mile; tel. 0131 225 5613; www. thewitchery.com; lunch noon-4:30pm, afternoon tea 3pm-4:30pm, dinner 4:30pm-11:30pm daily; entrees £10

The Witchery's rich baroque dining room is one of the most romantic places to dine in the city, and the restaurant's Angus beef steak tartare is the stuff of legend. On warmer nights, **The Secret Garden** is a lovely little enclave hidden in a historic courtyard with its own terrace. Whenever you come, you will inevitably see well-dressed locals and travelers splashing out and tucking into fresh seafood platters and rich dishes of game, beef, lamb, or fish, all served in the most theatrical of settings.

TOWER RESTAURANT

National Museum of Scotland, Chambers Street; tel. 0131 225 3003; www.tower-restaurant.com; brunch 10am-12:30pm, lunch noon-5pm, afternoon tea 2pm-6pm daily, dinner 5pm-10pm Sun.-Thurs., 5pm-10:30pm Fri.-Sat.; entrées £12.95

The city's first rooftop restaurant with views across the Old Town (including of the castle, of course), the Tower Restaurant is open for brunch, lunch, and dinner and is a good spot for cocktails too. A celebrity haunt—J. K. Rowling has been known to visit when she's in town—it's a special occasion kind of place that specializes in seafood and delicious steaks.

Seafood
ONDINE

2 George IV Bridge; tel. 0131 226 1888; www. ondinerestaurant.co.uk; noon-3pm and 5:30pm-10pm Mon.-Sat., closed Sun.; entrées £15

Ondine is the place to go to for sustainable and fresh seafood. Huge windows offer superb views of the Old Town, and tempting sharing dishes include the roasted shellfish platter and the more standard fruits of the sea. There are a couple of meat mains for those averse to seafood, but it would be a crying shame not to try the crab risotto, lemon sole, or lobster.

Steak
CHOP HOUSE MARKET STREET

Arch 15 East Market Street; tel. 0131 629 1551; www. chophousesteak.co.uk; noon-5pm and 5pm-10:30pm Mon.-Fri., 10am-3pm (brunch) and noon-10:30pm (main) Sat.-Sun.; entrées £8.50

A simple concept, this very cool brickwork restaurant serves up big cuts of beef cooked over hot coals, leaving them charred on the outside and tender on the inside. It's not for vegetarians: meat is the order of the day here. The cocktails are pretty tasty too. There are also branches in Leith (102 Constitution Street) and Bruntsfield (88 Bruntsfield Place).

Indian
MOTHER INDIA'S CAFÉ

3-5 Infirmary Street; tel. 0131 524 9801; www. motherindia.co.uk; noon-2pm and 5pm-10:30pm Mon.-Weds., noon-10:30pm Thurs., noon-11pm Fri.-Sat., noon-10pm Sun.; dishes £4.95

Serving tapas-style Indian food, this is a very wallet-friendly option that is popular among the student population. Service is swift yet friendly, and dishes are well-sized—4-6 dishes are usually plenty for two, meaning you could have a tasty meal for under £15 a head.

Afternoon Tea
COLONNADES AT THE SIGNET LIBRARY

Signet Library, Parliament Square; tel. 0131 226 1064; www.thesignetlibrary.co.uk/colonnades; 1pm-5pm Mon.-Fri.,11am-5pm Sun., closed Sat.; afternoon tea £34 per person

Perhaps the grandest place in the whole city for afternoon tea, this 19th-century building has been restored to all its fine glory, complete with fluted Corinthian columns around the salon and neoclassical balustrades. The food is of the utmost quality and provided by one of Her Majesty The Queen's very own caterers no less. Afternoon tea is served on silver trays and starts with a selection of savories (ham, pea and truffle pie, and smoked applewood and tomato chutney finger sandwiches), followed by a sweet selection (such as a rosewater Battenberg cake and a strawberry and basil tart), plus freshly made scones with the obligatory clotted cream and jam.

The type of tea you choose will depend on preference—would you rather black tea with milk added as is most common, or perhaps white tea with no additions to counter the richness of the food? Your waiter or waitress will gladly guide you.

Light Bites
LUSCIOUS

261 Canongate; tel. 0131 556 9363; 8am-6:30pm daily; breakfast rolls £3.25

A good pit stop before or after the trek up to Arthur's Seat, this is a no-thrills but clean and homely little café where you can get good coffee, brunch classics such as bacon and poached eggs, plus omelets and toasties.

CAFÉ AT THE PALACE

Palace of Holyroodhouse; tel. 0131 652 3685; afternoon tea noon-4pm Apr.-Oct., noon-3pm Nov.-Mar.; afternoon tea £18.95 per person

End your visit to the Palace of Holyroodhouse with lunch or afternoon tea here. Lunch options include soups, sandwiches, and one or two hot options. You can eat outside on tables in the historic mews or retreat to the pleasant back room. The latter is best for afternoon tea, and at £18.95 (£27 with a glass of champagne) it's a fair bit cheaper than the offering at Colonnades, though it does lack a bit of the finesse.

NEW TOWN
Local Produce
★ THE WEE RESTAURANT

61 Frederick Street; tel. 0131 225 7983; www. theweerestaurant.co.uk; noon-2pm and 6pm-9pm Tues.-Fri. and Sun., noon-9:30pm Sat., closed Mon.; entrees £7.95

Just five minutes from Princes Street you'll come away from this reliably good restaurant feeling well fed and not ripped off. As the name suggests, it's compact but also bright and buzzy. Dishes (which come in generous portions) include Shetland mussels, Loch Duart salmon, and a choice of three steaks, all aged for a minimum of 28 days. There's also a good-value menu du jour at lunchtime from Tuesday to Saturday and on evenings from Tuesday to Thursday (£16 for two courses, £20 for three). On Sundays you can get two courses for £17.50 and three courses for £22.

THE GARDENER'S COTTAGE

1 Royal Terrace Gardens; tel. 0131 677 0244; www. thegardenerscottage.co; brunch 10am-11:45am Sat.-Sun., lunch noon-2:30pm daily, dinner 5pm-9:30pm daily; entrees £7

At the foot of Calton Hill in a charming 19th-century cottage, this restaurant encourages communal dining at long tables. Seasonal countryside dishes such as nettle soup and mackerel tartare, leave you feeling good from the inside out. Pop in for brunch (pastries from £4), lunch, or dinner but be warned: the latter comes as a five or seven-course tasting menu (£45/£60).

THE TABLE

3a Dundas Street; tel. 0131 281 1689; www. thetableedinburgh.com; 7pm seating Tues.-Sat.; £80 per person Tues.-Thurs., £90 per person Fri.-Sat.

At this cool concept restaurant there is just one table (which seats 10) and one seating each evening. All dinner guests can see their meal being prepared in the open-plan kitchen and ask questions of the chef as they go, making for a relaxed, dinner-party atmosphere. The menu is heavily European influenced but relies on Scottish ingredients to make dishes such as Isle of Mull cheddar ravioli or lobster with persimmon (edible fruit) and lime. The downside? There is no room to accommodate any allergies or dislikes, so you will have to be open to and able to try all the dishes put in front of you.

Seafood
THE MUSSEL INN

61-65 Rose Street; tel. 0843 289 2481; www. mussel-inn.com/seafood-restaurant-edinburgh; 12pm-3pm and 5:30pm-10pm Mon.-Thurs., 12pm-10pm Fri. and Sat., 12:30pm-10pm Sun., in July and Aug. the restaurant is open 12pm-10pm Mon.-Thurs., too; entrées £7.60

This casual, centrally located restaurant has a good selection of seafood dishes with a few meat dishes thrown in for good measure. The pots of mussels are hugely popular, while the seafood chowder is comfort food at its best. In summer, tables are placed outside, giving a very European feel.

Steak
THE DOME

14 George Street; tel. 0131 624 8624; www. thedomeedinburgh.com/grillroom; noon-late daily; entrées £8.50

Once the Commercial Bank of Scotland

headquarters, this is now a favored lunch spot where you can dine under the spectacular glass dome, which gives the building its name, in the **Grill Room**. Not as extortionate as you might imagine, the set menu (though a bit uninspiring) is well priced, but the à la carte menu is more exciting and includes ribeye steak or an option for Angus venison fillet. Afternoon tea (£18.50) is served in the opulent **Georgian Tea Room** (all crisp linen, cushioned ebony chairs, and chandeliers).

British
THE DOGS

110 Hanover Street; tel. 0131 220 1208; www. thedogsonline.co.uk; lunch noon-2:30pm Mon.-Fri., noon-4pm Sat.-Sun., dinner 6pm-10pm daily; entrées £4.95

An unpretentious place serving classic British dishes (sausage and mash, fish and chips) with a touch more class than your average pub. Despite being up a flight of stairs, it's light and airy with white walls and wooden tables and chairs, and the bar in the main room has a touch of the French bistro about it—albeit with a large portrait of a dog looming over proceedings. It's an affordable option among the tourist traps.

French
LE ROI FOU

1 Forth Street; tel. 0131 557 9346; leroifou.com; 5pm-10:30pm Tues.-Weds., noon-2:30pm and 5pm-10:30pm Thurs.-Sat., closed Sun.; entrées £11.50

In a fashionable part of the New Town toward Broughton Street, this newcomer to the dining scene opened in 2017 and is a good choice for a pre-theater dinner if you are seeing a show at the Edinburgh Playhouse. It's small or "bijou" if you ask the owners and a tad pricey, but the set menus help ease the blow: with dishes such as seared foie gras and homemade pork terrine and ingredients like Scottish lamb and Hebridean salmon, it's a good interpretation of French-style cooking with Scottish flair. Opening and closing times may vary in August.

CAFÉ ST HONORE

34 Thistle Street; tel. 0131 226 2211; www. cafesthonore.com; lunch 12-2pm, dinner 5:15pm-10pm Mon.-Fri., 5:30pm-10pm Sat.-Sun.; entrees £10, express lunch £18.50 for three courses

The daily changing menus at this classy French-inspired restaurant include gluten-free and dairy-free options. The à la carte selection is at the high-end, but the Express Lunch Menu (three courses for £18.50) is a good alternative. You could be forgiven for thinking you've been transported all the way to Paris were it not for the Scotch ox tongue and Borders roe deer on the menu.

POMPADOUR BY GALVIN

Waldorf Astoria Edinburgh—The Caledonian Princes Street; tel. 0131 222 8975; www.galvinedinburgh. com/s/3/restaurants-edinburgh; lunch 1pm-3pm Sun., dinner 6pm-9:30pm Weds.-Sun.; entrees £12.50; Sunday lunch £29.50 for three courses

This restaurant within the confines of "the Caley" hotel in the West End is nothing short of luxurious. Hand-painted wall panels provide an elegant backdrop, while views of the castle never fail to please. The menu from the Michelin-starred Galvin brothers uses British ingredients cooked in a French style, such as sea trout from Loch Etive served with an emulsion of Jersey Royal potatoes, leek hearts, and celery. Even the cheese selection is a mix of French and British. The best time to visit is on Sunday lunchtime for its tempting three-course set menu (£29.50), which includes a Bloody Mary.

Indian
DISHOOM

3a St. Andrew Square; tel. 0131 222 8975; www. dishoom.com/edinburgh; 8am-11pm Mon.-Weds., 8am-midnight Thurs.-Fri., 9am-midnight Sat., 9am-11pm Sun.; dishes £5.50

The first restaurant outside London for this much-lauded chain, Dishoom pays homage to the Irani cafés of Bombay and is utterly sublime. Dip your toes into its culinary delights with a morning bacon naan roll or pop in for dinner to try the house black daal, which is cooked for over 24 hours. Dishes are well priced and memorable.

Pub Grub
THE CAMBRIDGE BAR

20 Young Street; tel. 0131 226 2120; www. thecambridgebar.co.uk; food served 12pm-10pm daily; entrées £3.25

Just a few doors down from the famous Oxford Bar, this pub doesn't have quite the same charm as its neighbor, but it does do decent homemade burgers with a dizzying number of toppings and options. You could try the haggis with whisky sauce, rocket and mayo, or the Smokehouse—a pulled pork burger with coleslaw and BBQ sauce.

Light Bites
L'ALBA D'ORO

7 Henderson Row; tel. 0131 557 2580; www.lalbadoro. com; 5pm-10:30pm daily; fish supper £7.70

This Edinburgh mainstay is renowned for its tasty fish and chips, particularly the fish supper, which uses fresh haddock (with a delicious crispy batter) and good quality potatoes. It has a few surprises up its sleeve, too: expect to see guest seafood such as monkfish, pollack, and halibut. It also does good pizza and pasta dishes, and the 1970s décor offers a nice bit of nostalgia plus reassurance that things don't change here very often.

Coffee
LOWDOWN COFFEE

Ardmore House, 40 George Street; tel. 0131 226 2132; 8am-6pm Mon.-Fri., 9am-6pm Sat., 9:30am-6pm Sun.; coffee £2.60

Set in the basement of a Georgian townhouse on one of the New Town's main shopping drags, this minimalist café serves good coffee (and tea) well. There's also a selection of pastries and cakes to choose from, which you might want to take with you to enjoy in nearby Princes Street Gardens.

WEST END
Local Produce
★ FORAGE & CHATTER

1a Alva Street; tel. 0131 225 4599; www. forageandchatter.com; noon-2:30pm and 6pm-11pm Tues.-Sat., closed Sun.-Mon.; entrées £8

This basement restaurant tucked away in the West End has earned such a good reputation that you'd be lucky to get a table on a weekend. Bare-brick walls and low lighting create an intimate feel, and dishes such as aged beef sirloin and ox tongue with wild leeks are a delight. It feels very much like you've stumbled upon the real Edinburgh.

TIMBERYARD

10 Lady Lawson Street; tel. 0131 221 1222; www. timberyard.co; noon-2pm and 5:30pm-9:30pm Tues.-Sat., closed Sun.-Mon; entrées £7.50

This ethical restaurant is one of the most inventive to hit the Edinburgh food scene in recent years. All the wine is organic, edible herbs and flowers grown in the restaurant's very own raised beds feature heavily on the menu, and everything else is sourced from artisan growers and producers. Tasting menus include a pescatarian option, and the setting in a former warehouse adds to the very cool ambience. As food is seasonal, options change all the time, but you can expect to see a good selection of seafood dishes (scallops with apple and parsley, for example) alongside the likes of sweetbreads and lamb or beef options.

Light Bites
SOCIAL BITE

131 Rose Street; tel. 0131 220 8206; social-bite.co.uk; 7am-3pm Mon.-Fri.; breakfast bagels £2.50

This sandwich shop has a big ambition: to end homelessness in Scotland. Part of a franchise of socially minded cafés across the country, 100 percent of its profits go to charity. Plus, it uses a pay-it-forward scheme whereby customers can buy a meal for a homeless person who can come in to claim a free meal in the same way that a paying customer would, thereby removing some of the stigma. The breakfast bagels are outstanding value and pretty tasty too.

Vegan and Vegetarian
ROOTS CAFÉ

18 William Street; tel. 0131 225 6376; www. rootsedinburgh.co.uk; 7:30am-5:30pm Mon.-Thurs., 7:30am-3pm Fri., 9:30am-3:30pm Sat.; sandwiches £4.75

Opened in 2017, this ethical café focuses on healthy and mainly vegan food and is an affordable lunch stop when perusing the shops of the West End. During the week it caters mainly to office workers, while on Saturdays it is a quiet spot for some healthy fare. The salad bar (from £3.50 for a small bowl) has more adventurous offerings than most, including elderflower tomatoes with mint, red onion, and cucumber as well as couscous with sultanas, peas, and hemp seeds, proving that you don't have to compromise on flavor when it comes to vegan and vegetarian food.

STOCKBRIDGE
Modern Scottish
THE SCRAN AND SCALLIE

1 Comely Bank Road; tel. 0131 332 6281; scranandscallie.com; lunch noon-3pm, bar food 3pm-5pm, dinner 5pm-10pm Mon.-Fri., breakfast 8:30am-11am, full menu noon-10pm Sat.-Sun.; entrées £9.50

Part of the Kitchin group of restaurants, this is a gastropub in the real sense of the word—simple pub grub (or scran as the Scottish like to say) cooked very well. The Sunday roasts are renowned (so much so that you must book at least a few days in advance). Other highlights include the Highland burger and chips and The Scran and Scallie fish pie. It has a relaxed atmosphere and is loud but not so much that you can't hear the person seated opposite. Families are well looked after, with a living room aimed at children, with a sofa and TV, so parents can take their time over their meal when the kids get fidgety.

Fine Dining
PURSLANE RESTAURANT

33a St. Stephen Street; tel. 0131 226 3500; www.purslanerestaurant.co.uk; noon-2pm and 6pm-11:30pm Tues.-Sun., closed Mon.; entrees £10 lunch menu £14.95 for two courses

Stockbridge locals are a laid-back crowd, thus Purslane Restaurant's casual approach to fine dining makes sense. The lunch set menus with wine pairings (£26.95 for two courses with wine/£35.95 for three courses) are an excellent value, and even the seven-course tasting menu is a lot cheaper than you would find elsewhere (£60/£90 with wine pairing). Lunch menus include Teriyaki pork or mackerel to start, followed by corn-fed chicken or baked hake. With just 10 tables, it's an intimate restaurant with staff who know their stuff, and it's becoming a trusted place for Edinburgh's ever-increasing foodie population to frequent.

★ THE STOCKBRIDGE RESTAURANT

54 St. Stephen Street; tel. 0131 226 6766; www. thestockbridgerestaurant.co.uk; 7pm-9:30pm Mon.-Fri., 12:30pm-2pm and 7pm-9:30pm Sat.-Sun.; entrées £9.45

This high-spirited neighborhood restaurant is everything a good local should be: welcoming you in from the wet and cold and providing you with good food, wine, and company. The basement restaurant has a slight Gothic feel, with bare black walls, a fireplace overflowing with melted wax, and the soft glow of candlelight.

Established in 2004, it's run by couple Jason and Jane (he's the chef, she manages the front of the house), who have built up strong relationships with Scottish suppliers, including Danny of Neptune's Larder, who updates the restaurant as to which fish are available by contacting his dad in the galley of the family's fishing boat berthed in Port Seton. Meat dishes include rump steak with wild mushrooms, sauteed potatoes, and jus, and all meat comes from the local Gilmore butchers.

Food Markets

There are so many good independent food and drink shops in and around Edinburgh that it makes sense that several food markets now cater for the huge interest locals and visitors have in buying from small-scale producers.

LEITH MARKET

Dock Place; tel. 0131 261 6181; www.stockbridgemarket.com/leith.html; 10am-4pm Sat.
This is a great place to sample some of the best Scottish produce. Plus, on the first Saturday of the month it even has its own Vegan Quarter.

EDINBURGH FARMERS' MARKET

Castle Terrace; tel. 0131 220 8580; www.edinburghfarmersmarket.co.uk; 9am-2pm Sat.
Peruse some of the finest produce from Scotland's natural larder at Edinburgh Farmers' Market held just below the castle on Castle Terrace. There's a casual vibe about the place with lots of time to pick the brains of stallholders, most of whom grow or rear what they sell themselves. Stallholders from across Scotland include Arbroath Fisheries from Angus, Arran Cheese, based in the Firth of Clyde, and Seriously Good Venison, which sells meat reared on its farm less than 50 miles away in Fife.

Brunch
★ THE PANTRY

1 North West Circus Parade; tel. 0131 629 0206; www.thepantryedinburgh.co.uk; 9am-5pm daily (last orders 3:30pm); cooked breakfasts from £8.75
This is the go-to place for the residents of Stockbridge looking for breakfast or a lazy brunch on the weekends. With white tiles behind the counter, colorful artworks on the wall, and a variety of mid-century tables and chairs to sit upon, it has a cool, retro feel. House favorites include the Sunshine on Stockbridge brunch (£9.50)—a vegetarian cooked breakfast with sweet potato and grilled courgette, but the waffles and the millennial favorite of smashed avocado on sourdough are also tempting.

SOUTHSIDE
Fine Dining
FIELD

41 West Nicolson Street; tel. 0131 228 3322; fieldrestaurant.co.uk; noon-2pm and 5:30pm-9pm daily; entrées £6.75
There's a small and friendly team behind this hidden Southside gem, which presents a superb menu with all the hallmarks of a future Michelin contender at very reasonable prices. But the best bits? The wine list is priced fairly—almost unheard of in a city center restaurant—and the service is effortless with a no-rush approach. It's the kind of place locals don't want you to know about, and who can blame them with soul-warming dishes like roasted rabbit loin, followed by a jam roly-poly with crème Anglaise for dessert?

French
BIA BISTROT

19 Colinton Road; tel. 0131 452 8453; www.biabistrot. co.uk; noon-2pm and 5pm-10pm Tues.-Sat.; entrées £6
If you're craving French-style cooking in a family environment, then this Morningside secret is worth a try; if it feels like too much a schlep, then fret not: it's just a 10-minute bus ride from Princes Street (no. 11, 16, or 101). The menu is reassuringly small yet features meat, fish, and vegetarian options, all homemade. Prices are reasonable, particularly if you opt for the daily changing set menu.

Indian
TUK TUK INDIAN STREET FOOD

1 Leven Street; tel. 0131 228 3322; tuktukonline.com; noon-10:30pm Sun.-Thurs., noon-10:45pm Fri.-Sat.; plates £4.85
With flavorsome Indian dishes that taste

like they've come straight from a market in Mumbai, you'd be hard-pushed to get tastier comfort food for less. The curries are particularly well priced, and the gulab jamun (warm milk dumplings served with pistachio and cardamom syrup and ice cream) are every bit as delicious as they sound.

Coffee
★ **THE COUNTER**
Corner of Morningside Park and Morningside Road; www.facebook.com/TheCountered; 7:30am-3pm daily; coffee from £2
This small chain of coffee shops includes three housed in old police boxes—the Morningside one is next to Marks & Spencer on Morningside Road, and there is also one by Usher Hall and one in Tolcross—plus a new canal boat coffee shop on the Union Canal, which is fueling (quite literally) the trend for pavement coffee drinking. The flat whites are good, and, frankly, I just really like their attitude.

LEITH
Local Produce
A ROOM IN LEITH
1A Dock Place; tel. 0131 554 7427; teuchtersbar.co.uk/ a-room-in-leith-scottish-restaurant-leith-edinburgh; 4pm-9pm Mon.-Thurs., noon-9pm Fri.-Sun.; entrées £16.50
The focus at this small restaurant is on locally sourced seafood and game without the hefty bill at the end. The "room" is reminiscent of a Highland pub, and service is relaxed. You can order mugs of haggis, neeps and tatties, haggis stovies, and warming Cullen skink—a traditional comforting dish of creamy fish soup.

Fine Dining
KITCHIN
78 Commercial Street; tel. 0131 555 1755; thekitchin. com; noon-2:30pm and 6pm-10pm Tues.-Sat.; entrees £21, set lunch £33 for three courses
The ethos at this award-winning, Michelin-starred restaurant from Tom Kitchin's ever-growing portfolio is "from nature to plate." Dishes such as the rockpool of local seafood

and the fillet of North Sea turbot with raw vegetables use the freshest ingredients and are served with Tom's signature finesse. Adventurous diners might want to brave the Surprise Tasting Menu (£85, vegetarian option available) for an education in Scottish seasonal cooking. The purple chairs and low lighting give the restaurant a slightly decadent feel, which is perhaps why so many fail to resist the whisky trolley at the end. Set menus (from £33 for three courses) offer much better value than à la carte.

RESTAURANT MARTIN WISHART
54 Shore; tel. 0131 553 3557; restaurantmartinwishart.co.uk; lunch noon-1:30pm Tues.-Sat. (no lunch menu or eight-course tasting menu on Sat.), dinner 7pm-9pm Tues.-Thurs. and 6:30pm-9:30pm Fri.-Sat.; lunch menu £32 for three courses, six-course tasting menu £85/£75 for vegetarian option, lunch menu £32 for three courses
One of the many fine restaurants lining Leith's Shore, nevertheless, this is one of the best—as proven by its Michelin Star—and its elegant dining room with spotless white tablecloths and glinting glasses makes you feel that you're in for a special meal. At £32, its three-course lunch menu isn't the cheapest, but with a choice of roast fillet of scrabster or navarin of lamb it is more adventurous than most. The tasting menus are what Wishart is really known for, though the six-course menu also has a slightly cheaper vegetarian option.

Seafood
★ **FISHERS IN LEITH**
1 Shore; tel. 0131 554 5666; www.fishersrestaurants. co.uk/fishers-leith; noon-late Mon.-Sat., 12:30pm-late Sun.; entrées £9
Housed in a 17th-century watchtower, the original Fishers has been serving fresh shellfish and seafood to Leith residents for 20 years. There are tempting surf and turf options, or go for the Fishers paella for two, which includes pork belly, prawns, Merguez sausage, squid, langoustines, and mussels. If you can, eat upstairs in the round room for views of the water. **The Shore Bar &**

Restaurant next door, owned by the same people, continues the theme and has live jazz on Sundays to accompany your meal. There's now also a city center offshoot called **Fishers in the City** at 58 Thistle Street.

Coffee
WILLIAMS AND JOHNSON

Custom Lane, 67 Commercial Street; tel. www. williamsandjohnson.com; 8:30am-5pm Mon.-Fri., *10am-5pm Sat. and Sun.; coffees from £2.20*

It only opened in 2016, but already this no-nonsense micro roastery has won a loyal following. This spot is for travelers who take their coffee seriously. Set just back from the Shore (the bustling waterfront in Leith), it's a good pit stop when pottering around the waterside in Leith or visiting the weekly market.

Accommodations

A wide range of places to stay in Edinburgh suit all budgets and time frames. Types of accommodations range from good-value hostels and budget hotels and apartments to smart B&Bs, chic guesthouses, five-star establishments, and grand hotels. There are, of course, lots of well-known hotel brands in the city, many of which offer good rates, but I've tried to give an overview of some of the more unique and personal properties you can stay in for a memorable stay.

It's worth noting that if you book online direct with the hotels you often get hidden extras such as a free bottle of prosecco on arrival, and often this is how you'll get their cheapest rate too. The prices I've quoted are for high season (July), but you can expect to pay even more in August (festival time) and during Hogmanay. Or you can get much reduced prices at other times of the year.

There will often also be minimum-stay requirements of two to three nights, particularly over weekends. Smaller establishments (particularly B&Bs) may accept cash only, and some require payment up front for stays of more than two nights. Unless otherwise mentioned, all rooms and apartments come with en suite bathrooms, and breakfast is included.

Where to Stay

If you are only here for one or two days, then it makes sense to stay in the Old Town to allow enough time to see the main sights. For trips of a few days or more, the New Town with its classic Georgian properties is a good option, while the West End and Haymarket are still within reasonable walking distance of the Royal Mile, and they provide a little respite from the hordes of tourists and offer much more value for money.

The port suburb of Leith is a good choice for foodies as dozens of restaurants line its buzzing Shore, plus the Royal Yacht Britannia is permanently docked here. For a hip crowd, independent shops, and chilled coffee culture, you can't beat Stockbridge, the neighborhood everyone is talking about.

OLD TOWN
Under £100
CASTLE ROCK HOSTEL

15 Johnstone Terrace; tel. 0131 225 9666; www. castlerockedinburgh.com; £13 dorm, £55 d

Situated beneath the castle at the bottom of Castle Wynd North steps, this hostel is a great base for solo travelers to Edinburgh. Staff organize pub crawls and ceilidhs for guests, plus the posh lounge with its free book exchange (and piano) and the groove lounge are great places to make new friends over a free tea or coffee. Accommodation is in dorms or double and triple rooms.

SAFESTAY EDINBURGH

50 Blackfriars Street; tel. 0131 524 1989; www. safestay.com; dorm beds from £31

Just off the Royal Mile, this hostel is perfectly

located for seeing the city's main attractions and enjoying its famous nightlife. Accommodation is in dorms (you'll share a bathroom), and while there are some private rooms sleeping two or four, there are no private doubles. Rooms are basic but fine, and beds have reading lights, power sockets, privacy curtains, and lockers. Dorms are mixed, though they will try to accommodate single sex where possible.

£100-200
STAY CENTRAL HOTEL
139 Cowgate, Royal Mile; tel. 0131 622 6801; staycentral.co.uk; £153 d
This fun city center hotel has 37 rooms, catering to parties of all sizes, and has an urban-cool feel about it. But with a number of private dorms, including in-room entertainment such as table tennis and darts boards, it can be a bit of a party hotel when the hen and stag parties descend on the weekend.

★ THE NATIONAL TRUST GLADSTONE'S LAND APARTMENTS
477B Lawnmarket, Royal Mile; tel. 0131 226 5856; www.nts.org.uk/Holidays/Accommodation/ONeill-Flat-Gladstones-Land; from £130 per night for a one-bed apartment
Set in one of the oldest tenement buildings on the Royal Mile, these small apartments with kitchens for self-catering feel very much like secret hideaways. In truth, they're not that secret, and they book up fast—not surprising since they do offer good value for money and a cozy retreat from the hectic Royal Mile outside. The steep turnpike staircase does render it out of bounds for some, and there is a three-night minimum stay.

Over £200
THE INN ON THE MILE
82 High Street, Royal Mile; tel. 0131 556 9940; www.theinnonthemile.co.uk; £252 d
This boutique hotel housed in a 1920s building offers reasonable prices considering the central location. The nine individual rooms feature high ceilings, cornicing, and sash windows, plus they come with iPod docks, Nespresso machines, rainfall showers, and even GHD hair straighteners to fight back against the inevitable Edinburgh winds. Breakfast is extra, but mid-week deals can be good here.

★ THE WITCHERY BY THE CASTLE
352 Castlehill, Royal Mile; tel. 0131 225 5613; www.thewitchery.com; suites from £395
The nine suites in this enviably located hotel, at the top of the Royal Mile by the castle are famously indulgent. Choose between the fairytale romance of The Turret, with its oak-paneled bathroom and tapestry-lined entrance, and the rich furnishings of the seductively Gothic Vestry, with its silk walls, organ-piped headboard, and red and gold décor. Guests are greeted with a bottle of champagne on arrival and can also opt for a breakfast hamper in the room or start their day by dining in the **Witchery Dining Room.** It's not cheap, but you are unlikely to stay anywhere quite like this ever again.

NEW TOWN
Under £100
★ THE BAXTER
5 West Register Street; tel. 0131 503 1001; thebaxter.eu; dorm beds from £26
This hostel feels much more boutique than many. Its classy lounge area with a cool day bed, modern kitchen, fake fur throws, and Sonos sound system will make you feel like you're staying in a trendy apartment. It's definitely a lot more hipster than hippie. Even the dorms with their custom-built beds, personal night lights, power sockets, and French-style tiled bathrooms have an air of sophistication, and breakfast is included. This is hosteling for millennials and Generation Z who expect more, so much more.

14 HART STREET
14 Hart Street; tel. 07795 203 414; 14hartstreet.co.uk; £80 d (minimum two-night stay)
This Georgian guesthouse is the epitome of understated elegance and is nestled in a side

street off the New Town's hidden quarter of Broughton Street with its lively cafés and independent shops. Run by husband-and-wife team Angela and James, with just three bedrooms, all on garden level, it offers a truly personal touch. There is a decanter of whisky, tea, coffee, short bread, and even wine in the room, while communal breakfast is served in the formal dining room whenever guests choose to have it.

HUB BY PREMIER INN

Rose Street; tel. 0333 321 3104; www.premierinn.
com/gb/en/hotels/scotland/lothian/edinburgh/hub-
edinburgh-rose-street.html; £87 d

Located on a lively street with myriad bars and restaurants, this is a fab base for making the most of Edinburgh's nightlife or its many shops. Rooms are compact but well serviced, with Hypnos beds, monsoon showers, and smart TVs. Breakfast is extra, but tea and coffee are free and there is a deli and bar on site.

£100-200

THE STEVENSON HOUSE

17A Heriot Row; tel. 0131 556 1896; www.
stevenson-house.com; £115 twin, £135 d

Once the home of Robert Louis Stevenson, this heritage building is still a family home but also operates as a B&B year-round. The two rooms to let (a double and a twin) are like something from a time warp. In the double, there is a resplendent four-poster bed and William Morris wallpaper, while the twin is dressed like a Georgian boarding room. Breakfast is included and comes with homemade bread and jam.

SIX BRUNTON PLACE GUEST HOUSE

6 Brunton Place; tel. 0131 623 6405; www.
sixbruntonplace.com; £139 d

A five-star guesthouse with just four rooms, this elegant townhouse designed by the famous William Playfair is just a short walk from Calton Hill for some of the best city views. Period features such as the wonderful cantilever staircase and marble fireplaces

remain, and rooms are sensitively decorated to reflect their Georgian heritage.

ROYAL SCOTS CLUB

29-31 Abercromby Place; tel. 0131 556 4270; www.
royalscotsclub.com; £144 d

This private members club by Queen Street Gardens has little of the stuffiness you might expect and just the right balance of nostalgia; its bedrooms are open to the public. It's a genteel, quiet place, and guests can make use of the club rooms, including the cocktail bar and lounge and the Abercromby dining room. For special occasions, ask for one of the four-poster bedrooms.

NO 11

11 Brunswick Street; tel. 0131 557 6910;
www.11brunswickst.co.uk; £155 d

This is a sly choice for those looking for luxury accommodation at a snippet of the price as there are often good deals to be had (particularly in low season). Once the Black Watch Regimental Club (the private club of the oldest Highland regiment), the building was originally commissioned by William Playfair and completed in 1822. Today, it is a small, refined hotel that makes the most of its former grandeur, including its cupola, which lords over the sweeping staircase. Georgian suites include four-poster beds, freestanding baths, and floor-to-ceiling sash windows.

ROCK HOUSE

28 Calton Hill; tel. 0131 556 9358; rockhouse-
edinburgh.com; Terrace Apartment or Photographer's
Studio from £155 per night, Rock House from £328
per night

This exquisite holiday home at the foot of Calton Hill is brimming with character, 18th-century features (not to mention great views of the castle and New Town), and a sense of seclusion. It was once home to David Octavius Hill, who is considered one of the founding fathers of photography. With cast-iron beds, Arts & Crafts wallpaper, and floor-length curtains, the house has been thoughtfully restored to its Victorian heyday. Accommodations include the four-bed Rock House, the two-bed Terrace Apartment, and the one-bed Photographer's Studio.

Over £200
24 ROYAL TERRACE

24 Royal Terrace; tel. 0131 297 2424; www.24royalterrace.co.uk; £210 d

This stylish B&B includes oodles of modern art works on its walls. Designed by master architect William Playfair (again), it's set within the longest continuous row of Georgian properties in the city, which was once named "whisky row" due to the number of spirit merchants who lived here. It's a prestigious address. With Egyptian cotton sheets and lambswool throws, you can rest assured that comfort is taken care of too.

★ THE BALMORAL

1 Princes Street; tel. 0131 556 2414; www. roccofortehotels.com/hotels-and-resorts/the-balmoral-hotel; £510 d

Standing at Edinburgh's most prestigious address, this grand dame of a hotel is a prominent feature of the city's skyline. Inside, you can dine in the Michelin-starred **Number One** restaurant, relax in the spa, or simply soak up the timeless glamour of one of the 168 bedrooms, each individually designed by Olga Polizzi with definite nods to the hotel's Scottish heritage.

WEST END
£100-200
B&B EDINBURGH

3 Rothesay Terrace; tel. 0131 225 5084; www. bb-edinburgh.com; £110 d

This private B&B with fully licensed bar in a listed building is just a few minutes from Princes Street, to the west of the city center. The contemporary rooms are immaculate, and a full Scottish breakfast (which is included and comes with haggis and square Lorne sausages) is served in the ground-floor breakfast room. The website might look a bit cheap, but don't let that put you off—the

guest bar and library with open fire, guest laptop, and daily newspapers more than make up for it.

Over £200
★ DUNSTANE HOUSE

4 West Coates; tel. 0131 337 6169; thedunstane.com; £204 d

Despite being set on a main road, you don't hear a peep from the cars outside at this sophisticated hotel. Rooms have Nespresso machines, huge flat-screen TVs, and Roberts radios, and those at the front of the house are even equipped with telescopes. Downstairs there is a Mad-Men style bar, **the Ba' Bar,** with velvet wingback chairs and a lounge where you can order from the brasserie-style menu until 9:30pm. There are books to borrow, framed prints on the wall, and everything about it is achingly chic.

THE RUTLAND HOTEL

1-3 Rutland Street; tel. 0131 229 3402; www. therutlandhotel.com; £220 d, apartments from £350

This quirky but top-notch guesthouse is set across several Georgian houses. The ceilings are incredibly high, and the pristine rooms have huge sash windows. Alongside chic bedrooms, swish apartments complete with living room, kitchen, and gigantic bedrooms are available. The vibrant décor may not be to everybody's taste, but it is unapologetically fun.

WALDORF ASTORIA EDINBURGH– THE CALEDONIAN

Princes Street; tel. 0131 222 8889; www. waldorfastoriaedinburgh.com; £303 d

This former railway hotel, affectionately known as "the Caley" by locals, has been a fixture on Edinburgh's skyline for over a century. Renovated in 2012, it boasts large bathrooms and bedrooms that are bedecked with bespoke furniture and intriguing artwork. The Carriage Queen Rooms have even been restored to evoke the Victorian train carriages that first brought people from across the world to stay in "The Old Lady of Princes Street." But its allure—aside from its first-class service—is surely the incredible views some rooms have of Edinburgh Castle, particularly in the evening when it positively glows against the fading daylight. The rooms have enormous windows to make the best of that view, but while the spa is a nice addition, it feels a little basic for a five-star hotel.

SOUTHSIDE
Under £100
BROOKS HOTEL EDINBURGH

70-72 Grove Street; tel. 0131 228 2323; www. brooksedinburgh.com; £99 d

This charming B&B that lies halfway between Haymarket and Southside features peculiar interiors, where stag heads meet contemporary artworks on the walls and vintage furniture abounds. Rooms are fresh and clean, while the lounge, honesty bar, and pretty courtyard make it feel a lot more boutique than budget.

£100-200
ALBYN TOWNHOUSE

16 Hartington Gardens; tel. 0131 229 6459; albyntownhouse.co.uk; £149 d

At this Victorian listed property, formerly St. Oswald's Church Manse, the bright and bold rooms are set across three floors. Family run, you can expect a warm welcome as well as a comfy room and a hearty breakfast to set you up for the day. You'll need it because Lydie and David will arm you with lots of insider knowledge to help you make the most of your time. Book well ahead and you could even get a double in spring or autumn for just £55.

23 MAYFIELD

23 Mayfield Gardens; tel. 0131 667 5806; www.23mayfield.co.uk; £155 d, minimum two-night stay on weekends

This Victorian guesthouse a mile from the city center is the embodiment of Scottish elegance. It's a little way out, but it's a quiet and harmonious part of town and still within walking distance of Pickering's and Summerhall. Bedrooms feature solid hand-crafted mahogany furniture and Penhaligon's toiletries, while the Club Room has Chesterfield sofas and a selection of games, including a Georgian chessboard, and a selection of rare books. Breakfasts (which are included) are cooked to order, and local buses (nos. 3, 7, 8, 29, 31, 37) run from the opposite side of the road into the Old Town and the castle in less than 20 minutes.

Over £200
PRESTONFIELD HOUSE

Priestfield Road; tel. 0131 225 7800; www. prestonfield.com; £355 d

In 2003 this Southside baroque mansion on the edge of Holyrood Park was taken over by the team behind the Witchery who turned the 18 bedrooms in this glamorous boutique hotel into some of the most seductive imaginable, making it well deserving of its five-star status. The Churchill Suite, named in honor of the former British prime minister who frequented Edinburgh, includes a tapestry-laden four-poster and views toward Arthur's Seat, plus a separate sitting room. Breakfast specialties (which of course come as standard) include Finnan Haddie (cold smoked haddock) and kippers, plus treats from the in-house pastry chefs. Plus, if you book direct, you get a complimentary bottle of champagne, not prosecco, champagne.

LEITH
Under £100
A-HAVEN TOWNHOUSE HOTEL

180 Ferry Road; tel. 0131 554 6559; a-haven.co.uk; £79 d

Set in a smart Victorian townhouse, this B&B is better value than most, and its owner, David, will regale you with tales of the city and the best places to visit. Rooms are brimming with charm, and guests can relax in the ever-so-chintzy bar in the evening and look forward to a cooked Scottish breakfast including delicious Lorne sausages.

£100-200
MALMAISON HOTEL

1 Tower Place; tel. 0131 285 1478; www.malmaison.
com/locations/edinburgh; £135 d

Sited right on the waterfront in Leith's popular Shore, you know what you're getting with this trendy hotel chain. Fluffy fabrics, lights that dim, beds you sink into, and modern bathrooms can be found across all 100 rooms, while suites at the higher end of the scale also come with stunning city views.

★ MILLERS64

64 Pilrig Street; tel. 0131 454 3666; www.millers64.
com; £120 d

Set on a residential street between Leith and the city center, where every other property seems to be a guesthouse, Millers64 stands out for its unfussy yet genuine welcome. The two rooms have Noble Isle toiletries in their private en suites, bedside radios, and a decanter of whisky waiting for you on arrival. Louise, whose family home it is, will serve you tea or coffee downstairs (there is also a good selection of beverages in the room) and give you advice on where to go. This is still a family home, and nice touches include good reading material in the communal room downstairs and a bound book on Edinburgh to borrow for excursions.

THE PAVILION AT LAMB'S HOUSE

11 Water's Close; tel. 0131 467 7777; www.nts.org.
uk/Holidays/Accommodation/The-Pavilion-Lambs-
House; from £1,140 for a three-night stay

This three-bed property has been built in the style of an 18th-century house within the curtilage of 17th-century Lamb's House—once a tenement rented out to the merchants who controlled trade in and out of Leith. Today, it offers Old-English style accommodation with modern comforts. It sleeps six, so, despite the hefty-seeming price-tag, it's reasonable if you're traveling with friends.

Over £200
MV FINGAL

Alexandra Dock, Leith; tel. 0131 357 5000; www.
fingal.co.uk; £300 d

This floating hotel, which opened in January 2019, doesn't come cheap, but it offers luxury accommodation in 23 cabins within strolling distance of two Michelin Star restaurants. The hotel, set aboard a former lighthouse tender, is being run by the same people behind the Royal Yacht Britannia, so I expect to see some guest deals for visitors to the Royal Family's former yacht too.

GREATER EDINBURGH
Under £100
MORTONHALL WIGWAMS

38 Mortonhall Gate; tel. 0131 664 1533; www.
meadowhead.co.uk/parks/mortonhall; wigwams £60
per night (minimum stay two nights), tent pitch £27

If you want to combine city exploration with carbon-neutral living, then this place, just four miles south of the city center, offers a good compromise (albeit with a TV room). Glamping is available in eco-friendly wigwams, shepherd's huts, and even dedicated bell tents during festival season. Sleeping bag and pillow hire is available. There are play areas, along with a games room and on-site bar and restaurant—during the festival there's even a breakfast van to help you emerge from the fog of the previous night.

Information and Services

TOURIST INFORMATION

This is Edinburgh (26 Frederick Street; tel. 0131 473 3666; edinburgh.org,) is the official guide to the capital and is a particularly useful reference when it comes to events taking place across the city.

The main tourist office, **Edinburgh iCentre** (3 Princes Street; tel. 0131 473 3868; 9am-5pm Mon.-Sat., 10am-5pm Sun., open later in summer) is right by Waverley Station on top of Princes Mall and is impossible to miss. It's a good place to pick up lots of free leaflets and maps of the city. Staff can also provide information on day trips from the city and suggest itineraries if you want to travel farther afield. You can also purchase tickets for many of Edinburgh's attractions, including city tours and the Royal Edinburgh Ticket. There is also an outlet at the airport if you can't wait until you reach the city.

Historic Scotland (tel. 0131 668 8600; www.historicenvironment.scot) manages many of the heritage buildings across Scotland and can be a useful port of call for discovering historic buildings worth visiting a little farther away.

Haggis Adventures on the Royal Mile (60 High Street; www.haggisadventures. com) is a good source of information on Edinburgh's highlights, but their primary focus is on running minibus tours of the city and budget backpacker excursions, so be prepared for the hard sell on these.

SIGHTSEEING PASSES

The **Royal Edinburgh Ticket** (adult £55, child £30) allows unlimited travel aboard three Edinburgh Bus Tour routes over two days, plus entry to Edinburgh Castle, the Royal Yacht Britannia, and the Palace of Holyroodhouse. The ticket is available at Edinburgh iCentre or from Edinburgh Bus Tours (tel. 0131 220 0770; edinburghtour. com). If you include the bus tours, which are £15 each, then this does work out cheaper, but only if you are planning to do a bus tour and visit each of the three attractions above.

The **Historic Scotland Explorer Pass** (tel. 0131 668 8095; www. historicenvironment.scot/visit-a-place/ explorer-passes), which can be bought direct through Historic Scotland or in person at any of the Historic Scotland attractions, gives you access and fast-track entry to up to 77 heritage sites (40 in winter) for a set fee. Prices start at £35 for a five-day pass that can be used at Edinburgh Castle, Linlithgow Palace, Melrose Abbey, and Jedburgh Abbey. It's particularly worthwhile if you are planning to venture farther out of the city to places like Stirling Castle during the time frame.

Getting There

BY AIR

Edinburgh Airport (EDI, www. edinburghairport.com) is located eight miles (12km) west of the city.

From the United States

Edinburgh Airport has direct international flights from a number of U.S. cities, including New York and Chicago **(United Airlines)**. American Airlines also flies to Edinburgh via London Heathrow from several U.S airports, including JFK, and Delta offers flights from JFK via Paris and Amsterdam. **Icelandair** runs routes via Iceland from Boston, Minneapolis, and Chicago to Glasgow, just a short train ride from Edinburgh.

From the United Kingdom

Most overseas visitors to Edinburgh come into London first. From here, there are several easy options for onward travel. Several budget airlines, including **easyJet** and **Ryanair,** offer many daily flights from each of London's airports. Flight time is just over an hour, and, if you fly on a weekday outside school holidays, you can pick up a brilliant bargain.

Airport Transportation

There are two main options for public transport from Edinburgh Airport into the city: tram or bus (www.edinburghairport.com/transport-links). The tram has only been operating for a short while but is hugely popular with locals (they are very proud of their tram service, which was a bit of an ordeal getting up and running but is now much-loved). Transport links are all fairly well signposted, and staff are only too happy to point you in the right direction.

TRAM

To reach the trams it's a two-minute walk out of the airport's main entrance. At £8.50 for an open return, trams are slightly more expensive than buses but they are also less crowded and a bit quicker, and you are not at the mercy of city center traffic. The trams run all the way from the airport to York Place in the east end of the city, stopping at Haymarket and Princes Street en route.

From the moment you land you are greeted by the famous Scottish humor, so don't be surprised if the ticket officers make jokes at your expense—it is all meant in a friendly way. A few minutes into the 30-minute tram journey into the city, you can see stags grazing in fields and it is clear: you have arrived in Scotland. Another benefit of the tram: compared with the train, it stops at a greater number of stations in town.

BUS

Airlink 100 buses that go directly to the city center wait right outside the main entrance to the airport and are a smidgen cheaper than the tram (£4.50 single, £7.50 return). They are incredibly regular, making the roughly 30-minute journey into the city center every 10 minutes between 4:30am and 12:35am and then every 30 minutes or so until they start again fully for the day. Similarly, **Skylink 200** buses (also £4.50 each way, £7.50 for an open return) go from the airport to Leith via north Edinburgh

(from 4:10am-midnight every 30 minutes, journey time 40 minutes).

TAXI

You'll find taxis on the ground floor of the multi-story car park opposite the main terminal building. **City Cabs** is the official taxi provider and does not need to be booked. The cabs seat five to six people with a reasonable amount of luggage, take on average 25 minutes to the city center, and cost around £20-30, depending on your city center location.

BY TRAIN

Edinburgh Waverley (Princes Street; www.networkrail.co.uk/stations/edinburgh-waverley) on Waverley Bridge, which overlooks Princes Street Gardens, is the city's main station and is the departure and arrival station for trains from London and Glasgow, among other destinations.

Flying may be quicker (and sometimes cheaper), but traveling by train is virtually stress-free. **Virgin Trains East Coast** (www.virgintrainseastcoast.com) provides high-speed trains between London and Edinburgh, which take about five hours and cost anywhere from £40 to £80 for a single. The earlier you can book your ticket, the better in terms of price.

Perhaps the most romantic way to travel is on the **Caledonian Sleeper train** (tel. 0330 060 0500; www.sleeper.scot), which departs London's Euston at night (except Saturdays) with just enough time for a spot of dinner in the Club Car before bedding down for the night in your cabin and waking up in Scotland in the morning. Tickets cost from £45 for a standard seat (one way) to around £125 each way for a cabin.

It's also really easy to travel between Edinburgh and Glasgow by train. Edinburgh Waverley has several trains an hour from Glasgow Queen Street. The journey takes a little more than 50 minutes and prices start at £13 for a day return.

By Car

If you're driving from London, you need to allow a good eight to nine hours, and you're best to split your journey into two days, perhaps stopping at the Lake District (260 mi/418km from London) or the Yorkshire Dales (230 mi/143km from London). The full distance from London to Edinburgh is 400 miles (644km). Your route will very much depend on your starting point in London, but the main options include taking the M1 and then joining the A1 (M), which takes you close to Leeds, in Yorkshire, or following the M40 past Oxford before taking the M6 up through the Lake District and then joining the A702. From Glasgow, the quickest route (from one hour, depending on traffic) is to take the M8 and then the A71 into Edinburgh, a distance of 47 miles (76km).

Getting Around

ON FOOT

By far the most enjoyable way to explore the city is on foot because this way you'll see incredible buildings you didn't know about (there are too many to mention) as well as discover the city's secret passageways and hidden corners. It's a great way to get your bearings too, particularly in the New Town, which is laid out neatly with parallel streets. The Old Town, with its many twists and turns, is a little harder to fathom.

BY BUS

The main bus provider in Edinburgh is **Lothian,** which runs 50 routes in and around the city, including the Airlink and Skylink buses from the airport and the nos. 43 and X43 buses to South Queensferry. To get to the port district of Leith, you can take the no. 22 or no. 300 buses, which will get you to Leith in 15 minutes.

The main **bus depot** is just north of St. Andrew Square, and the vast majority of buses run along Princes Street. Prices are £1.70 for a single or £4 for a day ticket. A NIGHTticket, which covers travel on buses from midnight to 4:30am is £3. You can pay in exact change on the bus (feed through the slot at the top of the ticket machine or the bus driver will just stare at you blankly), or you can download the **Transport for Edinburgh** app (tfeapp.com) and buy your tickets in advance, though you must make a minimum purchase of £10.

BY TAXI

Taxis are in abundance. Hail a black cab from the street, or go to one of the designated taxi ranks (such as the one outside Waverley Station). There are three main black cab firms in Edinburgh: **City Cabs, Central Taxis,** and **ComCabs.** They are all metered with their prices regulated by the council. Step-in charges start at £2.60 for two people (rising to £4.60 at peak times with a small surcharge for additional people). You can pre-book these cabs, but there is a small fee for this and it is rarely necessary.

Average taxi journeys from the New Town to the Old Town cost around £5, while from Princes Street to Leith expect to pay around £10. There are private mini cabs too, and, though these are occasionally cheaper, they are nowhere near as reliable.

Day Trips from Edinburgh

Escaping the hustle of Edinburgh is easy. To the east of the capital is the seaside suburb of Portobello, where on sunny days (or at least ones when it's not raining too much), locals make the most of the beach cafés and ice cream parlors and saunter over its golden sands.

The harbor town of **South Queensferry,** just a 15-minute train ride away north of Edinburgh, is seeing a resurgence in visitors due to the opening of the new Queensferry Crossing, which affords incredible views of the famous Forth Bridge, plus the area's starring role in the *Outlander* TV series.

Alternatively, you can visit the haunting ruins of **Linlithgow Palace,** the birthplace of Mary, Queen of Scots, or venture to the enigmatic 15th-century Rosslyn Chapel to the south of the city, made famous in the *Da Vinci Code* films and home to innumerable mysterious stone carvings.

★ SOUTH QUEENSFERRY

A little less self-aware than Portobello, Queensferry is turning into a charming little weekend spot, with a terrace of colorful houses, front-seat views of the Forth Bridge, and a nice collection of shops and restaurants on the narrow high street that runs just behind the waterfront.

The success of the TV series *Outlander* has also brought a new generation of visitors who come to follow in the footsteps of Jamie and Claire as several of the locations were shot right here.

Sights
FORTH BRIDGE

It's a pretty special sight as you approach South Queensferry and the Forth Bridge comes into view. Spanning the Firth of Forth and connecting Edinburgh with Fife, the Forth Bridge (sometimes called the Forth Rail Bridge to distinguish it for the Forth Road Bridge) is a true icon of Scotland.

Work on the triple cantilever bridge, which includes an unbelievable 6.5 million rivets, began in 1882 but befell many tragedies before its completion in 1890 with 78 workers (possibly more) dying during the build. But

Forth Bridge, South Queensferry

despite this, or perhaps because of it, the mammoth engineering project is seen as an act of human endeavor. The Forth Bridge was celebrated as the world's foremost steel structure when it opened in 1890, and it was designated a UNESCO World Heritage Site in 2015.

It's well worth getting the bus or driving yourself over the new Queensferry Crossing, which opened in August 2017, to see the Forth Bridge in all its glory. The Queensferry Crossing will soon replace the ailing Forth Road Bridge that is frequently forced to close in less than favorable weather conditions. It is also a vital upgrade to the cross-Forth transport links and will open up more of Fife and Aberdeenshire to Edinburgh.

If you are driving, there is no toll to pay. If traveling by bus, take the bus from Queensferry Street, just two minutes from Princes Street, over the Queensferry Crossing to the Ferrytoll Park and Ride. Several buses do this route (nos. X54, X55, X56, X58, X59, X60). They are run by **Stagecoach** and cost £5 each way or £9 return; tickets can be purchased on board.

From here you can get the bus (89 or 89) for a few minutes to the free Harbour Light Tower—the smallest of its kind in the world—or come back over the bridge and get off at the slip road the other side of the bridge and stroll down to South Queensferry for a bite to eat and more fabulous views. The Queensferry Crossing is not open to pedestrians or cyclists, but the Forth Road Bridge is.

The best places to get views of the Forth Rail Bridge from South Queensferry are from one of the restaurants, such as **The Boathouse** on the waterfront.

HOPETOUN HOUSE

Queensferry, EH30 9RW; tel. 0131 331 2451;
hopetoun.co.uk; 10:30am-5pm (last entry 4pm)
daily mid-April.-late Sept.; adult £10.50, child £5.50,
family £28

One of Scotland's grandest stately homes, this 17th-century palace has been home to the Hope family for generations. Designed by William Bruce, the house was later extended in the 18th century by William Adam, who added the huge colonnades and the north and south pavilions. Its interiors were completed by his sons, Robert Adam and John Adam, following his death.

So spectacular was the finished house that King George IV visited here at the end of his state visit to Scotland in 1822, which was the first time an English monarch had visited Scotland in 200 years. Recently, people have come to Hopetoun for an altogether different reason—to see some of the locations that appeared in the TV series *Outlander.*

In the first season, scenes set in the Duke of Sandringham's house were filmed in the house's resplendent **Red Drawing Room.** Elsewhere, the **Sea Trail** and **West Lawn** were settings for a dual between the Duke and the head of the MacDonald Clan, while the courtyard behind the tearoom also features.

MIDHOPE CASTLE

Accessed via the Hopetoun House entrance;
hopetoun.co.uk/access-midhope-castle; car permits
£10 per car

For years this 16th-century tower house in the hamlet of Abercorn on the Hopetoun estate was out of bounds to tourists. However, with the success of TV's *Outlander,* in which the castle doubles as Lallybroch, Jamie's family home, visitor interest shot up. It's not officially open to visitors, but owners have relented to pressure from *Outlander* fans and now charge a small fee to cover security costs. Because it is located on a private part of the estate, the house is only accessible by car. To be permitted entry, you'll need an access pass, which can be purchased from the Hopetoun Farm Shop on the estate or the ticket kiosk at Hopetoun House, both of which are open daily from April to September. Please note, you will only be able to see the exterior of the property.

INCHCOLM

South Queensferry

The tiny yet beautiful island of Inchcolm is known as the east coast's Iona, a spiritual and calm retreat. Inchcolm's abbey, which dates back to the 12th century, is considered the best-preserved group of monastic buildings in the whole of Scotland; look out for the rare 13th-century fresco in the well. The abbey was supposedly founded by King David I after his brother King Alexander I had to seek shelter here following a terrible storm. The abbey is free to visit as are the coastal fortifications—remnants from when all the islands in the Forth were garrisoned to protect the road bridge and the Royal Navy's Rosyth base from attack during both the First and Second World Wars.

To reach Inchcolm, take a ride across the Forth aboard the **Maid of the Forth** (tel. 0131 331 5000, www.maidoftheforth.co.uk) for a three-hour landing tour of Inchcolm, including a 45-minute guided tour (£20 adult, £10.60 child, under fives free). Boats depart from **Hawes Pier** in South Queensferry at 10:30am, 12:15pm, and 2pm on most days, with additional departures in August (check the website for details). Look out for seals lazing on the rocks as you approach and perhaps even puffins, razorbills, and guillemots circling above. Booking is advisable.

Recreation
JOHN MUIR WAY
johnmuirway.org

This long-distance walking path named after the famous naturalist John Muir, stretches from coast to coast across the central belt of Scotland, from Muir's birthplace in Dunbar, East Lothian, all the way to Helensburgh near to where he set sail to America. Known as the Father of the National Parks, John Muir was a Scottish-born naturalist who emigrated to America aged 10, yet never forgot his early years in East Lothian, which no doubt inspired his later work. Muir was an early advocate for protecting America's wilderness by setting up national parks.

The 134-mile route passes through some of Scotland's most amazing attractions, including **Linlithgow Palace**, the Roman-built **Antonine Wall**, and the **Falkirk Wheel**. You can join the walk at South Queensferry. For Linlithgow, head west out of South Queensferry along Hopetoun Road before bearing slightly right on to Farquar Terrace and following this on to Society Road. From South Queensferry, it's 14 miles (23 km) to Linlithgow, along mainly quiet roads and tracks through rural countryside. It will take you past **Hopetoun House** and **Bo'ness** with its attractive 16th-century housing, before reaching the famous town of **Linlithgow**. In all it should take about seven hours to walk or three hours to cycle.

Food
THE BOAT HOUSE
22 High Street, South Queensferry; tel. 0131 331 5429; www.theboathouse-sq.co.uk; noon-9pm daily; entrées £5.95

The views of the **Forth Bridge** from this lower-deck restaurant are lovely, but the fish and chips are pretty good too. It's hard to argue with delicious homemade tartar sauce and a golden crispy batter.

DOWN THE HATCH
Port Edgar Marina, South Queensferry; tel. 0131 331 1387; www.downthehatchcafe.com; 8:30am-4pm Mon.-Sat., 10am-4pm Sun.; bagels £4.50

The ethos at this café-diner is on providing North American-influenced food featuring locally sourced ingredients. The coffee comes from Forth Coffee Roasters, and the portions are huge—try the popular Hatch Burger (£7.25) with an Angus beef patty, topped with bacon, cheese, onion, and pickles—and served on a toasted brioche bun. A great find for any North Americans—particularly Canadians—who are feeling a little homesick.

Accommodations
OROCCO PIER
17 High Street, South Queensferry; tel. 0131 331 1298; www.oroccopier.co.uk; Samphire restaurant open 12pm-10pm daily in spring and summer, 12pm-3pm for lunch and 6pm-10pm for dinner daily in winter; £134 d

This boutique hotel set within a 17th-century building has 17 bedrooms, some of which have uninterrupted views of the Forth Bridge. Bedrooms and bathrooms are contemporary, if a little business-like. There's also a good seafood restaurant, **Samphire,** which has floor-to-ceiling windows for great views of the bridge.

Getting There and Around

Trains depart Edinburgh's **Waverley Station** around every 15 minutes for Dalmeny, the nearest station to South Queensferry. The ride takes 15 minutes and costs from £4.70 return. From Dalmeny, it's about a 15-minute walk to South Queensferry, or you can take the no. 43 Lothian bus (every 20 minutes Mon.-Sat., every 30 minutes Sun., £1.70) from the station and get off at Stonycroft Road less than 10 minutes later. Alternatively, you can get the no. 43 bus all the way there from St. Andrew Square, for a journey time of 40 minutes. Buses are every half an hour and are considerably cheaper than getting the train and bus as you just need to pay the standard Lothian bus fee of £1.70 each way or £4 for a day ticket.

If you are driving, it takes about a half hour from the city center to South Queensferry (traffic depending), a distance of 9.5 miles (15 km) along the A90 and then B924.

PORTOBELLO

This seaside suburb, known affectionately as "Porty," is home to street after street of stunning period properties in a mix of styles—from double-fronted houses with upper gabled windows to huge Georgian properties on **Pittville Street,** which leads down to the beach. There is a smattering of artisan shops, cafés, and ice cream parlors on the main road, too.

Sights
PORTOBELLO BEACH

This huge sweep of sand is the perfect place to wear out the kids. In summer and basically any time when it's not bucketing down, locals come here to chill out, walk the dog, and let the kids run wid. Some mad people even swim in the icy waters. There's something pretty cool about walking along a sandy beach with

blue skies overhead and snow-capped mountains in the distance. Well, no one said it would be warm. There's tons of space, so it never feels too busy.

PROMENADE

Walk off the whisky from the night before with a brisk wander along the promenade. It's a great people-watching spot with lots of places to stop for refreshment en route, including the cute **Little Green Van,** usually parked on the promenade at the end of Pittville Street, that serves coffee and ice cream. The promenade runs alongside the seafront for the whole of the beach's two miles and is pedestrian only (plus cycles). There are lots of play areas running off it too and an old arcade.

THE VELVET EASEL GALLERY

298 Portobello High Street; tel. 07813 916 684; velveteasel.co.uk; 10am-5pm Thurs.-Sat. and 12pm-5pm Sun.

This contemporary gallery specializes in modern pieces by both Scottish and international artists and prides itself on championing new artists. Browse the paintings, ceramics, jewelry, and sculptures on show, or buy a print or postcard to take home.

PORTOBELLO MARKET

Brighton Park; www.pedal-porty.org.uk/food/portobello-market; 9:30am-1:30pm first Sat. of every month except January

Portobello Market, in Brighton Park, is just a five-minute walk from the main strip. More than 20 traders sell the best of local produce, including organic food, fruit, fish, and meat, along with local crafts.

Food
THE BEACH HOUSE

57 Bath Street; tel. 0131 657 2636; www.thebeachhousecafe.co.uk; 8:45am-9:30pm daily; light bites £6.95

Perfectly positioned by the beach, this is a great spot to stop for a gelato, a light lunch, or even a gin and tonic—go for the Seaside from Edinburgh Gin, which has ground ivy and bladderwrack seaweed among its botanicals, inspired by this stretch of coastline. From mid-May until September, it's open in the evenings too.

MONNY
3 Brighton Place; monnyicecream@gmail.com; 8:30am-6pm daily
When the people of Porty want good ice cream, this is where they come—an authentic Italian gelateria on the corner of High Street just a couple of minutes from the promenade. There are always around 30 flavors to choose from (freshly made on site with no colors or additives), and the brave may even want to try the brioche con gelato, which, just as its sounds, is ice cream in a brioche roll. Monny also serves good coffee.

Accommodations
ABERCORN GUESTHOUSE
1 Abercorn Terrace; tel. 0131 669 6139; www. abercornguesthouse.com; £100 d
This charming period property just a two-minute walk from the beach features gorgeous wooden shutters, a large walled garden, and open fires. Plus, rates start at just £60 out of season, and somehow that includes breakfast.

Getting There and Around
There's a direct train from Edinburgh Waverley to Brunstane Station, which is about a 15-minute walk away from Portobello beach. Trains run every half an hour and take just seven minutes (£2.70 each way). Taxis from the city center take just 10 minutes and cost around £10, but the best way to get there is to jump on the no. 26 bus from Princes Street (about every 20-30 minutes), which will take you all the way to Portobello High Street in around 30 minutes for just £1.70 each way.

To reach Portobello by car, head east out of the city along Queen's Drive, which runs through Holyrood Park, turn right onto the A1140, and follow all the way to Portobello High Street. It's less than four miles (6km) from the city center and should take about 15 minutes by car.

★ LINLITHGOW PALACE

Kirkgate, Linlithgow; tel. 01506 842 896; www. historicenvironment.scot/visit-a-place/places/ linlithgow-palace; 9:30am-5:30pm Apr.-late Sept., 10am-4pm Oct.-late Mar.; adult £6, child £3.60, under fives free

Ensconced in the Scottish Lowlands, Linlithgow (around halfway between Edinburgh and Falkirk) is the proud protector of the haunting ruins of one of Scotland's most significant royal castles—Linlithgow Palace. With its stunning elevated position overlooking the loch and peel (park) below, it is arguably the most outstanding of all of Scotland's medieval palaces. It's famous for being the birthplace of Mary, Queen of Scots, and her father, James V, and remarkably the exterior has remained much as it was in the 15th century, though its once grand halls have been ravaged by fire and time. Last entry is 45 minutes before closing.

History
Linlithgow Palace was built to replace an earlier structure, devastated by fire in 1424, on the orders of King James I of Scotland. The new palace was a chance for the Royal Family to show off their extraordinary wealth and power. Linlithgow's location was both beautiful and easy to defend—Robert Burns called it "sweetly situated." It was developed by successive monarchs over the next 200 years with the layout evolving until it became the quadrangular palace with four ranges around a central courtyard that you see today.

The palace was a popular retreat for many of the Stuart queens and consorts. It formed the marriage dowry of both Margaret Tudor of England (James IV's wife) and before that James III's queen, Margaret of Denmark. In fact, its sense of tranquility and peace may be the reason that two Scottish sovereigns were born here—first King James V in 1512 and then Mary, Queen of Scots, on December 8, 1542, who was named queen just six days after (though it was several months before it was made official). Mary was whisked away from here at just seven months old to the safety of

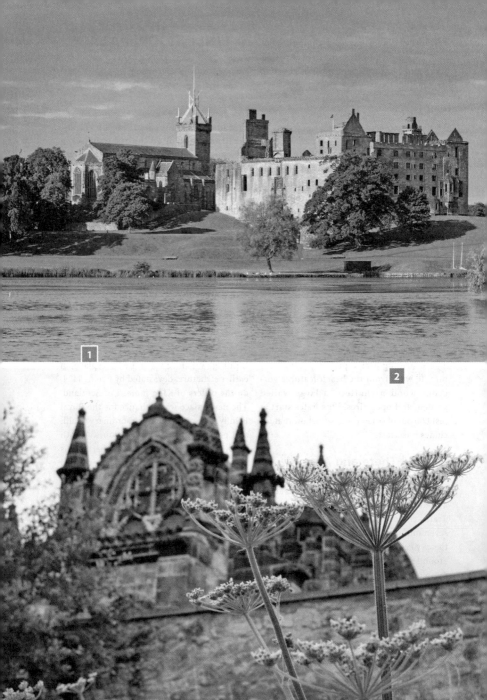

Stirling Castle and shortly afterward crowned Queen of Scotland. Even though Mary did not return to the castle for 20 years—and even then, just for short visits—it is still closely associated with her.

Sadly, the house fell out of royal favor in the late 16th century, and by 1600 it was in decline with the north range collapsing in 1607. James VI did attempt to restore it and rebuilt the north wall, but it never returned to the same level of prestige. When Charles I spent one night here in 1633, he became the last reigning monarch to sleep in the palace. Oliver Cromwell and his roundheads lodged at the palace in 1650. In 1745 the Young Pretender, Bonnie Prince Charlie, stopped at Linlithgow en route to Edinburgh to claim the crown of Scotland for the Stuart dynasty. It then suffered a devastating fire in 1746 during the last Jacobite Rising.

Since the early 19th century the castle has been actively preserved, and today it is looked after by Historic Environment Scotland and is open to visitors year-round.

Visiting the Palace

On entry to the courtyard, the first thing that strikes you is the flamboyant fountain in the center. Commissioned by King James V (father of Mary, Queen of Scots) around 1538, it features three tiers of sculptures surmounted by a crown, which presumably represents the king's superiority over his subjects. Other recognizable symbols are those of a drummer, a man holding a scroll, and a mermaid demonstrating eloquence. These figures were a nod to James's role as a patron of the arts. Though staff dismiss the rumors, it's been said that the fountain once flowed with red wine to celebrate Bonnie Prince Charlie.

Inside, Linlithgow Palace is a spooky place to explore, with lots of hidden rooms, low passages, and turnpike staircases that climb up towers. It's surprisingly quiet, too, and you do often find yourself alone in some of the rooms, with the faces of unicorns and ancient

angels staring down at you. **The Great Hall,** originally added by James I but later remodeled, still dominates the layout and is a highlight of a visit to Linlithgow. Flanked by huge galleries on either side, this once ostentatious room is where magnificent medieval banquets took place, and, though its walls are now bare, the size of the room gives some indication of the scale of the events.

Take yourself all the way to the very top of the palace to **Queen Margaret's Bower,** a tiny room often linked to the wife of King James IV, which boasts far-reaching views across the surrounding countryside. Popular myth says that this is where the queen sat in the autumn of 1513, waiting in vain for her husband, who was slain at the Battle of Flodden, to return.

Food and Accommodations
THE FOUR MARYS
65-67 High Street, Linlithgow; tel. 01506 842 171; www.fourmarys-linlithgow.co.uk; noon-9pm daily; entrées £4.29

This stone-walled inn by Linlithgow Cross, a short walk from the castle, is named after the four ladies in waiting who were sent with Mary, Queen of Scots, to France. Inside you'll find low ceilings, tartan carpet, and plenty of pub grub at good prices, including tasty burgers and staples such as steak and chips. There are meal deals Sunday to Thursday.

CHAMPANY INN
Linlithgow, EH49 7LU; tel. 01506 834 532; www.champany.com; £119 d

This cozy inn within converted farm buildings is as traditional as they come. The décor is a little outdated and the floorboards a little creaky, but there's no denying the charm of the place. Rooms are spacious and feature tartan bedspreads and curtains. In truth, Champany Inn is more of a restaurant with rooms than a typical inn.

The slightly chintzy **restaurant** (12:30pm-2pm, 7pm-10pm Mon.-Fri., 7pm-10pm Sat.; entrées £17.50), where carpets are patterned with the hotel's logo and there are fruit

---

1: Linlithgow Palace 2: Rosslyn Chapel

bowls on the table, nevertheless serves good (though pricey) food, and you should try the house speciality of hot smoked salmon. The **Chop and Ale House** (noon-2pm and 6:30pm-10pm Mon.-Thurs., noon-10pm Fri.-Sat., 12:30pm-10pm Sun.) next door is a low-key, bothy-style room with a stone fireplace and offers good burgers (£13.50) and steaks (£24.95). No bookings are taken in the Chop and Ale House.

Getting There and Around

There are about four trains an hour from **Edinburgh Waverley** to Linlithgow. The roughly 20-minute journey costs £5.40 each way. The station is centrally located in the town, and it's a five-minute walk to the palace. The 20-mile (32-km) drive from Edinburgh to Linlithgow takes 30 minutes. Follow the M8 west out of the city to join the M9 after 20 minutes. Take Exit 3 off the M9, and take the A803 to Linlithgow.

Once here, you could make use of the **Bike & Go** service (www.bikeandgo.co.uk, £10 annual subscription plus £3.80 a day) available throughout Scotland. You will need to sign up before you leave home. Bikes are available outside Linlithgow Station, and you can follow the towpath all the way to Falkirk (11 mi/17.7 km) in one direction or Edinburgh in the other (24 mi/38.6 km). The route to Edinburgh is relatively flat (though the path can be rough in places) and takes just over two hours, so a return trip could conceivably be done in a day. The journey to Falkirk is a tad more exciting and will see you traverse tunnels, aqueducts, and old settlements before arriving at the famous **Falkirk Wheel.**

AROUND LINLITHGOW
Bo'ness and Kinneil Railway

Bo'ness Station, Union Street; tel. 01506 822 298;
www.bkrailway.co.uk; 11am-4:30pm daily late
Mar.-late Oct.

This heritage railway is just a 15-minute bus ride from Linlithgow and offers a slice of railway nostalgia. Trains run on weekends, Tuesdays, and select school holidays from late

March to late October. You can grab lunch in the station buffet, and there's even a **Gauge O' Model Railway** that will delight children (open weekends and holidays only) as well as a **Museum of Scottish Railways,** which features old locomotives, carriages, and wagons. You can also enjoy afternoon tea and days out with Thomas the Tank Engine.

TRAIN RIDES

Adult £10, child £6, family £28, under fives free

Return train rides from Bo'ness to Manuel take around 1.25 hours; return train rides from Bo'ness to Birkhall take just over 1 hour. Tickets give you the freedom to hop on and off the train throughout the day, though, so you can explore the areas around any of the stations, such as Kinneil Halt where you can walk along the banks of the Firth of Forth through a nature reserve. The highlight of any visit are the trains themselves. You can watch them being coupled to their coaches, meet the driver on the footplate, or just sit back in one of the heritage carriages—the corridor coaches with sliding doors are very Harry Potter—and hark back to the Golden Age of travel.

MUSEUM OF SCOTTISH RAILWAYS

Bo'ness Station; 11am-4:30pm daily Mar.-late Oct.;
adult £5, children free

This museum, just a short walk over the footbridge from the train station, houses over 200 locomotives, wagons, and carriages. It has several interactive displays, such as the sorting office where you can help organize the mail, and the signal room where you can pull levers. A good exhibition tells the story of how Scotland's railways helped ferry injured soldiers home on special ambulance trains during the First World War as well as transport troops north to Scapa Flow. It's not huge but should keep you entertained for an hour or so.

GETTING THERE

From Linlithgow, take bus no. 45 (Mon.-Sat. with Prentice Westwood Coaches, www.prenticewestwoodcoaches.com), which leaves from just outside the train station once an hour to reach the railway. The trip takes about a half hour and costs £2.70 each way (£4.90 return). On Sundays the service is run by FirstGroup (bus no. F45) and it is still hourly. Drivers should head 4.3 miles (6.9 km) north on the A706 to reach the railway from Linlithgow.

Beecraigs Country Park

West Lothian Civic Centre, Howden South Road; tel. 01506 280 000; www.westlothian.gov.uk/beecraigs; 9am-7pm late Mar.-late Sept., 9am-5pm Oct., 10am-4pm Nov.-Mar.

High in the Bathgate Hills, this gorgeous 913-acre (369 hectare) green space is free to visit and open year-round. You can see red deer and Highland cattle, plus the Sutherland Way walkway provides access between the fields for views across the landscape and of Belted Galloways (a heritage breed of cattle) grazing dozily. The viewing shed is a definite must in spring as it is used for lambing and calving cows.

There is also an adventure playground, cycling trails, and free orienteering maps to download to test your navigational skills throughout the park. You may spot some horseback riders in the park, but unfortunately these are all the owners' own—it's a popular place for riding.

GETTING THERE

To get here, you can take the **Taxibus 7** service (adult £2, child £1), which runs on demand from 7:30am to 7:30pm, from any bus stop in Linlithgow High Street. You must pre-book by calling **All the Fours** (tel. 01506 444 444).

By car, it's less than a 10-minute drive south of Linlithgow, from the High Street; turn left onto Preston Road and follow it for just over 1.5 miles (2.4 km) before turning left again. It's the first road on your right.

★ ROSSLYN CHAPEL

Chapel Loan, Roslin; tel. 0131 440 2159; www. rosslynchapel.com; 9:30am-5pm Mon.-Sat Jan.-May, 9:30am-6pm Mon.-Sat. June-Aug., 9:30am-5pm Mon.-Sat. Sept.-Dec., noon-4:45pm Sun. year-round; adults £9, concessions £7, under 18s (with adult) free

This beautiful 15th-century chapel, known for its elaborate masonry, has seen visitor numbers soar since its appearance in the *Da Vinci Code* films, but it has actually been wowing visitors for centuries. Regular talks take place within the chapel (10am, 11am, 12:15pm, 2pm, 3pm, and 4pm Mon.-Sat.; 1pm, 2pm, and 3pm Sun.) to explain the significance of the many stone carvings around the church.

History

Rosslyn Chapel was founded in 1446 by William Sinclair, 1st Earl of Caithness, who saw it as his way into heaven. Sinclair was of Norman origin; his family is believed to have come to England from France around the same time as William the Conqueror (1066) before heading north into Scotland. Originally intending to build a "Bible in stone," Sinclair wanted a place of worship of cathedral proportions, but sadly work stalled following his death.

By the 1590s, following the Scottish Reformation, the Sinclair family was forced to abandon the chapel as a place of worship. In the 1650s Oliver Cromwell's army used it as a stable, and by the 1850s it had fallen into such a state of disrepair and was so overrun with foliage that it became known as the garden chapel. In 1862, Queen Victoria, who had fallen in love with Rosslyn, ordered its repair, and it opened as a Scottish episcopal place of worship.

Since the late 1980s, there has been a lot of speculation that the chapel was in some way connected to the Knights Templar and the Holy Grail. These theories and the excitement around them reached fever pitch following the filming of the *Da Vinci Code* here in 2006, and now conspiracy theorists as well as fans of Dan Brown's book and the subsequent film come here in their droves.

Visiting the Chapel

The master masonry on display in the chapel is incredible. Carvings all around depict what seem to be scenes of the crucifixion and resurrection alongside symbols of fertility and the natural world, including the famous green men, which are dozens of faces etched into the stone that have foliage coming out of their mouths. There even appears to be what looks like sheaths of maize and corn, which are native to North America, giving some weight to a theory that founder William Sinclair's grandfather actually made it to the Americas before Christopher Columbus.

There is much debate over what all of the carvings mean. Do they tell just a biblical story, or do they reference the Sinclair family's Norse heritage? Or maybe, just maybe, they are secret messages from the Knights Templar. Many people point to symbols in the crypt, which predates the chapel by some 100 years, as evidence of the latter.

Notice the carving of a man, the master mason, by the door of the chapel. Legend has it that, after building one intricate pillar for the chapel, the mason was determined to build another that was even more imaginative and traveled to Europe to find inspiration among the Renaissance architecture. While he was gone, his apprentice dreamed of an incredibly beautiful pillar; he told William, who ordered him to make it. When the master mason returned and saw the pillar, he flew into a jealous rage and whacked the apprentice over the head with his mason's hammer. The apprentice died, and the mason was hanged for his crime. As punishment, the figure of the mason is forced to look out over the apprentice's pillar (as it is called) for all of eternity.

Macabre tales aside, the chapel contains a good visitor center with a café, gift shop, and free leaflets giving an overview of the chapel and its highlights in a number of languages. The café serves hot drinks, soups, sandwiches, and cakes. The gift shop sells green man-themed gifts and soft cuddly cats (the resident cat has been here for 13 years or more).

Food
THE ORIGINAL ROSSLYN INN GASTROPUB

2-4 Main Street; tel. 0131 440 2384; http://theoriginalrosslyninn.co.uk/gastropub; 12pm-3pm & 5pm-11pm Mon.-Fri., 12pm-11pm Sat. and Sun.; entrées £5.95

This is a good lunch or dinner spot after you've looked around the chapel before getting the bus back to Edinburgh. All produce is locally sourced; the fish (including the house special of haddock) comes from Clark Brothers of Musselburgh, while the Scottish beef is supplied by local master butcher John from J Gilmour. There are light bites for lunch (sandwiches and soup of the day), or, if you're famished, try the haggis clapshot.

The Rosslyn Chapel carvings are intricate and mysterious.

Getting There and Around

The village of Roslin and Rosslyn Chapel are just seven miles south of Edinburgh, making it a very easy day trip. The no. 37 bus (make sure it has Penicuik/Deanburn on the front) from Edinburgh leaves from Princes Street or North Bridge, takes 45 minutes to 1 hour, and costs £1.70 each way. It drops you just outside the Original Rosslyn Inn Gastropub from where it is just a short walk down a lane to the chapel. There are only two buses an hour, so check times before you set off to ensure you're not waiting around for ages.

It is possible to reach Rosslyn via the newest train route in Britain, the **Borders Railway**, if you want to combine your visit with one to the Borders Abbeys. Trains from Edinburgh Waverly leave for Eskbank every half an hour and take just 18 minutes (£4.70 each way). From Eskbank, take the **East Coast Bus** service no. 140 from the main road to Roslin (every half hour with a journey time of 30 minutes, just £1.70 each way), or take a short taxi ride from here with **Dalkeith Taxis** (tel. 0131 654 1212) or the **Midlothian Taxi Hire Company** (tel. 0131 440 2985), which would cost around £12.

There are also lots of tour companies that travel here, including **Rabbie's** (tel. 0131 226 3133; www.rabbies.com), **Highland Experience** (tel. 0131 226 1414; www.highlandexperience.com), and **Go Scotland** (tel. 0131 258 3306; goscotlandtours.com), but it is very easy to do independently.

Roslin is just a half-hour drive south of Edinburgh (8 mi/12.9 km) via the A701. There will be brown tourist signposts as you approach the village, and there is free parking at the chapel.

Glasgow

While not as visually arresting as Edinburgh,

what Glasgow lacks in old-world charm it makes up with culture, which it has in spades. It is known for its exceptional museums (which are largely free) and its architecture, which encompasses both the handsome red sandstone buildings of the Victorian era and the Art Nouveau-inspired "Glasgow Style" developed in the early 20th century by the city's famous son, Charles Rennie Mackintosh. As Scotland's largest city, Glasgow also has one of the best shopping scenes in Britain and has world-leading live music venues—it is a UNESCO City of Music, after all.

Glasgow is a master of reinvention: although economic turmoil in the 1930s followed by the virtual collapse of its shipbuilding industry in the 1960s and the closure of its steelworks, coal mines, and factories in

Highlights

Look for ★ to find recommended sights, activities, dining, and lodging.

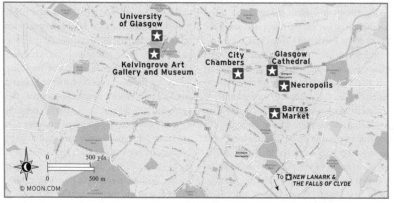

University of Glasgow ★

Kelvingrove Art Gallery and Museum ★

City Chambers ★

Glasgow Cathedral ★

★ Necropolis

★ Barras Market

0 — 500 yds
0 — 500 m

© MOON.COM

To ✛ NEW LANARK & THE FALLS OF CLYDE

★ **City Chambers:** This elaborate palazzo with its white marble staircase gives the Vatican a run for its money, and its free tours are one of Glasgow's best-kept secrets (page 137).

★ **Glasgow Cathedral:** Visit Glasgow's oldest building—the finest medieval large church to survive the Scottish Reformation with its roof intact (page 142).

★ **Necropolis:** Along with your visit to the cathedral, don't miss the chance to wander around this elegiac city of the dead (page 144).

★ **University of Glasgow:** Tour this grand neo-Gothic university, said to be J. K. Rowling's inspiration for Hogwarts, and poke through the treasures at the Hunterian Museum (page 145).

★ **Kelvingrove Art Gallery and Museum:** Set in a stunning late-Victorian building that looks more like a palace than a museum, this treasury of Scottish art and natural history is a must for any visit (page 148).

★ **Parks:** Explore the hidden gardens, open spaces, and woodland walks that give Glasgow its nickname "Dear Green Place" (page 154).

★ **Live Music in Glasgow:** From world-class concert halls to underground clubs jammed with up-and-coming bands and low-key pub sessions, you haven't experienced Glasgow until you've heard it sing (page 162).

★ **Barras Market:** Meander the warren of stalls at this historic working-class market, where the first green shoots of gentrification are sprouting, to hear Glasgow patter like nowhere else (page 171).

★ **New Lanark and the Falls of Clyde:** Just 30 miles out of the city center, this World Heritage site is a perfectly preserved mill village with pretty riverside walks through a wildlife reserve to spectacular waterfalls (page 188).

the 1970s saw unemployment levels escalate, it wasn't down for too long. By the 1980s it had started the process of picking itself up and dusting itself off to such an extent that it was named the first European City of Culture in 1990 and UK City of Architecture & Design in 1999.

Today, it is an exciting, innovative metropolis where the old warehouses of the 18th-century Merchant City have been turned into swish restaurants and bars. Finnieston in the West End is experiencing something of a food awakening, and the once down-trodden East End is emerging as a hipster haven. In the south of the city you can see hairy coos (Highland cattle) a-wandering, while to the north, the city's once thriving industrial heritage is celebrated along the banks of the Forth and Clyde Canal where old factories have been converted into dynamic art spaces. And no trip to Glasgow (or Glesga as locals would have it) is complete without a visit to the city's West End—home to some of its most historic attractions as well as a spirited student population and traditional pubs, where you can discover for yourself why Glasgow is considered the friendliest city in the world. If all that liveliness has taken its toll, then take the train out of the city to the 230-year-old World Heritage site of New Lanark, a conservation mill village surrounded by fertile woodland that is home to the cascading Falls of Clyde.

Glasgow is a lot more down to earth than Edinburgh (many Glaswegians describe Edinburgh as "Aw fur coat an nae knickers," which loosely means that despite appearances Edinburgh is no classier than Glasgow), and some visitors can be put off by Glasgow's grittier, post-industrial look. But it is the city's working-class roots that give it a steely determination that ensures it is never down at heel for too long and you're unlikely to ever encounter a more authentic city.

HISTORY

St. Kentigern (or St. Mungo as he is more widely known), Glasgow's patron saint, founded a church near where Glasgow Cathedral sits today circa AD 560 and it is here that he is believed to have been buried in AD 612; by the 10th and 11th centuries the region was one of the biggest and richest bishoprics in the Kingdom of Scotland. In 1136 the first stone of Glasgow Cathedral was laid, and the medieval settlement ran from here, along the high street, through the Saltmarket, and all the way to the River Clyde.

Sadly, little of this old town survives, save the cathedral, Provand's Lordship, and the Tolbooth Steeple at the old Glasgow Cross where the city's oldest streets converge. The Great Fire of Glasgow in 1652 destroyed almost a third of the city's buildings, and then untold riches brought to the city in the 18th century through trans-Atlantic trade led to many buildings being pulled down and replaced with the rich dwellings and huge warehouses of the Merchant City. Following the Act of Union between England and Scotland in 1707, new trade opportunities opened up to Scotland, and Glasgow's proximity to the west coast proved very attractive as it was faster for ships to come here than to go to London. Before long, Scottish agents were sent to the states of Virginia, North Carolina, and South Carolina in search of tobacco supplies; soon Glasgow was the center of the international tobacco trade.

You can see remnants of this time in many of the city's street names, which are named after the enormously wealthy Tobacco Lords—Buchanan, Glassford, and Ingram streets to name a few. However, to Glasgow's shame, its newfound wealth had a human cost: ships that left Glasgow made their way to Africa where they were loaded with slaves who were taken to the Americas and used to work the plantations—the very plantations that supplied the city's tobacco. It was the American War of Independence that finally spelled the end of the tobacco trade, but by this time Glasgow had established itself as a center of commerce and switched its attentions to cotton, sugar, ironworks, and shipbuilding.

Previous: Riverside Museum and Tall Ship; Ashton Lane; Kelvingrove Art Gallery and Museum

By the mid-19th century Glasgow was the shipbuilding center of the world and known as the Second City of the Empire, a status made possible by the deepening of the River Clyde; it is oft said that Glasgow made the Clyde and the Clyde made Glasgow. The city's boom period on the back of the Industrial Revolution in the late 19th and early 20th centuries meant there was a huge market for people who wanted beautiful things in their homes and on their ships, so the Glasgow School of Art was expanded to provide the artisan products so desired. The man tasked with developing the college was a relatively unknown designer and architect by the name of Charles Rennie Mackintosh, who would go on to shape the look of the city in the early 20th century with his trademark Art Nouveau-influenced style. However, this period of prosperity was not to last. Glasgow witnessed a huge period of decline post-war, further deepened by the closure of many of the shipyards from the 1960s onward.

Where once a fifth of the world's ships were built along the River Clyde, today shipbuilding is confined to the BAE Systems yards in Govan and Scotstoun, which still produce warships, and Ferguson Marine, much further out in the Port of Glasgow. However, the once-deserted region of Clydeside is now being revived with new buildings, such as the Clydeside Distillery, and more planned, creating a destination of note. In 2018 the city of Glasgow was tested again when there was a second devastating fire at the Glasgow School of Art, less than a year before the carefully restored Mackintosh masterpiece was due to reopen. While the future of the building is now uncertain, one thing is for sure—the city will once again rise from the ashes because no matter how many times Glasgow is down, it is never out.

ORIENTATION

Built on a grid system, Glasgow's city center, around Buchanan Street and the rest of the Style Mile that bleeds into the Merchant City, is surprisingly easy to navigate. And while much of the central attractions can be explored on foot, the brilliant Subway system connects you to other parts of the city in mere minutes too.

City Center

It can be a little tricky trying to work out exactly where the city center is in Glasgow. When most people talk about the city center, they are referring to the streets north of the River Clyde as far as the M8, which curves around the north and western fringes. The eastern boundary is marked by the Saltmarket and High Street. The city's principal plaza, George Square, is Glasgow's civic heart and home to the majestic City Chambers, a stately presence on its eastern side. It's a good place to start your exploration of Glasgow, with most of the city center's main attractions—the Style Mile, Mackintosh at the Willow, and the Gallery of Modern Art (GOMA)—lying to the west of George Square. Meanwhile, the cathedral and the Necropolis are just a 15-minute walk northeast of the square.

Merchant City

The Merchant City cuts through the city center and offers an air of sophistication to the area, with chic restaurants and bars that are buzzing with after-work drinkers and smartly dressed visitors any night of the week. Amid its cobbled lanes, which roughly speaking stretch west from the High Street all the way to Queen Street (home to the neoclassical Gallery of Modern Art) from below George Square and as far south as Trongate, you'll also find some incredible architecture and some real hidden gems, such as the Britannica Panopticon, the oldest surviving music hall in the world. It's also a hub of creativity; you can see great shows at places like the Tron, plus the city's very own "pink triangle", just south of George Square, which is home to Glasgow's growing gay scene that has everything from low-key dive bars to classy cocktail lounges and raucous cabaret nights and clubs.

Glasgow

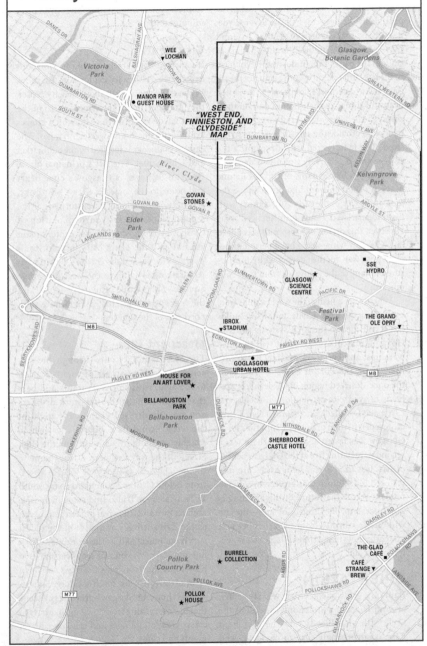

SEE "WEST END, FINNIESTON, AND CLYDESIDE" MAP

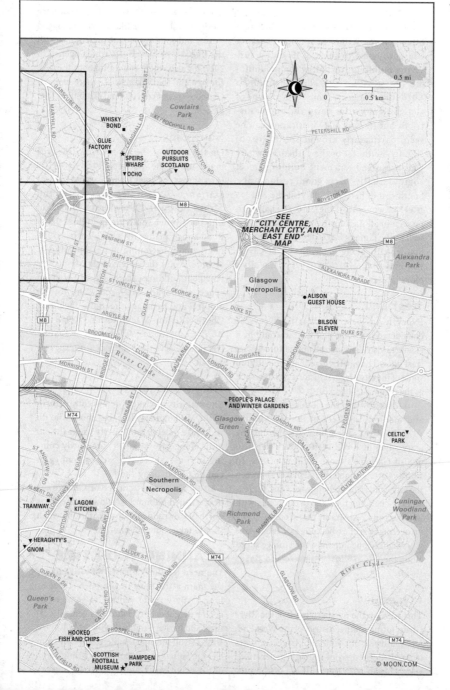

© MOON.COM

East End

To the east of the city center, from the High Street on, you'll find the medieval heart of Glasgow, home to some of its oldest surviving buildings, including the indomitable **Glasgow Cathedral** and **Provand's Lordship.** For generations, this was one of Glasgow's more run-down and poorer districts, but flickers of gentrification can be seen, particularly around **Dennistoun,** slightly southeast of the cathedral, where well-preserved tenement buildings meet some actually very good restaurants. Southwest of here you can visit the **Barras Market** where working-class Glasgow can be seen in all its colorful and brash glory, as well as the famous **Barrowland Ballroom.** South again, along the banks of the Clyde, you will find **Glasgow Green,** the city's oldest park.

West End

Everything west of Charing Cross is considered the West End, and it would be a shame to visit Glasgow and not venture west at least once. Though it's here that you will find some of the city's biggest historic charms, such as the magnificent **Kelvingrove Art Gallery and Museum** and the Gothic revival allure and medieval mystery of the **University of Glasgow,** which both sit around the leafy edges of **Kelvingrove Park,** it's also one of Glasgow's most exciting places. In **Finnieston,** a neighborhood that sits between the city center and Kelvingrove Park, there is an ever-changing food and drink scene, with new bars and restaurants that seem to spring up overnight, while who knows what bargains you might happen upon in the vintage shops along the **Great Western Road** and **Byres Road.**

Clydeside

This area, on the northern bank of the River Clyde, forms another district of the West End, just southwest of Finnieston. In recent years it has benefited from much regeneration, which began with the building of the now iconic **Riverside Museum** in 2011, whose modern design looks like a series of jagged waves, and continues to the present day with the **Clydeside Distillery,** which opened in 2017. It's also where you'll find both the **SEC Centre** and the **SSE Hydro,** where many of Glasgow's major concerts and exhibitions take place.

Southside

On the south of the River Clyde, this area made up of the districts **Pollokshields** (just across the river from Glasgow Central Station), **Govan** (farther west), and **Strathbungo and Shawlands,** which lead into each other south along Pollockshaws Road (once primarily a residential area), is gradually becoming more appealing to visitors. Amid the streets of tightly-packed tenement buildings, there is plenty of green space, a buoyant café scene, and lots of cultural and heritage attractions, including Charles Rennie Mackintosh's **House for an Art Lover** and **Pollok House.** Several bus routes serve the Southside from the city center.

North Glasgow

The majority of visitors don't venture north of the M8 boundary line, but those who do will find a quiet part of the city where the old mills along **Speirs Wharf** are slowly coming into use as creative spaces, and calm can be found along the **Forth and Clyde Canal.** This secret corner of Glasgow is best reached on foot by following the signs north of Cowcaddens Subway Station, which should take about 10 minutes.

PLANNING YOUR TIME

You need to allow at least **two days** to see the main attractions in Glasgow—three or four if you want to venture to some of its cooler neighborhoods and less central cultural and heritage sights. **If you only have a day,** a stroll through the Merchant City from George Square is a must, as is visiting some of the major Mackintosh buildings, such as the newly restored Mackintosh at the Willow on Sauchiehall Street or The Lighthouse. You won't want to miss the Gallery of Modern Art either, if only to take a photo of the cone-headed Duke of Wellington statue, an example of Scottish self-determination that won through. The **hop-on hop-off bus** is great for taking in the main attractions if you're short of time, including the cathedral, Necropolis, Riverside Museum, and Kelvingrove Art Gallery and Museum, though you won't have much time to explore them in a day.

For two days or more, spend one day in the city center, incorporating the cathedral and Necropolis in the East End, and then give yourself a full day in the West End, so you have plenty of time to look at specific exhibitions and gallery rooms in the Kelvingrove (such as the very good Glasgow Boys collection), as well as the Hunterian, the University of Glasgow, and some of the area's very cool thrift stores. If you're in Glasgow a little longer, venture to the Southside but not before you've visited the famous Barras Market over east.

Itinerary Ideas

DAY ONE IN GLASGOW

It's difficult to do Glasgow justice in a day, but you will at least have a lot of fun trying. Spend your day visiting some of the major sights, mostly clustered in and around the city center and East End.

1 Start your day with a hearty breakfast at **McCune Smith,** right on the cusp of the city center and East End, an ethical café where the coffee and breakfast rolls are as good as their morals.

2 Take the 10-minute walk to **Glasgow Cathedral,** the city's oldest building and one of the most impressive pre-Reformation churches in the whole of Scotland.

3 Stroll up behind the cathedral to the "city of the dead," the **Necropolis.** From the Victorian cemetery's lofty position above the city you can get some of the best views of Glasgow's skyline.

4 From here, it's a 30-minute walk or a short bus ride (no. 38 or no. 57) to the newly restored **Mackintosh at the Willow** on Sauchiehall Street, where you can eat finger sandwiches, scones, and cakes and sip tea from Mackintosh-designed crockery.

5 For more insight into the mark Mackintosh left on the Glasgow landscape, visit **The Lighthouse,** his first public commission and now Scotland's National Centre for Design and Architecture.

6 Before dinner, make sure to pass by the **Gallery of Modern Art** and doff your hat (or cone) to the Duke of Wellington outside.

7 Step back into the 1930s for dinner in an Art Deco setting at **Rogano,** Glasgow's oldest surviving restaurant.

8 If you're not totally worn out from your day of sightseeing, then put on your dancing shoes and head to the East End for a night of revelry at **Barrowland Ballroom.**

Glasgow Itineraries

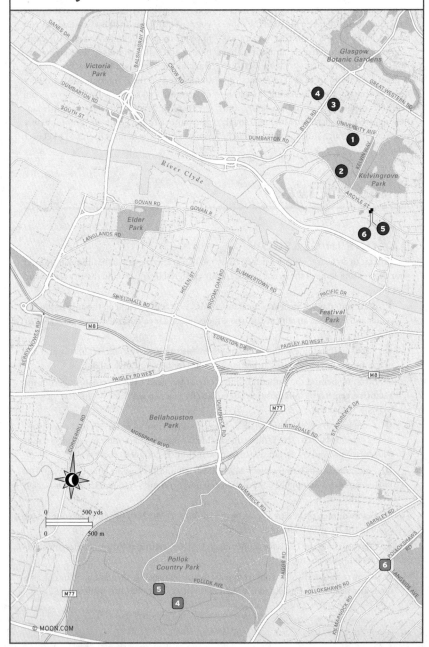

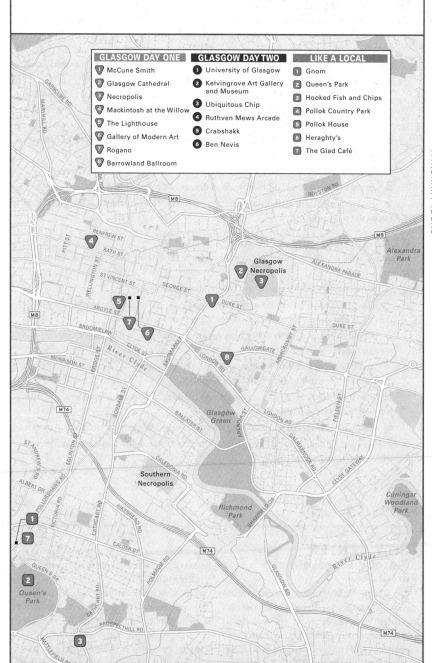

GLASGOW DAY ONE
1. McCune Smith
2. Glasgow Cathedral
3. Necropolis
4. Mackintosh at the Willow
5. The Lighthouse
6. Gallery of Modern Art
7. Rogano
8. Barrowland Ballroom

GLASGOW DAY TWO
1. University of Glasgow
2. Kelvingrove Art Gallery and Museum
3. Ubiquitous Chip
4. Ruthven Mews Arcade
5. Crabshakk
6. Ben Nevis

LIKE A LOCAL
1. Gnom
2. Queen's Park
3. Hooked Fish and Chips
4. Pollok Country Park
5. Pollok House
6. Heraghty's
7. The Glad Café

DAY TWO IN GLASGOW

If you have a second day in Glasgow, head to the hip West End for a morning of art and history followed by an afternoon of vintage shopping and good food.

1 Have a leisurely breakfast at your hotel, and then head to the West End for the late morning tour around the grounds of the neo-Gothic **University of Glasgow,** which some say inspired J. K. Rowling's Hogwarts.

2 Visit the cultural powerhouse that is the **Kelvingrove Art Gallery and Museum,** making sure to see the Glasgow Boys' works displayed here and hopefully even catching some of the daily organ recital.

3 For a late lunch, venture to cobbled Ashton Lane and see if the **Ubiquitous Chip** lives up to its exemplary reputation.

4 For some post-lunch vintage shopping, pop into the **Ruthven Mews Arcade.**

5 Enjoy a delicious and laid-back seafood dinner at **Crabshakk.**

6 End your night with a traditional music session and a few wee drams at the **Ben Nevis** across the road.

GLASGOW LIKE A LOCAL

Do as the locals do, and spend your day exploring the lesser-visited Southside and its green spaces.

1 Enjoy a street-food-inspired breakfast and coffee at **Gnom.**

2 Head to **Queen's Park** for a brisk walk up Camp Hill. Enjoy the sweeping views of the city as you lounge about reading the newspaper or a good book.

3 Stop into **Hooked Fish and Chips** for an interesting spin on a classic chippy—the mac and cheese balls are a must.

4 You'll need the fuel for a walk through **Pollok Country Park,** Glasgow's largest park. Look out for the herds of Highland cattle as you go.

5 Stop into **Pollok House** for a walk around the beautiful manicured gardens, and treat yourself to a scone and coffee at the café.

6 You're probably ready for something stronger, so head to **Heraghty's** for a pint or two.

7 Unwind with dinner and live music at **The Glad Café,** a down-to-earth, local venue with a distinctly bohemian vibe.

Sights

CITY CENTER
Glasgow School of Art
167 Renfrew Street

The Glasgow School of Art was once widely considered Charles Rennie Mackintosh's greatest achievement, with the wooden library the pinnacle of his Art Nouveau showpiece, but sadly it was devastated by a second major fire in the summer of 2018, less than a year before it was due to reopen following a painstaking restoration process after an earlier fire in 2014.

This most recent fire has blindsided the city and those involved in the project; at present it is really not known what future, if any, there is for the building (or at least Mackintosh's design). The Glasgow School of Art says it is still committed to restoring the building; the priority of the council is to stabilize the ruins, dismantle the building, and ensure the businesses around the university complex can re-open and run as normal.

In the meantime, the tours of both the famous Mackintosh building at the university (his alma mater) as well as walking tours of other Mackintosh sites around the city usually run by the university are on hold. If you are hungry to see some Mackintosh buildings, then you can visit the excellent **Lighthouse,** just off Buchanan Street, the newly opened **Mackintosh at the Willow** on Sauchiehall Street, or **House for an Art Lover** in Bellahouston Park in the Southside.

★ City Chambers

George Square; tel. 0141 287 4018; www.glasgow.gov.uk; 9am-5pm Mon.-Fri.; free

Step inside this magnificent building on George Square for a taste of the Victorian fashion for opulence. Built to house the city's council chambers following the closure of its former tolbooth, it is at times unnecessarily decorative to modern eyes, but to 19th-century society it was deemed absolutely necessary to showcase the wealth and power of Glasgow to the rest of the world.

The building, which was opened by Queen Victoria in 1888, is the creation of William Young and came at great expense—at £500k it far exceeded the original £100k budget, but you don't have to look far to see where the money was spent. In the foyer there is a mosaic floor decorated with the Glasgow Coat of Arms, which depicts the miracles of St. Mungo (versions of which you will see throughout the city), while the ceiling here is embellished with 1.5 million half-inch Oppenheimer ceramic tiles.

The three-story Italian white marble staircase is the building's real draw. The largest of its kind in the western world, it has often stood in for the Vatican on screen. All of the above can be explored on your own during council opening hours if you're short of time, but much better is to join one of the two daily **free tours** (10:30am and 2:30pm Mon.-Fri.) run by knowledgeable guides, who will explain the history of the building, tell tales on some of its famous past guests, and shed a little insight into the workings of the city council. Tours last about 45 minutes.

In the actual chamber itself (which you can only visit on a tour) you can sit in councilors' chairs or have your photo taken in the Lord Provost's seat—the city's elected figurehead. Look carefully by the seats in the chamber, and you will see a small hole on each shelf in front. For many years the council upheld a tradition of holding a flower in each one when the council was in session. One story behind the flower is that when Victoria came into the chamber as part of the opening ceremony, there were some members of the public here, and she is said to have preferred the smell of the flowers to them.

The **Banqueting Hall** is enormous, with many paintings on the wall, an abundance of leather-embossed gold leaf, and huge chandeliers. It was in this room that Billy Connolly was given the Freedom of the City of Glasgow as was Nelson Mandela when he visited in 1993. Glasgow was the first UK city to give Mandela the Freedom of the City, and so the statesman came to Glasgow to accept the honor. While here, Mandela also collected the keys to other British cities that had belatedly got round to making the same gesture. Overall it is a remarkable place. The tours are delivered with wit and panache, and everywhere you look there is another stunning detail to take in. It really is a work of art.

City Centre Mural Trail

www.citycentremuraltrail.co.uk; open 24/7; free

One great way of seeing the city is by following the mural trail, where you can see colorful and often fun street art round many a corner; it may just be the first official trail of its kind in the world. The murals have helped rejuvenate the city and add splashes of color and humor to vacant buildings and derelict sites.

The full route covers almost six miles, from the cathedral in the East End through to the M8 on the edge of the West End, and from

City Centre, Merchant City, and East End

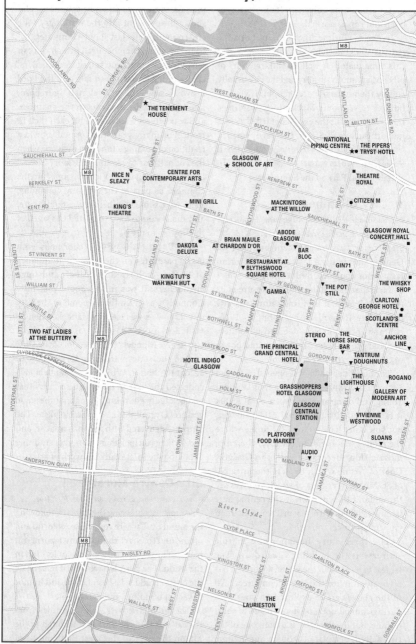

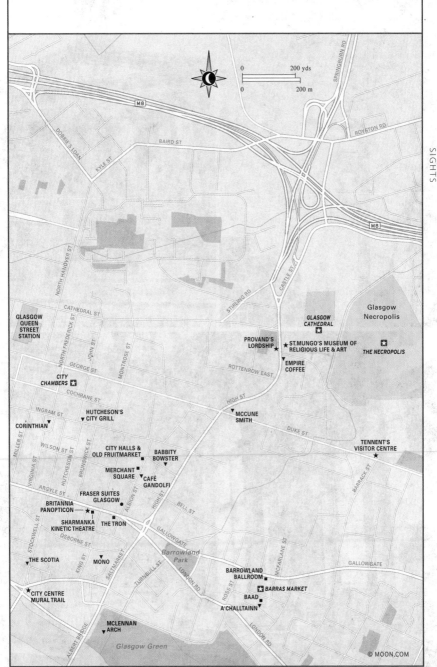

© MOON.COM

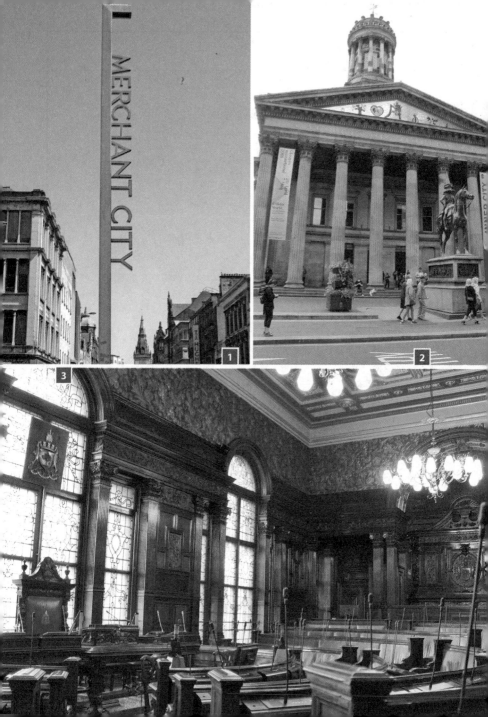

the banks of the River Clyde in the south of the city center, right up to Cowcaddens at the north of the city. It includes 24 pieces and counting, so it might be a bit much for an afternoon, but there is no reason you can't split it up over a couple of days. Many of the most famous pieces of graffiti can be found in the city center, and plotting a route to take them in (along with breaks for refreshments or other sightseeing) is a great way to orient yourself, especially if you like street art. Download a map from the website, or simply let your eye guide you as you wander around the city center.

Locals each have their favorites, but the few that are must-sees include the **Fellow Glasgow Residents** mural on Ingram Street, which transformed a run-down car park into something quite beautiful by bringing some of the nature and wildlife that can be found in and around the city to colorful life, and the famous **Glasgow Panda** (the black and white animal brings smiles to all who search him out in a secret corner on Gordon Lane, just off Buchanan Street), born out of the phrase (and still firmly believed in some parts) that there's more pandas in Glasgow than Conservatives. And make sure you visit each of the three murals added to celebrate the 75th birthday of one of Glasgow's favorite exports, the Big Yin, Billy Connolly, which depict the comedian at different stages of his career and can be seen at Osborne Street, Dixon Street, and Gallowgate.

The Tenement House

145 Buccleuch Street; tel. 0141 333 0183; www.nts. org.uk/visit/places/the-tenement-house; 11am-5pm Mon.-Sat., 1pm-5pm Sun. July-Aug, 1pm-5pm daily late Mar.-Jun., Sept.-Oct.; £7.50, family £18.50

This rather inconspicuous late Victorian tenement house contains a fascinating collection of archive materials that sheds valuable insight into what life was like living in Glasgow for women in the first half of the 20th century. The house was once lived in by

one Miss Agnes Toward, a shorthand typist who seemed something of a hoarder—albeit a very neat and ordered one. The four restored rooms give a glimpse into the domestic habits of Toward, who resided here between 1911 and 1965. It's a kid-friendly place, with a table of odd artifacts for little ones to play with and see if they can figure out what they are for, and a homely time capsule for the rest of us.

The National Piping Centre

30-34 McPhater Street; tel. 0141 353 0220; www. thepipingcentre.co.uk; 9am-7pm Mon.-Thurs., 9am-5pm Fri., 9am-noon Sat.; adult £4.50, child/ concessions £2.50, intensive five-day courses £330

It's hard to think of Scotland without thinking of the bagpipes—they are used to pipe the guests in for dinner on Burns Night and they are a common feature of the Highland Games—so the collection here, which encompasses over 300 years of piping history, is very important.

Make sure you view the chanter of Iain Dall (Blind John) Mackay who lived from 1656 to 1754. It is the oldest surviving chanter of a Highland bagpipe anywhere in the world, as well as the bagpipes of John MacColl, one of Scotland's finest piping composers. You will also get the chance to have a go on the bagpipes yourself when you visit the museum. If you like what you hear and have several days to spare, you can even book an intensive workshop to learn how to play the bagpipes, and there is a very good gift shop for equipping yourself with all that's necessary after your visit.

MERCHANT CITY
The Lighthouse

11 Mitchell Lane; tel. 0141 276 5365; www. thelighthouse.co.uk; 10:30am-5pm Mon.-Sat., noon-5pm Sun.; free

Designed by Charles Rennie Mackintosh, this building was once home to the *Glasgow Herald* newspaper and is today home to Scotland's National Centre for Design and Architecture. It takes its name from the tall

1: Merchant City 2: Gallery of Modern Art 3: Council Chamber, City Chambers

tower that glowers out over the city and is seen as a beacon of Scotland's creative industries.

Though sections of the building are sometimes closed off for public functions, on the whole the Lighthouse is one big creative space where you are free to wander. The permanent **Mackintosh Interpretation Centre** tells the story of the building, Mackintosh's part in it, and how it was transformed into what you see today on either side of a curved glass panel that stretches for much of the length of the room. A highlight of the building is undoubtedly the exposed stonework of the **tower,** which can be ascended via a dizzying spiral—or helical—staircase. At the top is an external viewing platform where you stand beneath the ogee arch of the roof. To access the tower stairs, go past the Mackintosh Interpretation Centre. The indoor viewing platform on floor 6 has floor-to-ceiling windows and is also worth a gander—if you're lucky someone may even be playing the piano as you take in the city views.

Gallery of Modern Art (GOMA)

Royal Exchange Square; tel. 0141 287 3050; www. glasgowlife.org.uk/museums/venues/gallery-of-modern-art-goma; 10am-5pm Mon.-Wed., Sat., 10am-8pm Thurs., 11am-5pm Fri. and Sun.; free

Housed in the former mansion of one of Glasgow's richest Tobacco Lords, William Cunninghame, this contemporary art gallery is sometimes maligned for offering style over substance. Nevertheless, it is popular with locals, and, with four galleries, a café, and a shop, it is a good place to while away a couple of hours. In particular, it is a good place to see works by the "New Glasgow Boys"—a generation of figurative painters who studied at the Glasgow School of Art in the 1980s and whose work tends to focus on the working-class side of Glasgow.

Truth be told, though, many people who head to GOMA don't actually come inside at all. Instead, they are drawn to the **statue of the Duke of Wellington** outside, which is distinctive because the Duke is wearing a bright traffic cone on his head. Of course,

this wasn't the intention of the sculptor Carlo Marochetti but appeared as part of a student prank in the 1980s; despite repeated efforts to remove it, it was always returned, so much so that the council gave up (there was even a popular online campaign to keep it). And so it remains, one of the most photographed spots in the whole of the city and a sign of the subversive nature of some residents. You'll even find it on postcards around the city.

Britannica Panopticon

117 Trongate, 1st Floor; tel. 0141 553 0840; www. britanniapanopticon.org; tours noon-5pm Tues.-Sat.

This beautiful building on Trongate, with arched windows supported by columns, is home to the oldest music hall in the world. If you can, join one of the free tours to peek behind the exterior and learn more about how audiences would cram into the hall in the Victorian era, armed with old turnips and other vegetables, ready to throw at performers who didn't have them rolling in the aisles. There are also occasional cabaret performances that really bring the venue to life, though throwing things these days is strictly forbidden.

EAST END
★ Glasgow Cathedral

Castle Street; tel. 0141 552 8198; www. glasgowcathedral.org; 9:30am-5pm Mon.-Sat., 1pm-4:30pm Sun. Apr.-Sept., 10am-3:30pm Mon.-Sat., 1pm-3:30pm Sun. Oct.-Mar., mornings Sun. for those attending 11am service only; free

To the east of the city center, the mighty Glasgow Cathedral, known by many names—the High Kirk of Glasgow, St. Kentigern's and, most affectionately, St Mungo's after the patron saint of Glasgow, who is believed to have built a church on this very site—has been a place of worship for more than 800 years. The first stone of the cathedral was laid in 1136 and dedicated to King David I, with the current building consecrated in 1197.

It is considered the best preserved large

1: Glasgow Cathedral 2: The Necropolis

medieval church in the whole of Scotland, surviving the turbulent Scottish Reformation remarkably intact—indeed, it is the only church on the Scottish mainland to have survived the uprising without losing its roof. Glasgow Cathedral remained unscathed during both the Battle of Glasgow in 1544 and the Reformation not because it was overlooked by would-be attackers but because it was so loved by the people of Glasgow that the tradespeople of the city organized themselves and took up arms to protect it.

Today, it is a splendid example of a medieval cathedral, its grey stone darkened with age and adorned with dozens of arched windows. The central stone spire (added after an earlier wooden spire was destroyed) is the pinnacle of this most precious building.

Inside, the rood screen (a rarity to still be found in Scottish churches) acts as a partition between the long nave and the chancel at the head of the building, where you will find the altar. A flight of stone steps takes you down into the dark crypt, where you will find the symbolic burial place of St. Mungo, while throughout the building there is beautiful stained glass, though much if it is more modern than you might think. Revealed in 1999, *The Millennial Window* by John Clark is on the north wall of the nave and includes text from the New Testament etched into pictures of birds taking flight, seen as a symbol of hope for the new millennium.

As with all cathedrals and places of worship, keep noise to a minimum, and please note that only visitors attending the morning service should come on Sunday mornings (11am); for everyone else, the cathedral opens at 1pm on Sundays. Guided tours, which last around an hour, are sometimes available with volunteer guides on site if you ask nicely. They are free, but donations are always welcome.

★ The Necropolis

Castle Street; www.glasgownecropolis.org
Overlooking the cathedral on the second highest hill in Glasgow, this sprawling cemetery dates back to 1832 when it was built

as a burial place for the rich merchants of the city. At the time, Glasgow's population was near a bursting point, having soared from 83,000 in 1800 to around 200,000 by 1830—a problem that brought both cholera and typhoid epidemics.

The wealthy residents wanted a place that reflected the status of Glasgow at the time, and so they took inspiration from Paris's Père Lachaise cemetery; many of the tombs and monuments were designed by Alexander "Greek" Thomson, known for his extravagant Greco-Egyptian style. It covers 37 acres (15 hectares) with more than 50,000 past residents of Glasgow buried here, although just 5 percent have a memorial erected. Look out for the Celtic headstone of one Andrew McCall, a close friend of Charles Rennie Mackintosh's father, thought to be the designer's first ever creation. Also here is the grave of William Miller, known as the "Laureate of the Nursery"—his most famous rhyme is "Wee Willie Winkie." The prominent statue of Scottish Reformer John Knox actually predates the cemetery.

The **free tours** each month are often fully booked, so be sure to book your place a couple of months in advance during peak months by emailing tours@glasgownecropolis.org. Tours on Friday nights are the most atmospheric and will tell of the past lives of Glasgow's anatomists, inventors, writers, and artists. The Necropolis is a Weegie (slang for people from Glasgow) favorite for views of the city, and you can easily visit here and the nearby cathedral in a few hours.

Provand's Lordship

3 Castle Street; tel. 0141 276 1625; www.glasgowlife. org.uk/museums/venues/provands-lordship; 10am-5pm Mon.-Weds. and Sat., 11am-5pm Fri. and Sun.; free
The oldest house in Glasgow, one of the few remaining examples of medieval architecture across the city of Glasgow, and known affectionately as the "auld hoose," Provand's Lordship is dressed much as it would have been during the 17th century (with furniture

gifted by shipping magnate and art collector Sir William Burrell himself). One of the highlights is the serene and pretty Tudor-style St. Nicholas Garden, a lovely place to escape the city's noise and read a book or just take in the history of the place. Look out for the carved faces in the cloistered walkway known as the Tontine Heads, which were once scattered across the city but were reunited here in 1995. Though it is free to enter, there are no facilities as such, but you are free to use the toilets and café across the road at St. Mungo's Museum.

St. Mungo's Museum of Religious Life and Art

2 Castle Street; tel. 0141 276 1625; www.glasgowlife.org.uk/museums/venues/st-mungo-museum-of-religious-life-and-art; 10am-5pm Mon.-Weds. and Sat., 11am-5pm Fri. and Sun.; free

Fitting for a city that was founded as a place of worship, this unusual museum explores the significance of religion on people's lives both in Scotland and across the world. It's at times poignant because religion has formed the basis of many of the divisions across the city, from the Scottish Reformation to the bitter rivalry between football fans—the mainly Catholic Celtic and the predominantly Protestant Rangers. A short walk from Provand's Lordship, the cathedral, and the Necropolis, it is feasible to see all four places in one day.

Tennent's Visitor Centre

161 Duke Street; tel. 0141 202 7145; www.tennents.com/tour; 9am-6pm Mon.-Sat., 10am-4pm Sun.; £10, concessions £8

Craft beer may be sneaking its way into more and more Glasgow pubs, but there are some that will never sway from what they know and what they know is Tennent's. At the Wellpark Brewery in the East End, where brewing in some form or other has taken place for 450 years, you can learn all about how this much-loved Scottish beer—brewed since 1885—is made, plus gain some insight into how methods have changed and adapted throughout history.

Tours, which take around 90 minutes, are well worth the fee, and you (of course) get to try some of the beer at the end. It also offers a slice of nostalgia for anyone who spent their youth in Scotland as there is an impressive collection of vintage packaging as well as footage of some classic old adverts. It's located just in front of the Necropolis and Glasgow Cathedral, too, it so could be a great way to lift the dour mood. Wear flat shoes as you'll be entering working areas.

WEST END
Glasgow Botanic Gardens

730 Great Western Road; tel. 0141 276 1614; www.glasgowbotanicgardens.com; 7am-dusk daily, glasshouses 10am-6pm daily Apr.-Sept., 10am-4:15pm daily Oct.-Mar.; free

These lovely gardens, originally opened to assist the teachings of the university, are free to roam. A delightful mix of formal gardens and more remote paths that venture into wooded areas, the Botanic Gardens are where most Westenders come for a brush with nature.

Amid the grounds you'll find several striking glasshouses, including the huge domed Kibble Palace, which extraordinarily once lived on the banks of Loch Long—a sea loch in Argyll and Bute—but which was transported here in the late 19th century. Inside Kibble Palace are lots of exotic plants and flowers, including a tree fern collection and orchids, and hidden among the fauna are some elaborate marble sculptures, not least the statue of Eve by Italian sculptor Scipione Tadolini.

★ University of Glasgow

University Avenue; www.gla.ac.uk; guided tours 11am and 2pm Tues.-Sun.; guided tours adult £10, child £5, concessions £8, under 5s free; family ticket £25

Could this be the inspiration behind J. K. Rowling's Hogwarts? The neo-Gothic design of the University of Glasgow with its crow-stepped gables, pointed turrets, and soaring spire that can be seen for miles around, attracts admiring glances from all that pass.

West End, Finnieston, and Clydeside

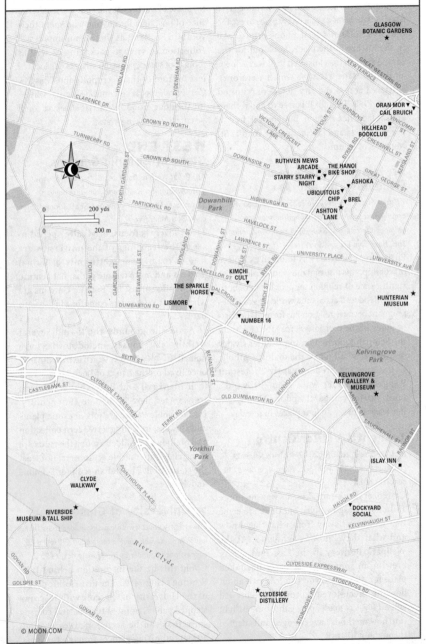

GLASGOW BOTANIC GARDENS ★

GREAT WESTERN RD

KEW TERRACE

HYNDLAND RD

SIDENHAM RD

CLARENCE DR

HUNTLY GARDENS

ORAN MOR ▼
CAIL BRUICH ▼

VINICOMBE ST

CROWN RD NORTH

VICTORIA CRESCENT LANE

SALTOUN ST

BYRES RD

HILLHEAD BOOKCLUB ■

CRESSWELL ST

KERSLAND ST

TURNBERRY RD

NORTH GARDNER ST

CROWN RD SOUTH

DOWANSIDE RD

RUTHVEN MEWS ARCADE ■

THE HANOI BIKE SHOP ▼

GREAT GEORGE ST

STARRY STARRY NIGHT ■ ▼

ASHOKA ▼

PARTICKHILL RD

Dowanhill Park

HIGHBURGH RD

UBIQUITOUS CHIP ▼

BREL ▼

HAVELOCK ST

ASHTON LANE ★

0   200 yds
0   200 m

LAWRENCE ST

FORTROSE ST

GARDNER ST

STEWARTVILLE ST

HYNDLAND ST

DOWANHILL ST

ELIE ST

LAWRENCE ST

UNIVERSITY PLACE

UNIVERSITY AVE

BYRES RD

KIMCHI CULT ■

CHANCELLOR ST

CHURCH ST

HUNTERIAN MUSEUM ★

THE SPARKLE HORSE ▼

DALCROSS ST

DUMBARTON RD

LISMORE ▼

NUMBER 16 ▼

DUMBARTON RD

Kelvingrove Park

BEITH ST

BENALDER ST

BUNHOUSE RD

CASTLEBANK ST

CLYDESIDE EXPRESSWAY

OLD DUMBARTON RD

KELVINGROVE ART GALLERY & MUSEUM ★

ARGYLE ST

SAUCHIEHALL ST

RADNOR ST

FERRY RD

Yorkhill Park

ISLAY INN ■

CLYDE WALKWAY ▼

POINTHOUSE PLACE

HAUGH RD

DOCKYARD ▼ SOCIAL

RIVERSIDE MUSEUM & TALL SHIP ★

KELVINHAUGH ST

GOVAN RD

River Clyde

CLYDESIDE EXPRESSWAY

STOBCROSS RD

GOLSPIE ST

CLYDESIDE DISTILLERY ★

STOBCROSS RD

GOVAN RD

© MOON.COM

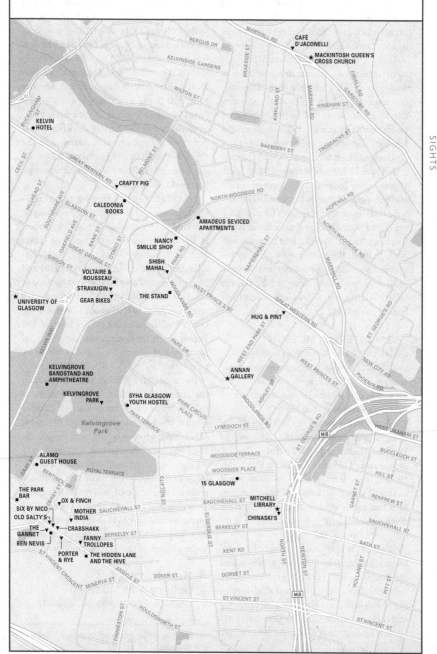

It's small wonder—it has more listed buildings than any other British university, including the beautiful vaulted cloisters with fluted columns, which have taken a recent starring role in TV's *Outlander*.

Indeed, it is one of Scotland's four ancient universities, second in age only to St. Andrew's in Fife and it has seen many special alumni graduate from here, including the inventor of the TV, John Logie Baird, and famous explorer, David Livingstone. The building that you see today was designed by Sir George Gilbert Scott in 1870, with the spire added later by his son, Sir John Oldrid Scott. However, one lodge and the decorative Lion and Unicorn staircase by the memorial chapel were taken from the university's former building on the high street, long since demolished. You can take a self-guided tour from the welcome point in the McIntyre Building by the university's main gate (look out for the iconic red telephone boxes, designed by George Gilbert Scott's son, Giles Gilbert Scott), or book a guided tour.

THE HUNTERIAN MUSEUM

University of Glasgow, Gilbert Scott Building; tel. 0141 330 4221; www.gla.ac.uk/hunterian; 10am-5pm Tues.-Sat., 11am-4pm Sun.; museum and art gallery free, special exhibitions adult £6, child £3; Mackintosh House adult £6, child £3

This compact museum in the University of Glasgow was created from the collections of William Hunter, an 18th-century Glasgow physician and obstetrician, and is filled with fascinating objects. Hunter collected many anatomical and pathological specimens to help him in his work—you can even see his death mask—and the collection has been carefully added to over the years.

Items in the main museum building focus on paleontology, archaeology, geology, and medicine, though many of Hunter's other collections have been dispersed elsewhere in the university; his zoological collections, for instance, are in the Graham Kerr Building, while his collection of books and manuscripts

are kept in the University of Glasgow Library. Young visitors will love seeing Scotland's first dinosaur footprint as well as a life-size plesiosaur on display. In the **Main Gallery** look out for the ancient mummy of Lady Shep-en-hor, which dates back 2,500 years, and the fossilized remains of the "Bearsden Shark," which is an astounding 330 million years old. Another highlight is the **Antonine Wall: Rome's Final Frontier exhibit** in the entrance gallery, which tells the story of the Roman border that once ran across Scotland from the Clyde to the Firth and Forth, much like the more famous Hadrian's Wall, which separated Scotland from England.

In a different building on the university campus, across University Avenue, you will find the **Hunterian Art Gallery,** home to the largest permanent display of James McNeil Whistler works in the world, bequeathed to the university in the 1930s and 1950s for several reasons, not least because of the American-born artist's Scottish ancestry and his support of the famous Glasgow Boys. Other highlights in the gallery include *The Entombment* by Rembrandt, a moving oil painting that depicts the burial of Christ by torchlight.

For a small fee you can also visit, within the same building, **Mackintosh House,** a re-creation of the Glasgow home of Charles Rennie Mackintosh and his wife Margaret Macdonald, which was very near the university. Look out for Mackintosh's personal writing desk—one of his most luxurious creations, made of ebonized mahogany and sycamore with mother-of-pearl, silvered metal, and glass. There is often an impressive series of special exhibitions held at the museum too, including a recent one celebrating some of the leading figures of the Scottish Enlightenment.

★ Kelvingrove Art Gallery and Museum

Argyle Street; tel. 0141 276 9599; www.glasgowlife.

1: University of Glasgow 2: Kelvingrove Art Gallery and Museum

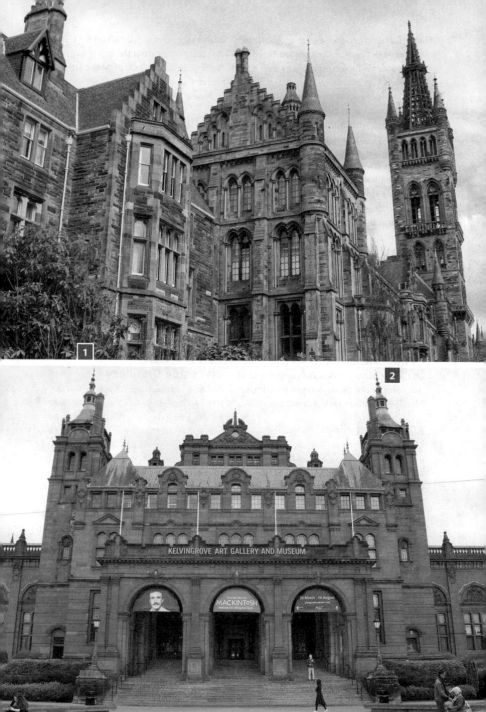

org.uk/museums/venues/kelvingrove-art-gallery-and-museum; 10am-5pm Mon.-Thurs. and Sat., 11am-5pm Fri. and Sun.; free (though some temporary exhibits may charge)

This stunning museum is one of the city's most popular attractions and is not to be missed. Set within the lovely Kelvingrove Park (designed by the former head gardener of Chatsworth House) and just a short stroll from the University of Glasgow, its grand exterior—with numerous red sandstone towers topped with finials—is one of the city's most recognizable landmarks.

Inside it doesn't disappoint either, with 22 galleries displaying some 8,000 objects. The interior is effectively split into two, with art galleries on one side displaying an impressive collection of Dutch and Flemish Masters, as well as the foremost collection of Glasgow Boys' works, while the museum on the other side focuses on natural history and world culture. The Kelvingrove organ in the center hall is also a highlight: In 2016 footage of organist Chris Nickol playing David Bowie's *Life on Mars* on the day of the musician's death went viral. Attending one of the daily organ recitals (1pm Mon.-Sat., 3pm Sun.) is highly recommended.

Mitchell Library

North Street; tel. 0141 287 2999; www.glasgowlife. org.uk/libraries/venues/the-mitchell-library; 9am-8pm Mon.-Thurs., 9am-5pm Fri.-Sat.; free

One of the largest libraries in Europe, this beautiful building is identifiable by its distinct copper dome. The city's archives are kept here, and it is an invaluable resource of information into Glasgow's past. In theory, anyone can access many of the materials (though copying restrictions do apply), but in practice it's often used by people tracing their family tree due to its collection of birth, marriage, and death registrations as well as census and burial records.

Annan Gallery

164 Woodlands Road; tel. 0141 332 0028; www. annanart.com; 10am-5:30pm Tues.-Sat., noon-4pm Sun.; free

This modest gallery in the West End has been a supporter of Scottish art for 150 years. Its pieces range from the bright canvases of Stanley Bird, alongside romantic landscapes and idyllic coastal scenes. It's a reputable place to browse or pick up some affordable art.

Ashton Lane

Ashton Lane

This cobbled backstreet in the student mecca of the West End is very pretty and is a living example of the city's ability to reinvent itself. Once a run-down, largely forgotten street, with the move of one of Glasgow's most popular restaurants, the Ubiquitous Chip, here in the 1970s, other independent businesses soon followed foot. It has since become a bustling passageway of bars and restaurants, firmly on the tourist trail. Follow the lane north and you'll come onto Creswell Lane, a similarly attractive cobbled lane that has lots of small boutiques and shops and that, for some reason, fewer tourists seem to find.

CLYDESIDE
Clydeside Distillery

The Old Pump House, Queen's Dock; tel. 0141 212 1401; www.theclydeside.com; 10am-4pm (4:30pm July-Aug.), tours every hour Mon.-Thurs., every half hour Fri.-Sun.; adult £15, concessions £13, child £5

This shiny new whisky distillery (it only opened in 2017) is part of the heralded redevelopment of the Clydeside area of the city and uses traditional techniques, such as hand-distilling to create its single malt. And the ambition here is personal—owner Tim Morrison, who has a background in whisky-making across Scotland, wants to revive whisky-making in Glasgow, in the very dock built by his great grandfather. Visitors on one of the tours (which last 80 minutes) will hear all about this personal journey and the history of the whisky industry in Glasgow, take a tour around the distillery, and be able to enjoy views of the Clyde from the gleaming glass Still House. At the end of the tour you'll also be able to sample three drams from across Scotland. There is also a good café and shop on site.

Riverside Museum and Tall Ship

Pointhouse Place; tel. 0141 287 2720; www. glasgowlife.org.uk/museums/venues/ riverside-museum; museum 10am-5pm Mon.-Thurs., 11am-5pm Fri. and Sun., tall ship 10am-5pm daily Feb.-late Oct., 10am-4pm late-Oct.-Jan.; free

Described as "Glasgow's Guggenheim," this award-winning transport museum is every bit as famous for its stunning exterior, which gives a modern nod to the pleated sheds of the Clyde's heyday, as it is for what's inside. The work of the revered late architect Zaha Hadid, though its striking design has added an exciting landmark to the city's skyline, Hadid actually designed the building from the inside out and its interactive displays celebrate Glasgow's engineering traditions while offering lots of hands-on exhibits. Jump aboard a vintage Glasgow tram or take a walk through Glasgow streets of old.

Plus, moored outside is the city's tall ship *Glenlee*, which is also free, and with its steel hull and trio of powerful masts, it recalls the Clyde's once thriving shipbuilding industry. On board you can explore life below decks, including the Captain's Cabin, and there is a good play area for under-fives. A short audio guide tells of the history of the ship.

SOUTHSIDE
Pollok House

2060 Pollokshaws Road, Pollok Country Park; tel. 0141 616 6410; www.nts.org.uk/visit/places/ pollok-house; 10am-5pm daily; £7.50, concession £5.50

It was at this elegant 18th-century stately home, set within Pollok Country Park, that discussions first took place to set up a National Trust for Scotland to care for some of the nation's most special heritage places in the 1930s. Like something from the pages of a Jane Austen novel, though the current house was designed by William Adam in 1752, the site and grounds were the ancestral home of the wealthy Maxwell family for 700 years.

Two giant lion sculptures greet you as you ascend the steps into the stunning Georgian gardens. Inside there is a magnificent collection of paintings on view, including a stunning array of Spanish art, plus pieces by Scottish artists Raeburn and Guthrie as well as beautiful silverware and furniture to admire. Refuel with a scone or cake and a coffee in **The Edwardian Kitchen** café.

Burrell Collection

Pollok Country Park; tel. 0141 287 2550; www. glasgowlife.org.uk/museums/venues/the-burrell-collection; closed until 2020

Though this extraordinary art collection is closed until 2020, it's worth a mention because of the sheer breadth of pieces that it contains, and it should still be on your radar. The collection was bequeathed to the city of Glasgow in 1944 by Sir William Burrell, a rich businessman and art collector, and his wife Constance. It includes 9,000 objects from Asian art to French impressionists, and highlights include the world's largest collection of tapestries, including the Wagner Garden Carpet.

However, the building in which it has been housed since the 1980s, in Pollok Park in the Southside, has been struggling over recent years, and it took a committed campaign to overturn a proviso by Burrell that the collection never be carried over water—the collection is out on tour while crucial improvement works to the building take place.

House for an Art Lover

Bellahouston Park, 10 Dumbreck Road; tel. 0141 353 4770; www.houseforanartlover.co.uk; 10am-4pm daily; adult £6, child £4.50

Set within the magnificent grounds of Glasgow's Bellahouston Park and originally designed as a grand country-style retreat, today this exciting art space celebrates the best of art, design, and architecture. Built in the late 1980s from designs by Charles Rennie Mackintosh on the site of 18th-century mansion Ibroxhill House, it is a multi-use venue where you can come for a lovely lunch, see art by emerging Glaswegian

Charles Rennie Mackintosh

Artist, designer, and architect Charles Rennie Mackintosh left an unparalleled imprint on the city of Glasgow, and when you hear the term Glasgow Style in reference to architecture, it is pretty much all down to this one man. Challenging the very staid Victorian expectations of how buildings should be, he created some of the city's most exquisite edifices, from the famously stylish Mackintosh at the Willow tearoom (although very touristy, it is still worth a visit) to his masterpiece, the Glasgow School of Art, of which little remains following two terrible fires. However, Mackintosh's legacy is far more than just architecture. He was an artist and designer with true vision and a talent for the aesthetic that has rarely been seen since. He was ahead of his time—even today Mackintosh's designs don't look dated.

Mackintosh was born in the city's poor East End in 1868 to a working-class family. In 1889 he took on a job as a trainee draftsman at architectural practice Honeyman & Keppie. In 1892, while still working at the practice (he later became a partner in the firm), Mackintosh became a night student at the Glasgow School of Art, where he met his future wife, fellow artist Margaret Macdonald, as well as her sister Frances Macdonald and Herbert MacNair (Frances and Herbert later married, too). They collectively came to be known as The Four—a group of artists who went on to define what is known as the Glasgow Style. In 1897 Mackintosh won a competition to remodel and develop his alma mater; his winning design caused his reputation to rocket.

In 1903 Mackintosh's friend Kate Cranston, herself a forward-thinker, asked him to build her a brand-new tearoom at Sauchiehall Street (he had already remodeled other tearooms in her emporium). The resulting Willow Tea Rooms (now **Mackintosh at the Willow**), in which Mackintosh and Margaret designed every minute detail together, right down to the waitresses' uniforms, became the place to be seen. This was the time of the Temperance Movement—a concerted effort to reduce the consumption of alcohol—and tearooms were one of the first places that ladies could come to socialize in public on their own; therefore, these tearooms needed to be very stylish.

Sadly for Mackintosh, his true genius was not really recognized until after his death. Today he has some very famous fans—Brad Pitt led a campaign to raise the £20 million needed to restore the Glasgow School of Art after the first fire, but it's thought a lot more money will be needed to get the Mackintosh building built again following the most recent fire of 2018.

artists in the galleries and studios, admire the design flourishes of Mackintosh and his wife, Margaret Macdonald, and wander the sculpture garden right outside the house.

All visitors are given an audio guide, plus you can access the **Heritage Centre,** located in the former stables of the house, which showcases the local history of Bellahouston Park and its surrounding area. Make time to stroll the grounds of the park itself, which includes a Victorian walled garden, a good playground, and an Alice in Wonderland-style maze for children. Please note that hours of operation may differ due to private events.

Govan Stones

Govan Old Church; tel. 0141 440 2466; www.

thegovanstones.org.uk; 1pm-4pm daily Apr.-Oct.; free but donations welcome

Possibly one of the most humbling experiences you can have in Glasgow is visiting this small church in the south of the city. On display are some of the city's most ancient artifacts, which were discovered here in 1855. Comprising 31 early medieval stones, first carved between the 9th and 11th centuries, the Govan Stones feature intricate etchings of warriors and crosses that tell the story of the Viking rulers of the Kingdom of Strathclyde. The collection's outstanding piece is undoubtedly the **Govan Sarcophagus**, which may have been intended to hold the remains of the founder of the previous church on the site.

Holmwood House

61-63 Netherlee Road; tel. 0141 571 0184; www.nts. org.uk/visit/places/holmwood; noon-5pm Fri.-Mon. early Mar.- late Oct.-Mar.; £7.50, child/concessions £5.50, family £18.50

The finest surviving villa by revered Scottish architect Alexander "Greek" Thomson, who—as his nickname suggests—took much inspiration from the buildings of ancient Greece, this former house is worthy of an hour or two of your time. When it came to elaborate design, Thomson couldn't help himself. The home, which is set back from the banks of the White Cart Water (the same river that flows through Pollok Country Park), has pretty grounds and a Victorian kitchen garden to wander. To the left of the entrance, a circular temple encloses full-length windows, giving a sense of the scale of grandeur inside. The classical exterior is a contrast to the bright colored walls of the interior: Some of Thomson's Egyptian influences are on display, and friezes depict scenes from *The Iliad*. If you ever doubted Thomson's ability to be bold, come see this house, which is full of architectural surprises.

Glasgow Science Centre

50 Pacific Quay; tel. 0141 420 5000; www. glasgowsciencecentre.org; 10am-5pm daily late Mar.-late Oct., 10am-3pm Wed.-Fri., 10am-5pm Sat.-Sun. late Oct.-late Mar.; adult £11.50, child £9.50, Glasgow Tower additional £3.50 (£6.50 on its own), planetarium additional £3 (£5.50 on its own)

A little away from the city center (it costs about £5 in a taxi) on the south side of the River Clyde, this huge attraction is spread across three floors and has over 300 interactive exhibits to get hands on with. It's a great place to amuse children (particularly on a rainy day), who will love the Bodyworks exhibition where they can burn off some energy on the hamster wheel or even perform a virtual autopsy. In a Question of Perception, both adults and kids will enjoy the mind-boggling illusions where you can grow or shrink and see the whole universe tilted. The center is also home to a planetarium, an IMAX cinema, a good shop, and a café. Many people head

out this way to ascend the 417-foot (127-meter) Glasgow Tower, which is the tallest fully rotating freestanding structure in the world and affords panoramic views across the city.

Scottish Football Museum

Hampden Park; tel. 0871 200 2233; www. scottishfootballmuseum.org.uk; 10am-5pm Mon.-Sat., 11am-5pm Sun.; museum £8, concessions £3, stadium tour £8, concessions £3.50

Get some sense of what the game of football (or soccer) really means to the people of Scotland at Hampden Park, Scotland's national stadium. In the museum you can sit in the old dressing room and listen to a rousing address from Craig Brown, the nation's most celebrated football manager, and see the original Scottish Cup, the first national football trophy in the world. Meanwhile, stadium tours will give you the chance to sit in team dressing rooms, walk the down the tunnel, feel the excitement and pride that players walking onto the pitch have with the full support of the "Hampden Roar," and even let you take a shot on goal. Make time for the Hall of Fame too where you can learn about some of the true greats of Scottish football.

NORTH GLASGOW
Speirs Wharf

A little-known location along the Forth and Clyde Canal, this sweet spot is just over a 10-minute walk from Cowcaddens Subway station. Once the heart of industrial Glasgow, this canal-side area has seen the old grain mills and sugar refineries turned into smart offices and trendy apartments. From here you can walk along the banks of the canal or simply stop for coffee or brunch at the Ocho deli (ochoglasgow.co.uk) and watch the world go by.

Mackintosh Queen's Cross Church

870 Garscube Rd.; tel. 0141 946 6600; mackintoshchurch.com; 10am-5pm Mon.-Fri. May-Oct.; adult £4, child free, concessions £2

One of the city's hidden architectural gems,

this is actually the only church designed by Mackintosh to be built and is now home to the Charles Rennie Mackintosh Society, which also owns it. When it was completed in 1899, it was praised for its simplicity but also for the mysticism of the motifs used by Mackintosh. Regular events and art installations are held here, or you can book one of the regular tours to learn more about this special place.

Sports and Recreation

TOP EXPERIENCE

★ PARKS

Glasgow has over 90 parks and green spaces, living up to its nickname of "Dear Green Place", so there are lots of opportunities to walk, cycle, and run or to just sit and get away from the hustle and bustle of the city for a few hours. Many of the parks also have museums, art galleries, and other sights worth visiting.

GLASGOW GREEN

Greendyke Street, Saltmarket; www.glasgow.gov.uk/ glasgowgreen

While by no means the prettiest of Glasgow's parks, Glasgow Green, a 136-acre (146-hectare) site of open land in the East End that reaches down to the River Clyde, is pretty hard to beat in terms of history. It was here that Bonnie Prince Charlie and his Jacobite army camped between 1745 and 1746 and where the Suffragette Movement regularly met in the 1870s. The Green is dominated by a column celebrating the victories of Admiral Horatio Nelson, and you can still see the cast-iron washing poles, which look like neatly arranged tree saplings from a distance, used by women from the poor East End to hang their washing out to dry right up until the 1970s.

To the west of the washing poles, you'll find the **People's Palace and Winter Gardens** (tel. 0141 276 0788; www.glasgowlife.org.uk/ museums/venues/peoples-palace; 10am-5pm Mon.-Weds. and Sat., 11am-5pm Fri. and Sun.; free). An incongruous French Renaissance-style building with attached glasshouse, it first opened in 1898 to provide a cultural space for residents of one of the city's most cramped and destitute areas. Upstairs, you can take a trip through Glasgow's social history through a thoroughly engaging series of exhibits that includes everything, from footage of Glaswegian comedians sending themselves up to memories of going "doon the watter," the Glasgow tradition of families going down the Clyde for day trips or holidays at the seaside. Downstairs, you can have coffee and cake in the Winter Gardens, or just have a gentle walk amid the tropical flowers.

On the edge of Glasgow Green, you'll see the **Mclennan Arch,** a triumphant arch framed by a pair of Ionic columns. Its presence often baffles visitors. What building was once here? The arch actually once formed part of the old Assembly Rooms, the fashionable place to be seen in Georgian society, a few streets away on the north side of Ingram Street. When the Assembly Rooms were demolished in the late Victorian period, the arch was saved and first moved to Greendyke Street and then moved to this spot in 1922, creating Glasgow's very own "Arc de Triomphe."

Today Glasgow Green still provides green space for the people of the East End, but people are more likely to come for a run or to sit and read among the foliage of the Winter Gardens than hang their washing out.

POLLOK COUNTRY PARK

2060 Pollokshaws Road

The largest park in Glasgow (360 acres/146 hectares in total) and also the only one that

---

1: People's Palace and Winter Gardens 2: Riverside Museum 3: Georgian buildings around Kelvingrove Park 4: Queen's Park, a popular green space for Southsiders

can be described as a country park, this haven of tranquility on Glasgow's Southside is made up of 140 acres (57 hectares) of woodland, along with more formal gardens that include perfectly clipped yew hedges and herbaceous borders, around Pollok House—a reminder that it was once a grand estate. Today it's most renowned for being the location of the **Burrell Collection** (a major art collection temporarily closed while renovations to its building take place, and it is due to reopen in 2020). However, many people also come here to see the herd of Highland cattle in the fields to the southwest of the museum building, and many more come to have a go on one of the three mountain bike tracks. Avid *Outlander* fans may also note that key scenes from the TV show were filmed here.

QUEEN'S PARK

520 Langside Road

When Southsiders want a lazy afternoon lying around reading the papers, catching up with friends over a picnic, or going for a walk, this is generally their place of choice. Set along the busy Pollokshaws Road, the 140-acre (57-hectare) park is easily accessible, yet it doesn't take long to escape the sound of traffic and climb deeper into the park, far away from city stresses. Laid out in the mid-19th century by revered landscape architect Sir Joseph Paxton, this mix of neatly manicured lawns and more natural grassy slopes was named after Mary, Queen of Scots (a battle was fought here in her name), and its grand style is typical of the Victorian era, with a boating lake, glasshouses, and aviary. Make time to climb up **Camp Hill** for views over the city; on a clear day you can see Ben Lomond beyond the Campsie Fells if you know what you're looking for. And don't be afraid to sneak a shortcut through some leaf-covered trails—it's all part of the fun.

KELVINGROVE PARK

6 Professors' Square

Over in the West End and connecting some of the area's biggest sights, including Kelvingrove Art Gallery and Museum and the University of Glasgow, and with the River Kelvin running through it, this possibly wins the prize of Glasgow's prettiest park. It was also designed by Sir Joseph Paxton, but at only 85 acres (34 hectares) it is tiny compared with its Southside cousin. However, what it lacks in size it makes up for in splendor. Part of the appeal of Kelvingrove is that, whether you're walking by the river or catching some shade beneath the Suffragette Oak—a tree planted a century ago to honor the women who made women's suffrage possible—you're never far from some beautiful architecture, such as the salubrious **Park District** that curls around the northeast corner of the park and is redolent of Edinburgh's New Town, though it was built some time later. The **Kelvingrove Bandstand and Amphitheatre** in the park is also a great place to watch summer concerts.

BELLAHOUSTON PARK

16 Dumbreck Road

Another giant of a park in the Southside, within this 169-acre (68-hectare) green site, just north of Pollok Park, you'll find bowling greens, a Victorian walled garden, a sunken garden, an Alice in Wonderland-style maze, and a pitch and putt; its wide open spaces also make it a popular choice for large outdoor concerts. However, it's a little tired compared with some of Glasgow's green spaces, and the highlight is without a doubt the incredibly stylish **House for an Art Lover,** an art gallery and exhibition space inspired by the designs of Charles Rennie Mackintosh but built long after his death.

WALKING

POLLOK COUNTRY PARK

Pollokshaws Road; www.walkhighlands.co.uk/ glasgow/pollok-park.shtml

While you could quite happily meander in Pollok Country Park in Glasgow's Southside with no defined route for an hour or two, this route takes you along south Glasgow's river, the White Cart Water, and then through shaded woodland areas. From Pollokshaws West train station, turn left and follow the driveway past the gatehouse before bearing left to follow the riverside path. Keep left and look out for Highland cattle that are often seen grazing in the field on your right. Soon you will reach the formal gardens, which you can detour into, or, if you keep to the riverside path, you can bypass them and get superb views of **Pollok House** from the front before entering the stately home grounds through an archway. Once you've perused the house (or stopped for a coffee in the café), head straight up past the house and bear left to take a path to the left of Lime Avenue. This surfaced path is known as the Highland Cattle Way, and its route is marked with red cow signs and will take you through woodland, past two ponds. Turn right at the far end of the second pond to return to a waterside path, and now you will be looking for blue signs, which will direct you left through a path marked by tall pine trees. If you follow the blue signs, the path will take you past the **Burrell Collection.** After the building, turn left and the path brings you along a driveway, past a car park and kids play area. At the junction, turn left again to return to the gatehouse and Pollokshaws Road. The full route covers 3.25 miles (5.25 km) and should take 1.5 hours, not allowing for any stops or detours.

CLYDE WALKWAY

Riverside Museum; www.southlanarkshire.gov.uk/ downloads/download/258/clyde_walkway

At some 40 miles (65 km) long altogether, this riverside route takes you from the center of Glasgow all the way to the tumbling Falls of Clyde in New Lanark. Most people won't attempt it all, but those who do will find the route quite straightforward and will probably stop at Cambuslang, Strathclyde Loch, Maudslie, and New Lanark. The stretch of this route in Glasgow, starting at the

Riverside Museum and tall ship and heading east, is a novel way to see much of the city. The route is waymarked and mainly paved and takes you along the river, past the SEC Centre opposite Glasgow Science Centre and its tower, through the heart of Glasgow's once busy shipbuilding and cargo centers, and all the way to Glasgow Green in the East End. This section of the route covers about four miles (6.4 km) and should take about two hours to walk, not accounting for stops and detours.

CYCLING
FORTH AND CLYDE CANAL PATH

Cowcaddens Subway Station or Speirs Wharf; www. sustrans.org.uk/ncn/map/route/route-754

This canal path, which runs all the way from Glasgow to Edinburgh, offers lots of opportunity for cycling along a flat, traffic-free route. If you're just after a little afternoon exploration, then the section from Cowcaddens Subway Station in the north of the city center to the canal-side village of Kirkintilloch, northeast of Glasgow, offers a reasonable nine-mile (15-km) route (18 mi/30 km round-trip) through gentle countryside and allows for a pit stop at the **Stables Pub** in Kirkintilloch, which was built to serve the watermen and horses who worked the canal. The route follows a section of the National Cycle Network (route 754) and is well signposted from Cowcaddens or Speirs Wharf; though the path is narrow (about 3.3 ft/1 m across), it's an easy ride across tarmac, gritted tarmac, and some cobblestones.

GEAR BIKES

19 Gibson Street; tel. 0141 339 1179; gearbikes.com; 10am-6pm Mon.-Sat. and noon-5pm Sun.; £20 a day, £80 a week

At this bike hire place in the city's West End, all bikes—currently Ridgeback hybrids, but they do update the range regularly—come with lights, a tool kit, pump, helmets, and locks all included in the price.

The Old Firm Rivalry: Celtic vs. Rangers

It's no secret that the rivalry between Glasgow's two biggest football teams, Celtic and Rangers, runs deep. While many Glaswegians treat it as a bit of fun, many others don't, so you're best avoiding the topic if it comes up in the pub. Traditionally, Celtic fans come from the Catholic side of the community, largely made up of the descendants of Irish immigrants who began arriving in Glasgow in droves in the 19th century, as they fled the Great Famine, while Rangers fans tend to hail from the Protestant community. Often rivalry among fans has been entwined with politics.

It hasn't always been the case that the two clubs don't get on. When Celtic was first formed in 1888, the two clubs seemed to be friendly enough; however, as Celtic, an outwardly Catholic club with a strong Irish Republican outlook started to establish itself as a serious contender in the game, the rivalry stepped up, leading to larger crowds in the stands. A satirical cartoon in 1904 first used the label "Old Firm" and hinted that the rivalry was seen as a money-spinner by the two clubs. However, it was the 1912 opening of a shipyard on the Clyde by Belfast shipbuilder Harland & Wolff (who built the *Titanic*) that is largely thought to have brought Irish politics into play. Harland & Wolff was notorious for excluding Catholics from its workforce, so it brought scores of Protestant workers over from Ireland, who gravitated towards Rangers. As sectarian violence spread across Ireland between Republicans (mostly Catholics) and Unionists (mostly Protestants), football supporters in Glasgow allowed their vitriol to spill out onto the stands. Indeed, such was the strength of belief that for many years Rangers had an unspoken rule that it would not knowingly sign a player from the Catholic community.

On Derby days police presence in Glasgow is stepped up, and, though the heady days of sectarian clashes seem to be fading into memory, there are still frictions. Celtic fans, for instance, still like to wind Rangers fans up about the fact Rangers' holding company went into liquidation in 2012 and the club had to apply to enter the third division of the Scottish League. Celtic fans joke that the Old Firm Derby is no more, since Rangers is now a new club. And so the war rumbles on.

GLASGOW BIKE TOURS

Meet at Drygate Brewing Company, 85 Drygate; tel. 0778 668 3445; glasgowbiketours.co.uk

If you want to explore Glasgow on two wheels but don't really know where to begin, then these guided tours, which set off from the East End, could be a good option. The standard three-hour Sightseeing Tour (10:30am or 2:30pm daily; adult £35, child £20) takes you from the city center, along the Clyde waterfront, and through leafy Kelvingrove Park to the trendy West End, taking in all the major sights, from the cathedral through to the People's Palace, Barrowland, and the Botanic Gardens. The 4.5-hour Sightseeing & Whisky tasting tour (by request with a 2pm start; £55) does all of the above but also incorporates a stop-off at a Glasgow pub for a few wee drams. Private tours are also available.

SPECTATOR SPORTS

Spectator sports are taken seriously here, particularly when it comes to football, so be careful about ribbing anyone about their team. But, if you happen to be in town when there's a match, do go and see the famous Scottish passion firsthand.

CELTIC PARK

Parkhead; tel. 0871 226 1888; www.celticfc.net; tours 11am, noon, 1:45pm, 2:30pm Mon.-Sun. (except home matchdays), matchday tours 9:30am, 10am, 10:30am, 11am Sat.; tours adult £10, child £6

This football stadium in the Parkhead area of Glasgow's East End is Celtic's home ground and has been since 1892. It is oft referred to simply as "Parkhead" or sometimes "Paradise." You can purchase tickets for home matches online or by calling the ticket line. Some tickets are available on the day of the match at Celtic ticket office, but queues can be enormous. To reach the ground, get the train from Glasgow Central to either Dalmarnock or Bridgeton, both of which are within 15 minutes' walk of the ground. There are guided tours Monday-Sunday.

IBROX STADIUM

150 Edmiston Drive; tel. 0871 702 1972; rangers.co.uk; tours 10:30am, 12:30pm, 2:30pm Fri.-Sun. (except home matchdays); tours adult £15, child £5

Rangers' home ground is in the Southside of the city in the Govan area and is served by Ibrox Subway Station. Tickets for home games can be purchased online or by calling the hotline. There are also tours of the grounds, during which you can visit the changing rooms and climb the marble staircase to the trophy room.

WATERSPORTS

OUTDOOR PURSUITS SCOTLAND

Pinkston Watersports, 75 North Canal Bank Street; tel. 0781 064 4877; pinkston.co.uk; £40pp for half a day

Did you know you could go white-water rafting in Glasgow? It may sound a little absurd, but at this artificial white-water course—the only one in Scotland—you can do just that. Outdoor Pursuits Scotland runs white-water rafting courses out of Pinkston Watersports, a flat water basin

at the end of the Forth and Clyde Canal (just round the corner from Speirs Wharf), which is one surefire way to wake yourself up after a night on the whisky.

TOURS

GLASGOW CENTRAL STATION TOUR

www.glasgowcentraltours.co.uk; £13

This fascinating walking tour takes you underneath the city proper into the railway vaults of this iconic station and through the basements and boiler rooms while telling the story of the city through the context of its main station. You will even visit the eerie deserted old Victorian platform. The brilliant guides know how to tell a story and will have you in both floods of laughter and floods of tears. The tours are popular, so book well in advance.

WALK THE GLASGOW MUSIC MILE

glasgowmusiccitytours.com; adult £17, child £12

Immerse yourself in the sound of the city on one of these insightful tours that take in some of Glasgow's most influential music venues. The two-hour tours will take you from the Royal Concert Hall to King Tut's Wah Wah Hut where you can take a selfie on the very stage where Oasis and Blur played as young unknowns.

Nightlife and Entertainment

There are no two ways about it. Glaswegians love a drink. Scottish writer Jack House, known as Mr. Glasgow, famously declared, "The Glasgow invention of square-toed shoes was to enable the Glasgow man to get closer to the bar." It's also a young city—almost a quarter of its population is aged between 16 and 29, and it has far fewer residents aged over 60 than its slightly more serious and less rebellious big sister of Edinburgh.

Perhaps because of its youthful inhabitants,

in terms of sheer variety of nightlife, Glasgow is rarely bettered. At the **Teuchters' Triangle,** a collection of convivial pubs with Highland roots in the West End that includes the Park Bar, the Islay Inn, and the Ben Nevis, you can experience the famous Glasgow good humor and hospitality, while for clubbing try the high-octane venues on Sauchiehall Street. When it comes to live music, the SSE Hydro attracts international talent, but those in the know go to King Tut's Wah Wah Hut

Speaking Glaswegian

Known as the Glasgow patter, the Scots dialect spoken in Glasgow is often indecipherable to anyone outside the city boundaries. However, familiarize yourself with a few well-worn phrases, politely ask people to slow down a "wee" bit, and you'll soon be conversing with everyone, from your taxi driver to the waiter, to the barman, with ease.

Be warned, though, swearing or cursing is common parlance in Glasgow, and more often than not, it's used endearingly or to describe something with passion. Glaswegians are also religiously sarcastic, so try not to take them too literally.

- **Whits happenin:** Short for "what's happening?" this gets used at nearly every opportunity, whether you're chatting to close friends or you've just bumped into someone you've not seen for months, and it's basically an open question to bring up whatever you think is noteworthy.

- **Mad way it:** You're likely to hear this in many a Glasgow pub or club. It essentially means really drunk.

- **Did ye aye:** Glasgow sarcasm at its best, this is used when someone starts bragging about something, and you want to show you don't really care.

- **Check the nick:** People say this if they want to alert someone to something going on (particularly if it's really bad). If you see someone that is "mad way it," you might say, "check the nick ae that."

- **Baltic:** This is a common term for really cold weather.

- **Pure and heavy:** These are two words that take on a completely different meaning in Glasgow. *Pure* emphasizes a point, much like "really" (e.g., "it's pure Baltic"). *Heavy,* meanwhile, suggests something is really bad, for example, "that's heavy" in response to bad news.

- **How:** This term is used often and pretty much means "why." For instance, if someone asks you to come back in five minutes, you might ask "how?"

- **Bolt:** This is Scottish slang for "go away" or "get lost". Sometimes other words are tagged on the end to really drive the point home, such as "bolt, ya rocket", meaning "get lost, you idiot" (**rocket** means an annoying or crazy person).

- **Taps aff:** This refers to weather so hot that Scottish males take to walking around with their tops off.

- **Growlin:** This refers to someone behaving in a confrontational way. While Glaswegians are generally friendly, if you stare at a stranger, you may be asked, "whit you growlin it?" (or, "what are you looking at?").

- **Aye:** This simply means "yes."

- **Tae:** This means "to."

- **Dae:** This means "do," for instance, "whit dae you dae?" or "what do you do for work?"

- **Shut your geggy:** Shut up.

- **Havnae a scooby:** I don't know.

- **Gaun yersel:** "Go on yourself," which basically encourages someone who is being passionate about something.

- **Wee:** This means "little" but is regularly used as simply another adjective when describing something.

- **An dinnae ken:** I don't know.

for an intimate (if rather sweaty) gig or the sprung dance floor of the 1960s Barrowland Ballroom. Be warned, though—neither venue is for the fainthearted.

Sauchiehall Street has long been considered the nucleus of late-night debauchery, and, with a seemingly endless array of bars, it offers a good pub crawl; because of this, though, it can get a bit too raucous, and you may tire of the stream of hen and stag parties.

Merchant City in the smart city center has top-name chain restaurants as well as a sprinkling of independents in indoor market Merchant Square (which also hosts regular events), plus the area is home to a fantastic gin restaurant.

Finnieston, just west of the city center, is known as the Shoreditch of Glasgow, a slightly lazy comparison perhaps, but you get the gist. In among the student digs and charity shops you'll find understated pubs serving cheap but good food.

Ashton Lane is a cute cobbled street with a boutique cinema, cool bars, and great food—Ashoka is a good Indian restaurant, and the Ubiquitous Chip is often voted the best restaurant in Glasgow (and it has a brasserie too if you don't want to remortgage your house).

Wherever you end up, make sure you are dressed for the occasion; while there is a cool, understated vibe at many bars and clubs, the term Glasvegas refers to the fact that many Glaswegians like to get dolled up for a night on the tiles (particularly on a Saturday night), and you wouldn't want to feel underdressed. And avoid getting your round in at your peril. The average cost of a pint is £3.60, while a small glass of wine is anything upward of £3.50.

CITY CENTER
Bars and Pubs
THE SCOTIA

112 Stockwell Street; www.scotiabar-glasgow. co.uk; tel. 0141 552 8681; 11am-midnight Mon.-Sat., 12:30pm-midnight Sun.; pints of beer from £2.95, single-malt whiskies from £2.30

It was here that a wide-eyed young man by the name of Billy Connolly first cut his teeth on the comedy circuit before going on to international acclaim. Reputedly Glasgow's oldest pub—it's been around since 1792—it's located on one of the city's original streets and it has all the fixtures of a traditional pub: wood beams, barstools, and brass pumps. Plus, aside from the regularly scheduled music, there are also some impromptu sessions.

NICE N SLEAZY

421 Sauchiehall Street; tel. 0141 333 0900; www. nicensleazy.com; 12pm-3am Mon.-Sat., 1pm-3am Sun.; entry often free, some gigs from £6; pints of beer from £3.30, cocktails from £3

Let's get one thing straight: you're not coming here to be wined and dined, so take a clue from the name. This dive bar has an amazing jukebox and booths, and it's a bona fide jumping joint. There is hand-scrawled graffiti on the walls and a disco ball, and, although it wouldn't kill bar staff to break into a smile every now and then, it's still one of the most fun nights out you can have in Glasgow.

Live Music
★ KING TUT'S WAH WAH HUT

274a St Vincent Street; 0141 221 5279; www.kingtuts. co.uk; 12pm-1am Mon.-Fri., 4pm-1am Sat., 3pm-1am Sun.; gigs from £8; pints of beer from £3.25

As the place where Oasis was discovered, this dark, underground (literally) gig venue has achieved cult status. But don't let that put you off—it still fires off fist-pumping bands on a regular basis. Every band starting out wants to play here because they know they'll be playing to a captive audience (as well as some record company spies), and you do get the sense that any minute you might just see the next big thing.

★ MONO

12 King Street; tel. 0141 553 2400; www. monocafebar.com; 11am-11pm Sun.-Thurs., 11am-1am Fri.-Sat.; many events free, other gigs from £8; beer from £4, small wine from £4.50

This stripped-back café-bar on the eastern side of the city center has an exposed

Best Places to Hear Live Music

Glasgow without music is simply impossible to imagine. No matter what night of the week you arrive in the city, you can be assured of an exceptional array of music taking place in pubs and clubs across Glasgow (much of which is free). There's simply no such thing as a quiet night out in Glasgow, Heaven forbid. Here are some of the top places to hear live music, whatever mood you are in.

- **King Tut's Wah Wah Hut:** It's over 25 years since a little-known band called Oasis was signed by Alan McGee here in 1993, but this 300-capacity venue is still considered at the forefront of new music (page 161).

- **Mono:** With live music most nights of the week (mostly up-and-coming bands, with free entry), this is a slightly cooler, more left-field venue on the eastern fringes of the city center. There's a good variety of music, from funk and soul, through to indie rock and dance (page 161).

- **Barrowland Ballroom:** Set in a 1930s music hall, this slightly kitsch and utterly retro venue in Glasgow's East End, with its sprung dance floor, is like a time machine back to the heady days of early rock 'n' roll. You can't miss it—just look for the huge neon sign (page 165).

- **Ben Nevis, Islay Inn, and Park Bar:** While there are lots of pubs around the city where you can hear Scottish folk, nowhere does it better than the trio of pubs that make up what is known as the Teuchter's Triangle on Argyle Street in the West End (page 166).

microbrewery and an award-winning vegan restaurant—the macaroni and cheese is especially good. During the day it is a cool place to chill out or browse the record store (run by Stephen McRobbie from indie band The Pastels), while from 7:30pm onward it's a good place to catch new music, often for free.

BABBITY BOWSTER
16-18 Blackfriars Street; tel. 0141 552 5055; babbitybowster.com; 11am-12am Mon.-Sat., 12:30pm-12am Sun.; pints of beer from £4, single malts from £3.50

What a special find. This pub comes alive on Wednesday afternoons with folk music from 3:30pm as guitars, accordions, and fiddles come out to play. Anyone who plays an instrument or sings is welcome to come along and join in. On Saturday afternoons (from 4pm) it's even livelier, and you may want to get down an hour or so earlier to bag a seat. Delicious Scottish grub (think Cullen skink and beef collops) is available in the bar noon-10pm. Or book a table in the upstairs Schottische Restaurant for a more formal affair with Gallic influences

from the French chef; in winter the peat fire is set too.

Theater
THEATRE ROYAL
282 Hope Street; tel. 0141 332 9000, box office 0844 871 7677; www.glasgowtheatreroyal.org.uk

Despite appearances (the building was massively redeveloped in 2014 so looks a lot newer than it is), Scotland's longest-running theater is also home to Scottish opera and ballet. Opera season runs October-June with the new program announced each April. Ballet season is year-round. There are also often special ballet and opera performances during the Edinburgh Festival. While on the outside the building may look ultra-modern, inside its auditorium, where the Victorian horseshoe wall remains, all the grandeur of yesteryear is still apparent. It's a beautiful setting for some world-class performances.

KING'S THEATRE
297 Bath Street; tel. 0844 871 7615; www.atgtickets.com/venues/kings-theatre

This historic theater, designed by renowned

theater architect Frank Matcham, who designed many London theaters, including the London Coliseum, presents an unusual façade with both Art Nouveau and baroque features and is the go-to place for touring productions in Glasgow. Forthcoming shows include *Avenue Q* and *Doctor Dolittle the Musical.*

The Arts
CENTRE FOR CONTEMPORARY ARTS

350 Sauchiehall Street; tel. 0141 352 4900; www. cca-glasgow.com; 10am-12am Mon.-Thurs., 10am-1am Fri. and Sat., noon-12am Sun.

Set in an 1868 building by Glasgow's greatest neoclassical architect, Alexander "Greek" Thomson, it's always worth seeing what's on here during your stay. It's diverse program includes photography shows, music recitals, short films, and carefully curated art exhibitions and is frequented by high-brow residents in the know.

MERCHANT CITY
Nightclubs
AUDIO

14 Midland Street; www.musicglue.com/ audioglasgow; times vary depending on the night, 7pm-11:30pm, till 3am on club nights; prices vary, from £7, some events free; beer & wine from £3

This tiny venue underneath the railway arches is a great place to see loud punk and metal bands. The crowd is dressed down, which is just as well as it's a little grotty, but with acoustics this good no one seems to care. You have to shout to be heard at the bar, though, or else get good at miming and mouthing your order.

BAR BLOC

117 Bath Street; tel. 0141 574 6066; www.bloc.ru; 11am-3am daily; free; pints of beer from £2.90, cocktails from £4.95

Refreshingly, all the gigs and events at this city center bar-club are free and the lineup is varied. There is live music or DJs seven nights a week playing an eclectic range, from

rockabilly to indie, to folk and jazz. It looks the part too, with neon lights and records stacked behind metal cages, giving it both an anarchic and disco fee.

Bars and Pubs
CORINTHIAN CLUB

191 Ingram Street; tel. 0141 552 1101; www. thecorinthianclub.co.uk; 10am-2am Sun.-Thurs., 10am-3am Fri.-Sat.; pints of beer from £4.50, cocktails from £7.50-12.50

One of Glasgow's most elaborate and richly decorated buildings both internally and externally, this gargantuan venue is spread across five floors. **Teller's Bar & Brasserie** under the dome is a superb setting for afternoon tea, or slink back in one of the booths for a cocktail or glass of bubbly, while the first-floor **Club** is a popular late-night venue for Friday and Saturday revelers.

ANCHOR LINE

19 St. Vincent Place; tel. 0141 248 1434; www. theanchorline.co.uk; 9am-11pm Mon.-Tues., 9am-midnight Weds.-Thurs., 9am-1am Fri.-Sat., 10am-11pm Sun.; gins (50ml serve) £7.50-11.50 (mixers extra), cocktails £7.75-11.95

This stylish cocktail bar just off George Square, takes its name from the trans-Atlantic liner company whose first-class ticket office was once housed in this building; the setting harks back to the ocean-liner heydays of the 1920s and 1930s. Celebrating the connection between Scotland and the United States, there is a good selection of both Scotch and bourbons, and, if none of the classic cocktails take your fancy, bartenders will happily mix you your own drink. There's also a good restaurant.

THE HORSESHOE BAR

17-18 Drury Street; tel. 0141 248 6368; www. thehorseshoebarglasgow.co.uk; 9am-midnight daily; pints of beer from £3.50, wine from £11.99 a bottle

Fancy it is not, but this Victorian bar, which, as you might have guessed, is shaped like a horseshoe, is nothing short of a Glaswegian institution—if the football is on, the place is heaving. Once one of the city's grandest gin bars, it is now one of its busiest pubs and an easy pit stop when shopping on nearby Buchanan Street. Be prepared to hang around the enormous bar, the longest in Europe, until a table becomes available, and, with daily deals such as two meals for £8, there are few places offering better-value food.

SLOANS

108 Argyle Street; tel. 0141 221 8886; www. sloansglasgow.com; 11am-midnight Mon.-Thurs. and Sun., 11am-1am Fri.-Sat.; pints of beer from £4, single-malt whiskies from £3.50

One of the oldest pubs in the city (it dates from 1797), Sloans is hidden down an alleyway just off Argyle Street. Inside, the oval bar is a good place to meet friends, while in summer drinkers spill out onto the cobbles. The biggest attraction of Sloans, however, is the weekly ceilidh held every Friday in the ballroom across the cobbles. It's a lively party where you'll be swung about to shrieks of laughter and the fun is undeniably infectious.

THE POT STILL

154 Hope Street; tel. 0141 333 0980; www.thepotstill. co.uk; 11am-12am daily; pints of beer from £3.45, single-malt whiskies from £2.95

This whisky bar is well and truly on the tourist trail, but it's still worth a nose in because the staff are friendly, the whisky is plentiful, and there's lots of paraphernalia to snoop at on the walls. Food is simple yet hearty and includes pies (from £2), soup, toasties, and wedges. Perfect stuff to soak up your single malts.

Concerts

GLASGOW ROYAL CONCERT HALL

2 Sauchiehall Street; tel. 0141 353 8000; www. glasgowconcerthalls.com/glasgow-royal-concert-hall; box office 10am-6pm Mon.-Sat.

Seen as a symbol of the regeneration of Glasgow following its City of Culture status in 1990, this concert hall is now home to the Royal Scottish National Orchestra. It's a high-tech space to hear music from the genres of classical, pop, folk, and rock, and everyone from B. B. King to Johnny Cash and Van Morrison have graced its stage.

statue of Donald Dewar, Scotland's inaugural First Minister, outside Glasgow Royal Concert Hall

CITY HALLS AND OLD FRUITMARKET

Candleriggs; tel. 0141 353 8000; www.
glasgowconcerthalls.com; box office 10am-6pm
Mon.-Sat.

As its name suggests, these dual venues once formed part of a market complex in Victorian Glasgow and were used to host large public gatherings, with the likes of Charles Dickens and Benjamin Disraeli holding court. The Old Fruitmarket was a working market until the 1970s, but since 2006 both venues have been operating primarily as performance spaces, with the Grand Hall of the City Halls auditorium home to the Scottish Symphony Orchestra, while the Old Fruitmarket has leaned more toward the experimental side of contemporary music.

Performance Art and Theaters
THE TRON

63 Trongate; tel. 0141 552 4267; www.tron.co.uk

With three performance spaces, there's always something going on at the Tron, a vibrant theater in the Merchant City. It is both a presenting and producing theater and has helped launch the careers of both Alan Cumming and Peter Mullan. Glaswegians are very protective of the Tron.

SHARMANKA KINETIC THEATRE

103 Trongate; tel. 0141 552 7080; www.sharmanka.
com; 5pm Wed., 5pm and 7pm Thurs., 1pm Fri., 3pm
Sat., 3pm and 5pm Sun.; 40-minute show adult £8,
concessions £6, child £3, 60-minute show adult £10,
concessions £8

This inventive place, which is part theater of the absurd, part museum, is like nothing you have ever seen. Hundreds of figures and pieces of mechanical scrap metal have been fashioned and choreographed into a magical yet surreal performance that feels like some kind of mad robotic ballet. The work of Russian-born Eduard Bersudsky, who has made Glasgow his home, it's the kind of place that leaves you smiling while also asking "what on earth have I just seen?" Choose between a 40-minute show

or the 60-minute extravaganza. Children can only attend the 40-minute show.

CLYDESIDE
Bars
CHINASKI'S

239 North Street; tel. 0141 221 0061; www.chinaskis.
com; 11am-midnight daily; bottle of house wine
£14.95

The height of decadence, this low-lit bar is often referred to as Bukowski's, after the American author's alter ego from whom it takes its name. Henry Chinaski was one of Charles Bukowski's most memorable characters, and many consider him based on the writer himself. In homage to Chinaski, who is known for his love of alcohol but also all things beautiful, the bar is dressed like an elegant drawing room.

Concert Venues
SSE HYDRO

Exhibition Way; tel. 0141 248 3000; www.
thessehydro.com

Designed by Foster & Partners (the same people behind the incredible Great Court in the British Library), this huge stadium has been part of the regeneration of the former docks. The arena has a capacity for 12,500, making it ideal for hosting big-name acts such as Katy Perry and Pink Floyd's Roger Waters, as well as other major events.

EAST END
Concerts
★ BARROWLAND BALLROOM

244 Gallowgate; tel. 0141 552 4601; barrowland-
ballroom.co.uk; times vary, but often 7pm-11pm

Built by "Barras Queen" Maggie McIver, the original Barrowland opened in 1934. Though that building burned down in 1958, the rebuilt ballroom opened in 1960 and has been one of the city's favorite music venues ever since. Everyone from David Bowie to The Clash, U2, and the Foo Fighters have been drawn here, attracted no doubt by the famous sprung dance floor, fantastic acoustics, and faded glamor. Today gigs are played out in the main hall or in the smaller Barrowland 2 bar downstairs, with big names (both contemporary and old school) regularly on the set list.

WEST END
Live Music
★ THE PARK BAR

1202 Argyle Street; tel. 0141 339 1715; 11:45am-12am daily; pints of beer from £3.50, single malts from £3.50

At the west end of Argyle Street you will find the city's largest number of proper pubs, including this gem, which forms part of what is known as the Highland (or Teuchter's) Triangle. It's famed for its ceilidh music—Thursday is the regular traditional music night and is an informal affair, followed by band nights on Friday, Saturday, and Sunday. Music starts around 9pm each night.

TOP EXPERIENCE

★ BEN NEVIS

1147 Argyle Street; tel. 0141 576 5204; www.facebook.com/TheBenNevisBar; noon-midnight Mon.-Sat., 12:30pm-midnight Sun.; pints of beer from £3.50, single malts from £3

This is one of the city's best bars for whisky and traditional music, a winning combination. With wooden floors and bare stone walls, it has a very old-school Scottish charm and is small enough to make you feel a part of things once the gathered musicians get going on one of the side tables. It's the kind of place you can come into on your own and soon make friends for the evening.

★ ISLAY INN

1256 Argyle Street; tel. 0141 334 7774; www.islayinn.com; 11am-12am daily; pints of beer from £3.50, single malts from £3.50

During the day this traditional inn is a little on the sleepy side, but come evening time it wakes from its slumber with good music and a typically talkative group of locals. If you're peckish, you can tuck into one of the homemade burgers, but it's the music that really draws the punters. There are jam sessions on Mondays and Thursday evenings, an open mic on Sundays, and live bands play on Friday and Saturday nights.

Bars and Pubs
ORAN MOR

Top of Byres Road; tel. 0141 357 6200; oran-mor.co.uk;9am-2am Mon.-Weds., 9am-3am Thurs.-Sat., 11am-3am Sun.; pints of beer from £3.80, single malts from £3.50

This old church has been converted into a unique venue, bar, and restaurant. Aside from the Whisky Bar, which offers 280 single malts, there is also the late-night brasserie and two restaurants. Most visitors come here to see the incredible mural ceiling in the auditorium by artist and writer Alastair Day, but, if you can, try to attend one of the *A Play, A Pie, and A Pint* shows, which are legendary.

LISMORE

206 Dumbarton Road; tel. 0141 576 0102; 11.30am-11pm daily; pints of beer from £3.80, single malts from £3.50

This is an old whisky bar, with lots of dark wood, an inglenook fireplace, and some stained glass depicting the Highland Clearances as a mark of respect to the ancestors of many of the locals. Although it may look a lot older, it only opened in 1996, but staff know their stuff and will advise on good single malts—try the Balvenie 14 Caribbean infused and slink into one of the bench seats by the door for a spot of people-watching. There are regular folk sessions and even the occasional jazz band.

THE SPARKLE HORSE

Dowanhill Street; tel. 0141 562 3175; thesparklehorse.com; noon-midnight Wed.-Sat., noon-11pm Sun.-Tues.; pints of beer from £4, bottle of wine from £14.95

Just a short walk from the Lismore, this is a funky, cool bar with black and white tiles on the floor, very good music on the stereo, and a fun crowd. The food is good and cheap too, with mains from £5. A very relaxed chatty

1: Lismore pub 2: Brel, Ashton Lane

group of trendy not-quite-so-young-things anymore are more than happy to bring you into their mix.

HUG & PINT

171 Great Western Road; tel. 0141 331 1901; www. thehugandpint.com; noon-12am daily; pints of beer from £3.50, bottle of wine from £14.95, main courses from £5

A firm favorite with Finnieston locals, not only does this pub do comfort vegan food with aplomb (dishes are typically designed to be shared and will make you wonder why you ever needed meat), but it also has an exciting music schedule. The highlight of the week here, though, is No Place to Fall, an "open stage" held each Sunday from 1pm-4pm in the basement, where pretty much anything goes, be it spoken word, photography, art, or music. It's this sense of support to the artistic community that really leaves you all warm and fuzzy.

BREL

Ashton Lane; tel. 0141 342 4966; www.brelbar.com; noon-midnight Mon.-Thurs. and Sun., noon-1am Fri.-Sat.; pints of beer from £4.60, bottle of wine £18.95

Among the many cool little restaurants and bars in and around Ashton Lane, this little gem stands out, not least because of its fab beer garden with tiered seating of fake grass, a student hub come summertime. In summer months there are also regular barbecues and a good lineup of live acts, while in winter hide away indoors and indulge in one of their regular fondue and raclette nights. It's not the cheapest pub around but it's a cool place to be.

Clubs
HILLHEAD BOOKCLUB

17 Vinicombe Street; tel. 0141 576 1700; hillheadbookclub.co.uk; 11am-midnight Mon.-Fri., 10am-midnight Sat. and Sun.; pints of beer from £3.75, cocktails from £7.50

Hillhead Bookclub is a case in point of quite how cool the West End has become.

This multi-faceted venue hosts some of the city's best DJs from Wednesday through Sunday, but it is so much more than just a club. Pop-up vintage fairs are held regularly, and on Sunday mornings, nay afternoons, you can often see trendy twenty- and thirty-somethings trying to undo the damage from the night before as they flop about drinking Bloody Marys and trying to read the newspaper—all against a rockabilly-rock 'n' roll soundtrack. There are also "mate's rates" drink deals Monday-Thursday.

Comedy Club
THE STAND

333 Woodlands Road; tel. 0141 212 3389; www. thestand.co.uk; tickets from £3

Like its sister venue in Edinburgh, this venue is a popular place for established comedians to try out their new material. Keep an eye out for Glaswegian comics such as Kevin Bridges coming back to home turf; the atmosphere is electric (even though the air is often blue).

Theater
KELVINGROVE BANDSTAND AND AMPHITHEATRE

Kelvin Way; tel. 0141 353 8000; kelvingrovebandstand.org.uk; ticket prices vary

The only original bandstand left in Glasgow, this outdoor stage has recently been revived and is attracting an incredible array of world talent—from the godfather of funk George Clinton, to original Beach Boy Brian Wilson and contemporary stars such as Jake Bugg. Its summer schedule, understandably, is hugely in demand but offers one of the most special concert experiences of anywhere in the city.

SOUTHSIDE
Live Music
GLASGOW'S GRAND OLE OPRY

2-4 Govan Road; tel. 0141 429 5396; www. glasgowsgrandoleopry.co.uk; 7pm-midnight Fri., Sat., and some Sun.; cover charge £5; pints of beer from £3.50, wine from £4 a glass

Taking inspiration from the famous Nashville bar from where it gets its name, this country and western dive bar first opened its doors in the 1970s, and, though it's become a little more ironic than in its 70s heyday, with fantastic live music and typical entertainment including bingo, a shoot-out, and line dancing, it's still an awful lot of fun.

THE GLAD CAFÉ
1006a Pollokshaws Road; tel. 0141 636 6119; www.thegladcafe.co.uk; 9am-11pm Mon.-Weds., 9am-midnight Thurs. and Fri., 10am-midnight Sat., 10am-11pm Sun., gigs usually start at 7:30pm; tickets from £5

There's always a steady flow of locals at this casual not-for-profit event space and café near Queen's Park. Like many Glasgow cafés, it curates its own music lineup and is a good place to see break-out musicians as well as internationally renowned acts. Open for breakfast, lunch, and dinner, this is a nice place to enjoy a meal or a coffee among the hipsters.

Pubs
THE LAURIESTON
58 Bridge Street; tel. 0141 429 4528; www.facebook.com/TheLaurieston; 11am-11pm daily; pints of beer from £3.50, single malts from £3.50

Stepping into this weathered but warm pub is like stepping into the set of a 1960s British cop show. Little has changed in the intervening years—the circular bar with Formica tables remains and the pub still has a separate lounge area, with wood paneling, red bench seats, and tartan carpet. Indeed, vintage touches abound, including a machine for heating pies and old Glasgow photos on the wall. It's well located for pre- or post-drinks at the nearby Citizen's Theatre and a friendlier bunch of punters you never did find.

HERAGHTY'S
708 Pollokshaws Road; tel. 0141 423 0380; 11am-12am Mon.-Sat., 12:30pm-midnight Sun; pints of beer from £3.45, single malts from £3.50

In the popular Strathbungo neighborhood, this family-run Irish pub, which first opened its doors in 1890 and has been in the Heraghty family since the 1970s, claims to pour the best pint of Guinness in the whole of Glasgow. It's moved with the times too and stocks a good range of craft beer as well as several Scottish gins.

Theater
TRAMWAY
25 Albert Drive; tel. 0141 276 0950; www.tramway.org ; exhibitions noon-5pm Tues.-Fri., noon-6pm Sat. and Sun., show times vary, but often 7pm-11pm

Housed in a former tram shed and originally opened to host Peter Brook's *Mahabharata,* this venue has lost little of its avant-garde reputation. Considered one of the most exciting theaters in Glasgow, it's a top-notch place for seeing contemporary and risk-taking shows. It also hosts regular day-time contemporary art exhibitions.

NORTH GLASGOW
The Arts
THE WHISKY BOND
2 Dawson Road; tel. 0141 345 2140; www.thewhiskybond.co.uk

Once home to the Highland Distillers, this former warehouse near Speirs Wharf is now a bubbling creative hub that hosts regular talks. **Glasgow Sculpture Studios** has its home here, but, unfortunately, its exhibition program has been halted.

GLUE FACTORY
22 Farnell Street; 0141 237 4845; thegluefactory.org

This venue, on the opposite side of the canal to the Whisky Bond, is also worth keeping an eye on for cutting-edge theater shows, poetry performances, and avant-garde shows as well as more left-field club nights.

Festivals and Events

CELTIC CONNECTIONS

Various city center venues; tel. 0141 353 8000; www. celticconnections.com; January; prices vary by performance

Lifting the post-Christmas gloom is this annual celebration of Celtic music across the genres of folk, roots, and world music that takes place over 18 days across numerous venues, from Oran Mor to The Tron to the City Halls. Over 300 events take place, from collaborative shows, to exhibitions and ceilidhs, all continuing late into the night, from formal concerts to more spontaneous sessions.

GLASGOW WHISKY FESTIVAL

Hampden Park; tel. 0141 204 5151; glasgowswhiskyfestival.com; November; £40

Held at Hampden Park each autumn, this drinks festival features over 60 stalls with the onus on distilleries close to Glasgow plus many of the city's independent bottlers. There are whiskies from other parts of Scotland too, however, as well as gin and rum producers. The day is split in two—a morning session and an afternoon session—and there are lots of tastings available. You also get vouchers alongside your tickets to get money off some of the spirits on sale.

SOUTHSIDE FRINGE

Various locations; www.southsidefringe.org.uk; May; prices vary

This community festival held each May takes place across several Southside venues, including The Glad Café, and includes around 100 events. There are theater performances, special tastings across the area's many bars, cafés, and restaurants, and lots and lots of live music. Many events are free.

WEST END FESTIVAL

Various locations; tel. 0141 341 0844; www. westendfestival.co.uk; June; prices vary

The city's largest cultural event takes place in its coolest quarter each June with as many as 400 events across 80 venues. With individual tickets for many events, and lots free, it's a great chance to dip in and out and see what this bustling area has to offer.

COUNTER FLOWS FESTIVAL

Various locations; www.counterflows.com; April; prices vary

This underground festival of experimental music that takes place every April at venues across the city, such as Tramway and The Glad Café, is one for the young ones or those looking to have their eyes and ears opened to new music.

Shopping

Glasgow is the undisputed shopping capital of Scotland, with everything from major brands, independent boutiques, and designer labels along its Style Mile. The **Style Mile** refers to a z-shaped mile-long route between Argyle Street and Sauchiehall Street that takes in the Buchanan Galleries, Buchanan Quarter, St. Enoch Centre, Ingram Street, and Princes Square. You'll find leading British stores here, including House of Fraser at one end of the main thoroughfare of Buchanan Street, which has the largest beauty hall in Scotland.

For more high-end one-off items, head to the **Merchant City,** home to many luxurious stores, while for quirkier, edgier stuff—particularly clothing and funky jewelry and furniture—you can't beat the **West End,** in particular **Ruthven Mews** with its plethora of antiques shops.

Take note that shops in the center are generally open Monday-Friday until at least 7pm and 10am-6pm on Saturdays and Sundays (smaller independents may have reduced hours). Late-night shopping is on Thursdays.

MERCHANT CITY
VIVIENNE WESTWOOD

Princes Square, 48 Buchanan Street; tel. 0141 222 2643; www.princessquare.co.uk/shopping/fashion/ vivienne-westwood; 10am-7pm Mon.-Fri., 9am-6pm Sat., 11am-5pm Sun.

The queen of alternative British fashion, Vivienne Westwood is the place to go for couture fashion if you have deep pockets. This shop in the pretty Princes Square is also close to other British brands such as Whistles, Ted Baker, and Karen Miller.

THE WHISKY SHOP

220 Buchanan Street; tel. 0141 331 0022; www. whiskyshop.com; 10am-7pm Mon.-Wed., Fri.-Sat., 10am-8pm Thurs., 10am-6pm Sun.

Once you've worked your way round some of Glasgow's many whisky bars and have found a dram you like, come here to pick up one to take home or arrange for international delivery to your home address.

MERCHANT SQUARE

71 Albion Street; www.merchantsquareglasgow.com; market runs 11am-6pm Sat., 12pm-6pm Sun.

Each weekend this covered courtyard hosts a craft and design fair, which is a great chance to browse handcrafted goods, all made right here in Glasgow. It's perfect for picking up authentic souvenirs.

EAST END
★ BARRAS MARKET

244 Gallowgate; tel. 0141 552 4601; www. theglasgowbarras.com; 10am-5pm Sat. and Sun.

This old East End market sprouted up in the

early 20th century when an entrepreneurial young lady by the name of Margaret Russell (known as the Barras Queen) and her husband James McIver began renting out horses and carts to traders who would fill them with goods for sale in some of the more affluent parts of the city. Eventually, they moved on to static barrows or *barras,* and so the market was born. Despite developing something of a negative reputation over recent decades, the Barras is still a popular destination for tourists, plus hip young things who come to peruse the stalls of bric-a-brac, vinyl, and secondhand clothes.

BAAD

54 Calton Entry; tel. 0141 237 9220; baadglasgow. com; noon-midnight Tues.-Sat., 11am-10pm Sun.

For something a bit different and to get a feel of the creative communities in Glasgow, head to Barras Art & Design (BAaD), a cool space near the old market with huge graffiti murals and home to lots of start-ups, including pop-up studios for picking up local art work and a record shop. This is certainly a place to watch—you may even catch one of the gigs that take place here sporadically.

WEST END
Shopping Streets
THE HIDDEN LANE AND THE HIVE

1081 Argyle Street; www.thehiddenlaneglasgow.com; hours vary, most businesses open Sat. 12pm-5pm, with some weekday hours, Hidden Lane Tearoom 10am-4pm Mon.-Fri., 10am-5pm Sat., noon-5pm Sun.

This secret lane in Finnieston features works from over 100 artists' studios and has a real local feel. You can shop for unique pieces at Shona Jewellery or stop off in the Hidden Lane Tearoom before perusing one of the many craft workshops. Meanwhile, The Hive, also hidden behind the main throng of Argyle Street, is a four-story building home to lots of independents.

Bookstores
VOLTAIRE & ROUSSEAU
12 Octago Lane; tel. 0141 611 8764; 10am-6pm Mon.-Sat.

You need to possess a certain level of patience to browse the messy and chaotic shelves and piles of books at this bookshop in Kelvinside, but you will be rewarded with lots of amazing finds and plenty of things that you never knew you needed.

CALEDONIA BOOKS
483 Great Western Road; tel. 01141 334 9663; www.caledoniabooks.co.uk; 10:30am-6pm daily

For rare books, including out-of-print titles, come to this shop in the Hillhead area of the West End, which has lots of publications on Scottish history and literature. It's a great place to stock up on books to swot up on (or study intensely).

Gifts and Souvenirs
NANCY SMILLIE SHOP
425 Great Western Road; tel. 0141 334 0055; nancysmillieshop.com; 10am-5:30pm Mon.-Tues., 9:30am-5:30pm Weds., 9:30am-6pm Thurs.-Sat.,

11:30am-5pm Sun.

Just by Kelvinbridge Subway Station, this boutique sells a range of ceramics, jewelry, and hand-blown glass as well as some lovely tweed throws. It's a good place for picking up Scottish gifts that aren't too tacky.

Antiques and Vintage
RUTHVEN MEWS ARCADE
57 Ruthven Lane; www.visitwestend.com/shopping/ruthven-mews-arcade; 11am-5:30pm Mon.-Sat., noon-5pm Sun.

A small arcade featuring just 10 outlets, it nevertheless has a good ratio of antiques and vintage goods, from mid-century furniture to subversive art and memorabilia.

STARRY STARRY NIGHT
19 Dowanside Lane; tel. 0141 337 1837; www.starrystarrynightvintage.co.uk; 10am-5:30pm Mon.-Sat., 11am-5pm Sun.

This Aladdin's cave has retro and vintage clothing dating all the way from the Victorian era, right up to the 1980s, including bejeweled flapper dresses and dazzling costume jewelry.

Food

As Scotland's largest city, Glasgow is where you can eat cuisine from all over the world. You may have heard of the deep-fried Mars Bars (which are exactly as you might expect—Mars Bars covered in batter and deep fried until crispy on the outside and sweet and gooey on the inside), but did you know that Glaswegians are partial to deep-frying all manner of foods? Deep-fried pizzas and deep-fried chips are all fair-game too.

But you would be wrong, so wrong, to think that Glaswegian food is all unhealthy, indeed far from it. Known as the vegan capital of Britain, you can expect to find really tasty healthy super foods in Glasgow, and, as there is a large student population, a lot of it is very well priced. If you do want to splash out, there are lots of lovely fine dining offerings (particularly in the city center and Merchant City), and the new Platform at Argyle Street Arches market is worth checking out if you want to try a variety of foods before booking a table somewhere (lots of the city's best dining rooms pop up here).

If it's local dishes you are after, then look out for some of the modern Scottish menus, while you can also experience some of the outside influences that have made their way onto the food and drink scene, including Indian food. After all, Glasgow's Shish Mahal was one of Britain's first Indian restaurants and it

1: Princes Square forms part of the Style Mile **2:** Buchanan Street Subway

may even be where the popular dish chicken tikka masala was invented.

CITY CENTER

RESTAURANT AT BLYTHSWOOD SQUARE HOTEL

11 Blythswood Square; tel. 0141 413 9236; www. phcompany.com/principal/glasgow-blythswood-square/dining/restaurant-blythswood-square/; 7am-10pm daily; entrées £8

It feels a bit more cocktail bar than sit-down restaurant here with more than a hint of the Mad Men about it. Private booths are perfect for an intimate meal, though, and the Harris Tweed seat covers are gorgeous. Mains include the likes of salt-cured cod or Kintyre smoked cheddar and truffle macaroni (with added lobster), or you can choose a steak from the grill.

Steak and Seafood
MINI GRILL

244A Bath Street; tel. 0141 332 2732; www. minigrillglasgow.co.uk; noon-10pm Mon.-Thurs., noon-11:30pm Fri.-Sat., noon-9pm Sun.; entrées £7

Not for vegetarians, it's all about meat at this city center grill. House specialties include a 40-ounce (1.1 kg) rib-eye steak for two, a "celebration of swine," which includes black pudding, pork belly, and swine cheek, and some of the best burgers in the city.

GAMBA

225A West George Street; tel. 0141 572 0899; www. gamba.co.uk; noon-2:15pm, 5pm-9:30pm Mon.-Sat., 5pm-9pm Sun.; entrées £10.50

If seafood is more your thing, then check out this award-winning restaurant that serves up fresh seafood in a French style with a bit of an Asian twist (think sashimi starters and fish served with sesame dressing). It's not cheap so best to save for a special meal.

Fine Dining
BRIAN MAULE AT CHARDON D'OR

176 West Regent Street; tel. 0141 248 3801; www. brianmaule.com; noon-2:30pm, 5pm-10pm Tues.-Sat.; entrées £11.75

The menu at this smart city center restaurant focuses on the abundance of natural produce available in Scotland, from hand-dived scallops to wild game and Scottish beef. Dishes are undeniably fresh with a French classic style such as spiced pork belly, garlic squid, and cumin jus or roast Scotch sirloin with crushed turnip.

Afternoon Tea
★ MACKINTOSH AT THE WILLOW TEA ROOMS

217 Sauchiehall Street; tel. 0141 332 7696; www. willowtearooms.co.uk; tea rooms 9am-5pm daily (afternoon tea served noon-4:30pm), exhibition 10am-4pm Mon.-Sat., 10am-3:45pm Sun., tours 9am, 10am Weds.-Sat., 10am Sun.; afternoon tea £19.03, exhibition adult £5.50, child £3.50, concessions £5.50, guided tours £7.50

Mackintosh designed these famous tearooms for his friend Miss Cranston in 1903-1904 and, though the building has changed hands several times, it remains resolutely Mackintosh—indeed, in June 2018 it reopened having been closed for several years while the Willow Tea Rooms Trust undertook major restoration work to return the tea rooms to their heyday after the building began to deteriorate.

Mackintosh and his wife designed everything, from the chairs to the menus, and even the waitress uniforms and cutlery; everything has been carefully restored to bring to life this detailed vision. Set across three floors, the 200-seater restaurant is the height of Edwardian elegance. There is a front and back saloon, a billiards room, and a gallery that floods with light, but the most beautiful room and the best place to have afternoon tea is the famously opulent Salon de Luxe, where once you had to pay a penny extra to enter (today the surcharge is £5). In this room you will find original Mackintosh stained-glass doors with purple paneling and leaded frieze decorated in the Art Nouveau style, there are grey silk dados, and the chairs, taking Mackintosh's signature high-backed form, are silver with nine glass square purple inserts in each. Margaret designed the tearoom with her husband and a gesso panel with the quote 'O ye, all ye that walk in Willowwood' (from the sonnet

"Willowood" by Dante Gabriel Rossetti) by her hand takes pride of place opposite the fireplace.

Afternoon tea includes a choice of a good range of white, black, green, and fruit teas, while the selection of finger sandwiches (egg, cucumber, and ham and mustard), scones, and cakes come presented on a tiered stand. The price is even a nod to the year the tea rooms first opened—1903.

Next door, at **no. 215,** a shop sells Mackintosh souvenirs and hosts a good exhibition. You can also book one of the 45-minute tours of the tea room, which will detail some of the design flourishes and talk you through the restoration process. Tours are run by volunteers from the Charles Rennie Macintosh Society, who can also advise on the Mackintosh walking trail and other Mackintosh buildings to visit.

Vegan
STEREO

22-28 Renfield Lane; tel. 0141 222 2254; www. stereocafebar.com; 11am-1am Mon.-Thurs., 11am-3am Fri.-Sat., noon-1am Sun.; small plates £4.90

One of the city's best-loved vegan restaurants, it also doubles as a gig venue and occupies the basement and lower floors of the former Daily Record building, designed by Charles Rennie Mackintosh. Choose from light bites such as sticky cauliflower wings, sharing platters, or one of the cakes (all baked in house). If you're really hungry, it's hard to resist one of the seasonal pies (mushroom and spring vegetable, for instance), and you can rest assured everything is completely free of animal produce.

MERCHANT CITY
Traditional Fare
CAFÉ GANDOLFI

64 Albion Street; tel. 0141 552 6813; www. cafegandolfi.com; 8am-10:30pm Mon.-Sat., 9am-10.30pm Sun.; entrées £7

This Glasgow institution serves delicious food using the freshest Scottish ingredients. The revolving doors lead to a beautiful room of heavy oak furniture designed by the late Glasgow School of Art graduate, Tim Read, and the food

is worthy of such a grand setting. Classic dishes include Stornoway black pudding to start, followed by house-smoked venison. There is also a good choice of pasta dishes.

Steak and Seafood
★ ROGANO

11 Exchange Place; tel. 0141 248 4055; www. roganoglasgow.com; noon-11pm daily; entrées £10.50

Now over 80 years old, Rogano is a Glasgow institution. Located just off the grand Royal Exchange Square, it was famously created in the same Art Deco style as the ship the *Queen Mary* (which was being built on the Clyde at the same time) and is the oldest surviving restaurant in the city. The **Oyster and Cocktail Bar** is a must, while dishes such as the chilled Scottish Fruits de Mer have been served in the restaurant since 1935.

HUTCHESON'S CITY GRILL

158 Ingram Street; tel. 0141 552 4050; www. hutchesonsglasgow.com; noon-12am Sun.-Thurs., 10am-1am Fri.-Sat.; entrées £12

Housed in a stunning, 200-year-old former hospital building, this restaurant is the brainchild of James Rusk, who honed his craft at Balthazar in New York. The double-height ceiling creates a sense of grandeur, while the olive-green velvet seats are exquisite. Each cut of meat is aged for a minimum of 35 days, and the seafood is all sourced off Scotland's shores.

Food Market
★ PLATFORM AT ARGYLE STREET ARCHES

The Arches, 253 Argyle Street; tel. 0345 241 6253; argylestarches.com/platform.; noon-10pm Fri.-Sat., noon-6pm Sun.; dishes £5

Once home to a world-renowned club, the Arches has been transformed into an independent street food market, open every Friday and Saturday night and Sunday afternoon, and it has proved a hit since opening in 2018. Freshly cooked food is served in a hidden urban underground market (the doorway under Central Station's arches is very discrete), with cool tunes being spun by a DJ, and a microbrewery

on site ensures a good footfall of hipsters as well as foodie travelers. Many of the stallholders already have establishments in Glasgow, so it's a good chance to try a variety of dishes under one roof before you book a table somewhere; it's a darn bit cheaper too.

GIN71

4 Virginia Court, tel. 0141 553 2326, www.gin71.com; 5pm-12am; entrees £7.50

This restaurant secreted away in a small courtyard in the Merchant City, specializes in gin-tasting menus—that's food that's designed to be complemented by carefully chosen gin pours. Even if you choose to drink wine with your dinner, the taste of gin won't be far away—it features in glazes, in sorbets and foams. There are two other GIN71 restaurants in the city (on Renfield Street and Buchanan Street) but this is my favorite as The Gin Spa is next door, and after a day pampering it's nice to not have to go far.

Light Bites
TANTRUM DOUGHNUTS

Gordon Street; tel. 0141 248 1552; www. tantrumdoughnuts.com; 8am-7pm Mon.-Fri., 9:30am-7pm Sat. and Sun.; doughnuts £2

This donut shop is so popular it has two venues (the other is in the West End), and the premise is simple: delicious, indulgent donuts that are handmade. The donuts, which are made by actual pastry chefs, are made using brioche dough that is proofed for 16 hours. Try the peanut butter and jam one or the "old fashioned" almond glaze buttermilk donut.

EAST END
Fine Dining
BILSON ELEVEN

10 Annfield Place; tel. 0141 554 6259; bilsoneleven. co.uk; five courses from £50

This lovely restaurant is housed in one of the oldest properties in the East End—a 19th-century townhouse on Annfield Place—which has actually been carefully restored by the

chef, Nick Rietz, and his family. There is little choice when it comes to dining (a five-course or six-course tasting menu), but Nick knows what he is doing, so let him guide you. At present there is no vegetarian option.

Seafood
A'CHALLTAINN

54 Calton Entry; tel. 0141 237 9220; baadglasgow. com/achalltainn; noon-midnight Tues.-Sat., 11am-10pm Sun.; entrées £8

Serving up seafood alongside a good choice of meat and vegetarian dishes, this restaurant located above the creative BAaD space by Barras Market is a cool place for a long lunch or dinner. The cold fish counter has lobster and langoustines, while mains include torched Scottish salmon and beer-battered haddock and chips.

Light Bites
MCCUNE SMITH

3-5 Duke Street; tel. 0141 548 1114; www. mccunesmith.co.uk; 8am-4pm daily; breakfast rolls £2.60

This ethical coffee and sandwich shop is run by a pair of brothers who grew up in the Hebrides. They are committed to serving local and sustainable produce, and the coffee is locally roasted by Dear Green from single-source Rwandan beans. Rather oddly, the café takes its name from one of the leading abolitionists of the slave trade, James McCune Smith, who was also the first African American to gain a medical degree in the United States. Elsewhere on the menu there are references to leading figures of the Scottish Enlightenment, but my pick has to be the Hebridean cooked breakfast, which includes a slow-roasted tomato and a tattie scone.

Coffee
★ EMPIRE COFFEE

Cathedral Square; tel. 07547 628 158; www.facebook. com/empirecoffeebox/; 8am-3pm daily; coffee £2.30

Not only is this miniscule coffee and sandwich shop brilliantly located for visitors to the cathedral, but its owner is also one of the friendliest people you'll meet in Glasgow.

1: Step back to the 1930s with dinner at Rogano
2: Ubiquitous Chip is on pretty Ashton Lane.

GLASGOW
FOOD

Served out of a Tardis-style booth, it's great for coffee on the run or sitting in Cathedral Square when the weather allows.

WEST END
Traditional Fare
WEE LOCHAN

340 Crow Road; tel. 0141 338 6606; www.an-lochan. com; noon-3pm, 5pm-10pm Mon.-Sat., noon-7pm Sun.; entrees £7, two-course Sunday lunch £17.95

If you are craving a Sunday roast, then this is the place to come as they serve it all day (noon-7pm), so it rarely (if ever) runs out. It's not your run-of-the-mill roast either: The beef is slowly braised for 16 hours topside, while the roast chicken is stuffed with chorizo and bacon mousse—but then at £17.95 a head I guess it should be.

Modern Scottish
FANNY TROLLOPES

1066 Argyle Street; tel. 0141 564 6464; www. fannytrollopes.co.uk; 5pm-9pm Tues.-Thurs., noon-10pm Fri.-Sat., noon-9pm Sun.; entrées £6.50

Using seasonal Scottish produce, this well-known restaurant in Finnieston specializes in seafood, Scottish beef, lamb, fowl, and game dishes. It was named after a local immigrant from Brazil who became a bit of a legend in the area and was known for her colorful costumes and lively dancing. Don't be put off by the diner-like appearance—the food is fabulous.

THE GANNET

1155 Argyle Street; tel. 0141 204 2081; www. thegannetgla.com; 5pm-9:30pm Tues.-Wed., noon-2pm,5pm-9:30pm Thurs.-Sat., 1pm-3pm, 5:30pm-9pm Sun.; six courses from £39

This Finnieston favorite offers a tantalizing six-course tasting menu featuring delicacies such as mutton as well as monkfish poached in buttermilk. At £39, it's not the cheapest, but you will be eating in a very cool setting—all bare wood and exposed brick—and afterward there are lots of hip bars nearby to check out.

OX & FINCH

920 Sauchiehall Street; tel. 0141 339 8627; www. oxandfinch.com; 12pm-10pm daily; plates from £7

This 2018 Michelin Bib award-winning restaurant in Finnieston serves up small plates of immaculately presented food for sharing. There is slow-cooked lamb shoulder served with an almond and mint yogurt, or charred leaks with poached egg as well as a really good choice of vegetarian and vegan dishes.

Traditional Fare
UBIQUITOUS CHIP

12 Ashton Lane; tel. 0141 334 5007; www. ubiquitouschip.co.uk; entrées £9.95, brasserie £7.45

Arguably Glasgow's most famous restaurant, this Ashton Lane stalwart, with its cobblestone floors, nooks, and crannies and covered courtyard (with fish pond), is an unforgettable place to eat. The food showcases the best of Scotland too, from homemade haggis to Orkney smoked salmon and scallops from Islay. There is a brasserie-style menu too, with slightly more affordable prices.

TWO FAT LADIES AT THE BUTTERY

652-654 Argyle Street; tel. 0141 221 8188; twofatladiesrestaurant.com/buttery; lunch 12pm-3pm Mon.-Sat., dinner 5:30pm-10pm Mon.-Thurs., 5:30pm-10:30pm Fri.-Sat., 12pm-9pm Sun. entrées £9

Ignore the name for a moment; this old-school Finnieston restaurant offers the archetypal fine dining experience, with mahogany walls and tartan carpet creating a very grand feel. Mains err on the traditional side (grilled lemon sole or Scottish beef fillet), but this is one place where you'll definitely want to leave space for dessert—opt for the Grand Dessert and you'll be presented with a sharing platter of all the desserts on the menu (bar the cheeses), so you may want to loosen your belt.

STRAVAIGIN

28 Gibson Street; tel. 0141 334 2665; www.stravaigin. co.uk; 11am-1am daily; entrées £7.95

This boundary-pushing restaurant, which offers a more casual approach to fine dining, has won a Michelin Bib Gourmand every year straight from 2012. Its vegetables are grown on its own small holding in Ayrshire, and, alongside its à la carte menu, it also offers a good pre-theater menu at £15.95 for two courses.

CAIL BRUICH

725 Great Western Road; tel. 0141 334 6265; cailbruich.co.uk; lunch noon-2pm Wed.-Sat., dinner 6pm-9pm Mon.-Sat., 1pm-7pm Sun.; entrees £8

Named one of Britain's 100 Best Restaurants by the *Sunday Times* in 2017, the menu at this West End restaurant is resolutely fresh, and flavor combinations are well thought out. There are seasonal tasting menus (two courses from £22), the service is effortlessly discrete, and mains include things like rabbit with black garlic, violet artichoke, foie gras, and white asparagus.

NUMBER 16

16 Byres Road; www.number16.co.uk; tel. 0141 339 2544; noon-2:30pm, 5:30pm-9pm Mon.-Sat., 1pm-2:30pm, 5:30pm-8:30pm Sun.; entrées £7.50

This local top pick prides itself on bringing an unusual take to Scottish cuisine. Salmon—a regular feature on Scottish menus—is glazed with maple and served with wasabi mayo, while the iced raspberry parfait with honeycomb and a honey and yogurt foam is anything but ordinary.

Seafood
★ CRABSHAKK

1114 Argyle Street; tel. 0141 334 6127; www.crabshakk. com; noon-midnight daily; entrées £9.95

This established restaurant that was in Finnieston long before it was cool, sticks to doing what it does well: serving seafood and fish suppers with finesse. Seared scallops with anchovies or salt and pepper squid are good for sharing, and everyone should try the Crabshakk fish club sandwich at least once.

Steakhouse
PORTER & RYE

1131 Argyle Street; tel. 0141 572 1212; www. porterandrye.com; noon-12am Sun.-Thurs., noon-1am Sat.- Sun.; entrées £8

At this premium steak house in Finnieston, the beef is aged for 50 days—even 100 days in some cases. Foraged foods also feature highly and portions are big, so come hungry. It also serves seasonal cocktails and has a good wine selection to accompany the steaks.

Fish and Chips
OLD SALTY'S

337 Byres Road; tel. 0141 334 3334; www.oldsaltys. co.uk; 8:30am-11:30pm daily; entrées £3.95

Fish suppers in Glasgow are taken very seriously, which is why new pretenders are taking a risk, particularly when they veer (even slightly) from tradition. Old Salty's gets the balance mostly right. It has all the hallmarks of a Glaswegian fish supper: "chippy" chips, battered fish, gravy, mushy peas, pickled onions, even deep-fried black pudding and haggis, and the famous chicken curry pie—plus a few fancier additions. Some Glaswegians might balk at the "posh" menu items, and this fish-and-chip shop is pricier than some, but for the rest of us, it's nice to have a bit of variety. Portions are huge, and Old Salty's is also open for breakfast.

Fine Dining
SIX BY NICO

1132 Argyle Street; tel. 0141 334 5661; www.sixbynico. co.uk; noon-9:45pm (last sitting) daily; six-course tasting menu £28

The menu at this Finnieston restaurant—indeed, the whole concept—changes every six weeks, so, even if you've been before, it will offer a completely new experience. Glasgow-born chef Nico Simeone has a talent for producing unexpected, but tantalising dishes. Previous six-course tasting menus have focused on Vietnamese street food, New York cooking, and even the rather abstract theme of childhood.

Asian

MOTHER INDIA

28 Westminster Terrace; tel. 0141 221 1663; www. motherindia.co.uk; noon-10pm Mon.-Thurs., Sun., noon-10:30pm Fri.-Sat.; entrées £7.45

Offering its unique "twist on tapas," this casual dining restaurant in Finnieston is one of Glasgow's most popular. It's recommended you choose three or four dishes between two people, but with everything on the menu sounding good, it's hard to stop yourself from going overboard.

THE HANOI BIKE SHOP

8 Ruthven Lane; tel. 0141 334 7165; https:// hanoibikeshop.co.uk; noon-11pm Mon.-Thurs., noon-12:30pm Fri., 11am-12:30am Sat., 11am-11pm Sun.; entrées £6.65

Tucked away on the quirky Ruthven Lane in the city's West End, this no-frills eatery serves fresh, vibrant Vietnamese street food with a menu designed for sharing.

ASHOKA

19 Ashton Lane; tel. 0141 337 1115; ashokarestaurants. com; noon-11pm Mon.-Sat., 5pm-11pm Sun.; entrées £5.25

There are several of these restaurants dotted around the city, and their ethos is on serving good Indian street food with some local influences (haggis pakora anyone?). They also offer a very good-value two-course option for £6 Monday-Saturday noon-4pm.

SHISH MAHAL

60-68 Park Road; tel. 0141 334 7899; www. shishmahal.co.uk; noon-2pm, 5pm-11pm Mon.-Thurs., noon-11:30pm Fri.-Sat., 5pm-10pm Sun.; entrées £4.95

This restaurant proudly boasts that chicken tikka masala was created here. With this in mind, it's nigh on impossible to resist sampling the restaurant's take on the dish, but, if you can, there is a range of Punjabi and South Indian dishes to choose from as well.

KIMCHI CULT

14 Chancellor Street; tel. 0141 258 8081; www. kimchicult.com; noon-9:30pm daily; entrées £4

The first of its kind in Scotland, this Korean fast food joint specializes in spicy fermented cabbage, which it uses to top off everything, from burgers to rice bowls, even fries. The bao (steamed buns) are also worth a try.

American

CRAFTY PIG

508 Great Western Road; tel. 0141 237 4040; www. crafty-pig.com; 11am-midnight daily; entrées £3.50

With more than a nod to American diners and sports bars, this restaurant has nailed the trend for pulled pork and slow-cooked meats, all served with a side order of fries and washed down with lashings of milkshake. The lunch menu here is really good value as well with a burger and soft drink or coffee for just £5.95.

Food Market

DOCKYARD SOCIAL

95 Haugh Road; dockyardsocial.com; 5pm-11pm Fri., noon-11pm Sat., noon-8pm Sun.

It was only a matter of time before Finnieston got its own street food market, and as you might expect, this one, which opened in December 2018 just a short walk from Kelvingrove Park, comes with a side serving of conscience. While for regular customers, the focus is on different vendors serving global comfort food—there are 12 different stalls and food allergies and dietary preferences are well catered for—organizers also hope to create a training school to help disadvantaged people in the city get on their feet.

But good karma aside, housed in an old warehouse building with a rolling program of live music and DJs providing a musical backdrop as you kick back and choose between an array of Scottish pop-ups while you sip on craft beer or a seasonal cocktail, it's a pretty cool hangout, too.

SOUTHSIDE
Breakfast and Brunch
★ GNOM

758 Pollokshaws Road; www.gnomfood.com; 9am-4pm Fri.-Wed.

This is the first permanent premises for the team behind Chompsky, street food vendors who have taken the city by storm. It has a small menu but still manages some good vegan and vegetarian options, and for meat-eaters, the crispy pork *bao* with fried egg are very messy but so worth it.

LAGOM KITCHEN

76 Victoria Road; tel. 0141 237 2424; 9am-5pm Mon. Weds.-Sat., 10am-4pm Sun.

Specializing in coffee, cake, and pancakes, this restaurant has proved such a hit that it has opened a new branch in Clydeside. It has a very natural, earthy feel inside, and, if the layered pancakes smothered in maple syrup with banana and granola, don't make you feel good, I don't know what will.

Fish and Chips
HOOKED FISH AND CHIPS

1027 Cathcart Road; tel. 0141 649 3994; noon-10pm Mon.-Sat., 4pm-10pm Sun.; entrées £2.95

This fish-and-chip shop near Mount Florida rail station is really handy for Hampden Park and features some interesting spins on normal chippy classics, including breaded haddock with pesto, sweet potato fries, and homemade mushy peas and tartare sauce. Don't miss the melt-in-your mouth mac and cheese balls either.

Cafés
CAFÉ STRANGE BREW

1082 Pollokshaws Road; tel. 0141 440 7290; 9am-5pm Mon.-Sat. , 9am-4pm Sun.

Set in the Shawlands area of Southside, this café serves up good coffee as well as a range of yummy brunch dishes. Don't be put off by the long queue—it does move fast and is worth it for the tasty cakes (many of which are gluten-free) and the baked eggs.

NORTH GLASGOW
Breakfast and Brunch
OCHO

8 Speirs Wharf; tel. 0141 332 6229; ochoglasgow. co.uk; 10am-4pm Sun.-Thurs., 10am-late Fri.-Sat.; brunch from £7.25

On the banks of Speirs Wharf is this cozy, laid-back eatery open for breakfast, brunch, and lunch; its bring-your-own brunch on Saturdays, Sundays, and bank holidays are popular and basically see you build your own open sandwich, or rosti, with toppings that include haggis, spinach, and kale. In the evening Thursday-Saturday, Ocho turns into Tomillo, a new vegan restaurant.

Ice Cream
CAFÉ D'JACONELLI

570 Maryhill Road; tel. 0141 946 1124; 9am-5:30pm daily; ice cream £2.60

This artisan ice cream parlor and café has been in the neighborhood since the 1920s and is such a staple of the city that it even featured in the cult movie *Trainspotting*. With an American diner look—be sure to play some tunes on its jukebox—it has a real nostalgic feel, and, while the breakfasts are lauded, it's really all about the ice cream.

Accommodations

This being a major city, accommodation options are wide. As expected, you pay more the more central you are, but prices are a lot more reasonable than you might find for similar places to stay in Edinburgh. Most guesthouses and hotel rooms come en suite, but, if you are staying in a hostel, then you will have to share a bathroom and often leave your room to do so. It will be made clear to you if this is the case.

If you are just in Glasgow for a couple of days, you will probably want to stay in and around the Merchant City or the city center for a chance to see the main attractions, plus explore one or two other areas. Many well-known hotel chains have places within easy reach of either Glasgow Central Station or Queen Street, and, if you can stay mid-week, then prices will drop substantially. Likewise, try to avoid school holidays (Easter and late July-early September) as these are peak times. If you're most interested in the city's cultural highlights, such as the Hunterian and the Kelvingrove, then it makes sense to stay in the West End, while the Southside is a good option for a relaxing few days where you can tap into the laid-back café culture.

CITY CENTER
Under £100
THE PIPERS' TRYST HOTEL
30-34 McPhater Street; tel. 0141 353 5551; www. thepipingcentre.co.uk/stay; £78 d, £90 with breakfast

This small hotel within the National Piping Centre offers superb value for money for a city center hotel, with clean and welcoming rooms (a wee dram comes as standard) if not the most exciting décor.

£100-200
HOTEL INDIGO GLASGOW
75 Waterloo Street; tel. 0141 226 7700; www. hinglasgow.co.uk.; £155 d

Housed in one of Glasgow's first-ever power stations, this smart and colorful hotel is a lot more inviting than you might expect. Minibars are stocked with free soft drinks (pay a little more and you'll get free beer and wine too), beds come with Egyptian cotton sheets, and you'll find Aveda toiletries and rainfall showers in the bathrooms. There's also a mini gym on site, plus a checkout time at noon is much more accommodating than most.

★ ABODE GLASGOW
129 Bath Street; tel. 0141 221 6289; www. abodeglasgow.co.uk; £114 d, £134 with breakfast

This 59-bed hotel is housed in an attractive converted townhouse. In the center of the hotel is an amazing cage lift, and rooms are bright and clean with large bathrooms. Breakfasts are tasty—the full Scottish is recommended, and you can even order a smoothie on the side. Plus, it's just a 10-minute walk to Glasgow Central Station and within staggering distance of King Tut's Wah Wah Hut.

CITIZEN M
60 Renfrew Street; tel. 0203 826 8623; www. citizenm.com; £170 d

This neat chain is ultra-modern, and, while rooms are a little too snug for an extended stay, it works well as a weekend stopover. Self check-in, tablet-controlled lights, window blinds, and TV may be fun for some, but others may miss the more personal touch. Make good use of the trendy communal areas and don't be put off by the buffet breakfast—it's a lot better than the name suggests.

DAKOTA DELUXE

179 West Regent Street; tel. 0141 404 3680; glasgow.
dakotahotels.co.uk; £180 d

This impeccably appointed grown-up hotel with décor in muted colors offers quietly assured concierges and comfy beds to sink into. The cocktail bar and grill are stylish places to hang out, and there's even a champagne room for special occasions. Perks include full Sky TV packages in even the Classic rooms, while guests in Executive Rooms or Suites can make use of the free transfers to and from Glasgow Airport, although it's a shame it doesn't apply to weekends.

MERCHANT CITY
Under £100
GRASSHOPPERS HOTEL GLASGOW

87 Union Street; tel. 0141 222 2666; www.
grasshoppersglasgow.com; £98 d

If you're arriving into Glasgow by train, you couldn't find a much more convenient place to stay. Rooms feature period details such as high ceilings and cornicing, and the bright décor is more cheerful than in many places of this price. It's a good affordable option if you want to stay central.

£100-200
★ THE PRINCIPAL GRAND CENTRAL HOTEL

99 Gordon Street; tel. 0141 413 9115; www.
phcompany.com/principal/glasgow-grand-central-
hotel; £123 d

Also very close to Glasgow Central but with a bit more gloss is this historic railway hotel, which has hosted many an illustrious guest, including Frank Sinatra and Winston Churchill. The hotel's Champagne Central bar harks bag to the Golden Age of Travel with views over the station. Rooms are tastefully decorated.

CARLTON GEORGE HOTEL

44 West George Street; tel. 0141 353 6373; www.
carlton.nl/en/hotel-george-glasgow; £126 d, £158
with breakfast

A highlight of a stay at this vibrant boutique hotel is having afternoon tea (from £14.95 per person) in the Windows Restaurant, which has splendid views of George Square. Another plus, which does make the price a lot more appealing, is complimentary minibars in all the rooms, plus decanters of gin, whisky, and vodka. Oh and all beds are king size.

FRASER SUITES GLASGOW

1 to 19 Albion Street; tel. 0141 553 4288; glasgow.
frasershospitality.com; £180 per apartment

These contemporary apartments, all located in an 1850s building in the Merchant City, have the look and feel of a four-star hotel while offering you the freedom to cook and prepare food in your own kitchen. The décor is a little cold—you have to really stretch your imagination to believe you actually live here—but it offers relatively affordable accommodation in a central location.

EAST END
Under £100
★ ALISON GUEST HOUSE

26 Circus Drive; tel. 0141 556 1431; www.thealison.
co.uk; £40 d

If you want to visit the cathedral and other historic sites in the East End, then this budget guesthouse is a steal. With doubles from £40 (with breakfast) and a genuinely personal reception from hosts Ann and Kenny, this Victorian villa offers budget accommodation that is clean, comfy, and welcoming. Plus, breakfast is cooked to order and the couple and their family will be only too happy to guide you to the best places to visit. Be warned though, they don't respond much to emails so ring to book.

WEST END
Under £100
SYHA GLASGOW YOUTH HOSTEL

7-8 Park Terrace; tel. 0141 332 3004; www.syha.org.
uk/where-to-stay/lowlands/glasgow; £59 private twin,
£26 shared room, cooked breakfast £7

This hostel overlooking Kelvingrove Park is basic but within walking distance of both the university and the Kelvingrove Art Gallery and Museum. Beds are wooden framed and rooms (including bathrooms) are clean.

Wireless Internet is patchy and is not available in the dorms, so you have to use one of the communal areas to get online.

MANOR PARK GUEST HOUSE

28 Blashagray; tel. 0141 339 2143; www.themanorpark.com; £65 d

Just minutes from Victoria Park, this family-run three-star B&B offers sweet, if a little tawdry, rooms. It's a little away from the main attractions, but Fiona and Scott are only too happy to give suggestions on visiting the city. Rooms are spacious and the cooked Scottish breakfast is generous too.

KELVIN HOTEL

15 Buckingham Terrace; tel. 0141 339 7143; www.kelvinhotel.com; £67 d, £84 with en suite

Set within a listed building, this B&B is quite bare-boned and rooms are more akin to private hostel rooms, but this is reflected in the price. Rooms do come with toiletries and tea and coffee-making facilities, and they make for a great base in the heart of the West End. Check yours is an en suite before you book.

★ ALAMO GUEST HOUSE

46 Gray Street; tel. 0141 339 2395; www.alamoguesthouse.com; £95 d

This impeccably presented family-run guesthouse offers astounding value for money. Set in a Victorian building, it is effortlessly refined, with period cabinetry, Victorian carved armchairs, and even four-posters in some rooms. Plus, breakfast, which is included, can be enjoyed while admiring views of Kelvingrove Park and the University of Glasgow.

£100-200

AMADEUS SERVICED APARTMENTS

411 North Woodside Road; tel. 0141 339 8257; www.amadeusguesthouse.co.uk; £340 for a two-night stay

If you want to Glasgow like a local, then having your own pied-à-terre is useful. Amadeus offers well-priced doubles in its guesthouse, plus it has a two-bed apartment to rent in a Victorian conversion by the university that is stylishly decorated, with animal print throws, bright furnishings, wall art, and a fabulously modern kitchen. Minimum stays apply.

15 GLASGOW

15 Woodside Place; tel. 0141 332 1263; http://15glasgow.com; £130 d

This luxurious B&B comes with super king beds and is immaculately presented with many of the 19th-century property's original features, including wooden shutters and fireplaces. Guests also have access to the private residents' garden opposite and considering breakfast is included, it's a pretty good price.

HOTEL DU VIN AT ONE DEVONSHIRE GARDENS

1 Devonshire Gardens; tel. 0141 378 0385; www.hotelduvin.com/locations/glasgow; £144 d

Uber-cool rooms veer on the decadent side with this trusted hotel brand. Beds come with hand-sprung mattresses and Egyptian cotton sheets, and room are decorated in warm hues with sumptuous fabrics. Bathrooms include free-standing baths and walk-in monsoon showers. The hotel is also located on a pretty tree-lined Victorian terrace, and you can retire to the sophisticated whisky room at the end of the day.

SOUTHSIDE
£100-200
SHERBROOKE CASTLE HOTEL

11 Sherbrooke Avenue; tel. 0141 427 4227; www.sherbrookecastlehotel.com; £176 d

This beautiful baronial four-star hotel in acres of its own grounds is not actually as expensive as you might think. Its turrets offer a fairy-tale feel to the place, but rooms aren't overly romantic with classic colors and no superfluous furnishings. Afternoon tea (£39.90 for two) can be taken each day between 1pm and 4pm in the lounge, library, or Morrisons Room.

GOGLASGOW URBAN HOTEL

517 Paisley Road West; tel. 0141 427 3146; www.crerarhotels.com; £183 d

Well located for the Ibrox Stadium if you are considering going to watch a match or do a tour of Rangers' ground, these modern rooms are cool and minimalist (though lacking a little character), but beds are fitted with Egyptian cotton sheets and there are full-length mirrors in each room. This hotel attracts a business crowd and sports fans.

Information and Services

VisitScotland iCentre (tel. 0141 566 4083; www.visitscotland.com/info/services/glasgow-icentre-p332751) is located at the south entrance of Buchanan Street Subway Station. Staff can advise on everything, from accommodation providers to travel to entrance tickets for attractions. There are also lots of leaflets if you are looking for ideas of where to go while you're here, and you can ask about possible day trips from Glasgow.

People Make Glasgow (peoplemakeglasgow.com) is the official guide to the city and is packed with tips and inspiring articles. It's also kept well abreast of events and festivals taking place across the city, so it is worth checking for up-to-date news. Similarly, **Glasgow Life** (www.glasgowlife.org.uk) is a charity that aims to inspire people to get out and explore and is particularly insightful when it comes to museums and cultural spaces.

As you travel round town, be sure to make good use of the many fliers and freebie magazines in the pubs and cafes, particularly in the West End and Southside. The two best magazines for gigs and exhibitions are *The Skinny* and *The List*.

Getting There

BY AIR

With two airports, Glasgow is extremely well served for air travel.

GLASGOW AIRPORT

Paisley, www.glasgowairport.com

Located just eight miles (12.9 km) west of the city, most people arriving into Glasgow will come into the city's main airport. It has direct flights from North America with **United Airlines** and from Canada with **Air Transat.**

A flight from London will take just an hour, and there are several flights to each of the main airports every day (in total there are 28 flights from London every day). **Ryanair** (www.ryanair.com) flies direct to Glasgow Airport from London Stansted; **British Airways** (www.britishairways.com) flies from London Gatwick, London Heathrow, and London City; and **easyJet** (www.easyjet. com) flies from London Gatwick, London Stansted, and London Luton.

The **Glasgow City Express** is the official airport bus and leaves from stance 1, just outside the terminal building every 10 minutes with a journey time of just 15 minutes. Buses run 24 hours a day, seven days a week, with the only exception of Christmas Day (adult £8, child £4). From the city center, you can get the return bus from Buchanan Bus Station or George Street.

You can also pre-book a taxi with **Glasgow Taxis** (tel. 0141 429 7070; www.glasgowtaxis.co.uk) or pick one up just outside the terminal building (although the former is cheaper, around £27).

GLASGOW PRESTWICK AIRPORT

Aviation House, Prestwick; www.glasgowprestwick.com

Located 32 miles (51 km) southwest of the city center, this airport has inbound flights from many European destinations but none from London. From Glasgow Prestwick Airport you can catch a train three times an hour to Glasgow Central Station, which takes around 50 minutes (£8.30 one-way).

BY TRAIN

Many people traveling from London choose to travel by train. **Glasgow Central** (Gordon St., www.scotrail.co.uk/plan-your-journey/stations-and-facilities/glc) and **Glasgow Queen Street** (North Hanover Street, George Square; www.scotrail.co.uk/plan-your-journey/stations-and-facilities/glq) are both centrally located stations.

There are over 20 direct trains from London Euston with **Virgin Trains** to Glasgow Central each day (www.virgintrains.co.uk) that take around 4.5 hours and cost anywhere in the region of £30 to £80 each way.

More romantic (though a little more expensive) is the **Caledonian Sleeper train** (www.scotrail.co.uk/plan-your-journey/travel-connections/caledonian-sleeper). The train journey takes 7.5 hours, but, as it's overnight, you hardly mind. It costs from £45 one-way (though it can cost a lot more last minute, particularly if you want a cabin). There is just one sleeper train per day.

From Edinburgh, a train runs every few minutes into either Glasgow Queen Street or, less regularly, Glasgow Central. Journey time varies from 50 minutes to 1.25 hours, and tickets cost just £12.90 one-way. From Inverness, roughly one train runs per hour into Glasgow Queen Street (3.5 hours, from £8.30 one-way).

Four trains a day run from Fort William to Glasgow Queen Street (3.75 hours, from £23.50 one-way), while there are trains half hourly from Balloch in Loch Lomond to Glasgow Queen Street (45 minutes, from £5.60

one-way). All tickets can be booked through **ScotRail** (www.scotrail.co.uk).

Watch yourself as you come out of Glasgow Central Station—buses pull onto what many presume is a pedestrian walkway.

BY CAR

Of course, you can also drive to Glasgow. From **London,** the most direct route is to take the M40 to just outside Birmingham where you'll join the M6 all the way to Gretna Green, just across the Scottish border, and then take the A74 up to Glasgow for a total journey time of 7.5 hours (415 mi/668 km).

From **Edinburgh** follow the M8 west for 47 miles (76 km, one hour). From Stirling, Glasgow is a 27-mile (43 km) drive southwest along the M80, which takes just 30 minutes.

From **Mallaig** on the west coast of Scotland (the main jumping off point for Skye), it's 152 miles (245 km), first east along the A830 to Fort William where you need to pick up the A82, which takes you all the way down through Loch Lomond before joining the M8 into the city. All in all this should take around 3.5 hours. From Fort William, the journey time is just 2.5 hours (109 mi/175 km).

From **Oban,** it's 98.5 miles (159 km), first east along the A85 to Crianlarich in Loch Lomond and The Trossachs National Park before heading south on the A82 and eventually joining the M8 into Glasgow. Expect a journey time of 2.25 hours. From **Balloch** in Loch Lomond it's just 26 miles (42 km) southeast along the A82 and then the M8, which should take around 35 minutes.

If you're coming all the way from **Inverness,** it's actually quite straightforward as you can take the A9 all the way down to Stirling and pick up the M80, which, despite covering 169 miles (272 km), only takes just over three hours.

Getting Around

Glasgow is a hilly city, built on a series of drumlins (hills), hence the names of many of its suburbs (Hillhead, Govan Hill, etc.), so, while walking is a good way to orient yourself, you may find it takes more exertion than you might like.

BY SUBWAY

By far the best way to get from area to area, though, is on the circular Subway (www.spt.co.uk/subway) system, which is similar to Paris's and is actually one of the oldest underground systems in the world. Tickets, which can be purchased in a machine at the Subway station, need to be tapped in and out at the card reader panels as you enter and leave stations, and with just two lines—one going clockwise and the other counterclockwise—it's virtually impossible to get lost. Journeys cost just £1.50 one-way, while an all-day ticket costs £4.10 adult (child £2, under fives free). If you are going to be here for a few days or more, you might want to think about getting a Subway Smartcard, which acts like a top-up card—you put money on and then travel with ease without needing to stop to buy a ticket each day. However, you will need to supply a passport-size photo for this and register on the SPT website (www.spt.co.uk/travelcards/subway-smartcard). Once obtained, you can top up your card on the Bramble-powered website (mybramble.co.uk) or in a ticket machine at a Subway station.

Subway stations are dotted around the city center, West End, and East End, with a few in the more northerly reaches of Southside. With just 15 stations on the circuit, it takes just 24 minutes to go around them all. Buchanan Street is the most popular stop for shopping on the Style Mile, while Hillhead is in the epicenter of the West End. If you're looking for a Subway station above ground, you should look for the logo, which is an orange S against a white background within a gray circle and then an outer orange circle.

Those with a head for drink might even want to attempt the Sub crawl—a variation on the typical pub crawl in which you must have a drink in a pub by each of the 15 stations. Officially, it's said it should be a pint, but that sounds either impossible or like a very, very bad idea.

BY TRAIN

In addition to the Subway, there are also lots of train stations connecting different parts of the city. An SPT Roundabout ticket (adult £7, child £3.50) gives you unlimited access to all the Subway and train stations throughout Glasgow and is valid after 9am on weekdays and all day on weekends or public holidays. You can buy these tickets at the ScotRail train stations or Subway stations.

BY BUS

A very good bus system reaches all of the spots that the Subway doesn't serve (particularly handy if you are staying in the Southside). The main bus company is First Glasgow (www.firstgroup.com), which operates over 100 routes through the city, connecting all its corners with the city center. Buses are a mix of double-deckers and single-decks, and they will always have the bus number and final destination displayed on the front. You can pick up a timetable at the Travel Centre in St. Enoch's Square or, better, download the FirstBus app, which will help you plan your journey with timetables and real-time bus updates. You can pay on board using your contactless debit card (overseas cards are usually accepted) or buy in advance through the app.

If you're traveling as a family and planning to use public transport, a Daytripper ticket (£21.80 for two adults and up to four children, £12.30 for one adult and up to two children) can be quite useful as it gives unlimited travel on most buses, Subway trips, and trains and can be purchased online from the **SPT Store** (zonecard.online), though it can only be used after 9am on weekdays.

Many first-time visitors like to use the **City Sightseeing** (https://city-sightseeing.com/en/92/Glasgow; one day £15, two days £16; 9:30am-4:30pm) hop-on hop-off bus to get around. With 21 stops taking in the biggest attractions and unlimited rides within a set time frame, it can be prudent. Two tours are offered: the live guide, which allows you to interact and ask questions, and the audio guide. Headphones are provided for the latter, so you can just plug in and chill out or jump off if somewhere sounds interesting. You can't miss the buses—big red double-deckers with the City Sightseeing logo emblazoned on the side. Main stops include George Square, Glasgow Cathedral, the Riverside Museum, the Buchanan Galleries, and the Kelvingrove Art Gallery and Museum. Tickets can be bought on the City Sightseeing website.

BY TAXI

You can hail a black taxi from anywhere in the city, and you'll recognize legitimate taxis as they will have a telling "taxi" sign—when this is lit up, you know the taxi is free to hail. Glasgow isn't huge, so you can expect to pay around £10 to travel from the Southside to, say, the West End. There are also taxi ranks outside both Glasgow Central and Queen Street stations.

BY CAR

As with most major cities, you should avoid driving in Glasgow where possible—parking is a nightmare and pricey. There's always traffic, so with an excellent Subway system, good buses, and plenty of places within walking distance of each other, there's really no need. If you are traveling out of Glasgow and would like to hire a car, there are numerous companies to choose from at Glasgow Airport. It's wise to go with a familiar name, such as **Hertz** (www.hertz.co.uk) because hidden costs are less likely. Lots of companies also rent out cars from the city center, such as **Avis** (www.avis.co.uk).

Greater Glasgow

★ NEW LANARK AND THE FALLS OF CLYDE

This perfectly preserved old mill town is a remnant of the busy cotton industry brought to Glasgow and its surrounds on the River Clyde. New Lanark was founded in 1786 by David Dale, a local businessman, and Richard Arkwright, the famous entrepreneur who had already transformed the cotton industry in England. Though Dale, who soon took over the running of the mill town, was considered enlightened for his time, nevertheless, the majority of his workforce was made up of children alongside Highlanders who had been removed from their land during the notorious clearances.

You can visit the World Heritage site of New Lanark and the Falls of Clyde for free, but, if you would like to see the museum exhibits and inside the many buildings that make up the visitor center, which is a little like a living history museum, you will need to pay the entry fee.

New Lanark Village

New Lanark Road; tel. 01555 661 345; www.newlanark.org; visitor center 10am-5pm Apr.-Oct., 10am-4pm Nov.-Mar.; adult £12.50, child £9

Today, you can tour many of the mill buildings, including the schoolroom where Dale's successor, his son-in-law Robert Owen, created the world's first infant school. You can also see the historic spinning mule in operation and visit the village store where you can learn about Owen's revolutionary idea of selling quality goods at affordable prices to workers. Make sure you try some of the New Lanark ice cream too.

Falls of Clyde

New Lanark; scottishwildlifetrust.org.uk/reserve/
falls-of-clyde; free

The Falls of Clyde are a series of linns, or waterfalls, which are located in a wildlife reserve that runs from the south of the heritage village of New Lanark and have attracted such famous visitors as William Wordsworth and J. M. W. Turner, who were mesmerized by their beauty. The four waterfalls that make up the Falls of Clyde are the upper falls of Bonnington Linn, Corra Linn, Dundaff Linn, and the lower falls of Stonebyres Linn (not included on this route); they are spaced out amid the serene wildlife reserve that follows the path of the River Clyde—at times rumbling, sometimes rushing—and the route is softly shaded by trees. En route, look out for birdlife, including dippers, ravens, and kingfishers, as well as otters along the riverbank and signs of badgers who forage here. In the evenings Daubenton's bats are known to feed along the river.

The route is clearly signposted from the village of New Lanark. Follow the badger signs south through the village with the river on your right until you reach the first of the waterfalls at the far end of the village, Dundaff Linn, which is where the woodland walk to Corra Linn, the tallest and most impressive of the waterfalls, and beyond begins.

Dundaff Linn is nice but not overly exciting, so continue on along the river's edge and let the path lead you through fertile woodland. Though the path is well laid out and sturdy for the most part, there can be some steep climbs, and you'll need to be wary of the wooden boardwalks that can be slippery following heavy rainfall (sometimes they are even submerged). It's worth it, though, for the views and the sense of calm. The path is rocky and muddy in places too.

Corra Linn is the second waterfall you come to (after about 45 minutes), and you can choose to walk back the way you came from New Lanark here or continue following the path up and over the river before coming back on the opposite bank past Bonnington Linn to New Lanark. This full route should take around two hours.

Getting There and Getting Around

There are two direct trains from Glasgow Central Station to Lanark Station every hour, and they take around 50 minutes (£7.30 one-way). From Lanark Station you can get the no. 135 bus right into New Lanark village with

Dundaff Linn, New Lanark

Stuarts Coaches (tel. 0155 577 3533; www. stuartscoaches.co.uk, £3.50 each way), which takes around 10 minutes and runs every hour at 27 minutes past the hour (subject to change). Make sure you check return times for the bus with **Traveline** (www.traveline.info), so that you can make your returning train.

To drive from Glasgow, it's just 32 miles (51 km) southeast to Lanark. Leave the city on the M8, heading east, before joining the M74 south. Leave the M74 at junction 9 and take the B7086 into New Lanark.

DUMBARTON CASTLE

Castle Road, Dumbarton; tel. 0138 973 2167; www. historicenvironment.scot/visit-a-place/places/ dumbarton-castle; 9:30am-5:30pm daily Apr.-Sept., 10am-4pm Sat.-Wed. Oct.-Mar. adult £5, child £3

In the heart of the ancient Kingdom of Strathclyde, just 15 miles (24.1 km) from Glasgow, lies this former stronghold, which sits on a volcanic plug (much like Edinburgh Castle). Once known as "Alt Clut" or "Rock of the Clyde," and later renamed "Dun Breatann" from the Gaelic for "fortress of the Britons," it was a significant fortress in the Middle Ages that initially stood to protect from Norwegian

Vikings, whose frontier lay just 10 miles downriver (and who once ruled the Western Isles as well as islands in the River Clyde), and later the English.

Today, not much is left of the 13th-century castle, built by Alexander II of Scotland, but you can still climb the 557 steps to the top of White Tower Crag for views as far as Ben Lomond. Plus, it offers good insight into 18th-century military tactics, and you can see some of the artifacts from the castle in the Georgian Governor's House. Grab a coffee by the main entrance to keep your hands warm as you walk around, as much of the site is exposed.

Getting There

It's just a 20.5-mile (33 km) drive west of Glasgow to Dumbarton Castle along the M8 and then the M898 before joining the A82 at Old Kilpatrick. Journey time is half an hour. Alternatively, you can get the train with **ScotRail** www.scotrail.com from Glasgow Queen Street to Dumbarton East, from where it is a 12-minute walk to the castle. Trains runs every 5-10 minutes and take 30 minutes (£4.60 one-way).

Loch Lomond and the Southern Highlands

While the romance of the western and northern

Highlands is inarguable, Loch Lomond and the more southerly Highlands are not to be missed. It was here that Sir Walter Scott was inspired to write his *Lady of the Lake* ode, a literary sensation that prompted the Highland Revival of the 19th century. Today, Loch Lomond and the Trossachs National Park encompasses 220 miles (354 km) of lochs, glens, mountains, and woodland, which in turn are home to 25 percent of Britain's threatened bird, animal, and plant species. To the west of the park lies Oban, the seafood capital of Scotland and gateway to the isles including Mull, one of the greenest places you will ever visit and a fantastic place to spot native wildlife such as red deer,

Highlights

Look for ★ to find recommended
sights, activities, dining, and lodging.

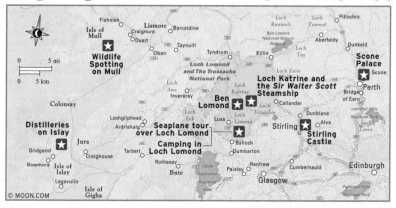

★ **Loch Katrine and the *Sir Walter Scott* steamship:** Take a tour of this stunning freshwater loch surrounded by lush woodland, aboard a Victorian-era steamship (page 203).

★ **Seaplane tour over Loch Lomond:** Get a bird's eye tour from the national park, all the way along Scotland's west coast, for a real sense of adventure (page 208).

★ **Ben Lomond:** Scale to the top of Scotland's most southerly munro for unparalleled views of Loch Lomond and the Trossachs National Park (page 210).

★ **Camping in Loch Lomond:** Go deep into the national park and pitch up for the night in absolute tranquility (page 215).

★ **Wildlife spotting on Mull:** Spot eagles soaring above you on land, or take a cruise and look for whales, dolphins, and more on the water (page 228).

★ **Distilleries on Islay:** Hop from distillery to distillery on this beautiful isle and enjoy drams of peat-tinged whisky, aged to perfection (page 235).

★ **Stirling Castle:** History permeates in this medieval royal court, where Stuart monarchs once reigned, and which played a pivotal role in the Wars of Independence (page 244).

★ **Scone Palace:** This grand estate was once the coronation site of Scotland's kings, from Macbeth to Robert the Bruce (page 252).

seals, otters, golden eagles, and even (if you're lucky) rare white-tailed sea eagles.

Islay, to the southwest, is renowned for its concentration of whisky distilleries known for their distinct peaty flavor, but it's also home to some of the friendliest people you are ever likely to meet. To the east of the park, a visit to Stirling is a must to see the mighty fortress from which many of the nation's monarchs ruled and to learn more about Rob Roy MacGregor and William Wallace—heroic figures whose stories are still passionately told. To the northeast of Stirling, Scotland's ancient capital of Perth is one of its prettiest cities and is a good base for venturing into the Highlands or visiting Scone Palace, where for centuries Scotland's kings were crowned.

ORIENTATION

Loch Lomond and the Trossachs National Park, just 25 miles (40 km) north of Glasgow, crosses the diagonal Highland Boundary Fault, which many people take as the division between the Highlands and the Lowlands, so you might say that the southern part of the park (from Luss to Callander and below) lies in the Lowlands and the rest forms part of the Highlands. The park is expansive, covering 720 square miles (1,865 km) in total. To the west, the port town of Oban, from where you can access many of Scotland's islands, including Mull, is just 36 miles (58 km) from the north end of the park. Islay is best accessed from Kennacraig on the Kintyre Peninsula, which lies southwest of the park, although to reach it, you'll have to take a bit of a detour

north into the park as far as Arrochar before turning west and then south (a journey of 106 mi/171 km from Glasgow). The city of Stirling, home to one of Scotland's finest castles, lies about 20 miles (32 km) east of the southeast corner of the park, while the city of Perth is around 40 miles (64 km) east of its northeast corner.

PLANNING YOUR TIME

Loch Lomond and the Trossachs National Park is large, and, though many travelers simply pass through it as they journey on up to Fort William and on to Mallaig to cross over to Skye (either by train or car), it really is worthy of a few days of your time, particularly if you are partial to walking or camping. The southern and west side of Loch Lomond itself, around Balloch and Luss, are very touristy, and while they are useful places to stock up and have some good restaurants and cafés, aim to travel to the north and east side of the park if you want a little more seclusion and some great walking and cycling trails. From the east of the park, it's an easy journey to either Stirling and Perth, which are both attractive cities with plenty of historic attractions, though a day or so in each is probably enough. If you're heading west, you will want to give yourself more time. Both Islay and Mull should be taken slowly (particularly if you want to see wildlife); you will also need to factor in ferry timetables and crossings to each, so allow for a minimum of around three days in each place, though a week is better.

Loch Lomond and Southern Highlands

Coll

Tobermory

Loch Linnhe

A828

A82

Fishnish

Lismore

Isle of Mull

Craignure

Duart

Barcaldine

Oban

A85

Taynuilt

A816

A85

Loch Awe

SEE
"OBAN AND THE
ISLE OF MULL"
MAP

Inveraray

Colonsay

A816

A83

Loch Eck

Lochgilphead

Ardrishaig

Jura

A83

Craighouse

Tarbert

Kames

Bridgend

Bowmore

Rothesay

A78

Isle of
Islay

Bute

Largs

Lagavulin

SEE
"ISLE OF ISLAY"
MAP

Isle of
Gigha

Isle of
Arran

Ardrossan

Brodick

A83

Firth of
Clyde

Campbeltown

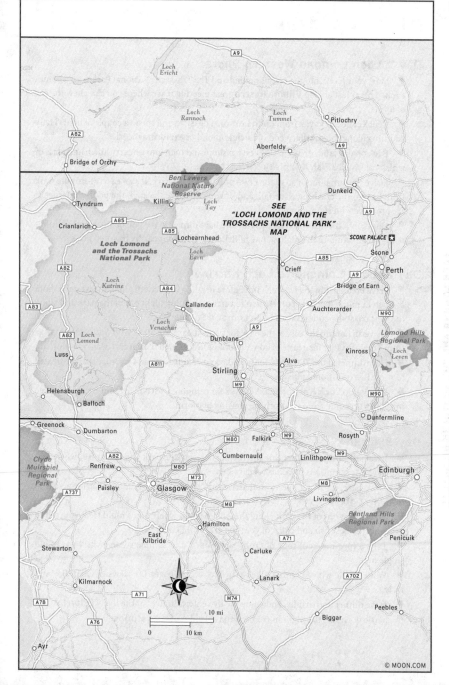

SEE
"LOCH LOMOND AND THE
TROSSACHS NATIONAL PARK"
MAP

© MOON.COM

Itinerary Ideas

Day 1: Loch Lomond Western Shore

- Start your foray into the Loch Lomond and The Trossachs National Park with a home-cooked breakfast at **The Village Rest,** a great meeting place where you can chew the ear of locals.

- Rent a canoe or kayak from **Loch Lomond Leisure** and spend a couple of hours lazily paddling along the southern end of Loch Lomond or exploring the isles.

- Back on dry land, drive up the western shore and tuck into a hearty lunch and glass of whisky at **Mr. C's Fish & Whisky Bar/Restaurant**

- Drive the half hour or so to the **Falls of Falloch** car park. It's an easy 10-minute walk from here to the crashing waterfall, and, if you can brave the cold, the pools underneath are great for wild swimming.

- Check into the nearby **Drover's Inn** and have dinner in the pub before seeing if things really do go bump in the night at one of Britain's most supposedly haunted places.

Day 2: Loch Lomond to Loch Katrine

- Have breakfast in the Drover's Inn before heading back south along the western shore of Loch Lomond to **Cameron House** to catch a morning flight out of the park and along the west coast of Scotland with **Loch Lomond Seaplanes.**

- Drive an hour to the east of the park for a trip aboard the *Sir Walter Scott* **steamship** from Trossachs Pier for a taste of how Victorians first viewed the natural beauty of the park.

- Have dinner at the **Pier Café** (only Fridays and Saturdays), and you may even be treated to some live traditional music.

- Check into **Loch Katrine Eco Lodges** for camping with added comfort, and indulge in some stargazing from your private viewing platform.

Day 3: Oban

- It's a half-hour drive first thing to the northeast of the park and **Mhor 84,** where you can have a scrumptious breakfast of eggs Benedict.

- From here, it's just a five-minute drive into the village of Balquhidder for a visit to **Rob Roy's grave.**

- Travel west out of the park along the A85 to Oban where you should treat yourself to probably the best fish and chips of your life at **Oban Fish & Chips.**

- Take a (pre-booked) tour of **Oban Distillery** and sample some of its 14-year-old single malt.

- Walk off the whisky with a hike up to **McCaig's Tower** for views of Oban Bay and its isles.

- Have dinner and drinks, and enjoy the live entertainment at the lively **Oban Inn.**

- Settle down for the night in the baronial splendor of **Greystones.**

Loch Lomond and Southern Highlands

BEST OF LOCH LOMOND
AND SOUTHERN HIGHLANDS

1 Day 1: Loch Lomond
Western Shore

2 Day 2: Loch Lomond to
Loch Katrine

3 Day 3: Oban

4 Day 4: Southern Mull and
Mull Eagle Watch

5 Day 5: Tobermory

Colonsay

Craighouse

Jura

Kames

Ardrishaig

Lochgilphead

A83

A816

A83

Inveraray

Loch
Awe

Loch
Fyne

Loch
Eck

Helensburgh

Greenock

Dumbarton

Balloch

A811

A82

A83

Luss

Loch
Lomond

The Village
Rest

Mr C's Fish
and Whiskey

Loch Lomond
Leisure

2 Cameron House

1

The Drovers
Inn

Falls of
Falloch

A82

Crianlarich

Tyndrum

Loch Lomond
and the Trossachs
National Park

Loch
Katrine

The Pier
Cafe

2

Loch
Venachar

Sir Walter Scott
Steamship
Loch Katrine
Eco Lodges

Callander

Rob Roy's
Grave

Lochearnhead

A84

Mhor 84

Loch
Earn

A85

Killin

Loch
Tay

Ben Lawers
National Nature
Reserve

A82

A85

A828

A85

Barcaldine

Taynuilt

Oban

Loch Linnhe

Lismore

Greystones
Oban Inn
McCaig's Tower
Oban Distillery
Oban
Fish & Chips

A816

3

Duart
Castle

4

Craignure
Inn

Craignure

Fishnish

Isle of
Mull

Mull Eagle
Watch

4

Glengorm
Castle

Calgary
Bay

Bellachroy
Hotel

Tobermory

5

MacGochan's
Strongarbh
House

0
10 km
0
10 mi

© MOON.COM

Day 4: Southern Mull and Mull Eagle Watch

- Have a hearty breakfast at Greystones before taking a morning ferry with CalMac over to the **Isle of Mull.**
- Pay a visit to the ancient seat of Clan Maclean at **Duart Castle.**
- Have lunch in the cozy and historic bar of the **Craignure Inn.**
- Book a trip with **Mull Eagle Watch** to view majestic sea eagles in their natural habitat.
- Check into one of the Tower rooms at the turreted **Glengorm Castle,** a 15-minute drive outside Tobermory.

Day 5: Tobermory

- After breakfast in the hotel, spend your morning exploring the colorful town of Tobermory before taking a whale-watching cruise with **Sea Life Surveys.**
- Have lunch a few miles from Tobermory in the **Bellachroy Hotel,** a typical Highlands inn, but be sure to check opening times.
- Pay a visit to the beautiful beach of **Calgary Bay** where you can visit the old crofting community of Invea.
- Head back to Tobermory for dinner and music at the lively **MacGochan's.**
- Bed down for the night at boutique hotel **Strongarbh House,** set just above the harbor.

Loch Lomond and the Trossachs National Park

For outdoor enthusiasts, there is little not to like about this sprawling national park that takes up large parts of Argyll and Bute as well as encroaching into parts of Perthshire, Stirlingshire, and the region just north of Glasgow, West Dunbartonshire. Way back in the 18th century, the Trossachs was a largely unknown enclave in the center of the country, but a chance visit here at the end of the century by Sir Walter Scott, who was regaled en route with tales of heroics of the local Robin Hood, Rob Roy, resulted in his poem, *Lady of the Lake* in the early 19th century. The poem tells the tale of three men (one of whom is an incognito King James V) who fight for the affections of local woman Ellen Douglas, interspersed with descriptions of a war between the Lowland Scots and rival Highland clans.

Building on the already fashionable "cult of the picturesque," that had taken flight in England's Lake District, the poem was one of the first examples of literary tourism, and soon large groups of tourists began to descend on the Trossachs in search of the landscapes Scott had so eloquently described. Back then the infrastructure for such large numbers of visitors wasn't in place, but it sure is today. In 2002 Loch Lomond and the Trossachs was made a national park, and today it has lots of places to stay amid its glistening glens and fertile forests, as well as large areas of space for wild camping, boat cruises across the famous loch and its sister lochs, and lots of bike-hire places, hiking trails, and adventure sports to try. It's a land of marked contrasts, with the relatively gently rolling lowland landscape of the south giving way to steep mountains in the north and myriad lochs, rivers, woodland, and forests in between. Munro-baggers are spoiled with 21 munros to choose from (that's a lot more than Skye), including Scotland's most southerly, Ben Lomond.

ORIENTATION

The national park stretches over 720 square miles (1,865 sq km), with a boundary length of 220 miles (350 km). It is divided into four distinct areas. **Breadalbane** in the northeast, which runs into Perthshire, is home to small villages with a real local feel, forest walks, and dramatic views of its many mountain peaks. It's a tranquil place, where you can visit the grave of celebrated outlaw Rob Roy (who Sir Walter Scott immortalized) in the village of Balquhidder or trek to the roaring Falls of Dochart.

The **Trossachs,** just south of Breadalbane encompasses both the Queen Elizabeth Forest Park and the Great Trossachs Forest National Nature Reserve, both of which offer Narnia-like trails beneath huge canopies of trees. **Loch Lomond** itself, the park's centerpiece, is the largest stretch of inland water in Britain, and though this is the most touristy of all four areas, it is still very beautiful. Pretty villages such as Luss, a heritage town that once housed workers from the nearby slate mines, and Tarbet farther north, are all overlooked by the mighty Ben Lomond.

The fourth area is the **Cowal Peninsula** in the west of the national park, on the far side of Loch Long, which includes the Argyll Forest Park, home to magical forest trails such as Puck's Glen, and the Arrochar Alps, where you will find the oddly shaped peak of Ben Arthur, known as the Cobbler.

VISITING THE PARK AND PLANNING YOUR TRIP

Unlike many of the national parks in the United States and elsewhere, Loch Lomond and the Trossachs National Park has no gates or fences. The main entry point to the park is **Balloch** in the south (particularly if you're traveling from Glasgow), but many people also come into it from Tyndrum and Crianlarich in the north, **Killin** in the northeast and either

Callander or **Aberfoyle** in the east (these latter two are particularly popular for visitors coming from Edinburgh or Stirling).

The national park's **official website** (www.lochlomond-trossachs.org) is a hugely useful resource. As well as offering tips of places to camp and advice on where to access services, it also has really handy maps and inspiring scenic routes that can be downloaded for free. The **VisitScotland iCentre** (The Old Station Building; tel. 01389 753 533; 10am-5pm daily) is located just opposite Balloch train station. Staff will furnish you with a map and give you some ideas of how to spend your time here.

If you are planning to attempt one of the munros or longer mountain hikes, then familiarize yourself with some safety measures. **Mountaineering Scotland** provides an easy-to-follow guide on the essential skills (www.mountaineering. scot/safety-and-skills). Meanwhile, **Walk Highlands** (www.walkhighlands.co.uk) has detailed route maps of some of the most popular walks in and around the park. If you are planning to **camp** in one of the park's hotspots between March and September, then **book a permit** well in advance as spaces are limited (www.lochlomond-trossachs. org/things-to-do/camping/get-a-permit). And, if you are coming during the summer months, keep one step ahead of the fearsome midges (groups of irritating flies that tend to travel in swarms) by checking out the **midges forecast** (www.smidgeup.com/ midge-forecast).

The park is geared up to visitors: there are picnic benches, barbecue stands, toilets, and scenic viewpoints all around (mostly well waymarked). It's a huge park best enjoyed on foot, by bike or on the water, though a car is really useful if you want to cover bigger distances. You really should allow yourself a few days here. If you are planning to explore the northeast of the park, Killin and Balquhidder are good places to base yourself. For the Trossachs, both Aberfoyle and Callander are good entry points. Luss

Loch Lomond and the Trossachs National Park

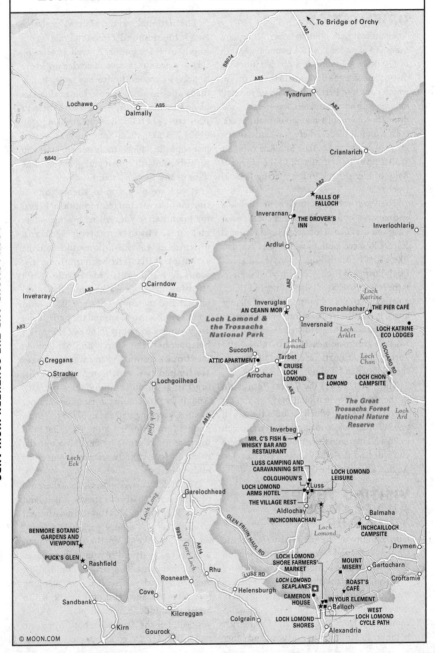

To Bridge of Orchy

B8074

A85

A85

Lochawe

Dalmally

Tyndrum

A82

B840

Crianlarich

A82

★ FALLS OF FALLOCH

Inverarnan
☆ THE DROVER'S INN

Inverlochlarig

Ardlui

A82

Cairndow

A83

A83

Inveruglas
AN CEANN MOR ★

Loch Katrine

Stronachlachar ★ THE PIER CAFÉ

Inveraray

Loch Lomond & the Trossachs National Park

Inversnaid

LOCH KATRINE ECO LODGES

LOCHARD RD

Creggans

Strachur

Lochgoilhead

Succoth
ATTIC APARTMENT ●

Loch Lomond

Tarbet
★ CRUISE LOCH LOMOND

Arrochar

Loch Arklet

Loch Chon

Loch Ard

BEN LOMOND

LOCH CHON CAMPSITE

A814

Loch Goil

Inverbeg

The Great Trossachs Forest National Nature Reserve

MR. C'S FISH & WHISKY BAR AND RESTAURANT

Loch Eck

Garelochhead

LUSS CAMPING AND CARAVANNING SITE
COLQUHOUN'S
LOCH LOMOND ARMS HOTEL
THE VILLAGE REST
Aldochlay
INCHCONNACHAN

Luss
LOCH LOMOND LEISURE

Loch Lomond

Balmaha

INCHCAILLOCH CAMPSITE

Drymen

BENMORE BOTANIC GARDENS AND VIEWPOINT ★

PUCK'S GLEN ★ Rashfield

Loch Long

B833

A814

GLEN FRUIN HAUL RD

LUSS RD

Gare Loch

Rhu

Garelochhead

MOUNT MISERY

Gartocharn

Croftamie

ROAST'S CAFÉ

Cove

Rosneath

Helensburgh

LOCH LOMOND SHORE FARMERS' MARKET

LOCH LOMOND SEAPLANES
CAMERON HOUSE

IN YOUR ELEMENT

Sandbank

Kilcreggan

Colgrain

Balloch

WEST LOCH LOMOND CYCLE PATH

Kirn

Gourock

LOCH LOMOND SHORES

Alexandria

© MOON.COM

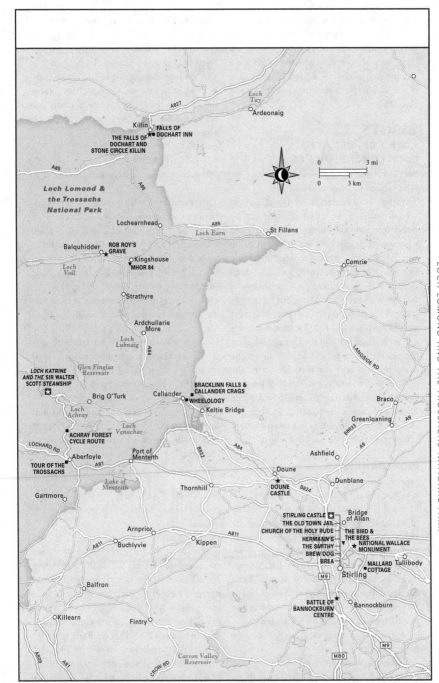

Loch Tay

A827

Killin

FALLS OF DOCHART INN

THE FALLS OF DOCHART AND STONE CIRCLE KILLIN

Ardeonaig

A85

A85

Loch Lomond & the Trossachs National Park

Lochearnhead

A85

Loch Earn

St Fillans

Balquhidder

ROB ROY'S GRAVE

Kingshouse

MHOR 84

Comrie

Loch Voil

Strathyre

LANGSIDE RD

Ardchullarie More

Loch Lubnaig

A84

Glen Finglas Reservoir

LOCH KATRINE AND THE SIR WALTER SCOTT STEAMSHIP

Brig O'Turk

Callander

BRACKLINN FALLS & CALLANDER CRAGS

WHEELOLOGY

Braco

Loch Achray

Keltie Bridge

Greenloaning

A9

Loch Venachar

Ashfield

A9

B8033

ACHRAY FOREST CYCLE ROUTE

LOCHARD RD

Aberfoyle

A81

Port of Menteith

B822

A84

Doune

B824

Dunblane

TOUR OF THE TROSSACHS

Lake of Menteith

Thornhill

DOUNE CASTLE

Gartmore

Bridge of Allan

STIRLING CASTLE

THE OLD TOWN JAIL

CHURCH OF THE HOLY RUDE

HERMANN'S

THE SMITHY

BREW DOG

BREA

THE BIRD & THE BEES

NATIONAL WALLACE MONUMENT

Arnprior

A811

Kippen

MALLARD COTTAGE

Tullibody

Buchlyvie

M9

Stirling

Balfron

BATTLE OF BANNOCKBURN CENTRE

Bannockburn

Killearn

Fintry

Carron Valley Reservoir

CROW RD

A809

A81

M80

M9

0   3 mi
0   3 km

and Tarbet are the best bases for the western shores of Loch Lomond (which, though busy, is the prettiest side of the loch), while on its eastern shores, Balmaha has some good camping. Arrochar is a good place to stay if you would like to venture into the Cowal Peninsula.

SIGHTS
Loch Lomond Area
LOCH LOMOND SHORES

Ben Lomond Way; www.lochlomondshores.com; 10am-6pm daily, outdoor areas never close

This tourism center is by far the most visited place in the whole park. It can be rather overrun in the height of summer, and some people might balk at the idea of going shopping in such a naturally beautiful setting (it has a large shopping mall, Jenner's, which is open 9:30am-6pm daily). Nevertheless, it does serve as a very useful nucleus for getting around the park on public transport (most buses stop here, and Balloch train station is a short walk away), and it's also a good place to stock up on necessities and book one of the many tours or services available across the park. You can look out for birds of prey, or swing through the trees (from £25 in the Tree Zone), and there's free parking. Most people come here to shop or hire equipment before venturing farther into the park proper.

INCHCONNACHAN

Near Inchtavannach, Loch Lomond

A visit to this little island on the west of Loch Lomond is a must, if only to see the colony of wallabies that have lived here since the 1940s—it's one of the very few places outside Australia where the marsupials run wild. Of course, the wallabies are not indigenous, meaning their presence does cause some controversy: some locals want them culled as they say they threaten the native capercaillie population (the island is one of the few places in Scotland where the giant grouse can be seen in the tree tops).

Passenger boats don't stop here, but you can reach it by hired motorized boat (with

skipper) or kayak from **Loch Lomond Leisure** in Luss, which also runs guided speedboat tours. A boat trip through The Narrows, the strait between Inchconnachan and the neighboring isle of Inchtavannach, is thought to be one of the prettiest places to cruise on the loch. Once on the isle, you are free to wander at leisure or simply paddle around its tranquil shores.

AN CEANN MOR

Inveruglas, on the northern banks of Loch Lomond; free

This viewpoint, which means large headland in Gaelic, was introduced to the park in 2015 and gives incredible vistas over Loch Lomond. It's part of a major government project to install viewing points throughout the park to help visitors engage with their surroundings more. Set off from the visitor center car park in Inveruglas, and follow the well laid out path through the trees for a couple of minutes until you find the strange wooden pyramid structure that is An Ceann Mor. You can either pass through it (best for those with limited mobility) or climb the 31 steps to the top of the structure for panoramic views from an elevated position along Loch Lomond and over to Ben Lomond to the southeast and the Arrochar Alps to the west. You can also walk down to the shoreline from the front of the structure if you fancy a little stone skimming.

FALLS OF FALLOCH

One mile north of the Drover's Inn, Inveranan, Arrochar

In the north of the park, these falls, the bottom of which are reached via a very easy 10-minute amble from the small car park, are often known by the slightly more romantic name of Rob Roy's Bathtub. The falls spill into pools below from a height of 30 feet (9 m), and, even following a particularly long dry spell in summer 2018, they were still in spate. Whether the bandit himself ever bathed here, we'll never truly know, but today the deep plunge pool beneath the waterfall is popular with wild swimmers who can cope with the freezing waters. Please don't attempt to jump or dive in from above the falls as this can be dangerous—the waterfall juts out a bit. There are plenty of other, safer spots from where you can plunge in from, such as the rocks that you can carefully climb down to the right of the falls (as you look at the waterfall).

The new "Woven Sound" viewing platform (made of a long trellis of woven-together steel rods) provides shelter for those who simply want to photograph or admire the thundering falls; etched into the dappled steel are some poetic words from Dorothy Wordsworth (sister of William Wordsworth), which begins: "Being at a great height on the mountain, we sate down, and heard, as if from the heart of the earth, the sound of torrents ascending out of the long hollow glen."

The Trossachs and Loch Katrine
THE GREAT TROSSACHS FOREST NATIONAL NATURE RESERVE
Enter at Inversnaid or Brig O' Turk; www.lochlomond-trossachs.org/things-to-see/great-trossachs-forest-national-nature-reserve

Within the confines of the park is this, one of the UK's largest nature reserves. Here a huge woodland regeneration plan is unfolding right before your eyes by returning heavily grazed land and plantation forestry to more natural landscapes through a mix of planting and natural regeneration; Highland cattle have even been brought in to trample the ground and spread the seeds from the trees, including birch, oak, willow, and Caledonian pine. Incredibly, the 200-year project, begun just a decade ago, aims to restore native woodland—unlike modern forestry, it is not densely packed with trees but has decent amounts of space in between too—as well as moorland, grassland, and montane scrub and thus encourage back indigenous wildlife. Already, dragonflies, golden eagles, and pine martens can all be seen, but it's also hoped that rare species such as the Scottish wildcat and red squirrels

will thrive too. So far, since the start of the project, black grouse numbers have soared by 700 percent.

But, while work goes up to improve the ecosystem, there is much to be enjoyed here too, including Loch Katrine, which sits in the center of the reserve and was the inspiration for Sir Walter Scott's *Lady of the Lake* poem, in which he wrote: "The Summer dawn's reflected hue / To purple changed Loch Katrine blue; / Mildly and soft the western breeze, / Just kissed the lake, just stirred the trees."

Camping is possible along the shores of the loch, though in summer there are a few by-laws in place, which means you may have to get a permit. The reserve is best entered from either Inversnaid to the west or Brig O'Turk to the east. The forest is crossed by the 30-mile (48 km) **Great Trossachs Path**—a walking or cycling route between Callander in the east of the park and Inversnaid at Loch Lomond in the west—from which many other routes snake off into looped trails through woodland and along lochside paths. You can choose to just do a small section of the Great Trossachs Path or walk or cycle its length. The path is waymarked, and, although it is rough or stony in places, it's easy to follow with lots of good smooth sections too (around Loch Katrine, it's tarmac). The path also connects to the West Highland Way, which links Glasgow to Fort William, and the Rob Roy Way, which goes all the way to Pitlochry in Perthshire, meaning long-distance walkers and cyclists can plot an epic trail.

★ LOCH KATRINE AND THE *SIR WALTER SCOTT* STEAMSHIP
Trossachs Pier; tel. 01877 376 315; www.lochkatrine.com/cruises/loch-cruises; two-hour return cruises from Trossachs Pier at 10:30am daily and Stronachlachar at 11:30am daily; round-trip tickets: adult £18, child £10, under 5 free, concessions £16.50, family £46, one-way tickets from adult £15, child £8.50, under 5 free, concessions £13.50, family £38, bikes £2 extra

This freshwater loch hidden away in the center of the park at the heart of the Great Trossachs

Forest National Nature Reserve—an area the size of Glasgow—is where you can board the famous steamship that has carried Victorian passengers across its waters since 1900. The loch itself, just eight miles (13 km) long—miniscule compared with Loch Lomond—is in many ways much prettier than its bigger sibling. Thick clumps of forestry line its banks, and its waters often glisten a vivid blue, reflecting the surrounding hills and mountains in their surface.

The Clyde-built *Sir Walter Scott* steamship, powered by a triple-expansion engine, is the last of its kind still in operation in Scotland. Passengers can view its workings as they glide across the loch just as Victorian day-trippers once did. The cruise from Trossachs Pier, at the southern end of the loch, to Stronachlachar on the northwest bank takes two hours round-trip; one-way trips also available. On the cruise, look out for Queen Victoria's Royal Cottage, a Gothic stone building intended to house the monarch when she visited the loch in 1859 but was not destined to be used because the 21-gun salute to welcome Her Majesty shattered all the windows. Also en route you can see the peaks of Ben A'an and Ben Venue, and at the northwest tip of the loch you can alight at Glengyle, the birthplace of Rob Roy MacGregor.

Bikes can be taken on board (though you should book them in advance), and there is a car park at Trossachs Pier. Many people book a one-way ticket from Trossachs Pier to Stronachlachar and cycle back along the scenic northern shore of the loch, where there is very little traffic. Bike hire is available with **Katrine Wheels at Trossachs Pier** (katrinewheelz.co.uk; £20 per day).

Breadalbane
ROB ROY'S GRAVE
Balquhidder Old Kirk

In the northeast of the park in this otherwise unremarkable graveyard lies the remains of one of Scottish folklore's biggest heroes, Rob Roy MacGregor, alongside the bodies of his wife and two of his sons—or so we are led to believe. Thousands of tourists make the pilgrimage to this quaint stone church on the outskirts of the village of Balquhidder each year, but many locals, particularly those of the rival MacLaren Clan, say the grave is a fake and nothing more than another example of MacGregor propaganda. Clan loyalties run deep in these parts, even after all these years.

The grave is found ever so slightly to the east of the ruins of the old kirk—the new parish church, which can be visited and holds some interesting mementoes as well as a detailed account of William Wordsworth and his sister Dorothy's visit, sits just above. The graves of Rob Roy (real name Raibert Ruadh MacGhriogair) and his family are guarded by a low black rail and the headstone is etched with the words "MacGregor Despite Them" in reference to the clan name that was outlawed.

THE FALLS OF DOCHART AND STONE CIRCLE KILLIN
Killin

These waterfalls, which tumble along the River Dochart, creating white water as they break over the many rocks before crashing down under the bridge in the village of Killin, may not be as high as some but are nonetheless beautiful. The best place to view them is from the bridge, where the sound of the rushing water as it makes its way to Loch Tay can be deafening. Look out for the island in the middle of the river downstream from the bridge. Known as Innis Bhuidhe, it is home to the burial ground of the chiefs of Clan MacNab.

If you are going to visit the Falls of Dochart in the northeast of the park, then it's worth going the extra half a mile to the nearby stone circle of Killin. From the village, head east along the river to the stone circle (which is actually more an oval shape composed of six dark gray slabs covering an area of around 33 feet/10 m by 28 feet/8.5 m that sits in a sheep

---

1: Falls of Falloch **2:** Benmore Botanic Gardens **3:** the *Sir Walter Scott* cruising on Loch Katrine

Rob Roy

The name Rob Roy probably rings a bell (largely because of the Hollywood film of the same name starring Liam Neeson), but how much do you know about one of Scotland's most famous outlaws?

Rob Roy MacGregor was born in Glengyle on the shores of Loch Katrine in 1671 in an area that now comes under the Loch Lomond and the Trossachs National Park, in Inversnaid. He was part of the MacGregor Clan who had been ousted from their land over three centuries before by Robert the Bruce, who gifted their lands to the rival Campbell Clan, and were treated as outsiders from thereon in. Indeed for many years it was illegal to even bear the name MacGregor and in 1693 Rob adopted the name of Campbell.

He fought during the Jacobite Rising of 1689 and was a well-known and respected cattleman who knew the land well, but after defaulting on a loan from the Duke of Montrose he was declared an outlaw. He then set about trying to seek revenge on his nemesis, who he blamed for his downfall, by wreaking as much havoc on him as possible. It was tales of Rob Roy's exploits of brigandage (living the life of a bandit) that Sir Walter Scott first heard on his early visits to the Trossachs that inspired his novel, *Rob Roy*, which ensured Rob Roy's story was immortalized. Later, William Wordsworth also romanticized the outlaw in his prose.

Around the north end of Loch Lomond and beyond, there are lots of places that bear Rob Roy's name, such as **the cave** where he supposedly hid out in that is conveniently, though sadly rather garishly, marked with the word "cave" on the rock. The **Falls of Falloch** are also known as Rob Roy's Bathtub, and you can visit his grave in the understated churchyard in Balquhidder in the northeast of the park.

field on farmer's land to your right). There is little known about the stone circle, though some slabs have cup marks, suggesting it is prehistoric, and there is some evidence of restoration, probably in the 18th or 19th century. The landowner seems happy enough to let visitors come and stand in the field; just make sure you close the gate behind you.

Cowal Peninsula
PUCK'S GLEN

Dunoon; http://scotland.forestry.gov.uk/forest-parks/argyll-forest-park/pucks-glen

This dark and mysterious ravine on the Cowal Peninsula, which hides tumbling burns, sparkling rock pools, and cascading waterfalls, offers a good short (but strenuous) walk that has a little bit of everything. It is located within Argyll Forest Park and shares a name with the mischievous sprite from Shakespeare's *Midsummer Night's Dream;* fittingly, locals have come up with their own spirit, Poca Ban, which apparently disguises itself as a ball of wool and rolls around the woodland looking for victims to terrorize. The 1.75-mile (3 km) walk winds along a Victorian walkway up the

gorge and passes several waterfalls. The gravel paths are firm but uneven, and there are some steep slopes and a long flight of steps.

BENMORE BOTANIC GARDENS AND VIEWPOINT

Benmore by Dunoon; tel. 01369 706 261; www.rbge.org.uk/the-gardens/benmore; 10am-6pm daily Apr.-Sept., 10am-5pm daily Mar. and Oct., fernery 11am-5pm daily Apr.-Sept., 11am-4pm daily Mar. and Oct.; adult £6.50, children free, concessions £5.50

Often overlooked by visitors, these mountainside gardens, also on the Cowal Peninsula, are renowned for their avenue of gigantic redwood trees, which create a grand and dramatic entrance, as well as hundreds of spectacular rhododendrons (not much-liked in Scotland as they are invasive plants causing problems for native fauna, but here at least they are kept under control). There are little pockets of calm by serene ponds and in both the Bhutanese and Chilean pavilions. The gardens are splayed out over 120 acres (49 hectares) and, as well as the redwoods, you will find Douglas fir, monkey puzzle, and native Scots pine trees. A highlight of a visit is the

Victorian fernery, a heated stone building accessed via a winding path and restored and reopened in 2009, where ferns cascade down the walls and carpet the ground.

For fabulous views, make your way through the exotic plantings to the viewpoint at 450 feet (140 m) and look out over the gardens themselves or across the glen to Holy Loch. **West Coast Motors** runs the **no. 489 bus** (25 min; www.travelinescotland.com; Mon.-Sat; £2.85) to the gardens from Dunoon several times a day (check the website for times). **Taxi George** (07913 601 442) runs a service on Sundays.

FESTIVALS AND EVENTS

LOCH LOMOND HIGHLAND GAMES
Balloch Country Park; tel. 01389 757 616; llhgb.com; July; adult £5, child and concessions £3, family £13
At the southern entry to the park, in the village of Balloch, these traditional Highland games take place every July. In addition to the usual piping, dancing, and caber toss, it also hosts two tugs-of-war (you can enter if you can persuade some teammates) and the 262.5-foot (80 m) Scottish Sprint Championship. Not to be taken too seriously, it's a fun day out even if you are just spectating.

CRUISES AND TOURS

CRUISE LOCH LOMOND
The Boatyard, Tarbet; tel. 01301 702 356, www. cruiselochlomond.co.uk; adult from £13
Offering cruises on the loch aboard one of six vessels, this family-run business has a range of itineraries, which set off from one of four locations. The 90-minute Rob Roy Discovery (£15) from Tarbet on the western shores of Loch Lomond, near Arrochar, includes a whisky coffee (for adults, and just instant coffee at that), which you can sip while being regaled with legends of the outlaw who supposedly hid in some of the caves (it's rather tackily daubed with the word "cave" outside). The large passenger boats have twin decks with an enclosed saloon below as well as an open deck on top, and, though they can get busy in summer, there's plenty of room for everyone.

The company also has bird-watching cruises and runs a **waterbus** (one-way from £10) between the east and west of Loch Lomond; it's quite common for people to use the waterbus simply to get from one side of the loch to the other, rather than doing a cruise. Crossings

Take a trip on Scotland's largest loch with Cruise Loch Lomond

include Tarbet to Rowardennan (best for Ben Lomond) and also Luss to Balmaha, along with lots of other routes. Cruise Loch Lomond also rents out bikes, with helmets and repair kits included, at very reasonable rates (£13 for up to three hours, £17 per day).

★ LOCH LOMOND SEAPLANES

1 John Street Lane, Helensburgh; tel. 01436 675 030; www.lochlomondseaplanes.com; 9am-5pm daily Jan.-Mar., 8:30am-6:30pm daily April-Sept., 8:30am-5pm daily Oct.-Dec.; from for a Classic Discovery/£139 for a Premium Discovery, Classic Explorer £149/£169 for a Premium Explorer

Board one of these light aircrafts for a memorable tour from above. Taxiing off from Loch Lomond from outside Cameron House Hotel, at first these tiny seaplanes are like speedboats picking up momentum as they whizz across the water, but pretty soon the nose of the plane starts to rise and you are airborne. Once in the air, the pilot acts as a tour guide, pointing out some of the sights down below, from old ruined castles, to lochs, glens, and mountain peaks. Afterward, you can reflect on the experience over a glass of prosecco. Discovery tours (Classic ticket £119) last 40 minutes (30 minutes in flight) and cover a distance of around 70 miles (113 km), giving aerial views of the park. On an Explorer tour (Classic ticket £149, 60 minutes), you will cover a larger distance and may head all the way out to the west coast of Scotland. Trips are dependent on weather, and routes may change. Occasionally, flights do need to be cancelled at short notice, so, if you're restricted about rebooking, then it's worth going for a Premium ticket for an additional £20, which allows a full refund if your flight gets canceled.

WATERSPORTS

LOCH LOMOND LEISURE

Luss; tel. 0333 577 0715; lochlomond-scotland. com; kayak from £20, speedboat £70 per half hour, speedboat tours from £160, bike from £14 for two hours or £30 for the day

If you'd rather get out on the water on your own (rather than joining a busy cruise), then this hire company based on the shore in Luss is a good option. You can rent out kayaks for a laid-back, gentle experience, or, for a bit more excitement, get your own speedboat (which comes with its own skipper). Lifejackets will be provided as will paddles for kayaks, but wetsuit hire is an extra £2 per person. The company also offers guided speedboat tours to some of the islands within the loch, and bike hire from a few hours to several days is available too.

IN YOUR ELEMENT

Loch Lomond Shores, Balloch; tel. 0333 700 7004; two-person canoe £45 for one day, £37 per day for two or more days, shuttle fee £80, TreeZone adult £25, under 18 £18

Though this outfit no longer has a hire base on Loch Lomond, they can still shuttle canoes to wherever you are staying in the area or wherever you want to get on the water, such as at Aldochlay Marina, near Luss, giving you easy access to the islands. Alternatively, if you want to save on shuttle costs and you have a roof rack or want to hire an inflatable one, you can pick up the canoes yourself. In Your Element still operates the TreeZone on Loch Lomond Shores too, where you can whizz down zip wires, walk tight ropes, and generally just try not to fall from the tree tops.

CYCLING

There are infinite possibilities when it comes to cycling through the park, from well-worn cycle routes to more off-road options. There are plenty of places to hire bikes if you don't have yours with you, and most ferries will accommodate them if you want to travel from one side of the loch to the other at no additional fee. The **Loch Lomond and the Trossachs National Park website** (www. lochlomond-trossachs.org) offers lots of suggested routes, which all come with their own downloadable route card.

WEST LOCH LOMOND CYCLE PATH

Balloch; www.lochlomond-trossachs.org/ things-to-do/cycling/cycling-routes/west-loch-

lomond-cycle-path

This is an easy route for beginners or reluctant cyclists who nevertheless want to cover a lot of ground in the park. Starting at the visitor center in Balloch, it pretty much follows the west shore of Loch Lomond, through the heritage village of Luss, all the way to Tarbet. It covers 17 miles (27 km) in all—34 miles (55 km) if you want to come back again—but it is mainly flat along a waymarked path, though one section of it does run alongside the exceedingly busy A82.

TOUR OF THE TROSSACHS

Aberfoyle; www.lochlomond-trossachs.org/things-to-do/cycling/cycling-routes/tour-of-the-trossachs

For those who want to exert themselves a lot more, this hard 31-mile (50 km) circular route takes you in a counterclockwise direction from Aberfoyle, north through Queen Elizabeth Forest Park, before skirting the north and west coast of Loch Katrine and heading back south, past Loch Arklet, and along the eastern shore of Loch Chon and the northern shore of Loch Ard, to Aberfoyle.

Setting off from Aberfoyle, the route sorts the wheat from the chaff early on by launching riders straight into the steepest path of the day—the challenging **Duke's Pass,** a sweat-inducing 2.4-mile (3.8 km) climb that has gradients of 6-11 percent and lots of sharp ramps. Those who do manage it, though, are rewarded with fabulous alpine views, as they ride past numerous rocky crags before winding down a road that twists and turns before joining a single-track road (though be alert as traffic may still come from the opposite direction) to Stronachlachar. Adventurists can continue on by climbing another road to Loch Ard via Loch Arklet and Loch Chon, which brings you all the way back to the beginning at Aberfoyle. If this feels a bit much, you can take the ferry from Stronachlachar to Trossachs Pier to rejoin the start of the route back to Aberfoyle, effectively cutting out around 6 miles (11 km).

ACHRAY FOREST CYCLE ROUTE

Aberfoyle; www.lochlomond-trossachs.org/things-to-do/cycling/cycling-routes/achray-forest

This intermediate bike route covers 14 miles (24 km) and takes you through the pine-rich heart of the Trossachs all the way east to Callander. You'll still encounter the dreaded Duke's Pass (only for 0.25 mi/0.4 km though), but once that is over with, you should have enough breath to look up and around, between forest climbs and sweeping descents. Keep an eye out for red squirrels, deer, pine martens, ospreys, and woodpeckers as you ride. There are lots of lovely spots to pull over for a picnic too.

KATRINE WHEELZ

Trossachs Pier, Loch Katrine; tel. 01877 376 366; www.katrinewheelz.co.uk; bike from £20 per day, £90 per week

For a cycling tour of Loch Lomond and the Trossachs, this outfit, conveniently located where you take the *Sir Walter Scott* steamer, hires out bikes for up to a week or more. Electric bikes, tandems, and trailers, as well as a good selection of kids bikes, are available with helmets provided.

WHEELOLOGY

4 Ancaster Square, Callander; tel. 01877 331 052; www.cyclehirecallander.co.uk; 9am-5pm daily Mar.-Oct., 9am-4pm Fri.-Mon. Nov.-Feb.; four hours £15, full day £20

This outfit, based in Callander, just east of the Trossachs, hires out mountain bikes, plus a selection of electric bikes (booking these in advance is advisable). It can also arrange for a cycling guide if you're not sure you want to go it alone.

HIKING

You can take numerous walks in and out of the park—both the West Highland Way and the Rob Roy Way pass through it—where meandering streams, lush forest, and moss-covered rocks are yours to discover. But, though on the whole the routes are waymarked, it doesn't take you long, once you turn off a minor road or start to ascend a mountain, to feel very isolated. While this may be just the effect you are looking for, make sure you are properly equipped with lots of drinking water, a map, sunblock, a hat, and midge repellent (particularly in summer). Here is a taster of some of the best walking experiences to be had.

★ BEN LOMOND

Trailhead: *Rowardenanan car park*
Distance: *7.5 miles (12 km) round-trip*
Hiking time: *4.5-5.5 hours*
Information and maps: *www.walkhighlands. co.uk/lochlomond/ben-lomond.shtml*

There is an incredible 21 munros across Loch Lomond—that's almost 10 percent of Scotland's total—so it's an ideal place to bag your first one. Scotland's most southerly, Ben Lomond, which looms over Loch Lomond, is a popular munro to bag but also relatively straightforward. Though it is popular, if you set off early in the morning, there's a good chance you can take in views of the length of Loch Lomond from its summit on your own.

The path for the most part is clear (though it narrows in places) and starts from just behind the information building in the car park. From here you will climb through oak woods first, followed by an area of cleared forest (which is being regenerated) and then open hill. Soon Loch Lomond will come into view on your left, and as you ascend at a steady gradient the views of the loch will become more spectacular. Keep following the path, which starts to zigzag up the mountain (less steeply than before), and then follow the ridge of the mountain before a steep ascent to the top, when the eastern corrie will come into view.

BRACKLINN FALLS AND CALLANDER CRAGS

Trailhead: *Bracklinn Falls car park, off Bracklinn Road*
Distance: *4 miles (6.5 km)*
Hiking time: *2-2.5 hours*
Information: *http://incallander.co.uk/bracklinn-falls-and-callander-crags*

This walk takes you through pretty woodland, past waterfalls (of course), and atop crags for views over the town of Callander as well as toward Loch Lomond and the mighty Ben Lomond. Set off from the Bracklinn Falls car park, from where it is well signposted to the falls. You will cross the peat-tinged river by bridge, and then you need to look out for a path to the left that rises into the woods upstream of the river. The track curves around as it ascends the hill. As long as you don't turn right you shouldn't get lost. After half a mile the track will drop down and pass by a waterfall and the deep Scouts Pool beneath the bridge.

On the other side of the bridge go through the gate and follow the path all the way up to the road. Turn left here and follow it for around a mile. Keep an eye on the numbers of the telephone poles—shortly after number 34 you'll see the path for Callander Crags marked, which will take you all the way to a ridge at the top. The cairn here was built to mark Queen Victoria's Jubilee, but you won't care too much about that because you'll be too busy catching your breath and looking out toward Ben Lomond to the north or Stirling Castle to the southeast. Follow this path back down to the minor road, turn right, and follow it all the way back to the car park.

MOUNT MISERY

Trailhead: *Balloch train station*
Distance: *6.5 miles (10 km)*
Hiking time: *2-2.5 hours*
Information: *www.hill-bagging.co.uk/ mountaindetails.php?rf=5011*

For day-trippers from Glasgow who are looking to squeeze a walk into their visit, the ascent to Mount Misery—named for the women who gathered on its summit in vigil for the men who perished in the Battle of Glen Fruin of 1603—affords views over Loch Lomond and is very doable.

From Balloch train station, turn right along the platform. Go past the Tullie Inn and then turn right again and cross the bridge. Follow the road on past the Balloch House, on your left-hand side. Follow the signs for Balloch Country Park. Turn into the park on your left-hand side and walk up the path in the direction of Balloch Castle. Take the path to the right just before the castle, follow for a few yards, and then turn right again. Follow this path all the way to the North Lodge exit of the park and then turn left up the hill, past the children's hospice of Robin House, which will be on your right.

This road continues for around two miles (3.2 km) until Lorn Mill Farm, which will be on your right, while ahead is the peak of Mount Misery (also known as the summit of Knockour Hill) for superb views of the loch and its islands. In total (there and back) this route climbs around 400 feet (122 m). Most of the route is hard paths with no mud so can be done in trainers.

GOLF
CAMERON HOUSE
Loch Lomond; tel. 01389 310 777; www. cameronhouse.co.uk/resort/golf.html; Carrick 8:30am-2:30pm daily, Wee Demon, 9am-1:30pm daily; green fees: Wee Demon from £10, Carrick £30, golf break packages from £245 per person, one-hour golf lesson £75

It's fitting that Loch Lomond's most luxurious resort comes with not one but two golf courses. The nine-hole Wee Demon, which overlooks the south of Loch Lomond, may seem genteel enough, but, as its name suggests, it has a few sneaky hazards, including sand traps and water features that swallow up many a golf ball. The 18-hole Carrick, meanwhile, has nine holes on low ground and nine on the high road, offering great views of the surrounding mountains and, of course, Loch Lomond itself, a natural bunker you'll want to avoid. In addition, there are golf break packages available and even golf lessons for sharpening up your technique.

FOOD
There are lots of good places to eat within the national park, from humble cafés to stop in mid-walk to cozy inns to replenish following a major hike—there's even the odd fine dining option for when you've had enough of working up a sweat on muddy trails.

Loch Lomond Area
ROAST'S CAFÉ
Loch Lomond Homes and Garden Centre, Balloch; tel. 01389 752 947; www.lochlomondgc.co.uk/ roasts-cafe.php; 10am-5pm daily; full Scottish breakfast £6.50/£12 for two, afternoon tea for two £14

Located within a garden center on Loch Lomond Shores, this is an unpretentious and really rather decent breakfast or lunch stop. Service is friendly and prompt and everything is homemade—there's even an on-site baker—and it offers good-value deals for two.

★ THE VILLAGE REST
Pier Road, Luss; tel. 01436 860 220; www. the-village-rest.co.uk; 10am-9pm daily; entrées £6.25

This casual and inviting café is pretty hard to resist when you are visiting the heritage village of Luss. Set in one of the lovely slate-roofed cottages where workers once lived, it's a good coffee or lunch stop or a welcoming place to indulge in some comfort food later in the day. If you're in need of a pick-me-up, you'd be a fool not to try the gateaux of haggis, neeps, and tatties smothered in Cognac sauce. Handy for anyone staying at the nearby Luss Camping and Caravanning Park.

COLQUHOUN'S
Lodge on Loch Lomond, Luss; tel. 01436 860 201; www.loch-lomond.co.uk/dining; breakfast 7am-10am Mon.-Fri., 8am-10am Sat.-Sun., lunch noon-4pm Mon.-Thurs., noon-5pm Fri.-Sun., afternoon tea noon-5pm daily, dinner 6pm-9:30pm daily, early bird menu 4pm-6pm Mon.-Thurs.; entrées £7.50

This elegant waterfront restaurant, named after the clan who once ruled these parts, is a little fancier than most in the park, but the white linen tablecloths and attentive service make it a place worth getting dressed up for. If you can, have a drink at dusk on one of the outdoor terraces where you may be able to spot some local wildlife. Mains include wood pigeon with Luss wild greens or Speyside lamb. Colquhoun's is also open for breakfast and lunch and does a good afternoon tea.

★ MR. C'S FISH & WHISKY BAR/RESTAURANT

The Inn at Loch Lomond, Inverbeg; tel. 01436 860 678; www.innonlochlomond.co.uk/dining; lunch noon-5pm daily, dinner 5pm-9pm; entrées £6.95
Set within the Inn at Loch Lomond, a Victorian tavern with rooms just three miles north of Luss near the banks of Loch Lomond (sadly no interrupted views), this informal restaurant serves a good choice of burgers, steaks, and seafood. Kids are well served with mini pizzas or chicken goujons followed by an ice cream sundae, while grown-ups should try the calamari and chips or a battered haggis supper. It has an extensive whisky menu too, and staff can talk you through it in a unpatronizing way. It's just a shame the views of the loch aren't better.

The Trossachs and Loch Katrine
THE PIER CAFÉ

Loch Katrine, Stronachlachar; tel. 01877 386 374; www.thepiercafe.com; 9am-5pm daily, 6pm-8:30pm Fri.-Sat.; entrees £6.25
This café, taken over by the current owners in 2007, has become something of a community hub in the quiet setting of Stronachlachar overlooking the serene Loch Katrine. The menu includes full cooked breakfasts in the morning to set you up for the day (and porridge, naturally), filled sandwiches, and rolls for those who pop in mid-cycle or walk, right through to stews in the evening on Fridays and Saturdays. Look out for a regular program of live traditional music too, the perfect accompaniment to the views.

Breadalbane
★ MHOR 84

Balquhidder; tel. 01877 384 646; mhor84.net; 8am-9pm daily; entrées £7; £90 d
This café-cum-bar-cum-restaurant in the

northeast of the park serves food throughout the day, starting with its house special of eggs Benedict in the morning, through to steaks, burgers, and seafood chowders from lunch to dinner time. It's well-priced home-cooked fare that is good enough to warrant a bit of a detour from your normal route. There are also some clean, affordable, retro-styled rooms.

Markets
LOCH LOMOND SHORE FARMERS' MARKET

Ben Lomond Way; www.lochlomondshores. com/2012/01/farmers-market; 10am-4pm first and third Sunday of the month
Stalls are piled high with fresh local produce at this twice-monthly market, which is a great place to pick up some bits for a picnic in the park or some ingredients for dinner round the campfire. Get there early to get the best offerings, which include pies baked that morning and delicious smoked fish.

ACCOMMODATIONS
Loch Lomond Area
CAMERON HOUSE

Loch Lomond, Balloch; tel. 01389 310 777; www. cameronhouse.co.uk; Cameron Club Lodges from £180 d (three-night minimum)
For out-and-out luxury on the banks of Loch Lomond, Cameron House has always been the place to go. Sadly, a fatal fire in December 2017 caused extensive damage, and a large and sensitive restoration project is now underway, with the new hotel rooms set to open in late 2019. Until then, the spa, two miles away at the Carrick estate remains open (with a complimentary shuttle service between the two), where you can relax in the rooftop infinity pool with gorgeous views of the lodge resort and surrounding mountains. You can also stay in the self-catering Cameron Club Lodges here, many of which have private terraces and balconies and sleep up to eight people. Both the nautical-themed **Boat House Restaurant** at Cameron House and the **Claret Jug** at the Carrick remain open while work goes on, and Cameron House

Marina is also where you can take a flight with Loch Lomond Seaplanes.

★ LOCH LOMOND ARMS HOTEL

Main Road, Luss; tel. 01436 860 420;
lochlomondarmshotel.com; £195 d

This impeccably presented country house hotel, in an old 17th-century coaching inn, is adorned in Scottish fabrics, with pretty cushions and woolen throws on the bed. The best rooms in the house are the Colquhoun Room, whose name is a nod to the clan that has made Luss its home since the 13th century, and the Lomond room, which comes with a romantic four-poster and even has a separate dressing room. Hospitality trays include shortbread, and there are Cinq Mondes toiletries in the bathroom.

ATTIC APARTMENT

Main Street, Arrochar; tel. 01301 702 704; www.
atticapartment.co.uk; £110 d

For a few more home comforts than camping but still well placed for the lochs and trails of the park, particularly those of Arrochar and the Cowal peninsulas, this studio apartment above a fish-and-chip shop and just a five-minute drive from Tarbet is a great little base, as long as you don't need lots of space. It can sleep two adults comfortably or a family of four as long as you are prepared to share beds (double bunks). There is good wireless Internet, but the biggest draw is the stunning view from the kitchen of Loch Long and the Arrochar Alps—a lovely spot to sip your morning coffee. Be aware, though, there is a flight of steps up to it.

THE DROVER'S INN

North Loch Lomond, Inverarnan; tel. 01301 704 234;
www.droversinn.co.uk; £99 d (with en suite)

This historic tavern—it is believed Rob Roy and later Samuel Johnson and James Boswell all enjoyed hospitality here—has 15 rooms in the main building, plus an additional 16 chalet-style rooms across the road and three new rooms (2017) in the Old Stagger Inn. Aside from its traditional candlelit pub with dark-wood furnishings and regular music sessions on weekends, many tourists visit this inn because of its ghostly sightings. The inn is said to be haunted by the ghosts of a crofting family who, having been forced from their land, got lost on the misty trails outside and succumbed to the elements. It's not perfect; the pub grub is OK and it's more than a little creaky in places, but it's all about the atmosphere really and quirky touches such as a cabinet of curiosities to peruse in a corridor off from the main pub.

If things that go bump in the night don't put you off, the nightly rate is reasonable—the three nights for the price of two deal offers exceptional value—and the rooms, which range from standard (with shared bathroom) to a whirlpool tub room and even the haunted room, are tastefully decorated. Plus, the views are exceptional.

The Trossachs and Loch Katrine

★ LOCH KATRINE ECO LODGES

Trossachs Pier, Loch Katrine, Callander; tel. 01877
376 315; www.lochkatrine.com/accommodation/pods;
Loch lodges £80 d, Ben lodges £40 d

Camping pods are popping up all over Scotland, and these ones, secreted behind a veil of trees, are simply lovely. There are eight pods (or lodges) in total. The pricier Loch lodges have under-floor heating, en suites, and their own picnic benches and terraces (great for stargazing). Meanwhile, the more basic Ben lodges are still cozy, with electric heating, but you'll have to share toilet and shower facilities and linen is extra. Both options offer a 20 percent discount off the *Sir Walter Scott* steamship.

Breadalbane

FALLS OF DOCHART INN

Gray Street, Killin; tel. 01567 820 270; www.
fallsofdochartinn.co.uk; £90 d

This three-star hotel in a former blacksmith's house has fantastic views of the nearby waterfalls and is well priced, considering. Rooms are small, but they have a certain vintage

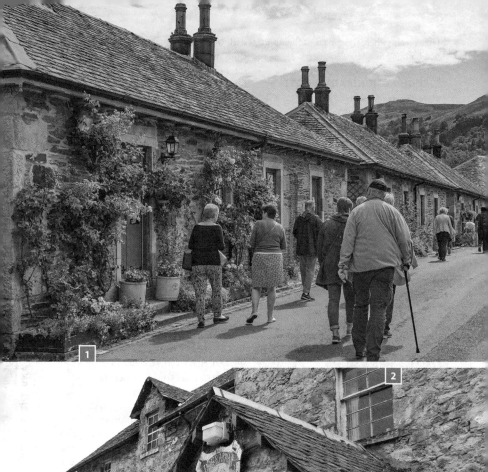

charm. Downstairs, there's a restaurant and an excellent bar with white stone walls, wooden floorboards, an open fire, and lots of Jacobean artifacts. If you're lucky, you may catch an impromptu folk music session; otherwise, there's usually some good Scottish music on the stereo in the pub.

★ Camping

Do you want to experience the ultimate freedom of pitching up under the stars? Thanks to the Scottish Outdoor Access Code, you can wild camp in most of the park as long as it is done responsibly (maximum of 2-3 nights in one place) throughout the year. From March to September some areas of the park are subject to bylaws, which means that, while you can camp there, you will need a permit, which costs £3 and allows you to camp anywhere within a designated area (though this only accounts for around 4 percent of the park in summer season). The bylaws are in place in some of the park's most popular lochside locations to protect the areas from environmental damage. Only a limited number of permits is given in each area to prevent overcrowding. For more information, visit the **Loch Lomond and Trossachs National Park website** (www.lochlomond-trossachs.org/things-to-do/camping).

For those who would prefer more structure, there are lots of good campsites that still offer a "wilder" experience with few amenities (just fresh water and composting toilets), many of which are lochside. For the camper who wants a little more comfort, lots offer full facilities with hot showers and electric hookup.

★ INCHCAILLOCH CAMPSITE

www.lochlomond-trossachs.org/things-to-see/inchcailloch; Mar.-Sept.; £5 per night

This pretty island on Loch Lomond is a nature

reserve and an idyllic camping spot. Only 12 people can camp here each night, and permits get booked up quickly. Access is by boat from Balmaha on the eastern shore of Loch Lomond, which must be arranged through **Balmaha Boatyard** (tel. 01360 870 214; www.balmahaboatyard.co.uk). The waterbus service from Loch Lomond Shores will also get you here. Once here, it offers a beautiful setting for remote camping, with forest trails through fields of wildflowers (the bluebells in May are particularly lovely). There is no drinking water, so stock up before you leave, and no refuse collection, so you will need to take any rubbish away with you. Public toilets are composting only.

LOCH CHON CAMPSITE

Aberfoyle; www.lochlomond-trossachs.org/things-to-do/camping/find-a-campsite/loch-chon-campsite; Mar.-Sept.; £7 per adult per night, under 16 free

This beautiful, tranquil campsite on the east side of the park, just outside the Great Trossachs Forest National Nature Reserve, is another example of a small, picturesque site with basic facilities and away from the tourist mass. Cloaked in woodland, it sits on the edge of Loch Chon, a sheltered water between Kinlochard and Inversnaid, which is said to be home to one of the world's largest population of fairies as well as a shape-shifting kelpie. There are 26 pitches (two of which are accessible), and, unlike many of the wilder campsites, you can bring your car here. Fire bowls are provided for making a campfire, and there are toilets and clean running water.

LUSS CAMPING AND CARAVANNING SITE

Luss; tel. 01436 860 658; www.campingandcaravanningclub.co.uk; late Mar.-late Oct.; £12.75 per adult per night, two-night minimum

If you are a more reluctant camper, then you may find comfort in numbers, which you will certainly find at this lochside campsite on the western shore of Loch Lomond. It's well facilitated too—there are proper toilets,

---

1: the heritage village of Luss, Loch Lomond 2: The Drover's Inn, Loch Lomond

showers, washing machines, and wireless Internet. It might lack some of the romance of wilder sites, but you'll be grateful of the pub within walking distance, particularly after a long drive. The site is run by the Camping and Caravanning Club, so only members can bring caravans and camper vans. However, anyone can book a tent pitch, though currently it has to be done by phone.

GETTING THERE
By Car
Loch Lomond is incredibly accessible from Glasgow. If you're coming by car, it's just a 35-minute drive (25 mi/40 km) from the city to the southerly entry point of Balloch along the M8 and the M898 to Erskine Bridge, where you will join the A82, which takes you all the way into the park.

Travelers setting off from Edinburgh can reach Balloch in an hour and a half (71 mi/114 km), also using the M8 to A82 route. Alternatively, it takes just over an hour to reach Callander in the east of the park from Edinburgh (54 mi/87 km). Take the M9 and B824 to Stirling and then the A84 to Callander.

From Oban you can reach Tyndrum in the far north of the park in an hour by following the A85 east for 36 miles (58 km). From Stirling, it's just 22 miles (35 km) west along the A811 (30 minutes) to Drymen in the southeast of the park, while from Perth, it's just 44 miles (71 km) west to Balquhidder in the northeast of the park, a journey time of 1.5 hours.

By Public Transit
The national park does try to encourage visitors to travel by public transport where possible. From Glasgow Queen Street, **ScotRail** (www.scotrail.co.uk) has trains every half hour to Balloch, with a journey time of 50 minutes (£5.60 each way). From Edinburgh, it takes two hours to reach Balloch by train, with trains every half hour and a change at Glasgow Queen Street (£17.60 one-way).

The **West Highland train line** (www.scotrail.co.uk/scotland-by-rail/great-scenic-rail-journeys/west-highland-line-glasgow-oban-and-fort-williammallaig) also passes through the park about six times a day (twice on Sundays) and stops at a number of stations. Alight at Arrochar and Tarbet (journey time 1.25 hours, £12.40 one way) to explore the western shores of Loch Lomond or the west of the park, while you should get off at Ardlui (journey time 1.30 hours, £16.30 one way) if you want to visit the north end of Loch Lomond.

GETTING AROUND
The best ways to explore the park are on foot, by bike, or by cruise. From Balloch station it's just a 12-minute walk through the park to Loch Lomond Shores from where you can catch a cruise or join one of the walking trails (pick up a map from the VisitScotland iCentre in Balloch).

By Car
You do not need a permit to drive in the national park, and parking is generally good and often free. There is a number of petrol stations throughout the park, including **Lomond Service Station** just outside Balloch, **Dreadnought Service Station** on the Stirling Road in Callander, and **MacTavish's** on Main Street in Arrochar.

The main A82 road links the towns along the western shores of Loch Lomond, including Balloch, Luss, Tarbet, and Arlui, all the way north to Crianlarich and Tyndrum. For Arrochar and the west of the park, turn west onto the A83 at Tarbet. From Crianlarich, you can turn east onto the A85 to explore the north and east of the park more fully. The main road east out of Balloch is the A811. Turn off at Drymen onto the B837 for Balmaha, or carry on for the left-hand turn for the A81 if you're heading to Aberfoyle.

By Bus
Bus routes through the park are relatively good (though far less regular than in the

cities, and some only run every two hours). A couple of operators run buses that go through the park, including **Scottish Citylink** (www.citylink.co.uk), which runs a service linking Balloch with Arrochar via Luss along the western shore (no. 976; £6 one-way) in just 25 minutes, though buses are infrequent (about three times a day). **Garelochhead Coaches** (www.garelochheadcoaches.co.uk) runs a direct service from Balloch to Luss (no. 305) roughly every two hours (15 minutes; £3.20 one-way).

By Boat

The main waterbuses in Loch Lomond are run by **Cruise Loch Lomond** (tel. 01301 702 356; www.cruiselochlomond.co.uk), which runs ferries out of Luss and Tarbet between mid-March through to the end of October (£10 one-way, £13 return, return tickets valid for five days). Both ferry ports run one service per day across to Rowardennan on the eastern shores of Loch Lomond, which is the jumping off point for Ben Lomond. From Tarbet the ferry leaves at 8:45am, arriving at Rowardennan at 9:30am, with the return ferry departing Rowardennan at 4:45pm, arriving into Tarbet at 5:30pm. For Luss, the ferry departs Rowardennan at 9:30am, arriving into Luss at 10am. The ferry taking you back to Rowardennan departs Luss at 4:15pm, arriving into Rowardennan at 4:45pm. There is also a service from Luss to Balmaha, farther south on the eastern shore, twice a day at 10:15am and 12:30pm, as well as waterbuses that connect Luss and Tarbet.

On Loch Katrine (tel. 01877 376 315; www.lochkatrine.com), there is a round-trip service from Trossachs Pier on the southern end of the loch, to Stronachlachar on the northwest shore, at 10:30am each day aboard the *Sir Walter Scott* steamship from late March to early January (£14 one-way, £17 round-trip). From late May until early October, there are also two additional trips (at 1:30pm and 4:15pm) aboard the modern cruiser *Lady of the Lake* (£11.50 one-way, £14 round-trip).

If you are cycling, it is possible to combine both lochs on a Two Lochs Tour via waterbus (www.cruiselochlomond.co.uk/two-lochs-tour) May-September, leaving Tarbet and traveling to Inversnaid and then cycling the four miles (6.4 km) to Stronachlachar to pick up the Loch Katrine ferry to Trossachs Pier. This is possible four times a day.

Oban and the Isle of Mull

This region just west of Loch Lomond is characterized by its lush greenery and miles and miles of coastline; there are lots of beautiful islands off the coast of Oban, plus numerous deep and alluring lochs within easy reach. There is a wildness about the place—a throwback to when much of the area was cut off from the rest of Scotland and ruled by the Lord of the Isles. In many ways this sense of separatism lingers in the many unique identities of the remote communities. But best of all, this adventure land where you can go hiking, wild swimming, and wildlife spotting is ridiculously accessible to Glasgow. When they're not working, this is where adrenalin junkie Glaswegians come to let loose.

OBAN

Oban is very much a gateway town. Most of the main amenities are clustered round the attractive and bustling harbor, and though it is a pleasant place to meander and watch the boats and ferries come and go in Oban Bay, there's little need to spend more than a day or two here while you are plotting routes to Mull and other islands that are nearby. Oban is well facilitated with several banks and shops to stock up at.

Oban and the Isle of Mull

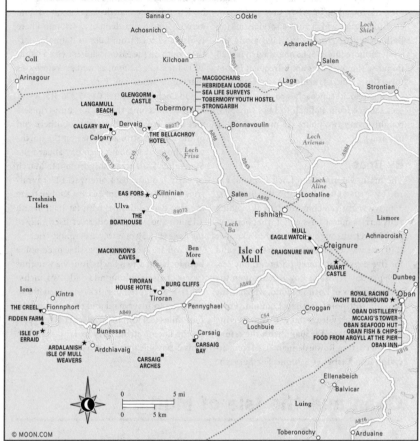

Sights
OBAN DISTILLERY

Oban; tel. 01631 572 004; www.malts.com/en-gb/ distilleries/oban; noon-4:30pm daily Dec.-Feb., 9:30am-5pm daily Mar.-Apr., 9:30am-7:30pm daily May-Sept., 9:30am-5pm daily Oct.-Nov.; Sensory and Flavour Finding Tour £10, Exclusive Distillery Tour £75

This small distillery in the center of Oban is one of the oldest single malt distilleries in Scotland, just set off from the harbor, and a good place to spend an hour or so, particularly if it's raining or you're waiting for a connection out to one of the islands. The distillery tours are popular so should be booked in advance. The one-hour Sensory and Flavour Finding Tour is a good introduction into the process of making Oban whisky and includes a tasting straight from the cask. Meanwhile, the Exclusive Distillery Tour (two hours) gives you access to the warehouse and includes an in-depth tasting in the manager's office. If tours are booked, it's still worth popping in for a tasting at the bar.

1: Pick up a bottle of single malt or do a tour at Oban Distillery. **2:** The Colosseum-like appearance of McCaig's Tower is an unexpected sight in Oban. **3:** Oban's busy harbor

MCCAIG'S TOWER

Duncraggan Road, Oban

This rather odd Colosseum-like landmark looks a little out of place towering over the traditional Scottish town. Often called McCaig's folly, it was built for local banker John Stuart McCaig in 1897 as a lasting monument to his family. McCaig intended for it to house an art gallery, but it was unfinished by the time of his death and his descendants refused to complete it. Only the outer walls were finished, and today, if you can cope with the steep 10-minute walk up here, it's a pleasant place to take in the views to Oban Bay and its many islands through the arched windows.

Tours

SEAFARI ADVENTURES

Easdale Village Shop, Easdale, Near Oban; tel. 01852 300 003; www.seafari.co.uk; tours from £42

If you are short of time, then these marine RIB (rigid inflatable boat) tours, which set off from the conservation area of Easdale, 16 miles (25.7 km) south of Oban, promise an exhilarating adventure. The company is based out of the village shop in the little village of Ellenabeich, on the isle of Seil (accessed by the Bridge over the Atlantic). Day trips include a two-hour trip to the Corrywreckan Whirlpool, the third largest whirlpool in the world (£42 per adult), a 2.5-hour whale-watching tour (£53 per adult, best booked in July and August when whales are in the area), or a full day trip to visit Iona and to see the puffins on Staffa (£90, best booked in spring and summer when puffins are in abundance). Wildlife tours run throughout the year, although from October to March you'll be aboard a cabin RIB.

Sailing

ROYAL RACING YACHT BLOODHOUND

Oban Marina, Isle of Kerrera; tel. 0131 555 8800; www.royalyachtbritannia.co.uk/exclusive-use/day-sailing-on-bloodhound; £222 for a day ticket, £2,220 for exclusive use

From August 2019, Prince Philip's 80-year-old Royal Racing Yacht *Bloodhound* will once again be available for summer sails from Oban Marina, crewed by the former yachtsmen who accompanied the Royal Family on their annual summer holiday around the Western Isles on *Britannia*. The 1930s sailing yacht was the very vessel on which Princess Anne and Prince Charles learned to sail. The yacht can accommodate eight people, and you can be as hands on or as hands off as your like. It's certainly not cheap, but it's a chance to explore the bays and inlets of some of the most beautiful Western Isles, including the isles of Lismore and Jura, aboard a historic yacht.

Food

Known as the seafood capital of the world, whether it's fish and chips to take away or lobster served in a posh restaurant, you have to try some of the seafood in Oban. But beware: if you opt for the former, you'll need to take cover (literally) as the seagulls here are vicious.

★ OBAN SEAFOOD HUT

Calmac Pier, Oban; tel. 07881 418 565; 10am-6pm daily; sandwiches from £2.95

Known by locals as the Green Shack, if you are getting on or off a ferry in Oban, you can't help but notice the gaggle of people huddled under a gazebo by this hut, tucking into trays of seafood. If you're rushing to get on a ferry, grab a ready-made prawn or fresh salmon sandwich, but if you have time (and are with a friend) get one of the seafood platters, which is just £12.50 for 2, or £25 for two for the Grand Platter, which includes lobster.

FOOD FROM ARGYLL AT THE PIER

Oban Ferry Terminal, The Ferry Pier, Oban; tel. 01631 563 636; www.foodfromargyllatthepier.com; 8am-5pm Mon.-Sat., 9am-4pm Sun.; bacon roll £3.90

Though there are a couple of tables, this is more a grab-and-go type of place than a sit-in café. A lot of people understandably stop in here before they board the ferry (though it's not open in time for the earliest ones) and it does simple breakfast items (porridge, bacon rolls, etc.) as well as coffees, toasties and chips.

★ OBAN FISH & CHIPS

116 George Street, Oban; tel. 01631 569 828; www. obanfishandchipshop.co.uk; 11am-11pm daily; entrées £6.30

I'd heard the hype (celebrity chef Rick Stein lauds it) and was skeptical but this is hands down the best battered fish I have ever tasted—perfectly seasoned and just the right side of crispy (still soft enough to bite into) without being too oily. The chips are good, too, but I've had better.

The fish tea special (£11), which is to be recommended, nay commended, comes with a thick cut of either haddock or cod, served with mushy (mashed peas, a common accompaniment to fish & chips across Britain) or house peas (it has to be the former, surely) and chips. You can also order white pudding, black pudding, Scotch pie, and specialties such as battered Isle of Mull scallops.

There is a dine-in restaurant, but they stop seating customers about 40 minutes before closing. If you're too late to eat in, don't be tempted to walk with your fish and chips to the harbor wall as you will be attacked by the relentless and aggressive seagull population;

stroll the streets away from the seafront instead.

THE WATERFRONT FISHHOUSE RESTAURANT

1 Railway Pier; tel. 01631 563 110; waterfrontfishhouse. co.uk; lunch noon-2pm, dinner 5:30pm-9:30pm daily summer, lunch noon-2pm, dinner 5:30pm-9pm daily winter; entrées £7.99

A little more upmarket than some of Oban's food establishments, this restaurant still manages to be more relaxed than its menu might suggest. Get stuck into a steaming bowl of local mussels or Isle of Mull scallops (a must) with smoked paprika butter. Oysters are also farmed locally, just north of Oban, and other dishes vary depending on what's been caught that day.

Pubs
★ OBAN INN

1 Stafford Street, Oban; tel. 01631 567 441; 11am-1am, food served noon-9pm daily; entrées £4.95

The Oban Inn—both the oldest and the best pub in town—is also one of its best meeting points and a good place to pick the brains of locals and other travelers. Thank goodness the Oban Inn reopened in 2016, having been closed for nine years. Still, it looks like it never

The battered fish at Oban Fish & Chips is second to none.

went away. The interior is reminiscent of Dickensian era (although it's actually the work of owner Maire Lynch and her vision of how it would have looked in the 19th century). Toby jugs and tankards dangle from the beams of the low-slung ceiling and a ship's wheel hangs on the wall. The pub's small size forces people to talk, so there is always a nice buzz about the place. There is music every weekend, and at other times you may find a guitarist or fiddle player sat on a bench willing to play if you buy him or her a pint. There's a real mix of tourists and locals, and, if you're looking for a whisky to try, you can't go far wrong with the Oban 14. There is a good pub food menu too. The pub forms part of a pretty terrace that includes a gallery, gift shop, handmade ice cream parlor, and a whisky merchant.

Accommodations

OBAN YOUTH HOSTEL

Corran Esplanade, Oban; tel. 01631 562 025; www. hostellingscotland.org.uk/hostels/oban; shared room £24 per bed (towels extra), private rooms £60 (including towels) d

Worth the trek out of town along the esplanade, this hostel is set within a Victorian villa and has waterfront views from its lovely lounge area. Staff are friendly and well informed, and, though the rooms are basic, they are clean. If you're staying in a dorm you need to pay extra for towels (£3 per person), and I'd skip the optional breakfast (which you need to pay for anyway) and head into town for something a little more appealing.

RANALD HOTEL

41 Stevenson Street, Oban; tel. 01631 562 887; theranaldhotel.com; £135 d

This smart, if a little bland, four-star hotel in the center of town is really handy for the train station and ferry terminal. The Ranald is part of the Metro chain and a continental buffet breakfast is included, which might not be to everyone's taste. Although the rooms are modern in terms of décor, they do lack character. Nevertheless this hotel is a good mid-range option.

★ **GREYSTONES**

1 Dalriach Road; tel. 01631 358 653; www. greystonesoban.co.uk; £135 d, The Turret £980 per week

Within an old baronial house with views of Oban Bay, this boutique B&B is more impressive than most. Breakfast, which is served in a spacious dining room with sea views, is good and options include smoked salmon and smoked haddock alongside a full cooked Scottish breakfast. Period features include cornicing, fireplaces, and stained glass, and there's also a luxury self-catering apartment, the Turret, which sleeps four.

Information and Services

Pop into the **VisitScotland iCentre** on the North Pier, where staff can help with accommodation and ferry bookings as well as day trips and free leaflets. The **Oban and Lorn Tourism Alliance** (www.oban. org.uk) offers useful tips on places to visit and where to stay. **Wild About Argyll** (www.wildaboutargyll.co.uk) is a tourism cooperative that represents lots of local businesses in Oban, on the isles, and in the surrounding area of Argyll and is jam-packed with local tips and ideas of how to spend your time here.

Getting There

BY TRAIN

Trains, operated by **ScotRail** (www.scotrail. co.uk) run six times a day from Glasgow to Oban, take just over three hours along the **West Highland Line** and cost from £19.80 each way. The route is spectacular: mountains peek over woodland and every now and then the lush greenery is broken by a loch, which appears for a few heavenly seconds before disappearing behind a bank of trees again, teasing you with its beauty. The trains are a little old and basic, but all that is forgotten when the scenery comes into view. You'll be willing the train to slow down so you can take it all in.

At Crainlarich in the north of Loch Lomond and the Trossachs National Park, the West Highland Line splits, with trains for Oban heading west and trains for Mallaig heading farther north. For Oban, as the train winds away from the water's edge near Crainlarich, the terrain becomes wilder and less predictable. Steep mountains reach up to the misty clouds, and the uneven ground gives way to lone boulders, broken up by the odd house, occasional stone wall, or field of sheep. There's no rush on this line—people (a mix of travelers and locals returning home) jump off at the small stations to get some fresh air and chat to the guards and everyone seems enraptured by the scenery.

If you're coming from Edinburgh, Stirling, or Perth, you'll need to get a train to Glasgow Queen Street and then take the train to Oban from there (52 minutes, 33 minutes, and one hour additional travel time respectively). Trains from Edinburgh cost £15.20 one-way and run five times a day, from Stirling they are three times a day and cost from £18.70 each way, and from Perth there are five trains a day and prices start at £26 each way. From Balloch, get the train to Dumbarton Central (nine minutes), where you can pick up the Oban train (five connections a day, from £13 one-way).

BY BUS

The no. 976 bus with **Scottish Citylink** operates three times a day between Glasgow Buchanan Bus Station and Oban (£13.70 one-way) with a journey time of just under three hours. The bus stops en route in Balloch, Luss, Tarbet, and Arrochar in Loch Lomond and the Trossachs Park. There are no direct buses from Edinburgh.

BY CAR

It's slightly quicker to drive from Glasgow (2.5 hours) rather than take the bus, and you'll still pass through Loch Lomond and the Trossachs National Park on your way. Just follow the M8 and the M898 from the city center to Erskine Bridge to join the A82, which takes you all the way to Loch Lomond and the Trossachs National Park. Follow the A82 north, all the way through the park until Tyndrum where

you will turn west onto the A85, which brings you all the way into Oban (total traveling distance is 97 mi/146 km).

From Tyndrum, north of the Loch Lomond and the Trossachs National Park, it's just 36 miles (58 km) west along the A85 (journey time 55 minutes). From Edinburgh, take the A90 west out of the city to join the M9 all the way to Stirling. From Stirling take the A84 northwest, into the Loch Lomond and the Trossachs National Park, via Callander and up to Lochearnhead in the northeast of the park, where you can take the A85 west all the way to Oban. The total distance from Edinburgh is 122 miles (196 km), with a journey time of just over three hours. From Stirling, it's 86 miles (138 km) and should take about 2.25 hours. From Perth, it's virtually a straight road along the A85 west for 94 miles (151 km) and should take around 2.5 hours.

MULL

Mull is perhaps the greenest island you will ever see, not to mention the most mountainous, and the natural beauty of its often wild landscape is balanced by its main town of Tobermory where colorful houses line its harbor. The most visited of all of Oban's islands, Mull is 36 miles (58 km) wide; by Scotland's standards, it's big, meaning there's plenty of space for all those tourists to share. It does take a long time to get around as most of the roads are single-track and winding, so, if you are driving, patience is a virtue.

It would take a lot to upset the air of calm on Mull. Otters roam its riverbanks, seals flop around in its sea lochs, and sheep often wander into the road, while cascading waterfalls are the only interruption to the thick slopes of pines and ferns. Highlights of a visit include the Burg Cliffs—dramatic basalt rock that look like terraces from the sea and where you can see the fossilized remains of trees or come across wild deer, goats, and eagles.

There's a good chance this tranquil isle will soon attract even more visitors as it was one of the places that the Duke and Duchess

Day Trips to the Isles from Oban and Mull

Oban is quite rightly known as the "Gateway to the Isles." Other than Mull, from its harbor you can also reach Lismore, Colonsay, Coll, Tiree, and Barra, and from Mull you can also travel on to Iona and Staffa. CalMac (www.calmac.co.uk) operates an extensive ferry service from Oban to the various isles. During the summer months the company also offers a range of day tours from Oban to some of the isles not served by their ferries—as do lots of other operators. Make sure you pick up a copy of the CalMac timetable at the Oban ferry terminal or train station, which is really useful (and a lot easier to decipher than the website).

LISMORE

Lismore, slightly north of Oban, actually sits in Loch Linnhe, the sea loch that marks the southern-most point of the famous Great Glen, which slices across Scotland all the way from Inverness down to Fort William at the head of the loch. Once a Celtic center for Christianity, today Lismore is best admired for its wildflowers (the Gaelic form of its name loosely translates as "great garden"). The ferry from Oban to Achnacroish on the eastern shore of the isle, only takes about an hour and costs £2.75 one-way for a foot passenger (£11.75 extra one-way if you are bringing a car). Once there, hire a bike and you will be able to explore most of the island (just 12 mi/19.3 km by 1.5 mi/2.4 km at its widest point), which includes numerous ancient brochs and cairns, with ease.

IONA

For a retreat from modern life, you can't beat the tiny isle of Iona—just 1 mile (1.6 km) by 3.5 miles (5.6 km)—which has been a place of religious retreat since St. Columba arrived in the 6th century and set up his monastery here. Iona is a very serene, spiritual place. The scent of the sea hangs in the air as does a sense of calm, and in between the day boats from Mull it's virtually empty, save a few sheep mingling in and around the abbey. If you can, spend a night here, or more, rather than cram it all into a day as most visitors do. It's just a 10-minute ferry ride from Fionnphort in southwest Mull (£1.70 each way).

of Sussex (Harry and Meghan) called in upon during their honeymoon aboard the *Hebridean Princess*. Hopefully, the royal connection will bring more of a trickle than an influx because a large part of Mull's appeal is the slow pace of life here and I wouldn't want it to change.

Orientation

Most visitors arrive into Mull at Craignure, the island's main ferry port on the southeast of the isle that connects with Oban. Tobermory, the island's main town, is on the northeast of the isle where many good restaurants and pubs and cute little gift shops can be found and is about a 40-minute drive from Craignure along the east coast.

Much of Mull's north coast is relatively

wild and inaccessible, which makes reaching the silvery sands of Calgary Bay on its northwest coast all the more special. Follow the main road (B8073) past Calgary a while, and you'll soon reach western Mull's most recognizable landmark, the distinct Burg Cliffs.

Fionnphort, the tiny little ferry slip from where you can catch the ferry to Iona, as well as meet boat trips out to Staffa, is located down on the southwestern corner of the isle. To reach it, you follow a long winding road from Craignure onto the Ross of Mull, a strip of land typified with black basalt cliffs that stand protectively over white sand beaches; here too you will find the venerable and spectacular geological feature known as the Carsaig Arches.

STAFFA

With its basalt columns and jagged terrain, Staffa is a distant cousin of Northern Ireland's Giant's Causeway. Most visitors come here to see its largest cave—**Fingal's Cave,** considered one of the wonders of the natural world—but it's also a great place to spot **puffins,** who breed here April-September. There are no ferry crossings here, just boat tours, such as the very good three-hour one from **Staffa Tours** (07831 885 985, www.staffatours.com) that departs from Fionnphort on Mull, or Iona's slipway.

COLL AND TIREE

The hidden gems of the dark sky island of Coll and its neighbor Tiree are not to be missed either. It takes 2.75 hours to reach Coll by ferry from Oban, and with just 200 residents it's easy to find peace and quiet among the many beautiful **beaches;** plus, with no street lights, it's one of the best places in Britain to enjoy **stargazing.** Tiree is a further hour crossing from Coll on the same ferry route. Tiree is renowned for its flatness (it's more like a raised beach) and its incredible **surf** as well as the annual **Tiree Music Festival** (tireemusicfestival.co.uk), which is a highlight of the calendar.

SEIL AND EASDALE

And last but not least, the "Bridge over the Atlantic," just a half-hour drive south of Oban, brings you to the island of Seil, from where you can get a short ferry over to Easdale. These two island communities, former "slate isles" (Easdale makes use of its surplus of slate by hosting the annual **World Stone Skimming Championships** each September), are celebrated for the defiance they showed in the face of the Dress Act of 1746. Brought in by the British government in the wake of the defeat of the Jacobites at the Battle of Culloden, the act effectively banned the wearing of Highland dress, including kilts. Residents of both Seil and Easdale refused to relent and continued to wear their kilts, only changing from their traditional attire at the inn by the bridge before coming to the mainland. The inn is still called the Tigh an Truish (www.tigh-an-truish.co.uk), or the "house of the trousers."

Sights
BURG CLIFFS

Tiroran, Mull; www.nts.org.uk/visit/places/burg; tel. 01681 700 659

If you do manage to take a boat trip out to Staffa from Mull, the sight of the Burg Cliffs as you pass along Mull's west coast is unmistakable. Millions of years of exposure to the Atlantic forces have shaped and sculpted the rock face here into what looks like perfectly lined terraces. However, while the view from the sea is special, you can't beat walking amid the wild and craggy landscape that makes up much of Mull's west coast and is a perfect example of Hebridean wilderness. A mix of rocky uplands, grassy lowlands, and wind- and sea-battered coast make it a unique place to explore; it is teeming with golden eagles, red deer, wild goats, and even otters along its rocky shoreline. In June look out for the rare Scotch burnet moth that lives here. Looked after by the National Trust, depending on the season, the cliffs could be a kaleidoscope of color thanks to an abundance of wildflowers or look barren and foreboding under heavy wintry skies.

Most visitors will want to see the ginormous **MacCulloch's fossil tree,** an imprint left in the cliffs some 50 million years ago, but this does entail a five-mile walk (10 miles there and back) from the car park at the Tiroran House Hotel. The route to the tree is along a rocky coastal path, which is not accessible for wheelchairs or buggies. Plus, at the time of going to press, the route was blocked following a huge landslide, with a detour including a tricky scramble across a boulder beach, so if you do want to visit it, check the current situation with the National Trust first.

DUART CASTLE

tel. 01680 812 309; duartcastle.com; 11am-4pm Apr., 10:30am-5pm May-Oct.; adult £7, child £3.50, family £17.50

The ancient seat of Clan Maclean, this castle is one of the first sights most visitors to Mull see as it seems to guard the entry to the island from the sea from its position atop a crag that juts out into the Sound of Mull. It's hard to believe it stood in ruin for years before being carefully restored in the early 20th century because it looks like a perfectly preserved clan castle, complete with a 14th-century keep with walls 10 feet (3 m) thick and huge curtain walls to ward off enemies. Inside, it's more grand stately home than medieval stronghold. The resplendent interiors, including the magnificent Great Hall, are filled with family heirlooms that give some insight into the lives of the Maclean Clan, while the ghostly dungeons are enough to prickle even the more conservative of imaginations. Though the castle is only open to visitors from April to October, you can visit the grounds and walk all the way down to the water's edge, past the lined-up canons, or just inspect the exterior at close quarters year-round.

ISLE OF ERRAID

Isle of Erraid, Fionnphort; tel. 01681 700 384; www. erraid.com

It is said that it was on this tiny island that Robert Louis Stevenson (author of *Treasure Island* and *Kidnapped*) first wished for a career as a writer (as opposed to that of a lighthouse man like his father who worked on the isle). Today people still make the pilgrimage to the "wishing stone" used by Stevenson in the hope that their wishes too will come true. However, others come to experience firsthand the sustainable lifestyle adhered to by a small spiritual community known as the Findhorn Foundation. Central to the beliefs of residents is the ethos of being with nature in its rawest form, helping them connect more fully with the land. Visitors are welcome too, with retreats of a week or more (from £250 a week) for all the family to explore the island and embrace the local environment. At low tide you can walk over to the isle from Knockvologan Farm on southwest Mull. At other times, access to the isle is by prior arrangement with the Findhorn Foundation, who will pick you up from near Fionnphort and ferry you over to the isle.

EAS FORS

A visit to this waterfall, which crashes into the sea from a height of 100 feet (30.4 m), is made doubly special when you drive via Salen, Gruline, and Ulva Ferry, along the shore of Loch Na Keal which is very popular for wildlife viewing. About two miles on from Ulva Primary School there is a large car parking area on the right, just before a bridge. Eas Fors flows under this bridge, and you will immediately see the upper falls. If you stay on the south side of the falls, you can access the lower falls and shore, but it is a bit of a scramble (and not suitable with children)—the safest way to access the lower falls (which are more dramatic than the upper falls) is to double back a half-mile or so, and walk along the shore from the field just beyond Laggan Ulva Farm, which will take you to a stony beach at the bottom of the falls (about 30 min.). Please note, when you reach the falls there is no barrier and the ground can be very slippery.

ARDALANISH ISLE OF MULL WEAVERS

Ardalanish Farm, Bunessan; tel. 01681 700 265; ardalanish.com; 10am-5pm daily summer, 10am-4pm Mon.-Fri. winter

In the southwest of the island, this sheep and cattle farm is where rural life and creativity using age-old techniques combine to produce beautiful and unique tweed and woolen products. The fleece from the Hebridean sheep on the farm and other farms on Mull is

1: Tobermory, Mull 2: Duart Castle, Mull

woven into beautiful items, from homewares to clothing and accessories, which can be bought in the on-site mill shop. Visitors can also take a tour of the weaving mill or try one of the homemade pasties that include some of the farm's own venison, lamb, and beef (meat can also be bought). From time to time, there are even short taster sessions if you'd like to have a go at hand-looming.

Beaches
CALGARY BAY

Dervaig; www.walkhighlands.co.uk/mull/ calgary-beach.shtml

This beautiful secluded beach, flanked by two craggy headlands, is a 30-minute drive from Tobermory on the northwest coast of Mull and faces toward the isles of Coll and Tiree. Its wide sands are backed by grassy machairs and dunes, and if you follow the path from the car park on the north side of the bay, you can see the remains of the old crofting community of Invea (the remains of around 20 houses can be seen), whose residents were cleared in the early 19th century to make way for more profitable sheep grazing. Calgary Bay has a sandy beach with shallow waters, making it safe for swimming. The nearby Art in Nature project in Calgary Wood makes for a good short excursion with beautiful artworks set amid the trees; plus, it has a lovely tearoom.

LANGAMULL BEACH

Mull; www.walkhighlands.co.uk/mull/ langamull-beach.shtml

This tricky-to-get-to beach on Mull's north coast has a wilder feel to nearby Calgary Bay (they're just over a mile apart). Its white sands are soft like flour, and it looks out toward Skye and the Small Isles. It's a bit of a walk to get here (you'll have to walk through a field of sheep at Langamull Farm), but it's worth it when you get here because the chances are you'll be the only person here. It's a great place to collect seashells too.

Park in the North West Community Woodland car park on the B8073 (marked with a colorful signpost) about halfway between Calgary and Dervaig). Follow the road through a gate on the left of the cattle grid, and then veer slightly left at the fork. Pass through a gate into a field—there's a good chance you'll be joined by grazing sheep or cattle; just keep a safe distance so as not to alarm them. Keep going straight ahead, going through another gate and veering to the left of the farm buildings. Keep left at all times, passing through several gates, until you see a sign directing you down to the beach. It's a lovely white sandy beach, with lots of rock pools to explore and one large pool that fills with water when the tide is in that is good for a dip, though swimming in the sea is fine too.

★ Wildlife Spotting
MULL EAGLE WATCH

Craignure Golf Club, Craignure; tel. 01680 812 556; mulleaglewatch.com; 11am and 2pm Sun.-Fri.; adult £8, child £4, family £20

These ranger-led tours are your best chance of spotting one of the swooping white-tailed eagles, which were reintroduced to Mull in the 1980s. You'll need to book in advance, pay in cash on the day, and come dressed suitably, with walking shoes and wet-weather gear if there's even the smallest chance it might rain.

SEA LIFE SURVEYS

Tobermory, Mull; Whalewatch Explorer 9:30am Tues., Thurs., and Sat. (adult £80, child £40, family £205) and 9:30am and 2pm Mon., Weds., Fri., and Sun. (adult £60, child £30, family £155), Ecocruz 1:45pm daily (adult £25, child £12.50, family £65)

These cruises set off from the pontoon in Tobermory between April and October and go in search of minke whales, common dolphins, and basking sharks as well as bottlenose dolphins, porpoises, and gray seals. Along the route, your skipper will regale you with tales of shipwrecks and clan battles. All sightings and findings are shared with the Hebridean Whale and Dolphin Trust, a conservation charity based in Tobermory. There are two options: the Whalewatch Explorer that lasts

4-6.5 hours (depending on the day of the sail) and the daily Ecocruz, which takes place in the sheltered waters of Tobermory and the Sound of Mull and lasts just two hours (best for small kids).

Hiking
BEN MORE
Trailhead: *Dhiseig*
Hiking time: *5-6 hours*

For a mountainous island, it's somewhat surprising that Mull has only one munro, but here it is: the mighty Ben More, which stands at 3,169 feet (966 m). It's a bit of a slog to the summit and very rocky in places, so not advisable for novices, but, if you are an experienced and skilled hiker, then Ben More is a rewarding experience. Many munro-baggers actually leave this climb till last because it's one of the few that you can reach from loch level, dipping your toes in the water before starting your ascent.

Park at Dhiseig by Loch Na Keal, which is a 45-minute drive from Tobermory taking the A848 south out of the town before turning right onto the B8035 at Salen for just under eight miles (12.9 km). Once parked, take the track up past the farmhouse (there's a sign that says helpfully "up"), follow the path of the burn Abhainn Dhiseig, and take the very steep path all the way up to the ridge for views to Ireland (on a clear day), Ben Nevis, and the Outer Hebrides. You'll feel on top of the world. The path is a mix of grass, stone, and scree and involves a fair bit of scrambling too along the ridge. You will ascend over 328 feet (1,000 m) and should allow 5-6 hours to go there and back. Beware that this volcanic rock is magnetic, so compasses are unreliable—come armed with a good map (OS Map Explorer 375) and make sure you know how to use it.

CARSAIG ARCHES
Trailhead: *Carsaig Pier, Mull*
Distance: *8.25 miles (13.25 km) round-trip*
Hiking time: *6 hours*
Information and maps: *www.walkhighlands. co.uk/mull/carsaig-arches.shtml*

On the south of Mull, these ancient sea arches are a genuine geological wonder, but getting here is no mean feat. Only to even be considered in the summer months, the 8.25-mile (13.25 km) trek here and back includes skirting the coastline and crossing rocky ground with narrow sections along a path where landslides are real possibilities. To reach the start point, turn off at the signed road just west of

Ben More caught with the evening light on the island of Mull

Pennyghael and follow signs to Carsaig Pier, where there is some parking. You'll then need to go back up the road on foot and turn left along the path marked "no through road." The Walk Highlands website has some good cautious instructions for following the path, including avoiding the high path and opting for the rocky shoreline instead. En route you'll pass the **Nun's Cave,** where apparently nuns cast off from Iona hid out, leaving their ancient markings inside. Today you're more likely to encounter a goat sheltering from the rain. You'll also pass a tall waterfall, and as the path evens out for a while you may even be able to enjoy views of the Paps of Jura and Islay, before eventually reaching the first of (and largest) of two craggy sea arches. The route there and back should take around six hours. (For an alternative route, consult *Walking in South Mull and Iona* by Olive Brown & Jean Whittaker.)

MACKINNON'S CAVES

Trailhead: *Balmeanach Farm*
Distance: *2.25 miles (3.5 km)*
Hiking time: *1.5-2 hours*
Information and maps: *www.walkhighlands. co.uk/mull/mackinnons-cave.shtml*

Is this the longest sea cave in the whole of the Hebrides? Perhaps—its immense depth has led to many a folk tale about the fate of 12 men here at some undefined time. Samuel Johnson wrote of some mysterious goings on in his *Journey into the Hebrides,* but he was short on detail. Versions vary, depending on who you speak to, but perhaps the most colorful is that a group of men from Clan Fingan led by a piper encountered a fairy in the depths of the cave. The fairy is said to have slain them all but spared the piper, who was promised he could keep his life if he continued playing as he retraced his steps out of the cave. He dutifully did so, but eventually, overcome with exhaustion, he could play no more and so the fairy killed him too. Whatever the truth, a journey here, though it involves some rock scrambling, is worth it to see if you dare go in as far as **Fingal's Table**—a

large flat stone in the deepest part of the cave that has its own legends.

Mercifully, this is actually a reasonably straightforward and short hike, covering a distance of 2.25 miles (3.5 km), which should take 1.5-2 hours, though you will have to cross some slippery boulders just before you reach the caves. Ideally, you should only really attempt this walk when the tide is still on its way out so check the tide tables to avoid a wasted journey. Park at Balmeanach Farm, and follow the tarmac lane, keeping to the left as it forks (it should be signposted). Go through the gate and climb the rough track to the left of the fence. Turn right and follow the path alongside the fence, which should now be on your right (it will be boggy). Eventually, you'll come to an iron gate to your right—go through this, go down through the grassy dip, and then follow the path round to your left. Soon there will be a ramp to your left, which will bring you to shore level; you should then cross the bay and look for a path up to your left just after the low section of cliff. That path will bring you to a grassy area that should take you round and over the boulders a bit more easily to an inlet just past the waterfall; by now you should see the cave entrance on your left. It's a long, dark cave (you'll need a flashlight to see inside) that narrows and widens in places.

Nightlife
MACGOCHAN'S

Ledaig, Tobermory; tel. 07733 794 535; macgochans-tobermory.co.uk; 9am-late daily; pints of beer from £3.50, single-malt whiskies from £3
This legendary local pub right in the harbor of Tobermory has good live music, with a rolling program of respected Scottish folk artists. There are few more rewarding ends to the day after a tour around the island than relaxing by the peat fire in the Bar-beag while sampling some single malts.

CRAIGNURE INN

Craignure; tel. 01680 812 305; www.craignure-inn. co.uk; 11:30am-11pm daily; pints of beer from £3.50,

single malts from £3

On the east coast of Mull, close to the ferry terminal, this drovers' inn may be petite, but it is big on character—it's the kind of place that you know would welcome you warmly in from the rain and pour you a drink, ignoring the mud on your boots. There is regular live music, from traditional jigs and reel to blues or folk.

Food

THE BOATHOUSE

Isle of Ulva, Dervaig; tel. 01688 500 241; theboathouseulva.co.uk; 9am-5pm Mon.-Fri. and Sun. June-Aug., closed Sun. Sept.-May; entrées £7.50

The Boathouse is just off the west coast of Mull on the isle of Ulva, and its commitment to serving local produce is impressive. The restaurant grows its own oysters, uses seafood caught by creel only, and bakes all its own bread. The menu is refreshingly small and simple: prawns served in their shell with garlic butter or oysters drizzled with lemon and tabasco, and all this in a quaint cottage setting. To reach Ulva, you need to take the small ferry across from **Ulva Ferry** (9am-5pm Mon.-Fri., Sun. June-Aug.). At all other times, you need to ring ahead to book it (tel. 01688 500 226).

TIRORAN HOUSE HOTEL

Mull; tel. 01681 705 232; www.tiroran.com; 6pm-9pm Mon.-Sat.; entrées £7.50

This is the only country house hotel on the whole of Mull, and, while the en suite rooms and three self-catering cottages are sweet with floral curtains and cute details, it's for owner Katie's Cordon Bleu cooking that most people come here. There's a venison cottage pie on the menu, and west coast smoked haddock fishcakes are very tempting. It's a little out of the way down some country lanes (it's not uncommon to have Highland cattle pass you on the road), so if you're here outside dinner service hours, pop into the **Whitetail Coffee Shop** behind the hotel (11am-5pm Sun.-Fri., check opening times in winter), which also makes its own gin and serves homemade snacks. A good food stop either before or after a walk on the Burg.

★ THE CREEL

Fionnphort Car Park; tel. 01681 700 312; 8am-late daily; entrées £4

A small shack perfectly positioned for day-trippers to Iona, it might not look like much, but you really don't want to miss the seafood here, most of which is caught by the owner Andrew. With langoustines, dressed

Buy fresh seafood from this hut by the ferry slipway in Fionnphort, Mull.

crab, kippers, and lobster—much of which is landed just the other side of the pier—it's hard to imagine a fresher catch elsewhere.

HEBRIDEAN LODGE

1 Baliscate, Tobermory; tel. 01688 301 207; www. hebrideanlodge.co.uk; 6:30pm-8:30pm Mon.-Fri.; entrées £7.50

Set on a mezzanine level above a gallery and shop, this restaurant, which is only open for dinners on weekdays is the go-to place for locals who want some home-cooked fare using local ingredients from the land and sea. The menu changes regularly, though it is always small, but it pretty much always includes half lobster with triple-cooked chips. There would be uproar if they removed it.

THE BELLACHROY HOTEL

Dervaig, Tobermory; tel. 01688 400 314; www. thebellachroy.co.uk; lunch 12:30pm-2:30pm Fri.-Tues., dinner 6pm-8:30pm Weds.-Thurs.; entrées £5.95

Dating from 1608, this is the oldest inn on Mull and began life as a stopping point for drovers (cattle herders). Set in the pretty village of Dervaig, it's not overly showy. The Bear Pit bar is atypical of a Highlands pub, but the food in the restaurant is good, honest Scottish cuisine: risotto, fish and chips, and steaks, served alongside local real ales, cheeses, and single malts.

Accommodations

★ FIDDEN FARM

Knockvologan Road, Near Fionnphort; tel. 01681 700 427; www.ukcampsite.co.uk; £10 per adult

Just two miles from Fionnphort, this campsite on the edge of another of Mull's white sandy beaches, Fidden, is a great place to get away from it all. There's little to do here except sit and watch the ebb and flow of the tide or look out for eagles above or dolphins and whales in the water, but isn't that the point? If you do feel the need to sightsee, catch the ferry to Iona, which has a similarly unhurried vibe. Toilets and showers are on site.

TOBERMORY YOUTH HOSTEL

Main Street, Tobermory; tel. 01688 302 481; www. hostellingscotland.org.uk/hostels/tobermory; bed in a shared dorm £20, four-person private room £96

Quite possibly the most photographed hostel in Scotland, this budget option is one of the bright properties that forms the colorful parade along Tobermory's harborside. It's well placed for the attractions of the town—shops, pubs, and restaurants—and many of the rooms have sea views. There's also a little garden out back for drinking your morning coffee.

★ STRONGARBH HOUSE

Tobermory; tel. 01688 302 319; strongarbh.com; £95 d, minimum two-night stay

This lovely period house overlooks Tobermory from up high, and, though it's set in its own spacious grounds, a private path will take you all the way down to the harbor. Inside, a curved staircase leads to the four stylish rooms: dressed in a contemporary take on Victoriana, two even have four-posters. The snug library is a lovely place to unwind after a day exploring, and, though there are tea- and coffee-making facilities in your room, you'll probably want to pop home for the complimentary afternoon tea served each day from 4pm-6pm.

GLENGORM CASTLE

Tobermory; tel. 01688 302 321; www.glengormcastle. co.uk, £195 d

Want to stay in a castle on your travels? Well, this baronial beauty may just be a little more affordable than you might think. Split up into five high-quality B&B rooms and one self-catering apartment, Glengorm offers Edwardian-style accommodation at a snip of the price elsewhere. In the Crannach Room, for instance, there's a wrought-iron bedstead and twin table lamps that look straight out of *Downton Abbey*; plus, it has both a Victorian bath and a walk-in shower. Guests at the B&B can also make use of the charming communal areas, such as the dining room (for breakfast), the main hall, and the library, where complimentary whisky is served.

DOBHRAN CROFT

Lochbuie; tel. 01688 400 682; www.
isleofmullcottages.com/cottage/dobhran-croft.html;
£750 per week

This quiet crofter's cottage sits alone in a field of sheep on the south of the island and has been renovated to a high standard while losing none of its rural charm. Outside it still retains its heritage look, while inside its walls are painted in vibrant colors and Scandinavian-style furniture adds a cool edge. The spiral staircase to the bedroom on the mezzanine level is stunning, though it certainly wouldn't be suitable for everyone.

Getting Here

Getting to Mull is fairly easy from Oban. **CalMac** (www.calmac.co.uk) runs a route from Oban to Craignure on the south of Mull, by far the most popular way to reach Mull, several times a day. The journey takes just over 45 minutes and costs £3.60 one-way, plus £13.40 if bringing a car. Arrive at the Oban ferry terminal (which is a bit like an airport lounge) a minimum of 10 minutes before your scheduled departure (longer if driving). Pick up a copy of the ferry timetables from Oban ferry port. It is invaluable because, as well as listing all sorts of ferry connections, it also shows how the buses on Mull link with each of the ferries. There is a good café on board serving cooked breakfasts and bacon or sausage rolls, as well as cereals and fruit for morning passengers and fuller meals at lunch and in the evening (burgers, macaroni and cheese, baked potatoes, etc.); plus, it has a decent kid's menu.

Getting Around

Many day-trippers who arrive on Mull are surprised to hear that they can't walk it all in a day, and, though there are buses—in particular, the ones that meet the ferries and transport people from Craignure to either the cute colorful port town of Tobermory to the north or to the miniscule ferry port of Fionnphort for crossing to Iona to the west— they are far from regular.

Buses on Mull are run by **West Coast Motors** (tel. 01586 552 319, www.westcoastmotors.co.uk). The bus takes about 1.25 hours from Craignure to Fionnphort (no. 496, four buses daily Mon.-Fri., three buses on Sat., no service Sun.), and from Craignure to Tobermory (no. 95 or no. 49), it takes just under an hour and buses are slightly more regular. Tickets cost £1.40 one-way, (£2.30 round-trip) for each route. If traveling by bus from Craignure, make sure you check the bus timetable before you book your ferry because only a select few are met by the bus, and this varies very much by the day and time of year. The timetables are available on the West Coast Motors website.

The best way to get around Mull is to drive; cars can be taken on the ferry from Oban with relative ease. If you do drive, you'll need to master the single-track roads quickly (learn when to pull aside to the left and when to go, and don't be too polite), but it's pretty hard to pick up any speed here, which should give you time to look out for some of the island's 5,000 wild red deer. In grassy areas hen harriers and short-eared owls are common, while golden eagles can sometimes be seen over the mountains in the center of the island. Don't despair if you get stuck behind one of the island's buses or coaches either—you can oft sneak in after them when traffic from the other direction invariably lets them pass. From Craignure to Tobermory it's a 40-minute trip north along the A849 and then the A848, while from Craignure to Fionnphort, it's an hour's drive west along the A849.

Some taxis are available if you don't have a car and would rather not be at the mercy of the infrequent buses. **Mull Taxi**, based in Tobermory (call Alan, tel. 07760 426 351; www.mulltaxi.co.uk), is reliable and will pick you (and your luggage) up from anywhere on the island and can take you on private tours too. Meanwhile, bike hire is available (also in Tobermory) from **Cycle Mull** (tel. 01688 302 923; www.cyclemull. co.uk) from £20 a day for a mountain bike or £25 for an electric bike; they will supply helmets, maps, and padlocks.

Isle of Islay

There is something of a paradox taking place on Islay at present. Tourism provides a brilliant injection to the economy, but locals fear that, with even more distilleries planned over the next few years—there are already eight across its 239 square miles (620 square kilometers) and a ninth set to open any day—it could turn into something of a whisky Disneyland. Whisky is a big draw for visitors here, it's true, but, with a wild landscape of bog and peat land as well as fertile farmland (though few trees), there's much more to the southernmost Inner Hebrides isle too, which is not known as the Queen of the Hebrides for nothing.

The people here are among Scotland's friendliest. The Ileach (plural Ilich), as they are called, have a strong sense of community and identity, and they're never too busy to stop to say hello or have a blether (idle chat). Other inhabitants include the red stags, whose bellows can be heard high on the hillsides in October, abundant birdlife, and the frequently spotted seals.

ORIENTATION

Islay lies just off the west coast of Scotland, accessed by ferry from the long arm of the **Kintyre Peninsula** of the mainland (the Mull of Kintyre that Paul McCartney sang of is just at the tip of this peninsula). There are two ferry terminals on Islay: Port Ellen on the south of the island and Port Arskaig on the northeast coast. CalMac runs services to both from Kennacraig on Kintyre.

If you land into the quaint town of **Port Ellen,** where there is a good hotel, some restaurants and shops for stocking up at, as well as a couple of nice-enough golden sand beaches, it's just a short drive east of the town to the three **"Kildalton Distilleries"** of the south: Laphroaig, Lagavulin, and Ardbeg, whose white-washed warehouses look out to sea along a pretty coastal road. Seven miles

(11 km) past the final of the three, Ardbeg, will bring you to the **Kildalton Cross,** a 9th-century Christian cross of note.

From Port Ellen it's also a relatively short drive (20 minutes) onto the stubby foot of the island (albeit largely by single track), a wild and fertile region known as the **Oa Peninsula** (you don't pronounce the *a*), an RSPB (Royal Society for the Protection of Birds) reserve, and also where you will find the commanding American Monument. To reach the peninsula, turn left at the Port Ellen Maltings on the outskirts of the town, follow the road for a few minutes, and then turn left onto the Oa (signposted).

The island's capital is **Bowmore,** home to a distillery of the same name, a 20-minute drive north on the A846 (past the airport), and built-up by Islay standards, though still attractive. From here, continue north to Bridgend, and then round Loch Indaal to your left to reach the **Rhinns,** an area once separated by sea but now connected to the rest of Islay by a thin strip of land. This peninsula, which juts out from the rest of Islay—some liken it to a witch's head—is home to arguably the island's prettiest village of **Port Charlotte** (all white-painted cottages tucked around a deep loch), as well as two of its distilleries: **Bruichladdich** on the east of the peninsula and the smallest enterprise, **Kilchoman,** on the west.

Northeast of Bridgend, along the A846, will bring you to the island's other port of **Port Askaig** as well as the northern distilleries of **Caol Ila, Bunnahabhain,** and the set-to-open **Ardnahoe** (as of 2018). Before you reach the ferry port, there's a turning for **Finlaggan** on your left, the ancient seat of the Lord of the Isles. A visit to the neighboring isle of **Jura,** where red deer outnumber humans by around 30 to 1, is also worth at least a day trip; a short car ferry ride can be taken from Port Askaig.

Isle of Islay

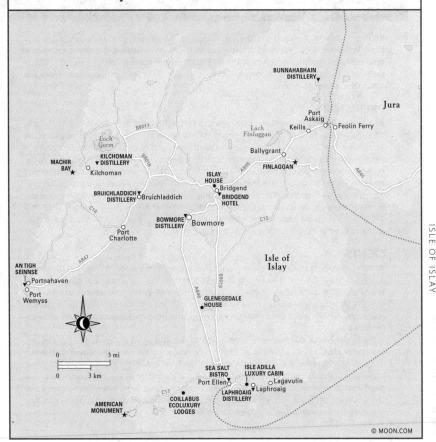

TOP EXPERIENCE

★ DISTILLERIES

Islay whiskies are generally renowned for being heavily-peated, a holdover from when the island's only abundant source of fuel was peat from the bogland, so it was used to dry out the barley during the malting process. The peat-tinged flavor proved popular and has come to define Islay whiskies ever since. However, while the whiskies of the south (Laphroaig, Lagaluvin, and Ardbeg) are known for their smokiness—they can

be a bit of an acquired taste, and some people find them too medicinal—the whiskies of the north are a lot lighter. All distilleries are geared up for visitors, and each offers tours, which are competitively priced and include a tasting of at least one of the distillery's expressions.

Laphroaig Distillery

Port Ellen; tel. 01496 302 418; www.laphroaig.com; 9:15am-5pm daily Apr.-Sept., 9:30am-5pm daily Oct.-Mar. (closed weekends Jan.-Feb.); tours from £10
Some people find this whisky, made on the

Detour on the Road to Islay: Kilmartin Glen

If you're traveling to Kennacraig for the ferry to Islay, you'd be remiss not to make a short detour to Kilmartin Glen, near Lochgilphead, whether you are coming from Oban or Glasgow (the main road from the former passes through it). With over 350 ancient monuments within a six-mile (9.7 km) radius of the village (many of them prehistoric), this is one of the most important archaeological sites in the whole of Scotland.

PREHISTORY

People have lived here for at least 5,000 years; its first settlers may even have arrived as long as 10,000 years ago. By the 6th century Dunadd in Kilmartin was the capital of the kingdom of the Scotti people—Celtic-speaking people who ruled large parts of what now forms Scotland and Ireland and who ultimately gave Scotland its modern-day name. Today the region is home to the highest concentration of prehistoric sites in Scotland, with countless stone circles, cairns, and standing stones (some of which feature bizarre cup-and-ring stone markings) placed surreptitiously in fields across the landscape. We can only speculate on what all of these were used for,. However, there's no doubting that this landscape was once rich in meaning and power. Dunadd crag has carvings of a footprint and a basin that are among Scotland's most intriguing and were probably used by the Lords of the Isles to transfer power.

SIGHTS

Visitors can learn more about the region at the very good, if a little dated, Kilmartin Museum (tel. 01546 510 278; www.kilmartin.org; 10am-5:30pm daily Mar.-Oct., reduced hours Nov.-Feb., phone ahead to check; adult £7, child £2.50, concessions £6, family (two adults and up to four kids) £14.50, from where you can buy a basic map for £1; plans are afoot to create a new museum. Make sure you visit the churchyard next door too, where there are headstones with centuries-old carvings.

While here, take the mile-long walk north of the village to the ruins of 15th-century Carnasserie Castle, which sits on a hill in a dominant position over the region. Staff at the museum can direct you. If you're hungry, stop in to the Kilmartin Inn (tel. 01546 510 250; www.kilmartin-hotel.com; sandwiches £6.95) in the center of the pretty village of Kilmartin. There is a good light-bites menu of baked potatoes and sandwiches, plus some fuller meals (scampi and chips, burgers, etc.), but portions are huge: sandwiches come with crisps and a nice salad. You can also get takeaway coffee, or crisps or chocolate bars to go.

south of the island, a bit too peaty. It's a bit like marmite: People either love or hate it. It is popular though and one of the more familiar names, plus you get three drams on the one-hour Laphroaig Experience tour. It's also located just outside the town of Port Ellen, the main entry point to the island, and visitors here often combine a visit to stop-offs at both Ardbeg and Lagavulin, also in the south of Islay.

Ardbeg Distillery

Port Ellen; tel. 01496 302 244; www.ardbeg.com; 9:30am-5pm Mon.-Fri. early Jan.-Mar., 9:30am-5pm daily April-Oct., 9:30am-5pm Mon.-Fri. Oct.-mid

Dec., closed Dec. 21-Jan.6; tours from £6

The farthest of the three southern distilleries along the winding road of Port Ellen (though still manageable on foot for many), Ardbeg has been legally distilling whisky for 200 years, and like Laphroaig, its whisky is heavily peated. You can take the Distillery Tour and Wee Taste (1.25 hours, Mon.-Fri. 11am and 3pm, no tours Dec. and Jan.), which start by taking you down to the pier in front of the whitewashed warehouses, where you will hear tales of how this distillery has weathered the storms of the past two centuries. Inside, you'll

1: the town of Bowmore, Islay 2: Ardbeg Distillery

be guided through the whisky-making process step-by-step, before choosing a dram to sample in a charming hidden tasting room. Many visitors stop here for lunch in the very good **Old Kiln Café** (12pm-4pm when distillery is open), which serves well-priced mains, such as fish pie or haggis, neeps and tatties with a creamy pepper sauce.

Bowmore Distillery

School Street, Bowmore; tel. 01496 810 441; www. bowmore.com; tours 10am, 11am, 1:30pm, and 3:30pm Mon.-Sat., 12:30pm and 2pm Sun. Apr.-Oct., 10:30am and 2pm Mon.-Sat. Nov.-Mar.; tours from £10

The first legal distillery on the island, Bowmore in the center of the town of the same name, malts some of its own barley (about 30 percent) and has the oldest maturation warehouse in the world. Amid its stone walls, on the one-hour tour you'll learn how they've been making their whiskies since 1779 using traditions passed down through generations. There are also more in-depth tastings that incur a higher price, and you can stay on site in either **The Harbour Inn** (www.bowmore. com/harbour-inn, doubles from £115 d) across the road or one of the **self-catering cottages** (www.bowmore.com/bowmore-cottages, cottages from £105 d) within the distillery complex. Bowmore produces a medium-peated malt, which is one of the island's most popular exports.

Bruichladdich Distillery

Port Charlotte; tel. 01496 850 190; www. bruichladdich.com; 10am, 1pm, 3pm, and 4pm Mon.-Fri., 10am, 1pm, 2pm, and 3pm Sat., 11am, 1pm, and 2pm Sun.; distillery tours £5, Warehouse Experience £25, Botanist Tour £25 (all one hour)

There is a breathtaking array of whisky made at this distillery in the southwest of Islay, from the un-peated Bruichladdich, to the heavily peated Port Charlotte, the eye-watering smokiness of the Octomore, and the distillery's brand of dry gin, The Botanist. A departure from the signature style of Islay whiskies, the normal (un-peated) range here has

a more floral flavor. Tours are famously generous, and even on the £5 tour you should be able to try several whiskies; the Warehouse Experience will give you the chance to taste straight from the cask, and the Botanist Tour is a chance to learn about and try the distillery's gin.

Kilchoman Distillery

Rockside Farm, Bruichladdich; tel. 01496 850 011; kilchomandistillery.com; 9:45am-5pm daily late Mar.-early Nov., closed weekends early Nov.-late Mar. Distillery Tour £7

Scotland's second-most westerly distillery (beaten only by Abhainn Dearg distillery on Lewis) and Islay's renowned farmhouse distillery is a popular place for those wanting to see how whisky is made from start to finish—the distillery harvests its own barley, and even the bottling is done by hand on site. It's set on a pretty farm, there's a good **café** here, and, with two drams plus a free glass thrown in, it is exceptional value too. The result of its slow distillation process is an intense and smoky dram.

Bunnahabhain Distillery

Port Askaig; tel. 01496 840 557; bunnahabhain.com; 10am-4pm Mon.-Sat., noon-4pm Sun., tour times vary in winter and summer; Quick Look Tour £5, Production Tour £7, Warehouse 9 Experience £25

Near Port Askaig on the north of the island, the whisky distilled at Bunnahabhain is much milder than its southern counterparts, and many find it a better introduction to the distinct malts of Islay. If you're short of time, the Quick Look Tour (30 minutes) will give you an overview of the distilling process and a wee dram, while the Production Tour (50 minutes) goes into a little more detail. One of the most popular tours, though, is the Warehouse 9 Experience (one hour), which includes tastings straight from the cask.

SIGHTS
Machir Bay

Kilchoman

With 1.2 miles (2 km) of golden sands, Machir

Bay on the Atlantic west coast of the Rhinns is one of Islay's most spectacular beaches, especially when it comes to sunsets. It's very accessible too—just a short walk over a bridge and through the dunes from the small car park, making it a great option for kids or the less mobile. It's also a good stop-off before or after visiting Kilchoman Distillery.

Kildalton Cross

West of Ardmore; free

Reached by following the coastal road from the three southern distilleries for a few miles, this early Christian high cross in the churchyard of Kildalton Old Parish Church dates from the 8th century and has stood on the same spot for more than 1,500 years. It's even believed to be connected to three similar crosses on the tiny isle of Iona, where St. Columba first brought Christianity to Scotland. It's incredible to think how old this 8.7-foot (2.65 m) cross is; the gray-green chlorite schist stone of which it is made has weathered well, and you can still make out some of the details carved into the rock face, including four inward-facing lions, the Virgin and Child on the cross head, and rich spiral work.

Finlaggan

The Cottage, Ballygrant; tel. 01496 840 644; www. finlaggan.org; 10:30am-4:30pm Mon.-Sat. Apr.-Oct.; information center £3

It's hard to overstate the significance of this loch, which was once the seat of power of the Lord of the Isles, chief of the Clan Donald, who ruled much of western Scotland for centuries. The reverberations of clan warfare can be felt here still. Two main isles were once used by the Lord and his privy: Eilean Mor and Eilean na Comhairle. It was from the second that charters pertaining to how matters should be decided were issued, and two of these remain today.

To get here from the A846 (toward Port Askaig), turn left about one mile after Ballygrant. After half a mile turn left again onto Finlaggan Farm (look out for animals in your pathway) until you come to the information center. You should pay the small fee inside, where knowledgeable staff will also give you useful background on the site. Follow the small path down over a bridge and onto the first island of Eilean Mor, where you can walk amid the ruins of this once ancient seat and settlement, thought to have been destroyed in the 15th century by Clan Campbell on the orders of King James V in retribution to an earlier plot between the Lord of the Isles and the English King Edward IV to wrestle power from James III. If the visitor center is closed, you can still visit the island of Eilean Mor (Eilean na Comhairle is not accessible), but you should put your fee in the honesty box provided.

American Monument

Mull of Oa

This monument commemorates the huge loss of life of U.S. servicemen in two separate ship sinkings in 1918: the sinking of the passenger liner *SS Tuscania* on February 5, which was transporting over 2,000 troops to France, and just eight months later *HMS Otranto,* which was ferrying troops to Glasgow. Many of the over 600 people to lose their lives (British soldiers among them) in the two tragedies are buried at the military cemetery at Kilchoman.

Standing high on a cliff on the Oa Peninsula, the lighthouse-shaped monument is a tribute to those who lost their lives and includes a plaque with words from then president Woodrow Wilson. It's a half-hour walk to get here from the RSPB parking spot, through a well-marked but muddy trail that crosses a field of sheep before ascending the headland. Once here, it is an exposed but beautiful spot (stay well back from the edge) with views over to Antrim in Northern Ireland, just 25 miles across the sea. If you are planning to visit for sunset, leave with enough light to make your way back down to the car park.

FESTIVALS

FESI LLE

Various locations; tel. 07914 675 228; www.
islayfestival.com

This weeklong celebration of whisky, traditional music, and Gaelic culture held at the end of May each year at distilleries and other venues across the isle is getting more popular each year, so book rooms well in advance and come and immerse yourself in the fun and inclusive atmosphere—Ceud Mìle Fàilte ("a hundred thousand welcomes" as they say here, and yes, that is the correct spelling in Scots Gaelic).

FOOD

★ BRIDGEND HOTEL

Islay; tel. 01496 810 212; bridgend-hotel.com;
home-baking from 11am, lunch noon-2pm daily,
dinner 6pm-9pm; entrées £6.95

This utterly unpretentious restaurant with rooms (£135 d) uses the freshest of local ingredients, including game from the Islay Estates and vegetables from the restaurant's very own garden. Try the likes of medallions of venison or baked hake with shellfish risotto. You won't be disappointed.

SEA SALT BISTRO

57 Frederick Crescent, Port Ellen; tel. 01496 300
300; www.seasalt-bistro.co.uk; morning coffee
10am-noon daily, lunch noon-2:30pm, dinner
5pm-9pm, takeaway 5pm-9pm; entrées £5.50

At this busy bistro-takeaway place, you can stop for a morning coffee if you are on your way to the ferry, sit down for a full-on dinner, or get takeaway fish and chips for an evening stroll.

AN TIGH SEINNSE

11 Queen Street, Portnahaven; tel. 01496 860 224;
12pm-4pm Weds.-Thurs., 12pm-8pm Fri.-Tues.; entrees
£5.25

Once the center of the island's lively ceilidhs (its name translates as "house of singing"), this

pub on the Rhinns Peninsula that looks more like a private residence than a public place is one of the best places to experience Islay hospitality. It also sells great seafood (a pint of prawns in their shells or fresh crab), and you might even hear the seals outside "singing."

ACCOMMODATIONS

ISLAY HOUSE

Bridgend; tel. 01496 810 287; www.islayhouse.co.uk;
£295 d

A grand country house affair, set amid 28 acres (11 hectares) of glorious grounds and overlooking Loch Indaal, the allure of Islay House is hard to deny. Each of the rooms is bedecked with beautiful period furniture. Some have four-posters and roll-top baths, but all have luxury bedding. There's also a good **restaurant** with a Michelin-starred chef.

GLENEGEDALE HOUSE

Glenegedale; tel. 01496 300 400; www.
glenegedaleguesthouse.co.uk; £160 d

This award-winning guesthouse, halfway between Bowmore and Port Ellen and very close to the airport, has just four rooms in the lavish home of Graeme and Emma, who make you feel every inch as though you are their personal guests. Rooms come with Egyptian cotton sheets, plus Highland chocolates on the hospitality trays—you'll even be met with home-baking and tea if you arrive between 3:30pm and 5pm.

ISLE ADILLA LUXURY CABIN

The Old Excise House, Laphroaig, Port Ellen;
tel. 01496 302 567; www.islaycabin.co.uk; £100
(two-night minimum)

For those who want a feeling of seclusion while still visiting the whisky distilleries of the south, this cute little cabin with a fantastic port window for taking in the magnificent sea views should do the trick. Accommodation is basic in a wooden-pod-style room that can convert to a double or twin beds, but it has heating and a kitchenette as well as an en-suite shower room.

1: the American Monument, Islay 2: Finlaggan, Islay, with the Paps of Jura in the background

★ COILLABUS ECOLUXURY LODGES

The Oa Peninsula, Islay; tel. 07824 567 435; http:// coillabus.com; £1,700 per week

This duo of luxury lodges, hidden away in the wilds of the Oa, offer impeccable accommodation in a remote location. With turf-roofs that are designed to blend into the landscape, the floor-to-ceiling windows in their living rooms are perfect for sitting by and just watching and waiting for the wildlife to come, from pheasants, to golden eagles and buzzards—it's even possible to hear red deer at night during rutting season. While not cheap, the lodges can comfortably sleep four in two huge en suite bedrooms, which have a five-star private spa feel to them, with your own sauna and an outdoor bathtub (with hot water of course), perfect for an unforgettable stargazing experience. Owners can also book mobile holistic therapists and have seafood platters delivered to your door (by prior arrangement).

GETTING THERE
By Ferry

The ferry to Islay departs from Kennacraig on the mainland. From Glasgow, the best way to reach Kennacraig is to take the A82 up into Loch Lomond and the Trossachs National Park all the way to Tarbet, where you'll turn left onto the A83, which takes you all the way to Kennacraig. The full journey time is around two and a half hours and you'll cover a distance of 100 miles (161 km). From Oban, you can reach Kennacraig in an hour and a half by heading south on the A816 before picking up the A83 at Lochgilphead, a distance of 55 miles (88 km). From Edinburgh, it's a 3.75-hour drive (150 mi/241 km) along the M9 to Stirling, before turning west onto the A811 to Balloch and then coming up the A82 through Loch Lomond before joining the A83 at Tarbet. Alternatively, there are three buses a day from Glasgow to Kennacraig with **Scottish Citylink** that take 3.25 hours (£18.60 one-way).

From Kennacraig, the ferry crossing takes 2 hours to Port Asking on the east coast of Islay and 2.25 hours to Port Ellen on the south coast; there are around four ferries a day with **Calmat** (www.calmac.co.uk). Cars can be taken on both ferry routes (which are entirely separate). The Port Asking ferries take just under 2 hours, while the Port Ellen crossings take 2.25 hours. Prices are the same for both ferries: £6.10 one-way and £13.40 round-trip

Coillabus Ecoluxury Lodges

adult passenger, £3.35 one-way and £6.70 round-trip child, plus £33.45 one-way for a car.

By Air

You can fly to Islay from Glasgow with **Logan Air** (www.loganair.co.uk), the most charming airline in Britain, but flights do book up early. Flight time is just 45 minutes, and flights cost from £50 each way—though the earlier you book, the more likely you are to get these prices.

GETTING AROUND

Once on the island you can hire a car with **Islay Car Hire** (tel. 01496 810 544; www. islaycarhire.com) from the airport or from either of the ferry ports, but with little competition, prices are a lot higher than on the mainland and can cost as much as £50 per day.

Alternatively, you can hire a bike from **Islay Cycles** (tel. 07760 196 592; www. islaycycles.co.uk) from Port Ellen and cycle from place to place—this is a pretty good idea if you are planning to visit the three southern distilleries as they are easily reached by bike. Standard prices are £20 a day or £70 for a week for a mountain bike, but do make sure you book well in advance; it's a small outfit and at present it only has one electric bike in its fleet (which costs £30 a day or £120 a week).

There are just two **bus** routes on the island, run by the local council: no. 450, which runs from Bowmore in the center of the island to either Port Ellen or Port Charlotte on the Rhinos (£2.75 one-way, £5.50 round-trip), and no. 451, which runs from Port Askaig in the northeast, down to Port Ellen in the south, and then along past each of the three southern distilleries to Ardbeg (£3.85 one-way, £7.70 round-trip). However, buses are not frequent, with two, perhaps three a day, and not on Sundays.

Carol's Cabs (tel. 01496 302 155; www. carols-cabs.co.uk) is the longest-running cab firm on Islay and, in addition to offering a standard taxi service, offers island and whisky tours.

Stirling

Once the capital of Scotland, it was from Stirling that kings and queens of old once ruled—an infant Mary, Queen of Scots, was famously crowned here in 1543—and history can be encountered throughout the city. Stirling is an attractive place that in many ways is just like a smaller version of Edinburgh, with its cobbled main street and imposing ancient castle sat atop a crag that can be viewed from most points of the city; it's a wee town that packs a big punch.

Stirling is perhaps most famous for being the scene of one of the most significant victories of the Scottish over the English during the Wars of Independence in which William Wallace and Andrew Moray caught English forces off guard at the Battle of Stirling Bridge in 1297, proving that at times infantry could defeat cavalry and giving Wallace's campaign to keep Scotland independent of England a lot of momentum. Wallace is celebrated in the city with the huge imposing National Wallace Monument, located near where the famous battle took place.

While the castle, which stands at the north of the city center, leads downhill into the Old Town, where many of the city's other main sights, such as the **Church of the Holy Rude** and the **Old Town Jail** can be found (as well as myriad restaurants and pubs), the **National Wallace Monument** is a 1.5-mile (2.4 km) trek to the northeast of the city over the new bridge. If you don't fancy the walk, the no. 52 bus from Stirling Bus Station will take you there, or in summer the 1314 hop-on, hop-off bus connects the castle with the monument. As well as its historic sights, Stirling is a great base from which to explore Loch Lomond and the

Detour from Edinburgh: Falkirk

If you're driving from Edinburgh, stop by Falkirk to see the world-famous boat lift and the eye-catching Kelpies and have a bite to eat, before continuing on to Stirling.

FALKIRK WHEEL

Lime Road; www.scottishcanals.co.uk/falkirk-wheel

This feat of engineering that connects the Forth & Clyde and the Union canals is the only rotating boat lift in the world. It attracts crowds of tourists who come to marvel at its mechanical workings, which demonstrate how Scotland has long been at the forefront of industrial technologies. There is a café where you can sit and watch the boats go up and down, or you can hire a boat and get out on the canals yourself.

THE KELPIES

The Helix, Falkirk; tel. 01324 590 600; www.thehelix.co.uk; 9:30am-5pm daily; adult £7.50, concessions £6.50, child free

This pair of giant horse heads may be a relative new addition to the landscape, but they have quickly become one of Scotland's most loved sights. Located a short drive from the Falkirk Wheel, the 98.4-foot (30 m) sculptures are both a piece of art and a demonstration of Scotland's engineering prowess. You can view them outside for free or step inside the Kelpies on a 30-minute tour, which will explain artist Andy Scott's vision. Get tickets from the Visitor Centre at The Helix.

THE SHORE AT CARRONSHORE

195 Carronshore Road, Carron; tel. 01324 570 658; www.theshorefalkirk.co.uk; noon-11pm Tues.-Thurs. and Sun., noon-1am Fri.-Sat.; light bites £5.95, entrées £4.50

Just a 15-minute drive from the Kelpies, this casual eatery specializes in seafood (including fresh scallops or mussels) and succulent steaks; food is served throughout the day. The Thursday steak deal (two sirloin steaks with all the trimmings, plus a bottle of house wine for just £29.50) offers brilliant value.

Trossachs National Park to the west, and it is very easily accessible from Edinburgh.

SIGHTS
★ Stirling Castle

Castle Esplanade, Stirling; tel. 01786 450 000; www. stirlingcastle.scot; 9:30am-6pm late Mar.-Sept., 9:30am-5pm Oct.-Mar.; adult £15, child £9, concessions £12

While Edinburgh Castle may hold the crown of Scotland's most-visited stronghold, Stirling Castle rivals it in terms of admirers. Few can visit the 16th-century castle from where Renaissance monarchs ruled (an earlier castle also stood here) and not be wowed by the ostentatious interiors of its palace or stirred by its tales of heroics and royal rivalries. It was to here that a young Mary, Queen of Scots, was whisked as a young child; indeed, special slits were carved into the battlements to enable the toddling queen to look out over her realm.

The present building dates from the 16th century, but a castle has stood on this site since at least 1107 when we see the first written record of it during the reign of Alexander I. Soon after, the castle was handed over to King Henry II by William the Lion to meet the demands of his ransom and so began a lengthy tug-of-war between the Scottish and English for control of the castle, which reached its peak during the Wars of Independence. It was once said that, if you held Stirling, you controlled Scotland. One of the most famous retakes of the castle from the English occurred during the Battle of Stirling Bridge in which William Wallace and Andrew Moray executed a magnificent defeat of English forces; a few decades later Robert the Bruce defeated the English at the nearby Battle of Bannockburn. Like Wallace, Robert the Bruce is celebrated in the city of Stirling with a huge statue near the Battle of Bannockburn battle site.

On first appearances the castle is not unlike Edinburgh, surrounded as it is on three sides by steep cliffs, but look closer and it is prettier, grander even, with a pair of rounded towers marking the main entry in. Once inside the castle walls, you are spoiled for choice. The Royal Palace's suite of six rooms, restored in 2011 to how they would have looked during the reign of King James V in the mid-16th century at the height of its role as a Renaissance palace, are typically grand and decorated with flashes of rich color. Don't miss the Stirling Heads—3.2-foot-wide (1 m) carved oak medallions featuring the images of monarchs, gods, classical figures, and nobles that once hung on the ceiling in the chamber where the king received guests—or the recreations of the incredibly detailed Hunt of the Unicorn tapestries (the originals are on display in New York), the likes of which would have hung in the castle in the 16th century.

Meanwhile, the Great Hall, the largest ever built in Scotland, is utterly conspicuous, rendered on the outside in Royal Gold harling, giving it a distinct soft orange-pink hue. Inside you can see the gallery where minstrels and trumpeters once performed at famously lavish feasts played out below—during the baptism of James VI's son, Prince Henry, the fish course was reportedly served from a giant model wooden ship from which cannons fired. Outside in the peaceful and discrete Queen Anne's Gardens you can sit in the shade of a 200-year-old beech tree.

It's worth noting that many visitors come to the castle on a day trip, so it's much quieter at the end of the day, from around 4pm onward. There is also a discount available if you visit both the Wallace Monument and Stirling Castle; show your ticket from one attraction at the other attraction to receive 10 percent off. It's more expensive to visit the castle, so, if you're wise, you'll buy your ticket to the Wallace Monument first.

National Wallace Monument

Abbey Craig, Hillfoots Road, Stirling; tel. 01786 472 140; www.nationalwallacemonument.com; 10am-4pm Nov.-Feb., 10am-5pm Mar., 9:30am-5pm Apr.-June and Sept.-Oct., 9:30am-6pm July-Aug.; adult £10.50, child £6.50

Towering over the city is this lasting tribute to

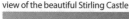
view of the beautiful Stirling Castle

one of the most celebrated figures in Scottish history, William Wallace, a patriot through and through. Though Mel Gibson's portrayal all those years ago may have romanticized the story somewhat, most Scots do still hail Wallace as a hero, not least for his role in the infamous Battle of Stirling Bridge, where bravery, balls, and a fair bit of luck saw rival Highland clans, united in their bid for freedom, win out against the English. The monument, which stands atop an old crag where William Wallace camped out before the battle with his army, was built in 1861 when the Highland Revival was in full swing—indeed, it's one of 20 or more Wallace monuments around Scotland.

Visitors to the monument often get here via the Wallace Way, a woodcarving trail that starts at the car park at the ticket office and continues up to Abbey Craig and the monument (15-20 minutes), though there is a free shuttle bus too. No expense was spared in the building of the monument, which stands 220 feet (67 m) high and is an example of Gothic grandeur, with a typical tower house topped with an elaborate crown spire (much like the one that stands atop St. Giles's Cathedral in Edinburgh) and a proud statue of Wallace beneath a crown, brandishing his sword victoriously.

If you just want to admire the monument from outside, there is no need to pay, but you would be missing out on fabulous views and the many treasures inside. Climbing the 246 spiral steps (which are very narrow and steep) is no easy feat, but with five stories in total, you can stop at each of the three galleries to break the journey up. In the **Hall of Arms,** on the first floor, you can learn about the Battle of Stirling Bridge, while in the **Hall of Heroes** on the next floor up, you can see Wallace's sword, protected by a glass case, as well as the busts of other Scottish heroes, including Robert Burns and King Robert the Bruce, though sadly no women; however, there is a slow-turning project to instate female figureheads such as Mary Slessor (a Scottish missionary) and Maggie Keswick Jencks (who, as she fought her own terminal cancer, devised a new approach to end-of-life cancer care).

The **Royal Chamber** on the next floor up is where you can learn about the construction of the monument (and there are some hands-on activities for kids), but other than catching your breath, you'll be eager to keep going to the pinnacle of **The Crown.** Stepping

The National Wallace Monument, Stirling

outside on top of the monument is a slightly dizzying experience, but, if you can handle it, you can see all the way to Ben Lomond and the Trossachs in the west and to the Pentland Hills to the east. If you can't manage the stairs, the **Keeper's Lodge** on the ground floor is a nice spot to rest or have a coffee.

Church of the Holy Rude

St John Street, Stirling; www.holyrude.org
This is the second oldest building in Stirling (after the castle), with the church founded in the 12th century (though the current building dates from the 15th century). Surely the most significant moment in the church's history was when King James VI was crowned here in 1567 with the sermon performed by none other than the pious John Knox who had campaigned for the overthrow of the king's mother, Mary, Queen of Scots. It's worth noting that James VI was just one year old at the time of his coronation. From its elevated position just downhill of the castle, at the top of the Old Town, the medieval church can be seen from throughout much of the city, but other than that, it looks like a fairly modest parish church and it still serves that purpose today. Inside, there is an impressive hammer-beam roof and some stunning stained glass. It's a good stop-off on your way up to the castle.

The Old Town Jail

St John Street; tel. 01786 464 640; oldtownjail.co.uk; 10:15am-5:15pm every half hour daily July-Sept.; adult £6.50, child and concessions £4.50, under 5 free
If you like your history played out for you in a dramatic fashion, then these performance tours of what was once labeled the "worst prison in Britain" should amuse you. Taking place over the summer months each year, the tours are a harmless foray into social history that, while hamming up certain aspects (horrible histories and horrific and gory punishments), are undeniably entertaining. It's an almost site-specific show; you'll be given a 25-minute tour and can then explore the cells and visit the observation tower for amazing

views of the city, which should take another half an hour or so. If you're not keen on over-acting, stay well away.

Battle of Bannockburn Centre

Glasgow Road, Whins of Milton; tel. 01786 812 664; www.battleofbannockburn.com; 10am-5:30pm daily Mar.-Oct., 10am-5pm daily Nov.-Mar.; adult £11.50, child and concessions £8.50, family £30.50
Learn more about this landmark victory for the Scottish during the first Wars of Independence at this 3D interactive experience, just two miles outside Stirling. At the Battle of Bannockburn, Robert the Bruce defeated the forces of the English King Edward II. The village of Whins of Milton, near the famous battle site, is just an eight-minute drive from Stirling, or you can get the no. 54A or no. 909 bus from Stirling Bus Station, which will get you there in minutes.

Doune Castle

Castle Hill, Doune; www.historicenvironment.scot/visit-a-place/places/doune-castle; 9:30am-5:30pm Apr.-Sept., 10am-4pm Oct.-Mar.; adult £6, child £3.60
This medieval stronghold eight miles outside Stirling has one of the best surviving great halls in Scotland, plus an impressive 100-foot-high (30.5 m) gatehouse. The castle was built in the 14th century to a courtyard design for the Duke of Albany and has changed very little since, a perfectly preserved slice of medieval history.

Its atmospheric timeworn walls, which, though slightly crumbling, are still intact, have led to it being featured on both the big and small screen. Firstly, it starred in the cult classic *Monty Python and the Holy Grail* in the 1970s (the audio guide is even narrated by Terry Jones of Monty Python fame). More recently, it has starred in both the pilot of *Game of Thrones* as Winterfell and in *Outlander* as Castle Leoch.

Once through the large gatehouse, you'll find another tower, slightly smaller, and a large courtyard enclosed by a high curtain wall. Explore cobbled tunnels, a cellar, and spiral staircases connecting the floors. The **Lord's Hall** (or Great Hall), with its double fireplace, carved oak screen, and musicians' gallery, is where lavish feasts would have taken place; in the kitchen, you can find out about the preparation that went into such boastful banquets.

GOLF

STIRLING GOLF CLUB

Queen's Road, Stirling; tel. 01786 464 098; www. stirlinggolfclub.com; 8am-5pm daily; green fees from £20

Located in the shadow of Stirling Castle, this 18-hole course certainly gets top marks for scenery. It's also one of Scotland's oldest and is kept in excellent condition. Staff are friendly and unstuffy too, offering a good all-round experience. Make time for a traditional Scottish lunch in the clubhouse.

NIGHTLIFE

CURLY COO

51 Barnton Street; tel. 01786 447 191; www. curlycoobar.com; 11:30am-11pm daily; pints of beer from £3.30, single-malt whiskies from £3.50

This small but perfectly formed whisky bar may be relatively new (2013), but it has the feel of a well-worn establishment. More living room than stand-off bar, it's the kind of place where chatter flows and folk mingle, both with bar staff and each other. There are 130 whiskies to choose from, plus a good selection of Scottish gins.

BREW DOG

7 Baker Street; tel. 01786 440 043; www.brewdog. com/bars/uk/stirling; noon-midnight Mon.-Thurs. and Sun., noon-1am Fri.-Sat.; pints of craft beer from £4.25

If beer is more your thing, then you won't want to miss this chain of craft beer pubs, which is one of Scotland's great success stories. You'll find Brew Dog bars in all of Scotland's main cities, and it does two things well—its own craft beer (there are 15 pumps here) and pizzas. Set up by two friends, who were in their twenties at the time, Brew Dog

has gone from a craft beer start up in 2007 to a major franchise with 46 bars (and counting) and 70,000 shareholders.

FOOD

THE BIRDS & THE BEES

Easter Cornton Road, Causewayhead; tel. 01786 473 663; www.thebirdsandthebees-stirling.com; lunch noon-2:30pm daily, dinner 5pm-11pm Mon.-Fri; food served noon-10pm Sat.-Sun.; entrées £5.90

In an old farm stead, this slightly grown-up take on pub grub—there's slow roast pork ribs and the fish and chips come with crushed minted peas rather than mushy—is a local hit worth heading a little out of town for. In winter cozy up by the fire in the bar, or in summer eat on the pretty garden terrace.

HERMANN'S

Mar Place House, 58 Broad Street; tel. 01786 450 632; www.hermanns-restaurant.co.uk; lunch noon-2pm, dinner from 6pm; entrées £5.90

Fusing Scottish ingredients with his Austrian hankering for schnitzel and strudel, chef and owner Hermann Aschaber seems to have hit a winning formula, which has proved pretty much impossible to top in over two decades. Try the pan-fried veal or the excellent-value set dinner menu. This is fine dining with affable and trouble-free service.

BREA

5 Baker Street; tel. 01786 446 277; www.brea-stirling. co.uk; noon-9pm Mon.-Thurs. and Sun., noon-10pm Fri.-Sat..; entrées £6.95

Just a five-minute walk from the Holy Rude church, this is a great place for a leisurely lunch once you've taken in the historic sights or a more extravagant meal with wine pairing come evening time. Using Scottish ingredients—seafood comes from the west coast—it serves a good choice of meat and fish dishes, plus there's a full vegan menu too.

LOVING FOOD

51 King Street; tel. 01786 357 953; www.loving-food. com; 8:30am-3pm Mon., 8:30am-5pm Tues.-Weds.,

8:30am-9pm Thurs.-Sat., 9:30am-4pm Sun.; cakes £4.50

This trendy bake shop delivers both on style and tasty grub. Fill up for the day with breakfast (served 8:30am-11:30am), or for lunch choose from the small but fine selection of sandwiches and flatbreads; fillings include harissa chicken with avocado and lime coriander. However, it's all about the cakes here really. Oh and the coffee, don't forget the coffee—quite possibly the best in the city.

★ THE SMITHY

73-75 St. Mary's Wynd; tel. 01786 449 142; 9:30am-4pm Tues.-Sun.; coffees from £2, pastries from £2:50

When it comes to coffee time in Stirling, most people agree that this little café in Stirling's Old Town is one of the best. Dating from 1595, the pub-like exterior hides a cozy interior that has a mix of high-back chairs and sofas to sink into. The most popular spot is in one of the two armchairs placed in front of the fireplace. Aside from freshly ground coffee, you can also treat yourself to some homemade pastries and cakes.

ACCOMMODATIONS

THE STIRLING HIGHLAND HOTEL

Spittal Street; tel. 01786 272 727; www. thecairncollection.co.uk/hotels/the-stirling-highland; £146 d

Part of the Cairn Collection of luxury hotels, this hotel is housed in a smart Victorian building on the site of a former convent founded by King James IV. Rooms are immaculate if a little soulless, but guests can make use of the well-equipped spa, gorgeously refined social areas, and even an old observatory, a relic from the building's former guise as a school.

PARK LODGE COUNTRY HOUSE HOTEL

32 Park Terrace; tel. 01786 474 862; www.parklodge. net; from £95 d

This beautiful Georgian mansion in an affluent part of Stirling, just a 10-minute drive (20-minute walk) from the city center, was restored and rebranded as a country house hotel, and it sure hits the mark. Four-poster beds, old writing desks, and a good restaurant make it feel like you have visited rich friends for the weekend. Plus, there are just nine bedrooms, giving it a much more personal feel than similar properties.

MALLARD COTTAGE

Bolfornought Farm; tel. 07712 824 269; www. gatewaycottages.co.uk; £765 per week

Just east of the city center, this two-bed cottage (sleeping up to six) sited in open farmland offers a rural escape while still close enough to visit the city attractions. Fitted out to a high standard, guests will also be treated to a welcome basket that includes home-baked scones or other treats, fresh flowers, and tea and coffee. In winter, an initial supply of wood for the wood-burning stove awaits you too.

FORTH GUEST HOUSE

23 Forth Place; tel. 01786 471 020; www. forthguesthouse.co.uk; £60 d

This lovely B&B in a Georgian stone townhouse is located slap bang in the middle of Stirling. The décor is borderline chintzy, with old-fashioned lampshades and patterned carpets, but you have to respect a place that still serves breakfast on bone china. Besides, at these prices you can cope with a few quirks.

★ CROMLIX

Kinbuck, near Dunblane; 01786 822 125; cromlix.com; £290 d, £595 suite

Owned by tennis superstar Andy Murray, this high-end hotel located just outside the star's hometown of Dunblane (only 10 miles north of Stirling city center), is a pretender to the throne of Scotland's best luxury small hotel—there are just 10 bedrooms and five suites, each elegantly dressed.

Rooms come with views of either the tennis courts (of course) or manicured gardens, while the five suites are named after famous Scots or in the case of the Eden suite (built into the turrets), after the former owners. You can play croquet or giant chess on the lawn, have dinner in the Chez Roux restaurant, take exceedingly good afternoon tea by the fireside or enjoy a nightcap in the snooker room. This is country house living at its finest.

INFORMATION AND SERVICES

The main tourist information center for Stirling is based in the **Old Town Jail** (tel. 01786 475 019). The **Your Stirling** tourism website (www.yourstirling.com) is a useful starting point with lots of inspiring ideas to help you shape your itinerary. For £25 (£14.95 for children), the **Stirling City Pass,** available from July to September only, gives you free entry to the town's major attractions (plus, no need to pay extra for audio guides, etc.) and lots of other local discounts. You'll also be given a free guidebook and map to help you navigate around the city. You can buy the pass online at www.yourstirling.com or at the Old Town Jail.

GETTING THERE

Stirling is easily accessible to both Glasgow and Edinburgh; you can get here from either city in under an hour.

By Car

From Glasgow it's just 26 miles (42 km), which should take you just 30 minutes in the car along the M8, M80, and then A872. From Edinburgh it's 36 miles (57 km), which should take about 50 minutes; take the A90, M9, and then the A872. From Perth, it's a 37-mile (60 km) drive southwest via the A9 to Stirling (about 45 minutes), while from Callander in Loch Lomond it's a 23-mile (37 km) drive southeast along the A84 (just under an hour).

By Train

If traveling by train, **ScotRail** has regular connections from Glasgow (three trains an hour, 27 min., £8.30 one-way) and Edinburgh (every half-hour, 50 minutes, £9.10 one-way). Stirling Train Station is located on Goosecroft Road, just a two-minute walk from the modern city center, longer to the Old Town.

To walk to the Old Town from the train station, go straight across the roundabout in front of the station onto Station Road, turn right onto Murray Place, turn left down Friars Street, and right onto Baker Street. Then take the first left onto Bank Street and right onto John Street, where you will find the Old Town Jail. It's just under 10 minutes altogether.

afternoon tea at the Cromlix

GETTING AROUND

The Old Town and Stirling Castle are both a bit of a walk from the modern city, but chances are it's in these more historic areas that you'll want to spend most of your time. Parking does fill up at the castle quickly in summer, and there is still a nice (but uphill) walk up to the castle.

If it's busy, use one of the city's **Park and Ride** bus services (www.parkandride. net/stirling/index.shtml), which will transport you to the castle and other main attractions. There are three Park and Ride car parks, which are well signposted as you drive into the city. The best one is probably **Springkerse Retail Park** to the east of the city center as buses are slightly more regular (every 12 minutes), but there isn't much difference between them all otherwise. Parking is free, but you'll need to pay £1.20 for an adult return on the bus, or 60p for a child return. Travel time is about 15 minutes, traffic depending.

From the bus station in Stirling (Goosecroft Road), which is adjacent to the train station, you can take the no. 52 bus to the Wallace Monument with **First Bus** (www.firstgroup. com), a journey of just 12 minutes (£1.60 one-way, 80p child). Over summer, the no. 1314 hop-on hop-off bus takes you from the castle to the National Wallace Monument (£2.50 each way single, £1.30 child, or £4.50 for a day ticket, £2.30 child's day ticket).

There are also taxi ranks at the train station, and **Saturn Taxis** (tel. 01786 811 111) is a trusted mini cab operator. Expect to pay around £4-5 for a taxi ride from the train station to the castle.

Perth

Known as the "Fair City" for its handsome location on the banks of the River Tay, the city of Perth, just 35 miles northeast of Stirling, is one of Scotland's most attractive centers. There are many culturally significant buildings to discover in and around the city, plus it's a good base for exploring the northern part of Loch Lomond and the Trossachs National Park.

It was near Perth that Kenneth MacAlp defeated the Picts, thus uniting two separate kingdoms and becoming the first King of Scots. The city's location near Scone Palace, where Scotland's kings were crowned for centuries, led to it being the effective ancient capital of Scotland, and it could even have become the modern-day capital were it not for the murder of King James I at the city's old Blackfriars monastery in 1437 (destroyed during the Scottish Reformation along with Greyfriars monastery following a rousing speech by John Knox in the city condemning Catholic idolatry in 1559).

The city was thrice occupied by Jacobite supporters during the various uprisings, but nevertheless it went on to become a center of major industries such as linen and whisky in the 18th century. Despite its continued prosperity, it has actually since been downgraded to status of "former city," much to the chagrin of locals who refuse to accept it (road signs still declare it the "City of Perth").

Its compact city center on the west bank of the River Tay is flanked by two areas of greenery: the larger North Inch, where the gory Battle of the Clans took place in 1396 (a deadly battle that seemed staged for the entertainment of King Robert III and his cronies), and South Inch, which also has a murky history as here witch trials took place in the 17th century. Thankfully, today you're more likely to see locals walking their dogs, picnicking or jogging in the two parks.

With streets of elegant houses and grand Victorian buildings, the modern city of Perth is a very appealing place to wander, and it is home to fantastic restaurants, good shopping, and a few very well-thought-of museums and galleries. It's location, just 14 miles (22.5 km) south of the Perthshire village of Dunkeld, also leads many people to refer to it as the "Gateway to the Highlands."

SIGHTS

★ Scone Palace

tel. 01738 552 300; scone-palace.co.uk; 9:30am-5pm May-Sept., 10am-4pm Mar.-April and Oct.; adult £12, child £8.50, family £40

Just 2.5 miles (4 km) north of the city center, this stately home, once the location for the crowning of Scotland's kings, is a must-see on any visit to Perth. Both Macbeth and Robert the Bruce were crowned on the famous Stone of Destiny (now kept in Edinburgh Castle) at the abbey that stood here until the 17th century. Like Blackfriars and Greyfriars, Scone Abbey was attacked by a mob following Knox's sermon, but it continued to function on some level for 90 years or so. The palace as it stands, originally built in the 16th century but restored in the 19th century, is more grand stately home than royal palace and has been the family seat of the Earls of Mansfield for almost four centuries.

Aside from the sense of history it's worth a day trip here to admire the stunning gardens and the splendid state rooms, some of the best in Scotland and home to exorbitant treasures such as fine porcelains, rare ivories, antiques, and paintings. It's like a history lesson in British period furniture too, with pieces by Chippendale and Robert Adams proudly on display. Ticket holders can explore the house and grounds at their leisure, though stewards all around can help answer any questions you might have.

Outside, **Moot Hill,** where you will find a small Presbyterian chapel, is the site of the historic coronations, and a replica of the famous Stone of Destiny sits in front of the chapel. There are beautiful walks through the grounds, including through the **Pinetum,** where you will find giant redwoods, noble firs, and conifers, and to the **Murray Star Maze,** planted with a mix of copper and green beech trees to resemble the tartan of the Earls of Mansfield. Though the palace

is only open March-October, there is free admission to the grounds, maze, café, and children's playground Friday-Sunday in February, March, November, and some parts of December.

Black Watch Castle and Museum

Balhousie Castle, Hay Street; tel. 01738 638 152; www.theblackwatch.co.uk; 9:30am-4:30pm daily Apr.-Oct., 10am-4pm daily Nov.-Mar.; adult £8, child £3.50, under 5 free, family £19, guided tour adult £12.50, child £7.50

Home to the most legendary of Scotland's Regiments, this museum and castle, adjacent to North Inch, is recommended for anyone with even the smallest interest in military history or Highland culture. Inside the museum, you can peruse diaries, weapons, and photographs of the regiment from the 18th century right up to the present day and also hear the story of the Black Watch regiment. The Black Watch regiment began life way back in 1725 when members of Highland clans loyal to the crown formed companies tasked with keeping watch for crime in the wake of the Jacobite Rising of 1715. Later, these companies formed a regiment that became renowned for its ferocity, and the distinct tartan of black and green is now one of Scotland's most recognizable. Located inside the baronial Balhousie Castle, the museum isn't huge, so you should probably allow an hour and a half, though there is also a café and gift shop on site. Guided tours, which take place at 11am and 2pm daily, are informative and give detailed analysis of the exhibits as well as personal stories of some of the members of the regiment. Book in advance.

Fergusson Gallery

Marshall Place; tel. 01738 783 425; www.culturepk. org.uk/museums-and-galleries/the-fergusson-gallery; 10am-5pm Tues.-Sat., noon-4:30pm Sun.; free

This gallery in the city's former waterworks is dedicated to the work of Scottish colorist

1: Scone Palace 2: beautiful riverside Perth

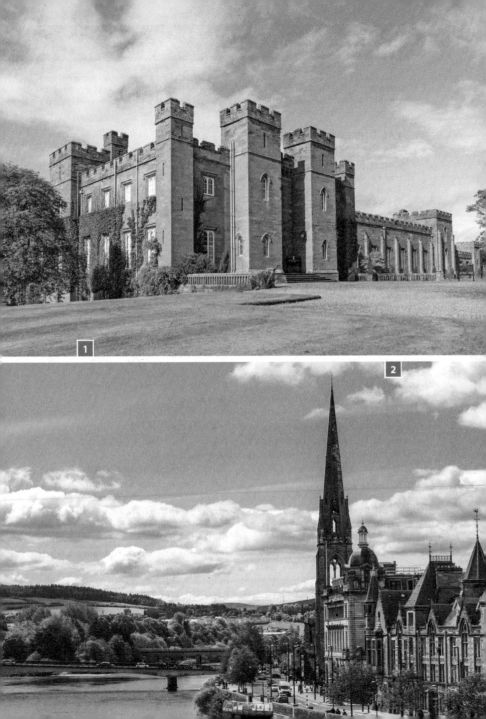

Side Trip: Crieff

Less than 20 miles (32 km) west of Perth is the town of Crieff, home to Scotland's oldest distillery and oldest library. Crieff is an easy side trip out of Perth—simply follow the A85 west out of the city for 18 miles (29 km, about 40 minutes)—or you can stop here on your way from Perth to the northeastern end of Loch Lomond and the Trossachs National Park.

FAMOUS GROUSE EXPERIENCE

Glenturret Distillery, Crieff; tel. 01764 656 565; experience.thefamousgrouse.com; 10am-6pm daily Apr.-Oct., 10am-5pm daily Nov.-Mar.; Distillery Tour £10, Warehouse Experience £40
Home to Glenturret whisky, this is the oldest legal whisky distillery still operating in Scotland. The general distillery tour lasts an hour and includes two wee drams. For something a bit more in-depth, try the Warehouse Experience where you get a tour of the distillery, plus access to the normally off-limits warehouses for a nosing and tasting of four whiskies. Tours run hourly from 10:30am, they can be booked online up to 48 hours before (after that you'll have to ring to check availability), and you must arrive 15 minutes before the start of the tour.

LIBRARY OF INNERPEFFRAY

Crieff, tel. 01764 652 819; innerpeffraylibrary.co.uk; 10am-5pm Wed.-Sat. and 2pm-5pm Sun. Mar.-Oct.; adult £7.50, under 16 free
Just a short drive from the Famous Grouse Distillery (6 mi/10 km southeast along the B8062) is Scotland's oldest library. It's a genuine treasure trove for anyone interested in Scottish heritage, with a captivating collection of literature on the Jacobite rebellions, plus excellent resources for those tracing family history.

J. D. Fergusson (although he was Edinburgh-born, he had many ties to Perthshire) and his lifelong partner, Margaret Morris, herself a pioneer of modern dance. Visitors can view thousands of pieces of work by prolific Fergusson, as well as many personal items, and the many costumes and artworks of Morris.

Perth Museum and Art Gallery

78 George Street, Perth; tel. 01738 632 488; www. culturepk.org.uk/museums-and-galleries/perth-museum-and-art-gallery; 10am-5pm Tues.-Sun.; free
This is another great gallery, this time housed in a resplendent neoclassical building with an exciting program of rolling exhibits. The gallery is just one small part of one of the oldest museums in Scotland, and among its highlights is a cast of the biggest salmon caught in Britain—a whopping 64-pound (29 kg) fish caught in the River Tay by one Georgina

Ballantine whose name is still revered by anglers across Britain.

RECREATION
KINNOULL HILL WOODLAND PARK

Perth; www.kinnoull.org.uk
This woodland park just two miles (3.2 km) east of the city has miles of nature trails to choose from and gives a little taste of what rural Perthshire has to offer. Look out for the wooden animal sculptures as you go, which show some of the very real wildlife you may be able to spot, including roe deer and red squirrels. If you have time, climb one of the five hills—Corsiehill, Deuchny Hill, Barn Hill, Binn Hill, or the park's namesake of Kinnoull Hill, which offers glorious views across the River Tay and Perthshire countryside.

Walks through native woodland such as Scots pines, oak, birch, and larch are very peaceful; look out for signs of nature, such as mushrooms, toads, and insects beneath your feet as you follow the grassy paths. There's a folly atop Kinnoull Hill, but stay clear of the edge of the cliff, which drops as far as 500 feet (152.4 m) in places.

SHOPPING
CONCORDE MUSIC

15 Scott Street; tel. 01738 621 818; www.concordemusic.com; 9am-4:45pm Mon.-Sat.

No self-respecting music fan can visit Perth without stopping off at Scotland's oldest family record shop, which has been keeping customers in vinyl since the 1960s. Today there are still lots of records to buy, alongside CDs, music books, and posters.

FOOD
DEAN'S AT LET'S EATS

77-79 Kinnoull Street; tel. 01738 643 377; www.letseatperth.co.uk; noon-2:30pm Weds.-Sat., dinner 6pm-8:30pm Weds.-Thurs., 6pm-9pm Fri.-Sat., noon-6pm Sun.; entrées £7.95

A contemporary and suave interior with high-back dining benches covered in lush red velvet, it's not all about looks here—the food is pretty good too. The modern Scottish cuisine uses seasonal produce: choose from pink roast rump of lamb or seared and blackened Atlantic cod, and don't miss the restaurant's signature Black Forest Baked Alaska for afters.

★ NORTH PORT RESTAURANT

8 North Port; tel. 01738 580 867; www.thenorthport.co.uk; lunch noon-2:30pm Tues.-Sat., dinner 5pm until late Tues.-Sat.; entrées £7.45

Located on a lovely cobbled street just behind the Perth Museum & Art Gallery, this small restaurant has attracted a big following since opening in 2011. From the tasty homemade bread through an impressive menu that features local-ish ingredients such as pork fillet served with Isle of Skye langoustine or Scrabster plaice, it rarely disappoints. The low-slung ceilings and intimate atmosphere simply round things off for happy diners.

63 TAY STREET

63 Tay Street; tel. 01738 441 451; www.63taystreet.com; lunch noon-1:45pm Thurs.-Sat., dinner 5:45pm-8:45pm Tues.-Fri., 6:30pm-8:45pm Sat.; entrées £9.50

For many years this was the place for fine food in Perth, but a slew of new competitors means it's had to stay on point and it has obliged fully. It has an extensive wine list, and good hearty food, such as roast quail with butterbean stew, keeps people coming back.

HINTERLAND

10 St. Johns Place; www.hinterlandcoffee.co.uk; 9am-5pm Mon.-Sat., 11am-5pm Sun.; coffee £2.75

This independent coffee shop in the center of Perth serves its own roasted coffee alongside some carefully selected teas. The shop's handcrafted coffee blends two Arabica beans and then uses a traditional drum method to roast them until they are the color of dark chocolate—try it in a mocha or good old americano.

ACCOMMODATIONS
ARDFERN GUEST HOUSE

15 Pitcullen Crescent; tel. 01738 637 031; www.ardfernperth.co.uk; £65 d

The owners of Ardfern are well known for making you feel like you are guests in their home. And what a lovely home it is too—a Victorian house split into eight comfortable rooms, many of which have lovely bay windows. Just check yours is not one of the rooms with a separate (though private) bathroom, unless you don't mind nipping into the hallway. You'll struggle to get a better bargain in Perth.

★ SCONE CASTLE APARTMENT

Balvaird Wing, Scone Palace; tel. 01738 552 300; www.airbnb.co.uk/rooms/5908470; £500 per night (sleeps six)

If you are traveling with friends, then this grand five-star apartment that sleeps six and is available through Airbnb, looks very tempting indeed. Located in the west wing of the palace, with unbeatable views of the parkland, it is like your own mini royal retreat. It's just a 10-minute taxi ride from here to Perth city too to see the rest of the sights, but there is a minimum stay of two nights.

THE SALUTATION

34 South Street; tel. 01738 630 066; www. strathmorehotels-thesalutation.com; £85 d

Perth's oldest hotel—in fact, it may be Scotland's oldest—is another of those places where the folk hero Bonnie Prince Charlie is said to have stayed. The gray and white façade is incredibly grand, with a huge arched window, and, though inside it doesn't quite live up to the high expectations (it's a little corporate), it nevertheless is a good standard of a hotel, well priced, and well placed in the city center.

INFORMATION AND SERVICES

Open year-round, the **VisitScotland Perth iCentre** (45 High Street; tel. 01738 450 600; 9:30am-5pm Mon.-Sat. and 11am-4pm Sun. in summer, 9:30am-4:30pm Mon.-Sat. and 11am-4pm Sun. in winter) is a good starting point for local leaflets and itineraries. There are also lots of advice on places to stay and visit on the **City of Perth website** (www.perthcity.co.uk).

GETTING THERE

Perched in the heart of central Scotland, it's pretty easy to get to Perth from anywhere in the UK. Indeed, as much as 90 percent of Scotland's population lives within 90 miles (144.8 km) of the city.

By Car

It's just an hour's drive here from Glasgow Airport (67 mi/108 km along the M80 and the A9), while both Edinburgh (M90, 41 miles/66 km, 50 mins) and Dundee airports (A90, 20 miles/12 km, 30 mins) are under an hour away. Aberdeen Airport is 92 miles (150 km, 2 hours) away. From Balquhidder in the northeast of the Loch Lomond and the Trossachs National Park, it's a 44-mile (70 km) drive east along the A85 to Perth, which should take around an hour and a half.

By Train

ScotRail (www.scotrail.co.uk) runs services from Edinburgh (1.25 hours, two per hour, £17.10 one-way) and Glasgow (1 hour, two per hour, £17.10 one-way) to Perth, and the **Caledonian Sleeper** (www.sleeper.scot) train from London also stops here once a day (8.5 hours, from £50 one-way). ScotRail also runs direct trains from Stirling to Perth that take 35 minutes (two an hour, £8.30 one-way).

Inverness and the Central Highlands

When one thinks of Scotland, it is undoubt- edly the endless skies, mighty mountains, and deep, dark lochs of the Highlands that come to mind. There is a mystique about this region that is hard to fathom. On the one hand, little has changed in millennia. On the other, with every rising sun and shift in cloud, the landscape reveals different sides to its character. It's a place interwoven with stories, from theories on Scotland's "unsolved mystery" of the Loch Ness Monster to tales of heroics of Scottish folk heroes such as Bonnie Prince Charlie and his gutsy Jacobites. And where better to hear them than round a campfire in sublime surroundings?

It was near Inverness, the region's main city, that the infamous Battle of Culloden took place in 1746, ending Jacobite ambitions forever and

Highlights

Look for ★ to find recommended sights, activities, dining, and lodging.

★ **Dolphin-spotting on the Moray Firth:** Just a few miles outside Inverness this is one of the best places in Europe to spot the playful mammals (page 273).

★ **Culloden Battlefield:** Stand on the site of one of Scotland's bloodiest and most decisive battles—the last stand of the Jacobites (page 279).

★ **Cawdor Castle:** Visit the medieval fortress that Shakespeare bound to King of Scots Macbeth forever more (page 281).

★ **Kayaking on Loch Ness:** Serenity can be found paddling on the waters of Scotland's deepest and most famous loch (page 291).

★ **Climbing Ben Nevis:** You'll feel on top of the world when you conquer Britain's highest peak (page 296).

★ **Mountain Gondola in Fort William:** For the best views of Ben Nevis and the Great Glen, take this cable car to the top of Aonach Mor (page 299).

★ **Driving the Glencoe Road:** As the A82 twists and curls through Scotland's most scenic glen, you'll want to pull over and take a thousand photos (page 305).

★ **Camping in Glencoe:** Pitching up by a gentle stream in the shadow of gargantuan mountains in Glencoe is a humbling experience (page 307).

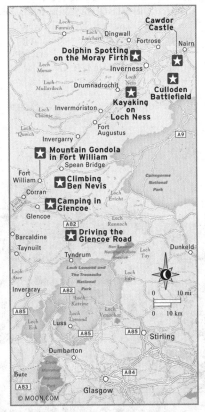

setting in motion a series of measures aimed to decimate Highland culture for good, resulting in a poignancy that is palpable all across the region.

Inverness, a pretty city set along the River Ness, is a good launch pad for visiting Loch Ness, the Moray Firth, and the Highlands generally. At the far end of the Great Glen, a diagonal fault line that runs from Inverness southwest to Loch Linnhe, you will find Fort William, home to Ben Nevis, the highest peak in the British Isles, and a mecca for outdoor adventure sports fans. And just a short journey south of that will bring you to Glencoe, a dramatic valley of epic proportions, where mountains rocket to the sky from abyssal gorges, making you feel but a small speckle on nature's great canvas.

HISTORY

Perhaps more than any other part of Scotland, the central Highlands will always be linked to the rise and fall of the Jacobites—supporters of the Stuart line to the throne who cast aside clan rivalries to rise up united in a series of attempts to overthrow English or British monarchs (first King William III and Queen Mary II of England, and later the House of Hanover) with the aim of returning the Stuart line of succession.

Tensions between the Jacobites and English crown began in 1688 when King James VII of Scotland (King James II of England and Ireland) was deposed over his Catholic leanings and replaced with his own daughter Queen Mary II and her overtly Protestant Dutch husband William III (known as William of Orange) during a period known as the Glorious Revolution. In 1689 the first of a series of Jacobite risings took place, in which supporters of King James VII rose up in an attempt to overthrow the coregency. The rising began to falter with the death of its leader, Viscount Dundee, at the Battle of Killiecrankie later that year but not before

government forces suffered a humiliating defeat at the hands of the Jacobites. Despite winning that battle, the Jacobites lost a subsequent one, and by the end of the year the rebellion was all but over.

In a bid to deter future uprisings, in 1691 William of Orange issued a pardon to all the Highland clans who had fought against his ascension but with a condition: they had to take an oath of allegiance to the crown before a magistrate by January 1, 1692. This order and its repercussions led to one of the worst acts of treacheries in Scottish history. Reluctantly, the MacDonald Clan Chief, MacIain of Glencoe, agreed to take William's oath, but a catalog of errors and unfortunate incidents meant that he was late getting to the designated place to swear his allegiance. Nevertheless, it was taken and MacIain mistakenly believed his clan was safe from King William's retribution. Unbeknownst to him, the force of 130 soldiers led by Captain Robert Campbell of Glen Lyon, whom MacIain's clan offered food and shelter to for 10 days the following month, were actually sent to kill the men in their midst, and this is exactly what they did on the morning of February 12, 1692. As many as 38 men were slaughtered—others who had run to the mountains succumbed to exposure and hunger—and while there were certainly larger death tolls in Scottish history, this is remembered for its shocking act of betrayal. The Glencoe Massacre has been the subject of many a poem, song, and work of literature and is often held up as an example of the brutal oppression of the Scots at the hands of the English.

Over half a century later, in 1745, Bonnie Prince Charlie (Charles Edward Stuart), grandson of King James VII, arrived in Scotland, ready to rouse his supporters to victory in a third major rebellion. However, though there were some promising moments for the Jacobites, it was not to be. In 1746, their bloody defeat at the hands of the far larger

---

Previous: The ruins of Urquhart Castle overlook Loch Ness; Memorial Cairn at the battlefield of Culloden near Inverness; Falls of Foyers, Loch Ness

Inverness and the Central Highlands

Loch Fannich

Kinlochewe

A832

A832

Achnasheen

Shieldaig

A890

Applecross

Strathcarron

Raasay

Lochcarron

A890

Inverarish

Stromeferry

Loch Monar

Scalpay

Kyle of Lochalsh

A87

A87

Loch Mullardoch

Broadford

Isle of Skye

A87

A887

Loch Cluanie

Armadale

A87

Loch Quoich

Invergarry

Mallaig

A82

ADVENTURE NEVIS

A830

Loch Morar

Loch Arkaig

Loch Lochy

A86

Arisaig

COMMANDO MONUMENT

Spean Bridge

WILDWOOD BUSHCRAFT

Lochailort

Glenfinnan

A830

ROCKHOPPER SEA KAYAKING

SEE DETAIL

NEVIS RANGE

MOUNTAIN GONDOLA

Loch Shiel

Fort William

BEN NEVIS

STEALL FALLS

VERTICAL DESCENTS

A82

GLENCOE FOLK MUSEUM

Corran

GLENCOE MASSACRE MONUMENT

NISA LOCAL

RED SQUIRREL CAMPSITE

DRIVING THE GLENCOE ROAD

Strontian

Glencoe

CLACHAIG INN

GLEN COE BUACHAILLE ETIVE MOR

A884

CRAFTS & THINGS

To Bridge of Orchy Hotel

THE BOATHOUSE BISTRO

A828

GLENCOE VISITOR'S CENTRE

LOST VALLEY

THREE SISTERS

A82

0   5 mi
0   5 km

© MOON.COM

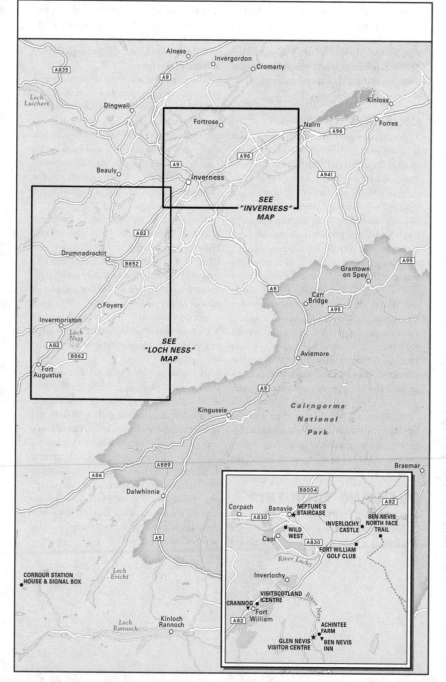

number of redcoats they met on the battlefield of Culloden Moor, just outside Inverness, spelled the end of the rebellions. Bonnie Prince Charlie limped off into hiding, and the British government spent the next few decades doing everything it could to undermine and obliterate Highland culture forever.

ORIENTATION

The main entry point to the central Highlands is **Inverness,** located on the Moray Firth coast at the north end of the **Great Glen**—a diagonal fault line that runs southwest from Inverness all the way to **Fort William** at the head of Loch Linnhe. Connected by a series of lochs and canals, including the legendary **Loch Ness,** it is possible to travel between Inverness and Fort William by boat, though it is also pretty straightforward to travel the length of the Great Glen by road or rail.

There are a few major towns along the shores of Loch Ness, most notably **Drumnadrochit** on its western shore, **Foyers** on its eastern shore, and **Fort Augustus** at its most southerly end. Just 16 miles (26 km) south of Fort William lies **Glencoe,** a monumental valley where craggy munros rise up to the skies, punctuated with green moorland and icy lochs. Together with Fort William, Glencoe forms part of the **Lochaber Geopark,** a region of incredible geological interest that actually stretches as far west as the Isle of Rum, which lies off the coast of Skye.

PLANNING YOUR TRIP

Inverness is the obvious first port of call or base for anyone wishing to explore the Highlands or the Great Glen. Inverness Airport has regular flights from London, and the Caledonian Sleeper train stops here too, so if it's the Highlands you wish to visit, you could bypass Glasgow and Edinburgh entirely and come right here.

The city itself is relatively compact and pretty easy to explore on foot; indeed, there's not a huge amount to see if truth be told—a couple of interesting museums and galleries and some decent restaurants. A day is all you really need to see Inverness and stock up for your trip into the Highlands, as Inverness's biggest attraction is its accessibility to the mountains, glens, and lochs for which the Highlands is famous.

Numerous tour companies in Inverness offer to take you monster-spotting on Loch Ness or adventuring in Fort William and Glencoe, but with so many bus routes setting off from here, plus car hire companies aplenty, it is very conceivable that you can go it alone. Make sure you're armed with a good road map—the *A to Z Scotland North & South* is the best—as well as Ordnance Survey maps of specific areas if you are planning to do any off-road walks.

If you do opt for a tour, try to avoid the day trips that promise multiple destinations; all you'll really get a chance to do is step out for a quick photo before getting back on the coach until the next place, which can feel very much like you're simply ticking things off a list. If you are planning a trip into the central Highlands on your own, whether its climbing Ben Nevis in Fort William, hiking and camping in Glencoe, or going in search of Nessie herself, leave yourself at least three or four days, though there is plenty to keep you busy here for a couple of weeks.

Itinerary Ideas

ONE DAY IN INVERNESS

The beauty of Inverness is that, even if you have less than 24 hours, you should still be able to see some of the city's most impressive sights, plus get out into the countryside and along the coastline to visit some truly special places.

1 Take a morning boat ride with **Dolphin Spirit** on the Moray Firth to see some of the resident bottlenose dolphin population. You may also see a rather awkward-looking seal or two lazing on the rocks, some cormorants, or other sea birds.

2 Back on dry land, walk the 25 minutes or so back to the city center, taking in views of the River Ness as you go, and stop for brunch at the family-run café of **Girvans.**

3 Tummy full, it's just a couple of minutes' walk to the excellent (and free) **Inverness Museum and Art Gallery,** where you can spend a couple hours immersing yourself in stories of the region's earliest peoples.

4 Next, follow Castle Wynd round to **Inverness Castle Viewpoint** and pay the small entrance fee to climb up the tower for some of the best views of the city.

5 Walk across Ness Bridge and head to the **Scottish Kiltmaker Visitor Centre** to catch a live demonstration and peruse the clothes made of beautiful Scottish fabrics in the ground-floor shop.

6 Round your day off with dinner and drinks at one of the city's most inviting and lively pubs, **Hootananny.**

BEST OF THE CENTRAL HIGHLANDS

With so much to see, it can be tricky to narrow down where to go and where to miss out, but for the best taste of what the Highlands has to offer you have to get out of the towns and cities and into the great outdoors.

Day 1: Cawdor to Culloden

■ After breakfasting at your hotel, set off northeast from Inverness and spend the morning exploring **Cawdor Castle.** Take the tour (reserve it in advance) to hear tales of the castle's former residents, which, sorry to say, doesn't include Macbeth.

■ Have a hearty Scottish lunch at the **Cawdor Tavern.**

■ Head to the **Culloden Battlefield** and take your time wandering through the exhibits in the visitor center before heading out to soak up the atmosphere of the battlefield itself.

■ Unwind at **Culloden House** with a whisky tasting at the Library Bar, before tucking into dinner and then sinking into bed for the night.

Day 2: Loch Ness

■ If there's even a tiny part of you that believes in magic and mysterious goings on, head to Loch Ness. To avoid the crowds, head down the eastern shores of the loch to camp or book one of the wigwams at the waterside **Loch Ness Shores.**

■ Once settled, walk to the nearby **Falls of Foyers** (around a two-hour round trip),

Inverness and the Central Highlands Itineraries

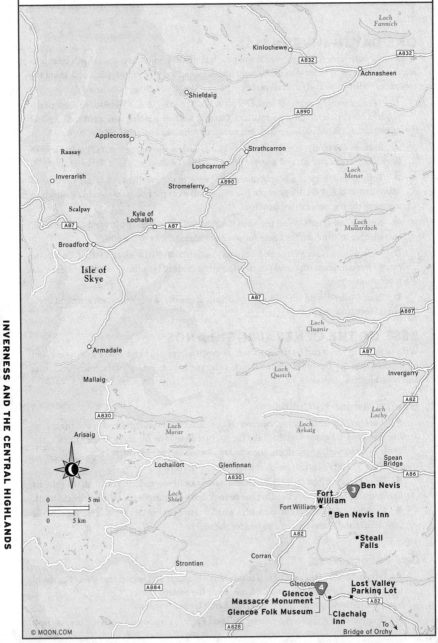

© MOON.COM

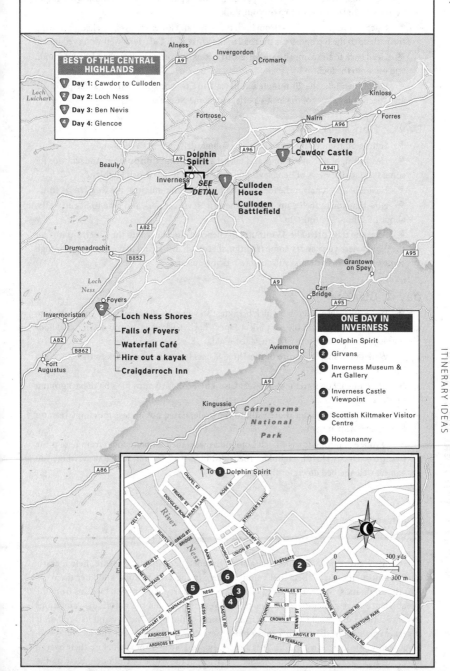

BEST OF THE CENTRAL HIGHLANDS

1 **Day 1:** Cawdor to Culloden
2 **Day 2:** Loch Ness
3 **Day 3:** Ben Nevis
4 **Day 4:** Glencoe

Alness
Invergordon
Cromarty
A9
Kinloss
Loch Luichart
Fortrose
Nairn
A96
Forres
Dolphin Spirit
A9
Beauly
A96
Cawdor Tavern
Cawdor Castle
Inverness
A941
SEE DETAIL
1 Culloden House
Culloden Battlefield
A82
Drumnadrochit
B852
Grantown on Spey
A95
Loch Ness
A9
Carr Bridge
Foyers
A95
2 **Loch Ness Shores**
Invermoriston
Falls of Foyers
A82
Waterfall Café
B862
Hire out a kayak
Aviemore
Fort Augustus
Craigdarroch Inn
A9
Kingussie
Cairngorms National Park
A86

ONE DAY IN INVERNESS

1 Dolphin Spirit
2 Girvans
3 Inverness Museum & Art Gallery
4 Inverness Castle Viewpoint
5 Scottish Kiltmaker Visitor Centre
6 Hootananny

↑ To 1 Dolphin Spirit

CHAPEL ST
FRIARS ST
ROSE ST
FRIARS LANE
DOUGLAS ROW
STROTHER'S LANE
River Ness
CELT ST
ACADEMY ST
HUNTLY ST
GREIG ST
GREIG ST BRIDGE
UNION ST
KING ST
BANK ST
CHURCH ST
EASTGATE
2
KENNETH ST
DUNCRAIG ST
6
NESS ST
5
3
CHARLES ST
4
GLENURQUHART RD
TOMNAHURICH
NESS WALK
ALEXANDER PLACE
CASTLE RD
ARDCONNEL ST
HILL ST
DENNY ST
SOUTHSIDE RD
UNION RD
KINGSMILLS RD
BROSTONE PARK
ARDROSS PLACE
ARDROSS ST
CROWN ST
ARGYLE ST
ARGYLE TERRACE

0   300 yds
0   300 m

which, though steep in places, has a proper wooden path through woodland. You might even spot a red squirrel or two on your walk.

■ Once you've seen the falls (from both the upper and lower viewpoints), keep following the path up to the top and cross the road to the **Waterfall Café** for a well-deserved lunch.

■ Head back to the campsite and **hire out a kayak** from reception for a late-afternoon trip out onto the loch.

■ For dinner, take the 20-minute uphill walk to **Craigdarroch Inn** for some pub grub and spectacular views of the loch—perfect for some Nessie spotting.

Day 3: Ben Nevis

■ Setting off from your campsite, it's a 1.5-hour drive to **Fort William.**

■ Head straight to Nevis Range and take the **mountain gondola** up Aonach Mor for some spectacular views of Ben Nevis and the surrounding Scottish Highlands.

■ Have a hearty lunch at the foot of Britain's highest mountain at the **Ben Nevis Inn.**

■ Now that you're fueled up, head to the Ben Nevis car park and hike to **Steall Falls,** about 1.5-2 hours round-trip.

■ After the trek, drive the 45 minutes to Glencoe, and check into the **Clachaig Inn** for the night where you can try some traditional Scottish dishes and make your way through some of the extensive whisky list before retiring upstairs.

Day 4: Glencoe

■ Wake up early and grab a quick breakfast so you miss the crowds for your hike into the **Lost Valley** (park in the car park at Piper's Layby), which takes you down to the floor of the glen in the footsteps of Clan Macdonald.

■ Walk done, snap a picture of the Three Sisters before heading back to the **Clachaig Inn** for a hearty lunch.

■ After lunch, pop into the very sweet **Glencoe Folk Museum** for a bit of background on the area.

■ From there, it's just a short walk to the understated but no less moving **Glencoe Massacre Monument.**

■ If you're planning to visit Loch Lomond as well, the best place to go from here is the **Bridge of Orchy Hotel,** a fabulous roadside inn, just a 25-minute drive away, where you can eat well and bed down for the night.

Inverness

For many visitors to Scotland, Britain's northernmost city marks their first venture into the Highlands. Sited at the head of the Great Glen, a huge geological fault line that bisects Scotland diagonally all the way from Inverness to Fort William, Inverness has long been a strategic stronghold. It is believed the legendary King of Scots Macbeth, immortalized by Shakespeare, held a castle here in the 11th century, and later the royal burgh was regularly raided by clans from the Western Isles and the notoriously ambitious Lords of the Isles. The city and its surrounds were common targets for the Jacobites too, who, in 1746 and shortly before their overall defeat at the Battle of Culloden, blew up the old Fort George in Inverness, which, ironically enough, was built to subdue them following the Jacobite rising of 1715.

As the main entry point into the Highlands, Inverness is undoubtedly a useful city. It provides an essential lifeline to the thousands upon thousands of visitors who travel through here each year; you don't have to look far for a tourist shop or signs promising to take you to some far-flung destination and back in a day (beware those who promise too much— the experience is generally disappointing). It also serves the inhabitants of the more remote towns and villages of the Highlands, who regularly travel here to shop.

But it's also not a bad-looking city. Inverness loosely translates as "mouth of Ness," in reference to the pretty river that winds its way through the city, with the pink sandstone of Inverness Castle on the east side and the red sandstone towers of St. Andrew's Cathedral on the west. Much of the city was built up in the Victorian era, and some fine 19th-century buildings can still be found here today.

ORIENTATION

The east side of River Ness is where you'll find most of the city's attractions and shops, all clustered on and around Castle Street, Church Street, and the High Street, including **Inverness Castle** and **Inverness Museum and Art Gallery.** The train station is just a couple of minutes' walk east of these attractions on Academy Street and the bus station is just a block farther north of this, tucked away at the end of Margaret Street in Farraline Park. The airport is nine miles (14 km) northeast of the city center, along the Moray Firth coast.

You will need to cross **Ness Bridge** in the city center to get to the renowned **Scottish Kiltmaker Centre** within the Highland House of Fraser shop on the west bank (turn right when you cross the bridge). Meanwhile, if you turn left when crossing **Ness Bridge** and follow the river south, you'll soon reach **St. Andrew's Cathedral,** and a block even farther south will bring you to the **arts center** of Eden Court. Back on the east side of the river, the older part of town, behind the castle in and around **Old Edinburgh Road,** is where you will find a good smattering of charming and well-priced B&Bs, while the more upmarket hotels tend to be along the banks of the River Ness.

Farther afield, the **Moray Firth** lies just to the north of the city center, while the **Merkinch Nature Reserve** and **South Kessock Pier** are just to the northwest. Both **Ness Islands** and the **Botanic Gardens** lie a short distance south of the city center. All of these destinations are accessible on foot, if you're reasonably fit.

SIGHTS
Inverness Museum and Art Gallery

Castle Wynd, Inverness; tel. 01463 237 114; www. highlifehighland.com/inverness-museum-and-art-gallery; 10am-5pm Tues.-Sat. Apr.-Oct., noon-4pm Tues.-Thurs. and 11am-4pm Fri.-Sat. Nov.-Easter; free

Don't let the ugly exterior of this museum and art gallery put you off (there are proposals to update the 1970s façade anyway). Set across two floors, it's a fascinating walk through Highland culture and history and a good use of an hour or two if you are planning to head out to Culloden too. The ground floor is given over to exhibits charting the geological development of Scotland through to its early peoples (including examples of Pictish stones) and the beginnings of clan culture. On the first floor, this history continues with the plight of the Jacobites, showcasing some of their traditional weapons (such as dirks) alongside bagpipes and other memorabilia. The first floor is also home to two art galleries that host temporary exhibitions, often from local artists, covering fine art, ceramics, and modern art, but it's the museum part that is of real interest. There's also a café, a shop, plus a useful exhibit (on the ground floor) where you can hear how Gaelic phrases are pronounced, so you can show off to your friends back home.

Inverness

A82

A82

CHAPEL ST

ROSE ST

RAILWAY TERRACE

FRIARS ST

DOUGLAS ROW

River

FRIARS LANE

LEAKEY'S SECONDHAND BOOKSHOP ■

INVERNESS BUS STATION ■

STROTHER'S LANE

CELT ST

HUNTLY ST

QUEEN ST

BALNAIN ST

GREIG ST BRIDGE

POST OFFICE AVE

QUEENSGATE

VICTORIAN MARKET

ACADEMY ST

HOOTANANNY'S ■

CHURCH ST

MUSTARD SEED ▼

UNION ST

BARON TAYLOR'S ST

MELLAMARKET

A82

GREIG ST

DUNCRAIG ST

KING ST

HUNTLY ST

Ness

BANK ST

LOMBARD ST

EASTGATE

GIRVANS ▼

TOURIST OFFICE ■

THE SCOTTISH KILTMAKER VISITOR CENTRE ■

BRIDGE ST

★ **INVERNESS TOWN HOUSE**

CHARLES ST

KENNETH ST

URQUHARTS RESTAURANT ▼

NESS BRIDGE

★ **INVERNESS MUSEUM AND ART GALLERY**

■ **CASTLE GALLERY**

HILL ST

REAY ST

DENNY ST

TOMNAHURICH ST

ROCPOOL RESTAURANT ■

INVERNESS CASTLE VIEWPOINT ★

★ **INVERNESS CASTLE**

ARDCONNEL ST

CROWN ST

GLENURQUHART RD

KENNETH ST

ALEXANDER PLACE

CASTLE RD

● **PITFARANNE GUEST HOUSE**

ARGYLE ST

ARGYLE TERRACE

ARDROSS PLACE

NESS WALK

CASTLE TAVERN ▼

MITCHELL'S LANE

PORTERFIELD BANK

A82

ARDROSS ST

● **BAZPACKERS**

CULDUTHEL RD

OLD EDINBURGH RD

BISHOPS RD

MAYFIELD RD

NESS BANK

HAUGH RD

EDEN COURT THEATRE ■

BISHOPS RD

● **GLENMORISTON HOUSE HOTEL**

★ **ST. ANDREW'S CATHEDRAL**

NESS WALK

INFIRMARY BRIDGE

● **ROCPOOL RESERVE**

CULDUTHEL RD

SOUTHSIDE RD

GORDONVILLE RD

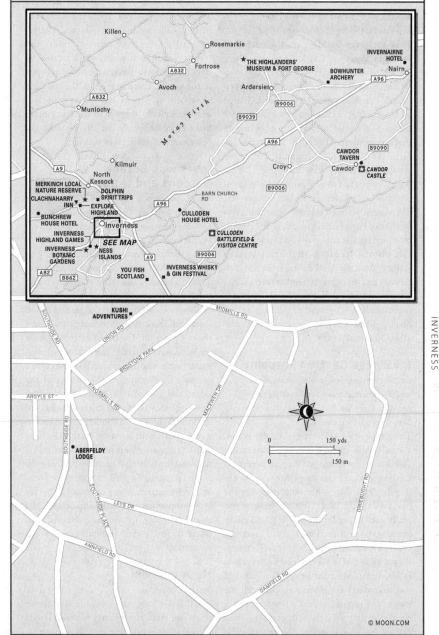

© MOON.COM

Inverness Town House

*High Street; tel. 01463 237 114; www.highlifehighland.
com/inverness-museum-and-art-gallery/inverness-
town-house-2; 2pm and 3:30pm Thurs. early
June-late Sept.; adult £7, child (under 12) £4*

This Victorian building on the corner of
the High Street and Castle Street was where
the Inverness Formula was agreed upon—a
strategy that arose out of a meeting between
British Prime Minister David Lloyd George
and his cabinet in 1921 and paved the way for
the Irish Free State (the 26 counties of Ireland
that separated from Britain in 1922 and today
form the Republic of Ireland). For many
years the baronial-style building with its
pretty turrets has merely provided a touch of
elegance to the Inverness streets, but now you
can join one of the weekly one-hour tours, run
by charity High Life Highland, of the elegant
interiors; it's the only way you can see inside
this historic building. Highlights include
stained-glass windows dating from the 17th
century and the council chamber where Lloyd
George and his cabinet met for that historic
meeting all those years ago. Make sure you
book in advance as numbers are limited, and
arrive 10 minutes early.

Inverness Castle Viewpoint

*Castle Street, Inverness; www.highlifehighland.
com/invernesscastleviewpoint; 11am-6pm daily
Apr.-May, 10am-7pm daily June-Aug., 11am-6pm daily
Sept.-Oct.; adult £5, under 12 £3*

Though you can follow round Castle Wynd,
a small lane to the side of Inverness Museum
and Art Gallery, and walk up to Inverness
Castle esplanade and its gardens, views are
largely blocked by other buildings. For the
best views of the River Ness and beyond you
really need to pay for the privilege and climb
the new visitor attraction (2017) of Inverness
Castle Viewpoint, which is only really worth
it on a clear day (a short video introduction
is also included in the price). One word of
warning: don't ask if you can climb all the
way to the top of the castle tower as you'll
simply be met with the witty retort—"You
can try, but it's a chimney." The castle itself is

a pastel palace of pink sandstone, built in its
current guise on a hill overlooking the city on
the eastern bank in 1847 (after the Jacobites
destroyed the medieval castle just before the
Battle of Culloden in 1746). In typical Scottish
baronial style, it has a series of towers and
turrets, and the viewpoint, which ascends 94
steps up the north tower, is the only part open
to the public. Once at the top, the rounded
viewpoint is narrow but rarely crowded,
so there's plenty of space to see everything;
however, come later in the afternoon for the
best chance of having it to yourself.

Inverness Botanic
Gardens and Nursery

*Bught Lane, Inverness; tel. 01463 713 553; www.
highlifehighland.com/inverness-botanic-gardens;
10am-5pm daily summer, 10am-4pm daily winter;
free but donations welcome*

This delightful garden, which is free to visit
(though donations are welcome) is small but
quaint. There are two main glasshouses and
a well-cared-for outdoor area. In the Tropical
House see colorful displays of plantings and
a waterfall that creates a soothing atmosphere
above a pond filled with koi carp; next door
see hundreds of cacti. In the outdoor garden,
you'll find a wildflower meadow and carved
animals hidden among the shrubs of the
raised and ground-level beds. One surprise
find is the secret GROW garden at the back of
the formal gardens—a community project in
which adults with learning disabilities have
helped turn an urban waste ground into a
sustainable wildlife haven. After perusing the
plants, pop into **Cobb's tearoom** for some
light refreshment. If you do make it this far
(a 20-minute walk from the city center), you
should definitely visit the nearby Ness Islands,
where there are some tranquil nature trails
to wander.

Ness Islands

Great Glen Way; free

You'll feel a long way from the city center
when you reach these pretty islands planted
with mature Scots pine and fir, sycamore,

Detour: Speyside's Malt Whisky Trail

The isle of Islay off Scotland's west coast may be the top place of pilgrimage for Scotch lovers, but its whiskies are something of an acquired taste, with a peaty, often smoky flavor, and in terms of number of distilleries, it is small fry compared with Speyside, which boasts the largest concentration of single malt distilleries in the world. It's an easy detour from Inverness, some 50 miles (80.5 km) or so east and can either be explored independently or on a reputable tour.

Whisky has been distilled in Scotland for hundreds of years—some say it was introduced to the country by Christian monks, while others believe it could simply have been a way for farmers in the Highlands to use up extra barley. But while we know it was well established in Scotland by the late 15th century, regularly used to help keep people warm through the brutal, long, Scottish winters and often used for medicinal purposes, most distilling took place in hard-to-reach places, lest the taxman would get wind of it. It was only in the late 18th century that distilleries began to apply for licenses, thus making them legal.

Stretching from Grantown-on-Spey in the Cairngorms to Dufftown along the River Spey, all the way up to Elgin and Forres on the Moray coast, Speyside encompasses a whopping 50 distilleries. Even the most dedicated whisky drinker visiting the region several times would never make it round all of the distilleries, so the trick is in choosing a few that appeal and mapping a route around them—one of the oldest more familiar names such as Glenfiddich (www.glenfiddich.com) can easily be combined with a trip to Balvenie (thebalvenie.com), which, despite sharing the same distiller, has a very different taste. Of course, if you are going to be tasting whisky, then you will need to leave the car where you are staying (unless you are happy to chauffeur your drinking companions around), and with a little planning this is perfectly doable.

GETTING AROUND

Taxi

Grantown-on-Spey, 15 miles (24 km) northeast of Aviemore, is one of the main entry points to the region, and a couple of local taxi firms will happily transport you between distilleries. Aviemore Taxis (tel. 01479 811 111) or Johnny's (tel. 01479 851 375) in Grantown-on-Spey itself are both reliable and friendly. Dufftown is probably the best-placed base for exploring several distilleries, including Glenfiddich, which is less than a mile (1.6 km) away (so perfectly walkable). Dufftown Taxis (tel. 07766 301 838) will arrange transfers between distilleries and point out places of interest en route. In addition, Stagecoach has a good network of bus routes in the area (www.stagecoachbus.com). For other routes, check Traveline (www.traveline.info).

Tours

But if that all feels a bit too arduous, then some very reputable chauffeur-driven tours will take you to several distilleries in a day. Speyside Whisky Tours (speysidewhiskytours.com; from £150 per person) is probably the most established, and, while staff can collect from Inverness, for the best value for money and use of your time, you're best to head to Aberlour in Speyside the night before. Finally, Moray Firth Tours (tel. 07724 095 739, www.morayfirthtours.co.uk) can plan bespoke tours to the distilleries for you (from £50 per hour or £350 for a day, but very dependent on what you plan to do), and even throw in some other attractions; they can collect you from Inverness.

and beech trees, but, in actual fact, you can get here in around 20 minutes. Connected by a series of Victorian footbridges, the islands, which sit in the River Ness and mark the start of the Great Glen Way, are free to wander. The best way to experience them is to set off from the castle and head upstream along the eastern shore of the River Ness, passing by the Inverness War Memorial and its pretty flower garden en route. Keep one eye on the river, though, as seals can often be spotted in its waters. Once on the islands, stop and enjoy the peace with a picnic or continue on to the Botanic Gardens and return to the city along the western bank. All in all, you should allow 1-2 hours to complete this city nature tour (including stops).

Merkinch Local Nature Reserve

South Kessock, Inverness; tel. 07795 253 727; merkinchlnr.org.uk; reserve open year-round, Old Ferry Ticket Office 2pm-4pm Tues.-Sat.; free

This wildlife reserve on an area of saltmarsh, bog, and scrub that was once an island to the north of the city center and is still partially connected to the sea, comes as a surprise to those who stumble upon it. The Old Ferry Ticket Office by South Kessock pier, the main entry point, has now been turned into an information center where you can learn about the history of the reserve and how it came to be connected to the mainland, as well as read about recent wildlife sightings, which regularly include roe deer, weasels, much birdlife, including owls, herons, and kingfishers, and even bottlenose dolphins on an incoming tide.

The main path to follow is the Sea Wall Path, which starts just by the car park at South Kessock, and will bring you past the mudflats (look out for waders and wildfowl as you go), down to the Muirtown Pools, and all the way to the edge of the Caledonian Canal where most of the wildlife can be seen. This route takes about 30 minutes each way. Alternatively, a couple of other trails, including the West Fields Loop Trail, take you through woodland and also set off from the car park.

The reserve is not overly pretty—indeed it can look quite desolate and forgotten—but birdlife thrives in this swampy corner of the city, so definitely one for twitchers. If you don't fancy the 20-minute walk from the city center, jump on the no. 8 bus from Academy Street in the city center (30 minutes; every 45 minutes Mon.-Sat.; £1.95 one-way, £3.60 day rider ticket).

FESTIVALS AND EVENTS

INVERNESS HIGHLAND GAMES

Bught Park, Inverness; tel. 01463 785 006; invernesshighlandgames.com; July; adult £8, child and concessions £2, under 5 free

There is an absolutely packed program each year at this stalwart Highland event, in a park on the west side of the river, which began way back in 1822. There are track and field events throughout the day for participants of all ages. The highlight, though, is the opening ceremony at midday, which features clan chieftains in full dress, followed thereafter by a mass Highland fling, which is fast, chaotic, and a lot of fun.

INVERNESS WHISKY & GIN FESTIVAL

Bogbain Farm, Inverness; tel. 01463 772 800; www. invernesswhiskygin.com; April; £30

At a 19th-century farm with views over the Moray Firth, this festival takes place on the first or second weekend in April each year and, in true Highland style, includes tastings of Scotland's two favorite spirits alongside delicious Scottish food, music, and a lot of craic (fun). In addition to the festival itself, lots of fringe events are also taking place in Inverness in the week leading up to the big day.

SHOPPING

LEAKEY'S SECONDHAND BOOKSHOP

Greyfriars Hall, Church Street, Inverness; tel. 01463 239 947; www.facebook.com/LeakeysBookshop; 10am-5:30pm Mon.-Sat.

There are bookshops and then there is Leakey's—on entering the former church you can smell the old pages of the thousands of tomes all stacked together, a little higgledy-piggledy, but in sections at least. That's beside the point, though; the joy here is in releasing yourself for an hour or two from the pressures of the real world and trawling for bargains or collectors' editions or even just reclining into a sofa on the gallery above to try before you buy.

THE SCOTTISH KILTMAKER VISITOR CENTRE

4-9 Huntly Street, Highland House of Fraser, Inverness; tel. 01463 222 781; www. highlandhouseoffraser.com; 9am-10pm daily summer, 9am-6pm daily winter, closed Sun. Jan.-Mar.; kilt-making exhibition adult £2.50, concessions £1.50, under 5 free

As well as a gorgeous array of bright knits and woolen garments from the likes of Harley of Scotland and Glen Appin, and Trinity caps and capes made from Harris Tweed—all sold to you by staff dressed in kilts—you can learn about the art of kilt-making here. Head upstairs to the kilt-making exhibition where you can see some of the shop's kilts being handmade and learn about the precision art, from how much cloth to cut to how to fold and pleat it correctly. Last entry is 45 minutes prior to closing.

VICTORIAN MARKET

Academy Street, Inverness; tel. 01463 710 524; www. facebook.com/victorianmarketinverness; 8am-6pm Mon.-Sat., 11am-4pm Sun.

This covered market, which can be entered through a doorway on Academy Street near the train station, has seen better days, but there are still a couple of pleasant cafés plus retailers selling traditional garb (including Prince Charlie jackets and waistcoats) and a fair few jewelers. It also offers a slice of 19th-century nostalgia, although it's not quite the original building—that one burned down in 1889 when the only fatality was a dog who refused to leave the shop it guarded. The mall was soon rebuilt, and a plaque remembering the dog's sacrifice still stands.

CASTLE GALLERY

43 Castle Street, Inverness; tel. 01463 729 512; www. castlegallery.co.uk; 9am-5pm Mon.-Sat.

Just a short walk from the city's main museum and gallery is this bright gallery with art works spread across two floors featuring a mix of contemporary pieces from both Scottish artists and artists from other parts of Britain. View paintings inspired by Scottish landscapes, alongside studio glass and even some pieces of jewelry from time to time.

ARTS AND CULTURE

EDEN COURT THEATRE

Bishops Road, Inverness; tel. 01463 234 234; www. eden-court.co.uk; cinema from £6.50, theater tickets from £13

Easily the Highlands' premier culture hub, this is a real meeting place for locals, who come to catch up over coffee, attend one of the many creative classes, watch a film, see a play, or poke their heads into one of the regular free exhibitions. Ticket prices are good compared with theaters in other major cities, and, while there are few West End names, a lot of the shows are critically acclaimed and give good insight into local culture and, more importantly, humor. Look out for touring shows from Scottish Ballet.

★ DOLPHIN-SPOTTING

DOLPHIN SPIRIT TRIPS

Inverness Marina, Stadium Road; tel. 075 800 620; www.dolphinspirit.co.uk; RIB rides 10:30am-12:30pm and 2:30pm-4:30pm Apr.-June and Sept.-Oct., 9:30am-11:30am, 12:30pm-2:30pm, and 3:30pm-5:30pm July-Aug.; cruiser rides 10am-11:15am, noon-1:15pm, 2pm-3:15pm, 4pm-5:15pm Apr.-Oct.; RIB rides adult £34, child £24, family £105, cruiser rides adult £18.50, child £12, family £55, under 4 free

If you want an exhilarating ride out to the **Moray Firth,** then book one of these two-hour RIB rides where, hopefully, you may be able to spot some of the resident dolphins or see some of the passing pods, even some whales. For something a bit calmer and kid-friendly, there's also a gentler cruiser option. You must arrive 30 minutes before your scheduled departure time for the RIB rides and 15 minutes before for cruiser trips. Most importantly, though, Dolphin Spirit is accredited by the Dolphin Space Programme, which means it adheres to a code of conduct

to ensure the dolphins don't endure any undue stress from the boats, particularly during breeding season.

Fishing
YOU FISH SCOTLAND

Inverness; tel. 01463 772 121; youfishscotland.com; year-round; salmon fly-fishing from £372 per day

The River Ness flows through Inverness and is renowned for its great salmon and trout fishing. Whether you're a complete beginner who would like to learn the basics or a more advanced fly-fisher keen to learn about the best tackles and methods for each fish, this small company run by the affable Wes and Roz will organize the best trip for you. Your guide, sometimes Wes, sometimes one of his very experienced hands, will collect you from your hotel. Day-trippers will be given a homemade lunch, plus all equipment is supplied. For longer, more relaxed angling adventures, book the company's cozy lochside cabin for the night too, where you can mull over your day's activities over a whisky tasting in the evening.

OUTDOOR ADVENTURES
KUSHI ADVENTURES

20 Union Road, Inverness; tel. 07833 462 707; www. kushiadventures.co.uk; year-round; three-day rock climbing courses £250

This outdoor activity provider can tailor walks into the Highlands hills and mountains to suit all levels of ability, whether you want an introduction to the region and its many wild flowers, scenic waterfalls, and forests under the watchful eye of experienced hikers, or you want a little more adventure and would like to camp under the stars. If you have your own navigation equipment, guides can give advice and training on how best to use it on one of the two-day Mountain Navigation courses, and for adrenalin junkies, rock climbing courses where you can really get to grips with

some of the many crags in the area are also available, as is abseiling.

FOOD
Traditional
URQUHARTS RESTAURANT

2 Young Street, Inverness; tel. 01463 233 373; www. urquharts-inverness.co.uk; lunch noon-2:30pm and dinner 5:30pm-9pm Tues.-Sat., noon-9pm Sun.; entrées £6.25

This small family-run restaurant is a great place for an early dinner if you are seeing a show at nearby Eden Court. The menu isn't the most daring—there's sausage and mash, steak, and Hunters-style chicken on offer—but the house special fish pie hits just the right spot and the haggis, neeps, and tatties pleases most visitors. My only criticism is the minimum charge of £10 per head, which is a bit restrictive.

★ HOOTANANNY

67 Church Street, Inverness; tel. 01463 233 651; www. hootanannyinverness.co.uk; lunch noon-3pm and dinner 5pm-8pm Mon.-Sat., noon-9pm Sun.; entrées £5.45

Make no mistake, most people come to Hootananny in the center of town for the brilliant atmosphere and Scottish traditional music sessions that take place round a table in the middle of the dining area every night Sunday-Wednesday 9:30pm-midnight. However, the menu is pretty decent too, with stews, tasty burgers, and homemade haggis meatballs to choose from. My tip is to book a table for dinner and settle in for the night. On Fridays and Saturdays live Scottish bands play on the main stage too.

Modern Scottish
MUSTARD SEED

16 Fraser Street, Inverness; tel. 01463 220 220; www. mustardseedrestaurant.co.uk; lunch noon-3pm daily, dinner 5:30pm-10pm daily, early evening menu 5:30pm-7pm daily; entrées £6.95, £14.95 for two courses on the early evening menu

Ask anyone in Inverness for their top three restaurants, and the chances are this will be

---

1: Highland House of Fraser, Inverness
2: Hootananny, Inverness **3:** Victorian Market, Inverness

one of them. The building itself is reason enough to visit: its former guise as a church affords it a double-height ceiling, and period features entwine with modern minimalist touches to give a fresh feel. That's not to undersell the food, though, which is consistently good, and dishes such as pan-seared Scottish salmon on shellfish gnocchi are realistically priced. In summer book a table on the terrace for lovely river views.

ROCPOOL RESTAURANT

1 Ness Walk, Inverness; tel. 01463 717 274; www. rocpoolrestaurant.com; lunch noon-2:30pm, dinner 5:45pm-10pm Mon.-Sat. Mon.-Fri., early evening menu 5:45pm-6:30pm Mon.-Fri.; entrées £9.95

This corner building on the west side of the river (just opposite the castle) might not look like much from the outside, but the inside reveals a chic restaurant with a superb standard of food. It's pretty pricey, but I bet you'll still be talking about dishes such as roasted Speyside venison with haggis, Parma ham, and creamed parsnips and crispy potatoes on the side long after you've left. There's a good cocktail menu too.

Pub Grub
CASTLE TAVERN

1 View Place, Inverness; tel. 01463 718 178; www. castletavern.pub; noon-10pm daily; entrées £5.75

A short hop from the castle, this lively pub is a nice enough place to stop for a pint or a bite to eat. If you're lucky, you'll find space at one of the tables in the bar area; if not, head upstairs to the restaurant, which has a slightly forgotten-about appearance—old carpet and bare tables, with the exception of a tiny glass bottle of flowers—but the menu is the same. The menu is OK pub food, with the odd more exciting special, such as west coast king scallops served with creamy pesto sauce, thrown in.

★ CLACHNAHARRY INN

17-19 High Street, Clachnaharry; tel. 01463 239 806; www.clachnaharryinn.co.uk; 12:30pm-9pm Mon.-Sat., carvery 12:30pm-8pm Sun.; entrées £4.95

This lovely inn, known to locals as "the Clach," is worth taking a little trip out of town for. It is located in the former fishing village of Clachnaharry, which is now a quiet backwater of Inverness; you can catch the no. 307 bus there from the bus station in Inverness. It's pub fare with a little flair: there's a grill section and a good few fish choices and portions are large, so come hungry. There's a nice beer garden, staff are great, and the bar is pretty much always humming with the chatter of locals. There's sometimes a reduced menu on Mondays and Tuesdays and don't arrive too late—they occasionally decide to close the kitchen a little early if it's quiet.

Light Bites
GIRVANS

2-4 Stephens Brae, Inverness; tel. 01463 711 900; www.girvansrestaurant.co.uk; 9am-6pm Mon.-Weds., 9am-7pm Thurs.-Sat., 10am-5pm Sun.; cooked breakfast £9.50

This is a popular brunch spot at weekends. You'll often find leisurely locals tucking into cooked breakfasts (served all day Sundays), which come with tea or coffee and toast. It's a good lunch spot during the week too, with lovely fresh filled sandwiches and baked potatoes or patisseries (though rather cheekily, there is a minimum spend of £4 per person noon-2:30pm).

ACCOMMODATIONS
Under £100
BAZPACKERS

4 Culduthel Road; tel. 01463 717 663; www. bazpackershostel.co.uk; £22 for a dorm bed, £65 d

You can't get much more centrally located than this hostel, which lies in the lee of Inverness Castle. Rooms are pretty standard for a hostel (dorms and some private doubles and singles are available), but there are some nice touches, including the real fire that awaits you on arrival and the full range cooker in the communal kitchen. Plus, for £5 staff will even wash and dry your clothes for you—beats waiting around all day in the laundry room when you could be out exploring.

Over £100
★ ABERFELDY LODGE
11 Southside Road; tel. 01463 231 120; www. aberfeldylodge.com; £110 d

This homely B&B is set in a grand detached Victorian villa, making it feel a lot less budget than its price may suggest. Inside, rooms are clean and bright; indeed, two of them have doors that lead onto the nice garden. It's also handy for the train station (just a 10-minute walk away); however, the building is old, so the hot water has a little knack to it and wireless Internet is only really good in the lounge. Nevertheless, if you can see past these things, you'll have a lovely wallet-friendly stay.

PITFARANNE GUEST HOUSE
57 Crown Street, Inverness; tel. 01463 239 338; www. pitfaranne.com; £130 d

Centrally located—the castle is just a five-minute walk away—this B&B on a quiet residential street is a real home from home. The new owners, Malcom and Maggie, took over the running of the six-bed property in 2018 and will go out of their way to help you make the most of your time here.

Over £200
ROCPOOL RESERVE
Culduthel Road, Inverness; tel. 01463 240 089; rocpool.com; £250 d

Not to be confused with the family-run restaurant with a similar name, this is an altogether bigger enterprise, which falls under the fabulously luxuriously ICMI collection of hotels. Housed within an attractive but understated Georgian mansion, each of the 11 rooms comes with a giant bed and in a range of styles, from the decadent to classic or hip. As well as Tassimo coffee machines and Bose Bluetooth sound systems, lots of extra perks can be added, including in-room massages. And it even has its own Chez Roux restaurant.

GLENMORISTON HOUSE HOTEL
20 Ness Bank, Inverness; tel. 01463 223 777; www. glenmoristontownhouse.com; £229 d, £269 river view room

Set back from the road along the riverbank, this townhouse hotel has a surprising 30 bedrooms, plus three posh self-catering apartments known as the Windsor Suites. In the hotel itself the Deluxe River View rooms with a huge trio of windows are the nicest, and it's hard to resist the lure of the Whisky and Piano Bar—all Italian marble and wood paneling—where you can dip into the city's largest whisky collection. On Saturdays you'll even be entertained by the resident pianist.

BUNCHREW HOUSE HOTEL
Bunchrew; tel. 01463 234 917; bunchrewhousehotel. com; £360 d

A little out of town, perched on the banks of the Beauly Firth to the west of the city is this pretty-in-pink castle that looks like something out of a fairy-tale book. Despite grand appearances, it's only four-star, though prices are certainly five-star. Still, if you want to have a romantic Highlands getaway, then this is the place; some rooms come with a four-poster (ask at booking), and in the expansive grounds you will find the Loving Tree, a 250-year-old Cedar of Lebanon tree, a popular backdrop for wedding photos. With its wood paneling and more oft than not crackling fire, the hotel is a lovely destination for afternoon tea—a good alternative if you can't afford the eye-popping overnight prices.

INFORMATION AND SERVICES

The main **tourist office** for Inverness is located near the castle (36 High Street; www. visitscotland.com/info/services/inverness-icentre-p333031) and is a good place to ask about the best tours (there are dozens of operators to choose from). Also, for a small fee they will even help you book accommodation, should you need extra assistance.

A few websites can help plan your visit. The **official city website** (inverness-scotland.com) is OK but obviously has to pander to certain local politics and keep people happy (that is, make sure everyone gets an equal footing with little critique). Slightly more useful is **Visit Inverness & Loch Ness** (www.visitinvernesslochness.com), which does assume that most visitors to Inverness want to visit the famous loch. Last, but certainly not least, **Highlife Highland** (www.highlifehighland.com) is a local charity that runs many of the local tours, helps support the heritage of the city, and is a good resource.

GETTING THERE

By Air

Inverness Airport (www.invernessairport.co.uk) lies 9 miles (14 km) east of the city and has several arrivals each day from London Heathrow, Gatwick, and Luton. **EasyJet** (www.easyjet.com) flies direct to Inverness from London Gatwick and London Luton, and **British Airways** (www.britishairways.com) has direct flights from London Heathrow. There are also flights from Manchester and around one flight a day from Stornoway on the Isle of Lewis with Logan Air (www.loganair.co.uk). The earlier you book flights the cheaper they will be—with easyJet it's fairly easy to pay just £30 each way if you can be a little flexible on dates and avoid weekends and bank holidays.

From the airport, you can take the no. 11 or no. 11A bus with **Stagecoach** (£4.40 each way) from Inverness Airport into the city center. Buses are fairly regular (every 40 minutes Mon.-Sat., slightly less regular Sun.), with a journey time of 20-25 minutes. Taxis are also available with **Inverness Taxis** (www.inverness-taxis.com), which take around 20 minutes and you can expect to pay £12 to reach the city. Car hire is available at the airport with a number of operators, including **Arnold Clark** (www.arnoldclarkrental.com/airport-car-hire/inverness-airport) and **Avis** (www.avis.co.uk) from around £140 per week.

By Train

The other main travel option into Inverness from London is aboard the **Caledonian Sleeper train** (www.sleeper.scot), which sets off the night before from London Euston and arrives into Inverness at around 8:40am. There is one train a day with a journey time of just around 11.5 hours, and tickets cost from £50 one-way or £185 with a single cabin.

There are also trains into Inverness from all major Scottish cities (Perth, Edinburgh, Stirling, and Glasgow). From Edinburgh around seven direct trains run a day, with a journey time of 3.5 hours (from £15.50 one-way). From Glasgow six direct trains run a day, with a journey time of 3.25 hours, and tickets cost from £11.80 one-way single. Go to **ScotRail** (www.scotrail.co.uk) for more information. The train station in Inverness is located on Academy Street in the city center.

By Car

Inverness is 157 miles (253 km) north of Edinburgh. Take the M90 north of the capital to Perth where you will join the A9, which will take you all the way into Inverness with a journey time of 3.25 hours. The journey time from Glasgow is the same as the one from Edinburgh, but this time you take the M80 out of the city, all the way to Stirling, where you can also pick up the A9 (169 mi/272 km). From Fort William it's a very direct route of 66 miles (106 km) northeast up the A82 (which follows the Great Glen) all the way to Inverness, with a journey time of 1.75 hours.

By Bus

Just a block away from the train station, **Inverness Bus Station** (Margaret Street) is also accessed from Academy Street and offers all manner of connections. The no. N19 from **Shiel Buses** (shielbuses.co.uk, two buses per day Mon.-Fri., one per day Sat., £10.40 one-way) and the no. 919 from **Stagecoach** (www.stagecoachbus.com, two buses per day Mon.-Sat., £10.40 one-way) travel from Fort William to Inverness Bus Station (two hours), stopping at Fort Augustus at the southern end of Loch Ness and Drumnadrochit and Urquhart Castle on its western shores. Stagecoach has also recently overtaken a service from Foyers on the eastern shores of Loch Ness to Inverness a few times a day Mon.-Sat. (no. 302, 50 minutes, £3.40 one-way).

The no. 917 from **Scottish Citylink** links Skye with Inverness (journey time 4.25 hours, four times per day, £26.40 each way single) and also passes along the western shores of Loch Ness. To reach Inverness from Glencoe you'll need to get the no. 915 or no. 916 bus with **Scottish Citylink** from Glencoe to Fort William (about four buses a day) and connect with one of the Inverness buses here (30 minutes to Fort William, £8.50 one-way).

GETTING AROUND

Once in the city, you can reach most of the main sights on foot. However, if you're short of time, jump on the **CitySightseeing** hop-on hop-off bus (www.citysightseeinginverness. com), which encircles the city and takes in major sights outside of the city center such as Ness Islands and Merkinch Local Nature Reserve (adult £10, concessions £8, child £3, under 5 free). Tickets last 24 hours, though the buses only run 9:30am-4:15pm.

To reach Merkinch Nature Reserve you can take one of a few buses that leave from outside the Farmfoods shop on Academy Street (near the bus station) to South Kessock, including the no. 8 with **Stagecoach** (12 minutes; £1.95 one-way single, £3.60 dayrider). Though some of the buses heading out to Loch Ness stop near Ness Islands and the Botanic Gardens, they really are so rare that you are best walking or getting a cab. **Inverness Taxis** (tel. 01463 222 222; www.inverness-taxis.com), which can be hailed or ordered, is the main taxi provider.

Vicinity of Inverness

The vast majority of visitors to Inverness come to visit Loch Ness, which lies just 13 miles (21 km) south of the city and can be reached easily by bus, car, or even boat tour. However, make time to explore some of the major attractions to the east of the city, not least Culloden Moor, scene of one of the most historic battles in British history, and also the seaside resort of Nairn, where you'll find Cawdor Castle and surely one of Scotland's most tourist-friendly coastal towns.

Fans of TV's *Outlander* are well served in the area too. The area's nearby ancient burial site of Clava Cairns was supposedly the inspiration for Craigh na Dun on the show. Talking of fictional connections, when Shakespeare wrote down his account of one of the most notorious of Scottish kings, Macbeth, he used more than a little poetic license by changing the setting to Cawdor Castle, just 15 miles (24 km) northeast of Inverness. The fact that the castle was built a couple of centuries after the

bloodthirsty king lived has done nothing to dampen the enthusiasm of visitors who come in search of literary links, no matter how dubious. However, while they may be disappointed to have many of the links dispelled, surely they can't find the beautiful castle, which has many more interesting stories to tell, a letdown.

And jutting out onto the Moray Firth with its own dolphin population, is the imposing Fort George, which some consider one of the finest military fortifications in the whole of Europe.

SIGHTS

TOP EXPERIENCE

★ Culloden Battlefield

Culloden Moor, Inverness; tel. 01463 796 090;
www.nts.org.uk/visit/places/culloden; 10am-4pm
Jan.-Feb., 9am-6pm Mar.-May, 9am-7pm June-Aug.,

9am-6pm Sept.-Oct., 10am-4pm Nov.-Dec. 23 and Dec. 27-30, 10am-2pm Dec. 31; visitor center adult £11, concessions £9.50, family £27, entry to the battlefield free

There are few experiences more emotive, particularly for members of the Scottish diaspora, than standing on the very battlefield where 1,600 men and boys (1,500 of whom were Jacobites) were brutally slaughtered in an hour, bringing the Jacobite dream crashing down and sending its leader, Bonnie Prince Charlie, running for the hills.

HISTORY

The Battle of Culloden, which ultimately changed the course of Scottish history, took place here, just six miles (10 km) east of Inverness, on April 16, 1746, and was the culmination of a rising first begun with Bonnie Prince Charlie's arrival in Scotland just months earlier.

Raising the Stuart standard at Glenfinnan near Loch Shiel on August 19, 1745, Bonnie Prince Charlie staked his family's claim to the British crown and thus began a hearty uprising to rid Scotland and England of Hanoverian rule (King George II sat on the throne at the time) once and for all. The cause united Highland clans (both Catholic and Protestant), many of whom had grown tired of the authoritarian rule from London and believed the Stuarts would give Scotland more control over its affairs, and the Jacobites looked on course to win their fight.

After declaring Charles's father, James Francis Edward Stuart, King of Scotland in Edinburgh and celebrating victories at both the Battle of Prestopans and Battle of Falkirk Muir, the Jacobites marched south in the hope of launching an invasion on London. They were making steady progress and made it as far as Derbyshire in England—just three days from the capital—but there an about-turn took place. When English and French reinforcements they had been promised failed to materialize, the Jacobite army got jittery and, against the wishes of Bonnie Prince Charlie,

decided to retreat. Sadly, this was to be their downfall. Unbeknownst to the Jacobites, King George II's son, the Duke of Cumberland, a fearsome and expert commander (his brutality earned him the nickname "Butcher"), was hot on their heels with a huge army, and it was at Culloden that he caught up with them.

The open moorland of Culloden did not suit the fighting style of the Jacobites, made up predominantly of Highlanders whose best weapon was the element of surprise, leaping down mountains to catch their enemies off guard. Faced with a much larger and much better organized army of redcoats, who were drilled and in line, the Highlanders did the only thing they could—they charged at the enemy, but as they did the redcoats released canon after canon. Since then, the battle site has become a place of pilgrimage for millions of Scots, many of whom became scattered around the globe in the wake of Culloden as a result of the subsequent emigrations.

VISITING TODAY

Anyone can step onto the moor itself for no charge, and it's an emotional experience, particularly for descendants of any of the clans who lost members that day. The battlefield, an area of generally flat (though lumpy) open boggy moorland, has been left much as it was prior to that fateful day; it's easy to see how the Jacobites, who favored charging downhill, were left vulnerable. On a cold and wet day when there are few visitors and an eerie sense of calm, it's not hard to imagine the battle cries of the clansmen as they charged forward, claymores in hand, bellowing their clan names as they ran to certain death.

Old Leanach Cottage, which was here back then (government forces burned down the barns that once stood near it when Jacobites hid there), still stands, and, though it has been closed for restoration, it is due to open, complete with a newly heather-thatched roof. Some sensitive additions have also been made to the landscape, including red and blue flags that indicate where each side stood, a six-foot (1.8-m) memorial cairn, and head-stones to mark the graves of hundreds of clansmen.

If you are at all unfamiliar with the lead-up to the battle or the significance of the Jacobite cause, then paying to enter the visitor center is a must. There's a lot to take in, so give yourself at least a couple of hours here; the audio guide is good, even if it doesn't always seem to tally with the exhibits, so feel free to pause at times to take in the extra bits of information.

There is an easy-to-follow path through the exhibits, spread out through one interconnected gallery, which use a mix of sound, stories, and artifacts to bring the Jacobite cause to life. About halfway round you can enter a separate room in which you can take part in an immersive experience. Hemmed in by screens with reenacted footage on all sides, and with surround sound, you really get a sense of the relentless combat in which the Jacobites armed with claymores and dirks were torn down by the better-equipped redcoats. This can make for uncomfortable viewing and is quite graphic in places, so it's not suitable for children. It's also worth paying the extra £2 for a tour of the battlefield and a really unforgettable experience in which your guide will reveal some of the personal stories of some of the men and boys who fought that day.

Clava Cairns

Near Inverness; tel. 0131 668 8600; year-round; free
With the earliest parts dating from around 2,000 BC, this collection of burial chambers in a woodland setting above the River Nairn is utterly beguiling. Two main sections, open to the public, once formed part of a larger complex. The first is Balnuaran of Clava, where an impressive central ring cairn is surrounded by standing stones and two passage graves and a curb ring cairn (a small circle of large curbstones, with the center filled in) was added some thousand years later. Because the graves are aligned with the three prominent cairns forming a line from northeast to southwest and the passages from

the two outer cairns are aligned toward the southwest, it's thought that the midwinter solstice would have been a significant time of the year for the people here.

The second area you can see is Milton of Clava where you can view the remains of a medieval chapel—little more than a collection of large stones today—as well as a prominent standing stone, which may have formed part of another cairn. Today visitors are also drawn to Clava Cairns due to its role in inspiring TV's *Outlander*.

Though a little tricky to reach by public transport, these prehistoric burial chambers are an easy detour from Culloden on your way back to Inverness by car (just a five-minute drive). Simply turn right onto the B9006 when you leave the Culloden Visitors Centre (rather than left to go back to Inverness), then turn right at Culloden Road, follow the road for a couple of minutes, and take the first road on your right (just past Clava Lodge Holiday Homes). The site will be on your right-hand side. The same route can be walked in around 30 minutes.

★ Cawdor Castle

Nairn; tel. 01667 404 401; www.cawdorcastle.com; 10am-5:30pm daily late Apr.-early Oct.; adult £11.50, child £7.20, family £33
Before I bring you the bad news, here's some good: Cawdor Castle is a well-preserved 14th-century castle in the style of a rectangular tower house that was constructed around a legendary thorn tree, which still exists and even has its own room in the castle. The story goes that the Thane of Cawdor decided he needed a more powerful castle. He was visited by an oracle who told him to strap all of his gold to the back of a donkey, and wherever that donkey rested he should build his castle. The donkey came to rest by a hawthorn tree, and that is where the castle was built.

Now for some not-so-welcome news: Macbeth never lived here—he couldn't have. He died some 200 years before the current castle was built. There was an earlier castle here, founded in the 12th century, but that was still way after his time. The link to Macbeth seems to have come from a little rewriting of history at the hands of Shakespeare as oft writers are want to do.

This news shouldn't put you off though; the castle, which is still lived in by the Cawdor family, is a fine stately home with all the exquisite paintings and priceless furniture that one might expect of the landed gentry. It's a sprawling palace, with 11 rooms in total to visit, and, though much of the splendor was added in the 17th century, it's incredibly preserved. The Thorn Tree room, where the fabled tree still stands, is relatively plain, with bare brick walls, but who can argue with the rich decoration of the Tapestry Bedroom, where you'll find a crimson velvet four-poster bed, with a 17th-century Venetian headboard, and huge tapestries on the walls? Outside, the expansive grounds include a walled garden, flower garden, and wild garden, where you can find displays of roses, blue poppies, and rhododendrons. A walk through the **Big Wood,** a remnant of the ancient Caledonian forest, is also a must, and on bright days, you should also stroll to the summer house of the Dowager Countess Cawdor, **Auchindoune House.**

Macbeth aside, Cawdor Castle has been home to one or two more dubious characters in its time. To hear scandals and stories of past residents, a tour of the castle with an expert guide (£110 for groups of up to 15, one hour) is recommended, but they only run on request, so book ahead. Express guided tours (just half an hour, from £30 per person) also run out of season if you ring ahead, and a new audio guide is said to be in the works for 2019.

The Highlanders' Museum and Fort George

Fort George; tel. 0131 310 8702; www. thehighlandersmuseum.com; 9:30am-5:30pm daily late Mar.-Sept., 10am-3:15pm daily Oct.-late Mar. (closed Sat.-Sun. Dec.-Jan.); museum free, Fort George adult £9, child £5.40, under 5 free

For those interested in military history, the Highlanders' Museum, set across three floors

of the former Lieutenant Governors' House within the confines of Fort George, is a must visit. The Highlanders are made up of the descendants of four historic Scottish regiments that were formed from clansmen of the Highlands and islands in the late 18th century: the Seaforth Highlanders, the Queen's Own Cameron Highlanders, the Queen's Own Highlanders (known as Seaforth and Camerons), and the Gordon Highlanders (they have their own museum in Aberdeen). Over 20,000 artifacts and 10,000 documents and photographs in 16 rooms chart the story of some of these Highlanders. In the neatly organized cabinet displays you can see campaign medals, including 16 of the regiment's 22 Victoria Crosses, the regimental uniform of King Edward VIII, and, rather unexpectedly, a box once used by Adolf Hitler to file personal papers.

Of course, if you've made it this far, then you'll want to explore the fort itself, which was constructed in the wake of the 1745 Jacobite rising to protect against future uprisings. Its most striking feature is the mile of wall that surrounds the fort—there's no doubt that the Hanoverians were serious about keeping the Jacobites out, though by the time they built it, the rising was over and not so much as a single shot has been fired at it. The ramparts provide a great viewing platform for views out to the Black Isle, and you can also sometimes spot dolphins, whales, and seals in the waters of the Moray Firth. Elsewhere in the complex, the grand Georgian military buildings are worth a gander, including the grand magazine, originally created to hold 2,672 gunpowder barrels and today filled with a huge weapon collection.

Today Black Watch, the 3rd Battalion the Royal Regiment of Scotland, are based here. An audio guide is available for the fort, and I've heard whispers of a virtual reality headset too. Please note the museum is closed on weekends in December and January, though the fort is open. The ramparts and most of the fort are accessible to wheelchair users, but the museum is largely inaccessible.

SPORTS AND RECREATION

BOWHUNTER ARCHERY

Balnagowan Woods, Ardesier; tel. 07923 111 997, 07753 426 141; www.bowhunterarchery.co.uk; daylight dependent but normally 9:30am-9pm summer and 10am-3pm winter; from £13 per hour

These live archery sessions veer somewhere between the riotously fun and the bit too weird. The chance to have a go at archery would appeal to most, but perhaps these sessions, which are open to all ages from eight up, are slightly more suited to the children in your midst. Not only will children get to run around for an hour firing arrows, but they will also have other less traditional targets, such as model dinosaurs, zombies, and dragons. Located somewhat between Cawdor Castle and Fort George, It's the type of place to take kids when you've dragged them round one too many heritage sights.

FOOD AND ACCOMMODATIONS

★ CAWDOR TAVERN

Cawdor, Nairn; tel. 01667 404 777; lunch noon-5pm Mon.-Sat., 12:30pm-5pm Sun., dinner 5pm-9pm; entrées £6.95

In the little village of Cawdor, not far from the castle, is this local tavern where you can eat hearty Scottish dishes such as roast rump steak and the famous chicken Culloden, in which chicken breast is stuffed with haggis, swede puree, and mashed potatoes as well as a delicious whisky cream sauce. It's a fair bit pricier than most pubs, but the quality is worthy of it. The pub itself, once the workshop for the Cawdor Estate, is exactly what you want inside, particularly in the lounge bar where there is a log fire and oak paneling that originally came from the castle's dining room.

INVERNAIRNE HOTEL

Nairn; tel. 01667 452 039; invernairne.co.uk; £140 d, Luxury King £350

Prices are deceptively low at this splendid boutique hotel, with an elevated position and sea views. It doesn't look like many other hotels you'll find in Scotland because its original owner took inspiration from his travels in Italy, hence the sunken garden. Inside it's a little surprising too—there's lots of period Scottish features (leather armchairs round a roaring fire and shelves filled with books) plus some more modern flourishes, including smart TVs. The Luxury King Rooms with mahogany four-posters, velvet cushions, and whirlpool baths are the best in the house, but this is reflected in the price.

CULLODEN HOUSE

Culloden Rd, Balloch, Culloden; tel. 01463 790 461; www.cullodenhouse.co.uk; £198 d

It was in this Palladian mansion (then a castle) during the Jacobite rising of 1745-1746 that Bonnie Prince Charlie lodged for three nights ahead of the fateful battle. Today the grandiose building, given a huge makeover following Culloden, still looks fit for royalty. In the drawing room there is plasterwork by renowned Scottish architect Robert Adam, from which chandeliers hang, and rooms feature sumptuous fabrics and the occasional marble fireplace. There's also a well-rated restaurant on the premises, and you can arrange for a whisky tasting at the **Library Bar.** It's a good base for visiting the battlefield, of course, but also Clava Cairns and Fort George.

GETTING THERE AND AROUND
By Car

To reach Culloden Battlefield it's just a six-mile (10 km) drive east from Inverness along the B9006, which takes about 15 minutes. There is a car park just outside. For Cawdor Castle, take the A96 east out of the city to Brackley, before turning right onto the B9090 to Cawdor (14 mi/23 km), which should take less than half an hour. For Fort George, you'll take the A96 east to begin with and then turn left onto the B9039 at Newton of Petty, which eventually leads onto the B9006 to Fort George (13 mi/21 km), with a journey time of

25 minutes. Nairn is a 20-minute drive east of Inverness along the A96 (16 mi/26 km).

By Bus

From Inverness, it's very easy to get to Culloden Battlefield by bus. Take the no. 5 bus from Queensgate to Croy and tell the driver you're going to Culloden Moor, not Culloden—the site is a further 10-minute bus ride from its namesake town (30 minutes, hourly, Mon.-Sat.; £3.15 one-way, £4.20 day-rider). On Mondays-Fridays the no. 252 with D&E Coaches (www.decoaches.co.uk) from Strothes Lane (just off Academy Street) in Inverness will get you to Cawdor in 45 minutes twice a day (£3.40 each way, £5.20 return). Get off at Cawdor Primary School, and it's just a 10-minute walk from here.

By Taxi

Located between Inverness and the airport, **Sneckie Taxis** (www.sneckietaxis.com) can organize tours to Cawdor Castle, Culloden, and Fort George, or work with you to create a bespoke itinerary such as a drive into the Highlands.

Loch Ness

Loch Ness is undoubtedly the tourist hub of the central Highlands. Most visitors come in search of the famous Loch Ness Monster, but, legends aside, this loch is one of nature's great enigmas. Stretching for 23 miles (36 km) and around one mile (1.6 km) at its widest, it's neither Scotland's largest loch (that is Loch Lomond) nor quite its deepest (Loch Morar in Lochaber claims that title), but it is certainly its biggest body of water—with a depth of 755 feet (230 m) in places, it holds more water than all the lochs in England and Wales put together.

Along the shores of the loch you'll find Urquhart Castle, with its thousand years of history, standing like a broken vase on the western shores, while to the northeast, the pink splendor of the Rapunzel-worthy Aldourie Castle peeps out from behind a curtain of trees. In the southeastern corner, visitors leaving Fort Augustus by boat may just make out a strange pyramid-style structure poking up from the land. The stone obelisk is known as the Hambro memorial, built by one Mr. Ro Olaf Hambro following the tragic drowning of his wife in 1932. His wife, Winifred, attempted to swim back to shore with her husband and two sons following an explosion on their boat, but, while they and the family's governess, who remained on board, survived, Winifred did not. For many, this was just a tragic accident, but, for others, questions abounded about whether Mrs. Hambro, a confident swimmer, was dragged under by some mysterious creature. This is, after all, Loch Ness.

ORIENTATION

The loch is served by the town of **Fort Augustus** in the south and the village of **Drumnadrochit** on the western shore, and the A82 runs from the outskirts of Inverness through both places. Both towns do get invaded by tourists (particularly in the height of summer in July and August), but they are useful places to restock and book tours and experiences. For a more sedate visit, head to the much quieter eastern shore of the loch along the B862 and then the B852, where the charms of villages such as **Dores** and **Foyers** are subtler and more genuine. There are a couple of good hotels, plus an excellent shore-side campsite, in Foyers.

SIGHTS

Loch Ness Centre and Exhibition

Drumnadrochit; tel. 01456 450 573; www.lochness. com; 9:30am-5pm daily Easter-June, 9:30am-6pm July-Aug., 9:30am-5pm Sept.-Oct., 10am-3:30pm

Loch Ness

Struy

A831

A82

FISHING ON
LOCH NESS

B862

ALDOURIE
CASTLE

DORES INN
Dores

B862

A82

B852

ACH NA
SIDHE

LOCH NESS CENTRE
& EXHIBITION

DRUMBUIE
FARM

CORRIMONY
CHAMBERED CAIRN

A887

Drumnadrochit

LOCH NESS GIFTS

CAFE
EIGHTY2

URQUHART
CASTLE

DIVACH
FALLS

A82

B852

B862

Ness

Inverfarigaig

LOCH NESS
SHORES

THE CRAIGDARROCH
INN

Foyers

WATERFALL
CAFE

THE FALLS
OF FOYERS

B862

Loch
Mhor

A82

Loch

Invermoriston

B862

SEE
DETAIL

Fort
Augustus

A82

0   2 mi

0   2 km

© MOON.COM

Detail inset:

BUNOICH BRAE

A82

MORAG'S
LODGE

Fort
Augustus

CALEDONIAN
CANAL CENTRE

CANAL SIDE

CANAL SIDE

CRUISE
LOCH NESS

THE BOTHY

STATION RD

THE CLANSMAN
CENTRE

GLENDOE RD

THE LOVAT
BRASSERIE

A82

B862

winter; adult £7.95, child £4.95, under 6 free

If you want to learn more about the myth of Nessie, then a stop here is worth an hour of your time. While it doesn't shy away from revealing some of the more daring hoaxes, it also puts forward a compelling argument that there is something lurking beneath the loch's surface. All visitors take part in a 35-minute audio-visual tour, using a mix of archive materials. To younger tech-savvy minds, it may look a little amateurish, so kids could get a little bored.

For the more cynical traveler, the exhibition also includes a lot of background on the geology of the loch, though granted, many of the displays are a little dated. It's not particularly ground-breaking stuff, but on a wet day it can fill in an afternoon and may even trigger a theory or two.

Divach Falls

Drumnadrochit; scotland.forestry.gov.uk/visit/divach-falls

Once the biggest tourist attraction in Drumnadrochit (before Nessie mania took hold), these waterfalls, which drop 100 feet (30.5 m), are just two miles south of the village and only a short walk from the small parking area (albeit at the end of a single-track road).

To get to the car park, follow the A82 south out of Drumnadrochit and turn left onto the Balmaccan Road (it should be signposted to Balmaccan and Divach). Then follow this road for around a quarter of a mile (0.4 km) before staying right to join a single-track unmarked road. The small parking area will be on your right after another mile (1.6 km). The walk to the viewing platform, though just 984.3 feet (300 m), is steep and muddy at times over rough ground. The falls, surrounded by ancient oakwoods, drop from a good height and appear pure and wild.

Corrimony Chambered Cairn

Glen Urquhart, off the A831; www. historicenvironment.scot/visit-a-place/places/corrimony-chambered-cairn

This ancient site is the perfect antithesis to Nessie, with not a monster motif in sight but plenty of historic intrigue surrounding who built it and why. Incredibly well preserved, this circular mound of stones—a sort of sibling to Clava Cairns—once formed part of a burial chamber dating from around 2000 BC and has a diameter of around 60 feet (18.3 m). At the center of the cairn is a round chamber that would once have been covered, and a long low passage runs from here to the edge of

Loch Ness

The Myth of the Loch Ness Monster

Of course, this most famous of Scottish lochs is now virtually synonymous with a certain monster called Nessie thanks to an ancient legend that gained a lot of traction in the 1930s and a clever tourism campaign thereafter. However, while its unimaginably deep waters are certainly mysterious—in many places Loch Ness is deeper than the North Sea—it's unlikely that a green diplodocus-like creature really lurks beneath its inky surface, and the magic is broken with every tacky toy and cartoon blazoned on shop windows.

FIRST TALES

The Loch Ness Monster story first reared its head way back in the 6th century when St. Columba is said to have banished a giant beast he came across on the River Ness after it attacked a local farmer. For centuries afterward, there were often tales of strange goings-on within the loch, perhaps fueled by Scottish myths of kelpies: shape-shifting spirits that often take on the form of a horse and are said to haunt many Scottish lochs.

THE PHOTO

It wasn't until the 1930s, though, that the notion of a creature living in the deep, dark loch drew interest from far and wide. Around this time, numerous sightings were recorded, and in 1934 a London surgeon by the name of R. K. Wilson even managed to take a photograph of what appeared to be the long neck of an unknown creature rising up above the water. It was published in the *Daily Mail* newspaper, and so Nessie became a tabloid sensation. Soon hundreds of people descended on the loch, determined to get more photographic evidence of the monster's existence or even to find Nessie and catch it.

THEORIES

Even though Wilson's photo was revealed as a hoax in the 1970s, the myth of Nessie refuses to die; to date, there have been around 1,000 sightings. Some say secret underwater caves lead out to sea and cause occasional whales to get lost in the loch, while others say that she is some kind of giant eel. One theory is that Nessie is actually a plesiosaurus that failed to die off with the rest of the dinosaurs and was somehow kept alive in the dark and deep waters of Loch Ness. Perhaps some people just like to believe in the impossible, or maybe, just maybe, there is something to the stories after all.

the cairn. Just like at Clava Cairns, its layout suggests some alignment with celestial events, and there is evidence of cup-marking (a sort of prehistoric rock art) similar to marks found at Clava Cairns. The cairn can be found amid pretty moorland beside Caledonian forest, which is a haven for birdlife. There is parking just before the cairn and it's just enough off the beaten path that it generally feels very calm and spiritual here, with few tourists spoiling the illusion. It's hard to believe it's just 8.5 miles (13.7 km) west of the tourist hotspot of Drumnadrochit.

Urquhart Castle

A82, Drumnadrochit; tel. 01456 450 551; www.

urquhart-castle.co.uk; 9:30am-6pm Apr.-Sept., 9:30am-5pm Oct., 9:30am-4:30pm Nov.-Mar.; adult £9, child £5.40

This ruined castle on the bonnie banks of Loch Ness has endured much warfare and unrest. Today, battle-scarred though it is, it retains a haunting beauty that offers just a hint of what this once great fortress was. With 1,500 years of history, it has drawn romantic poets and writers to its walls in search of some of the relics of its past that saw it host lavish royal banquets and withstand countless sieges. St. Columba is said to have visited in the 6th century, and it has spent 500 years as a medieval fortress—changing hands many times during the Wars of Independence

Still thro' the gap
the struggling river toils,
And still, below,
the horrid caldron boils

between the English and the Scottish, who fought over it like a dog bone, according to one chronicler. It was finally abandoned in 1692 when the last soldiers marched out, burning it on their way so it could not be requisitioned by Jacobite forces.

Today, some of the magic is lost among the throngs of people who come simply to tick it off or take well-cropped photos. There is a good visitor center though, and the short film particularly will give you a good overview of the history of the place before revealing a magnificent view of the castle. You can wander the grounds freely, nip in and out of the ruined segments, including the miserable-looking prison cell, and head down to a little pebble beach in front of the castle that looks out over Loch Ness. For the best views, though, climb the five-story **Grant Tower** and see if you can spot unusual ripples—large unidentified objects have shown up on sonar here. There's also a decent café and a large shop in the visitor center.

Falls of Foyers

This thunderous waterfall was a popular beauty spot among 18th- and 19th-century travelers, though it appears many visitors may have been quite scared of its awesome power. Robert Burns wrote of how the "roaring Foyers pours his mossy floods," and later in the same poem, "Still, through the gap the struggling river toils, and still, below, the horrid cauldron boils." There's little to fear today, though. The path is safe and well laid out with steps over steep parts and two viewpoints (upper and lower) with proper safety guards. It's pot luck too (depending how much rainfall there has been recently) whether the falls are gushing or merely trickling, but the woodland around them is a very pretty place to be anyway.

Most visitors enter from the top of the woodland park by the village of Foyers (where there's a good café and shop) and walk down toward the falls, see them, and simply return the way they came—10 minutes there, 10 minutes back. However, for more peace and a better chance of seeing some red squirrels, continue down the path once you've visited the falls, all the way along the walkway, and enjoy the increasing quiet as you go. The bottom part of the woodland park is where squirrels are most frequently sighted, so find a spot, lay down a blanket, sit in silence, and wait. The walk down and back up again should take no more than an hour.

SHOPPING

THE CLANSMAN CENTRE

Canalside, Fort Augustus; tel. 01320 366 444; www. clansmancentre.uk; 10:30am-6pm daily Mar.-Oct., restricted openings in winter

In this old 19th-century schoolhouse at the bottom of Fort Augustus's staircase of locks, you'll find a better-than-most souvenir shop, with good-quality tartan scarves (much better than across the canal at the Mill Shop) alongside the ubiquitous Nessie hats and fridge magnets. More interestingly, however, is the **Highlanders museum** hidden behind a door in the corner of the shop: a replica of a clansman's turf house where intermittent shows describe the traditional way of life in 18th-century Scotland. Sadly, at present these shows are only available by prior arrangement for groups of eight or more.

THE CALEDONIAN CANAL CENTRE

Ardchatten House, Fort Augustus; tel. 01320 366 493; 9am-5pm daily

This new café-cum-shop-cum-museum (it opened in summer 2018) is a great addition to the town of Fort Augustus. The gift shop has a higher-caliber selection of books, toys, and souvenirs than you'll find elsewhere, plus a small but well-presented learning section tells the story of the canal and the people who built it. The café offers a choice of sit-down light bites and hot drinks, or you can get a coffee and cake to go and sit and watch the boats go by outside.

1: Urquhart Castle stands on the shores of Loch Ness **2:** Robert Burns lyrics at the Falls of Foyers

LOCH NESS GIFTS

The Green, Drumnadrochit; tel. 01456 450 695; www. lochnessgifts.com; 9am-9pm summer, 9:15am-5:15pm fall, winter, and spring

Sometimes all you want is an unashamedly tacky gift shop where you can pick up all your presents in one swoop, and that's exactly what you'll find here. Keyrings and soft Highland cattle and Loch Ness Monsters are all here to tempt you, as are scarves in a wide choice of tartans.

TOP EXPERIENCE

★ KAYAKING

There's surely no better way to grasp the scale of Loch Ness than on a boat powered by pure elbow grease. You can take a kayaking tour if you'd like more guidance, or, if you're staying at **Loch Ness Shores,** you can rent one for a leisurely solo paddle.

EXPLORE HIGHLAND

Clachnaharry Works Lock, Clachnaharry Road, Inverness; www.explorehighland.com; one four-hour trip per week Easter-Oct.; adult £45, under 18 £30

These four-hour paddling trips are taken aboard tandem kayaks under the guidance of local expert Donald Macpherson. While at times the waters of the loch are eerily still, they can be precarious when the wind picks up; having Donald nearby is very reassuring. Trips are taken weekly from Dochgarroch Locks on the Caledonian Canal where they continue toward Loch Ness. They are typically offered in the afternoon (1pm-5pm), though evening trips are sometimes offered in summer.

BOAT TRIPS AND FISHING

CRUISE LOCH NESS

Canal Swing Bridge, Fort Augustus; tel. 01320 366 277; www.cruiselochness.com; 10am, 11am, noon, 1pm, 2pm, 3pm, and 4pm late Mar.-Oct., 1pm and 2pm

---

1: Fort Augustus 2: Cruise Loch Ness is based in Fort Augustus. 3: kayaking on Loch Ness

Nov.-late Mar.; adult £14.50, child £8.50, family £44

These child-friendly cruises are pretty hard to miss—you'll spot their kiosk and usually one of the large catamarans emblazoned with the company's branding when you cross the bridge in Fort Augustus. They are a lot of fun, though; while dispelling some of the Loch Ness myths, your guide for the 50-minute Daily Cruise will also intrigue you with tales of unexplained objects on the sonar with plenty of jokes thrown in too. Morning cruises are a lot quieter, and you can usually just walk up and buy a ticket a few minutes before; from 1pm onward (especially in July and August) you'd do well to book. They also run evening cruises and high-speed RIB rides.

FISH LOCH NESS

Dochgarroch Lock, Inverness; tel. 07793 066 455; fishlochness.com; Easter-Sept.; from £90 per person

On these private guided fishing trips on Loch Ness, local ghillie Stuart Macdonald takes you out on his little fishing boat, *Time Bandit*. He can take groups of up to seven and the more of you there are, the cheaper it is per head. Trips take place morning, afternoon, or evening and tend to last four hours to give you a reasonable amount of time to fish plus take in some of the Highland scenery. Wet-weather gear is recommended, and Stuart will provide licenses, rods, lifejackets, and tackle.

HIKING

SOUTH LOCH NESS TRAIL

Torbreck; www.visitinvernesslochness.com/ things-to-do/south-loch-ness-trail.aspx

For years, the southern and eastern shores of Loch Ness were largely ignored by visitors, who were drawn to the more famous destinations on the northern and western shores. In recent years there has been a concerted effort to redress the balance, and this trail, which leads from Torbreck just outside Inverness to Loch Tarff just outside Fort Augustus, takes in a quieter, slower pace of travel, away from the busy A82. The landscape is a little more unkempt, and, with fewer travelers, you're more likely to see deer wandering the woods, plus the villages of Dores and Foyers feel much more geared toward ramblers and cyclists than day-trippers.

You can download and print copies of the map from the Visit Inverness Loch Ness website and choose which section you would like to do, as the full route is over 26 miles (42 km) and would take you around nine hours to walk. There are seven lochs to explore and numerous forest trails, all waymarked, on this side of Loch Ness. One option is the first section from Torbreck to Dores, which covers six miles (11 km) and takes you through woodland, past a farm, and onto a forest track high up to Drumashie Moor before descending into the pretty village of Dores (which has a nice beach) and should take around 2.5-3 hours.

FOOD
THE BOTHY

Canalside, Fort Augustus; tel. 01320 366 710; noon-2:15pm and 5pm-9pm (5pm-8pm winter); entrées £5.50

This canal-side pub-restaurant in Fort Augustus is probably its most welcoming. There are a couple of good beers on tap, including Skye Red and Skye Gold, and the menu is reassuringly traditional, with haddock and chips and steak pie on offer. With its stone walls and fireplace, the pub area is cozier than the conservatory, but the whole place feels very rustic and unpretentious.

WATERFALL CAFÉ

Foyers; tel. 01456 486 233; foyersstoresandwaterfallcafe.co.uk; 9am-5pm Mon.-Thurs., 9am-7pm Fri.-Sat., 10am-3pm Sun. Apr.-Oct., 9:30am-4pm Mon.-Thurs., 9:30am-7pm Fri.-Sat., 10am-2pm Sun. Nov.-Mar.; sandwiches £7.50

In the village of Foyers, just across the road from the path that leads down to the famous falls, is this cute little café where you can buy delicious homemade cakes, sandwiches, and fresh tea and coffee or even read one of the

books available. While here, pick up supplies at the village store/post office next door, and in summer treat yourself to an ice cream from the hut outside where you can help yourself to free sprinkles and sauce. In the telephone box outside, there's even a resident gnome to whom you are encouraged to send postcards; all the postcards he receives are displayed here.

★ THE CRAIGDARROCH INN

Foyers; tel. 01456 486 400; www.thecraigdarrochinn. co.uk; noon-2pm and 6pm-8:30pm daily; entrées £4.35

It's worth the 15-minute uphill trek from the Loch Ness Shores campsite to this pub, if only for the views of the campsite and loch, where the more you indulge in the local ale, the more you may convince yourself you've seen Nessie. The food is pretty standard pub grub, but good all the same and there is a kids' menu. You may be tempted to cut through the overgrown trails on your way up to shorten the journey, but, if you want to avoid getting bitten by midges, take the main road up to the left and then take a sharp right once you see the sign after 1,500 feet (457.2 m) or so. Or you can even drive the car all the way up. There are also rooms available (£120 d).

THE LOVAT BRASSERIE

Fort Augustus; tel. 01456 649 0000; www.thelovat. com; 7:30am-9:30am Mon.-Sat., noon-2pm and 6pm-9pm Sun.-Thurs., noon-2pm and 6pm-9:30pm Fri.-Sat.; entrées £8.25

This upmarket restaurant in a former railway hotel (now an elegant four-star hotel) is probably Loch Ness's finest. Dishes are of the haute cuisine level and have been awarded three Rosettes and it shows. Ox cheek, roast grouse, and scallops all appear on the menu regularly and are given the light touch that lets their natural flavors come through. It puts other restaurants in the area to shame.

1: The Craigdorrach Inn is an uphill walk from Loch Ness but the views are worth it. **2:** Waterfall Café, Foyers **3:** The Bothy, Fort Augustus **4:** Loch Ness Shores is a fantastic campsite.

CAFÉ EIGHTY2

Lewiston, Drumnadrochit; tel. 01456 450 400; www. facebook.com/cafeighty2; 9am-5pm Mon.-Sat., 11am-5pm Sun.; coffee from £2, cakes from £2.75

Don't be a fool and underestimate this wee café in the center of Drumnadrochit; it might look like a slightly quirky thrift store—all pastel colors, mismatched chairs and tables, and bunting—but it serves the best coffee around. Plus, it has exemplary vegan and vegetarian food. Oh, and cakes. You must try the cakes.

★ DORES INN

South Loch Ness; tel. 01463 751 203; www. thedoresinn.co.uk; lunch menu noon-5pm, evening menu 5pm-8:45pm; entrées £4.95

With roses climbing its walls, this white stone building with slate-tiled roof is about as inviting as they come, and inside it just gets better. Sit by the fire as you fill up on home-cooked food, or take in the views of Loch Ness from one of the window seats. There's also a sun terrace and a large beer garden, and you may find yourself rubbing shoulders with locals who would much rather eat here than in Fort Augustus. Staff are very friendly—so much so there is a complimentary shuttle service to pick you up and drop you off if you are staying within a 10-mile (16.1 km) radius.

ACCOMMODATIONS

MORAG'S LODGE

Bunoich Brae, Fort Augustus; tel. 01320 366 289; www.moragslodge.com; £24.50 for a dorm bed, £62 private double

Just outside Fort Augustus, this hostel offers the normal dorm set up alongside doubles, twins, and family rooms and is something of a local legend in its own right. There's a self-catering kitchen (of course), but you can also order a well-priced home-cooked meal before you sample some of the single malt whiskies in the bothy-style bar and dance the night away to some of the live music. It's not your average hostel at all.

ACH NA SIDHE

Wester Drumashie, Dores; tel. 01456 486 639; www. visit-lochness.co.uk; £90 d

Just a five-minute drive from the village of Dores, this quiet B&B has both loch and mountain views, a relaxing lounge and TV area, and lovely grounds with horses in a paddock. Family-run, there's little husband-and-wife team Marsaili and Ian and their kids won't do to make you feel at home—including washing and drying your clothes if you've been caught out by the weather.

DRUMBUIE FARM

Drumnadrochit; tel. 01456 450 634; www. loch-ness-farm.co.uk; £90 d

There are three en suite rooms in this intimate B&B on a working farm; the family breeds Highland cattle, and you can often see cows and their calves grazing outside. In the morning, as you feast on smoked salmon, scrambled eggs, or a full Scottish breakfast, you can gaze out to Loch Ness from the dining room. In the evenings snuggle up by the log fire in the lounge.

ALDOURIE CASTLE

Loch Ness; tel. 01463 751 309; www.aldouriecastle. co.uk; cottages (sleeping two or more) from £1,000 per week, exclusive two-night use of the castle £20,000

If you've spotted this Disney-style castle from the water, then you no doubt have fantasies of staying here. The good news is that, if you are loaded and/or have lots of friends to share it with, you can—it is available for exclusive hire. For the rest of us, there are some lovely cottages in the grounds to hire, such as the romantic white-stone Ivy Cottage with pitched roof or the one-story Pier Cottage right on the shoreline. Each of the four cottages are brimming with charm, and you'll get to gaze up at the stepped gables and Rapunzel-style turrets every day during your stay, although the castle is closed for major refurbishment until summer 2020.

Camping

★ LOCH NESS SHORES

Monument Park, Lower Foyers; tel. 01456 486 333; lochnessshores.com; £20 for a tent pitch, wigwams from £65

The only campsite with direct shore access, if you want a campsite on Loch Ness, it has to be here. Owners Donald and Lyn have created a warm, lovely environment where it seems everybody is just delighted to work here, and everyone, whether you have brought your own tent or are staying in one of the onsite wigwams (more a wooden pod) or in a motorhome, is made to feel at home. The toilets and showers are pristine, you can hire one of the kayaks for just £10 per person to head out on the loch, or try your luck making it up the nearby River Foyers as far as the old Telford Bridge (if conditions are suitable). There is a nice pebble beach from where you can skim stones after a home-cooked dinner that can be purchased from the Airstream van. There are lots of books to read and a fab shop, fires are allowed, and there are even den-building workshops for kids. Need I go on?

INFORMATION AND SERVICES

A **VisitScotland iCentre** in the main village car park in Drumnadrochit (tel. 01456 453 165) is open 9am-6pm Mon.-Sat. late June-early September with opening times gradually reducing outside peak season. You can get information on local tours, attractions, and accommodation providers.

Likewise, for visitors who arrive in Fort Augustus, the **VisitScotland iCentre** is in the main car park (tel. 01320 345 156) and is the place to pick up maps and leaflets on local tours. Opening hours are 9am-6:30pm Monday-Friday and 9am-6pm Sundays from late June-early Sept. From September-June the center closes at 5pm.

A useful online resource for both Loch Ness and Inverness can be found at www.visitinvernesslochness.com, with lots of inspiration for things to do in the area and useful walking trails.

GETTING THERE AND AROUND

Most visitors to Loch Ness will arrive from Inverness; as well as having a well-served airport, it's where the closest train station is. Once here, it's time to get your walking boots on if you don't have a car as local buses can be unreliable. Alternatively, you could book a private tour with the likes of **Loch Ness Travel** (tel. 01456 450 550; lochnesstravel. com), which also offers a taxi service. You can expect to pay around £34 for a transfer from Inverness to Drumnadrochit, or, for a full day's excursion (eight hours) from Inverness to Loch Ness, it would cost £500, though you could bring seven friends with you.

By Car

It's just 16 miles (26 km) from Inverness along the A82 to Drumnadrochit (a journey time of half an hour) and 20 miles (32 km) along the B862 and B852 to Foyers (about 45 minutes). Fort Augustus can be reached by following either of these routes on for another 15-20 minutes. from Drumnadrochit, it's a further 19 miles (31 km) to Fort Augustus, while from Foyers it's a further 14 miles (23 km). From Fort William, it's a 50-mile (80 km) drive northeast up the A82 to Drumnadrochit (1.25 hours).

From Glasgow, it's 139 miles (224 km) to Fort Augustus at the foot of Loch Ness. Take the M8 north out of the city before picking up the A82 at the bottom of Loch Lomond, which will take you all the way up through the national park, through Glencoe, and up past Fort William toward Loch Ness. Expect this to take around 3.5 hours. The journey time from Edinburgh to Fort Augustus is similar (3.75 hours, 159 miles/99 km), but you'll take the M90 north to Perth and join the A9, which you'll follow all the way through Perthshire to Dalwhinnie, where you fork off onto the A889. Follow the A889 until it turns into the A86, which you continue on before turning right onto the A82 at Spean Bridge, bringing you to Fort William.

By Bus

A number of buses set off from Inverness Bus Station to Loch Ness, including the no. 513 (or N19) from **Shiel Buses** (shielbuses.co.uk, from £3.70 one-way to Drumnadrochit, 30 minutes, every two hours summer, twice a day winter, Mon.-Sat.) and the no. 919 from **Stagecoach** (www.stagecoachbus.com, from £3.70 one-way to Drumnadrochit, 30 minutes, twice a day Mon.-Sat.). Both these buses stop at Drumnadrochit, Urquhart Castle, and Fort Augustus. These buses also link with Fort William in the opposite direction (1.75 hours to Drumnadrochit). Stagecoach has also recently overtaken a service from Foyers on the eastern shores of Loch Ness to Inverness a few times a day Mon.-Sat. (no. 302, 50 minutes, £3.40 one-way). To reach Loch Ness from Glencoe, you'll need to get the no. 915 or no. 916 bus with **Scottish Citylink** from Glencoe to Fort William (about four buses a day) and connect with one of the Loch Ness buses there (30 minutes to Fort William, £8.50 one-way).

Fort William

Say Fort William to most people, and there's one place that naturally springs to mind: Ben Nevis—a beast of a mountain that soars over the town and whose head is usually, quite literally, in the clouds.

But the highest peak in the British Isles is just one reason to visit this vast region that falls under the even larger area of Lochaber—an area of huge geographical interest. It is a place of natural contrasts where menacing mountains glower over serene lochs, and the thing it has above all else is space, miles and miles of it, with very few people cluttering it up. It is one great big playground for adventure sports, whether you want to ride a mountain gondola, go kayaking, hill-walk till your heart's content, or even ski in winter.

While by no means Scotland's most appealing town, Fort William nevertheless serves a purpose as a gateway to those seeking adventure. Stock up on necessities here and remember that it's all about the great outdoors, so forgive them their overly tacky gift shops and disappointing modern buildings.

★ BEN NEVIS

Ben Nevis, Fort William; www.visitscotland.com/ see-do/iconic-scotland/ben-nevis

The highest mountain in the British Isles, it's rare that you can actually see the peak of Ben Nevis, hence its nickname, "the mountain with its head in the clouds." Still, this king of the Grampian Mountains, in the west of the mountain range that covers a huge region of the Highlands and spreads southwest to northeast on the eastern side of the Great Glen, also called simply "Ben," is always there looking over proceedings, asking to be photographed. Ben Nevis stands 4,411 feet (1,345 m) above sea level and was once an active volcano that collapsed in on itself millions of years ago—light-colored granite at its peak is evidence of this event. Today the dominant mountain, which lords itself over Fort William and Loch Linnhe below, is a craggy, stern presence, where the hard lines in its rock face seem to dare you to test them. Though it is not quite as high as the Alpine mountains, its high latitude means its summit, so frequently shrouded in mist, is also often capped in snow, thanks to the Arctic-like conditions. Don't be fooled by temperatures on ground level; if you are scaling Ben Nevis, you need to pack warm clothes, whatever the weather.

For those who do make it to the rocky plateau of its summit, look for a cairn (a carefully positioned pile of stones), about 10 feet (3 m) high, that serves as an Ordnance Survey trig point as well as the ruins of a Victorian observatory, which looks like a rather ramshackle shelter atop a mound of stones, that was once used to chart Scottish weather.

Visiting Ben Nevis

If you're planning to hike or climb Ben Nevis, then it's worth paying a visit to the **Glen Nevis Visitor Centre** (Glen Nevis, Fort William; tel. 01397 705 922). At least stop in to check on the daily forecast specific to Ben Nevis, which is updated each morning at 9am. You can also stock up on last-minute snacks here, and it is the best place to park (£3 per car) as most routes around or up the mountain start here. It can get very busy in summer, so the earlier you get here the better to nab a space. There are also events, such as the Three Peaks Challenge, held regularly in summer, which means the mountain and amenities can be even busier. If you're at all worried, ring the visitor center to see if you can book a car parking space.

Bring lots of water, food for the expedition, good walking boots, a compass, a map, and appropriate clothing (usually thermals and wet-weather clothes). Make sure you fill out a mountain safety route card too, and leave it with someone trustworthy before you set off. Unless you are incredibly experienced, don't even consider doing the walk in winter.

Hiking Ben Nevis
PONY TRACK

Trailhead: *Glen Nevis Visitor Center*
Distance: *10.8 miles (17 km) round-trip*
Hiking time: *7-9 hours*
Information and maps: *www.walkhighlands. co.uk/fortwilliam/bennevis.shtml*

Most visitors who ascend to the summit of Ben Nevis use the Pony Track (erstwhile known as the Mountain Path), which sets off from the Glen Nevis Visitor Centre and begins with a steep climb on a track to Lochan Meall an t-Suidhe, which roughly marks the halfway point, before following a zigzag route to the top. Suitable for beginners, this route is straightforward in the sense that there is a relatively clear path to the top. But it is strenuous with steep sections throughout and then stony and rough as you near the top. It is also sometimes possible for the path to disappear under snow, so you will need to be prepared to exercise some navigational skills. The visitor center has useful signs offering advice on how to approach this hike—read them. The route outlined by the Walk Highlands website is detailed and includes maps and GPS waypoints that you can download.

To start the walk, cross the new bridge over

hiking on Ben Nevis

the River Nevis, turn right, and then follow the riverbank for a short time before turning left when you see a sign, which will lead you up through a path between a fence and a wall. You'll soon come to a stile that you need to cross and then go forward to cross a track and meet a path coming up from the left. Turn right up this path and climb up the hillside; soon after another path joins (coming up from Glen Nevis Hostel), the path will start to do a wide zigzag. Keep on the path as it crosses some small streams and over the valley of the Red Burn.

As you near the head of the burn, take the track that turns sharply to your left, and this will soon lead to the right of Lochan Meall an t-Suidhe, or the "halfway lochan". Keep to the right on the path until you come to a junction. You need to take the path on your right, and though at first the path is good, shortly it will become a lot rougher. Take care as a well-worn path navigates around scree and boulders, all the time climbing up the mountain, and pay attention as you near Five Finger Gully, which can be perilous. Eventually, the gradient will start to ease off as you get ever closer to the summit. From Ben Nevis's peak you can see most of the Scottish Highlands, even sometimes over to Northern Ireland. Your descent is back along the same route, but extra care needs to be taken to avoid dangerous areas of scree.

BEN NEVIS NORTH FACE TRAIL

Trailhead: *North Face Car Park, near Torlundy*
Distance: *11 miles (17.5 km) round-trip*
Hiking time: *10-11 hours*
Information and maps: *www.walkhighlands. co.uk/fortwilliam/carnmordeargarete.shtml*

If you don't want to walk in the wake of millions of other tourists and you are a very experienced mountain walker, then this alternative route up the mighty mountain is worth considering. You need to come properly equipped (good boots, maps, compass, walking sticks, and ice-ax or crampons in winter) and be prepared for a lot of scrambling. Those who do come this way

will view the graceful arc of the Carn Mor Dearg Arete, a curvaceous mountain ridge, which you'll need to traverse by scrambling.

To reach the trailhead, park at the North Face Car Park and walk along the track until you reach a barrier. The track will shortly turn to the left, and you want to follow the path to the right signposted for the North Face Trail. Continue ahead uphill and keep left at a fork in the trees. Follow the path as it climbs up and swings to the right before leveling out. Keep straight ahead when another path joins, and soon you'll reach the edge of a forest. Carry on left along the path and look out for a sign to the right for "Allt a'Mhuillin and CIC Hut." Take this and keep on the path before joining a track. When you come to the junction, turn right and Ben Nevis will be in front of you.

From now on you will be walking toward the north face of Ben Nevis. Cross a stile and follow the path. Eventually, there will be a boggy path to the left; take this path to begin your ascent to Carn Mor Dearg, the first of two munros you will scale today. The higher you go, the more dramatic the views, and you'll be able to see the many crevices and gullies of Ben Nevis. You'll now climb on to the ridge of Carn Deag Meadhonach and see the pointed peak of Carn Mor Dearg. Next, you'll descend slightly to the crest of Carn Mor Dearg, which involves some scrambling, not too precipitous, though you will want to concentrate and try not to get too distracted by the awesome view beneath Ben Nevis's cliffs. Once across the ridge, it's a steep climb over boulders and scree to the summit. Your route down should follow the Pony Track.

Tours and Mountain Guides

If you're not confident enough to attempt Ben Nevis yourself—and there's absolutely no shame in that—then there are some very good mountain guides that can take you there.

ADVENTURE NEVIS

3 Bracara, Morar; tel. 01687 460 163; www. adventurenevis.com; year-round, check website

for organized tour dates; group tours from £70,
Mountain Path from £200 per day for two, North
Face Trail £220 for two

This outfit, run by experienced hill-walker Peter Khambatta—he has walked the Scottish hills for over 20 years and is a munro compleatist himself—will take you on guided tours along either the Pony Track or the North Face Trail. You can choose to join a small group or book Peter or one of his trusted guides to yourself. As well as telling you a little about the history of the area and pointing out geographical features you might otherwise overlook, your guide will also teach you how to read a map and navigate so you might have more confidence to go it alone in future.

OTHER SIGHTS
Commando Monument

Spean Bridge; aboutfortwilliam.com/things-to-see/
visitor-attractions/the-commando-memorial

Just a mile (1.6 km) north of Spean Bridge (a village at the southern end of the Great Glen, which acts as a bit of a crossroads between Inverness to the north, Fort William and Skye to the west, and Loch Laggan to the east) and set amid a patchwork of green fields, this monument commemorates the men of the original British Commando Forces, formed during the Second World War, who trained nearby. The Commando Monument, sculpted from bronze, depicts three triumphant soldiers, who tower 17 feet (5.2 m) high on a platform overlooking Glen Spean below, and is hard to miss as the A82 passes right by it.

In truth, though, the reason this statue is so snapped is that it's positioned high up with fabulous views of Ben Nevis as well as nearby Aonach Mor, another munro topping the 4,000-foot (1,219.2 m) mark and which the Fort William mountain gondola climbs up and down each day.

Neptune's Staircase

Banavie, Fort William; www.scottishcanals.co.uk/
locations/neptunes-staircase

A good spot to sit and watch the boats come and go (albeit very slowly) as they go up and down this "staircase" of eight locks at the start of the Caledonian Canal—it takes about 90 minutes for boats to traverse all eight locks. A feat of engineering from Thomas Telford, who built the Caledonian Canal between 1803 and 1822 to connect the many lochs of the Great Glen, Neptune's Staircase raises (and lowers) boats an astounding 62 feet (19 m) across a distance of a quarter of a mile so they can continue on their journey from Loch Linnhe up through the Great Glen all the way to Inverness (or vice versa). Once hand-powered, the eight locks are now operated by a hydraulic system. Choose a spot by the canal on the western side, and, as you watch the boats leisurely descend and ascend the locks, you can keep one eye on Ben Nevis in the background too.

★ Mountain Gondola

Torlundy, Fort William; tel. 01687 470 415; www.
nevisrange.co.uk; mountain gondola 10am-5pm
Apr.-June and Sept.-Oct., 10am-6pm July-Aug.
(10am-9pm mid-July-Aug.), 10am-4pm Nov.,
9:30am-dusk Dec.-Mar.; mountain gondola one-way
day adult £19.50, child £10.50

Fort William's cable car that ascends one of the region's other highest mountains (Aonach Mor) is not to be missed. Not only will you get incredible views of Ben Nevis and the Great Glen (and you'll be able to photograph them without fear of losing your footing on a cliff edge), but you'll also be able to reach the top in just 15 minutes, giving you plenty of time to walk one of the viewpoint trails—either the 45-minute Sgurr Finnisg-aig trail or the one-hour Meall Beag walk—and warm up with a hot drink at the Snowgoose Restaurant & Bar at the top station. For those who want a bit more excitement, you can try your hand at paragliding or mountain biking down one of the daring downhill tracks. In the summer, you can even join in the raucous fun of a ceilidh on Fridays and Saturday nights.

In the winter, this is a great place to try winter sports such as skiing and snowboarding (Dec.-Apr., adult ski passes from £273, equipment-hire extra), occasionally opening earlier on busy weekends, though do check the website before you go as the range does close for maintenance each year, usually mid-November-mid-December.

RECREATION
Walks
STEALL FALLS

Ben Nevis Car Park, Glen Nevis Road; www. walkhighlands.co.uk/fortwilliam/steallfalls.shtml

This brilliant short walk covers just 2.3 miles (3.5 km) and takes you through Nevis Gorge before arriving at Steall Falls. The path is clear and well-marked throughout, though you should be prepared for some steep drops and rough track underfoot. Park at the Ben Nevis car park at the end of Glen Nevis and look for the path at the far end of the car park, which is signposted to Spean Bridge, Corrour Station, and Kinlochleven. Allow 1.5-2 hours for the round-trip journey (once you reach the falls return to the car park by the same route). It's a wild walk along a rocky gorge, where you will see glimpses of the river below through gaps in the trees before crossing a grassy meadow to view the waterfalls, above which rises the munro of An Gearanach.

Cycling and Mountain Biking
COW HILL

Braveheart Car Park, Glen Nevis; www. ridefortwilliam.co.uk

This light woodland, where once crofters' cows would graze, is now home to a herd of Highland cattle that help keep the wildflowers just right to attract more wildlife and is a lovely place for an afternoon's cycle. Setting off from Braveheart Car Park, the route, which suits intermediate and advanced cyclists, includes a little road cycling at first before you reach Cow Hill, just behind the Lochaber Leisure Centre, where there's a steep climb. In fact, this 7.5-mile (12.1 km) circular route involves a lot of uphill cycling, but persevere and you'll be afforded amazing views of Loch Linnhe, Fort William, and the villages of Corpach and Caol. The good news is that the way back is pretty much all downhill. It should take 1-2 hours.

NEVIS CYCLES

Lochy Crescent, Inverlochy; tel. 01397 705 555; www. neviscycles.com; 9am-5:30pm daily; from £35 per day, £160 per week

This well-facilitated bike-hire company offers full-suspension enduro bikes (good for some of the rougher tracks at Nevis Range), road and touring bikes, cross-country bikes for adventure cyclists, and a good selection of electric bikes and downhill two-wheelers too. Kid's bikes and child's seats are also available, and there is an option for one-way bike collection if you're planning a long-distance route and don't intend to come back. Bikes are all pretty new and come with helmets, pumps, water bottles, tire levers, and a spare tube. If you're not sure what the best bike is for your trip, ask staff and they'll be able to advise you. The company also runs a **Witch's Trails** hire shop from the Nevis Range mountain gondola station that operates late March-October.

Water Sports
ROCKHOPPER SEA KAYAKING

Unit 17 Annat Industrial Estate, Corpach, Fort William; tel. 07739 837 344; www. rockhopperscotland.co.uk; day trips year-round, multi-day June-Aug.; half day from £50, full day £80, multi-day £225

This is the go-to place for sea-kayaking adventures in the Fort William area. Choose among half-, full-, and multi-day excursions to explore some of the stunning coastline, from the relative calm of the Sound of Arisaig, where you can look out for otters en route, to the lesser-known waters of Glenuig. Multi-day adventures include camping under the stars and beach combing along spectacular coastal waters. For sheltered bays and spectacular backdrops, a paddle along Loch Leven with the mountains of Glencoe to look back upon is pretty special, and, when you've built up your confidence, you can venture out to open water and perhaps even the tidal narrows of Corran.

Golf
FORT WILLIAM GOLF CLUB
North Road, Fort William; tel. 01397 704 464;
fortwilliamgolfclub.com; 9am-5pm Mon., 9am-10pm
Tues. and Thurs., 9am-6pm Weds., 9am-7pm Fri.,
8am-8pm Sat.-Sun.; green fees Mar.-Oct. £30 per
player for 18 holes, £15 for nine holes, Oct.-late Feb.
£15 per round

There are few more spectacular backdrops to a few rounds than here, in the majestic mountainous region of Fort William. A relatively new course by Scottish standards, this 18-hole course at the base of Ben Nevis only opened in 1976 and has a more relaxed approach than most, but don't be too sloppy—jeans and sports colors won't be tolerated. Visitors are always welcome.

Wildlife Safaris
WILD WEST
9 MacKay Crescent, Caol, Fort William; tel. 0333 123
2820; www.wildwest.scot; year-round; Big Five Safari
adult £69, child £42, Big Five with cruise adult £85,
child £50

These eight-hour tours not only take you into wild landscapes not far from Fort William where you can hopefully see Scotland's "big five" (golden eagles, harbor seals, otters, red deer, and red squirrels) in one day but also furnish you with practical tips on how best to spot them when you venture out on your own. On Wednesdays the Big Five Safari trip also includes a two-hour boat ride across Loch Shiel. Guide Ian McLeod also offers half-day excursions and can create bespoke itineraries.

Survival Training
WILDWOOD BUSHCRAFT
Roshven, Lochailort; tel. 01397 705 825; www.
wildwoodbushcraft.com; year-round; from £90 for
two-day courses

If merely visiting the wilds of the Highlands as a spectator is not quite enough for you and you want to learn how to survive if you were to ever get lost (a very real possibility), then these bushcraft and survival courses will appeal. Courses start from near Achriabach in the Fort William area or in the Moirdart region a little west of Fort William.

FOOD
★ CRANNOG
Town Pier, Fort William; tel. 01397 705 589; www.
crannog.net; lunch noon-2:30pm daily, evening meals
from 6pm; entrées £7.95

Set just by the town pier in Fort William, this red-roofed building (once a bait shed) has been providing top-notch Scottish seafood for over 26 years. The menu changes each season, but you can expect the likes of west coast mussels and peppered salmon fillet.

BEN NEVIS INN
Claggan, Achintee, Fort William; tel. 01397 701 227;
www.ben-nevis-inn.co.uk; food served noon-9pm
daily Mar.-Oct. and Thurs.-Sun. winter (closed Nov.);
entrées £5.95

Known as the "wee inn at the foot of the Ben," this is where most walkers of Ben Nevis come to reward themselves after their trek. All wooden benches, wooden floors, you won't feel bad walking a bit of mud in and the food is suitably hearty, with pub staples such as burgers and fish and chips as well as more unusual-sounding dishes such as chicken and haggis rumbledethumps, a sort of cheesy mashed potato. There's a good choice of vegetarian dishes too.

THE BOATHOUSE BISTRO
Kingairloch Estate, Ardgour; tel. 01397 701 227; www.
kingairloch.co.uk/restaurant; 11am-9pm Weds.-Sat.,
11am-3pm Sun.; entrées £6.25

Housed in an old boathouse on the western shores of Loch Linnhe, this charming little terrace restaurant offers superb lochside dining (when the weather allows). At lunch there's a decent choice of sandwiches, including hot smoked salmon, cream cheese, and cucumber, while for dinner you can start with a black pudding and haggis stack with whisky cream before tucking into a Scottish shorthorn rump steak.

ACCOMMODATIONS

INVERLOCHY CASTLE

Torlundy, Fort William; tel. 01397 702 177;
inverlochycastlehotel.com; £595 d

This beautiful country house hotel, surrounded by acres of greenery and housed in a 19th-century castle, is a must for royal fans. It was here that Queen Victoria stopped in 1873 en route to Balmoral and so enamored was she by her surroundings that she took to painting them. Each of the 17 rooms and suites, including the one Victoria stayed in, have views of the grounds or loch and are luxuriously appointed. Dinner at the **Albert and Michel Roux Jr restaurant** is also a great place for a special occasion (three-course set menus £67)—though men should pack a dinner jacket.

ACHINTEE FARM

Glen Nevis; tel. 01397 702 240; achinteefarm.com;
£80 self-catering apartment, £110 d

Self-catering rooms on this farm at the foot of Ben Nevis are pretty basic, but they are very cheap too. You'll have to make your own breakfast, but there's a shop a mile away and the Ben Nevis Inn is very near for dinner. The farm also has the charming Shepherds Cottage for hire (sleeps two, £550 per week), plus three B&B rooms in the farmhouse, which are available mid-May-early October.

★ CORROUR STATION HOUSE & SIGNAL BOX

Corrour Station, near Loch Ossian; tel. 01397 732 236; www.corrour.co.uk/station-house; closed Nov.-Mar.; £110 d

This stop-off is brilliant for those traveling the West Highland Line and who want to stop a while to take it all in. The Station House restaurant proudly calls itself the most remote restaurant in Scotland as it is only accessible by those disembarking the train at Corrour Station or anyone willing to walk a very long way to get here (entrees £7). It's worth it, though: a roaring fire awaits as does homemade food, and the three double rooms in the old signal box (right on the tracks) are cozy;

plus, guests can make use of the sitting room in the old lookout tower, for panoramic views.

INFORMATION AND SERVICES

Fort William's **VisitScotland iCentre** is located in the center of town (15 High Street; tel. 01397 701 801) and can advise on places to stay, bus tickets, cruises, and local activities. For tips and inspiration on walking in the area, you can't beat the **Glen Nevis Visitor Centre** (Glen Nevis; tel. 01397 705 922), where you can also pick up useful maps and get a local weather forecast—essential if you're planning to climb Ben Nevis. The center is currently being refurbished, but there are still cabins providing the necessary information.

GETTING THERE
By Car

From Inverness it's a 66-mile (106-km) drive south along the A82, with a journey time of around 1.75 hours, while from Glencoe, it's just a 16-mile (26-km) drive, which takes around half an hour. From Glasgow it's a 108-mile (174 km) drive north to Fort William pretty much all the way along the A82, which should take about 2.5 hours.

From Edinburgh it takes just over three hours (132 mi/212 km) to get to Fort William. The most direct route is to take the M9 to Stirling to join the A84 into Loch Lomond and the Trossachs National Park as far as Lochearnhead, before turning left onto the A85 and following this west to Crianlarich, where you can take the A82 all the way to Fort William (if you're coming from Loch Lomond, this leg of the trip takes just 1.25 hours).

By Bus

From Inverness you can take the no. 919 bus, with **Stagecoach** (www.stagecoachbus.com, two hours, two per day Mon.-Sat. one per day Sun., £10.40 one-way). **Shiel Buses** (shielbuses.co.uk) runs the no. 513 (N19) from Inverness to Fort William (two hours, two per day Mon.-Fri., one per day Sat., £10.40 one-way).

The Great Glen Way

The Great Glen Way follows a huge geographical fault line that bisects Scotland, cutting through the country via a series of canals, lochs, and rivers, all the way from Inverness to Fort William. To the southeast you'll find the Grampian Mountains while to the northwest the North West Highlands. The chasm that exists today was formed when the two sides of the line slid in opposite directions, with the melting of the glaciers during the last Ice Age creating much of the landscape we see today.

The Great Glen's location, slicing through the Highlands diagonally, played a large role in the region's history. It was used by English forces to control the clans during the Jacobite risings, as evidenced in many of the place names along its route: Fort Augustus, Fort William, and Fort George. Today, there are 79 miles (127 km) of towpath to explore, with plenty of woodland trails leading off, making it a great location for cycling and hiking holidays—indeed, it is virtually impossible to travel through the northern Highlands without passing through it. However, if what you really want to do is experience the waterways along the course of the Great Glen Way, which includes (from north to south) the River Ness, Loch Dochfour, Loch Ness, River Oich, Loch Oich, Loch Lochy, River Lochy, and Loch Linnhe, then there's no better way than from the water.

Boat charter along the route is available, and Le Boat (www.leboat.co.uk) is clearly the most popular company, judging from the large number of their boats you see along the waterways each day.

CALEDONIAN DISCOVERY CRUISES

For a taste of slow travel, you could book a seven-day cruise with Caledonian Discovery (www.caledonian-discovery.co.uk, from £985 per person) along the Caledonian Canal. The canal was built by the famous Scottish engineer Thomas Telford and runs along the Great Glen for 60 miles (95.6 km), linking Loch Ness, Loch Oich, Loch Lochy, and Loch Linnhe.

Cruises with Caledonian Discovery take place aboard one of two colorful barges—*Fingal of Caledonia* and *Ros Crana*—and you can opt to travel north to south or south to north. Huge meals are served on board, which you'll eat communally with other guests and crew. Days are spent cycling or walking along the canal path or detouring along wooded trails as the canal boat dozily sits at anchor awaiting your return or crawls ahead to meet you at your next destination. More adventurous passengers can opt to kayak on some of the waterways or do some off-road cycling, depending on what itinerary you book.

From Glasgow, the no. 916 with **Scottish Citylink** (www.citylink.co.uk, 3.25 hours, four per day, £18.70 one-way) takes 3.25 hours to reach Fort William from Buchanan Street Bus Station.

By Train

Many visitors arrive in Fort William on the overnight **Caledonian Sleeper train** from London. One train sets off each night from London and gets into Fort William in the morning (12.75 hours, £50 one-way, £185 with cabin). There are around four direct trains with **ScotRail** (www.scotrail.co.uk) from Glasgow Queen Street each day (3.5 hours,

£13.90 each way). Trains from Edinburgh and Inverness change in Glasgow.

GETTING AROUND

Once here, the best way to get around is by car, on foot or by bike. There are some **local bus and coach services** (www.lochabertransport.org.uk) but they are infrequent and are generally used to connect Fort William with other towns and villages, such as Glencoe.

Of course, if you've arrived by public transport and want to hire a car, that's possible too. **Practical Car & Van Rental** (www.practical.co.uk/locations/england/scotland/fortwilliam) will meet you at the train or bus station with your chosen vehicle.

Glencoe

Home to quite possibly the most beautiful glen in Scotland and flanked by mighty mountains, the deep valley of Glencoe provides one of the world's most scenic passes, and the landscape here is nothing short of sublime. Carved out by a series of volcanic explosions and icy glaciers, Glencoe is a vast place with oodles of space for adventure sports and a backdrop that is so jaw-dropping it's featured on the big screen in James Bond's *Skyfall*, several *Harry Potter* movies, *Braveheart,* and *Rob Roy* while effortlessly stealing the show from the human stars.

The journey to Glencoe is all part of the adventure, whether you're coming from Fort William or Loch Lomond. As you enter the glen it's impossible not to be taken aback by the drama of it all as steep slopes reach up to the skies and the emptiness, openness, and desolation of your surroundings enraptures you. Tree stumps left over from forestry as you approach the glen from Rannoch Moor look like scattered bones, adding to the moodiness of the place (especially when the rain comes in), water spills down the mountainside, and as you stare into the gnarly mountain rock it's hard not to start seeing faces. As you venture into the glen proper, the road twists and turns, revealing new scenes at every corner—isolated bridges, streams, gorges, and rocky outcrops with little human interference and lone white cottages that stand out like single crocodile teeth on the grass verges, giving a sense of the huge scale of this remarkable landscape.

SIGHTS

Glencoe Massacre Monument

8 Upper Carnoch, Glencoe; free

Set away on a little side street, this monument to the 38 men killed in the Glencoe Massacre is very discreet and understated. Erected by a descendant of the MacIain clan in the 1880s when monuments to significant Scottish events and people were very fashionable, the memorial has a Celtic design and honors those who fell to the sword in this most heinous of crimes. A far cry from the general Victorian trend for over-complicated design, this monument is quite simple: a large stone slab at the bottom explains what it is there for, and a slender pillar with a Celtic cross stands on top. It doesn't make it any less powerful, though, and in a way it's nice that it's tucked out of the way with no great queue of morbid tourists come to pore over it.

To reach the monument, it's just a short walk from the village. Go past the Nisa shop with the shop on your left and then turn right up the lane signposted Upper Carnoch. You can also drive to it, but parking is scarce. Immortalized in song and poetry for generations, the reverberations of the Glencoe Massacre of 1692 still hang in the air here, a remembering of when English forces betrayed their hosts and turned their sword on them in a horrific act of retribution.

Glencoe Folk Museum

Main Street, Glencoe Village; tel. 01855 811 664; www.glencoemuseum.com; 10am-4:30pm Mon.-Sat., reduced hours in winter; adult £3, under 16 free

Just next door to the village shop is this intriguing thatched property that houses a very sweet and informative museum. It's antiquated, sure, but it gives a good overview of the history of the area, with particular emphasis on the Glencoe Massacre. Exhibits are a little outdated, with prints-outs explaining the lead-up to events, but some of the artifacts (toys, old tools, etc.) give a useful slice of social history. It's definitely worth the very small entry fee.

Three Sisters

Glencoe; www.walkhighlands.co.uk/fortwilliam/ bideannambian.shtml

The ridges Beinn Fhada, Gearr Aonach, and Aonach Dubh form part of the highest mountain range in the region, Bidean Nam Bian, or the Three Sisters, which stands on the south side of Glencoe. This trio of giant rocks, each as magnificent as the next, stands side by side craggily and epitomizes the huge scale of Glencoe. It's one of the most photographed sights in Scotland and can be viewed from the A82, where most people pull into the Piper's Layby, on the left-hand side as you approach the mountains from the Rannoch Moor end, though the view is probably better from the old road before the gorge narrows (a sharp left just after the layby).

TOP EXPERIENCE

★ Glencoe Road

Bridge of Orchy to Glencoe village, A82

Setting off from the Bridge of Orchy, to the south of the Glencoe valley (the normal approach for anyone coming from Edinburgh, Glasgow or Loch Lomond), this drive is utterly unforgettable. It takes just half an hour to travel the 24 miles (39 km) to Glencoe village, and you'll pass by some of Scotland's most epic sights: to your right, the windswept peat bogs of Rannoch Moor, one of Scotland's most unforgiving landscapes sitting at an elevation of 1,000 feet (305 m), and to your left, the pointed peak of Buchaille Etive Mor and the trio of mountains that make up the Three Sisters. You will at times feel vulnerable to the elements and have to pay close attention to the road, as it twists and turns unexpectedly through Scotland's most stunning valley. Take your time, watch out for red deer, pull over into one of the large laybys to take photos, and just appreciate the sheer majesty of it all. This is Scotland in all its bare, naked glory.

HIKING

BUCHAILLE ETIVE MOR

Trailhead: *Layby at Altnafeadh*
Distance: *8.25 miles (13 km) round-trip*
Hiking time: *7-9 hours*
Information and maps: *www.walkhighlands. co.uk/fortwilliam/buchailleetivemor.shtml*

Standing guard to Glencoe valley and ending the barren landscape of Rannoch Moor is Buachaille Etive Mor, a giant pyramid-shaped munro and one of Scotland's most iconic and seemingly unassailable. Appearances can be deceptive, though, and it is indeed possible to climb this huge mountain, with a fair bit of preparation, of course.

Walkers should park in the busy layby at Altnafeadh to start the journey to the mountain's dual summits. Be prepared for a steep and rough climb up, before crossing a boulder ridge. There is a fair bit of scrambling on the way down too.

Follow the track to the footbridge, cross over, and bear right to the path toward Lagangarbh Hut, the striking white building dwarfed by the mountain, and continue up the path until it forks. Keep right and follow the path as it climbs more and more steeply, crossing the Allt Coire na Tulaich from where you can get great views of the neighboring mountain of Buachaille Etive Beag. Stick to the path as it veers high into the corrie, via boulders and scree until you meet the ridge. Turn left onto the ridge and follow the quite broad path until it starts to narrow as you near the summit of Stob Dearg, the highest of Buachaille's two munros. Once this one is bagged you'll need to cross the ridge to the mountain's second munro of Stob na Brioge.

If all this sounds too much, there are plenty of photo opportunities for Buachaille Etive Mor from the **Glencoe Mountain Resort,** an adventure sports center you'll pass as you drive to Glencoe from Rannoch Moor. Or you can simply enjoy the views as you drive along the A82.

LOST VALLEY

Trailhead: *Piper's Layby*
Distance: *2.5 miles (4 km)*
Hiking time: *2-3 hours*
Information and maps: *www.walkhighlands. co.uk/fortwilliam/lostvalley.shtml*

This is a good manageable hike that will give you a decent introduction to the Glencoe landscape. The deceptively deep valley is said

to be where the once ruling Macdonald clan hid any cattle they stole from neighboring farms and clans—it's also where some of them fled to following the Glencoe Massacre. Park in the large car park at Piper's Layby (get there early in the day to avoid the coaches) and follow the path down to your left into the glen, which is fairly obvious from the car park. Once you see a well-trodden path to your right, follow this until you reach a bridge that you need to cross over the deep gorge below. The path will now get a lot rockier, and you will need to scramble to keep on the path as it cuts through birch woods, round the base of Gearr Aonach, and along a wooded gorge.

You'll need to cross the stream over rough stepping stones, and then you will have to scramble up a narrow rake, which many people prefer to do on their bottoms. Shortly after this, the path improves, and you will start to descend into the Lost Valley, which is completely hidden from the rest of the valley. Explore the valley floor where huge rocks the size of houses lay undisturbed before returning along the same route.

ADVENTURE SPORTS
VERTICAL DESCENTS

Inchree Falls, Onich; tel. 01855 821 593; www. verticaldescents.com; canyoning £60o, £110 per person for two activities each

As the name suggests, these excursions are not for the faint of heart. If you want to try coasteering, gorge walking, river tubing, or whitewater funyakking (basically inflatable kayaks for two) in and around Glencoe, then these are the people for you.

TOP EXPERIENCE

★ CAMPING

There's no better way to spend your nights in Glencoe than pitching up in a tent near the water, or even in the Lost Valley, and

taking full advantage of being in one of the most naturally stunning places in Scotland, though do make sure you're following the **Scottish Outdoor Access Code** (www. outdooraccess-scotland.scot). There are also campsites, should you prefer something with more facilities.

RED SQUIRREL CAMPSITE

Glencoe; tel. 01855 811 256; redsquirrelcampsite. co.uk; year-round; £12.50 per adult for a pitch, £2 per child

At this well-facilitated campsite, there are clean toilets and showers but also lots of nature to play with. Pitch your tent by the stream in the family-friendly area where kids will love clambering across the fallen trees or hopping on stepping stones, or opt for a slightly wilder experience near the river. Campfires are allowed (pick up wood from the shop in Glencoe village), and, with acres of space here, you very rarely need to book. If you're going to be eating in the Clachaig Inn (a 15-minute walk), then take the path that runs alongside the road rather than walking in the road itself, and keep your eyes peeled for wild goats.

FOOD AND OTHER ACCOMMODATIONS
CRAFTS & THINGS

Glencoe; tel. 01855 811 325; www.craftsandthings. co.uk; 9:30am-5pm Mon.-Fri., 9:30am-5:30pm Sat.-Sun., opening times may vary in winter; hot filled rolls from £2.50

Housed in an old byre (cow barn) alongside a quirky crafts shop and clothes shop, this café is a useful pit stop that serves tea and coffee and light meals alongside cakes and other baked goodies. It's an informal place where cyclists decked in spandex are just as welcome as those wearing muddy boots. Fully sated, browse the gallery and bookshelves for interesting gifts to take home.

1: The Three Sisters, Glencoe **2:** Glencoe Monument **3:** Driving through Glencoe is an unforgettable experience. **4:** camping at the Red Squirrel Campsite, Glencoe

★ CLACHAIG INN

Glencoe; tel. 01855 811 252; clachaig.com; food
served noon-9pm; entrées £5.95, £100 d

In the heart of Glencoe is this local and tourist favorite. A short walk from a couple of nearby hostels as well as the Red Squirrel Campsite, it gets its fair share of weary walkers in need of some sustenance. Food is decent and portions generous. Try the Highland game pie or the haggis, neaps, and tatties. The **Boots Bar** (round the back) is where you go for music, while locals head straight to the small bar next door to it behind an unmarked door. If you don't have kids, don't eat in the lounge—the atmosphere is much better elsewhere. Black Gold (a Scottish alternative to Guinness) is on tap, and there is a huge whisky list to work your way through.

And if camping is a bit too rough for you, book a night or two here, which has a surprising 23 bedrooms across the Ossian Wing (the older part of the building), the Bidean Wing (which has mountain views), and The Lodge (good for dog owners), all of which are well priced. Plus, the Clachaig also manages 12 self-catering properties (from £725 a week for a cottage sleeping four) in and around Glencoe if you're looking to stay in the area a little longer.

BRIDGE OF ORCHY HOTEL

Argyll; tel. 01838 400 208; www.bridgeoforchy.
co.uk; breakfast 7am-9:30am, lunch noon-5pm daily;
entrées £6.95; £185 d

This is a popular stop-off point for people traveling between Loch Lomond and Glencoe. The beautiful white building stands out against the mass of green mountains that surround it, and all dishes in both the dining room or the more relaxed bar area are cooked to order using local ingredients. There are also good, neat rooms if you want to make a night of it.

INFORMATION AND SERVICES

Tourist Information and Tours

GLENCOE VISITOR'S CENTRE

Glencoe; tel. 01855 811 307; www.nts.org.uk/
visit/places/glencoe; 9:30am-5:30pm Mar.-Oct.,
10am-4pm Nov.-Feb.; adult £6.50, concessions £5,
family £16.50

While the Glencoe landscape is obviously free to all, the Glencoe Visitor's Centre does incur a fee, but it offers a very poignant introduction to the area and enables you to stand on the sites of the famous massacre as well as find out about the wildlife often found in and around the glen along with the families who once lived here. Plus, for a more immersive experience, you can join one of the **Land Rover Safaris** (from £20 per adult for a 1.5-hour tour) to explore the glen more fully. The **Historical Land Rover Safari Tour** (set dates each year, adult £25, child £15) takes 2.5 hours and takes you through some of the townships affected by the Glencoe Massacre as well as a site overlooking the isles where the clan chief is buried.

Supplies

En route to Glencoe from the south, shops are few and far between. If camping, stop at the **Green Welly Shop** (Tyndrum; www. thegreenwellystop.co.uk; 01301 702 089; main site 8:30am-5:30pm Apr.-Oct., 8:30am-5pm Nov.-Mar.; petrol station 7am-10pm May-Sept., 8am-9pm Oct.-Apr.) to stock up on any additional bits of gear you may need.

Glencoe village itself is small but surprisingly well facilitated. The good shop, **Nisa Local** (Glencoe; tel. 01855 811 156; www. nisalocally.co.uk/store/nisa-local-carnoch-ballachulish; 8am-7pm Mon.-Fri., 8am-6:30pm Sat.-Sun.) has an ATM and all the essentials, whether you're staying in a nearby hotel or camping.

GETTING THERE AND AROUND

By Car

From the south (Glasgow and Loch Lomond) you can take the A82 going north without fear of getting lost. It's just over two hours from Glasgow (92 mi/148 km) and 45 minutes from Crianlarich (35 mi/56 km) in the north of Loch Lomond. Visitors from Oban might prefer the slightly longer but definitely quieter route along the A828, which takes just over 50 minutes (34 mi/55 km). Meanwhile, those coming from Inverness can take the A82 going south for 82 miles (132 km), which takes about 2.25 hours. From Edinburgh it's a 117-mile (188 km) journey along the M9 to Stirling and then the A84, A85, and A82, which takes about 2.75 hours. From Fort William it's a simple 16-mile (26 km) journey south on the A82 and takes less than half an hour.

By Bus

If you don't have a car, the no. 916 **Scottish Citylink** bus (www.citylink.co.uk) from Glasgow (£17.10 one-way) will bring you to the Glencoe Visitor Centre in 2.75 hours and runs four times a day. Make sure you travel in daylight, so you can see the stunning pass in all its glory, and also ensure there will be someone available to give you advice at the visitor center. From Fort William, the no. 915 and no. 916 Scottish Citylink bus takes just half an hour and runs four times a day (£8.50 each way).

By Taxi

If you'd rather not leave too much to chance, **Alistair's Taxis** (tel. 01397 25 25 25; www.alistairstaxis.co.uk) serves the whole Fort William and Glencoe area. From Fort William to Glencoe, for instance, it should cost in the region of £40 and it's advisable to book in advance.

Isle of Skye and the Western Highlands

The enigmatic Isle of Skye was named Skuy (misty isle) by its Norse settlers, no doubt due to the almost constant veil of mist that shrouds its most spectacular landmarks before vanishing as though it was never there, thus revealing the island's full beauty to startling effect.

The Isle of Skye is a magical place of eerily still lochs, colossal mountains, and improbable geographical features, such as the dagger-like peaks of the Quiraing. So surreal is its landscape that it has spawned countless myths and legends—of giants turned to stone, lovelorn fairy queens, and mysterious kelpies. Many visitors to Skye come to bag (climb) one of its many munros (hills over 3,000 ft/914.4 m) amid the gabbro rock of the sensational Cuillin mountain range, swim in its

Highlights

Look for ★ to find recommended sights, activities, dining, and lodging.

★ **Jacobite Steam Train:** Board the *Harry Potter* train for a scenic journey along the West Highland Line to Mallaig before heading to the Isle of Skye (page 318).

★ **Glenfinnan Monument and Loch Shiel:** Take in the awesome Highlands scenery from this towering tribute to the many clansmen who died fighting for the Jacobite cause (page 320).

★ **Eileen Donan Castle:** En route to the Isle of Skye, visit one of Scotland's most photographed castles, made famous by the film *Highlander* (page 327).

★ **Loch Coruisk:** Take a boat to this hidden-away loch, flanked by the Cuillin Hills, whose raw allure left both J. M. W. Turner and Sir Walter Scott awestruck (page 339).

★ **Talisker Distillery:** Join a tour and have a wee dram at Skye's original, and best, whisky distillery. Be sure to leave room in the suitcase to bring a bottle of single malt home (page 340).

★ **Bla Bheinn:** The only one of Skye's munros not on the Cuillin Ridge, this bulk of a mountain is one of the Skye's most attainable (page 341).

★ **Hike to the cleared village of Boreraig:** This ghost village toward the south of Skye is a haunting reminder of the human impact of one of the darkest periods in Scottish history (page 343).

★ **The Old Man of Storr:** Instantly recognizable, this huge pinnacle is one of Scotland's most iconic landmarks (page 351).

★ **The Quiraing:** Hike this otherworldly

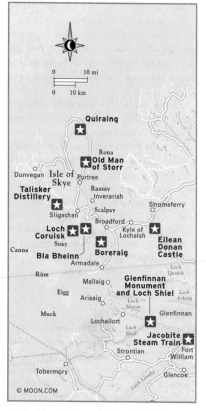

© MOON.COM

landscape on the Trotternish Peninsula of Skye, the result of a mighty landslide, and examine up close the incomprehensible rocks, crags, and lonesome boulders (page 352).

silent pools, and marvel at its myriad waterfalls and rugged coastline. While its dramatic landscape makes the largest of the Inner Hebrides isles also its most visited, it's not hard to escape the flock of day-trippers as long as you are open to leaving behind the main thoroughfare to explore the less ventured single-track roads and hidden walking trails.

Lying off Skye's east side and with awe-inspiring views across to Applecross on the northwest mainland, Raasay is an intriguing island where the repercussions of the Highland Clearances, a period in the 18th and 19th centuries when tenants were evicted from ancestral lands across the Highlands, can still be felt.

To the south of Skye are the Small Isles—an archipelago rich in local fauna, flora, and wildlife, where you can just as easily find solace amid the hillsides and cliff-top paths as you can be swept away by the friendliness of locals.

Though the pull is strong, don't rush your way to Skye. Plot a road trip that takes you past Eilean Donan Castle, which stands on an island at the point where three sea lochs meet and looks like a relic of a forgotten time, and over the bridge from Kyle of Lochalsh onto Skye. Alternatively, admire the scenery from a window seat aboard the West Highland Line, one of the most beautiful rail routes in the world, particularly in summer when the final stretch can be done by steam train. The rail route takes you all the way to Mallaig in Lochaber, from where it's a short ferry ride across to the island.

ORIENTATION

Skye is the largest isle in the Inner Hebrides, just off the northwest coast of Scotland. For a long time, it was only accessible by ferry, and the original crossing was from Kyle of Lochalsh on the shores of Loch Alsh on the mainland to Kyleakin on the southeast of Skye—a distance of around 1,640 feet (500 m). Since 1995, however, people can now drive onto the island at Kyleakin via the **Skye Bridge,** just a mile west of Kyle of Lochalsh, which has rendered the Kyleakin ferry obsolete. The other year-round way of reaching Skye is to take the ferry from **Mallaig,** farther south on the mainland, which comes into Armadale on the south of Skye. From Easter to October, you can also take a short ferry crossing from Glenelg, also on the shores of Loch Alsh, to Kylerhea, just a few miles south of Kyleakin.

Raasay is located between Skye and the northwest mainland. It is separated from Skye by the Sound of Raasay and is accessed by ferry from Sconser on the east coast of Skye.

The **Small Isles,** a collection of four islands also in the Inner Hebrides and just south of Skye, are accessed by boat charter from Skye or by ferry from either **Mallaig** or **Arisaig,** just eight miles south of Mallaig. **Eigg** is the closest isle to the mainland and, to its southwest, is the tiny isle of **Muck.** Northwest of Eigg is the largest isle in the archipelago, **Rum,** and just beyond this lies **Canna.**

Lewis and Harris is a large isle north of Skye, which forms part of the Outer Hebrides. It is renowned for its two distinct parts (hence the name), which leads many people to presume it is two isles. Harris has a varied landscape of Caribbean-esque beaches backed by swathes of machair (low-lying grassland rich with wildlife) in the west, with a rugged necklace of inlets to its east and mountains to its north. Lewis, in comparison, is much more desolate (despite having the larger population, most of whom live in the isle's main town of Stornoway) and home to flat peatlands that stretch into the horizon. Although the Outer Hebrides has a reputation for being very remote, Lewis and Harris is relatively easy to get to from Skye via the ferry from Uig on the **Trotternish Peninsula** on the north side of the island.

Previous: Approaching the Quiraing; Glenfinnan Monument and Loch Shiel; Eilean Donan Castle.

PLANNING YOUR TIME

As with anywhere in Scotland, the longer you give yourself, the deeper you'll be able to explore Skye and its surrounds. Both the main road routes to reach Skye (from Fort William to Mallaig, and from Inverness to Kyle of Lochalsh) are beautiful and deserve at least a full day each (preferably with an overnight stop) to ensure you can see the main sights. If you are coming by train, the chances are you will whizz through the route, but if traveling from Fort William, do ensure you get off at **Glenfinnan** for at least a few hours. Likewise, from **Inverness,** you'll kick yourself if you don't visit **Eilean Donan Castle.**

One of the biggest mistakes people make is to try to see all of Skye in a day or two. While you may be able to get some choice photographs this way, you really will miss the true allure of the place, and, if you don't schedule at least one major walk, you'll only really skim the surface.

You really need at least a week to do Skye justice—even then you'll have to compromise on visiting a few places. You'll want to visit **Portree** at least for an afternoon or dinner, and then the **Trotternish Peninsula** where you will find both **the Quiraing** and **the Old Man of Storr.** Skye is quite a large island and traveling around it takes time, so a good solution is to base yourself on the north of the isle for a few days, so you can venture into the **Waternish peninsula** too, and then stay on the south of the island for the remainder of your visit (or vice versa, depending on your overall route).

Raasay can easily be visited in a day, and, if you're venturing to the **Small Isles,** more often than not one or two isles can be done on a day trip, but spending a couple of nights on one of the isles will give you a better understanding of Hebridean culture.

If you do make it as far north as **Lewis and Harris,** aim to spend a minimum of four days there (two nights each at the two distinct parts of the island).

Itinerary Ideas

Day 1: Fort William to the Isle of Skye

Spend the day enjoying the route from Fort William to the Isle of Skye.

- Board the first **Jacobite Steam Train** of the day at Fort William and travel across the iconic Glenfinnan Viaduct, all the way to Mallaig.
- At Mallaig, tuck into a seafood lunch at the **Cornerstone Restaurant** (be sure to book ahead) overlooking the harbor.
- Pick up your hire car from **Morar Motors** at the **ferry terminal** (you'll need to arrange for them to leave your car at the ferry terminal for you).
- Catch a mid-afternoon car ferry to **Armadale,** on Skye.
- Once in Armadale, it's a 15-minute drive up the coast to **Eilean Iarmain** on the Sleat Peninsula, where you'll be staying for the night. Have dinner at the characterful pub downstairs, where, if you're lucky, you may catch some traditional Gaelic music.

Isle of Skye

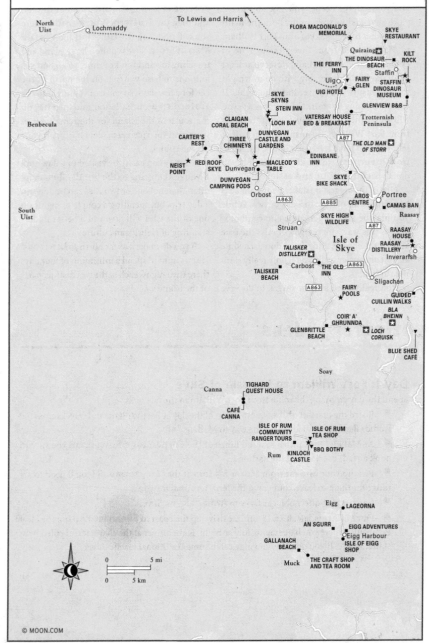

© MOON.COM

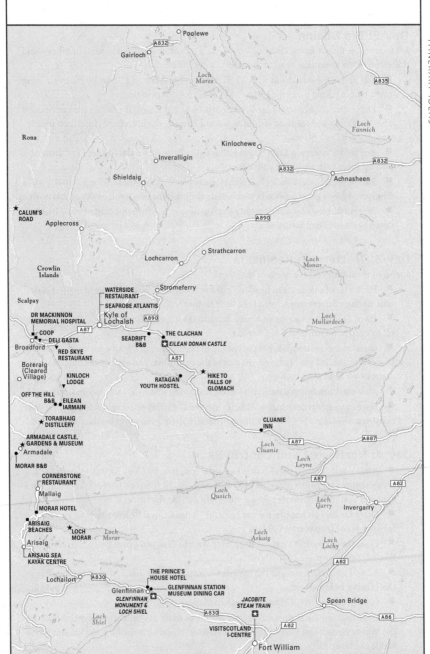

Day 2: Bla Bheinn

Set today aside for a hike into the Cuillin—Britain's most magnificent mountain range—and there's no better mountain to scale than the mighty Bla Bheinn.

- Fill up for the day ahead with a full Scottish breakfast in **Eilean Iarmain's** dining room before taking a morning stroll to look out for otters in the bay.
- Drive down the spectacular **Broadford to Elgol Road,** the B8083 (the second left after the Co-op in Broadford if driving toward Portree; the Broadford Hotel is on the corner), toward Loch Slapin.
- Just before you reach Loch Slapin pull into the **Blue Shed Café** to get a hot drink and pick up some sustenance for your hike.
- Park at the far side of the loch, which is where you'll pick up the trail for your trek up **Bla Bheinn.** Allow a good 5-6 hours to complete the hike; the views will be out of this world.
- Post walk, reward yourself with a slap-up dinner at **Kinloch Lodge** before bedding down again at Eilean Iarmain.

Day 3: Trotternish Peninsula

Spend your third day on the north of the island.

- Have a bit of a lie-in, then head to **Talisker Distillery** for a mid-morning pre-booked tour (though drivers will have to take their tasting with them).
- From Talisker, it's about an hour's drive to the Trotternish Peninsula. En route, stop off in Portree for lunch at **Café Arriba.**
- Once on the Trotternish, park at the top of the single-track road a few miles from Uig (the same road links to Staffin on the east of the peninsula) and explore the ethereal landscape of the **Quiraing** on foot.
- Afterward, head toward the **Stein Inn** on Waternish, where you can check in for the night.
- Have dinner next door in the Michelin-starred **Loch Bay** restaurant before ending your evening in the Stein Inn's cozy bar, dram in hand, watching the waves lap the shores outside.

Day 4: Northwest and Central Skye

- After a full Scottish breakfast at the Stein Inn, stop by **Skye Skyns** to see how this sheep tannery makes its gorgeous rugs and clothing. In summer, have tea (or coffee) and cake at a Scandinavian-style pop-up yurt right outside the tannery.
- Drive for half an hour to the car park for Claigan Coral Beach, stopping en route to take photos of **Dunvegan Castle.**
- From the car park, it's a good 40-minute walk to **Claigan Coral Beach,** so allow two hours for your visit.
- As you head back toward the mainland, stop for a late lunch of crab sandwiches at **Deli Gasta** in Broadford.
- Grab the ferry from **Armadale** back to Mallaig.
- Once back on the mainland, drive a few miles south of Mallaig to Morar, check into the **Morar Hotel,** and have dinner in the hotel restaurant overlooking the famous Silver Sands of Morar.

Isle of Skye Itinerary

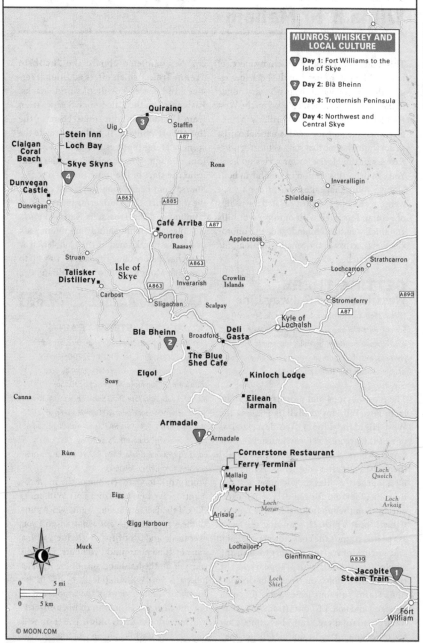

MUNROS, WHISKEY AND LOCAL CULTURE

1 **Day 1:** Fort Williams to the Isle of Skye

2 **Day 2:** Blà Bheinn

3 **Day 3:** Trotternish Peninsula

4 **Day 4:** Northwest and Central Skye

© MOON.COM

Road to the Isles: Fort William to Mallaig

This route, from the outdoor activity mecca of Fort William at the heart of the Lochaber region through to one of the main entry points to the Isle of Skye, is best enjoyed on the West Highland Railway Line—particularly in summer when the journey can be made aboard a steam train (the one that stars as the *Hogwarts Express* in the Harry Potter series no less). You can drive this section in around an hour along a route that takes you through what were once among the most isolated townships of Scotland, fringed with omnipresent hills and thick woodland inland, and with unbroken views across to the Small Isles along the coastal stretch.

GETTING THERE
West Highland Railway Line

Fort William train station, Tom-na-Faire, Station Square, Fort William; tel. 0344 811 0141; www.scotrail.co.uk/scotland-by-rail/great-scenic-rail-journeys/west-highland-line-glasgow-oban-and-fort-williammallaig; four trains per day Mon.-Sat., one on Sun.

The most obvious and most traveled route from Fort William to Mallaig is along the West Highland Line. Often described as one of the greatest railway journeys in the world, where cinematic backdrops reveal themselves one after another like a film reel, it's a journey you'll want a window seat for. En route, look out for red deer, often camouflaged on the mountainsides, the famous **Glenfinnan Viaduct**, stunning sea views as the line rounds the coast toward Mallaig, and Loch Morar—the deepest loch in the whole of Scotland, which appears to the right shortly before you reach your destination. Trains run four times a day (once on Sundays) and take 1.5 hours (from £7.20 one-way). Standard diesel trains have toilets but few other amenities; in summer the journey

can be completed aboard the **Jacobite Steam Train,** which offers additional services and serves hot drinks and snacks. Passengers on the Caledonian Sleeper train from London can join this section of the line at Fort William. To fully appreciate the scenery along the West Highland Railway Line though, you should catch the train from the start of the route in Glasgow (5.5 hours, from £26.60 one-way), and gawp as the train skirts the glimmering lochs of Loch Lomond and the Trossachs National Park, past the eye-catching lumpy mountain peak of Ben Arthur, known as the Cobbler, near Arrochar, before chugging all the way up to Rannoch Moor and on to Fort William.

★ JACOBITE STEAM TRAIN

Fort William train station, Tom-na-Faire, Station Square, Fort William; tel. 01524 732 100; www.westcoastrailways.co.uk/jacobite/jacobite-steam-train-details.cfm; morning service at 10:15am Mon.-Fri. late Apr.-late Oct., Sat.-Sun. early May-late Sept.; afternoon service at 2:30pm Mon.-Fri. mid-May-mid-Sept., Sat.-Sun. mid-June-early Sept.; adult £31.75 one-way, child £18.75 one-way; first class adult £59.95 round-trip, child £32.90 round-trip (no one-way first class available)

From April to October, one of the most romantic ways to travel from Fort William is aboard the Jacobite Steam Train, which runs all the way to Mallaig, and will transport you over the iconic **Glenfinnan Viaduct,** with a journey time of around two hours. Position yourself on the left-hand side of the train as it departs Fort William (ideally by one of the doors) for the best views of the famous crossing and also the **Glenfinnan Monument,** which overlooks **Loch Shiel.** The train will stop here for a while, giving you time to visit

Highland Clearances and Cleared Villages

Few periods of Scottish history have had such a lasting impact on the people and landscape of Scotland as the notorious Highland Clearances, and western Scotland was one of the worst hit areas.

Following the defeat of the Jacobites at the Battle of Culloden in 1746, the British Government wanted to ensure such an uprising would never happen again, and so they introduced a series of measures that aimed to decimate Highland culture forever. While many travelers may have heard of the banning of kilts, the public executions of Jacobite supporters, forced transportations to the colonies, and the Disarming Act of 1746 (which effectively outlawed the carrying of a broadsword), fewer seem aware of the much more damaging practice of displacement known as the Highland Clearances.

The Highland Clearances refers to a period in the 18th and 19th centuries when clansmen and tenants were removed from their homelands—lands that they and their ancestors had lived and worked on for generations, often centuries. Central to the clan way of life was the principle of Duthchas, a belief that the ancient lineage of a clan meant they were rooted to a place and that place was communally owned by the clan.

After Culloden, many Jacobite clan chiefs saw their lands forfeited to the Crown, but moreover the clan culture was eroded by the changed role of the clan chief—once a powerful leader with recognized powers both in and outside the clan, the clan chief was stripped of autonomy and became little more than a landlord. In time, as land became seen as an asset, the needs of the community came second to the desire to make money: the undermining of clan culture was complete.

Sometimes the clearances, which began on a small scale following the Jacobite defeat of 1715, prior to the 1745 Jacobite Rebellion and Culloden, and became more widespread from the 1760s on, were blatant, with people forcefully evicted to make way for more profitable sheep farming. Sometimes tenants were threatened, burned out of their homes, or herded to less hospitable areas were eking out a living or any form of subsistence was virtually impossible.

Tactics were often subtler too, with promises of new lives overseas, in America, Canada, or Australasia, and ships waiting to take them away, but promises rarely stacked up. This practice continued for a century or more until the Crofters Act of 1886 brought a level of security to tenants and allowed land to be passed on from one generation to another once again. Many Scottish laments are written from the perspective of emigrants, sent to live thousands of miles away, longing to return to the land of their home, their people.

When people left, their townships often fell into a state of disrepair. While little remains of many cleared villages, such as those in Sutherland in northwest Scotland, which suffered some of the most brutal evictions, in some, such as Boreraig on Skye and Hallaig on Raasay, you can still see the ruins of the houses people once lived in and imagine the communities that once toiled the land. Today, utterly deserted, save for a few sheep wandering amid ghostly stone outlines of former homes, a visit to one of these villages is one of the most poignant things you can experience on a visit to Scotland.

the station museum. When the journey resumes, look out to sea as you approach Arisaig; on a clear day the Small Isles should come into view. First-class tickets come with free tea and coffee, and there are also options for afternoon tea and a cheese board. The best seats are either the private tables for two on the left-hand side in Carriage A or in the "Harry Potter" seats in Carriage D, which are in vintage compartments that seat six (you'll need a first-class ticket for both these options). However, there is no each-way option for first-class (you need to book a return ticket), so if you want the luxury of first-class and the choice of seats but plan to travel on to Skye, you will need to forfeit your return ticket.

If you are not headed to the Isle of Skye, you can still complete the 84-mile round-trip from Fort William to Mallaig and back again in a day. Adult day-return tickets are £59.95 first class and £37.75 standard, and round-trip tickets for children are £32.90 first class and £20.75 standard.

By Car

Driving offers some spectacular scenery too. Follow the A830 (43 mi/69 km; 1 hour) as it bends and winds its way through the heart of the Rough Bounds—a wild, largely uninhabited region that encompasses the areas of Knoydart, north Morar, Arisaig, and Moidart. On the main route to Mallaig there are few places to stop (apart from Glenfinnan itself, of course), unless you simply want to pull into one of the laybys to take in your breathtaking surroundings of mountain sides and glens, heather-covered moorland, and dashing chunks of lush greenery or make a scenic detour to the Ardnamurchan Peninsula when you reach Lochailort. Historically, this region was renowned for its inaccessibility—the road from Lochailort into Moidart and Ardnamurchan didn't even exist until the 1960s—and it was here that Bonnie Prince Charlie found his last piece of sanctuary in Scotland following Culloden, before departing to France.

You can hire a car from **Morar Motors** (tel. 01599 534 329, www.morarmotors.co.uk, from £54 per day, including insurance), based just outside Mallaig, who will deliver it to the ferry port for you.

By Bus

It is possible to travel this route by bus too. **Shiel Buses** (01967 431 272, shielbuses.co.uk) runs a service between Fort William and Mallaig twice a day Monday-Friday, with one bus a day on weekends. Journey time is around 1.5 hours and costs £6.10 one-way or £7.95 round-trip.

GLENFINNAN
Sights
★ GLENFINNAN MONUMENT AND LOCH SHIEL

Glenfinnan; tel. 01397 722 250; www.nts.org.uk/ visit/places/glenfinnan-monument; 10am-4pm daily Nov.-Feb., 9am-6pm daily Mar.-June, 9am-7pm daily July-Aug., 9:30am-6pm daily Sept.-Oct.; adult £3.50, concession £2.50, family £9

Standing on the banks of Loch Shiel, the Glenfinnan Monument is a poignant tribute to the moment Bonnie Prince Charlie arrived in Scotland in 1745, raising his standard to launch a rebellion that came close to overthrowing the monarchy. The monument stands 15 feet (18 m) high and features a lone kilted clansman on top—a reminder of all those who lost their lives in the ensuing rebellion, fighting for the Jacobite cause.

A good exhibition in the **Glenfinnan Visitor Centre** tells the story of the '45 rebellion, or you can join one of the guided tours, included in the visitor center price and available when there is available staff, to the top of the monument; in winter you will need to ring ahead to book. It's 62 steps to the top (with no disabled access unfortunately), and there is a fairly narrow hatch to pass through, but if you can manage it, the views of Loch Shiel and its surrounds, including the **Glenfinnan Viaduct,** are amazing. Be warned, the monument and car park can be saturated with Harry Potter fanatics in summer due to the viaduct's starring role in the movies, so if you are coming here to absorb the history, it's best visited out of season.

GLENFINNAN VIEWPOINT

A muddy walking trail behind the visitor center leads up a small hill where you can get another great viewpoint of the viaduct in one direction and Loch Shiel in the other. Some travelers prefer to walk down the main road and follow a path that leads under the viaduct for close-up shots of the trains passing by.

1: Glenfinnan Monument and Loch Shiel 2: the Jacobite Steam Train crossing the Glenfinnan Viaduct

Harry Potter Locations

While any bona fide Harry Potter fan will no doubt hotfoot it to platform 9 ¾ at London's King's Cross, there is no shortage of Harry Potter filming locations right here in Scotland too.

THE BRIDGE TO HOGWARTS

The most famous of all is of course the **Glenfinnan Viaduct,** known as the Bridge to Hogwarts, which the *Hogwarts Express* crosses in *Harry Potter and the Chamber of Secrets* (when Harry and Ron narrowly miss a collision with it in their flying car). The best way to experience it is aboard the **Jacobite Steam Train** (Apr.-Oct., from £31.75 adult/£18.75 child). Book a first-class seat in Carriage D, which features in the films, for a true Harry Potter experience. For the more budget wary, return tickets from Fort William to Glenfinnan aboard a boring diesel train cost just a fraction of the price at £9.40 per adult/£4.70 child.

Once you alight at Glenfinnan, be sure to pop into the **Glenfinnan Station Museum Dining Car,** and then follow the walking trail down to the **Glenfinnan Viewpoint** where in summer (if you time it right with the trains) you can watch the Jacobite Steam Train crossing the viaduct and take plenty of photos in the process—be warned though, you'll be far from on your own.

NATURAL SETTINGS

If Loch Shiel looks familiar it may be because it (as well as Loch Morar, close to Mallaig) are often used to represent Hogwarts Lake in the films.

Other incredible natural landscapes have starred in the films, including **Loch Eilt,** not far from Glenfinnan, which has regularly been used for scenes of Hogwarts' grounds and has provided the island location, Eilean na Moine, of Dumbledore's grave. The West Highland Line passes by the loch, as does the A830, and views are best from up here, but if you would like to stand on the shoreline, it's just a 10-minute walk from the roadside, or 30 minutes from Lochailort train station.

The dramatic mountains and valleys of **Glencoe** have frequently provided backdrops in the films; most memorably, it was opposite the Clachan Inn that Hagrid's Hut was placed in the spring of 2003 for filming of *Harry Potter and the Prisoner of Azkaban*, while it is on the northern banks of Loch Etive in Glencoe that Hermione, Harry and Ron go on their camping trip in *Harry Potter and the Deathly Hallows Part 1*.

Food and Accommodations

GLENFINNAN STATION MUSEUM DINING CAR

Station Cottage, Glenfinnan; tel. 01397 722 300; glenfinnanstationmuseum.co.uk; 9am-4:30pm Mon.-Sat., 10am-4:30pm Sun May-Oct.; evening meals may be available on occasion; sandwiches £6.60, cakes £2.80

What could be more quintessentially British (ssshhh, don't say it too loud, you're in Scotland after all) than dining in an old railway carriage? This sweet little restaurant harks back to the Golden Age of travel of the late 19th and early 20th centuries. Visitors can get toasted sandwiches (egg mayonnaise or pulled pork with honey and mustard), served with salad and coleslaw, homemade soup, or

traditional cakes and treats, such as all-butter shortbread and fruit cake.

THE PRINCE'S HOTEL HOUSE HOTEL

Main Road, Glenfinnan; tel. 01397 722 246; www. glenfinnan.co.uk; bistro 6pm-9pm daily mid-Mar.-end of Oct., dining room 7pm-late daily mid-Mar.-Oct.; £165 d

This old coaching inn, just a few minutes' walk from Glenfinnan station and dating from the 17th century, once provided respite for weary horseback travelers along the Road to the Isles. Today, you can still stay in the oldest part of the building, where there are two bedrooms, including the splendid four-poster Stuart room, but there are also a further seven comfortable rooms in the newer part of the building. Downstairs, the antiquated dining room is not the kind of place you can just casually dip into, though (you'll need to nip into the bistro and bar area for that); here it's all about the five-course fine-dining menu, which is decided each morning (£55pp), while small plates in the bar start at around £6.95. The hotel and restaurant and bistro are open seasonally mid-March-late October.

GLENFINNAN HOUSE

Main Road, Glenfinnan; tel. 01397 722 235; www. glenfinnanhouse.com; bar dining noon-9pm daily, '45 Room 6pm-8:30pm daily; entrées £7.95; £145 d, £245 Jacobite Suite

Just a short walk from Glenfinnan station, this smart hotel in an 18th-century shooting lodge (albeit one with a Victorian makeover) on the banks of Loch Shiel, is a good lunch or dinner spot once you've explored the wealth of attractions nearby. The bar snack menu offers great value for money, with sandwiches from £7.95, all served in the lovely traditional bar with wooden stools and floorboards. For an altogether grander affair (entrées from £7.95), you can have homemade venison sausage or a platter of Inverawe smoked salmon in the smart '45 dining room where chef (and owner) Duncan really goes to town with his classic French style of cooking. This being Jacobite country—the Glenfinnan Monument is just over a 10-minute away, indeed you should be able to spy it across the loch—paintings of affluent supporters hang on the walls and the Jacobite Suite has a high four-poster. Downstairs, fires roar in each of the public rooms.

ARISAIG, MORAR, AND MALLAIG

The little village of **Arisaig** is sited in a sheltered bay at the western end of the North Morar region, and is one of the launch pads for visiting the Small Isles. It is the most westerly point on the West Highland Railway Line as it chugs towards Mallaig; though if you're traveling here by train, it's a good idea to let staff know in advance if you want to stop.

North Morar's coastline, which stretches from Arisaig all the way north to Mallaig (about 8 mi/13 km) through the village of Morar itself, is characterized with acres of pearl-white sandy beaches, rocky islets, and aquamarine waters, which can be seen from the train or the picturesque coastal road route.

Morar village is a relatively sleepy place, thanks to the fact that the main A830 now bypasses it, with a smattering of good restaurants and an excellent hotel. It's also a good access point for the shores of **Loch Morar**—the deepest loch in all of Scotland. **Mallaig,** by comparison, is a busy fishing and ferry port but a great place to catch your breath before you venture out to Skye or the Small Isles.

Sights
LOCH MORAR

Morar; www.walkhighlands.co.uk/fortwilliam/ morar-tarbet.shtml

This sprawling loch, which runs east from the outskirts of the village of Morar, is famed for being the deepest freshwater body of water in the whole of the British Isles. At its deepest, it plunges over 1,000 feet (300 m) below the surface of the water, and its dark waters have inspired its own mythical creature: Morag. Victorian depictions of Morag presented her as some kind of foreboding presence that was only seen when someone died or when the local clan had lost a battle. One early 20th-century folklore chronicler described her as a half-fish/half-woman creature, with long flowing lochs of hair. However, more contemporary descriptions paint her as more of a serpent-like creature—a distant cousin of the famous Loch Ness Monster. You can take a good scenic walk (5.75 mi/9 km) along the shores of Loch Morar from the road end of Bracorina (where there is also parking), which takes you all the way to Tarbet on the southern shore of Loch Nevis. In summer (Apr.-Oct.), there is a **ferry** from Tarbet to Mallaig (Mon.-Fri at 3:30pm), which must be pre-booked with **Western Isle Cruises** (tel.

01687 462 233). Much of the walking route to Tarbet follows a rocky path along the shoreline, which is lined with native woodland and surrounded by mountains (though, if you're walking from Morar village, the first section is road and this will add on an extra hour and 10 minutes); there is an eerie calm about the place, which makes it very special indeed.

Beaches
SILVER SANDS OF MORAR
Arisaig to Morar
This gorgeous chain of white sand beaches and small coves that pepper the coast all the way from Arisaig to Morar are collectively known as the Silver Sands of Morar. If you're driving, take the slower coastal road via Portnaluchaig (as opposed to the faster A830 to Mallaig), which allows you to see the beaches and rocky islets of the region fully, most of which can be easily accessed from the roadside. One of the most special beaches is **Camusdarach,** where parking is available; here, scenes from the Burt Lancaster comedy film *Local Hero* were shot and the views out toward the Small Isles are beautiful. The slightly more hidden-away beaches of **Bourbach** and **Sgeir Mhor** can both be visited on foot from Morar village and should take no more than an hour and a half there and back. Ask locals for directions on visiting these beaches.

Sports and Recreation
ARISAIG SEA KAYAK CENTRE
Arisaig; arisaigseakayakcentre.co.uk; beginner half-day tours (3 hours)£50, £35 child/full-day tours (6.75 hours) £85, £55 child
There are few better ways to explore the indented Morar coastline than by kayak. This company offers half-day trips suitable for beginners around the sheltered sea loch of Loch nan Ceall, where you can land at beaches and get up close to the local seals, or longer day trips for more experienced kayakers that go farther out to explore hidden lagoons and local sights, such as the ruins of Castle Tioram on Loch Moidart, or the abandoned settlements along the shores of Loch Ailort.

The company also offers a six-day wilderness adventure tour of the Small Isles, that will give you a unique introduction to the archipelago's best assets (£795 per person). You'll spend just shy of a week with an expert guide exploring the waters around the islands by kayak, seeing wildlife such as minke whales and shearwaters in their natural habitats and wild camping on beaches or staying in bunkhouses. The company can only be visited in person or contacted through the website, and there are no set opening times, though it is usually open April-September. Check the website for scheduled trips.

Entertainment and Events
MALLAIG AND MORAR GAMES
Lovat Field, Morar; tel. 07920 563 248; early Aug.
On the first Sunday of August each year, this compact and intimate Highland games is a family-friendly affair and includes piping in full dress, alongside dancing, a cross-country race, some heavy-lifting competitions, and the highly competitive Tug of War. It's a great place to meet locals, who come out to support friends and families, and the location, with sea views, is pretty special too.

Food and Accommodations
CORNERSTONE RESTAURANT
Main Street, Mallaig; tel. 01687 462 306; seafoodrestaurantmallaig.com; lunch noon-2:45pm daily, dinner 4:45pm-9pm, mid-Mar.-Sept. opening times may shorten out of season; entrées £6.95
At this seafood restaurant you can tuck into freshly landed prawns, langoustines, mussels, salmon—the list goes on—while enjoying harbor views. Entrées are well priced, with good-sized portions—if you're starving, go for the excellent fish and chips. The restaurant fills up quickly when the Jacobite Steam Train comes in, so you'd be wise to book, just in case.

MORAR HOTEL

Columba Road, Morar, Mallaig; tel. 01687 462 346;
www.morarhotel.co.uk; £72 d

Simple yet clean rooms await you at this three-star hotel. But while you can look forward to a comfy night's sleep, it's for the location that you'll be glad you find yourself here. Overlooking Morar Bay and its beautiful beach (part of the Silver Sands of Morar), views are best enjoyed from the on-site restaurant.

INFORMATION AND SERVICES

The **VisitScotland iCentre** in Fort William (15 High Street, Fort William; tel. 01397 701 801; 9am-6pm Mon.-Fri and 10am-5pm Sun. in summer, 9am-5pm Mon.-Fri. and 10am-3pm Sun. in winter) can give you advice on traveling this route. However, the official **Road to the Isles website** (www.road-to-the-isles.org.uk) probably offers more than enough local information and inspiration. Once in Mallaig, pop into the **Mallaig Heritage Centre** (11am-4pm late Mar.-June and mid-Sept.-Oct., 11am-6pm July-mid-Sept.; adult £2.50, kids free) for a local history lesson. You can hire a car from Morar Motors (tel. 01599 534 329, www.morarmotors.co.uk, from £54 per day, including insurance), based just outside Mallaig, who will deliver it to the ferry port for you.

Road to the Isle of Skye: Inverness to Kyle of Lochalsh

This route, which again can be easily completed by rail or road, takes you into the heart of the western Highlands, to the road bridge crossing to the Isle of Skye.

There are few places to stop en route for sustenance or petrol, so plan accordingly. You'll also want to take your time, to savor the views as clumps of forests huddle round the empty shorelines of forgotten lochs overlooked by lonesome cairns and broken with patches of golden sand. On the heather or gorse-strewn mountains, look out for stags on the horizon, who seem to appear out of nowhere as though responding to some ancient battle cry.

By Car

By car there are two main routes from Inverness. The most popular and probably most scenic is via the A82 along the shores of Loch Ness before joining the A887 at Invermoriston and then the A87. This route is incredibly picturesque as it skirts the shores of Loch Cluanie under the mountainous protection of Glen Shiel. It covers a distance of 80 miles (129 km) and takes around two hours.

Alternatively, the less traveled more northerly route takes you up through the Black Isle to join the A835, past Achnasheen and Strathcarron. For this route you will have to do a little detour along the A87 when you get to Auchtertyre if you'd like to visit Eilean Donan Castle. The distance covered and time traveled is similar.

By Train

Arcing all the way from Inverness to the shores of Loch Alsh for a distance of 80 miles (129 km), the **Kyle Line** is a spectacular route to travel between the two (2.75 hours, £13.90 one-way) and is known as the Great Highland Railway journey. As you approach the west coast you can see the dramatic Torridon Peaks to the north, while Skye comes into view to the south. There are some fabulous places to alight en route, including the small fishing village of Plockton—a place full of charm, where new faces are embraced,

Detour: Ardnamurchan, the West Coast's Beautiful Secret

I love this place so much, I almost don't want to tell you about it. A remote and untouched peninsula, Ardnamurchan has thus far been missed off most tourist lists and is all the better for it. Though Ardnamurchan proper refers to the peninsula west of Salen, it has come to encompass the other areas in and around this most westerly part of Britain (Ardnamurchan Point, the western tip of the peninsula, indeed claims to be the most westerly point on the British mainland, although it will have to fight the nearby headland of Corrachadh Mor for the title), including Moidart, Morvern, and Ardgour. This region was hit hard by the infamous Highland clearances. Today, just a few small close-knit communities remain (many residents have migrated here from elsewhere), and they are hugely proud of their home and more than happy to share its secrets—just don't go telling anyone.

GETTING TO SALEN

There is pretty much one road in and one road out of the peninsula—the B8007 from Salen that twists and snakes for 25 miles (40 km) along a mostly single track to Ardnamurchan Point— the western tip of the peninsula. There are two options for reaching Salen: from the A830 at Lochailort, turn left onto the A861, which bends and curls for 22 miles (35 km) to Salen. On the way you can detour off the main road by taking a road to your right down to the evocative ruins of Castle Tioram by Doirlinn, burned down by Jacobite sympathizers during the 1715 rebellion. The castle stands on a rocky islet, and there is a car park at the bottom if you want to take photos, or (if the tide is out) stroll over to examine the castle exterior more closely.

Alternatively, Salen can be reached quite easily from Fort William, by taking the Corran Ferry (£8.20 each way, five-minute crossing) a few miles south of the town, the short way across Loch Linnhe. Once on the other side at Ardgour, turn left and drive for 25 miles (40 km) along the pretty A861 in the other direction.

SALEN TO THE PENINSULA

Once you reach Salen you join the B8007, a road that can be tiresome but oh so worth it. To begin, you'll pass the protected ancient oakwoods of Sunart, which gives the region a wilder, more natural feel. There are a few very good places to stay, including Sunart Adventures (sunartadventures.com), where you can book one of two luxury cabins (£995 per week for a cabin sleeping six) on the unspoiled shores of Loch Sunart and arrange kayaking and wildlife-spotting trips (from £100 per person) direct from the beach by the cottages. Farther into the peninsula, lush woodland makes way for raw moorland and some of the most pristine white sandy beaches you have ever seen, but not before you cross the crater of an ancient volcano.

ARDNAMURCHAN POINT

Once you reach Ardnamurchan Point, marked with a lighthouse, you'll want to drive on to the heavenly shores of Sanna Bay, overlooked by volcanic rock and dunes thick with machair— grasses endemic to western Scotland and some parts of Ireland. Fully exposed to the Atlantic, it's rugged and windswept here and you will want to pay close attention, lest you miss the tail of a whale disappearing beneath the waves or a golden eagle swooping down to snatch up its unsuspecting prey. It's the kind of place where it feels as though the sunsets have been created for you alone.

particularly at the very good **Plockton Inn,** which hosts regular traditional music nights.

INVERMORISTON AND GLENMORISTON

Sights

Invermoriston Falls

Village Hall Car Park, Invermoriston

It's a pleasant riverside walk shaded by Scots pines to these waterfalls from the village car park in Invermoriston, a sweet village just six miles from Fort Augustus on the southwestern shores of Loch Ness, which seems comparatively unblemished by tourism. There are steep drops to the waters below though, so keep little ones close and watch your footing. The walk to the falls themselves—which you'll often have to yourself—is only a few minutes, but if you'd like to visit the old summerhouse, which has the best views of both the old Telford bridge and the falls and is a bit downriver from the modern road bridge, allow 30 minutes to an hour.

Food and Accommodations

GLENMORISTON ARMS

Invermoriston; tel. 01320 351 206; www. glenmoristonarms.co.uk; £140 d, £195 for the Moriston Four Poster and Jacuzzi room

This mid-price inn at the main junction to Fort William and the Kyle of Lochalsh from Loch Ness, has 11 rooms—8 of which are in the main building and traditional in style, while 3 separate rooms with a more contemporary finish can be found in the Old Tavern. The best room of all is the Moriston Four Poster and Jacuzzi room, for obvious reasons. The bar and restaurant are popular with hikers along the Great Glen Way, who receive a warm welcome (the stag head in the bar even has a name: Angus). Try the Glenmoriston Highland Sharing Plate (it includes both black pudding and haggis bon bons, smoked salmon, and local terrine), which at £18.95 is a good value for two. The hotel is closed mid-December-February.

GLEN ROWAN CAFÉ

Skye Road, Invermoriston; tel. 01320 351 208; 9am-6pm Tues.-Sat., 10am-5pm Sun. April-Oct.; cakes £2.75

This fanciful little café is a good place for a farewell cup of coffee and a perfectly decorated (and yummy) cupcake or healthy slice of carrot cake before leaving the vicinity of Loch Ness, on your way west to Kyle of Lochalsh. Breakfasts are good too, as are the lunches (homemade burgers and smoked salmon salads), but for me it's all about the cakes. There are some local gifts for sale too.

CLUANIE INN

A87, Glenmoriston; tel. 01320 340 238; www. cluanieinn.com; £140 d

If you take the main route from Invermoriston along the A887 and then the A87, you will pass by this essential roadhouse once you near the end of Loch Cluanie. With rooms, a petrol station, and a halfway decent restaurant serving modern Scottish dishes such as Balmoral chicken, it's a good place to collect yourself before continuing on to the west coast (plus it's new refurbishment should be ready by spring 2019). It also does coffee to take away.

DORNIE AND KYLE OF LOCHALSH

Sights

★ EILEAN DONAN CASTLE

Dornie, by Kyle of Lochalsh; tel. 01599 555 202; www. eileandonancastle.com; 10am-4pm daily Feb.-late Mar., 10am-6pm late Mar.-late Oct., 10am-4pm late Oct.-late Dec., opens at 9am July-Aug. and 9:30am Sept.; adult £7.50, child £4, family £20, under 5 free

Undoubtedly one of Scotland's most photographed sights and definitely one of its most romantic castles, a stop off here on your way to Skye is a must. It's located on its own little island at the point where three great sea lochs converge in the Kintail National Scenic Area, just a few miles from the bridge to Skye.

Though this 13th-century castle was all but destroyed by the Jacobites, it was carefully restored in the early 20th century and looks every bit the medieval fortress, complete with

Detour: Scotland's Last Wilderness of Glen Affric

From Drumnadrochit, on the western shores of Loch Ness, head west on the A831 for a distance of 12 miles (19 km) and you enter a region known as Glen Affric—a place of untamed beauty, unsullied by man, where the River Affric tumbles down from the Hills of Kintail via a series of rapids and burns to two freshwater lochs.

At the first, Loch Beinn a Mheadhoin, you can go wild swimming in utter peace, with just the otters and osprey for company. Loch Affric is equally tranquil and isolated. There are few roads here—if you want to explore the mighty hills and glens of this area, home to ancient Caledonian pinewoods, you need to be prepared to walk, although a car is handy for getting here. Taxis will take you here (though drivers will think you're mad), and there is a bus three times a day from Inverness to Cannich, which has a good campsite and hostel.

Just outside Cannich you will find Affric Lodge (glenaffricestate.com), a Victorian shooting lodge that now operates as an exclusive use hotel (just eight rooms) and is a prime place to find out about deer stalking and trout fishing. Make sure you pop into the reading room, which is painted with Highland scenes by Sir Edward Landseer, the artist behind the famous *Monarch of the Glen* painting on display in the Scottish National Gallery in Edinburgh (the painting was set here).

Other nearby sights include Plodda Falls, reached via a waymarked forest trail from Plodda Falls car park, just three miles south of the conservation village of Tomich. The trail to one of Scotland's most spectacular waterfalls is shaded by Douglas firs.

Glen Affric might just be Scotland's finest glen, just don't tell Glencoe I said that.

---

a fearsome portcullis and noble keep, reached via an arched stone bridge. Its atmospheric location has given it starring roles in over 30 films, including the original *Highlander*, the James Bond film *The World Is Not Enough*, *Loch Ness*, and *Rob Roy*.

Many simply stop here for the photo opportunity—particularly at sunset or sunrise when the colors of the sky add another level of beauty—and the best shots are taken over the road bridge. However, it's also worth paying the entrance fee, crossing over the stone bridge and exploring the castle, all of which is open to the public. It's good for families too; kids can swing a claymore, peer through spy holes, or make up adventurous games within the ancient battlements and terrifying portcullis. Re-opened in the 1930s, having been restored under the direction of Lieutenant Colonel MacRae-Gilstrap, who bought the ruined castle, it is very much an Edwardian reimagining of what a medieval castle would have looked like and is dressed much as it was when MacRae-Gilstrap and his family lived

here. Inside, bare stone walls are adorned with all manner of memorabilia, including cannonballs that the Jacobites fired on the castle in 1719, alongside dirks and dueling pistols and family portraits. The Banqueting Hall, with its timber-framed ceiling is typically grand and dominated by a huge fireplace above which hangs a stag's head. You can picture members of Clan MacRae (whose descendants still come here to show their respects at the war memorial to lost clan members during WWI, erected by MacRae-Gilstrap) tucking into lavish feasts.

Outside, you can walk around much of the castle exterior via a pathway that branches off to meet narrow staircases and courtyards and fully appreciate the architectural niches and the romantic setting. Before you enter the castle, look out for the plaque above the main entrance with a Gaelic inscription that refers to the kinship of the clans who share common ancestry. It roughly translates as: "As long as

---

1: Eilean Donan Castle 2: below decks on the Seaprobe Atlantis

there is a MacRae inside, there will never be a Fraser outside."

Check the website before coming because the castle is occasionally closed in winter for special events and weddings.

Sports and Recreation
HIKE TO FALLS OF GLOMACH

Kintail Ranger Office, Morvich Farm, Inverinate; tel. 01599 511 231; www.nts.org.uk/visit/places/ falls-of-glomach; open all year; free

This waterfall, which slices through some of Scotland's most unexplored countryside, is one of Britain's highest and one of its hardest to get to. It's Gaelic name, Glomach, roughly translates as hazy, perhaps in reference to the blanket of mist that often covers the falls. If you want to visit this waterfall, you have to be prepared to put on your walking boots and hike the 12 miles (19.3 km) from the ranger office on Morvich Farm via the Bealach na Sroine pass. Parking is available at the ranger office and staff can advise you on the walk, but you should pick up a copy of **Ordnance Survey Explorer map 414** (Glen Shiel and Kintail Forest) before you head here too. The trek, though long (it takes about six hours there and back), is relatively straightforward with a good path (though rough to start) that is well marked. It does climb to altitudes of 1,800 feet (550 m) though, and at times the path skirts steep drops to the valley below, so good fitness and some hillwalking experience are advised. The route takes you through some of the most remote countryside in Scotland, and it's a breathtaking sight when the falls finally come into view, piercing through a narrow cleft between the rocks.

SEAPROBE ATLANTIS

The Car Park, Kyle of Lochalsh; tel. 01471 822 716; www.seaprobeatlantis.com; 1-hour boat trip adult £14, youth (ages 13-15) £9, child (ages 4-12) £8, toddler (ages 1-3) £5, family £42; 1.25-hour trip adult £17, youth £10, child £9, toddler £6, family £50; 2-hour boat trip adult £26, youth £16, child £14,

toddler £8, family £76

These tours aboard a glass-bottomed boat (with windows in the hull) are unforgettable. Squeeze downstairs at the start of the trip to peer out as the boat slowly makes its way out of the harbor through tall sea grasses and seaweed—a great place to spot crabs, small fish, and jellyfish. Once out on the water you'll be beckoned upstairs to see seals up close and even the occasional passing dolphin or other marine wildlife. The skipper is knowledgeable and candid in his descriptions, and there is a choice of cruises for 1 hour, 1.25 hours, and 2 hours; on the longer two you'll also be able to view the shipwreck of a WWII vessel from underwater.

Food and Accommodations
THE CLACHAN

13 Francis Street, Dornie; tel. 01599 555 366; www. theclachan.com; meals served 6pm-9pm Easter to Oct.; entrées £5.75

Straightforward traditional dishes (steak and Guinness pie or poached salmon served with seasonal vegetables) are served at this pub, just a 10-minute walk from Eilean Donan Castle. You can't book—it's first come, first served—and the menu won't set the world on fire, but food is well cooked and presented, and well priced too.

WATERSIDE RESTAURANT

Railway Buildings, Station Road, Kyle of Lochalsh; tel. 01599 534 813; www.watersideseafoodrestaurant. co.uk; 6pm-9pm Mon.-Sat. and noon-2:30pm Wed.; entrées £6.95

If you love seafood, then this place is for you. Owners Jann and Neil MacRae handpick their local suppliers, with Isle of Skye mussels and peat-smoked salmon featuring on the menu alongside "queenie" scallops, though the menu is dictated by what the fishermen have hauled in. Neil also runs seafood cruises aboard his own fishing boat, *Green Isle*, cooking the daily catches on board. Seafood doesn't get much fresher than this and it's right near where you board the Seaprobe Atlantis.

RATAGAN YOUTH HOSTEL

Glenshiel, Kyle, Ross Shire; tel. 01599 511 243; www.
hostellingscotland.org.uk/hostels/ratagan; bed in
shared room from £21, private room £78

From the outside, this looks less like a hostel and more like an inviting guesthouse. For starters, it's on the far edge of Loch Duich and guests are free to wander down to the little pebble beach at the end of the garden. Inside though, it's pretty standard for a hostel—there's a big kitchen and a large communal chill-out area, and rooms are clean enough but could do with one or two more shared bathrooms. Dorms are well priced, but private rooms are a tad pricey for what you get.

SEADRIFT B&B

Avernish by Kyle of Lochalsh IV40 8EQ; tel. 01599
555 415; www.seadrift.co.uk; £180 d per night,
minimum two-night stay

Just a few minutes from Eilean Donan and only a 10-minute drive to the Kyle of Lochalsh bridge, it's perfectly possible to base yourself at this intimate and luxurious B&B while you explore Skye and Scotland's west coast up to Plockton and Applecross. The three light and airy rooms, two of which have loch views, have big beds with Egyptian cotton sheets, Nespresso machines and fancy toiletries. The excellent breakfast includes eggs laid by the owners' own hens and homemade granola.

INFORMATION AND SERVICES

Pick up maps and mine for as much info as possible at the **VisitScotland iCentres** in Inverness and Fort Augustus before heading along the A87 because, once you're on the road, services are sparse. For online inspiration and tips ahead of travel, check out the **Lochalsh & the Isle of Skye guide** (www. lochalsh.co.uk). You can also pop into the **visitor center at Eilean Donan Castle** (tel. 01599 555 202, www.eileandonancastle.com/ visit/visitor-centre), which can direct you to other local attractions and give you some insight into the history of the area.

Isle of Skye

Often touted as everyone's favorite island, the drama of Skye's landscape—all jagged peaks and startling pinnacles, where shimmering lochs and pools are hidden high up in mountain ranges amid secret gullies—seems otherworldly, impossible even.

It's home to Britain's most magnificent mountain range, the Cuillin, which covers much of the center of the island, including the taller, sharper, formidable main **Cuillin Ridge** to the west (known sometimes as the Black Cuillin), as well as the slightly more rounded slopes of the Red Cuillin to the east of Glen Sligachan. Remarkably, the Cuillin, weren't fully explored and mapped out until the early 1900s, and since then they have become a mecca for mountaineers.

Skye is a land that has fired imaginations for generation after generation, with tales of fairies, sprites, and kelpies passed down through folklore to help explain the unexplainable. It is now also home to some of the best stargazing spots in the British Isles.

Headlines purporting over-tourism may have taken a little of the shine off, but you'd be a fool to fall for the lie that Skye is busy. Yes, if you want to visit the same five or six sights (the Quiraing, the Old Man of Storr, Fairy Pools, etc.) as everyone else, then you will find yourself admiring beauty spots surrounded by strangers, but it really doesn't take much to find peace and serenity on this most varied of islands.

ORIENTATION

Most visitors to Skye will arrive into either **Armadale** in the southwest of the island on the **Sleat Peninsula** or **Kyleakin** in the southeast. The terrain of the south is much gentler and more fertile than the melodramatic bare rock of other parts of the island, and on the Sleat Peninsula at least you'll be able to find space away from the tourist crowds.

The main town of the island is **Portree,** a pretty harbor town where colorful houses line the quayside and from where tours can be booked and provisions collected. To reach Portree you'll join the A87, the busiest of a handful of main roads that connects the corners of the isle. The A87 passes through **Broadford,** another relatively large town with a large supermarket and petrol station.

Portree sits at the bottom of the protruding **Trotternish Peninsula** on the northeast of the island, which is where you will find some of Skye's most famous sights, including **the Quiraing, the Old Man of Storr, Fairy Glen,** and **Staffin's dinosaur beach.**

West of Portree, the A850 brings you past the entry point to the **Waternish peninsula** on the northwest of the island (the B886), or you can continue on to **Dunvegan Castle.** Further west, taking the B884 via the A863 will bring you to **Glendale** and **Neist Point.**

While north Skye may get the most visitors, it's in the center of Skye that you'll find its best assets—the monumental **Cuillin** peaks. To reach the Cuillin, you can turn off the A87 at Sligachan and enter the mountains from here—Glen Sligachan acts as a natural boundary between the Black Cuillin in the west and the Red Cuillin in the east. Alternatively, from Sligachan, continue west to Carbost (where you'll also find **Talisker Distillery**) before turning south toward Glen Brittle, another popular entry point for climbers. The final option is to turn off the A87 at Broadford and take the B8083 toward **Elgol** (which also has boat trips to the Small Isles), for entry to the range from the south.

The A87 also goes through Sconser, from where you can take the ferry across to **Raasay.**

GETTING TO THE ISLE OF SKYE

By Car

Once only accessible by a ferry crossing from Kyle of Lochalsh, today Skye is one of the easiest islands to get to by car due to the Kyle of Lochalsh bridge, which opened in 1995, and links the mainland to Kyleakin in the south of the Isle of Skye. Just 10 miles west of Dornie on the A87, the bridge, which has no toll, has made it much easier for islanders to head to the mainland for work; it's also encouraged a whole wave of day visitors who whizz over to the island and try to tick off as many of the most famous sights and destinations as possible in 12 hours or so.

To reach Skye, it's around a two-hour drive from Inverness (81 mi/130 km) along the A82 and then A87, or via the route of the Kyle railway line along the A835, the A832 and the A890 (similar time and distance). The bridge takes just five minutes to cross.

From Fort William the journey time is just under two hours (74 mi/119 km) to Kyle of Lochalsh; follow the A82 north to Invergarry from where you can pick up the A87 all the way west to Kyle of Lochalsh and simply drive over the bridge. Most people driving from Fort William though simply follow the A830 west to Mallaig (43 mi/69 km) for about an hour and get the ferry from there to Armadale.

By Bus

Citylink (www.citylink.co.uk) runs bus services between Glasgow and the Isle of Skye and between Inverness and Skye. From Inverness bus station, there are two direct buses a day to Portree on the Isle of Skye (the no. 917). The trip takes 3.5 hours and costs £26.40 one-way. Tickets can be booked online or bought from the ticket office at the bus station. There is also an option to take the bus from Inverness to Invergarry (no. 919) and change for the bus to Skye (no. 916) if times don't suit, but this does take longer and is more expensive.

There are at least three buses from Glasgow

to Skye each day, from Buchanan Bus Station to Portree (no. 915 or no.916). The trip takes 6.75 hours and costs £44.30 each way. Spaces can book up, so book a seat online in advance.

From Kyle of Lochalsh, bus numbers 917 (twice a day) and 915 (once a day) set off from the harbor slipway in Kyle of Lochalsh (near the Seaprobe Atlantis office) and will get you over the bridge and to Portree in just over an hour. Tickets are £7.50 one-way.

By Ferry

By far the most utilized ferry crossing to Skye is from Mallaig, where the West Highland Railway Line ends. Ferries with CalMac (www.calmac.co.uk) depart several times a day (roughly every hour). The crossing to Armadale in south Skye takes 45 minutes and costs just £3 each way for a foot passenger, plus £9.95 one-way for a car (you'll need to pay for each passenger on top).

The Glenelg Ferry crossing (Easter-Oct.), a small independent operation, is considered the more scenic route, and the ferry crossing is much shorter than the one from Mallaig. To reach Glenelg, turn off the main road from Invermoriston to Kyle of Lochalsh (the A87) at Shiel Bridge and follow the Old Military Road for nine miles (14 km). If you do opt for this route, you're in for a treat as you'll get to ride on Scotland's last manually operated turntable ferry. This ferry route operates every 20 minutes or so (as much as it's needed) 10am-6pm daily April-May, September-October and 10am-7pm June-August. It costs £15 one-way for a car with up to four people. The crossing takes mere minutes and lands in Kylerhea, just a few miles south of Kyleakin on Skye.

GETTING AROUND THE ISLE OF SKYE

At 639 square miles (1,656 sq km), Skye may not sound huge, but, with much of the rocky landscape not navigable to road vehicles and just a clutch of main roads, it can take a long time to get from A to B here. Because you'll be astounded at the landscape as you

drive (particularly when you get off the main thoroughfares, which will keep you occupied), it's not a place to rush.

By Car

To really see as much of the island as possible, get off the beaten track, and travel at your own pace, you need a car to see Skye. The biggest joy to be had on Skye is when you leave the main roads behind and turn onto one of the narrow single-track roads where there will be far fewer cars to break the illusion of peace and plenty of sheep to keep you company.

You'll need a map—the Scotland Visitors' Atlas & Guide A-Z is good—and try to get into the habit of filling up the tank when you see a petrol station (there is a 24-hour one at the Co-op in Broadford) because you never know when you might see one again.

If you didn't travel to the Isle of Skye with a car, you can rent one in Portree with Jans (jans.co.uk) and Morrisons Car Hire (www.morrisoncarrental.com).

By Bus

There is a sporadic bus service operated by Stagecoach (www.stagecoachbus.com) on the Isle of Skye, and in theory it is possible to move around the island this way, particularly if you base yourself in one area for a few days before moving on to the next as bus connections do link all of the main towns and villages. The no. 52 bus links the two main towns of Broadford and Portree with the ferry terminal at Armadale (£4.20 from Armadale to Broadford, £7.70 from Armadale to Portree). If you are planning to get more than one bus in a day, a Day Rider ticket at £9.20 will save you money and can be bought on board or through the Stagecoach app.

By Taxi

If you want to pop out for dinner or even arrange a bit of a whistle-stop tour of some of the main attractions, then Gus's Taxis (tel. 01478 613 000; skye-taxis.co.uk) based in Portree can arrange either lifts or more bespoke tours. The fleet of five minicabs can also collect you from the ferry port in Armadale or at the Kyle of Lochalsh train station and bring you over to the island.

ISLE OF SKYE TOURS

SKYE JEEP TOURS

Pickup in Broadford or Portree; tel. 01599 522 270 or 07976 238 862; skyejeeptours.com; £225 for a seven-hour tour (£75 pp if booking for three)

What a cool adventure: on these road trips aboard a vintage jeep, your driver (usually one half of husband-and-wife team Lynne and Sam) will take you pretty much wherever you want—from the famous sights to a more in-depth exploration of lesser-known places, all while entertaining you with stories, legends, and memories. Tours are limited to three passengers in the vintage jeep and Wrangler, and four in the Cherokee. Tours last a minimum of seven hours, and they will pick you up from either Broadford or Portree. Occasionally, you'll be joined on board by the couple's friendly (and well-behaved) half lab half border collie, Brymer. For the truly adventurous, you can stay in the couple's military pod, Boris, for £66 per night with a minimum stay of two nights.

SKYE ADVENTURE

Pickup in Portree or Sligachan; tel. 07785 962 391 or 07818 884 609; www.skyeadventure.co.uk; from £57

Skye is a real place to unleash your intrepid side and some of the best experiences are had when you pit yourself against its awesome landscape, which makes these outdoor tours so worthwhile. Tours include munro-bagging (the term used for climbing a munro, a mountain over 3,000 feet/914 meters high), traversing the Cuillin Ridge, or gorge walking—think scrambling, climbing, and swimming in crystal-clear pools and jumping, sliding, and climbing down amazing waterfalls. Tours are adapted to match your ability. Tour guides will pick you up from Portree or Sligachan and will provide all equipment (including wet suits), but those wanting to go for a dip will need to wear swimming clothes underneath.

SKYE HIGH WILDLIFE

Pickup from hotel on Skye; tel. 01471 855 643 or 07809 580 253; skyehighwildlife.com; half day £60 pp, full day £120 per person

For a slow adventure with a difference, join professional photographer Stewart Dawber on one of his wildlife photography courses in some of the most remote parts of the island (often taking you off road). Stewart is an expert in stealth photography, and with his expertise in tracking wildlife, as well as a lot of patience, you'll be able to get up close to pine martens, otters, red deer, and Highland cows and take photos worthy of a magazine cover—as long as you bring your own camera. Each course is tailor-made to your requirements, and Stewart will pick you up from where you are staying. Tours are offered year round, and in winter Stewart will even take you to an out-of-the-way bothy where you can have lunch cooked on a wood burner and sample some local whiskies.

ARMADALE AND SOUTH SKYE

Fools are they who discount the south of Skye—in particular, the **Sleat Peninsula**— and roar through it when they get off the ferry at Armadale, determined to reach Portree and the far reaches of the Trotternish. Known as the "garden of Skye," it's much greener than most of the isle, with its rocky shoreline punctuated with pretty meadows of wildflowers, forests, lonely beaches, and heather-clad hills. There's a slower air about the place too, mainly because it gets far fewer visitors, and there's not actually an awful lot to do here other than sit and listen to the birds, take bracing walks, or watch out for otters or seals, but that's half the appeal.

Armadale Castle is worth an afternoon of your time, and there are some pretty and deserted **beaches** as well as a brand-new **distillery,** which is a small sign that this region is waking up to itself. Plus, with a Gaelic college and a hotel that only employs staff who speak Gaelic, it's a great place to learn about this integral part of local culture.

Armadale ferry terminal—where the Mallaig ferry lands onto Skye, is located on the southeast of the peninsula.

Sights
ARMADALE CASTLE, GARDENS, AND MUSEUM

Armadale, Sleat; tel. 01471 844 305; www. armadalecastle.com; gardens daily 9:30am-5:30pm, museum 10am-5:30pm, café 9:30am-3:30pm, plus Thurs., Fri., and Sat. evenings, late Mar.-late Oct., 10am-3pm Weds.-Sun. Mar. and Nov.; adult £8.50, concessions and child £6.95, under 5 free, family £25

Once the family seat of the Macdonalds of Sleat, part of the formidable Clan Donald, this castle, which now stands in ruin, is set amid 40 acres (16 hectares) of well-kept woodland gardens. The castle ruins date from the 19th century, though Macdonalds lived here in an older mansion house from the 1650s onward. History lovers will no doubt be intrigued that Scottish heroine Flora Macdonald was married here in 1750 and just over 20 years later Samuel Johnson and James Boswell visited it.

Inside, the museum tells the story of Clan Donald across six galleries, from their position as powerful Lords of the Isles to the subsequent diaspora in the wake of Culloden.

On display are broadswords (one of the weapons of choice of clansmen), bagpipes, and a 17th-century firearm reputedly fired at Culloden.

You can't step inside the castle itself because the crumbling walls that remain are fenced off for safety, but you can walk around the splendid gardens (though you'll need a ticket) where 100-year-old trees stand watch over beautiful displays of bluebells and orchids, plus herbaceous borders and pretty little ponds. Take a seat on one of the well-placed benches for views across the Sound of Sleat toward the mountains of Knoydart and Moidart.

It's an easy stop-off for anyone arriving or departing by ferry at Armadale, particularly those with kids—there's a playground and special trails to follow. Visiting times for November 2019 are not yet confirmed, so check the website.

TORABHAIG DISTILLERY

Teangue, Sleat; tel. 01471 833 447; torabhaig.com; 10am-4pm Mon.-Fri. and 10am-3pm Sat. and Sun. Mar.-mid-Oct., 10am-4pm Mon.-Fri. mid-Oct.-Feb (except Christmas and New Year's); tours £10

Skye's newest distillery and part of the new **Hebridean Whisky Trail,** this distillery

Armadale ferry terminal

has only been making whisky since January 2017 so there's not much to taste . . . yet. Housed in an old farmstead (built from stone from the ruined castle you can see below the distillery) the water necessary to make the whisky comes from the nearby Allt Breacach burn. Visitors can learn all about the whisky-making process—from the mashing to the fermenting to the distilling—as well as try a dram of Mossburn Island Blend, a whisky similar to the finish and flavor the distillery is going for: a well-tempered peat. Unusually, the wash backs used by the distillery are made of Douglas firs, and the whisky is then distilled in custom-made copper stills. Only time will tell the quality of the whisky produced—the earliest it will be available is 2020, but until then the 45-minute tour is an interesting way to spend an hour, get good insight into the distilling process, and have lunch in the nice café.

Beaches
CAMAS DARAICH
Road end of the Aird of Sleat
While tourists head to Claigan Beach in northern Skye, locals know that this is Skye's other best beach. It takes a little while to get here, but with golden sands and sparkling turquoise waters, it's worth the effort. The trail starts at the road end of the Aird of Sleat, reached via Newton Bank (left when you come off the Armadale Ferry), where parking is available. Follow the path straight ahead as it crosses boggy moorland. You'll reach a bridge where there is a sign pointing to the left to "sandy beach." Follow this direction as the path leads steeply uphill, a little rough in places, but follow close to the fence and you should be OK. In total the walk should take about 1.5 hours there and back.

Food and Accommodations
KINLOCH LODGE
Sleat; tel. 01471 833 333; kinloch-lodge.co.uk; breakfast 8:15am-9:45am, lunch noon-2pm, dinner 6:30pm-9pm daily; five-course menu £80, afternoon tea £24, three-course Sunday lunch £40; cookery courses from £25; £340 d
This is grand-style dining in a resplendent room where you slide into period chairs and eat beneath the approving stares of the expensively framed portraits on the wall. Tables are dressed in white linen with candles in the center, and the food by chef Marcello Tully is superb, with shellfish, game, and seasonal vegetables and herbs prepared imaginatively and matched with good wine. Afternoon tea is also available, and from late October to the end of February the elegant Edwardian hotel (you can stay too, if you can afford it) hosts Sunday roasts, followed by a whisky tasting in the bar. Look out too for sporadic cookery courses with Marcello.

★ EILEAN IARMAIN
Isleornsay, Sleat; 01471 833 332; eileaniarmain.co.uk; Am Birlinn 5:30pm-8pm, Am Praban 5:30pm-9pm, daily ring ahead to check in winter; entrées £6; £191 d
This hotel, with 12 bedrooms and suites, a pub, and a restaurant, is in a fabulous waterside location and you'll be so glad you found it—next door to the hotel you can sample Gaelic whiskies at **Pràban na Linne** Monday-Friday (though it's hard not to buy some too) and browse a shop selling Scottish cashmere and tweed. Resolutely Gaelic in its approach—speaking the language is apparently a prerequisite to working in the hotel—dishes are satisfyingly Scottish (rack of Scottish lamb and the hotel's own fish pie). You can have a more relaxed, walk-in dinner (though from the same menu) in the **Am Praban Bar,** where traveling Scottish musicians can often be found setting up a Ceilidh session. It's not so much a restaurant and hotel as it is a community.

MORAR B&B
2 Calgary, Ardvasar, Sleat; tel. 01471 844 378; www. accommodation-on-skye.co.uk; £95 d
Not your average B&B, this one, just a mile outside Armadale, it comes with its own indoor heated swimming pool. Set on a croft within a family home, guests can enjoy views from the terrace or wander down amid the

meadows where there are rare orchids. The nearby bay is a prime place to spot otters, and the family's chickens will keep you company. Rooms are bright and tastefully decorated with statement wallpaper and big prints, giving them a thoroughly modern feel. A steal at this price.

OFF THE HILL B&B

1 Duisdale Beag, Isleornsay, Sleat; tel. 01471 833 305; www.offthehillskye.com; £85 d/£75 South Room, minimum two-night stay

On the northeast of the Sleat Peninsula, this B&B has three spacious rooms, which have dual or triple aspects. Rooms are big, if a bit of a mishmash of styles, but hosts Elaine and Chris will make you feel so at ease that you really won't care. The country setting is pretty idyllic too. One note: the South Room's bathroom, though private, is across the corridor, so may not be for everyone.

Information and Services

In recent years Sleat has got its act together and pulled together a really useful portal of tourist information at **Visit Sleat** (www. visitsleat.org); how very helpful of them.

Getting There
BY CAR

From Portree, it's an hour's drive to Armadale south along the A87 for 25 miles (40 km) before turning right onto the A851 just past Harropool for a further 15 miles (24 km). From Broadford it's just 25 minutes, south on the A87 before taking the same turning onto the A851.

BY BUS

From Portree, the no. 52 **Stagecoach** bus will take you to Armadale in 1.25 hours (£7.70, three times a day in summer and timed to meet the ferries, less out of season). From Broadford, it's just a 30-minute bus ride on the no. 52 to Armadale (£4.10 one-way).

Getting Around

Take a left out of the ferry terminal and head four miles (6 km) along the east coast of the peninsula to the Aird of Sleat, the end of the road, via Newton Bank, from where you'll need to get your walking boots on to reach the tip of the peninsula. Take a right out of the ferry terminal onto the A851, also along the east coast, to get out of Sleat and explore the rest of Skye.

Few people venture to the west coast of Sleat, but if you would like to, you'll need to take one of the two roads that cross through the Sleat: the first is on your left by Kilbeg as you travel north, the second a short while after, just past Torabhaig Distillery. For traveling around the region or a little further afield, both **James's Taxi and Tours** (tel. 01471 844717) and **Nicolson Hire Taxi Service** (tel. 01471 844338) are reliable cab firms and can take you on bespoke tours too.

CENTRAL SKYE AND THE CUILLIN

Cutting through the center of Skye, the Cuillin is considered Britain's most magnificent mountain range and is a mecca for walking enthusiasts. There are 11 munros within its fold—12 if you count Bla Bheinn right on the cusp of the Cuillin Ridge—but even if you don't think you can manage scaling one of its peaks, the views of the craggy gray mountains towering over you are still very pleasing.

A largely uninhabited region of the isle, the center is where Skye is at its most awesome. You'll lose track of the number of eagles you spot swooping down to snatch up prey or hovering in the sky above you, and you'll need a little patience as the resident sheep wander into your path and refuse to budge, seemingly as mesmerized by the sublime beauty of it all as you are.

The mountains hide no end of waterfalls, some trickling and some thunderous, streams, gorges, and lochs, and it's easy to feel free in the vastness of it all. You may come across the odd hiker coming in the opposite direction—be friendly, you never know when you may need to call upon their help—and if the idea of total isolation leaves you a little nervous,

Hebridean Whisky Trail

Launched in 2018 this whisky trail across some of Scotland's most far-flung isles aims to detract attention from the whisky regions everyone knows about (Speyside, Islay) and show them that here in the outer regions of Scotland some pretty good whisky is being made too. It's also hoped that it will encourage travelers to flit between the isles a little more, thus sharing the benefits of tourism.

At the moment the trail includes stalwart **Talisker Distillery,** which has proven itself a world-class whisky maker; however, the other distilleries are virtual unknowns. The **Isle of Harris Distillery** in Tarbert on the Isle of Lewis and Harris may be familiar to anyone who has arrived on the island by ferry (it's bang opposite the ferry terminal), but few others seem to know about its Hearach single malt in the making—though a few more may know about its maritime-infused gin (featuring nine botanicals), which has been winning plaudits.

The **Isle of Raasay Distillery,** on the Isle of Rasaay, just off Skye's east coast, only opened its doors in 2017, so its single malt won't be ready for a while yet, though it did have the foresight to start distilling elsewhere a couple of years ago so people can still sample and buy its While You Wait whisky. **Torabhaig Distillery,** Skye's second-ever legal distillery, hidden away on the Sleat Peninsula in the far south of the island, doesn't even have that. It's hoping that its passion, knowledge, ambition, and stunning location overlooking a ruined castle and rugged bay are reason enough for people to stop by.

then you are best booking a tour to guide you through the region. Only experienced walkers and climbers who have safety measures in place should attempt trekking or climbing in the Cuillin alone.

Orientation

The center of civilization in these parts is in **Broadford,** a reasonably big town by Skye's standards on the east coast, where you can get online, pick up food, and send your postcards. From Broadford, the single-track B8083 to Elgol passes southwest through the village of **Torrin** before rounding **Loch Slapin** and then winding up and down on the edge of the Cuillin all the way to the fishing village of **Elgol** at the bottom of the **Strathaird peninsula.** Elgol is where you can take a boat trip to the **Small Isles** and also **Loch Coruisk** in the heart of the Cuillin.

The other ways of reaching the Cuillin are from farther north. **Sligachan** is pretty much where you would hit if you were to put a pin in the center of a map of Skye. It's 16 miles (26 km) northwest of Broadford along the A87 and has a hotel, a bar, and a good restaurant and is probably the most popular entry point into the mountain range.

From Sligachan, it's 8 miles west to **Carbost** (home to **Talisker Distillery**), and if you turn left just before you reach Carbost (by the Carbost Caravan Park) and follow this road for four miles (6.4 km), it will drop down into **Glen Brittle,** a beautiful valley where serious walkers come to explore the Cuillin from the west. This is also where you can access the famous Fairy Pools, as well as some good alternatives.

Sights
BROADFORD TO ELGOL ROAD
B8083 from Broadford
To fully appreciate the majesty of the Black Cuillin, take the main road from Broadford to Elgol. The no. 55 bus comes down here too four times a day from Broadford on Mondays to Fridays (50 minutes, £5.25).

As the road winds through a natural landscape of hills and unkempt fields where sheep wander or mill about by boggy lochs, there are plenty of passing places to pull over and take in the astounding views as Bla Bheinn, the mountain that marks the eastern edge of the Black Cuillin, comes into view, making you feel wholly insignificant in comparison.

In total the drive through Torrin, round **Loch Slapin**—definitely stop here for photos, you might even want a cuppa at the **Blue Shed Café**—up round the eastern side of the Black Cuillin and down into Elgol takes 35 minutes and covers 14.5 miles (23 km). It being a single-track road, though, you'll want to take your time; there's no need to rush scenery like this.

FAIRY POOLS

Carbost, Glenbrittle; www.isleofskye.com/skye-guide/top-ten-skye-walks/fairy-pools

Probably the most visited sight on Skye, this collection of pools fed by a series of waterfalls is an Instagram favorite: at times the color of the water is like emerald green.

Unfortunately, the pools have become a victim of their own success, with thousands upon thousands of people visiting them each year. The ecosystem simply can't cope, and the Highland Council has already had to widen the path to accommodate the tremendous footfall. There are other, less visited and equally special pools to see. If you must visit the pools, follow a couple simple rules to prevent even further degradation of the area: stick to the path (don't be tempted to take off-road shortcuts), and where possible take one of the local tours (too many cars is another problem, and this will cause less impact) with someone like **Tour Skye** (tel. 01478 613 514; www.tourskye.com).

If you want to appreciate the atmosphere of the area, it's also advisable to visit outside high season, or come early in the morning or late at night. The Fairy Pools can be a special place to be under Skye's famously dark skies.

COIR' A' GHRUNNDA

Glenbrittle Campsite, Carbost; www.theskyeguide.com/walking-mainmenu-32/34-stretching/156-coir-a-ghrunnda

The route to this hidden-away pool is not too hard to follow, but it can take some organizing to find, although the description from the Skye Guide website should make it easier. First up, grab yourself a copy of Ordnance Survey Explorer Map 411: Skye—Cuillin Hills, which you can buy online or again from Inside Out in Portree, and only attempt this trek on a fine day.

Setting off from Glenbrittle Campsite, follow the main path that goes up behind the toilet block and then take the path that branches right across the burn. From here the path is relatively easy to follow as it takes you up, rising steeply to the left (cairns are there to help mark the way) into the lower corrie (steep-sided hollow). Once in the lower corrie the ground becomes trickier, with scree and large boulders to navigate. Stick left and high as much as possible; once you reach the waterfall you should be able to scramble up it and over into the upper corrie. And there you have it, your own private pool, with no other tourists spoiling your view. Inexperienced walkers should have no problem finding a local guide to take them there.

★ LOCH CORUISK

Reached from Elgol with Bella Jane boat trips; tel. 01471 866 244; www.bellajane.co.uk; adult £28, child £16, under 4 free

If you've ever heard *The Skye Boat Song*, you might be interested to hear that it was while being rowed across the waters of this secret loch—it's hidden in the Cuillin—in the 18th century that Miss Annie MacLeod first had its melody sung to her by boatmen. She quickly wrote it down (lyrics were added later by Sir Harold Boulton), and it is now a song that invokes a strong sense of patriotism and longing. The loch is also said to have its own kelpie (water spirit), which isn't very surprising because there is something ethereal about the place.

Walking round the edge of the loch (the south is easiest and offers the best views), it's hard not to spend the entire time looking up at the enormous mountains that encircle it and feeling at the utter mercy of nature. Truly remote and once a volcanic bowl (its Gaelic name translates as cauldron of waters), over time it was shaped by

Overtourism on Skye–Do Your Bit

Let's get one thing clear: Tourism is absolutely key to Skye. If it goes, the impact would have a devastating effect on the local economy. You only have to go to the empty pits of Ayrshire or see the effect the demise of shipbuilding had on Glasgow and the fall in value of oil in Aberdeenshire to see the impact a loss in tourism could have on places like Skye.

However, there is a bit of a problem with people visiting the same places. By simply widening your net, you will not only have a more unique experience (and the photos to match), but you can also sleep easy at night, safe in the knowledge that you are contributing to safeguarding and protecting this most special island for future generations.

Overtourism threatens the most popular sights in Skye. Social media has played a key role: Posts of scenic places, Photoshopped out of recognition in some instances, on social media convince people they have to visit them. The challenge is to persuade people that there is more than just the social media side of things and that having a genuinely unique experience far outweighs impressing other people.

For instance, the Fairy Pools are beautiful, but will your experience really be that special when you have to fight for position on your iPhone to capture the same photos as everyone else? Why not venture to some of the other stunning pools on Skye instead, such as Coir' a' Ghrunnda? It may take a little more organizing than a trip to the Fairy Pools, and anyone who wants to go there will have to have a degree of fitness and a willingness to get their feet wet and have a scramble. But isn't that all part of the adventure?

Some useful blogs, such as Quiet Skye (quietskye.com), really promote some of the benefits of slower tourism and less visited places in Skye and will enrich your experience of the isle.

glaciers. Though at times it's a sinister, bewitching place with ink-black waters, and it must be terrifying in a storm, when the sun is out, the loch glimmers a bright blue, and it's tempting to go for a dip, until you touch its surface and its coldness scolds you.

Bella Jane runs trips here from its base in Elgol every day (when weather allows) at 9am, 10:45am, 12:15pm, and 2pm. The standard round trip lasts three hours and gives you the chance to see seals (and possibly other marine wildlife) before spending an hour and a half ashore. Experienced hikers can also opt for a one-way trip and walk back to Elgol, though they will need to traverse at least one river and the aptly named Bad Step—a precariously balanced huge boulder that has a huge drop down to sea. Many hikers opt to get the boat here and then use the loch as a starting point for a walk to Sligachan, traversing the Black Cuillin and the Red Cuillin, a trek of eight miles (13 km).

★ TALISKER DISTILLERY

Carbost; tel. 01478 614 308; www.malts.com/en-gb/distilleries/talisker; 10am-4:30pm Mon.-Fri. Jan.-Mar., 9:30am-5pm Mon.-Sat. and 10am-5pm Sun. Apr.-June and Sept.-Oct., 9:30am-5:30pm Mon.-Sat. and 10am-5pm Sun. July-Aug., 10am-4:30pm Mon.-Sat. and 11am-4:30pm Sun. Nov.-Dec.; Classic Distillery Tour £10, Talisker Flight Tour £25

The granddaddy of Hebridean distilleries, Talisker single malt whisky is renowned for its full-bodied flavor, inspired by its coastal windswept location. It's a great whisky brand, and this distillery runs like a well-oiled machine. There are tours throughout the day, though, to ensure you get on one (especially in summer), book at least 3-4 days in advance. The Classic Distillery Tour (45 minutes) will talk you through the process of making Talisker whisky and give you the chance to have a wee dram, while the Talisker Flight Tour (1.5 hours) gives you a tasting of several different Talisker whiskies. If tours are booked up, you can stop by and have a dram at the bar, or buy a bottle to take home with you if you're the designated driver.

Beaches
TALISKER BEACH
Near Talisker Distillery; www.isleofskye.com/ skye-guide/top-ten-skye-walks/talisker-beach

There is a certain rawness to this black and white sand beach in Talisker Bay. Park on one of the verges at the end of the tarmac road into the settlement of Talisker and follow the sign that reads "to the bay." The track runs behind Talisker House, a smart house that was one of Samuel Johnson's and James Boswell's stop-offs on their epic Hebridean journey in the 1770s. The track, which rises slightly, soon emerges at the southern end of the bay. Though the beach is largely sandy, there are stones here too and a waterfall on the north side of the bay pours down the rock face. The beach's most impressive facet, though, is its irregular sea stack to the south. The walk takes just 20-30 minutes, and swimming is possible here.

GLENBRITTLE BEACH
Glenbrittle, Carbost

The up side of this beach, on the shores of Loch Brittle and in the shadow of the Cuillin, is that there is sand here at all states of tide, so you'll often find locals walking dogs or flying kites. There's parking plus a campsite shop for picking up hot drinks or ice creams on the odd day that the sun is out. Strong swimmers may even want to venture to the lower cliffs to the left of the beach where a series of waterfalls drops to the water, creating pleasant showers.

Hiking
If you are considering a hike, then ensure you have a good map—obviously, you should not rely on a mobile phone and even compasses often fail to work here. Also, tell someone where you are going and be prepared to turn back if conditions change. Climbing the Cuillin is not for beginners: you will often be scrambling over scree, debris, and bare rock at perilous heights, so you need to know what you are doing.

TOP EXPERIENCE

★ BLA BHEINN
Trailhead: *Car park off B8083 road near Loch Slapin*
Hiking Time: *5-6 hours*
Information and maps: *www.walkhighlands. co.uk/munros/bla-bheinn*

As you approach Loch Slapin from Broadford, the hulk of Bla Bheinn, one of Britain's mightiest mountains, glares down at you. It marks the entry to the Black Cuillin proper and is separated from the rest of the range by Glen Sligachan, making it the only one of Skye's munros not to be part of the Black Cuillin. Nevertheless, its mass of gabbro displays all the characteristics of the nearby mountain range, and it is relatively easy to ascend—as long as you are prepared for a bit of scrambling—though inexperienced walkers are advised to go with a guide.

Start your walk at the car park on the far side of the loch if coming from Broadford; you'll need to look out for it because it's easy to miss. From the car park, cross the stream and turn left. The path is well-marked initially, is mostly gravel, and follows the river, which turns into quite a deep gorge punctuated with several waterfalls. The path gradually starts to wind up and become less clear, following a somewhat zig-zag path to the top as you round big boulders. Don't forget to stop to look behind you once the boulder section is complete for stunning views of Loch Slapin and to see how far you've come. En route you'll pass mountain streams and surprise corries (steep-sided hollows). The higher and higher you go, the more spectacular the views become: with some mild scrambling, go past the vertical rock wall of the Great Prow as you near the top to see the Cuillin range to the northwest and the Red Cuillin to the northeast.

★ HIKE TO THE CLEARED VILLAGE OF BORERAIG

Trailhead: *Kilchrist Church on the Broadford to Elgol road*

Hiking time: *4 hours*

Information: *www.isleofskye.com/skye-guide/top-ten-skye-walks/boreraig*

One of the saddest mars on Scotland's past are the notorious Highland Clearances, in which communities were forced from their land to make way for more profitable sheep farming. On this walk, which sets off from the ruins of Kilchrist Church on the Broadford to Elgol road and climbs high into the mountains before descending on to the shores of Loch Eishort, you can visit one of the cutoff communities that suffered this fate.

The church is located on the Broadford to Elgol road itself (you can't miss it); it's just a six-minute drive from Broadford, and parking is available in a layby (or turnout) opposite. To start the walk, walk back in the direction of Broadford and take the first right after the cattle grid. A well-worn path crosses a muddy field. As you near the end of the field the path turns to gravel and will lead up a grassy slope, where you will turn right onto the main path. As it rounds the corner, it becomes quite steep for a while, and after 20 minutes or so you will reach the remains of the old turn table of the now defunct marble quarry. Take the path slightly to the left, which climbs uphill and becomes increasingly muddy. After a good while you will come to a gate with a stile to cross, and once through here the path evens out for a while. Continue on the well-marked path. Gradually, the left-hand side will drop away to reveal a loch and valley below and the path will become much narrower and at times sodden underfoot but still easy to follow. The path will rise up then down again, and there are some narrow sections along the edge of

the valley, so tread with care. Eventually, there will be another gate to pass over, and once on the other side the path starts to steadily go down. Soon you'll reach a grass-covered wall, and shortly after this you will see the remains of the first house marking the entry into Boreraig.

From here, it's a direct route down into the township. Houses are then spread out to the far left of the bay and a little over to the right, so explore the ruins and stone outlines of former homes and imagine what once was. One point of warning: Before you go too far, get your bearings because it is a little too easy on the way back up to get disoriented and lose the path.

While here, head to the waterfall at the far left end of the village as you look out to sea. You can swim in the pools at the bottom, which is a lovely way to refresh yourself before starting the walk back. The walk takes around four hours there and back and is grueling at times, so pack water and snacks for your trek.

GUIDED CUILLIN WALKS

Skye Guides, 3 Luib; tel. 01471 822 116; skyeguides. co.uk; three-day 1:1 traverse £800, four-day 1:1 traverse £1,060, five-day 1:1 traverse £1,350

Though this group of tour guides offers more introductory walks that will take you into the heart of Skye on wildlife-spotting adventures (even camping overnight for the chance to see the Northern Lights), their specialty is to traverse the Cuillin Ridge. The Cuillin Ridge is no mean feat and takes 3-5 days to complete; even with experienced guides, around a quarter of those who start it won't be able to complete the mammoth task. If you are a highly experienced mountaineer and ready to take on this challenge, then these are the people to help get you there.

Food

BLUE SHED CAFÉ

Elgol Road, Torrin; tel. 01471 822 847; theblueshedcafe.magix.net/website; 10:30am-5pm Mon.-Sat. and noon-5pm Sun.; cakes £2.80

The Blue Shed Café is a fantastic coffee-break stop for anyone en route to Elgol from

---

1: Bla Bheinn is one of Britain's most magnificent mountains. 2: The walk to Boreraig can be rather wet underfoot.

Broadford. The tea, coffee, cakes, and sandwiches are all decent, but it's for the spectacular views of Loch Slapin and Bla Bheinn that you should really stop here to catch your breath. Food service stops at 4pm, but you should still be able to get a drink and a slice of cake for the last hour (there's normally at least one gluten-free and one vegan option available). It's a small enterprise, so it does sometimes close at short notice.

DELI GASTA

The Old Mill, Harrapool, Broadford; tel. 01471 822 646; www.deligasta.co.uk; 8:30am-5pm daily; sandwiches £6.45

Opened in 2016 in an old mill on the outskirts of Broadford, this café has brought a little bit of gentrification to the town that's been embraced by locals. The coffee, which comes from Dear Green in Glasgow, is delicious, and the sandwiches, filled with fresh crabmeat, smoked salmon, and venison, are a step above your normal over-the-counter light bites.

RED SKYE RESTAURANT

The Old Schoolhouse, Breakish; tel. 01471 822 666; www.redskyerestaurant.co.uk; café noon-3pm daily, restaurant 5:30pm-late; entrées £7.50

This family-run restaurant, in an idyllic location with views of both the Cuillin and the Applecross hills, has a tempting menu of local dishes as well as a good drinks menu, with plenty of Scottish whisky and gin alongside the wine. Alcohol seems to be a strong theme as even the mussels are whisky-infused, but Scottish staples such as cullen skink and Stornoway black pudding will soon soak it up.

Accommodations
★ 10 TORRIN

10 Torrin, Broadford; tel. 01478 612 123; www.ihcottages.com/property/?id=161879; £575 per week

This well-equipped old crofter's cottage still retains a lot of its original features and charm. It's been in the same family for generations and is a lovely holiday home, secreted away on a short single-track road in the village of Torrin (about halfway between Broadford and Elgol) and a short walk away from both the Blue Shed Café and Loch Slapin. With two good-sized bedrooms and a huge bathroom, it's a great base for families (there are lots of books and games to borrow), and in the evening you can snuggle under a blanket on one of the sofas to watch a film as the real wood fire crackles away—pure bliss.

SKYE HOBBIT HOUSE

9 Torrin, Broadford; tel. 4401471 822 078; skyehobbithouse.co.uk; Barrel House £15 pp, Round House £20 per person

Tucked away on a little road just before you come into Torrin is this little gem of a place, which offers two options: the cute-as-anything Barrel House, which has twin beds, a table, a bench, and not much else, and the Round House, which sleeps up to four. Prices include pillows and pillow cases (you'll need to bring sleeping bags), drinking water, solar electricity, and use of a compost toilet and communal cooking area. There's wireless Internet in a little shed and even a games room with a pool table; plus, you have amazing views of Bla Bheinn and a fire pit and BBQ to make the most of those long summer evenings.

THE OLD INN

Carbost; tel. 01478 640 205; www.theoldinnskye.co.uk; B&B £100, Bunkhouse £23 per person

At this inn, right by Talisker Distillery, you can stay in the lodge (which offers reasonable B&B rooms) or in the more basic bunkhouse. The inn itself is a music pub, with a jam session every Friday and a more traditional session every Wednesday.

Information and Services

There are a few main towns in central Skye to pick up supplies, get online, and get that all-important phone signal. **Broadford** is

---

1: Skye Hobbit House 2: ferry from the Isle of Skye to the Isle of Raasay 3: view from the Co-op in Broadford

probably the best facilitated and is just seven miles (11 km) from the Skye Bridge; visitors arriving into Armadale will also pass through it on the way to Portree. It has a large **Co-op** directly on the A87 (Main Street, Broadford, 7am-10pm daily) with the finest view of any supermarket I've ever come across and an essential 24-hour petrol station. Broadford is also where you will find Skye's main hospital, **Dr MacKinnon Memorial Hospital** (High Road, tel. 01471 822 491).

Getting There
BY CAR

Broadford is located on the A87, and it's pretty much impossible to visit the center or north of Skye without traveling through it. From Portree it's a 26-mile (42 km) journey south along the A87 to Broadford (35 mins). From Armadale the distance to Broadford is 16 miles (26 km)—take the A851 north up the Sleat Peninsula and then turn left onto the A87 and you should reach Broadford in 25 minutes.

BY BUS

The no. 52 bus from **Stagecoach** (www.stagecoach.com) passes through Broadford from both Portree and Armadale. From Portree the journey time is 45 minutes (£6.10), and there are three buses a day in summer (two in winter) Monday-Saturday. From Armadale it's a 25-minute journey (£4.10) three times a day (twice in winter and no Sunday service in winter either).

Getting Around

From Broadford, you can take the main A87 road for 16 miles (26 km) to reach Sligachan, which should take around 25 minutes. To reach Carbost, turn off the A87 at Sligachan onto the A863, from where it's another eight-mile (13 km) drive, for a total journey time of 35 minutes from Broadford.

A skeleton bus service run by **Stagecoach** (www.stagecoachbus.com) operates between the towns. From Broadford, you can jump

on the no. 917 or no. 52 buses, which will get to Sligachan in just over 20 minutes (£4.10). There are no direct buses to Carbost from Broadford, and connections from Sligachan and Portree are sporadic at best. Check **Traveline** (www.traveline.info) for the best route at your intended time to travel.

PORTREE

The pretty-as-a-picture town of Portree is the main hub for Skye. It's from here that most tours set off, and it is also a good launch pad for many of the main sights on the island, in particular those north along the **Trotternish Peninsula** (where you will find the Quiraing, the Old Man of Storr, and the famous dinosaur footprints of Staffin), and west toward Waternish and Glendale, where you will find Neist Point.

The town itself hugs the harbor and has some useful shops, from gift stores to places to pick up walking gear, plus lots of places to stay and some very good restaurants and cafés.

Sights
HARBOR
Off the Sound of Raasay, Portree

A clutch of colorful buildings lines the harbor front, where boat cruises set off daily and there is also a reasonable amount of traffic from leisure craft. Pick up fish and chips from the **Harbour Fish and Chip Shop** on Quay Street and sit and watch the boats come and go, or walk up the hill (known locally as the Lump) for the best views of this typical Scottish harbor.

AROS CENTRE
Viewfield Road, Portree; www.aros.co.uk; 9am-5pm daily; free but some events may charge

This cultural center at the southern fringe of Portree is part performance space (there are regular concerts and theater shows), part cinema, and part general meeting place. There's a good restaurant, frequented by locals, and a gift shop, plus a large indoor soft play area for kids for all those rainy days.

Beaches
CAMAS BAN

Portree

The only sandy beach within reasonable access of Portree, Camas Ban is by no means the prettiest beach in the Hebrides (see Harris for that), or indeed Skye's most attractive—Claigan Coral Beach in the northwest and Camas Daraich in the far south compete for that crown—but it is often deserted, so it is a nice place for a paddle or for a picnic if you feel the need to have sand under your toes. To get here you need to walk from the end of the Penifiler Road on the far side of Loch Portree, but there is no obvious path. To start, go through the gate that stops cars from going farther and then climb up the slope to your right. You basically then need to follow the ridge round before finding a safe place to descend into the valley to your right. You'll cross a burn and then head uphill until the beach appears in view. Head toward the right end of the beach where you can follow down some slightly easier sheep tracks. Alternatively, you could organize a kayak trip there—three-hour excursions are available with **Whitewave**

(www.white-wave.co.uk), based a few miles north of Uig on the Trotternish Peninsula, with prices starting at £45 per person.

Shopping
INSIDE OUT

Varragill House, The Green, Portree; tel. 01478 611 663; www.inside-out-skye.com; 9am-6pm Mon.-Sat. year-round, Sun. in summer

If you're planning to hike while you are here or even if you're just ill-prepared for Scotland's unpredictable weather, then this place will doubtlessly come in handy. You'll find big-name brands (Haglofs, Marmot, and Keela) alongside lesser-known U.K. brands, and you can pick up everything from wet-weather gear to walking boots, those all-important walking poles, and the vital Ordnance Survey walking maps.

SKYE BATIKS

The Green, Portree; tel. 01478 613 331; skyebatiks. com; 9am-6pm Mon.-Sat., 10am-5pm Sun.

This quirky new-age shop has been brightening up the lives of Portree residents and visitors since the 1980s. You can browse and buy batik-style clothing (handmade in Sri Lanka using traditional methods to wax and dye the cloth) or homewares and

Portree

bright bags. It's a good place to indulge your hippy side and staff are extremely friendly. They may even offer you a coffee if you smile nicely.

Food
CAFÉ ARRIBA

Gladstone Buildings, Quay Brae, Portree; tel. 01478 611 830; www.cafearriba.co.uk; 8am-5pm Tues.-Sat.; flatbreads £4.25

Arguably the best coffee on Skye (made of 100 percent Arabica beans) is to be had at this vibrant and laid-back café—you can't miss the loud blue and orange sign—where you could just as happily pore over your guidebook while nursing a hot drink as you could tuck into a hearty breakfast or good home-cooked lunch. The flatbreads are nice and affordable, and comfort food such as creamy macaroni and cheese or sausage and mash will cheer up the rainiest of days. There are good views of the harbor too, and vegetarians and vegans are well catered for.

SEA BREEZES

2 Marine Buildings, Quay Street, Portree; tel. 01478 612 016; www.seabreezes-skye.co.uk; lunch noon-2pm, dinner 5pm-9:30pm daily Apr.-late Oct.; entrées £6.50

In a Victorian stone building that forms part of a conservation area, this small friendly restaurant serves delicious straight-up seafood. Here the freshness of the dishes speaks for itself—there's a squeeze of lemon here and splash of white wine there but no heavy sauces—and the seafood platters, whose content depends on local supply, are good for sharing. Some tables have harbor views too.

★ SCORRYBREAC

7 Bosville Terrace, Portree; tel. 01478 612 069; www.scorrybreac.com; 5pm-9:30pm Weds.-Sun.; three courses £42, six courses £60

This absolute find of a restaurant above the harbor is intimate and inventive. Chef Calum Munro opened his first restaurant in his parents' front room, and it soon became so popular that he found himself here, in prime position in Portree. Fine-dining dishes such as cod, polenta, samphire, and lemon use the best local and seasonal ingredients (the seafood comes from Skye-based fishmonger Just Hooked) and work perfectly. It's the type of place you want to settle in for the evening and savor each mouthful—just as well as there's a minimum three courses.

Accommodations
ROSEDALE HOTEL

Beaumont Crescent, Portree; tel. 01478 613 131; www.rosedalehotelskye.co.uk; £125 d

The layout of this hotel seems a little odd at first until you realize its quirks (a maze of stairways and corridors and lots of low beams) come from combining three separate fishermen's cottages. Rooms are good, if a little on the plain side, and some have nice harbor views. There's a decent Scottish Tapas restaurant on site and you feel well looked after from the get go, with a wee dram presented to you on arrival along with some homemade shortbread.

BOSVILLE HOTEL

9-11 Bosville Terrace, Portree; tel. 01478 612 846; www.bosvillehotel.co.uk; £210 d

Showing off the results of its recent makeover, the Bosville is all minimalist seaside chic with a slight Scandinavian-cool edge, right in the center of town. Book a premium double room for harbor views. Downstairs, the Dulse & Rose restaurant serves a good modern Scottish menu, and the Merchant Bar with its wood burner has a good selection of Scottish gins to tempt you.

THE OLD COTTAGE

Suladale, near Portree; www.sykescottages.co.uk; £553 pw

This former crofter's cottage, about 10 miles west of Portree, is brimming with character. There's a four-poster bed in the bedroom and the rest of the accommodation, which includes a cozy living room with wood burner and pitched roof, is spread neatly across one

What's a Munro?

Many visitors to Skye come to bag one or more of its 12 munros—mountains (or hills as they often call them in Scotland) whose summits are **3,000 feet (914 m) or higher.** Skye's munros are considered some of the most challenging munros to complete in the whole of Scotland, making them high on the lists of real adventurists.

With 282 munros across the whole of Scotland, **munro-bagging** (climbing to the top of a munro) is a popular pastime in Scotland and a real achievement when you can scale these huge mountains, for spectacular views and unblemished scenery en route.

Munros get their name from Sir Hugh Munro, a mountaineer who set about surveying and scaling them in the late 19th century and who inspired generations of others who set about following in his hard-worn footsteps.

Those who complete all 282 are known as **Munroists** or **Compleatists** (there are some 6,000 people who have earned the right to these monikers to date) with the current record time for reaching all the munro peaks set by Stephen Pyke in 2010, who completed the feat in a staggering 39 days, nine hours, and six minutes—that's over seven munros a day.

If you do manage to complete them all (or even one), you might want to move on to some of the other hills in Scotland, which are classified as follows: Corbetts (hills between 2,500 ft/762 m and 3,000 ft/914.4 m with a drop of at least 500 ft/152 m on all sides), Grahams (hills of 2,000 ft/610 m-2,500 ft/762 m with a drop of 150 ft/46 m on all sides), and Donalds (hills in the Lowlands of over 2,000 ft/610 m).

---

floor. The kitchen is small but functional, and the owner will start you off with enough fire wood for at least your first evening. This romantic hideaway is well placed for exploring the north of Skye.

Information and Services

The **VisitScotland iCentre** for Portree is located in the town center (Bayfield House, Bayfield Road, Portree, tel. 01478 612 992, 9am-5pm Mon.-Sat. and 10am-4pm Sun. Apr.-late Oct., 9:30am-4:30pm Mon.-Sat. late Oct.-Mar.). They will help you book boat cruises and tours; plus, you can make use of their free wireless Internet access. **Portree Filling Station** on the A87, shortly before you enter the town from the south, is open from 7:30am-9pm Monday-Saturday and 9:30am-6pm on Sundays.

Portree Medical Centre (tel. 01478 612 013), near the harbor, is open 8:30am-5:30pm Monday to Friday for minor complaints. The **Portree Community Hospital** (tel. 01478 613 200) is also based here, though it is under threat of closure. At present it does have a Minor Injury Unit,

which operates from 8am-11pm. For more serious conditions it is likely you will be transferred or admitted to **Dr Mackinnon Memorial Hospital** in Broadford (26 mi/42 km away).

Getting There
BY CAR

Portree is a 35-mile (56 km) drive from Kyle of Lochalsh over the Skye Bridge and along the A87, with a journey time of just under an hour. From Armadale Ferry Terminal (where ferries from Mallaig arrive), it's a distance of 42 miles (68 km), first north along the A851 before joining the A87, with a journey time of just over an hour. From Broadford it's 26 miles (42 km) north along the A87 to Portree, which should take about 40 minutes.

BY BUS

From the Armadale Ferry Terminal, you can catch the no. 52 bus with **Stagecoach** (www.stagecoachbus.com) to Portree, which takes 1.25 hours (£7.70, three times a day in summer, less out of season). It does stop at Broadford for a short time, but there's no need to get off. From Broadford, it's just under 40 minutes on the no. 52 to Portree (£6.10 each way).

From the harbor slipway in Kyle of Lochalsh, there are several buses a day with Scottish Citylink (www.citylink.co.uk), including the no. 915, no. 916 and no. 917, which cost £7.10 each way and take just over an hour. The first bus sets off at 11am, and there are around five in total each day.

Getting Around

Portree itself is perfectly manageable on foot. All the main amenities, restaurants, and bars are centered around the harbor in the heart of town, or a few streets back from it, with the main exception being the Aros Centre, which is about a 20-minute walk from the harbor. If you want to venture further afield and you don't have a car, there are plenty of trip boats operating from here and most tour guides will pick up from Portree too.

If you want to get around by bike, bike hire is available from Skye Bike Shack (The Old Croft House, 6 Carbost, tel. 01470 532 375; www.skyebikeshack.com), which hires out a range of road and mountain bikes from one day (£30) to a week (£125). The company also supplies helmets, saddle bags, pumps, and repair kits and can deliver to you or collect from you in north Skye.

TROTTERNISH AND NORTHEAST SKYE

The craggy landscape of the Trotternish Peninsula that pokes out above Portree like a scolding finger is like nothing you have ever seen before and is a haven for hikers and explorers. Amid its dream-like landscape that seems to defy all logic are two of Skye's most famous and visited hikes (which are much more achievable than the munro climbs of the Cuillin): The Old Man of Storr, an unmistakable pinnacle that stabs at the sky and can be seen for miles around, and the Quiraing, a supernatural place, often shrouded in mist, where unbelievable rock formations jut out, that look like they have been placed here by the gods themselves.

Orientation

The Trotternish Peninsula extends for 20 miles north from the town of Portree. From Portree there are two routes onto the peninsula by road—the old faithful A87 that you can follow for 16 miles (26 km) to the town of Uig on the west coast, set around a horseshoe bay, from where you can get the ferry across to Lewis and Harris, and the A855, which travels along the more dramatic east coast of the peninsula all the way to Flodigarry (21 mi/34 km) before curving round and coming back south along the west coast to meet the A87 at Uig. So in theory, if you're driving, you could plot a circular route.

If starting along the east coast on a round trip, the first major site you will come to is the Old Man of Storr, six miles (10 km) north of Portree. A further 10 miles (16 km) will bring you to Staffin, which is not only where you need to head to see the dinosaur footprints, but also one of the main access points to the befuddling rocky wilderness of the Quiraing (it can also be accessed from Uig). A further 11 miles (18 km) along the same road will bring you to to turning for Kilmuir Graveyard (just behind the Skye Museum of Island Life) where you will find a huge monument to the woman who helped Bonnie Prince Charlie escape, Flora Macdonald. Four miles (6 km) south from Kilmuir is Uig, which is the best entry point for the famous Fairy Glen.

Sights
KILT ROCK AND MEALT FALLS
Staffin Road, 1.24 miles (2 km) south of Staffin

On the Staffin Road on the east coast of the Trotternish (about 9 mi/15 km north from Portree) is this dual viewpoint where you can see both the vertical basalt columns of Kilt Rock (as you might expect, they look like the pleats of a kilt; in the right light the colors look a little like tartan too), and Mealt Falls, which crash down from the rocks to the sea below. Parking is free; though there's not much of it, it's worth a 10-minute stop, if you can find space, if only to hear the soft hum as wind travels through the pipes of the rocks. If not, in summer there's a chance a bagpiper may be here to interpret it for you.

STAFFIN DINOSAUR MUSEUM

6 Ellishadder, Staffin; www.staffindinosaurmuseum. com; 9:30am-5pm daily; adult £2, child £1, family £5
If you want to see dinosaur footprints at the beach in Staffin, stop by this esoteric museum where staff will be able to guide you. Run since 1976, the miniscule museum has a staggering collection of dinosaur fossils, all of which can be explained to you by the man who collected and catalogued them, Dugald Ross, including a cast of the smallest dinosaur footprint found on Skye. Through his research, Ross was able to ascertain what dinosaurs once walked here, including the mighty Stegosaurus. He also offers tours to see the footprints in situ at the beach and can shed light on the most recent dinosaur footprints discovered at nearby Brothers Point but these are by request and should be booked in advance.

FLORA MACDONALD'S MEMORIAL

Kilmuir Graveyard
Not all legends in Scotland are mythical (though surely the art of storytelling has embellished even the historically true ones). Flora Macdonald is a heroine, not only here in Skye, but across the whole of Scotland for the part she played in helping Bonnie Prince Charlie flee government forces in the wake of Culloden. Disguising Charlie as an Irish maid by the name of Betty Burk, she transported him to Skye from the Outer Hebrides Isle of South Uist from where he made good his escape (her role is mentioned, albeit partly down-played, in *The Skye Boat Song:* "Flora will keep watch by your weary head"). At this small graveyard on the west coast of the Trotternish, a large memorial stands for Flora Macdonald (who is buried here) and commemorates her act of sheer bravery with the words: "Her name will be mentioned in history and if courage and fidelity be virtues, mentioned with honour."

Hiking
★ THE OLD MAN OF STORR

Old Man of Storr car park, A855; www.isleofskye. com/skye-guide/top-ten-skye-walks/old-man-of-storr
Seen from miles away as you drive around the Trotternish Peninsula, particularly on the east side, the Old Man of Storr is a true symbol of Skye.

Its unusual formation, in which it stands out slightly separate from the other spires around it, have spawned many a folktale. One

Old Man of Storr

story says that it is a giant's thumb, the only bit still seen of him after he was buried in the earth, another that it is the remnant of a giant who was turned to stone when he disobeyed orders not to turn back.

Many visitors simply view it from the road, but there's a relatively straightforward 30-45-minute walk to the foot of the pinnacle (allow 1.5 hours there and back) via a graveled footpath that leads from the Old Man of Storr car park on the A855. Walk through the gate at the end of the car park and follow the trail up the hillside. Once this section would have taken you through woodland, but now forestry is well underway and you may see some saplings among the recently felled trees. Don't worry when the path splits; you can take either side (it re-converges later), but the path on the right-hand side is probably best. After a while the gravel finishes and it becomes muddy underfoot, before becoming rougher. When the path splits again, take the left-hand trail and watch out for uneven rocks. Soon the Old Man will appear on your right and the path too will turn right, bringing you ever closer to the iconic crag. Standing at the foot of the Old Man of Storr is a wondrous place to drink in the rest of the spectacular scenery of the Trotternish. Only the brave and sure-footed should attempt to climb to its summit, which, while offering far-reaching views of the Cuillin, Raasay, and the mainland, is very steep and requires some scrambling.

TOP EXPERIENCE

★ QUIRAING
Accessed from Staffin or Uig

The result of a giant landslide, this natural arena, which soars above the Trotternish Peninsula, is best experienced on foot when you can really get a sense of the scale of the large pinnacles and spires of bare rock that protrude from its surface. Found at the northern end of the Trotternish, the Quiraing was formed when the upper volcanic layers of the Trotternish Ridge caused the lower layers to slip. Over time, erosions and glaciers sculpted the rock into the bizarre pillars and formations you see today, which have names that give some indication of their appearance, such as **the Needle**—a sinister spiky rock that could be a needle but looks more like a pointed witch's finger beckoning you over, and **the Table**—a smooth, plateau that seems out of place amid the craggy scenery.

There's a straightforward walking route to the escarpment, which can be accessed quite easily from a single-track road at Brogaig, just after Staffin. If coming from the south, take the road to your left just after the Staffin post office. Stay on this road, taking care round the hairpin bends, for 2.5 miles (4 km), ignoring the road that leads off to the left, until you reach the car park. The same unmarked road can be accessed from Uig by taking the first right after you round the huge hairpin bend after the ferry terminal. If coming from this direction, you'll reach the car park after around four miles (6 km).

Opposite the car park is the **Flodigarry Path,** which will take you all the way through the 1.25-mile wild rocky fortress of the Quiraing. The path is narrow and mainly level, though it will start to drop away steeply to your right, revealing views of Raasay and Applecross. You will cross a burn and then about half a mile later the path will become steeper as you enter the Quiraing, with the foreboding prison to your right. It's then up to you how much you explore the individual features of the Quiraing before following the same path back down; you'll need to leave the main path to ascend the slopes to the Needle and, if you keep the Needle to your left, you'll soon reach a gully where there is another path that will take you to the Table.

FAIRY GLEN
Uig

It was in this ethereal landscape near Uig that movie director Steven Spielberg chose to film the 2016 fantasy adaptation of Roald Dahl's classic, The BFG. It's not hard to see why: its cone-shaped hills easily convince one that they could be home to magical beings, hence the name (though Skye is home to many fairy legends, there are none specific to it). It's an easy 1.5-mile (2 km) hike from the Uig Hotel, but leave yourself plenty of time to ascend the many hillocks and really immerse yourself in the strange scenery of the glen. Parking is limited in the glen, so park in Uig itself and walk from here. From the south, turn right before the Uig Hotel, signposted for Sheader and Balnaknock, and follow the narrow lane up for about 30 minutes. You'll know when you've arrived, as the road creeps through the magical landscape, which is like the Quiraing in miniature. There's no specific trail to take as such, though a few well-trodden areas, but don't worry as the road is always nearby; however, with it being a grassy region, it can get very muddy. Once you've ascended some of the small hills, you'll want to head to the odd looking peak in the distance on the left-hand side of the road. Called Castle Ewen, it may look like a ruined castle, but it is in fact just a bizarre-shaped lump of basalt. Ignore the tenuous claims by some guides that moving some of the smaller rocks in the glen to create spirals is an offering to the fairies; all this does is serve to undermine the natural state of the glen.

Beaches
THE DINOSAUR BEACH
An Corran, Staffin
It was on this beach, just outside the old crofting community of Staffin (where you will find a good and useful café and Gaelic is still spoken by many locals), that fossilised dinosaur footprints, believed to belong to a family of Ornithipods, were discovered in 2002. Today, many people make the visit to this pretty but otherwise fairly nondescript beach to see the prints. Visit at low tide and look to the right of the big boulders on the flat mud stone (at the bottom of the slipway). There is a map in the car park, which shows you where to look; if you still can't find them, it's worth asking a local—there's normally one or two around walking their dogs.

Food
SKYE RESTAURANT
Flodigarry Hotel, Flodigarry; tel. 01470 552 203; restaurant-isleofskye.co.uk; 12:30pm-3pm and
6:30pm-9pm daily; entrées £8.50
Within the Flodigarry Hotel, this fine-dining restaurant presents classic dishes in a relaxed environment, with stunning views of both the Torridon mountains on the mainland and the Quiraing. The menu is lighter and less fancy at lunchtime—try the Highland beef stew served in a big bun, which should set you up for a big walk—while for dinner you can eat salmon caviar of venison cured in heather honey. Delicious.

THE FERRY INN
A87, Uig; tel. 01470 542 300; theferryinnskye.com; 5pm-10pm Mon.-Sat.; £27 for two courses/£35 for three courses; £170 d
This 19th-century inn has been given a warm and contemporary refurb, which still makes it feel utterly inviting. Seafood comes fresh—it's landed at nearby Uig Pier—and meat and vegetables are also as local as possible. Dishes are on the fine-dining side, yet with more stomach-filling portion sizes. Alongside dishes of roast salmon with mussels, there's also a hearty cote de boeuf to share. Rooms are also exquisite.

Accommodations
GLENVIEW B&B
Culnacnoc, Portree; tel. 01470 562 248; glenviewskye.co.uk; £95 d
There's a little bit of everything at this charming B&B tucked away in the Trotternish hills. There are three cozy but good-sized rooms with iron bedsteads, floral prints, and vintage radios; plus, it's now also a place to peruse hand-dyed yarns using foraged plants or take a breather in the yoga studio. Sadly the Skye Pie Café next door is now closed, but keep your eyes peeled for pop-ups—the pies are good and great for a picnic when you're going into the hills.

UIG HOTEL
A87, Uig; tel. 01470 542 205; www.uig-hotel-skye. com; £75 s/£165 d
Just a five-minute drive from Uig Bay on the western side of the Trotternish, this old coaching inn is now a warm hotel with 11

rooms, which are comfortable if a little plain. Isle of Skye red deer plus scallops from the Hebridean Uist isles are served in the on-site restaurant, which overlooks the bay. This hotel is the obvious choice if you want to visit the nearby Fairy Glen.

VATERSAY HOUSE BED & BREAKFAST

Glenhinnidsal; tel. 01470 542 284; www. vatersayhouse.com; open Apr.-end of Aug.; £100 d

This small B&B in a glorious countryside setting is LGBT friendly and has just one room for two, ensuring a very personal experience. Accessed down a single-track road off the A87, turn off for Glenhinnisdal a few miles before Uig if coming from Portree and it's two miles down a single-track road. The room is smart with tartan carpet and a comfy memory foam bed but few thrills. You can make use of the lounge area too, from where you can borrow local maps, or sit in the lovely garden.

Information and Services

If you want to walk amid the unearthly landscape of the Trotternish, then get a copy of the indispensable **Ordnance Survey map** (Explorer 408, Skye—Trotternish & The Storr), which can be picked up in the **Inside Out** shop in Portree.

Uig Filling Station, right by the ferry terminal, is the only place to refuel on the Trotternish and is open 8am-8pm Monday to Saturday and 10:30am-5pm on Sundays. There is no visitor center on the Trotternish itself, but the **VisitScotland iCentre** in Portree (tel. 01478 612 992) will be able to advise you on travel in the area.

Getting There and Getting Around

BY CAR

From Portree it's straightforward to do a circular drive either clockwise or counter-clockwise, round the peninsula, giving you a good overview of the area and letting you take in the main sights. You can do the loop starting on the west coast of the peninsula or on the east coast; my preference is for the latter. From Portree, take the A855 up the east coast, through Staffin, round the top via Flodigarry, and back through Uig (joining the A87) to Portree. The full distance is 49 miles (79 km), and, if you were to do the route without stopping, it would take 1.5 hours, though obviously you should factor in some time to stop and enjoy the sights.

From the ferry terminal at Armadale it's 59 miles (95 km) to Staffin and a similar distance to Uig, which takes about 1.5 hours. To reach the Trotternish, take the A851 north from Armadale for about 15 miles (24 km) before turning left onto the A87 that will take you all the way into Portree. From Portree you can choose to take either the A855 to Staffin, or continue on the A87 to Uig. From Broadford, it's around 42 miles (68 km) to either Uig or Staffin, following the A87 to Portree before making the same decision between the A855 to Staffin or the A87 to Uig. The journey time to either is just over an hour from Broadford.

BY BUS

There are also a couple of daily **Stagecoach** (www.stagecoachbus.com) buses from Portree that follow the same route. The 57A stops at Staffin (£4; 30 minutes), Flodigarry (£4.60; 35 minutes), and Uig (£5.35; 1.25 hours) and runs around four times a day (twice on Saturdays and no Sunday service), while the 57C (which travels from west to east) stops in Uig (£5.35; 30 minutes) and Kilmuir (£5.35; 35 minutes) and also runs four times a day with two buses on Saturdays and none on Sundays. Check Stagecoach (www.stagecoachbus.com) for timetables.

If you are traveling from Broadford or Armadale, get the no. 52 bus to Portree and change here for the Trotternish.

NORTHWEST SKYE AND WATERNISH

Most of the main draws to the northwest of Skye lie in and around the **Waternish peninsula,** just northeast of the region's famous **Dunvegan Castle,** where there are

This island, often treated as though it were two separate islands, lies to the north of Skye and is the most northerly island in the Outer Hebrides. The southern part, **Harris,** where ferries from Uig on Skye arrive into Tarbert, is the most visually stimulating, with high mountains inland, indented lochs and some of the most beautiful beaches in the world. It's also where the famous Harris Tweed is made, from the homes of weavers, using time-old techniques.

As you head north and enter **Lewis,** the landscape changes quite dramatically. Though it is also quite mountainous at first, the further north you go, the more lunar-like and barren everything becomes. Wide-open peat moors stretch into the horizon, and at times the sense of desolation is so consuming that it's as though you have stepped into some post-apocalyptic world. Signs of civilization do eventually reveal themselves, with Iron Age brochs (hollow stone structures), ancient standing stones, and 17th-century blackhouses (traditional Hebridean houses) offering clues into the region's rich and varied past. This part of the island is most easily accessed by ferry from Ullapool on the northwest coast of the mainland to Stornoway, the island's main town.

WHAT TO DO ON LEWIS AND HARRIS

- Visit the **Standing Stones of Callanish** (callanishvisitorcentre.co.uk), a pretender to Stonehenge's claim as the U.K.'s most alluring stone circle.

- Continue your journey west to **Uig Sands,** where the famous Lewis Chessmen were discovered in 1831—a decorative 12th-century chess set carved from walrus ivory, which is now split between the National Museum of Scotland in Edinburgh and the British Museum in London.

- If it's beaches you're after, they don't come much more magical than **Seilebost** in southwest Harris, which stretches for miles when the turquoise tide is out.

- Meet a traditional **Harris Tweed** maker. Rebecca Hutton is a traditional Harris Tweed maker and she weaves her carefully chosen dyed and spun wool in a shed in her garden. Her house is the first on the left as you enter the little village of **Northton** in south Harris. As long as her van is outside, you can be pretty sure she's home and happy to show you around. She also sells her wares direct from her shed through her website, **Taobh Tuath Tweeds** (www.taobhtuathtweeds.com) or through a local shop in **Leverburgh.**

some excellent restaurants and some eclectic art studios and craft workshops. A narrow strip of land, it's a quite untouched place where green hills gently sweep down to the blue sea below and corncrakes can be heard (but not seen) making their distinct "crex-crex" mating call under cover of tall grasses.

The entry point to Waternish is marked by a little blink-and-you'll-miss-it bridge known as **Fairy Bridge** shortly after you turn off the main road from Portree to Dunvegan onto the B886. Many people stop here to take photos because of the dubious story that says it was here that the fairy lover of the chief of Clan MacLeod bid him farewell to return to her own people. According to the legend, she wrapped their son in the Fairy Flag, which it is said held special powers to protect the clan in battle. The flag can still be seen in Dunvegan Castle, but there's no real reason to stop at the Fairy Bridge; instead, venture farther into the peninsula where you can find some real hidden treasures, including the sleepy village of **Stein** on the northeastern shore of Loch Bay, from where you can witness some spectacular sunsets.

Further west of Waternish, the steep cliffs of **Glendale** are alive with seabirds, while its wild meadows are filled with vibrant flowers, from orchids to primroses and bluebells. Look out too for the duo of flat-topped hills known as **MacLeod's Tables,** which can be hiked.

According to folklore, the tips of these hills were cut off by St. Columba, the Irish missionary who brought Christianity to Scotland in the 6th century. The tale goes that Columba arrived on Skye seeking shelter but received a hostile reception from the chief of Clan MacLeod, who ruled much of northern Skye at the time, and so he created the flat beds on top of the hills so he could have a table at which to dine and a place to lie down to rest.

Sights
DUNVEGAN CASTLE AND GARDENS

MacLeod Estate, Dunvegan; tel. 01470 521 206; www.dunvegancastle.com; 10am-5:30pm daily Easter-mid-Oct.; adult £14, child £9, concessions £11, family £34

The oldest continuously inhabited castle in Scotland, Dunvegan Castle is the ancestral home of the chiefs of Clan MacLeod and looks romantic in its picturesque loch-side setting, elevated on a basalt outcrop, particularly when covered in a misty haze. It is possible to admire the Victorian revamp of its exterior, which includes battlements that run the full length of the roof line, and sweet pepper-pot towers, as you drive down to Claigan Beach. However, to see the older parts of the castle, including the 14th-century keep, you need to pay the entry fee, step inside the castle walls, and peer behind its streamlined veneer. Inside, it's palatial, both in terms of size and design, and it is decorated in opulent 19th-century style. Artifacts on display are designed to stir up a sense of Scottish patriotism—there's a lock of Bonnie Prince Charlie's hair here— as well as clan loyalty. The most famous item on display is the fabled Fairy Flag, an ancient banner, which according to one legend was gifted to a chief of Clan MacLeod by his fairy wife at the nearby Fairy Bridge and which when unfurled in battle helped the MacLeods defeat their enemy. Take time too to walk the castle's grounds; laid out in the 18th century, they include five acres (two hectares) that are a riot of color, in stark contrast to the largely barren landscape of Skye. Traipse

through wooded glades and cross over pretty bridges where gushing waterfalls feed pools below. Boat rides out on the loch to see seals and other wildlife are also available for an additional fee (25 minutes, adult £7.50, child £5.50, under 3 free).

SKYE SKYNS

17 Lochbay, Waternish; tel. 01470 592 237; www.skyeskyns.co.uk; 9am-6pm daily Apr.-Oct., 9:30am-5:30pm daily Nov.-Mar.; free

One of the only sheep tanneries in the United Kingdom, this place is a must for anyone interested in seeing how time-old traditions of leather-making are used to make beautiful sheepskin rugs and clothing. Free tours of the workshop (no need to book, just turn up; they last around 20 minutes) show the implements used and describe the process from start to finish, including the laborious Highland tradition of hand-combing fleeces. Upstairs in the showroom you can buy rugs, mittens, and slippers, and in summer there is a very cozy pop-up yurt outside where you can have a cup of tea and slice of cake on sheepskin-covered seats.

NEIST POINT

Duirnish, Glendale; www.glendaleskye.com/neistpoint.php

Skye's most westerly point, Neist Point at the tip of the remote peninsula of Duirnish, is one of the best places on Skye to see whales, dolphins, and even the occasional basking shark. It's the only real reason to venture this far over (unless you're seeking seclusion) and offers splendid views of the jagged Waterstein Head, and from its stunning cliff-top location you can look over the Minch (Atlantic sea channel) toward the Western Isles. It's possible to walk down to the lighthouse, which stands at Neist Point; just follow the signs to Neist Point and park up at the car park at the end of the road. The path starts just

1: Dunvegan Castle, Skye **2:** Torabhaig is Skye's newest distillery. **3:** Skye Skyns, northwest Skye **4:** the rural village of Torrin on the shores of Loch Slapin

past the weather-beaten shed in the car park. The path itself is well laid out with concrete, steps, and handrails, though it is steep. You may be tempted by some of the well-worn trails leading up grassy banks to your right, and, though these will take you to fabulous viewpoints, care must be taken due to exposed cliff-top sections that are unfenced and steep in places. Once you reach the lighthouse, take a moment to examine the bizarre rocks upon which it sits, akin to those at the Giant's Causeway across the sea. Some believe the Causeway continues under the sea, all the way from Northern Ireland to Skye.

Hiking
MACLEOD'S TABLES

Orbost; www.walkhighlands.co.uk/skye/ macleodstables.shtml

Much gentler in their incline than most of Skye's hills, this pair of hills is instantly recognizable as it looks as though their peaks have been chopped off, which is indeed how locals have explained them through folklore for centuries.

To begin the seven-mile (11 km) circular walk to take in both the **North Table** and the **South Table** outlined by the Walk Highlands website, you need to set off from where the road bends round to the left upon heading north from the village of Orbost. Follow the bank alongside the stream, just before this bend, to the west, which passes along the edge of a ravine. Above the ravine you'll need to keep to the height of the land in a southwest and then south direction toward Beinn Bhuide, where you'll cross rough moorland to reach An Cruachan to the southwest; from here, you should be able to see your way to the highest of the tables, **Healabhal Beag (South Table)**, which looks more conical than flat on the approach. To reach its summit, you will need to round a rocky prow, but there is an eroded path to the right to bypass it. Enjoy views of the Cuillin from atop the plateau and then descend the steep grassy slope to cross over and begin the steep ascent to **Healabhal Mhor (North Table)**.

The full route, bringing you back to Orbost, takes 5-6 hours and should not be attempted without first arming yourself with **Ordnance Survey Explorer map 407 Dunvegan, Waternish & MacLeod's Tables,** which can be bought online before you travel or at **Inside Out** in Portree.

Afterward, reward yourself with dinner at the nearby **Red Roof Skye** restaurant.

Beaches
CLAIGAN CORAL BEACH

Dunvegan

This beach—one of Skye's finest—is just a short drive past Dunvegan Castle down a single-track road that passes by windswept hills strewn with heather until you reach a car park. From the car park it's a good mile-long trek along a cliffside path to reach the beach, and you'll inevitably meet sheep and the odd cow blocking the path en route. Walking boots are advised as you will have to cross a couple of streams, but it's utterly worth it. The water looks clear enough to drink and the "coral," which looks like sand at first, is actually sun-bleached algae. At low tide you can also walk over to the tidal island of **Lampay.**

Food
★ STEIN INN

Macleods Terrace, Stein, Waternish; tel. 01470 592 362; www.stein-inn.co.uk; Easter-Oct.: lunch noon-3pm Mon.-Sat. and 12:30pm-3pm Sun., supper 6pm-9:30pm Mon.-Sat. and 6:30pm-9pm Sun.; winter: lunch noon-2:30pm Tues.-Sat. and 12:30pm-3pm Sun., supper 5:30pm-8pm Tues.-Thurs. and Sun. and 5:30pm-8:30pm Fri. and Sat.; entrées £6.95; £125 d

In the little township of Stein on the eastern shore of Loch Bay is this, Skye's oldest inn. Inside the whitewashed building you'll find a traditional inn—all low ceilings, with a pub area with an inglenook fireplace in the center of the room and a slightly more formal restaurant in a separate room. There are lots of really tempting meat and fish dishes, such as Highland venison pie or Isle of Skye scallops, and with some good ales on tap, you won't want to leave, so think ahead and book into one of the five rooms.

LOCH BAY

1 Macleods Terrace, Stein; tel. 01470 592 235; www.lochbay-restaurant.co.uk; Easter-Oct.: lunch 12:15pm-1:30pm Weds.-Fri. and Sun., dinner 5:30pm-8:45pm Tues. and Sat., 6:15pm-8:45pm Weds.-Fri.; Nov.-22 Dec.: 6:15pm-8:45pm Weds.-Sat.; three-course lunch £34, three-course dinner £43, five-course fruits de mer £70

Next door to the Stein Inn, this restaurant, which gives a contemporary Scottish twist to classic French cooking, is one of Skye's best, as proven by its recent (2018) Michelin Star. Well worth the drive here down winding roads (all the better if you're staying in the Stein Inn), you can expect the freshest seafood—try the Fruits de Mer menu if you want a tantalizing walk through local seafood delicacies—in a traditional crofter's cottage (the seats are even covered in Harris Tweed). Staff are down to earth and friendly too, making for an altogether fantastic culinary experience.

THREE CHIMNEYS

B884, Colbost; tel. 01470 511 258; www. threechimneys.co.uk; lunch noon-1:45pm daily (may be some winter reduction), dinner 6pm-9:15pm daily, closed mid-Dec.-mid-Jan.; tasting menu £68 pp; £360 d

Another of Skye's finest restaurants, the Three Chimneys (signposted on the B884) has retained its reputation for producing delicious Scottish dishes using carefully sourced ingredients for years—it has held three AA red rosettes for 18 years, and in 2018 it was named U.K. restaurant of the year in the Good Food Guide. Of course, the menu is dependent on what's in season, but expect such delights as slow-cooked Wester Ross salmon or lemon sole with lobster ravioli. Next door the restaurant also runs an excellent guest house, the House Over-by, with six luxuriously and feminine rooms, if you want to make a night or two of it.

RED ROOF SKYE

Off the B884, Holmisdale, Glendale; www.redroofskye. co.uk; dinner 7:30pm (welcome drinks from 7pm) early June-mid-Oct.; three-course menu £35

Restaurants don't get much more off the beaten track than this one, an intimate little venue near MacLeod's Tables, which is just open for a few months every year. Understated, homely, it offers the best of farmhouse cooking (all produce is either grown here or sourced from other crofts)—think rustic fare such as free-range eggs, homegrown kale, and turnips served alongside Hebridean lamb. The three-course menu also includes nibbles, breads, and petit fours, so it is remarkably good value. Drinks are extra but well priced. Unfortunately, it's not suitable for vegans or anyone with any allergies; it's very much a get-what-you're-given ethos.

Accommodations

EDINBANE INN

Off the A850, Edinbane; tel. 01470 582 414; www. edinbaneinn.co.uk; £140 d

Halfway between Portree and Edinbane, this is a great place to stay if you like traditional music. Sessions take place on Sunday afternoons year round and on Tuesday and Friday evenings (9pm-11pm) in high season. More a pub with rooms than a hotel, it can be a little noisy at times, but rooms are freshly decorated and comfortable. There's also a good bar menu. Wireless Internet is available, but mobile phone service is virtually nonexistent. Only children over 14 are allowed.

DUNVEGAN CAMPING PODS

Dunvegan (behind the post office); tel. 01470 521 469; dunvegancampingpods.co.uk; open year-round; £110 per night, minimum two-night stay

Unlike many similar pods, these camping pods in the village of Dunvegan (just behind the post office) are all en suite. The pine interiors are fitted with a bed, a little kitchenette, and a settee (which can also fold down to sleep two kids). There's a small seating area outside each one, and the site is a short walk

What's in a Number?

As you travel around Skye, look closely at some of the house numbers, particularly in more rural locations, and you may notice something a bit odd. While some are labelled simply "8" or "12," others have strange numbering, such as "¼ of 10."

Though the anomaly leaves many observant travelers scratching their heads, the reason behind it is really rather simple. It all comes down to when these regions were fully functioning crofting areas; the numbering system basically has enabled landowners to sell off plots of their land, while ensuring the future of crofting communities. The Crofter's Commission is tasked with deciding how the land gets split—for instance, sometimes the house number apportions the house land around it where crofters might milk cows or shear sheep or grow fruit and vegetables.

So if someone who owns, say, croft number 7, decides to downsize, they can divide a quarter of the croft and give it to someone else—thus the divided area would be called ¼ 7 and the remainder of the croft ¾ 7.

from local shops. This is camping with a few home comforts (including heating).

CARTERS REST

8/9 Upper Milovaig, Glendale; tel. 01470 511 272; cartersrestskye.co.uk; £140 d (minimum two-night stay)

This smart boutique guest house has gorgeous views of Skye's west coast—the dining room and lounge looks out over Loch Pooltiel and you really feel like you are on the edge of the isle. The neutral yet sophisticated-styled bedrooms boast beautiful textiles and modern en suites, and while certainly not the cheapest, they are perfectly appointed. Owners Julie and Steve will take care of you like you are old friends and the rural location feels far off the tourist trail.

Information and Services

The main source of information for this side of the island is the very good website **Visit Waternish** (www.visit-waternish.co.uk), which can point you in the direction of all the main attractions and places to stay and dine, as well as tell you where you can best experience the region's dark skies—there isn't a single street light on the whole peninsula.

For petrol, **Atholl Service Station,** just south of Dunvegan, is open 8am-8pm Monday-Saturday and 8am-5pm on Sundays.

Getting There
BY CAR

From Portree, it's a 30-minute drive to Dunvegan along the A850 (21 mi/34 km). From Armadale, it's an hour and 20-minute drive to Dunvegan, taking the A851 for 15 miles (24 km) before turning left onto the A87 for 18 miles (29 km) and then turning left onto the A863 at Sligachan, which you follow for 23 miles (37 km) all the way to Dunvegan. From Broadford the journey time is 55 minutes, again following the A87 to Sligachan and then joining the A863, a total distance of 39 miles (63 km).

BY BUS

From Portree, you can take the no. 56 bus, run by **Stagecoach** (www.stagecoachbus.com), to Dunvegan. The bus runs four times a day (no service on Sundays), takes 45 minutes, and costs £5.35. Take the no. 52 from Armadale and Broadford and change at Portree.

Getting Around

As with all of the Isle of Skye, having a car makes traveling to and around this region easier. While it is possible to get to Dunvegan by bus, once you're here you really need a car, a bike, or a good set of walking boots to explore fully. The main roads in the region are the A850, which links Dunvegan with

Portree, and the A863, which links Dunvegan to Sligachan. The B884, which you can pick up just south of Dunvegan at Lonmore, will take you all the way to Glendale and Neist Point.

Another smaller road is also pivotal to exploring the region fully: the right-hand turn halfway down the A850 from Portree that takes you onto the Waternish peninsula.

Isle of Raasay

This island, between Skye and the northwest mainland by Applecross, has long been overlooked by tourists. But with the opening of a new distillery, which forms part of the **Hebridean Whisky Trail**, this looks set to change.

Aside from its natural attractions—beautiful beaches, ruined castles, and a sense of calm that its neighbors on Skye must sometimes yearn for—the biggest lure to Raasay are the stories of inhabitants who endured some of the toughest repercussions of the dreaded Highland Clearances. In the 1840s, the clan chief sold the island to one George Rainy. Rainy pushed the island's residents off the land surrounding his property to make way for more profitable sheep and built a wall to ensure that they, and more importantly their cattle, couldn't wander in. He also banned marriage to prevent procreation, presumably because it would place more demands on "his" land. The result was catastrophic. Family after family left and the population dwindled—a sad state of affairs immortalized in the poems of Raasay native Sorley MacLean.

Over time, people started moving back to Raasay, and in turn buildings on the island, including Raasay House, once Rainey's home, were eventually bought back for the community. Today there is a sense of solidarity among folk who live here that is both admirable and infectious.

The island is 14 miles (22.5 km) long and just 3 miles (4.8 km) across, and on a map it looks as though someone has taken a big bite out of the northeast of the isle. The north end of the isle has historically been less hospitable than the south and for a long time was cut off from the rest of the isle until Calum MacLeod

began building his road in the 1960s. It's a wild uninhabited part of the island that is worth exploring.

The main village of the isle, if you can even call it that, is **Inverarish**, just a 20-minute walk east of the ferry terminal. This is where most of the 160 island inhabitants live, but there's not much else here besides homes. The island's only restaurant is in **Raasay House** and is just a few minutes walk from the ferry terminal on the south of the isle at Kyle (turn right and follow the path; you'll see the grand house very soon), and the new **distillery** is a further 5-10-minute walk.

Sights
ISLE OF RAASAY DISTILLERY
Borodale House, Raasay; tel. 01478 470 178; raasaydistillery.com; hourly tours 10am-5pm daily in summer, fewer in winter; tour with tasting £10

This new distillery, which only opened its doors in September 2017, is like a beacon of hope for islanders—a tenth of the population of 160 or so are employed here, so there is a real incentive for it to succeed. The first signs are good: the distillery's single malt *While You Wait* (filling in until its new spirit matures) is very good. The ultra-modern building, extended from a former hotel that locals tell me was bad, has absolutely beautiful views across to Skye of the Red Cuillin from both its bar/restaurant and tasting room. Everything about this distillery feels local and loyal; even its logo depicts the island's most famous landmark, Dun Caan, with its highest peak that looks a little like a volcano as you view it on the way over from Skye. Some very nice, if a little overpriced, rooms make it one of less than a handful of places to stay on the island.

CALUM'S ROAD
Brochel, Raasay

This road, which links the far reaches of the north of the island, two miles past Brochel, to the south is pretty much the life's work of one man: Calum MacLeod. Fed up of waiting for the council to respond to his repeated requests to build a road connecting the cutoff north of the island—a problem that had caused all of his neighbors to leave—in the 1960s Calum put shovel to the ground and pretty much built this two-mile road himself over the course of 20 years. It's an incredible tale of one man's defiance and commitment to keep his way of life alive, brilliantly told in a book by Roger Hutchinson, and a journey here is a great way to experience his endeavor. To get a real sense of the sheer grit and determination Calum put into creating the road, it's best to drive it. Only by motoring round its cliff-skimming bends, up its steep inclines, and down its sudden descents do you really understand that this is no ordinary road. It's worth noting too that the road has since been finished in tarmac by the council, so it's not quite as rough and ready as Calum's original road. This route will also take you past the ruins of **Brochel Castle**—a former stronghold of Clan MacLeod.

Hiking
HALLAIG

Start at North Fearns; www.raasay-house.co.uk/activities/raasay-walks-hallaig

Once the biggest settlement on Raasay, Hallaig on the southeast coast was one of the places that bore the brunt of the Highland Clearances. Today, it's a moving experience walking amid the stone remnants of what was once an active community. It's a place of ghosts, as described in Sorley MacLean's poem *Hallaig,* in which he implores: "They are still in Hallaig, MacLeans and MacLeods, all who were there in the time of Mac Gille Chaluim: the dead have been seen alive."

1: view from the top of Raasay distillery 2: Raasay House 3: North Bay beach, Raasay

To reach it, follow the narrow footpath from the end of the public road at North Fearns as it hugs the coastline. En route look out for the cairn memorial to Sorley MacLean. This marks the start of the village, and shortly afterward you will see the first stone walls of one of Hallaig's former houses. Follow the path up through birchwood, and you'll discover the enclosures of more homes—a sad and small reminder of the lives once lived here.

Allow at least two hours there and back (3.75 mi/6 km in total), more if you want to linger at Hallaig. The path is good and well marked, although the ground around Hallaig itself is quite rough.

Beaches
NORTH BAY AND THE PICTISH STONE
Kyle

This lovely beach, accessed by a small path round the back of Raasay House, is very pretty and more often than not empty. The water is reasonably calm, making it a good place to swim if you can cope with clambering over the large pebbles until it's deep enough. The pebbles in question are very pretty—a mix of dusty pink, blue, and gray. On the opposite side of the main road from the path to the beach, look out for the Pictish stone, one of only nine symbol stones from this period discovered in the whole of Scotland. A slab of gray stone, it looks a bit like a headstone carved with a Christian cross and other decorative, perhaps symbolic, motifs.

INVER BEACH
Near Brae; www.walkhighlands.co.uk/skye/bagh-an-inbhire.shtml

This pebble beach was supposedly a favorite of the Queen and the Royal Family when they used to sail around the Western Isles aboard the Royal Yacht Britannia (decommissioned and now moored in Edinburgh). It is certainly secluded and safe to swim, and to reach it you need to follow a walk through native woodlands, past several waterfalls. The route starts about halfway up Raasay's north-south road, near the cleared township of Brae—look out for a wooden sign reading "Inver 1.5 km." Start your walk by passing through the gate and follow the clear path downhill for two miles (3 km), but be mindful that it will be uphill on the way back.

Food and Accommodations
RAASAY HOUSE

Raasay; tel. 01478 660 300; www.raasay-house. co.uk; light meals and lunch 10am-2pm daily, evening meals 6pm-8pm,; entrées £6.95; £140 hostel-style twin, £285 d hotel room

The only place to eat on the island (so make sure you reserve a table), the historic Raasay House has a good relaxed café for day-time dining and a smarter dining room for more substantial meals. Local produce is used to create homely and filling meals such as the house specialty of venison casserole. When it comes to staying over, there are hotel rooms plus hostel-style rooms (you'll need to book the whole room), which still have access to all the house's other amenities.

Raasay House is also a very active **outdoor center,** and you can sign up to lots of activities, including kayaking, gorge walking, abseiling, sailing, and coasteering. Sessions should be booked in advance. Sailing sessions around the bay aboard a traditional Hebridean fishing boat, including a lesson in old drop-fishing techniques, cost from £50 per person. Loch kayaking sessions cost £35 per person.

Information and Services

The undoubtable hub of the island, the reception of **Raasay House** is the best place to go for information and maps or leaflets. Make sure you pick up the local leaflet to Raasay on the **ferry** over to the isle because it has useful maps and some suggestions of things to do.

Getting There and Getting Around

It's actually a lot easier to get to Raasay than you might think. From Sconser on the east coast of Skye, there are several ferries a day with **CalMac** (three on Sundays). Ferries take just 25 minutes and cost £3.90 return per adult, plus £12.60 if you are bringing a car. Once on the isle, it is possible to walk around much of the isle in a day if you don't have a car, or you can hire a bike from **Raasay House** (www.raasay.com).

Small Isles

The Small Isles refers to a collection of compact islands that lie to the south of Skye—Eigg, Rum, Muck, and Canna—that form part of the Inner Hebrides. **Eigg** is the nearest isle to the mainland, and the little isle of **Muck** lies just south of it. Northeast of Eigg is **Rum,** the largest isle in the archipelago, and beyond this is **Canna.** Each isle has its own character, with natural features such as high basalt cliffs, rocky shores, and sandy beaches and dunes, making the region a haven for wildlife.

Easily reached from the mainland by ferry from Arisaig and Mallaig, there are also plenty of boat tours from Skye offering to take you to one or several of the islands in a day.

EIGG

The strong sense of community on this teeny isle (islanders bought it in 1997) assures only the friendliest of welcomes. There is just one main road on the island, and in summer it is often lined with vibrant orchids. Most visitors come to climb the oddly shaped ridge of **An Sgurr,** and there is a good **café** for a bite to eat afterward. Look out for minke whales and dolphins on the ferry ride over here in summer.

Hiking
AN SGURR

Trailhead: *Eigg Ferry Pier*
Distance: *5 miles (8 km)*
Hiking time: *3-4 hours*
Information and maps: *www.walkhighlands. co.uk/islands/an-sgurr.shtml*

This big bulk of volcanic rock, which rises sharply from a plateau, is the island's most prominent landmark. The route to the top is waymarked with red paint and sets off from the pier uphill. You'll cut round the much-photographed house at **Galmisdale,** which stars in many a postcard as the Sgurr rises dramatically behind it. The path takes you over bracken and moorland, and though relatively straightforward it is steep and boggy in parts. From the top there are splendid views of Muck and Rum, as well as over to Skye and Ardnamurchan. Allow 3-4 hours to complete the 5-mile (8km) trip there and back. There is a steep path and some rocky scrambling is required, making it a medium to difficult walk.

Recreation
EIGG ADVENTURES

The Adventure Hut, Eigg Pier; tel. 01687 347 007; www.eiggadventures.co.uk; year round; walks from £15

This small adventure company is run by husband-and-wife team Owain and Laraine and based out of a little hut near the An Laimrhig complex by the pier. The company offers all sorts of activities—from bike hire (it also offers bike servicing if you've brought your own bike), kayaking, archery, and sailing trips. There are guided walks with resident and committed walker Craig Lovatt, who will take you to some very special places and reveal the stories and legends behind them, such as the cleared village of **Grulin,** or to **Massacre Cave** where the entire population of Eigg was once suffocated as an act of retribution by a rival clan. Activities should be booked in advance as they take place only when there is demand for them.

Food and Accommodations
ISLE OF EIGG SHOP

An Laimrhig, The Pier; tel. 01687 482 432; isleofeiggshop.com; 10am-5pm Mon., Weds., and Fri., 11am-3pm Thurs., noon-5pm Sat.

It's pretty much impossible to visit Eigg and not stop by here, at the island's only shop. Not only can you pick up groceries (freshly baked bread, meat from the butcher, and fresh seafood), but you can also send your postcards from the post office inside, and U.K. bank-holders can withdraw money too.

Opening hours are limited, and, if the ferry to Eigg is cancelled, it often closes at 3pm. Similarly, it may close for an hour on a Monday from about 11:30am if it is receiving stock.

★ SWEENEY'S BOTHY

Cleadale, northwest Eigg; www.eiggtime.com/ sweeneys-bothy; £85 d, two-night minimum stay

This eco-friendly bothy (a remote shelter) offers cozy, sustainable living in the quietest of surroundings. Completely off grid, the hot shower, though outdoors, is heated by either solar panels or the wood-burning stove inside. For half the year this bolt-hole is given over to week-long artist residences; hence, it's only open to guests for six months. Inside, it's stylish and contemporary with clever uses of space—there's even a reading corner—and everything is set up to help you switch off from modern life completely.

LAGEORNA

Eigg; tel. 01687 460 081; lageorna.com/restaurant; dinner 7pm Tues., Weds., and Fri.; three-course set menu £30; £110 d minimum two-night stay

Just a few minutes' walk from Sweeney's Bothy, this restaurant with rooms uses local and fair-trade ingredients in all its dishes, and the Friday night Scottish small plates menu is a local favorite. It's a small team and in summer it gets busy, so table sharing is the norm. Outside the summer season, the restaurant is only open to B&B residents, who have a choice of two double bedrooms—each one has a bed made by a craftsman right here on the island.

RUM

The largest of the Small Isles, Rum is most notable for its striking southern mountain range—a mass of fearsome volcanic peaks that reputedly inspired J. R. R. Tolkien's *Lord of the Rings* (his holiday home on Eigg overlooked them). It's also run as a National Nature Reserve, so look out for sea eagles (reintroduced to the island in the 1980s) as well as red deer, Manx shearwaters, and the island's own breed of pony. Most of the island's inhabitants live in Kinloch, a village on the east coast, near where ferries to the island land.

Sights
KINLOCH CASTLE

Kinloch; www.isleofrum.com/isleofrumheritag.php; one tour a day Apr.-Oct., times vary but usually mid-afternoon; adult £9, child £4.50, concessions £8

The incredibly intricate design of Kinloch Castle cost its Victorian owners dear: £15 million in today's money. But it's unlikely they cared—Lancashire-born industrialist George Bullough was set on creating a lavish home before its time, and the red sandstone palace was also the first home in Scotland to have electricity. Bullough and his wife, society beauty Lady Monica, used Kinloch to host fashionable shooting parties in the heady Edwardian era. Though much of the grandeur has now faded, stepping through the castle doors is like entering a portal to a bygone time: it's been hauntingly left much as it was, as though the Bulloughs may return at any moment. The tours, which last 45 minutes, are entertaining and informative and timed to be between boats. There is no need to book, but latecomers will not be tolerated. It's a 20-minute walk from the ferry pier, or there is a paid-for shuttle service.

Tours
ISLE OF RUM COMMUNITY RANGER TOURS

Set off from Village Hall, Kinloch; tel. 01687 462 404; www.isleofrum.com/wildliferanger.php; times vary; day tours from £15 for adult, £5 child

These guided walks with your own experienced ranger offer exceptional value for money and will really help you understand the land in which you walk. Tours are dependent on season, but you could visit the red deer rut in autumn or go in search of wild flowers in spring.

Food and Accommodations
ISLE OF RUM TEA SHOP

Village Hall, Kinloch, tel. 01687 498 247; www. isleofrumteashop.co.uk; 10am-4pm Mon.-Fri., 10am-3pm Sat., 6pm-7:30pm Mon., 6pm-7pm Tues. and Thurs., 6pm-8pm Weds. and Fri., 6:30pm-7:45pm Sat.; main dishes £15

This little café in the village hall just a short walk from Kinloch village (past the castle), serves good coffee and sandwiches and light bites during the day, plus a fuller menu of venison steak and beer-battered fish and chips (only on Fridays and must be booked in advance) in the evenings. Sit inside, or, if the weather allows, on the picnic benches outside and enjoy views over to Skye.

BBQ BOTHY

Rum Campsite, Kinloch; tel. 01687 460 328; £50 per night

The price for this bothy, which is really a wooden cabin, is for as many people as you can squeeze in, although you'd be hard-pushed to get more than four. But with raised sleeping platforms covered in reindeer hides and a barbecue in the center with a hole in the roof for the smoke, it sure beats sleeping in a tent. You can use the campsite's toilet and shower facilities too.

MUCK

Smallest of the small, this virtually tree-less isle is flat and fertile. It's just two miles (3.2 km) long and one mile (1.6 km) wide and is home to 38 people. There are no cars on the isle (aside from a handful of local vehicles), so look out for the red tractor (owned by Lawrence), a bit of a local icon, which can frequently be seen transporting luggage and goods across the island.

Wild Camping

You can camp anywhere on Rum at any time of year and it can be a very memorable experience, but ensure you keep to the **Scottish Outdoor Access Code** and conduct yourself appropriately (www.outdooraccess-scotland.scot). It's a good idea to chat to the Community Ranger before you set off for a little advice, and remember no fires are allowed.

There are also two bothies, in Guirdhil and Dibidil, that are about a three-hour walk away from the village of Kinloch. It's not possible to book—you simply turn up with sleeping bags and carry mats and make the most of the rustic shelter on offer.

There's not an awful lot to do here, save plodding about, walking, or swimming in the clear waters (or even natural pools), but that is rather the point. Look out for the Highland ponies as you walk the island and also porpoises in the water—Muck's name comes from *muc*, the Gaelic word for pig, which some believe is a reference to the many "sea pigs" found in its waters.

Hiking
BEINN AIREIN

Set off from Port Mor ferry pier; www.walkhighlands. co.uk/islands/beinn-airein.shtml

At 452 feet (138 m), this hill isn't overly lofty, but it still offers beautiful panoramic views of the Inner Hebrides from its summit. The walk here, outlined by **Walk Highlands** (see the website), also takes you past the nicest beach of the island—**Gallanach.** The route takes you across grazing land, where you'll no doubt encounter some native wildlife, and is pretty straightforward. Allow 2.5-3 hours to do the 4.5-mile (7 km) return journey there and back.

Beaches and Pools
GALLANACH BEACH

Gallanach, north Muck

This lovely beach can be reached by traversing Muck's only road from the ferry slipway by Port Mor to the north of the isle—a walk of just 30 minutes. It's a minor track, and you may be joined by wandering ponies. Once you reach the fine sandy beach, right by Gallanach Farm, you can enjoy views across to Rum and the Black Cuillin, and of course swim in its clear waters.

Food and Accommodations
THE CRAFT SHOP AND TEA ROOM

Port Mhor; tel. 01687 462 990; www.isleofmuck.com; 11am-4pm Mon.-Weds. and Fri. Apr.-Sept.; cake £2.50

Almost an attraction in its own right, this lovable café and gift shop is the place to come if you need local tips, a friendly welcome, and general bearings. Gorgeous gifts and souvenirs include Muck mugs and colorful knits.

YURT

Godag House, Muck; ; tel. 01687 460 264; yurt@ isleofmuck.com; May-Sept., adult £15/child £5

It might not be what you expect to find on a miniscule island off the coast of Scotland, but this Mongolian yurt is a beautiful alternative to camping. On the north of Muck, in a secluded spot near Blah Mhor, it offers a few more home comforts than standard canvas stays—camp beds, pillows, and pillowcase are supplied (bring your sleeping bag), and a wood burner in the middle provides heating. There is also a stone for cooking, and utensils can be borrowed. There is a compost toilet, or you can use the one in the café. Showers are available in the community hall (for a fee).

CANNA

This is the westernmost of the Small Isles, and the longer ferry or boat ride here means more opportunity to spot wildlife, such as whales, dolphins, and some of the 20,000 seabirds that inhabit the isle (including puffins and Manx shearwaters). The whole island is a Special Area of Conservation and is run as a sustainable farm with traditional Hebridean customs at its core—just as its benefactor folklorist John Lorne Campbell requested when he handed it over to the National Trust of Scotland in the 1980s. Thus, expect to see wandering livestock on your travels. Canna quite possibly may be the safest place in the British Isles too, with just a few crimes here recorded in decades.

Sights
A'CHILL
Keil

Known as the "Punishment Stone," it is said misbehaving islanders once had their thumbs wedged in the small hole on the top of this standing stone, which stands six feet, four inches (1.93 m) above the ground, and were left to dangle while they thought about what they had done. To reach it, go through the gate before the square by St. Columba's Chapel and follow the sign. The path also takes you past the grave of John Lorne Campbell and an old Christian cross, sadly missing two arms, which locals say is due to cannonball practice during the Napoleonic Wars.

Food and Accommodations
CAFÉ CANNA
The Bothy; tel. 01687 482 488; www.cafecanna. co.uk; 11am-10pm Mon. and Weds.-Sun. (dinner 6pm-8:30pm except Tues.) May-Aug., 1pm-9pm Mon. and Weds.-Sun. (dinner 5pm-7pm, except Tues.) Sept.; entrées £5.90

The sole café on Canna, this lovely café in Canna Harbour offers light refreshments throughout the day and home-cooked meals in the evening, including west coast salmon and local rabbit. The Arisaig moules frites are particularly good, as is the lobster. Daily specials depend on local catches but could include mackerel, octopus, or crab. Make sure you book in for dinner.

TIGHARD GUEST HOUSE
Canna; tel. 01687 462 474; www.tighard.com; £85 d

At this guest house within an Edwardian house, there are three lovely bedrooms all decorated to match the period of the house, with iron bedsteads and tiled fireplaces. Rooms come stocked with tea, coffee, and shortbread, plus complimentary toiletries,

which is great for this price. Hosts Iain and Fiona will take good care of you: Fiona will ply you with home-baked cakes as well as share her knowledge of local flora and fauna, and you can admire some of craftsman Iain's handiwork around the house.

INFORMATION AND SERVICES

For a relatively small collection of islands, there are a lot of good resources for the Small Isles. The main source, **Visit Small Isles** (www.visitsmallisles.com) is a font of information, but then each of the isles has more specific visitor info too. **Visit Eigg** (www. isleofeigg.org), run by the local community is particularly useful and will have you throwing your support behind the ethos of the isle. **The Isle of Rum** (www.isleofrum. com), **Visit Muck** (www.isleofmuck.com), and **Visit Canna** (www.theisleofcanna.com) also offer useful introductions to the isles. However, my advice is to get on the phone to your B&B or campsite before setting off to find out about some of the intricacies of these little communities and, while here, make small talk with everyone you meet—you'll be surprised with how much they are happy to help you.

GETTING THERE
BY PUBLIC FERRY

To travel at your own pace, ferry crossings leave from Mallaig or Arisaig on the mainland. From Mallaig there are ferry crossings with **CalMac** (tel. 0800 066 5000; www. calmac.co.uk) year-round, but keep in mind that there's a maximum of one ferry per day and not all the isles will be visited daily. Travel times are as follows: Eigg 1.25 hours, Muck 1.75 hours, Rum 2.5 hours, Canna 3.5 hours. Round-trip ticket prices from Mallaig are as follows: Eigg £8, Muck £9.20, Rum £8.60, Canna £10.90. You can bring a bike but no cars.

From Arisaig, **Arisaig Marine** (tel. 01687 450 224; www.arisaig.co.uk) operates a service from late April to mid-September and drops you off on the isles for a set number of hours (usually at least four hours unless you request a shorter return time). Round-trip prices are as follows: Eigg £18, Muck £20, Rum £25. There is currently no ferry from Arisaig to Canna. Travel times from Arisaig are as follows: Eigg 1 hour, Rum 2.5 hours, Muck 2 hours.

BY PRIVATE BOAT TOUR

Most visitors to the Small Isles come on day trips, which is perfectly reasonable if a little rushed. **Bella Jane Boat Trips** (tel. 0800 731 3089; www.bellajane.co.uk) based at Elgol on the Isle of Skye runs super-fast trips out to the isles aboard their RIB *AquaExplore* or in more comfort cruising on motorboat Island Cruiser. The Puffin Run trip (£60 adult, £48 child) is their most popular and offers fabulous wild-life-spotting opportunities (3.5-4 hours, offered twice a day). The company also offers more specific trips to Eigg and Rum and even drop offs.

Getting Around

The easy answer to getting around the individual isles is to walk—in theory they are all are do-able in a day (although on Rum you won't be able to see everything). Cycling will obviously allow more time to see the sights, but cabs and buses don't run. You can bring your bike across on the ferry for free if you hire one in Mallaig (**Mallaig Pool and Leisure,** www.mallaigleisure.org.uk) or Arisaig (**West Coast Cycles,** www.westcoastcyclehire. co.uk). If you'd like to travel between the isles without returning to Mallaig or Arisaig, you can catch one of the **CalMac** ferries (www. calmac.co.uk) when it comes into dock on the isle you are on while en route elsewhere. You'll need to check the timetable on the website because not all ferries visit all the isles each day.

Background

The Landscape

GEOGRAPHY

Located at the top of the British Isles and connected to England by land, Scotland covers an area of 30,421 square miles (78,789 sq km). It has somewhere in the region of 790 islands (most of which are uninhabited), creating thousands of miles of coastline, and around 40 of these form a string of islands known as the Hebrides, which lie off Scotland's west coast. The most northerly part of the United Kingdom, Scotland occupies about a third of the land mass that makes

up the island of Great Britain and is home to some of the wildest and least inhabited parts of Europe.

Some time between 25,000 and 10,000 years ago Scotland was covered in ice, the weight of which caused much of the land to be pushed into the earth's crust. A warming period between 13,500 and 11,000 years ago caused the ice to melt, shaping the landscape of Scotland as we know it today as mountains rose and valleys once carved by ice now began to fill with water, creating numerous inland lochs—on Skye's Cuillin mountain range geologists can even tell the direction the ice sheet took thanks to deeply etched scars in the bedrock.

Scotland is divided into three main topographic areas: the Highlands, the Central Lowlands, and the Southern Uplands. The latter two are generally grouped together in an area known as the Lowlands. This area, as you might guess, comprises much lower land in comparison to the Highlands, though it is certainly not flat—here you will find fertile rolling hills and narrow, more gentle valleys. Meanwhile, the east coast of Scotland has a much smoother outline, which is again distinct from the more rugged and craggy west coast of Scotland.

The Highlands, which covers much of north and west Scotland, is bisected by the fault line of Glen Mor, or the Great Glen. To the northwest of the Great Glen you'll find an ancient plateau where peaks have been eroded over time and dramatic glens have been sculpted by glaciers. The far northwest of Scotland is particularly barren, and the rocks of the Lewisian Complex—the oldest in all of Scotland—have been worn down to create a mountainous region where the imposing sea cliffs sweep down to vast sea lochs and numerous inlets.

To the southeast of the Great Glen are the slightly more rounded Grampian Mountains, home to Britain's highest mountain of Ben Nevis. The southeastern fringe of the Highlands is marked by the Highland Boundary fault line, which runs from Stonehaven, just south of Aberdeen, to Helensburgh, just south of Loch Lomond.

Edinburgh and Glasgow lie in an area known as the Central Belt, a region that lies between the Southern Uplands and the Highlands, while Skye is an island off the west coast of Scotland that is part of the Highlands but also forms part of what is known as the Inner Hebrides. The Hebrides comprises two main archipelagos—the Inner Hebrides that lie closer to the mainland and the even more remote Outer Hebrides.

CLIMATE

Ah, where to begin. The saying goes that in Scotland you can see four seasons in a day, but some might argue that you could see four seasons in an hour. Though it is sometimes hard to tell the difference between the seasons—it is perfectly possible to have bright, warm days in autumn, and it often rains in spring and summer, while in certain high terrains you can see snow on the mountains throughout the year—they roughly occur at these times: spring (March-May), summer (June-August), autumn (September-November) and winter (December-February).

Spring is when many flowers come into bloom (daffodils, bluebells, cherry blossoms), setting the meadows and mountainsides ablaze with color, and it's also when many baby animals are born, so you will see lambs frolicking in the fields, calves feeding on their mothers, and plenty of fluffy rabbits hopping about. On the last Sunday in March the clocks go forward in Scotland for British Summer Time (BST), creating more daylight in the evenings, less in the mornings. Scotland has a high latitude, which means you can enjoy long summer days; indeed, in the far north of Scotland there's sometimes no complete darkness at all in summer.

In autumn (fall) Scotland is often at its most beautiful, as the green leaves of summer start to fade to orange or brown, falling from the trees and decorating the ground like golden confetti. It's a great time of year for woodland walks; it's also the time of year when Scotland's deer breed, and you can often hear their rutting mating call. Clocks go back an hour on the last Sunday in October, bringing the UK back in line with Greenwich Mean Time (GMT).

Winter is the coldest time of year in Scotland, and it can get very cold indeed, causing ice and snow to fall and making getting to and from some of the more remote parts very tricky. It's not uncommon for Highland passes to become impassable or for people to become stranded in one place as single-track roads get blocked up. It's worth noting that, though across Scotland snow fall averages 15 to 20 days a year, in the Highlands this rockets to as much as 100 days of snow. However, this is a good time of year to try snow sports in Scotland with ski resorts in both Glencoe and Fort William. It's also the best time of year to enjoy Scotland's dark skies and possibly even see the Northern Lights.

In spring average maximum temperatures range 45-55°F (7-13°C); in summer this increases to around 59-63°F (15-17°C) (though in summer 2018, temperatures got a lot higher). Autumn temperatures drop again to around 46-57°F (8-14°C), and the average maximum temperature in winter is about 41°F (5°C).

The other thing to remember is that, although Scotland is a reasonably small country, its terrain is varied, and so weather can be very changeable between the regions. It also rains a lot, but people are philosophical about it; as they say here, "today's rain is tomorrow's whisky."

ENVIRONMENTAL ISSUES

Scotland's allure is also its curse. Its wild, open spaces, with unbelievably beautiful beaches that go on for miles and natural landscapes that look as though they have been plucked out of Eden, have certainly turned the heads of visitors over recent years, and tourism is on the up, particularly in certain big-name areas such as Edinburgh and Skye.

It's not without its problems, though, with the old cities and eco-systems of the natural landscape not necessarily cut out for vastly increased footfall. This is one reason it's good to get off the beaten track where possible and find your own adventure. You should also listen to the guidelines when it comes to hiking and wild camping to ensure you leave as small a footprint as possible.

Much of Scotland's once raw landscape has been affected by too much sheep farming and deforestation, with trees often cut down to provide first agricultural land and later charcoal for the country's busy ironworks. There are many concerted efforts across parts of Scotland to return the landscape to its natural state, such as the major project underway at the Great Trossachs Forest National Nature Reserve. It's hoped that, by restoring and regenerating natural areas, wildlife that was once driven to extinction can return. There have already been successful projects to reintroduce sea eagles to Mull; some people are even calling for the reintroduction of wolves to rebalance the food chain (deer are prolific, and with nothing to hunt them their numbers will continue to grow) and even brown bear, which were once native to these shores, or Scottish lynx.

PLANTS AND ANIMALS
Trees

There has been a long history of deforestation in Scotland, which is complex to say the least. Native trees such as ancient oakwoods, Scots pine, and birch do still exist, but they are found in pockets on more remote peninsulas or in protected areas rather than all over as they once would have been. And, while the vision of Highland mountains thick with pines may look beautiful, these woods are often too densely packed and don't allow enough room for wildlife to grow and thrive.

Projects are underway to restore the

once sprawling Caledonian Forest to parts of Scotland, which has suffered immensely from over-grazing from sheep and deer. Conservation charity Trees for Life (treesforlife.org.uk) is committed to expanding and relinking the remnants of these ancient woodlands through a programme of natural regeneration (restricting access to grazing animals to allow seedlings to grow and mature properly), replanting native trees and removing non-native trees. It relies on a steady stream of volunteers to help it in its task to encourage young native trees such as Scots pine, oak, birch, rowan, hazel, and juniper, to grow in Scotland again and to revive this all-important eco-system.

Flowers

Spring is undoubtedly one of the best times to visit Scotland for flowers, when its meadows are carpeted with bluebells and other wildflowers, though to see the rich purple haze of its heather, contrasted against the lush greenery of the hillsides, late summer is best.

Other flowers to look out for include the thistle, the national flower of Scotland. This purple prickly weed has long been synonymous with Scotland and can be found on many heraldic symbols; however, there are several varieties, so it's difficult to decide which one is the actual symbol of Scotland. One legend of the thistle tells of how a sleeping party of Scots warriors were alerted to an ambush by Norse invaders when one of the Vikings stood on the spiky plant, and, though there is scant evidence to back it up, you shouldn't let that get in the way of a good story.

Mammals

There are many mammals to be found in Scotland, and, with much of the place uninhabited by people, it's not uncommon to spot them as you are driving through the countryside. Although, for the best sightings, you can't beat finding a quiet spot and setting up camp (or picnic) for an hour or two and letting them come to you.

Large red deer can be seen, most commonly in the Highlands, as well as smaller roe deer, red squirrels, pine martens, badgers, and foxes. Today, by far the most prolific mammal is the red deer—who doesn't think of Scotland and envisage a mighty stag silhouetted against a misty mountain top? However, there is some debate as to how much deer stalking is good to keep numbers down and give other wildlife a chance without damaging the deer numbers themselves.

Red deer stag stalking season runs July-mid-October, with the hind stalking season taking place mid-October-mid-February, though most commercial operations take place August-October. If you are planning to do any hill-walking during stalking season, it is worth checking if there is any shooting taking place on the estate at the same time so you don't risk disturbing any stalking activities. The best way to do this is to check with the Heading for the Scottish Hills access service (www.outdooraccess-scotland.scot/Practical-guide/public/heading-for-the-scottish-hills).

Sealife

With thousands of miles of coastline, Scotland's seas are teeming with marine wildlife. Along the west coast, many boat trips will take you out to see gray seals and common seals, often spotted lazily basking on rocks, as well as harbor porpoises, otters, dolphins (both common and bottle-nose), and minke whales, which are best seen May-September.

Birds

Scotland's skies are busy with birdlife. On Skye, Mull, and Islay, eagles are regularly sighted (Mull is particularly good for sea eagles, or white-tailed eagles as they're also called). Other sea birds, such as buzzards and puffins, are also abundant. Meanwhile, the elusive capercaillie can still be found in Loch Lomond and the Trossachs National Park, and here too the numbers of black grouse are currently on the rise.

Insects

Midges are by far the most complained about group of insects found in Scotland. Traveling in clouds or swarms, they can range from being mildly irritating to a downright nuisance. May-September is when they are mostly seen, although it's the biting females from June onward that you want to be particularly wary of. Midges tend to like the warm slightly damp air after it's rained, and they come out the most at dusk. If you're planning to do any camping at all, particularly in summer, you will want to protect yourself against the midges—Avon Skin So Soft spray is the protection of choice, but wear long trousers and long sleeves too.

In rural Scotland lots of other insects can be found too, including mosquitos, horseflies, ants, beetles, ladybirds, birch flies, and black flies (these last two can also be annoying), as well as bees, wasps, spiders, butterflies, dragonflies, and grasshoppers. However, while you may get the odd bite, there's not much to be worried about when it comes to Scottish insects, although a bite from a tick—a nasty little insect often found in wooded and bushy areas and which carries Lyme disease—can make you very sick if not treated. If you do get bitten by one of these tiny creatures, try to remove them using either a tick removal device or finely tipped tweezers. It's also worth familiarizing yourself with the symptoms (www.tickalert. org) if you have been bitten (similar to flu symptoms, they often show up a couple of weeks later) so you can get treated as soon as possible.

History

Scotland's history is emotive, long, and at times brutal and savage but often told with a sense of pride and patriotism. It has been invaded and settled more times than you can count and its people have been dispersed to all corners of the globe—as many as 29 million people in the United States claim some Scottish ancestry, with many more in Canada, Australasia, and South Africa. It is this sense of belonging and connection to the land that binds its people and has led to the many romanticisms of its famous heroes, from fearless warriors to enlightened thinkers. While in other parts of the UK patriotism is a thorny issue, it's rare to meet a Scotsman or Scotswoman, who either lives here or elsewhere, who is not proud of where they are from.

ANCIENT HISTORY

The first people to settle in Scotland, if you can even call it "settle," were hunters and

1: Thistle is the national flower of Scotland. 2: bottlenose dolphins in the Moray Firth

gatherers of the Stone Age around 10,000 BC, shortly after the last Ice Age. They were nomads who wandered the wild land, surviving on what they could—wild animals, seasonal berries, and fruits. It's likely that these wanderers were able seamen, and so the numerous isles off Scotland's west coast were undoubtedly attractive to them, with plenty of inlets to travel between. A stone arrowhead dating back 11,000 years found near Bowmore on the Isle of Islay proves that it was certainly one of these early islands visited, and this way of life subsisted for thousands of years. It's interesting to note that, despite the many different people who arrived in Scotland thereafter, DNA evidence shows that the bloodstock has changed little since these early hunter-gatherers arrived; thus, Scottish people are mostly descended from them. Eventually other people, the early farmers, did come but not until around 4,000 BC. They then began clearing forests for arable land, and so began Scotland's long story of deforestation.

It's thought that it's through these early Neolithic people, who began to rely on specific patches of land for survival, that the first signs of clan life sprung as people "belonged" to a certain home turf for the first time. These Neolithic people also built stone burial chambers (cairns) for their dead, the remains of which can be seen around Scotland, such as Clava Cairns near Inverness. These people also began creating tools and weapons using bronze, an idea that probably came to Scotland via Europe and was possibly brought up through Britain by the Beaker people (so named for the distinct shaped cups they would leave in burial chambers). This period from 2,000 BC onward is known as the Bronze Age.

ROMAN INVASION

The Romans first attacked Scotland in AD 79, and the country's recorded history began shortly after. Though the Romans tried to subjugate Scotland, or Caledonia as the Romans called it, ultimately, they failed. On arrival, they named the indigenous people, who they considered savages, Picts (meaning painted people). In reality, the Picts, pre-Christian people, were probably made up of lots of different tribes, but the Romans considered

them one. In AD 83 or 84 the Romans, led by Julius Agricola, fought the Caledonians, led by a fearsome chief known as Calgacus, at the Battle of Mons Graupius (the Grampian Mountains). Though, according to the Roman historian Tacitus, the Romans won this battle and colonized much of southern Scotland, their style of of attack was not suited to the terrain of the Highlands, and further attempts to bring the north of the country under control failed.

As a result, the Romans built the huge stone barrier between England and Scotland known as Hadrian's Wall largely to keep the northern savages out of their empire. They later built the 37-mile (60 km) Antonine Wall, another great hulk of a barrier, from the Clyde to the Forth, to try to exert control. Eventually, in AD 410, the Romans retreated from Scotland and Britain, having never really conquered the north and leading many to hail it the first episode of Scotland's unwavering might.

POST-ROMAN SCOTLAND

In AD 563 St. Columba arrived in Scotland, setting up a monastery on the tiny Isle of Iona, off the west coast of Mull, and

National Monument of Scotland

also visiting Skye, where he preached Christianity. Celtic people from Ireland, known as Gaels, had already settled in the west of Scotland. By the 5th century these early Celts (also known as Scoti) ruled a huge area of Scotland known as Dál Riata from the center of their kingdom in Kilmartin Glen, Argyll. By AD 800 Vikings, accomplished seamen from Scandinavia (mainly Norway and Denmark), began crossing the North Sea and settling in parts of Scotland, particularly in the west, around Skye, as evidenced in many of the Norse names that still survive. Later, the Picts and the Gaels began to forge a new kingdom known as the Kingdom of Alba. In 843 Kenneth MacAlpin became the first King of Scots, ultimately uniting the nation of Scotland into the country we see today.

Following MacAlpin, the role of king was passed down through a Gaelic system of tanistry (in which eligible men were elected to the role, though blood was often spilled too), which was largely adhered to. Macbeth, King of Scotland from 1040-1057, who Shakespeare painted as some kind of bloodthirsty social climber, was probably no worse than his peers. Although his reign was largely peaceful, Macbeth eventually got his comeuppance when he was killed in battle in 1057 by forces loyal to the future King Malcolm III (whose father, Duncan I, Macbeth had killed to claim his title). By the 12th century, Scotland, increasingly more influenced by England, became a feudal society, and under this new system the role of king became a hereditary right in Scotland.

WARS OF INDEPENDENCE

Scotland has long had a fragile relationship with its southern neighbor, England. The larger and more powerful country of England saw itself as superior, and its monarchs considered themselves overlords of Scotland, an idea that riled many a Scottish king or warrior. In 1286, there was a succession crisis in Scotland following the death of King Alexander III, which enabled power-hungry King Edward I of England to wrestle some control. A tussle for the Scottish crown between John Balliol and Robert the Bruce led the guardians of Scotland (a group of noblemen given temporary control of the country) to ask the English king to decide who should be king. Edward I dutifully chose Balliol but not before he had convinced the guardians to recognize him as overlord of Scotland.

John Balliol's reign was thwarted by Edward's constant demands, which undermined the Scottish king, and it soon became clear that Edward saw Scotland as nothing more than a vassal state. In 1294, seeing trouble on the horizon, Balliol formed a treaty with England's other enemy, France, that essentially agreed that the two nations would support each other against English attack. This partnership between two unlikely allies became known as the Auld Alliance and continued in some form or other until the 16th century.

On hearing of the Franco-Scottish negotiations, Edward was furious and in March 1296 he mounted an attack on Berwick, a town which then stood just across the Scottish border (today it forms part of England), and the following month the English defeated the Scottish at the Battle of Dunbar. By July, Balliol was forced to abdicate.

Edward I's bold move to take Scotland for himself infuriated many Scots people, not least a warrior known as William Wallace who managed to garner support for a fight for independence, with the aim of returning Balliol to the throne. Together with military leader Andrew Moray, Wallace led Scots troops, largely made up of clansmen from the Highlands, to a huge victory against English troops at the Battle of Stirling Bridge in 1297. Unfortunately, despite the Scottish victory, a determined Edward I continued a vicious assault on Scotland, eventually forcing William Wallace into hiding. By the time Wallace arrived back in Scotland a few years later, momentum had been lost and in 1305 Wallace was betrayed to English forces; he was captured just north of Glasgow, tried for treason in London's Westminster Hall, and hung, drawn, and quartered, with his head placed on a spike in London Bridge and parts of his body distributed among Scottish cities as a warning to future would-be revolters.

But the fight wasn't over. Robert the Bruce, himself a clever political maneuverer, was crowned King of Scotland in 1306, and in 1314 he and his army defeated Edward II at the Battle of Bannockburn, just outside Stirling. Six years later, in 1320, the Declaration of Arbroath, a letter on which the U.S. Declaration of Independence is thought to have been based, was signed by Scottish nobles and barons and delivered to Pope John XXII requesting that he acknowledge Scotland as an independent sovereign state from England. Though largely symbolic, its intent was clear: "As long as but a hundred of us remain alive, never will we on any conditions be brought under English rule. It is in truth not for glory, nor riches, nor honours, that we are fighting, but for freedom—for that alone, which no honest man gives up but with life itself." For a while Scotland was left largely alone.

THE LORD OF THE ISLES

Though much of Scotland now formed part of one country, for a long time much of the western isles and a large part of the western mainland were ruled by a separate entity known as the Lord of the Isles, whose ancient seat was at Finlaggan on the Isle of Islay. The title dates back to the Viking occupation of Scotland, when Somerled, the son of a Gael and a Norse settler, fought off the Norse ruler of the region, Olaf, securing the kingdom for himself and his descendants, the MacDonalds.

The power of the Lord of the Isles, which reached its peak in the 15th century, began to dwindle after one ruler, John Macdonald II, made a treaty with King Edward IV of England in 1462 in a bid to overthrow the Scottish king, James III. It was the beginning of the end for the powerhouse, and, when King James IV came to the throne a couple

of decades later, he began the process of dismantling the power structure of the Lord of the Isles for good.

THE STUARTS

In 1542, Scotland was thrown into turmoil when King James V of Scotland died, leaving his six-day-old daughter, Mary, Queen of Scots, the heir apparent. At the time, religious reform was sweeping across Europe; in England King Henry VIII had set up the Church of England following his divorce from Catherine of Aragon, making it a Protestant country. Nervous Catholics acted quickly, and Mary was crowned Queen of Scotland in the Chapel Royal at Stirling Castle in 1543, aged just nine months.

King Henry VIII of England saw a chance to unite the crowns of Scotland and England through the marriage of Mary and his son Prince Edward (later King Edward VI of England), who himself was aged just six. The Scots rejected the proposal, and the period of unrest that ensued, in which Henry sent troops to attack Edinburgh in December of that year, and later other parts of Scotland, in a bid to change their mind, became known as the Rough Wooing.

In 1558 Mary's mother, Mary of Guise, arranged for her to marry the Dauphin of France, in order to strengthen the Catholic line. Mary left for France and didn't return to Scotland until 1561, following the death of her husband. By this time Scotland was in a state of religious unrest. Mary quickly remarried, this time to Henry Stuart, Lord Darnley, a jealous man; in 1566 he entered into a Protestant conspiracy to have Mary's favorite and secretary David Rizzio murdered at the Palace of Holyroodhouse in Edinburgh. The following year Darnley himself was killed in an explosion in Edinburgh, and, when Mary then married the Earl of Bothwell, who many suspected of murdering Darnley, her fate was sealed.

Scotland turned against Mary, thanks in no small part to the vitriolic words of John Knox, leader of the Scottish Reformation and Mary's sworn enemy. Mary was arrested and forced to abdicate in favor of her son, King James VI, who was just 13 months old. However, she escaped to England, where for a while she lived under the protection of her cousin Queen Elizabeth I of England, though she never saw her son again. Eventually Elizabeth (who never actually met her cousin) grew scared that Mary could claim the throne of England for herself and had her executed at Fotheringhay Castle in Northamptonshire in 1587.

When Elizabeth died in 1603 with no children, King James VI of Scotland succeeded to the throne of England as King James I, thus uniting the two countries in what is known as the Union of the Crowns. In 1707, the Act of Union brought the two countries even closer by creating a single Parliament to rule Scotland and Britain from Westminster, effectively creating Great Britain.

THE JACOBITES

It was some years prior to the Act of Union that the wheels for the Jacobite cause began turning. During the Glorious Revolution of 1688 in which King James VII of Scotland (King James II of England) was deposed and replaced with William of Orange and his wife Mary II (James's own daughter), many Scottish patriots felt outraged. James, a Catholic, had hoped to return Catholicism to Scotland, but after William of Orange launched an attack on him, he had gone into hiding. It was now left to his supporters to retaliate, which they duly did in 1689. Led by Viscount Dundee, James's supporters (the name Jacobite means "supporter of James") mounted a successful Highland charge against William's forces at the Battle of Killiecrankie in 1689. However, Dundee was killed in the battle, and without a leader the cause simmered, for now.

William of Orange's government was characterized by a series of economic disasters and also proved unsympathetic to the needs of its Scottish subjects (in fact, many Scots felt humiliated by the way they were treated by the English Parliament), and so Jacobites who believed in James's hereditary right to the throne were soon joined by anyone who had a grudge against the king. The signing of the Act of Union with England in 1707 (this time under the reign of Queen Anne) brought yet more supporters.

There are two further noteworthy Jacobite risings: During the Jacobite Rising of 1715, one of Scotland's most influential politicians, the Earl of Mar, raised the standard for the Stuarts when George I of Hanover succeeded to the throne, in the hope of reclaiming it for James Francis Edward Stuart, the son of King James II who was known as the "Old Pretender." During the Jacobite Rising of 1745 (known as the '45), the "Young Pretender," Bonnie Prince Charlie, arrived from exile in Italy to raise his standard in Glenfinnan. Sadly, this final major uprising led to the overall defeat of the Jacobite cause at the Battle of Culloden, which took place just outside Inverness on April 16, 1746.

COLLAPSE OF THE CLAN SYSTEM

Following Culloden, the British government, by now under the reign of King George II, wanted to ensure no rebellions on such a scale could be mounted again, and so, many measures were put in place to undermine and eradicate traditional Highlands clan culture.

The Tartan and the Dress Act of 1746 outlawed the wearing of kilts and other Highland dress, but it was just the latest in a line of measures. The Disarming Act of 1716 some years earlier, though largely ineffective, had sought to outlaw traditional Highland weaponry and was followed by the slightly more successful Disarming Act of 1725. In addition, British forts were placed along the Great Glen to ensure British troops could leap into action as soon as possible, aided by the notorious "Wade's Roads" that were introduced throughout the Highlands. Highland clans were brought into the military fold, with Highland regiments in the British Army, such as the Black Watch, being created some years earlier.

But the most effective measure and also heartbreaking was the Highland Clearances that took place over the course of a century.

Through a mix of forced clearances (often brutal, sometimes subtler, by edging people off their land) and encouraged emigration, the Hanoverian government undid centuries of clan culture, in which a connection with the land as a sense of belonging was ingrained, in a spectacularly short space of time.

ENLIGHTENMENT

While many were being distracted by the Jacobite cause, others were quietly getting on with things, and an intellectual movement known as the Enlightenment took hold in Scotland in the wake of Culloden. From the 1750s onward, Scottish philosophers, scientists, engineers, doctors, and writers (such as David Hume, Adam Smith, and Robert Burns) were sharing and debating ideas in and around Edinburgh, many of which had a huge impact on the way the world works today. Indeed, so influential were the leading figures of the movement that French writer Voltaire was quoted as saying, "We look to Scotland for all our ideas of civilization."

HIGHLAND REVIVAL

One name that sprang up out of the Scottish Enlightenment was Walter Scott—a well-connected Scottish writer and historian whose historic fiction spawned a culture of literary tourism to places such as Loch Lomond and the Trossachs, which in turn was instrumental in the Highland Revival of the 19th century.

Keen to build on the union between Scotland and England and improve relations between the two nations, King George IV embarked on an ambitious state visit to Scotland in 1822, all stage managed by Sir Walter Scott. The first time an English monarch had visited Scotland since Charles I came for his Scottish coronation in 1633, George went all out, wearing a kilt for the occasion and improving his reputation in Scotland hugely. Later, Queen Victoria, who famously fell in love with Scotland and had the huge palace of Balmoral Castle built in Perthshire, cemented the role of Scotland as a fashionable place to be, and

people traveled all over to partake in Scottish customs, once maligned and outlawed that now became quaint and twee.

Interestingly, though Highland games and clan tartans are now symbolic of Scotland, it's unclear how popular these were with traditional Highland clans—indeed, the idea of a certain tartan being associated with a particular clan was probably a Scott invention.

BEGINNINGS OF INDUSTRIALIZATION

The union with England brought more trading opportunities to Scotland, and there was a real effort to improve agricultural practices in Scotland from the mid-18th century on. Around this time Glasgow became the center of the world's tobacco trade, and rich merchants built lavish buildings in the city center. Take a stroll through the Merchant City today to see many of the buildings. Over time too, the spread of people became much more centered on the cities, where industries such as mining and shipbuilding provided much needed work.

MODERN-DAY SCOTLAND

Much of the view of present-day Scotland has been romanticized by films such as *Braveheart*, and people are still drawn to its trove of historic sites, from ruined castles burned to the ground by the Jacobites to prehistoric relics. However, Scotland is also a hugely exciting and innovative country—without Scotland, we would have no flushing toilets (thanks to Alexander Cumming), telephones (thanks to Alexander Graham Bell), and no TVs (thanks to John Logie Baird).

It's also a cultural powerhouse, with world-class museums and art galleries, some of the best festivals in the world, and an increasing presence on the world stage. It's a progressive nation as happy to look to its past as it is to imagine a new future. All in all, it's a place that, once it has you in its hold, is very hard to forget.

Government and Economy

GOVERNMENT

Since 1999 Scotland has been devolved from the rest of the UK in some areas. This basically means it has its own government, elected by the people, which sits at the Scottish Parliament in Edinburgh and makes decisions over certain aspects of Scottish life, including how its budget is spent. The current leader is Nicola Sturgeon of the Scottish National Party (SNP), a center-left party with social democracy at its heart. The SNP is the largest political party in Scotland (it currently has 63 Scottish members of parliament and 35 who sit in Westminster) and had quite a monopoly on politics north of the border for a few years, but in 2015 the balance was redressed when it lost many seats in the general election.

The second largest party in Scottish politics is now the Scottish Conservative Party, a center-right party (known as the Tories). Despite dominating Scottish politics for the first half of the 20th century, for many years the Tories were virtually non-existent north of the border (they were virtually wiped out following the general election of 1997 when they won no seats whatsoever), but they are now experiencing something of a resurgence in Scotland. The third party in Scotland is the Scottish Labour Party, also center-left, which was the strongest party from 1959 until 2007. Since then, it has seen its fortunes wane as the SNP dominates.

In 2014 Sturgeon led a hearty referendum campaign for Scotland to vote for independence from the rest of the UK. It was a close-fought battle with the outcome 55 percent to 45 percent, but, ultimately, the people of Scotland chose to stay as part of the UK. Since then, the referendum on leaving the EU, referred to as Brexit, took place in 2016.

Despite the majority of people in Scotland voting to remain in the EU, as the majority of the UK did not (albeit by a small margin of 52 percent to 48 percent), as it stands, Scotland and the rest of the UK look set to leave Europe. On the back of this, Sturgeon is currently campaigning for a second Scottish referendum on independence.

ECONOMY

The uncertainty of Brexit (Britain's divorce from the EU) looms over the economy of Britain as a whole and means the value of the pound is currently low. It also leaves a huge question mark over future trade deals between Scotland and the rest of Europe as a large part of its GDP relies on its exports, particularly manufacturing exports.

In particular, the export of food and drink (Scotch whisky, Scottish salmon etc.) is considered four times as important to the Scottish economy as it is to the rest of the UK, and the Scottish government has repeatedly stated that it wishes to remain in the European Single Market, or at least the Customs Union. However, the labor market in Scotland is relatively strong, with unemployment levels nearing a record low.

Other main industries in Scotland are technology and engineering (which currently is more likely to mean software than ships), tourism (which accounts for around 5 percent of Scottish GDP), the financial services industry (which employs many people in Edinburgh and Glasgow and which contributes to around 7 percent of Scotland's overall GDP), and the oil and gas industries. Scotland has large oil reserves and is the biggest producer of petroleum in the EU, though the industry is in decline.

People and Culture

CLAN CULTURES

While Highland culture was largely detangled and picked apart from the late 18th century onward with restrictions placed on clans, and more importantly displacement and mass emigrations that saw people leave their ancestral lands, the sense of belonging to a place still rings true to many Scots people wherever they live in the world. Today, people travel the world over to visit places associated with their clan, from the battlefield of Culloden where they can pay respect to lost lives, to castles associated with their people. Thanks to the Highland Revival of the 19th century, there is now a tartan associated with each clan, which is worn like a badge of honor.

RELIGION

The largest faith in Scotland is Christianity, which accounts for 53.8 percent of all faiths according to the 2011 census. Scotland is a Presbyterian country, with the Church of Scotland recognized as the national church. The other main Christian denomination is the Roman Catholic Church (the dominant religion until the Scottish Reformation), which is still very popular in traditionally Gaelic areas, such as the Hebrides and western Scotland. The third most popular branch of Christianity is the Scottish Episcopal Church. There are also lots of smaller Presbyterian churches.

Other religions are gradually establishing here due to an increasingly ethnically diverse population, but they are still small in comparison (Islam: 1.4 percent, Hinduism: 0.3 percent, Sikhism: 0.2 percent, and Buddhism: 0.2 percent). In reality, though you will see cathedrals and churches in cities, and most towns and villages will have a parish church, Scotland is not an overtly religious country.

LANGUAGE

English is the main language spoken in Scotland, though in small pockets Gaelic is still spoken. The other main language is Scots, a variation of English, often referred to as Lowland Scots. English hasn't always been the main spoken language, though. When Norwegian Vikings arrived in the late 8th century, no doubt they would have had difficulty understanding the indigenous folk who spoke a mix of Old Irish (of which there would have been many varieties that evolved into Scottish Gaelic), Old English (which evolved into Scots), and some form of pre-Celtic language spoken by the Picts, which later died out.

The Norse, of course, spoke their own language, and many place names still bear evidence of this: the suffixes such as -*bus* or -*bost* that you'll see in places such as Carbost on Skye come from the Old Norse for farm (*Bolstadr*). After the Gaels (or Scoti) replaced the Picts as the most dominant people in the 9th century, Scottish Gaelic began to replace Pictish and later Norse as the main language in large parts of Scotland. However, the Lowlands of Scotland spoke a variation of northern Anglo-Saxon, which came to be known as Lowland Scots or simply Scots. In the lead up to the union with England in 1707, Scots became the widest spoken language in Scotland, but when Scotland and England formed a union, Scots and Gaelic were both suppressed, leading English to become the accepted norm to be spoken in courts and towns, where more commerce took place.

Today as many as 30 percent of the population speak Scots to some extent, and it is now being taught in schools once again. Similarly, Gaelic is still spoken in some areas of Scotland, particularly in the Outer Hebrides and parts of Skye. Indeed, there is a large movement to restore the Gaelic language to Scotland, which many people see as integral to its culture as, if not more so, the kilt, tartan, and whisky. You will see many place names written in Gaelic as you drive around, particularly in western Scotland, and it is once again being taught in many schools. Learning institutions such as Sabhal Mor Ostaig (www.smo.uhi.ac.uk) on Skye, which offers short courses over summer for an introduction to Gaelic, are determined to revive this very important part of Scottish culture.

LITERATURE

Sir Walter Scott is celebrated for having introduced literary tourism to Scotland with his depictions and romanticism of Highland clans and the landscape they called home, but he is also largely responsible for the romantic view we have of Highland culture, particularly through his novel *Rob Roy*, which tells of the plight of the Jacobites.

Scotland has long been associated with great works of literature, from the stirring poems of Robert Burns, where each word is excellently executed, to the incredible imaginings of Robert Louis Stevenson. Contemporary fiction is not to be overlooked either. Irvine Welsh may paint a slightly bleaker view of Scotland than Scott, but the dialect in which he writes and the honest depictions of inner-city life are no less captivating. Ian Rankin and Val McDermid rank among Scotland's best thriller writers, while Iain Banks, who writes under two guises (Iain Banks for mainstream fiction and Iain M. Banks for science fiction) is nothing short of a literary hero.

VISUAL ARTS

Henry Raeburn, portrait painter to King George IV, was an excellent portraitist, who captured the likenesses of key players of the day, including Sir Walter Scott, whom he painted in 1822, and the Reverend Robert Walker, the star of arguably his most famous work, *The Skating Minister*, on display in the Scottish National Gallery in Edinburgh.

Of course, Charles Rennie Mackintosh's contribution not only to the Glasgow landscape in his many buildings but also to its applied arts is huge. It's important to remember that Mackintosh was also keenly influenced by his wife Margaret Macdonald, her sister Frances Macdonald, and Frances's husband James Herbert MacNair. Together, they made up The Four, a group of accomplished and daring artists who met at the Glasgow School of Art in the 1890s and went on to create what was referred to as the Glasgow Style.

Around this time a group of artists known as the Glasgow Boys, featuring the likes of James Guthrie, who interpreted and expanded on impressionist and post-impressionist paintings of the day, also emerged from the school. Much later, the New Glasgow Boys of the 1980s also from the Glasgow School of Art became known for their honest, often gritty portrayals of daily life.

MUSIC AND DANCE

While contemporary Scotland, particularly in Glasgow and Edinburgh, is a melting pot of difficult musical styles and dance trends, from techno to thrashing guitar music, pop, and classical, folk music has long been at Scotland's heart. The bagpipes are a traditional instrument, long associated with the Highland clans; indeed, they were played when clans went into battle. There are two main styles of music played, the *Ceòl Mór* and *Ceòl Beag,* Gaelic for "big music" and "light music" respectively. The former is slower, featuring a simple melody, while Ceòl Beag features jigs and reels and is what you are more than likely to hear at ceilidhs—lively dance and music events that take place on occasion in the Highlands and more regularly in the cities.

Many inns in Highland villages, as well as pubs in Glasgow and Edinburgh, feature regular traditional music nights whereby gathering musicians sit and play round a table. Often it is improvised, and there are fiddles, accordions, and guitars as well as occasional singing—from laments to more rousing sing-a-longs—and the odd bagpipe. If you can sing or play and know a folk song or two, you are more than welcome to join in.

Essentials

Getting There

FROM THE UNITED STATES AND CANADA

Several airlines fly direct to Scotland from North America. From **New York (JFK)** you can fly direct to Edinburgh with **Virgin Atlantic** (www.virginatlantic.com) and **Delta** (www.delta.com). Delta also has flights from JFK to Glasgow via Amsterdam. **United Airlines** (www.unitedairlines.co.uk) runs flights from **Newark** to Edinburgh and Glasgow, from **Chicago** to Edinburgh, and from **Dulles** airport near Washington DC to Edinburgh.

Virgin Atlantic (www.virginatlantic. com) has flights from Orlando to Glasgow, and you can fly with American Airlines from Philadelphia to Glasgow, changing at London Heathrow.

From Canada, Air Canada (www. aircanada.com) flies from Toronto to Glasgow and Edinburgh. Air Transat (www. airtransat.com) also flies from Toronto to Glasgow and runs routes from Calgary and Vancouver to Glasgow. WestJet (www. westjet.com) has flights from Halifax to Glasgow.

Flight time from the east coast of the United States is around eight hours. From Toronto, flight time is around nine hours.

Some direct flight routes are just seasonal, and you will certainly find more options between May and October, although prices out of season (late October, November, and January-April) can be a lot cheaper if you book in advance.

FROM LONDON AND THE UNITED KINGDOM
By Air

There's absolutely no shortage of flights between London and Edinburgh, with several flights every day from each of the main London airports (Gatwick, Heathrow, and Stansted). There are also regular flights to Inverness from Heathrow, Gatwick, and Luton.

Unless you're staying in northeast London, steer clear of London Stansted as it's a bit of an ordeal to get to. London Heathrow is the busiest London airport, but London Gatwick probably has the best choice of domestic flights and is pretty well connected to central London. The Gatwick Express (www.gatwickexpress.com) has trains from London Victoria that get you to the airport in under half an hour.

The main budget airlines of easyJet (www.easyjet.com) and Ryanair (www. ryanair.com) are much of a muchness, and neither offers much in the way of comfort for travelers (seats are fairly cramped and all refreshments must be purchased). Plus, there's always a bit of a bun fight as passengers try to squeeze their hand luggage into the overhead hold. Still, with an average flight time of just under 1.5 hours, it's probably not necessary to go much fancier, and, if you book in advance and are happy to travel mid-week, you can usually get return flights for around £50-£100.

For a tad more comfort, British Airways (www.britishairways.com) is a bit better, staff are usually at least a little friendly, and flights from London to Scotland can usually be purchased for around £100-£150.

Loganair (www.loganair.co.uk) is Scotland's only airline, and, although most of its flights are within Scotland itself (the only one from London is from Stansted to Dundee), flights on these small passenger jets offer an unforgettable experience with staff who offer the most genuine of welcomes. From Glasgow you can fly to Islay.

Traveling between Ireland and Scotland is very easy. From Northern Ireland, there are regular flights from Belfast to Glasgow with both Flybe (www.flybe.com, a decent budget airline) as well as easyJet (www. easyjet.com), and there are also direct flights to the city from both the City of Derry and Donegal with Loganair (www.loganair. co.uk). Ryanair (www.ryanair.com) also flies direct to Glasgow from Derry.

Edinburgh can also be reached direct from both Belfast International with easyJet and Belfast City airport with Flybe. Dublin has direct flights to Edinburgh with Irish airlines Aer Lingus (www.aerlingus.com) and Ryanair. From Cork, in the south of Ireland, Aer Lingus flights take just over an hour and a half.

Sir Walter Scott's monument and Princes Street, Edinburgh

By Car

From London and other parts of the United Kingdom, it is perfectly possible to drive to Scotland as long as you are prepared for a fair bit of motorway driving. From London, it's an 8-hour journey up to Glasgow without stops, so you should allow 9-10 hours for one decent stop halfway.

The best route leaves London on the M40, which you stay on for just under 18 miles before joining the M6, which will take you all the way over the Scottish border (you won't even notice you're crossing it) where you pick up the A74 all the way into Glasgow.

By Ferry

There are just two ferry operators that run ferries between Ireland and Scotland: **Stenaline** (www.stenaline.co.uk), which operates a crossing from Belfast to Cairnryan in Dumfries and Galloway in southern Scotland, and **P&O Irish Sea** (www.poferries.com/en/cairnryan-larne), which runs a crossing from Larne in Ireland, also into Cairnryan.

By Train

Probably the most enjoyable way to travel between London and Scotland is by train, and ticket prices can be compared through Trainline (www.thetrainline.com), which includes services by all operators.

The main operator for Glasgow is **Virgin Trains** (www.virgintrains.co.uk), which leaves from **London Euston** to Glasgow Central and takes 4.5 hours. There are several trains a day, and seats (always reserve one when you book a ticket) are fairly comfortable. There is a buffet cart on board for refreshments (not included in the price) and wireless Internet (book direct with Virgin and this should be free). Tickets can be booked up to three months in advance and can cost as little as £30 each way, but be warned: last-minute ticket prices rocket to as much £125 each way. It's also worth checking out first-class tickets because often these are not much more than standard class but come with a free meal and drinks.

Trains to Edinburgh set off from **London King's Cross** with **London North Eastern Railway** (www.lner.co.uk), and prices, times, and amenities are similar.

For a little more adventure (and to save on a night's accommodation), book a seat on the **Caledonian Sleeper** (www.sleeper.scot) train that sets off from **London Euston** at night, arriving into Scotland in the morning. You can choose to disembark in Edinburgh,

The Jacobite Steam Train crosses the Glenfinnan Viaduct.

Glasgow, Aberdeen, Inverness, or Fort William. Anyone wanting to do the full train journey of the West Highland Line should go all the way to Fort William, where you can pick up a connection (the **Jacobite Steam Train** in spring and summer) to Mallaig for Skye.

Though the trains are a far cry from Orient-Express-style travel, there is still something terribly exciting about leaving London at night, having dinner on board before bedding down in your private cabin, and arriving into Scotland in the morning, fully rested and ready to start exploring. In recent years much criticism of the rickety old trains has resulted in a new batch of modern trains, with slightly more comfortable cabins and a snazzy new "Club Car" for drinks and dinner, and even—wait for it—wireless Internet, rolling out from spring 2019.

FROM EUROPE
By Air

There are excellent year-round flights from most major European cities, including Paris, Brussels, Berlin, and Rome, into both Glasgow and Edinburgh. In addition, you can fly to Inverness from Amsterdam, Bergen, Zurich, among others. The main European hubs for flight connections to Scotland are **London Heathrow, Paris Charles de Gaulle, Amsterdam Schipol, Frankfurt am Maine, Reykjavik-Keflavik Airport,** and **Madrid Barajas.**

By Car

While it is possible to drive to Scotland from Europe, it is a bit of a slog. From Brussels, for instance, it is just over a two-hour drive to reach the Euro Tunnel, which in itself is easy and takes just an hour to cross the English Channel. Once in England it's a short drive through Kent before skirting London to the east and heading up to Scotland via the M20 and then A1. Though straightforward enough, it's an 11-hour journey without stops, so you should definitely consider overnighting somewhere, such as York, en route.

By Train

Much of Europe is well facilitated by trains, making rail travel a real possibility. From Brussels, it's just a two-hour rail journey into London on the **Eurostar** (www.eurostar. com), from where you could pick up a connection to Glasgow, Edinburgh, or Inverness. Tickets can be excellent value too, starting at around £50 for a single ticket from Brussels to London. Eurostar trains from Paris to London take 2.5 hours, while there is now a direct route from Amsterdam to London that takes just 3.75 hours.

FROM AUSTRALIA AND NEW ZEALAND

Generally, the best way to get to Scotland from Australasia is to fly via the Middle Eastern hubs. Flight time is around 22 hours, perhaps more depending on transfers. It's likely you'll also have to change in either London or at another European airport. However, **Emirates** (www.emirates.com) offers lots of routes, including a daily flight from Auckland to Edinburgh, via Dubai, meaning there's no need for another changeover in London or Europe.

FROM SOUTH AFRICA

From Africa, the best way to reach Scotland is via one of the European or Middle Eastern hub airports, or come via London. **British Airways** (www.britishairways.com) has long-haul flights from **Johannesburg** to London Heathrow, from where you can connect to Scotland.

Getting Around

BY CAR

For maximum freedom and some of the best road journeys ever, you can't beat having your own car.

Car Hire

There are car hire companies at all major airports; it's best to go with a recognized name because, although other companies may offer what appear to be cheaper deals, by the time you add on insurance, it's likely you'll be out of pocket. It is possible to leave car hire until you arrive—it's very unlikely all the cars will be out on hire—but booking ahead usually gets you the best deal. If you want to get a good idea of prices, **Travel Supermarket** (www.travelsupermarket.com) is pretty trustworthy, and companies such as **Avis** (www.avis.co.uk) and **Europcar** (www.europcar.co.uk) are fairly reliable.

Consider a few things when hiring a car in Scotland. Because a lot of cars are stick, you will have to request an automatic, which tends to be more expensive, at the time of booking. While car hire itself can cost as little as £10 a day, you will probably want to include some decent insurance (from around £10 a day) should you have an accident (even a minor scrape), whether it's your fault or not, or in the unlikely event that the car is stolen; plus, you'll need to pay extra for GPS and additions such as child safety seats. You will need to have your driving license with you as well as a credit card, with a decent credit limit and in the main driver's name, which will be taken as a deposit, and you should also be prepared to show your passport.

Road Rules and Driving in Scotland

In Scotland (and the rest of the United Kingdom) you need to drive on the left-hand side of the road. Make sure you adhere to speed limits because speed cameras lurk in unsuspecting places, ready to catch you out. Usually, there will be a sign stating the speed limit in miles per hour. Where there is not, assume a speed limit of 30 mph in built-up areas and 70 mph on motorways.

Outside the main cities, there is not a huge amount of roads to choose from—normally one main route between the main cities and towns, with only the odd detour possible. While this does make it fairly easy to navigate, once you enter rural Scotland or more remote areas (particularly on Skye), there's a good chance you will have to drive down single-track roads. As the name suggests, these roads allow for just a single lane of traffic, meaning you'll have to anticipate the road ahead and pull over into passing places to allow other traffic to pass (sometimes this means even pulling over to let eager cars behind you overtake).

BY TRAIN

A relatively good train system in Scotland links the main towns and cities. **ScotRail** (www.scotrail.co.uk) has tickets and details on timetables and connections. You should always buy a ticket before you board a train, where possible.

BY FERRY

Though there are a couple of smaller operators (mentioned in this book where necessary), the main ferry operator is **Caledonian MacBrayne,** or **CalMac** (www.calmac.co.uk), which runs good services between the mainland and isles, most of which you can take your car on board.

BY BUS

The main bus service for traveling between cities is **Scottish Citylink** (www.citylink.co.uk). Local bus services (such as those on Skye) are served by **Stagecoach** (www.stagecoachbus.com). If in doubt about a journey, check **Traveline** (www.traveline.info), an excellent resource for planning your route from point A to point B via public transport.

Visas and Officialdom

You should always check the U.K. and Foreign and Commonwealth Office's website (www. gov.uk/government/organisations/uk-visas-and-immigration) before you book travel for the latest advice about entry and visa requirements into the United Kingdom.

UNITED STATES AND CANADA

At present, travelers from the United States and Canada do not need a visa to visit Scotland (or indeed any part of the United Kingdom) if they are visiting for six months or less. If you are planning to stay for more than six months, then you will need an entry clearance certificate, obtained from the British embassy in your home nation before you travel.

The American consulate is located in Edinburgh (3 Regent Terrace; tel. 0131 556 8315; edinburgh-info@state.gov). There is no Canadian consulate in Scotland, so all enquiries should go through the High Commission of Canada in London (Canada House, Trafalgar Square; tel. 0207 004 6000, ldn@international.gc.ca).

EUROPEAN UNION/ SCHENGEN

Though the United Kingdom opted out of the Schengen Agreement of 1985, which allows for free movement between much of Europe with no borders, at present citizens of European Union (EU) countries, non-EU member states of the European Economic Area (EEA; Norway, Liechtenstein, and Iceland), and Switzerland are all free to enter the United Kingdom with no visa. Members of the Overseas Countries and Territories (OCT) are also exempt from needing a visa to enter the United Kingdom. However, the future of visa requirements from the EU currently hangs in the balance as the United Kingdom negotiates its effective divorce from the EU under Brexit.

Consulates for several European countries can be found in Edinburgh, including the French Consulate (11 Randolph Crescent; contact.edimbourg-fslt@diplomatie.gouv.fr), the Consulate General of the Federal Republic of Germany and Honorary Consulates of Germany (16 Eglinton Crescent; tel. 0131 337 2323, info@edin.auswaertiges-amt.de), the Netherlands Consulate (Baird House, 4 Lower Gilmore Bank; tel. 07731 553 120, hon.consul@netherlands-consulate.co.uk), and the Spanish Consulate (63 North Castle Street, Edinburgh; tel. 0131 220 1843, cog. edimburgo@maec.es).

AUSTRALIA AND NEW ZEALAND

Visitors from Australia and New Zealand also do not need a visa to visit Scotland for six months or less. For stays longer than six months, you will need an entry clearance certificate, obtained from the British embassy before you travel.

The Consulate of New Zealand is located in Edinburgh (c/o Blackadders, 5 Rutland Square; tel. 0131 222 8109, nzconsulscotland@gmail.com), but as of 2014 there is no longer an Australian Consulate in Scotland. All enquiries must go through the Australia High Commission in London (Strand, London; tel. 020 7379 4334).

SOUTH AFRICA

Travelers from South Africa will need a Standard Visitor visa (www.gov.uk/ standard-visitor-visa) to enter the United Kingdom, whether you are coming for a holiday, to visit friends and family, or for business. The standard cost for this visa is £93 and will normally allow you to stay for up to six months. You can apply up to three months before you travel and will normally get a decision within three weeks of applying. There is no South African consulate in Scotland.

All enquiries should go through the **High Commission of the Republic of South Africa** in London (South Africa House, Trafalgar Square; tel. 020 7451 7299).

CUSTOMS

Most goods in Britain (except for food and books) are subject to Value Added Tax (VAT), which is not always obvious but included in the advertised price. Visitors from non-EU countries can claim a lot of this money back (though not on hotel bills unfortunately) before they leave the United Kingdom. To benefit from this, you should get a VAT 407 form from the vendor at the point of sale (a lot of bigger retailers geared toward overseas travelers will have these) and then show this and your receipt to Customs before you leave. For more information, see www.gov.uk/tax-on-shopping/taxfree-shopping.

Recreation

GOLF

Though St. Andrews in Fife is undoubtedly the home of golf in Scotland, there are prestigious courses all over, many of them ancient in origin; in fact, Scotland has over 400 golf courses.

The Scots are widely celebrated for having introduced the United States to the game of golf—it has been played here since at least the start of the 15th century, but, while early courses were often just simple tracks overgrown with bushes and heather, today they are generally a lot smarter. Though the game had trickled out to other parts of the world before then, golf only really became popular outside Scotland from the 19th century onward when a boom for tourism to Scotland began. Suddenly, it became fashionable to partake in traditional Scottish pastimes.

Today, most courses will allow visitors, and green fees are usually advertised on their websites. There are numerous courses around Edinburgh, a few on the outskirts of Glasgow, including the very good **Dullatur Golf Club,** which has two greens (www.dullaturgolf.com). Lots of tour companies offer trips to see some of the more famous and celebrated of Scotland's golf courses, such as **Golf Scotland** (www.golfscotland.com), which organizes transfers and trips to the famous Old Links course in St. Andrews.

HIKING AND TREKKING

There are infinite possibilities for walking and hiking in Scotland, whether you want a gentle amble through bucolic landscape, or to bag your first munro. If you are going it alone, then **Walk Highlands** (www.walkhighlands.co.uk) is an essential resource of routes and advice, with trails reviewed by people who have actually completed them.

However, hiking in Scotland—especially in the cut-off Highlands—is not to be taken lightly, and each year many people get into trouble because they are not experienced navigators. Even if you have printed off a trail description and are armed with an **Ordnance Survey** (www.ordnancesurvey.co.uk) or a **Harveys map** (www.harveymaps.co.uk), it is your responsibility to ensure you plan ahead, are realistic about your (and your group's) abilities, come equipped with a compass (which may not work in some areas, such as Skye Cuillin due to the magnetic pull), are dressed in the appropriate clothing (hiking boots, wet-weather gear, etc.), and have taken safety measures. Together with **Mountaineering Scotland** (www.mountaineering.scot), Walk Highlands has issued some essential safety advice at www.walkhighlands.co.uk/safety, which I recommend familiarizing yourself with before embarking on any hill-walking or climbing in Scotland.

If all this sounds a bit serious, then book a guide to escort you on your expedition. **West Coast Mountain Guides** (www. westcoast-mountainguides.co.uk) offers bespoke year-round trips.

Festivals and Events

Exciting cultural events take place across Scotland throughout the year, though some months tend to have more than others.

AUGUST IN EDINBURGH

August is the busy time for festivals in Edinburgh (www.edinburghfestivalcity. com), when five artistic and cultural festivals converge to create one almost non-stop extravaganza of music, comedy, dance, art, and literature. The biggest of the five are the **Edinburgh International Festival** and the **Edinburgh Fringe Festival,** and the others running at the same time are the **Edinburgh Military Tattoo,** the **Edinburgh Art Festival,** and the **Edinburgh International Book Festival.**

NEW YEAR'S FESTIVALS AND EVENTS

Hogmanay (www.edinburghshogmanay. com) is a big deal in Edinburgh, but it doesn't have the monopoly on New Year's celebrations. Throughout Scotland, lots of exciting events ring in the New Year, including the **Red Hot Highland Fling** in Inverness (invernessfestivals.com).

Even if you are not staying in a city on New Year's Eve, there is a good chance you will be brought into the Scottish fold with the tradition of **First Footing.** This tradition dictates that the "first-footing" (i.e., first person to take a step) across the threshold of a house in the new year should come bearing presents in the shape of a wee dram, a lump of coal, and a coin (though it does vary from place to place); I have known this to happen even in a remote cottage on the edge of a Highlands loch, so be prepared for visitors.

TRADITIONAL FESTIVALS AND EVENTS

Lots of traditional music and Gaelic culture festivals are also held throughout Scotland, including the huge **Celtic Connections** (www.celticconnections.com) festival hosted in Glasgow each January, and of course a busy calendar of **Highland Games** held each summer in towns and villages throughout the Highlands May-September.

Accommodations

A wide range of accommodations is available throughout Scotland, from high-end **hotels** to quaint **B&Bs** and cozy **self-catering properties.** This being a land of big open spaces, there are also plenty of places making the most of the incredible scenery and offering more rustic and basic places to stay, from **bothies** for the brave (simple shelters located in remote locations that offer a "camping with walls" experience) to cozier **camping pods** for those who still need a few home comforts.

Wild camping is possible pretty much all over Scotland thanks to the **Outdoor Access Code,** which in essence allows you to camp on most parts of unenclosed land, but you should adhere to the "leave-no-trace" motto, which means taking your rubbish with you and removing all signs of campfires. There are a few exceptions—parts of Loch Lomond and the Trossachs National Park are subject to bylaws in the summer months to avoid overcrowding—and common sense should prevail,

so don't camp right by someone's house or obscure someone else's view unless you want a hostile reception.

History lovers will revel at the chance to stay in a bona fide castle or Victorian shooting lodge, while those who long for comforts of a more traditional kind will be happy in an old crofter's house, as long as there is a real fire to warm up by.

Most hotels and B&Bs are happy for you to stay for just the one night (although this may vary on weekends, particularly in cities), while a lot of self-catering cottages have a minimum week-long stay in spring and summer and shorter stays of three nights or more out of season.

Breakfast is normally included unless stated otherwise (except in camping pods and self-catering places), and for the most part you can book your stay with a credit card with no funds taken until you leave (again not generally the case with self-catering).

Food

Scottish food has had a bit of a Renaissance in recent years; while during the 1980s and 1990s there was a drive toward international flavors that were considered more sophisticated, now there is a massive trend for serving local and wholly seasonal produce.

WHISKY AND GIN

Whisky is to Scotland what tea is to England. Whisky production takes place across five main regions: Campbeltown, the Highlands, Islay, the Lowlands, and Speyside. Each region brings its own flavors to the whisky. On the Isle of Islay, for instance, where whiskymaking goes back centuries, distilleries on the southeast of the island draw on heavily peated malt. However, whisky isn't the only

drink produced here—70 percent of the **gin** produced in the United Kingdom is made in Scotland, including James Bond's favorite tipple, Gordon's. And as gin is the fastest growing spirit in Scotland, new distilleries are popping up all the time, such as **Pickering's Summerhall** in Edinburgh, which when it opened in 2013 was the first gin-exclusive distillery to open in Edinburgh for 150 years.

SCOTTISH CUISINE

Scotland is quite rightly famed for its national dishes such as **haggis** (a dish of spiced sheep's heart, liver, and lungs, which tastes a lot nicer than it sounds and is the pinnacle of any Burns Night) served with **neeps** (swede, or rutabaga) and **tatties** (potatoes).

However, over the last decade Scottish cuisine has become somewhat more refined. The Isle of Skye boasts one Michelin-starred restaurant and a couple of others worthy of the honor too, and restaurants are responding to an increased interest in food provenance. Local fare now takes pride of place on menus, from Aberdeen Angus beef to shellfish still salty from the sea, to Stornoway black pudding and Arbroath smokies (a type of smoked haddock).

Other dishes you should look for are Cullen skink, a deliciously creamy fish stew, and Cranachan, a dessert made of oats, cream, whisky, and raspberries.

SEAFOOD

With miles and miles of coastline, it is fitting that seafood now features heavily on menus in Scotland, particularly along the coast and on the islands such as Skye and the Small Isles. For a long time, although the seas around Skye were rich with fish and shellfish, locals didn't get a look in as no sooner was it fished or plucked from the sea than it was ferried off elsewhere for a huge export business. Now, finally, locals (and visitors) are able to taste it too.

VEGANS AND VEGETARIANS

Vegans and vegetarians are excellently catered for in major cities, particularly in Glasgow, which is shedding its reputation for serving up deep-fried Mars bars and which actually has a thriving and hugely exciting vegan food scene.

Conduct and Customs

On the most part, Scottish people are very friendly and welcoming and keen to show off their homeland; however, there are some things you should be aware of. Though it is officially part of the United Kingdom, a large percentage of Scottish people consider themselves an independent nation and will take umbrage at being called British. Always err on the side of caution and be careful to make a distinction between the English and Scottish—the recent Scottish referendum over whether it should officially separate from the rest of the United Kingdom was a close-run thing and is still very raw for many.

In general, politics can be quite a divisive subject, particularly if heading into the murky waters of Brexit, so best steer clear. Similarly, sport can bring out the passionate side of even the meekest character.

Manners are important. Saying please and thank you and looking someone in the eye when you talk to them will take you a long way, whether it's someone you've stopped for directions or the taxi driver taking you back to your hotel.

Many Scottish superstitions center on traditional professions. Fishermen, for instance, observe many omens to keep them safe at sea. The words *rabbit, pig,* and *salmon* are deemed bad luck (perhaps because they were powerful symbols of Celtic gods), and many a sailor has turned around and headed back home after seeing a minister or even a woman on the way to their boat.

Health and Safety

As with all major cities, Glasgow and Edinburgh aren't without their problems. While Edinburgh particularly is relatively safe, you would do well to steer clear of the Meadows, Grassmarket, Cowgate, Tollcross, and Lothian Road after dark. Similarly, you'll need to keep your wits about you in Glasgow late at night, particularly around Sauchiehall Street when all the pubs and clubs kick out. The city does also have a bit of a drug problem, and neds (Scottish slang for gangs of men often looking for trouble) should be avoided. Social problems are less common in more rural areas where you will feel pretty safe; you'll be taken aback by how warmly local communities welcome you in.

Weather can be a hindrance in Scotland. In summer, midges (tiny flying biting insects that tend to travel in clouds) are very common, and you'll need spray to keep them at bay (particularly if camping). If you are planning to do a big trek in the wilderness, be warned that weather conditions can change quickly. Make sure you bring plenty of water and a map with you and let someone know where you are going and when to expect you back.

You do not need any vaccinations to visit the United Kingdom. At present all EU citizens are also entitled to free health care at National Health Service (NHS) hospitals and clinics on production of a European Health Insurance Card (EHIC). In addition, there are also reciprocal arrangements with residents of Australia and New Zealand. However, visitors from the United States, Canada, and South Africa, as well as lots of other non-EEA countries, do need to ensure they have travel insurance and/or health care to cover them for their visit.

If you are from a non-EEA country and have a medical emergency or accident and need to be treated by an accident and emergency department, you will not be liable for the initial urgent treatment, but it's possible that any further care, such as the admittance to hospital, would incur a charge.

Practical Details

WHAT TO PACK

There's a hackneyed phrase in Scotland: there's no such thing as bad weather, just the wrong clothes. With weather unpredictable to say the least, you need to be ready, whatever the weather. Unfortunately, this means packing lots. If you're visiting from April to September, you'll need jumpers (sweaters) and coats to keep you warm but also shorts and t-shirts (the sun does come out occasionally here, and you'll want to be prepared when it does). If coming in winter, a good range of thermals, jeans, trousers, and layers should serve you well. If you are planning to do any reasonably rough walking, you will need a good pair of hiking boots, some kind of insect repellent for the dreaded midges—locals swear by Avon Skin So Soft for keeping them at bay—and long sleeves to minimize the biting when they are at their hungriest (summer evenings).

You'll also want a good camera to capture the incredible sights, possibly some binoculars if you want to be able to identify some of the wildlife you do spot, and of course some swimwear for all that wild swimming.

MONEY
Exchange Rates and Currency Exchange
Like the rest of the United Kingdom, the currency is the British pound sterling. You may

notice a slight difference in some of the notes north of the border to those found in England; the Bank of Scotland prints its own notes, which feature prominent Scotsmen and the occasional Scotswoman. Although they look different to English notes, they are still legal tender in the whole of the United Kingdom, though you may have a problem trying to convince a bus driver or local shopkeeper in England of that.

As of late 2018, £1 was worth USD$1.30, €1.13, CAD$1.71, AUD$1.83, NZD$1.98, or R 18.9, but with constant fluctuations these rates change all the time. For the most up-to-date exchange rates, go to www.xe.com.

The best exchange rates can be found in banks, and most reasonably sized towns will have one (though not many villages—indeed some more remote places just have a mobile bank that visits once a week that aren't really geared up for currency exchange). You'll need to visit during business hours (usually 9am-4pm Mon.-Fri., with occasional Sat. morning openings in the cities). Post offices, which operate similar business hours to banks, are another option, and Marks and Spencer also does decent rates of exchange inside its stores. If you need to get cash outside normal business hours, you can visit a bureau de change, but these do give the worst rates (even if they make a big fuss about the fact you won't be charged to change your money).

Alternatively, you can take money out of an ATM (cash machine) connected to one of the main high-street banks (Royal Bank of Scotland, Lloyds, etc.) using a debit card that doesn't charge an overseas transaction fee (check with your home bank), which can be found all over Glasgow and Edinburgh.

Credit Cards and ATMs

Though you can pretty much pay for anything on card in Glasgow and Edinburgh, in more remote parts of Scotland (along the west coast and parts of Skye) where Internet access is sketchy to say the least, cash is king, so it is always an idea to carry just enough on you for a day or two. ATMs are everywhere in the cities, and there's one in most towns, but in some little villages locals rely on the little post office for money, which is only possible if you have a U.K. bank card.

VISA and Mastercard are the most readily accepted credit cards in Scotland. Some smaller enterprises don't accept American Express, although this is improving, and be prepared to be charged a small fee (around 50p) if you use your card to buy small purchases (such as under £10), particularly in smaller establishments.

Tipping

Tipping is only really necessary in restaurants (about 12.5 percent) and some high-end hotels where the amount is discretionary. Don't tip at a bar unless it's particularly posh.

OPENING HOURS

Normal shop opening hours are 9am-5pm Monday to Saturday, with a little variation either end. In cities, such as Glasgow and Edinburgh, you can expect most shops to be open from around 10am-4pm at least on Sundays too, but in more remote areas Sunday closing is common—indeed in the Western Isles where the Free Church of Scotland has quite a strong hold, it was virtually forbidden for shops to open (or for people to do any work at all) on Sundays until recently.

Thursday is often late-night shopping in cities, particularly when it comes to shopping malls and big department stores, and shops will often stay open until 8pm. Large supermarkets, such as Sainsbury's and Tesco, often stay open as late as 10pm, which is useful if you are arriving late and need to stock up for a cottage or house.

Traditionally, pubs open from 11am-11pm Monday to Saturday and from midday-10:30pm on Sundays; however, a relaxing of licensing laws back in 2005 means that pubs can apply for an extension to this, and most pubs will stay open until at least midnight (or 1am on Fridays and Saturdays) as long as there are enough customers.

PUBLIC HOLIDAYS

Each year a set number of days is put aside for public holidays across Scotland when lots of businesses will close (although in tourism hot spots many will still stay open), and hotels and restaurants may become busier and require a bit more forward planning. So raucous are Hogmanay celebrations across Scotland that both New Year's Day and January 2nd are deemed public holidays each year. If a public holiday (such as St. Andrew's Day, which is officially November 30th) falls on a weekend, it is normally substituted for a weekday, usually the following Monday. The Scottish public holidays are as follows (dates given are for 2019-2020, so verify for the year you are traveling to Scotland):

- **April 19:** Good Friday
- **April 21:** Easter Sunday
- **May 6:** Early May Bank Holiday
- **May 27:** Spring Bank Holiday
- **August 5:** Summer Bank Holiday
- **December 2:** St. Andrew's Day
- **December 25:** Christmas Day
- **December 26:** Boxing Day
- **January 1:** New Year's Day
- **January 2:** day after New Year's

COMMUNICATIONS
Phones and Cell Phones

Before you leave home, make sure your mobile phone is compatible with the United Kingdom's GSM technology as otherwise you may not be able to use a lot of your phone's functions. In Glasgow, Edinburgh, Inverness, and most big towns you are likely to have good phone reception. However, in large parts of the Highlands it is virtually non-existent, so, if you are traveling around, you need to get out of the habit of relying on your phone for navigation or as a point of contact. If someone might need to get hold of you, forward them the number of your accommodation.

Internet Access

Wireless Internet, 3G, and 4G and are all good in the cities, less so in smaller towns, and pretty terrible on the islands. Get into the habit of checking email when you are somewhere built up for a day or two (even if this means planning ahead a little), and then enjoy the fact that you are no longer ruled by that tiny machine in your pocket.

Shipping and Postal Service

You may be surprised to learn that even the

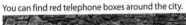
You can find red telephone boxes around the city.

Unique Gifts

Glasgow is the undisputed shopping capital of Scotland with everything from major brands, independent boutiques, and designer labels along its "style mile." However, for a more meaningful purchase, you can't beat buying something unique to Scotland. For those with a family connection to Scotland, tracing ancestry will reveal the traditional tartan of one's clan, from which a **kilt** can be made to measure by a number of reputable tailors. Scotland's only sheep tannery is on Skye, perfect for **woolly slippers,** and you will also want to pick up some **cashmere**—some of the finest in the world is made right here in Scotland—and of course it's almost criminal to leave without purchasing a bottle of whisky.

tiniest of villages tends to have a post office, albeit one that's just an adjunct to a local shop. You can normally find somewhere to get stamps to send postcards home, but for anything a bit more involved (wiring money, for example) you might have to do a little bit of research or head to a larger town.

While you are allowed to bring a liter of alcohol home with you in your checked luggage, you may prefer to take advantage of some of the shipping packages offered by whisky vendors, such as **Royal Mile Whiskies** (www.royalmilewhiskies.com), which can arrange for up to six standard 70 cl (23.7 oz) bottles of whisky to be sent to your home in one shipment (this is a legal limitation and more shipments can be arranged). At £49 for the shipment of one bottle, or £164 for seven, it's not cheap, but it can save you a lot of hassle when on holiday. Alternatively, you could wait until you get home—the United States has a good market of single malts and blended Scotch at the moment. In addition, many high-end kilt and tartan retailers also ship around the world.

WEIGHTS AND MEASURES

The United Kingdom uses metric measurements (grams, kilograms, milliliters, or liters) on all goods sold here, with a few exceptions. Beer and cider from the pump are still sold in pints or half-pint measures, milk in glass bottles normally comes in pints, and precious metals are measured by troy ounce.

TOURIST INFORMATION
Tourist Offices

VisitScotland operates satellite tourist offices throughout Scotland, which are known as **iCentres** and are open year-round. They are not located absolutely everywhere, but there is usually one not far from major attractions and it's a good place to book tours, find local restaurant and hotel recommendations, and even buy public transport tickets if you are not confident booking them online.

In **Edinburgh** the iCentre is in the heart of the city, right near **Waverley Station** (3 Princes Street, Edinburgh; tel. 0131 473 3868). **Glasgow's iCentre** is centrally located in the middle of the **Style Mile** (156a/158 Buchanan Street, Glasgow; tel. 0141 566 4083). In **Inverness,** you can book Loch Ness trips through the city's iCentre **near the castle** (36 High Street, Inverness; tel. 01463 252 401). On **Skye,** there is just one iCentre, in the main town of **Portree** (Bayfield House, Bayfield Road, Portree; tel. 01478 612 992.

Tourism Websites

The overriding tourist board for the whole of the United Kingdom is **VisitBritain** (www. visitbritain.com), but for more specific information on Scotland, **VisitScotland** is the place to go (www.visitscotland.org).

For Edinburgh, you can also visit www. edinburgh.org, while www.peoplemakeglasgow. com is an excellent source of information on Glasgow. And if you're visiting Loch Lomond, www.lochlomond-trossachs.org is a treasure trove of information on what to do, what to see, and where to stay in the park.

Maps

Ordnance Survey (OS) maps (www. ordnancesurvey.co.uk) are the most exhaustive and useful for hikes and long walks and absolutely essential if attempting any of the munros. **Harveys Maps** (www. harveymaps.co.uk) are also very useful, and some find them a lot clearer than the OS ones. Both sets of maps can be picked up from a good bookshop or a well-stocked outdoors shop, as well as purchased online before you travel.

Traveler Advice

OPPORTUNITIES FOR STUDY AND EMPLOYMENT

There are lots of excellent universities in Scotland; indeed, it is home to some of the oldest universities in the world. A good place to start your research is **Study in Scotland** (www.studyinscotland.org), which details Scotland's 19 universities and also has information on visas and available scholarships and bursaries.

In addition, **Work Away** (www.workaway. info) lists lots of work opportunities in Scotland that will pair you up with hosts offering jobs, from working on a croft in the Highlands to working at a hostel. Bear in mind, if you do plan to work or study here, you will need to get a visa.

ACCESS FOR TRAVELERS WITH DISABILITIES

While big attractions such as Edinburgh Castle and the Palace of Holyroodhouse are well adapted for disabled visitors, because of the nature of some of the sights in Scotland, not all of them are suitable for people with mobility issues, and Scotland does so far seem a bit slow on the uptake in terms of making places more accessible.

Tours are a good option for people with limited mobility, and obviously some are better than others. **Equal Adventure Developments** (www.equaladventure. org), based in Aviemore, is one organization committed to ensuring disabled travelers don't miss out on the sense of adventure in Scotland and can arrange outdoor activities and adventure sports. In Edinburgh, local guide **Margot McMurdo** has tours that cater for disabled travelers (www.aboutscotland. com/tour/guide/access.html).

Wheelchair users and blind or partially sighted travelers are eligible for a big discount on trains with the **Disabled Persons Railcard** (www.disabledpersons-railcard. co.uk), for you and a friend. In theory, all trains should have wheelchair assistance, but in practice this isn't always the case, especially in quieter stations that are not always manned (particularly out of high season).

Uneven ground around many ruins and cleared or abandoned villages have often been left as they were, and many of the walks and hikes are unsuitable for wheelchairs.

Most hotels and places to stay will try to have accessible rooms, and, where this is not possible, they normally make it clear on their website. However, it is advisable to ring and check if you are at all unsure.

TRAVELING WITH CHILDREN

Children love the wide open spaces and freedom that being in Scotland affords. Wildlife is abundant, in the skies, seas, grasses, and moors, much to their delight. Simply going for a woodland walk can be a huge adventure, searching for trails or faeries and obviously looking out for a certain mysterious monster along the shores of Loch Ness.

Most restaurants and pubs have tapped into family tourism and usually offer a kid's menu, though it can be a bit heavy on the nuggets and burgers. Children under three often go free into attractions, travel on buses and trains is free for children under five, and you are rarely if ever asked to prove it. If your children are over five, **ScotRail** offers a **Kids Go Free Ticket** that allows an adult to travel with two kids aged 5-15 for just the price of an adult fare.

WOMEN TRAVELING ALONE

Scotland is a relatively safe place to travel as a woman, with low crime rates in much of rural Scotland, but there are still some things you should do to stay safe.

Obviously in larger cities such as Glasgow and Edinburgh where social issues are more prevalent (petty crime, drug abuse, heavy drinking), it pays to be a bit cautious. Don't leave your drink unattended and don't walk alone at night if you can at all avoid it, particularly in an area you are unfamiliar with or if you are intoxicated. Don't accept a minicab off the street. If you need to get a cab, book one from a trusted number (better still, ask the pub or restaurant to ring one for you) or hail an official taxi, which are easy to identify by the "taxi" light on top.

SENIOR TRAVELERS

Travelers over the age of 60 can expect concessions at most paid-for attractions and leisure activities such as the cinema. If it's not offered to you, it's always worth asking.

Be aware that many of Scotland's more historic sights can have uneven ground around them, and a lot of attractions, particularly ruined castles and historic properties, do involve a fair bit of walking so require a good level of fitness.

LGBTQ TRAVELERS

Scotland is a relatively open-minded country, accepting people as they come, so LGBTQ tourists can look forward to a warm welcome like everyone else. Some hotels and B&Bs are very vocal about being gay-friendly, but don't take that to mean that those that don't aren't—it's a rarity that you will come across any hostility.

February in Scotland is LGBTQ month, and there are lots of events taking place in major cities to celebrate. In June, Edinburgh's vibrant and embracing Pride Scotia takes place, while Glasgow's Pride takes place in July in Kelvingrove Park. Both cities have bubbling gay scenes, with cool bars and clubs attracting diverse crowds.

If you want to find out more about the lesbian, gay, bisexual, and transgender scene in Scotland, go to www.lgbt.scot.

TRAVELERS OF COLOR

With major universities and a booming tourism industry, Scotland is increasingly a multicultural country. That said, it still falls way behind England in terms of geographical spread of different ethnicities. Most people of color live in busier, more built-up places such as Glasgow and Edinburgh, and the islands and more remote communities are still predominantly white. Scotland is generally very tolerant, and you should not expect to come across any racist behavior. If you do, report it to the police as it is a hate crime.

Resources

Glossary

To follow is a list of terms, together with an explanation of their meaning, that you will find used frequently within Scotland and the pages of this guide.

ben: a mountain, as in Ben Nevis

blackhouse: a traditional thatched cottage found in the Highlands or islands, usually with thick drystone walls; there was normally a fire in the middle of the room with no chimney, so the smoke went through the roof and caused the soot to blacken the interior, hence the name.

bothy: a Scottish hut or basic dwelling, usually located in the mountains or more remote areas, where rural workers once sought refuge but which are now often used by hikers or campers looking for shelter

broch: a circular stone tower, unique to Scotland, that dates from the Iron Age

burn: a stream, smaller than a river, that is often the main source of water for a village or settlement

cairn: found throughout Scotland, these mounds of stones are often used as a landmark (such as on the summit of a mountain); there are also lots of prehistoric chambered cairns, believed to have once been used for burials

ceilidh: a lively social event with Gaelic music, singing, and dancing

clan: a close-knit group of families, usually originating from the Scottish Highlands, who share a kinship and a connection to the same ancestral ground

coos: slang for cow, when referring to Highland cows (Heilan' coo)

coorie: a Scottish word meaning to snuggle, or get cozy, which is often now used to describe a wellness trend that encourages embracing small Scottish pleasures

corbett: the name given to mountains in Scotland 2,500-3,000 feet (762-914 m) high

corrie: a steep-sided hollow, often found on mountainsides or valleys

crannog: an ancient home, often built on stilts, found in Scottish lochs

crofter: a person who farms a croft (plot of land)

dram: a small drink of an alcoholic spirit—in Scotland, usually whisky

faerie: an alternative spelling of *fairy,* a mythical being that appears in many a folktale

first-foot: the first person to cross the threshold of a house on New Year's

firth: narrow inlet of the sea

gillie: someone who accompanies you on a fishing or hunting trip

glen: a narrow valley

howff: a welcoming meeting place, normally a pub

Highlands: This refers to a region that encompasses much of the northern two-thirds of Scotland and includes many mountain ranges. The Highlands was traditionally home to clans, many of whom descended from the Gaels. Since the mid-19th century, it has been sparsely populated.

Hogmanay: the name for New Year's Eve in Scotland; the term originated in the 17th century, perhaps of Norman French origin

Kelpie: a sinister water spirit that often pops

up in Scottish folklore, normally takes the form of a horse; there is said to be one in Loch Coruisk on the Isle of Skye—and often takes pleasure in the drowning of sailors

kilt: a knee-length pleated skirt of tartan, traditionally worn by Highlanders

kirk: a church; sometimes used to differentiate between the Church of Scotland and the Church of England

laird: estate owner

loch: in Scotland it can be used to describe a lake (often landlocked) or an inlet of the sea

Lowlands: a region of relatively low-lying land that lies south and east of the Highlands

machair: a fertile grassy plain enriched by sand blown in from the coast, where wildlife and wildflowers are in abundance

manse: the home or, more often, former home of a minister of the clergy

munro: a mountain in Scotland that is at least 3,000 feet (914 m) high

mushy peas: a side dish of mashed peas, which usually accompanies fish and chips

Scotch: Related to Scotch whisky, this is malt or grain whisky made in Scotland that must be aged for a minimum of three years. Most Scottish people do not respond well to being labelled "Scotch" themselves; they prefer to reserve the term for whisky or Scotch eggs (a hard-boiled egg wrapped in sausage meat, covered in breadcrumbs, and deep-fried; it isn't actually uniquely Scottish but eaten all over the UK)

single malt: whisky containing water and malted barley only (no other cereals) from a single distillery

sporran: part of Highland dress, this small pouch hangs from round the waist at the front of a kilt

tartan: woolen cloth woven in a pattern of checks or crossed lines that is usually associated with a particular Scottish clan or region

thane: a title often held by a clan chief, who was awarded land by the Scottish king

Tweed: a rough woolen cloth, renowned for its hardiness; originating from Scotland, it is typically woven of spun wool of different colors, giving it a speckled finish

Weegie: a slang term for someone from Glasgow, can sometimes be seen as derogatory so use sparingly

wynd: a narrow passageway

Scottish Phrases

The main language spoken in Scotland is English (or as some like to call it, Scottish English). It's much the same as standard English with the same spellings but has a lot of variation in slang and pronunciation (words such as *wee* and *muckle* are part of common parlance in Scottish English but not in standard English).

As many as 30 percent of the population speaks Scots, sometimes referred to as Lowland Scots, to some extent, and it is now being taught in schools once again. Similarly, Gaelic is still spoken in pockets of Scotland, particularly in the Outer Hebrides and parts of Skye. Of course, even if all the people you encounter speak English, different accents and dialects may still leave you baffled, and one thing you should bear in mind is that Scottish people like to abbreviate . . . a lot. Below is a list of common phrases and words you will undoubtedly come across regularly.

auld: old, as in "Auld Reekie," a nickname for Edinburgh

aye: yes

nay: no

blether: what the English might call "small talk," to blether is simply to chat about not very much; you'll always find someone happy to blether with you

boggin': something that's horrible, often used to describe wet and miserable weather

bonnie: something beautiful—the "bonnie" shores of Loch Ness

braw: something good or pleasing; it can also mean finely dressed

dae: do

dinnae: slang for "I don't"

dreich: dreary or bleak—usually used in reference to the weather

guid: pronounced "gid," it quite simply means "good"

havenae: have not

ken: know, as in "Ah dinnae ken," or "I don't know"

laddie: a young man or boy

lassie: a young woman or girl

mingin': really unpleasant—again, it is often used to describe the weather

muckle: a lot, or big

nae bother: not a problem

reek: bad smell as in "Auld Reekie"

roastin': really, really hot, as in "it's roastin'" on a sunny day

scran: food, usually something tasty

wee: little—a much-used adjective to describe pretty much anything

yer: your

Suggested Reading and Songs

There is a huge wealth of tomes dedicated to Scotland, its landscape, and its history. There is also a large number of books written by Scottish authors that in some way were inspired by the land of their home, from the brooding, gloomy graveyards, alleyways, and Gothic buildings of Edinburgh and Glasgow that helped shape J. K. Rowling's hugely popular series of *Harry Potter* books, to the childhood imaginings of J. M. Barrie, author of the magical *Peter Pan*. Below is a list of books, poems, and songs that I believe will enrich your travels in Scotland and give you a deeper understanding of its geography, history, culture, people, and perhaps most importantly its humor.

EDINBURGH

The Prime of Miss Jean Brodie, Muriel Spark, 1961. Set in 1930s Edinburgh, this novel penned by the famously wry Spark is a witty read that uses Edinburgh as its backdrop, perhaps even its heroine, in a tale about a teacher in her "prime" who singles out some girls to impart her wisdom on love, travel, fascism, and her subsequent downfall.

The Strange Case of Dr. Jekyll and Mr. Hyde, Robert Louis Stevenson, 1886. If you want a story to really bring to life the dark, Gothic mystery of Victorian Edinburgh, then this is it. Stevenson wrote several classic fictions, including *Kidnapped* and *Treasure Island*, but his tale of the dual character of Dr. Jekyll and his alter ego Mr. Hyde—perhaps based on someone known to Stevenson—is arguably his best.

The Inspector Rebus Books, Ian Rankin. There is something about Edinburgh, perhaps it's the brooding buildings or the constant threat of rain, that has led many a writer to set crime thrillers here. Ian Rankin's series of books about his detective, Rebus, have been hugely successful and usually begin with a murder or other crime that Rebus and the reader must solve together. There are 22 books in the Rebus collection of "tartan noir" mysteries and counting; start at the beginning with *Knots and Crosses*.

GLASGOW

No Mean City, H. Kingsley Long, 1935. Set in the Gorbals, a slum part of the city that is largely knocked down now, this gritty tale amid the city razor gangs doesn't paint the most flattering picture of Glasgow, but it does give a realistic portrayal of what life was like for the working classes in the city between the wars.

The Dear Green Place, Archie Hind, 1966. This novel, set in the Southside of Glasgow in the 1960s, also depicts working-class life in Glasgow, this time post-war. It mirrors the author's experiences of growing up in the city and his dilemma of whether he should follow the family into work in the slaughterhouse or find his way as a writer so much that it could even be considered part memoir. Either way, the sense of time and place depicted is unmistakable.

SKYE AND SURROUNDS

Over the Sea to Skye, Alastair Alpin MacGregor, 1930. This travelogue written by Scottish writer, photographer, and folklore expert, Alpin MacGregor (he wrote prolifically on Scotland) is a great introduction to the history and stories of the isle and is still hugely relevant nearly 100 years later.

Calum's Road, Robert Hutchinson, 2008. A fantastic account of the story of Calum MacLeod, the man who pretty much single-handedly built a road linking the far north of the isle of Raasay with the other islands. Told by journalist Hutchinson, who met with MacLeod many times and spoke with former neighbors, it's a great tale of endurance and one man's commitment to preserving the way of life he has always known.

HISTORY AND BACKGROUND

The History of Scotland, Neil Oliver, 2010. From its geological origins, through its early settlers, colonists, and bloody power battles, archaeologist Oliver weaves the story of Scotland together in a way that is both digestible and utterly enthralling.

Waverley, Sir Walter Scott, 1814. Scott's first foray into prose fiction, which tells the story of an English gentleman in the lead up to the Jacobite Rebellion of 1745, proved hugely successful. Other books followed, including *Rob Roy* in 1817, and so the romantic depiction of the Highlanders had begun.

A Journey to the Western Isles of Scotland, Samuel Johnson, 1775. This travelogue, written from the point of view of lexicographer Johnson (often called Dr. Johnson), depicts an 83-day journey that Johnson and his good friend, Scotsman James Boswell, took in 1773. The book is often published in one volume with Boswell's account, *A Journal of a Tour to the Hebrides,* to show the differing perspectives of the same trip.

HUMOR

Made in Scotland: My Grand Adventures in a Wee Country, Billy Connolly, 2018. Born and bred in Glasgow, Billy Connolly is one of the city's most famous exports. His unique, self-deprecating humor and art of storytelling have led to international recognition. In this book he tells of his travels in Scotland and why he is so proud to hail from here, even though he now lives in America.

Whisky Galore, Compton Mackenzie, 1947. This comic novel, turned into an Ealing comedy and remade in 2017, imagines what would happen if a small Hebridean isle were to run out of whisky. The island's menfolk go into a type of mourning until a government ship with thousands of cases of whisky runs aground off its shores. Cue lots of japes as the islanders plot to replenish their stores, and then some.

LANDSCAPE AND WILDLIFE

Findings, Kathleen Jamie, 2005. If you want to tap into the natural world of Scotland, then there really is no better book to encourage you to take your time and look, listen, and appreciate all that is going on around you.

POETRY

Robert Burns: The Scottish Bard, O. B. Duane, 1997. Scotland's national bard understood the character of Scotland more than any other and wrote of it so brilliantly in the language of Scots. This anthology, which includes some of his finest poems, is a great introduction to his work.

Hallaig and Other Poems: Selected Poems of Sorley MacLean, Angus Peter Campbell and Aonghas MacNeacail, 2014. This book's namesake poem, which hauntingly tells the story of the cleared village of Hallaig, invokes a sense of loss and longing that is so prevalent in MacLean's work—inspired so much as it was by the Highland Clearances.

SONGS

"The Skye Boat Song." This song, often quoted, stirs a sense of patriotism among listeners whenever it is played. It tells the story of Bonnie Prince Charlie's escape, aided by Flora Macdonald, from Uist to the Isle of Skye. The song only entered the folklore cannon in the late 19th century when Anne Campbelle MacLeod supposedly first heard the Gaelic air being sung by boatmen who ferried her across Loch Coruisk on Skye, with lyrics added by songwriter Sir Harold Boulton.

"Flower of Scotland." The unofficial national anthem of Scotland, this song, sung with gusto at many a wedding and sporting celebration, was written in the 1960s by Roy Williamson of the band the Corries and remembers Robert the Bruce's unexpected defeat of King Edward II of England at the Battle of Bannockburn in 1314.

Internet Resources

ACCOMMODATIONS
BOOKING.COM
www.booking.com
This resource is a good place to initially compare prices and availability. It's easy to navigate, with options for all budgets, and it allows you to book directly with small B&Bs, often at slightly lower rates than you would otherwise pay.

AIRBNB
www.airbnb.co.uk
A lot of self-catering apartments and houses for hire are now only bookable through Airbnb, but at least it offers a degree of security.

SYKES COTTAGES
www.sykescottages.co.uk
These good standard cottages and houses can be hired across Scotland and are realistically priced.

HIKING
WALK HIGHLANDS
www.walkhighlands.co.uk
Walk Highlands is an incomparable resource for hiking routes and trekking advice across Scotland.

TRANSPORTATION
SCOTRAIL
www.scotrail.co.uk
Visit ScotRail for details on train routes and connections across Scotland, as well as online tickets.

CALEDONIAN MACBRAYNE
www.calmac.co.uk
CalMac is the main ferry operator for trips to the islands.

CALEDONIAN SLEEPER

www.sleeper.scot

Take the Caledonian Sleeper for overnight train travel from London to Scotland.

STAGECOACH

www.stagecoachbus.com

Stagecoach provides the majority of local bus services throughout Scotland.

CITYLINK

www.citylink.co.uk

Use Citylink for buses between the main cities in Scotland.

TRAFFIC SCOTLAND

trafficscotland.org

Traffic Scotland provides up-to-date travel news for drivers.

MEDIA

SCOTSMAN

www.scotsman.com

The *Scotsman* is the main newspaper covering Scotland as a whole.

LGBT SCOTLAND

www.lgbt.scot

LGBT Scotland is a brilliant resource for lesbian, gay, bisexual, and transgender travelers in Scotland.

ANCESTRY

SCOTLANDSPEOPLE

www.scotlandspeople.gov.uk

Use this invaluable resource to research your Scottish family history.

BLOGS

TRAVELS WITH A KILT

travelswithakilt.com

An excellent blog by Scotsman and eternal traveler Neil Robertson, this site is full of local insight and inspiring travel tales.

Index

exports: 381

F

Fairy Bridge: 355
Fairy Glen: 352–353
Fairy Pools: 339
Falkirk: 244
Falkirk Wheel: 117, 122, 244
Falls of Clyde: 127, 188, 189–190
Falls of Dochart and Stone Circle Killin: 205–206
Falls of Falloch: 202–203, 206
Falls of Foyers: 289
Falls of Glomach: 330
Famous Grouse (Glenturret Distillery): 254
Fellow Glasgow Residents mural: 141
female solo travelers, tips for: 399
Fergusson Gallery: 252, 254
ferries: 368–369, 386, 388; Skye/Western
    Highlands 312, 326, 333, 335, 337, 368–369;
    Southern Highlands 217, 224–225, 233, 234,
    242
Fesi Lle festival: 241
festivals and events: 391; Edinburgh 84–87;
    Glasgow 170; Highlands 22, 207, 241, 272
Fingal's Table: 225, 230
Finlaggan: 239
Finnieston: 132, 161; map: 146–147
Fionnphort: 224
First Footing tradition: 391
fishing: 275, 291
Flodigarry Path: 352
Flora Macdonald's Memorial: 351
flowers: 373
folklore: 287, 323, 331, 355, 356
food: 392–393; Edinburgh 97–106; Glasgow
    173–179; see also specific place
football (soccer): 153, 158–159
forests: 372–373
Fort Augustus: 284
Fort George: 282
Forth and Clyde Canal Path: 132, 157
Forth Bridge: 115–116
Fort William: 25, 258, 296–303, 318, 325
Four, The: 152, 383
Foyers: 284
France: 33, 377
Fringe Festival (Edinburgh): 85–86

G

Gaelic (language): 382–383, 401
Gaelic festivals: 391
Gaels: 377
Gallanach beach: 367
Gallery of Modern Art (GOMA, Glasgow): 129, 142
Galmisdale: 365

gardens: Edinburgh 59, 70, 72; Glasgow 145,
    154–156; Highlands 206–207, 270, 335, 356
Gauge O' Model Railway: 122
gay and lesbian travelers, tips for: 129, 399
geography: 370–371
geology: 88, 303, 351–352
George IV, King of England: 380
George Square: 129
Georgian House, The: 62–63
Geowalks: 88
ghosts: 56–57, 88
gifts, shopping for: 94, 95, 173, 291, 397
gin distilleries and tasting: 10, 27, 32, 68, 71, 170,
    272, 392
Girvans: 276
Glad Café, The: 169
Gladstone's Land: 49
glamping: 111
Glasgow: 7, 18–19, 24, 28, 126–190, 371, 394;
    accommodations 182–185; festivals 170; food
    173–179; information/services 185; maps 130–
    131, 134–135; nearby 188–190; neighborhoods
    129–132; nightlife/entertainment 159,
    161–169; recreation/sports 154–159; shopping
    170–173, 397; sights 136–154; transportation
    22–23, 185–188
Glasgow Airport: 185
Glasgow Botanic Gardens: 145
Glasgow Boys: 148, 150, 383
Glasgow Cathedral: 127, 128, 142–144
Glasgow Central Station: 186
Glasgow Central Station Tour: 159
Glasgow Green: 132, 154
Glasgow Life: 185
Glasgow Panda: 141
Glasgow Prestwick Airport: 185–186
Glasgow Royal Concert Hall: 164
Glasgow School of Art: 129, 136–137, 383
Glasgow Science Centre: 153
Glasgow's Grand Ole Opry: 168–169
"Glasgow Style": 152, 383
Glasgow Tower: 153
Glasgow Whisky Festival: 170
Glaswegian phrases: 160
Glen Affric: 328
Glen Brittle: 338
Glenbrittle Beach: 341
Glencoe: 16, 25, 262, 304–309, 322
Glencoe Folk Museum: 304
Glencoe Massacre and Monument: 259, 304
Glencoe Road: 17, 28, 258, 305
Glencoe Visitor's Centre: 308
Glendale: 355–356
Glenfiddich Distillery: 27, 271
Glenfinnan: 320–323
Glenfinnan Monument: 14, 311, 318, 320

List of Maps

Front Map

Edinburgh

Glasgow

Loch Lomond and the Southern Highlands

Inverness and the Central Highlands

Isle of Skye and the Western Highlands

Photo Credits

Acknowledgments

Thanks to the many people who have provided useful hints and tips and guided me on my travels. From old friends who shared their favourite places, to chance meetings with locals, and more thorough chats and tours with people who went out of their way to walk me through unfamiliar areas (sometimes literally) and explain local issues.

Neil MacLeod of Caledonian Discovery (and general font of all knowledge), Alistair Danter of Skye Connect, Beth Thoms of Edinburgh Festivals, and local tourism providers Dan Klein, Alistair McQueen, and Rebecca Hutton particularly spring to mind.

VisitScotland was, of course, a useful resource, but more localised tourism organisations also proved invaluable. The team at Glasgow Life was super helpful, as were staff at Loch Lomond and the Trossachs National Park and Explore Islay and Jura.

And lastly, a big thanks to my soon-to-be husband Stephen's patience in keeping the home fires burning while I nipped off for yet another research trip, and our two sons, Arthur and Stanley, who took our epic summer Scottish road trip in their stride (even when mummy and daddy got engaged on a desolate beach on Skye).

Stunning Sights Around the World

BELIZE

COSTA RICA

FIJI

MACHU PICCHU

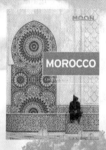
MOROCCO

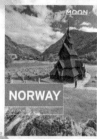
NORWAY

PATAGONIA

ROME, FLORENCE & VENICE

Guides for Urban Adventure

BUENOS AIRES

LISBON

MEXICO CITY

MONTRÉAL

NEW YORK CITY

OSLO

VANCOUVER

WASHINGTON DC

MAP SYMBOLS

▤ Expressway	○ City/Town	✈ Airport	⚲ Golf Course
▭ Primary Road	◉ State Capital	✈ Airfield	ℙ Parking Area
▭ Secondary Road	⊛ National Capital	▲ Mountain	▤ Archaeological Site
▭ Unpaved Road	★ Point of Interest	✛ Unique Natural Feature	♦ Church
▬ Feature Trail	• Accommodation		⛽ Gas Station
▬ Other Trail	▾ Restaurant/Bar	⚲ Waterfall	◎ Glacier
⋯ Ferry	▪ Other Location	▲ Park	▥ Mangrove
▥ Pedestrian Walkway	Λ Campground	▯ Trailhead	▥ Reef
▥ Stairs		⛷ Skiing Area	▥ Swamp

CONVERSION TABLES

°C = (°F - 32) / 1.8
°F = (°C x 1.8) + 32
1 inch = 2.54 centimeters (cm)
1 foot = 0.304 meters (m)
1 yard = 0.914 meters
1 mile = 1.6093 kilometers (km)
1 km = 0.6214 miles
1 fathom = 1.8288 m
1 chain = 20.1168 m
1 furlong = 201.168 m
1 acre = 0.4047 hectares
1 sq km = 100 hectares
1 sq mile = 2.59 square km
1 ounce = 28.35 grams
1 pound = 0.4536 kilograms
1 short ton = 0.90718 metric ton
1 short ton = 2,000 pounds
1 long ton = 1.016 metric tons
1 long ton = 2,240 pounds
1 metric ton = 1,000 kilograms
1 quart = 0.94635 liters
1 US gallon = 3.7854 liters
1 Imperial gallon = 4.5459 liters
1 nautical mile = 1.852 km

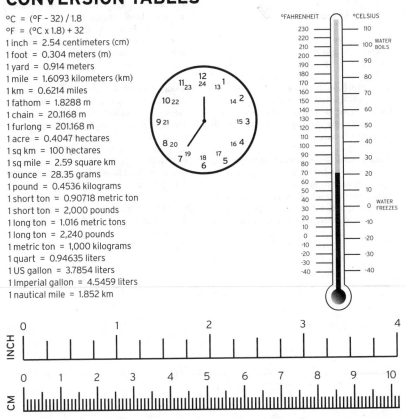

MOON EDINBURGH, GLASGOW
& THE ISLE OF SKYE
Avalon Travel
Hachette Book Group
1700 Fourth Street
Berkeley, CA 94710, USA
www.moon.com

Editor: Ada Fung
Series Manager: Kathryn Ettinger
Copy Editor: Amy Reff
Production and Graphics Coordinators: Krista
    Anderson, Ravina Schneider
Cover Design: Faceout Studios, Charles Brock
Interior Design: Domini Dragoone
Moon Logo: Tim McGrath
Map Editor: Mike Morgenfeld
Cartographers: Brian Shotwell, Karin Dahl
Indexer: Sam Arnold-Boyd

ISBN-13: 978-1-64049-015-4

Printing History
1st Edition — June 2019
5 4 3 2 1

Front cover photo: Ashton Lane in Glasgow's West
    End. © georgeclark | iStock.com
Back cover photo: Quiraing at sunrise. © Daniel_Kay
    | iStock.com

Printed in Canada by Friesens

Avalon Travel is a division of Hachette Book Group,
    Inc. Moon and the Moon logo are trademarks of
    Hachette Book Group, Inc. All other marks and
    logos depicted are the property of the original
    owners.